GUIDE MY STEADY
HAND AS I BASK UNDER
YOUR MAJESTY....

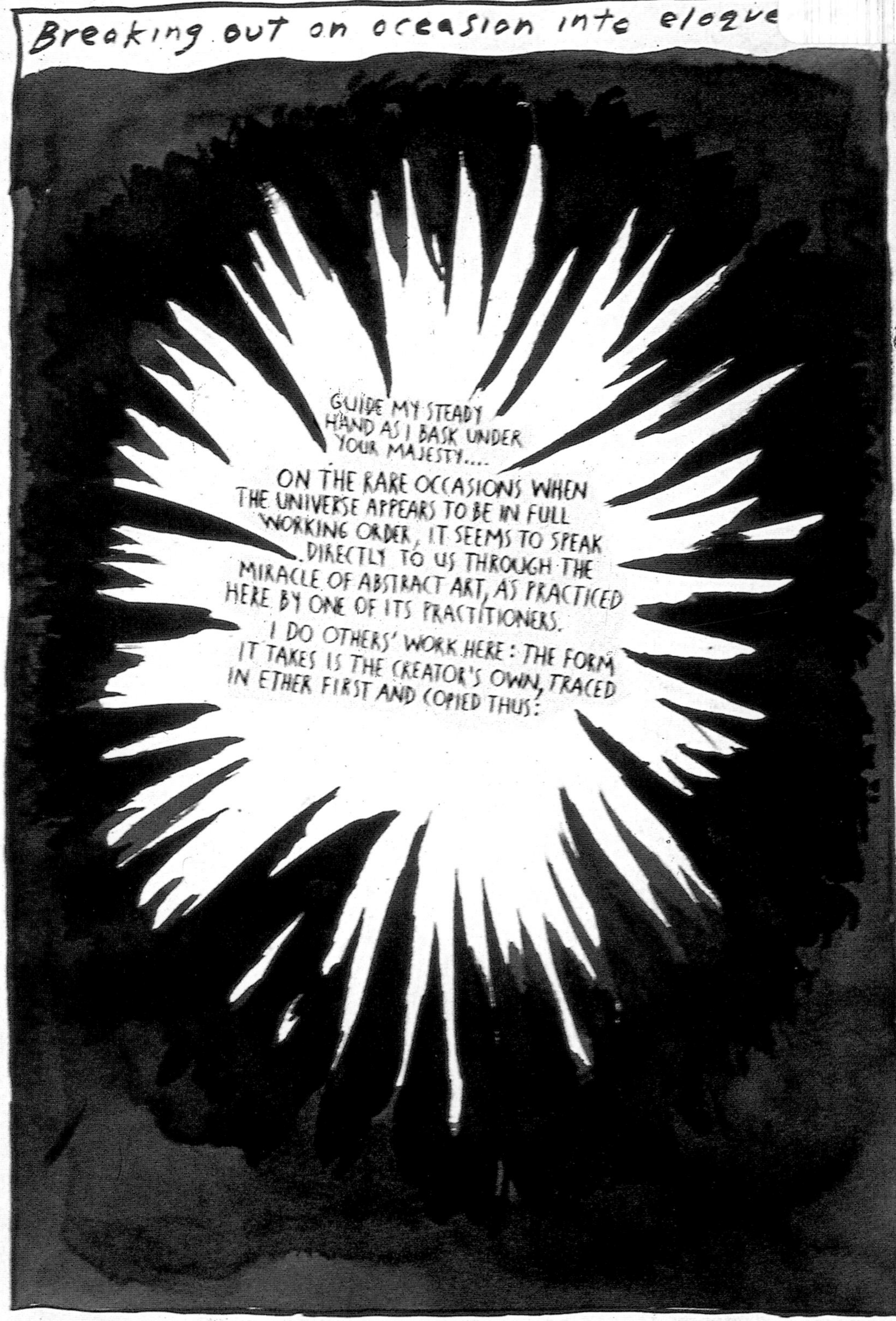

ON THE RARE OCCASIONS WHEN
THE UNIVERSE APPEARS TO BE IN FULL
WORKING ORDER, IT SEEMS TO SPEAK
DIRECTLY TO US THROUGH THE
MIRACLE OF ABSTRACT ART, AS PRACTICED
HERE BY ONE OF ITS PRACTITIONERS.

I DO OTHERS' WORK HERE: THE FORM
IT TAKES IS THE CREATOR'S OWN, TRACED
IN ETHER FIRST AND COPIED THUS:

DIE PARKETT-REIHE MIT GEGENWARTSKÜNSTLERN / THE PARKETT SERIES WITH CONTEMPORARY ARTISTS

Buchreihe mit Gegenwartskünstlern in deutscher und englischer Sprache, erscheint dreimal im Jahr. Jeder Band entsteht mit Künstlern oder Künstlerinnen, die eigens für die Leser von Parkett einen Originalbeitrag gestalten. Diese Werke sind in der gesamten Auflage abgebildet und zusätzlich in einer limitierten und signierten Vorzugsausgabe erhältlich.

Book Series with contemporary artists in English and German, published three times a year. Parkett choses to retain its authors' stylistic variations. Each volume is created in collaboration with artists, who contribute an original work specially made for the readers of Parkett. The works are reproduced in the regular edition and available in a limited and signed Special Edition.

PARKETT NR. 48 ENTSTEHT IN COLLABORATION MIT • GARY HUME, GABRIEL OROZCO, PIPILOTTI RIST • WILL BE COLLABORATING ON PARKETT NO. 48

JAHRESABONNEMENT (DREI NUMMERN) / ANNUAL SUBSCRIPTION (THREE ISSUES) SFR. 98.– (SCHWEIZ), DM 122,– (BRD), SFR. 115.– (ÜBRIGES EUROPA), US$ 75 (USA AND CANADA ONLY)

Zürichsee Druckereien AG (Stäfa)   Satz, Litho, Druck/Copy, Printing, Color Separations

Nachdrucke jeder Art sind nur mit Genehmigung des Verlags erlaubt, bei Besprechungen bitten wir um Belege.
No parts of this magazine may be reproduced without publisher's permission. We appreciate seeing any mention of Parkett in critical reviews.

PARKETT-VERLAG AG, ZÜRICH, SEPTEMBER 1996   PRINTED IN SWITZERLAND   ISBN 3-907509-97-8   ISSN 0256-0917

HEFTRÜCKEN / SPINE NO. 46–48: EMMA KUNZ

see also p. 6–18 in this issue / vgl. auch S. 6–18 dieser Ausgabe.

Umschlag / Cover: Ausschnitte von / Details of TONY OURSLER, SUBMERGED, 1995/96, RAYMOND PETTIBON, NO TITLE (BRING OUT WITH), 1990, and THOMAS SCHÜTTE, EHRHARD (OLD FRIENDS), 1992. – *Vordere Umschlagklappe / Front cover-flap:* THOMAS SCHÜTTE, GROSSE GEISTER,1996, and TONY OURSLER, SYSTEM FOR DRAMATIC FEEDBACK, 1994 – *page 1 /Seite 1:* RAYMOND PETTIBON, NO TITLE (BREAKING OUT ON), 1986.

Special thanks to Maika Pollack, Scott Rothkopf, Anton C. Meier and Minchie Huggler.

PARKETT Zürich New York Frankfurt

Bice Curiger Chefredaktorin/Editor in Chief; **Jacqueline Burckhardt** Redaktorin/Senior Editor; **Louise Neri** Redaktorin USA/Senior Editor US; **Susanne Schmidt** Textredaktion und Produktion/Editing and Production; **Trix Wetter** Graphik/Design; **Hanna Koller** Graphik Assistenz/Design Associate; **Catherine Schelbert** Englisches Lektorat/Editorial Assistant for English; **Frances Richard** Editing and Research US; **Claudia Meneghini** Korrektur/Proof Reading

Beatrice Fässler Vorzugsausgaben/Special Editions; **Beatrice Aschmann** Buchvertrieb, Inserate/Distribution, Advertising; **Vera Tremp** Abonnemente/Subscriptions; **Yvette Brackmann** Administration und Abonnemente USA/Administration, Research and Subscriptions US; **Adrian Koerfer** Deutsche Verlagsvertretung/German Representative

Jacqueline Burckhardt – Bice Curiger – Dieter von Graffenried Herausgeber/Editorial Board; **Jacqueline Burckhardt – Bice Curiger – Dieter von Graffenried – Walter Keller – Peter Blum** Gründer/Founders

Dieter von Graffenried Verleger/Publisher

**PARKETT-VERLAG AG, QUELLENSTRASSE 27, CH-8005 ZURICH, TEL. 41-1-271 81 40, FAX 41-1-272 43 01
PARKETT, NEW YORK, 155 AV. OF THE AMERICAS, N.Y. 10013, PHONE (212) 673-2660, FAX (212) 271-0704
PARKETT-VERLAG AG, TANNENWALDALLEE 17, D-61348 BAD HOMBURG, FAX 06172-937 444**

Gespenster-Realismus

Die ausgeprägte «Lebensnähe», der unübersehbare Realitätsanspruch der in dieser Ausgabe von PARKETT vorgestellten Kunst ist trügerisch. Immer wieder sieht man sich als Publikum zuerst von den einnehmenden Gesängen der Wiedererkennbarkeit umgarnt, um dann fatalerweise ins Leere zu laufen.

Da sind Tony Ourslers Lumpenkreaturen, deren aufsässige Präsenz uns martert, nicht nur weil ihre anrührenden Probleme an uns klebenbleiben wie schlechter Geruch, sondern weil ihre Stimmen aus dem Bodenlosen zu kommen scheinen. Mit unserer Aufmerksamkeit vergrössern wir nur noch die allgemeine Hilflosigkeit. In diesem Stelldichein von uns echten Kunstmenschen mit den artifiziellen Sozialfällen schnappt die Falle mehrfach zu: In welcher Realität befinden wir uns? Und ist das so glaubwürdig aus dem Leben Gegriffene vielleicht nur der verlängerte kalte Strom der Fernsehrealität, die vorgibt, sich zur allgemeinen Verwirrung mal auf die Strasse oder unter eine Matratze zu legen? Zum Glück macht sich auch «Erheiterung» breit, doch der alte Besserwisser-Vorsprung, mit dem man sich über die absurde Lage der Homunculi lustig macht, kehrt sich ja doch immer wieder gegen einen selbst.

Es ist ein fatales Hineinrutschen in mentale Zustände, die das Unheimliche der heutigen Realität widerspiegeln. So zwingen uns auch Raymond Pettibons Litaneien, hellsichtige Gedankensplitter und schlagende Bild-Refrains dazu, uns nicht einlösbaren Erwartungen hinzugeben. Sein Zeichnen zitiert ein Genre, das «Gröberes» verspricht und damit keinen Anspruch auf die Treibhaus-Sensibilität der Kunst zu fordern scheint. Aber die Sprachen und Codes verstellen sich; Wirklichkeit hat sich multipliziert oder verflüssigt.

Wenn lauter merkwürdige Stimmen sich zum Chor bilden, ist Offenheit angesagt. Thomas Schüttes Menschenfiguren nehmen in jüngster Zeit Science-fiction-Dimensionen an. Wie real sind Visionen des Zukunftsmenschen, wenn sie aus dem kollektiven Gedächtnis entsprungen scheinen? Man steht in jedem Fall nicht anders davor als vor Michelangelos David.

Sind die Mythen wahrer als die Wirklichkeit? Angesichts des INSERT von Zoe Leonard und Cheryl Dunye lässt sich studieren, wie tragfähig die Dokumentation einer Fiktion beziehungsweise die Fiktion einer Dokumentation ist. Wie mühelos glaubt es sich doch, dass die vorgespiegelten Spuren eines «öffentlichen» Lebens bereits Teil unser aller Geschichte sind!

Spooky Realism

The remarkably lifelike, unmistakable reality advanced by the art in this issue of PARKETT is deceptive. One finds oneself repeatedly ensnared by the seductive call of recognition, only to end up making the fatal leap into the void.

Take Tony Oursler's ragged beings: We are tormented by their rebellious presence not only because their emotional problems plague us like a swarm of mosquitoes, but because their voices seem to rise out of fathomless depths. By giving them our attention, we merely aggravate the prevailing aura of impotence. This rendezvous between real viewers and fake social welfare cases is a multiple trap. We are clearly part of reality—but which one? And is that eminently plausible slice of life simply an extension of the cold current of TV reality that confounds matters even more by taking to the streets and lying under a mattress? Fortunately, there is "comic relief," brief though it is, for the sense of superiority that makes us laugh at these homunculi's absurd situation inevitably turns against us. Inexorably we are drawn into the mindset that is spawned by today's spooky reality. Similarly, we are compelled by Raymond Pettibon's litanies, by his clairvoyant fragments of thought and shattering pictorial refrains, to cling to unrealizable expectations. Emulating a genre in his drawings that promises "coarser fare," he does not, it seems, advance the demand for the hothouse delicacy of art. But languages and codes may come in disguise; reality multiplies or evaporates.

When a host of peculiar voices rises in chorus, it is time to open wide the doors. Thomas Schütte's human figures have recently acquired the proportions of science fiction. How real are the envisioned people of the future if they seem to have sprung from collective memory? In any case, we stand before them as we do before Michelangelo's David.

Are myths truer than reality? The INSERT by Zoe Leonard and Cheryl Dunye displays the cogency of documented fiction, or rather fictional documentation, demonstrating once again how effortlessly we believe in the bogus traces of a "public" life, as if it had already become part of our common heritage!

Bice Curiger

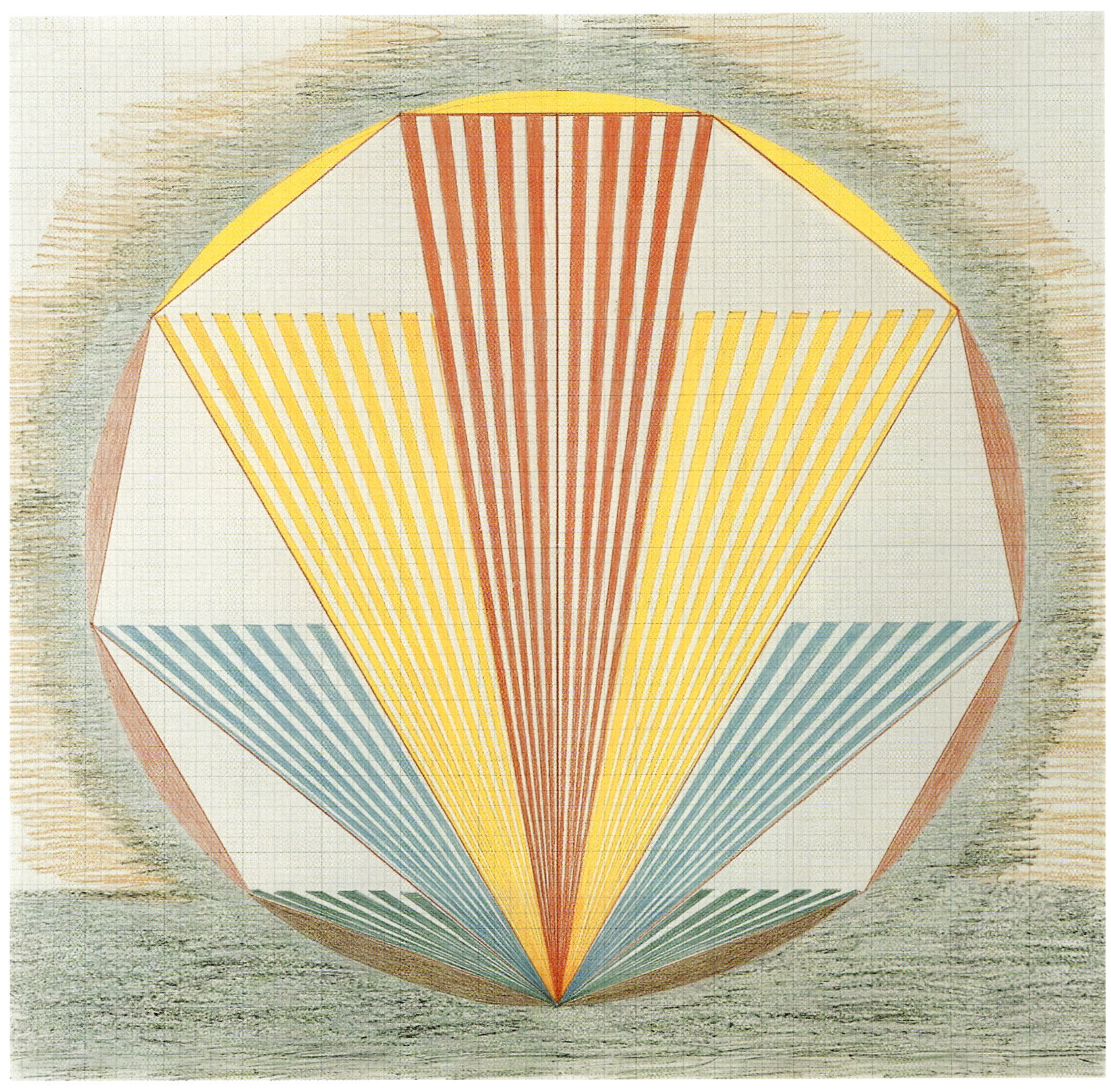

EMMA KUNZ, Werk Nr. 168, 1942, 70 x 70 cm, entstanden zwei Tage nach der Entdeckung des Heilgesteins Aion A und seiner Wirkung im physischen wie feinstofflichen Bereich. Grün steht für den physischen, erdverbundenen Körper, Blau für den energetischen Körper, Gelb für die biodynamische Sphäre, den Astralkörper und Rot schliesslich für die mental-geistige Sphäre / Piece no. 168, 1942, 27½ x 27½". Created two days after Kunz's discovery of Aion A and its healing powers. Green represents the earthbound human body, blue its energetic field, yellow the astral or emotional body, and red the mental and spiritual sphere penetrating them all.   (PHOTOS: EMMA-KUNZ-ZENTRUM, WÜRENLOS, SWITZERLAND)

JURI STEINER

Pentas Parabeln

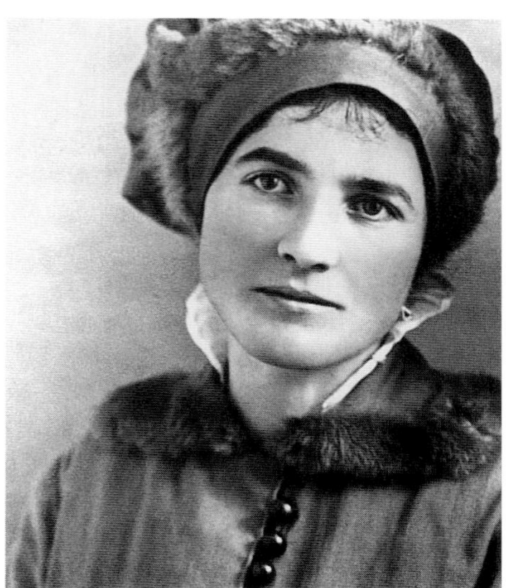

Emma Kunz, 1912.

Ich kann Ihren Buben heilen.   Emma Kunz

Am Busen von Emma Kunz ist das Menschenkind kristallrein und behütet. Alle seine Lebensfäden sind gewoben, um den strahlenden Menschen zu schaffen, Hingebung auszuströmen und Erleuchtung zu erlangen. Unsere liebe Frau aus dem Aargau war wundertätig und unbelesen. Sie heilte und prophezeite im Ärztekittel. Sie einsiedelte in ihrem zölibatären Körper und machte all jene verliebt in Gottesnamen, deren Gebresten sie vertrieb. Für manches sentimentale Beben war sie verantwortlich. Aber die animistische Schönheit war nicht André Bretons *Nadja,* das Luftgenie, das sich für obskurante Augenblicke binden liess. Emma Kunz zeichnete Ornamente der Seelenwelt. Aber sie war nicht *Hilma af Klint* (1862–1944), die als Geistermedium den Pinsel mit theosophistischem Gold und anthroposophistischer Tempera führte. Emma Kunz' Intention war jenseits des Artefakts. Der Geist steht im Zentrum, und nicht die Inkarnation, durch die er wirkt. Sie hat John F. Kennedys Ende vorhergesagt und wie Chiron, der mythologische Kentaur und Heiler, in ihrem Körper die Krankheiten anderer nachvollzogen, angenommen und kraft ihres Fühlens sympathetisch gebannt. Das ist schon bestürzend.

Geboren wurde Emma Kunz 1892 in Brittnau, Kanton Aargau. Der Vater, ein armer Handweber, trank, nahm sich das Leben, und als Zeugen des Jammers starben zwei Geschwister nach. Neunzehnjährig machte sich Emma, die Dorfschönheit, auf und davon, sie folgte den Spuren eines angehimmelten Pfarrerssohns nach Amerika. Bereits gebärdete sich ihre Liebe grenzenlos, doch sollte Emma ihren emigrierten Protestanten nicht bekommen. Reumütig war die Rückkehr ins Aargauer Nest. Man machte sich lustig über sie und rief sie nach ihrem Fluchtpunkt «Philadelphia». So ging sie wieder, diesmal nach Strengelbach in die Fabrik. Zwischen 1923 und 1939 wirkte sie als Bonne und Gesellschafterin in der Familie des Künstlers Jakob Friedrich Welti. Lasierend malte der Eklektiker seine haushaltende Muse. Vierzig Jahre alt, wurde Emma Kunz sich schliesslich ihrer Kräfte bewusst, begann mit Pendeln, dann mit Zeichnen und gab sich den Namen «Penta», entsprechend dem pythagoreischen Symbol für Gesundheit, klar wie das in einer Linie gezeichnete Pentagramm.

JURI STEINER ist Kunstkritiker in Zürich und mit Rudolf nicht verwandt.

Nachdem sie mit ihren beiden ledigen Schwestern in Brittnau jahrelang eine Art Konvent gebildet hatte, verbrachte Penta ihren letzten Lebensabschnitt in ihrem kleinen Haus in Waldstatt, Appenzell. Dort starb sie 1963.

Quadratmetergrosse Blätter pflegte sie auf ein über den Stubentisch gelegtes Brett zu nageln, nahm das Pendel, dessen Gewichte aus Jade und Silber an einer Kette schwangen, zur Hand und begann die Zeichenfläche auszuloten. *Plötzlich habe sie dann aufgemerkt, mit grosser Eile eine Linie gesetzt und erleichtert aufgeatmet. Dies geschah immer in dem Augenblick, da eine Formgestalt sichtbar vor ihr inneres Auge getreten war.*[1] So beschrieb es Heiny Widmer, Emma Kunz' frühester Exeget, anlässlich der ersten Ausstellung ihrer Arbeiten im Aargauer Kunsthaus 1973/74. Auf den Schwerlinien und Schwerpunkten aufbauend, entstanden in stunden-, gar tagelanger Konzentration und unter Zuhilfenahme von Zirkel und einer gehobelten Holzleiste geometrisch abstrakte Strukturen.

Über den Karrees des verwendeten Millimeterpapiers strahlen verflochtene Linien zu Rhomben, Polygonen, Hexagonen aus, repetieren sich symmetrisch oder lösen einander ab. Jede dieser mit Bleistift und Farbstift gezeichneten Formen, selbst Kreis und Parabel, entwickeln sich aus geraden Linien. Eine jede ist energetische Verbindung, Haargefäss des Lebensstroms.

Neuartige Zeichnungsmethode[2] nannte Emma Kunz ihr Verfahren in einem 1953 im Selbstverlag herausgegebenen Büchlein. Darin notierte sie den kryptischen Code zu ihrem verstrebten Bildwerk:

Das Wort als Wandlung (wenden), Entfaltung (entfalten); Die Zeichensprache als Symbol in Gleich und Mal; die Bildekräfte in Wesensart und Form als Kristall, Pflanze, Tier und Mensch… – die Wahl von zwei Zahlen miteinander verbunden und entfaltet, bestimmt die Art der Form und Gestalt. Das ist das Geheimnis als Schlüssel zu dieser Offenbarung.

Eine Grundform ist der Kreis. Auf ihrer solitären Bahn gebar Emma Kunz instinktiv das Mandala (Sanskrit: Kreis), das pankulturelle Urbild, das an die tiefsten Schichten des Unbewussten rührt und sich in der Natur, in den Bausteinen der Materie ebenso finden soll wie in den Gestalten der Psyche des Menschen. Von den altsteinzeitlichen Felsritzungen aus

Transvaal (Südafrika) bis hinein in die Carnets von Carl Gustav Jung schlägt das Zeichensystem sein Rad. Jung skizzierte, als er zwischen 1916 und 1918 Kommandant eines Internierungslagers für Engländer in Château-d'Œx war, jeden Morgen eine kleine Kreiszeichnung: *Anhand der Bilder konnte ich die psychischen Wandlungen von Tag zu Tag beobachten. Nur allmählich kam ich darauf, was das Mandala eigentlich ist: Gestaltung – Umgestaltung, des ewigen Sinnes ewige Unterhaltung.*[3]

Zeichnen: was der Psychoanalytiker zur kryptogrammatischen Investigation seines Selbst betrieb, das bezog Emma Kunz, altruistisch pur. Ihre Arbeiten waren Pendeltafeln, die, auf Patienten angewandt, seelische Probleme und körperliche Schwachstellen eruieren halfen. Emma Kunz zeichnete, weil sie Gesetzmässigkeiten in sich spürte, die sie nicht zur Ruhe kommen liessen. Der Modell- und Plancharakter schliesst das Affektive aus. Die Papierbogen halten Zustände grundlegend wirksamer, harmonikaler Prinzipien fest, «ohne eine eindeutig formulierbare Theorie zu illustrieren», wie Theo Kneubühler feststellte[4]. Nicht mit dem Instrumentarium des Verstandes seien die Bereiche des Unbekannten anzusprechen, sagte sie. Hier schafften nur Ahnung, Vision, Einklang mit dem eigenen Körper, genaues Hinhorchen auf die Natur, Hinsehen auf Gestalten und Gestaltveränderungen Kontakte.[5] Emma Kunz' Bilder sind, entsprechend der Kunstdefinition der Philosophin Susan K. Langer, der aktive Abschluss einer symbolischen Transformation von Erfahrung.[6]

Ihre Zeichnungen müssen auf die Patienten gewirkt haben wie Lacans Spiegel, in dem das Kleinkind sich zum erstenmal anblickt und ein imaginäres Bild seines Körpers entwirft. Im schwingenden Rhythmus des Pendels erkannten sie sich als vernetztes Abstraktum, begriffen sie sich raumgreifender und in die Schöpfung involvierter, als sie es sich je hätten träumen lassen. *Das ist das ursprüngliche Abenteuer, in dem der Mensch zum erstenmal die Erfahrung macht, dass er sich sieht, sich reflektiert und sich anders begreift, als er ist – die wesentliche Dimension des Menschlichen, die sein ganzes Phantasieleben strukturiert.*[7]

Die Emma Kunz geschenkte Aufmerksamkeit verlässt alsbald den Weg rationaler Argumentation und verliert sich in einem Labyrinth spekulativer Kunst-

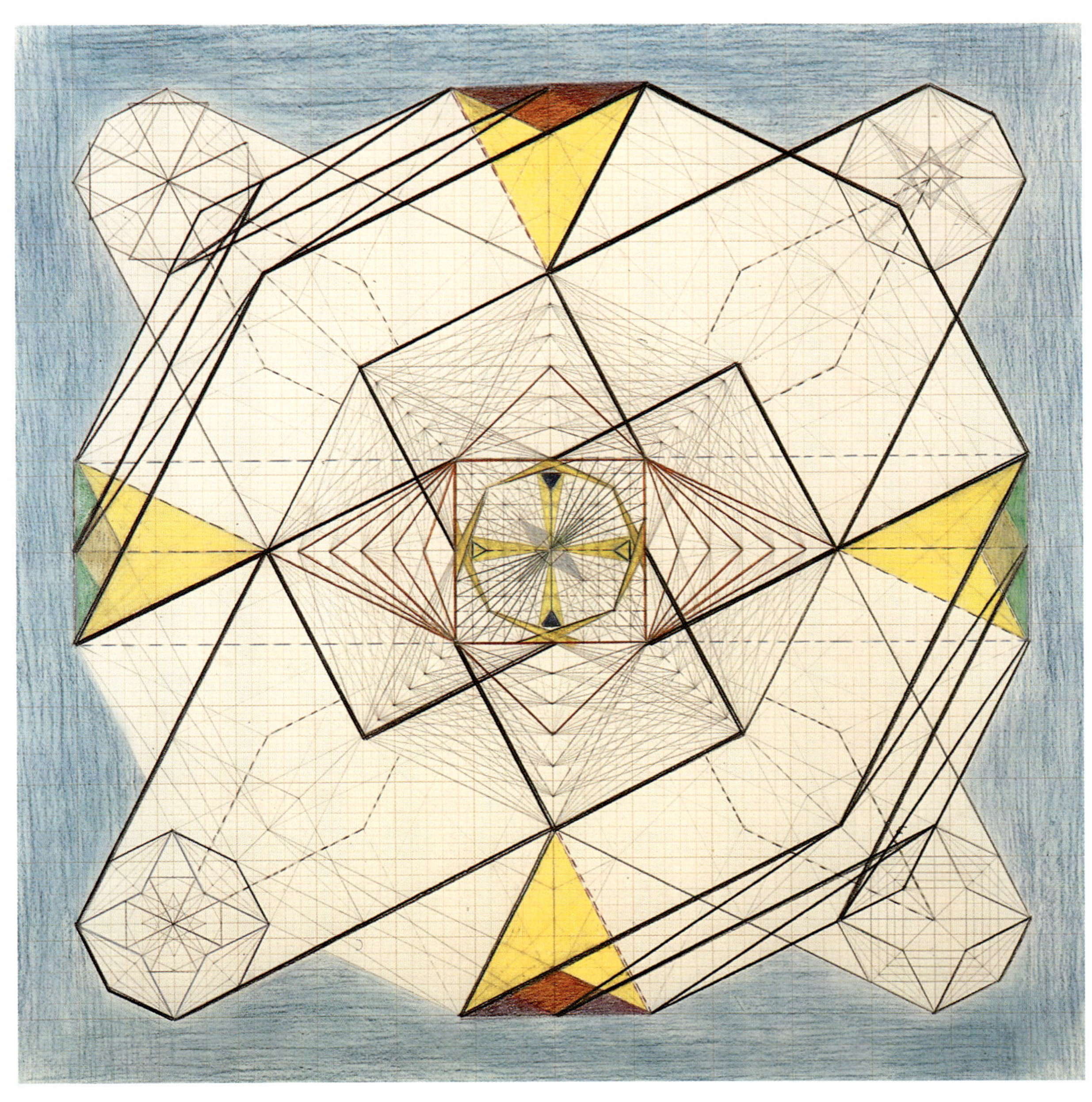

EMMA KUNZ, Werk Nr. 069, undatiert, 70 x 70 cm / piece no. 069, undated, 27½ x 27½".

theorie. Schwindelig tappt sie, zwischen Welt- und Einzelseele pendelnd, auf transzendenten Pfaden, die dem profanen Intellekt verschlossen bleiben. Im Begleittext zu der Emma Kunz gewidmeten Ausstellung «oh! cet écho!»[8] wurde auf das «Rhizom» von Deleuze und Guattari hingewiesen. Im botanischen Bild steckt die dezentrierte Mannigfaltigkeit, die so schön auf Emmas Welt passt: *Das Rhizom ist ein Kurzzeitgedächtnis oder ein Antigedächtnis... Es ist eine Karte. Die Karte ist offen, sie kann ständig neue Veränderungen aufnehmen. Man kann sie auf eine Wand zeichnen, als Kunstwerk konzipieren oder als politische Aktion oder Meditation begreifen*[9]

Im esoterischen Nebel, der sich um die Lichtgestalt legt, hält man sich am besten an den Mann, aus dessen Schriften Emma Kunz sich gerne vorlesen liess: «Philippus Aureolus Theophrastus Bombastus Paracelsus von Hohenheim, den Luther der Medizin und unsern grössten Schweizerarzt».[10] Er brachte im sechzehnten Jahrhundert eine erfahrungsbezogene und zugleich spekulativ-spirituelle Ganzheitsmedizin unter die Leute und betonte die Heilkraft der seelischen Imagination, auch die der Bilder und Signaturen. Er hielt es für möglich, «den Berg Olymp ins Rote Meer zu schmeissen oder den Ozean auf den Ätna zu entleeren und dergleichen».[11] Solch geistige Parforce macht den gläubigen Menschen Gott gleicher. Emma Kunz war ziemlich gleich. Gläubig, schien sie zu Christus ein eher mitempfindendes denn ein anbetendes Verhältnis gehabt zu haben; karfreitags litt sie physisch mit dem Rabbi aus Nazareth.

Der Kur-Segen über ihrem Werk relativiert jedes kunsthermeneutische Für und Wider. Ihr Werk fängt weder auf dem Papier an, noch hört es am Blattrand auf. Wie Paracelsus es definierte, ist die edelste, höchste und freieste aller Künste die Heiltätigkeit – Dürer und Leonardo reichen ihm die Hand. Als Heilpraktikerin und Forscherin unterhielt Emma Kunz einen grossen Pflanzengarten, der ihr die Kräuter für Salben und Tinkturen lieferte. Diese Naturmedizinen trugen ihren Teil bei zur Behandlung von an Veitstanz leidenden Frauen, augenkranken Theologen und Föten in Steisslage. 1942 erlöste die Heilkünstlerin einen Buben von der Kinderlähmung. Heute ist er ihr Nachlassverwalter und mehr. Er ist der jung gebliebene Lebendbeweis ihrer Kunstfertigkeit; *er* ist das eigentliche, von seiner Pygmaliondame befreite Kunstwerk.

Emmas Zeichnungen wurden, wie Widmer bemerkte, zur «Kunst wider Willen». Diese kann intrinsisch, in kanonisierten, ästhetischen Dimensionen wahrgenommen werden, weil sie von künstlerischen Solitären – Klee, Malewitsch, Ad Reinhard – umzingelt ist und weil die Mythologien der Abstraktion und die «Fälle» der Art brut (Adolf Wölfli, Anton Müller, Louis Soutter, Aloïse Strübin) ihren Platz in der Kunstgeschichte dieses Jahrhunderts haben. Harald Szeemann, der, zusammen mit Widmer, Emma Kunz' Werke ins Pariser Musée d'Art Moderne (1976) ausführte, verweist auf die «‹naiven› Konstruktivisten», auf die Visionen Auguste Herbins (1882–1960), auf die zahlengeometrischen Untersuchungen eines Alfred Jensen (1903–1981), kommt auf den erweiterten Kunstbegriff von Joseph Beuys zu sprechen. Emma Kunz selbst hat nur einen einzigen, formalen Bezug hergestellt, und zwar zur Illustration eines Zeitungsartikels von Professor Dr. Ginsburg, Leiter des Mathematischen Institutes der Yeshiva-Universität in New York: Sie war verdutzt, als sie unter dem Titel «Die Schönheit der mathematischen Formel» auf ein Kreisbild stiess, das sie gleichfalls schon gezeichnet hatte.

Penta lebte keine bewegte Existenz. Als ruhender Pol aber brachte sie die Welt um sich herum ins Rotieren, Spriessen und Wachsen. Einmal stellte sie sich im Beisein des Kantonschemikers von St. Gallen mit ihrer 63 cm langen Spiralrute vor die Rabatten und bependelte Ringelblumen, sie gab diesen den Auftrag, eine bestimmte Anzahl Tochterblüten hervorspriessen zu lassen. Und siehe, die polarisierten *Calendulae* gehorchten, so demütig wie die Elefanten Tarzan. Durchaus nüchtern und bescheiden, sah Emma Kunz diese mirakulöse Begebenheit als Forschungsarbeit. In ihrem Labor hatte sie wissenschaftliche Apparaturen stehen, ein Mikroskop, einen Geigerzähler. Diese dienten lediglich der Bestätigung, waren da für Skeptiker.

Immer hoffnungsfroher wurden die Visiten, nachdem Emma Kunz 1942 in Würenlos ein Heilgestein entdeckt hatte. In der aus dem Fels geschlagenen Grotte der dortigen Römersteinbrüche strahlen und schwingen starke positive Kräfte aus dem Berg, gute Vibrationen durchdringen das ganze Wesen des Besuchers, psychosonare Energie als Fruchtwasser im steinernen Uterus. Auf einem Vitalpfad durchschreitet man die Grotte – ganz wie in Lourdes – entlang der Felswand, lässt sich die anschwellenden «Bovis»-Werte durch den Körper jagen, die Chakras öffnen, und duscht in der Sphäre spiritueller Impulse.

Der Steinbruch gehört der Familie des Nachlassverwalters. «Ich kann Ihren Buben heilen. Dazu brauche ich ein spezielles Pulver, das ich im unmittelbaren Lebensbereich Ihres Sohnes finden werde.»[12] Dieser gesundete dank dem «gereinigten, verfeinerten und zu mehlfeinem Pulver verarbeiteten» Muschelkalk seiner Väter – heute unter dem Namen *Aion A* in Apotheken und Drogerien zu erstehen. Bauherren empfahl Emma Kunz, nur Materialien zu verwenden, die im gleichen Lebensraum wie sie selbst gewachsen oder entstanden sind. Das galt auch für die Nahrung. Als eine Gesandtschaft des Mystikers Sri Aurobindo (1872–1950) nach Brittnau pilgerte, um Emma Kunz als Meisterin nach Indien einzuladen, winkte sie ab: *Jeder Mensch sollte den ihm gestellten Auftrag im Rahmen seines Kulturkreises annehmen und erfüllen, aus dessen geistigen Ressourcen schöpfen und so innerhalb seiner Schwingungen wirken.*[13]

Der Grenzenlosen zeigen sich Limiten: Kultur aus und in der Heimat. Ihr Platz sei in der Schweiz, hat Penta gesagt. Auf einem hektographierten Flugblatt ohne Datum beschreibt ein Sekundarlehrer ihr Werk als «besondere Ausprägung schweizerischer Volkskunst» und beklagt die Vereinnahmung durch das internationale Kunstbusiness. Er befürchtet «den Ausverkauf der Heimat». In einer Zürcher Künstlerbar hört man, dass, weit weg von Würenlos, der Schah von Persien sich einst für Emma Kunz' Œuvre interessiert haben soll.

War es Bazon Brock, der darüber nachdachte, was die europäische Avantgarde in Asiens Museen verloren habe, so fern der eigenen Kultur? Ist da nicht die Gruppe der «Neunundachtziger» um Botho Straussens Bocksgesang, die eine Kantorei der neuen, spezifisch germanischen Innerlichkeit ins Leben ruft?[14] Glücklich sind wir autochthonen Kinder Helvetiens, die wir *Aion A* zwischen den Zähnen zerreiben können, mit Erfolg, weil wir von hier sind, die wir dank Sitzbädern und Wickeln nicht länger an *Tendovaginitis crepitans tibialis*, extrem schmerzhafter *Epicondylitis* oder Insektenstichen[15] leiden müssen, die wir Emma Kunz' Universal-Geometrie erfühlen können, aus dem Geiste der Identität. Unser Heil liegt wohl nicht in Philadelphia.

1) Heiny Widmer in: *Emma Kunz*, Katalog zur ersten Ausstellung ihrer Werke im Aargauer Kunsthaus in Aarau, 1973–74, S. 11.
2) Der ganze Titel lautet: *Neuartige Zeichnungsmethode. Gestaltung und Form als Mass, Rhythmus, Symbol und Wandlung von Zahl und Prinzip.*
3) Aniela Jaffé, *C.G. Jung: Bild und Wort*, Zürich 1979, S. 78.
4) *Emma Kunz, Forscherin, Naturheilpraktikerin, Künstlerin*, Emma-Kunz-Zentrum, Würenlos (Hrsg.), AT Verlag, Aarau 1993, S. 85.
5) Anton C. Meier, *Emma Kunz, 1892–1963*, Emma-Kunz-Zentrum, Würenlos 1994, S. 50.
6) Susanne K. Langer, *Philosophie auf neuem Weg. Das Symbol im Denken, im Ritus und in der Kunst*, Frankfurt 1992, S. 54. Die Originalausgabe erschien unter dem Titel *Philosophy in a New Key. A Study in the Symbolism of Reason, Rite and Art* bei Harvard University Press, Cambridge 1942.
7) Jacques Lacan, *Das Seminar von J. Lacan*, Buch I (1953–54), Freuds technische Schriften, Olten 1978, S. 10.
8) *oh! cet écho!*, Centre Culturel Suisse, Paris 1992.

9) Gilles Deleuze, Félix Guattari, *Tausend Plateaus*, Berlin 1992, S. 19.
10) Laut dem Paracelsus-Biographen Dr. Hans Locher, 1851, zitiert nach: Pirmin Meier, *Paracelsus. Arzt und Prophet*, Zürich 1993.
11) ebenda, S. 171.
12) Anton C. Meier, op. cit., S. 7.
13) ebenda, S. 26.
14) Seit den 60er Jahren propagiert der deutsche Publizist und Kulturphilosoph Bazon Brock (geb. 1936) einen in allen wesentlichen Wissensdisziplinen situierbaren Ästhetikbegriff. Als Vermittler beherrscht der Generalist die Praxis der Mediation wie kein anderer («action Teaching»). Der in Berlin lebende Schriftsteller Botho Strauss (geb. 1944) wurde mit seinem Essay über das Scheitern linker Utopien, «Anschwellender Bocksgesang» (1993), zur kontrovers rezipierten Figur der rechten Intelligenz Deutschlands.
15) Laut den Erfahrungsberichten aus der Praxis alles Anwendungsbereiche des Heilgesteins *Aion A*.

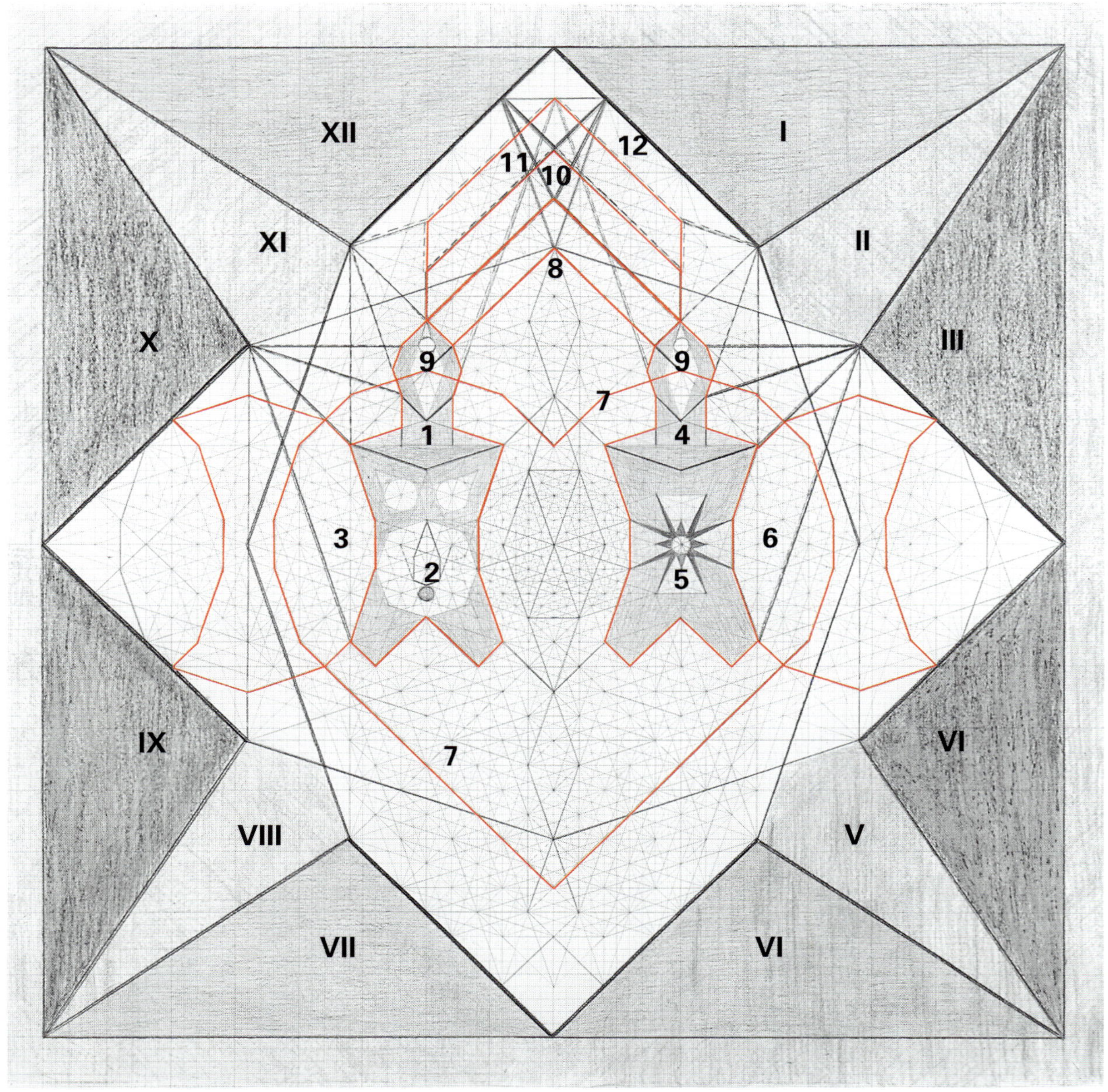

EMMA KUNZ, DAS MENSCHLICHE PAAR IM KOSMOS, 1940, Werk Nr. 086, 90 x 90 cm.

Die Frau (1) mit dem Embryo (2) steht für Verantwortung. Sie steht im Zeichen des zunehmenden Mondes, also der aufsteigenden Entwicklung. Der Mann (4) mit dem Malteserkreuz (5) entwickelt sich im Zeichen des abnehmenden Mondes (6). Menschliche Liebe und Herzensbindung (7) kulminieren im Schnittpunkt (8). Das Dritte Auge (9) steht für die geistige Ebene (Verbindung im Schnittpunkt 10). Darüber stehen noch zwei höhere geistige Ebenen (11, 12). Die Verbindung zum Kosmos wird durch die zwölf astrologischen Häuser (I–XII) dargestellt. Dieses Bild vermittelte Emma Kunz umfangreiche Kenntnisse, die leider nicht schriftlich erhalten sind.

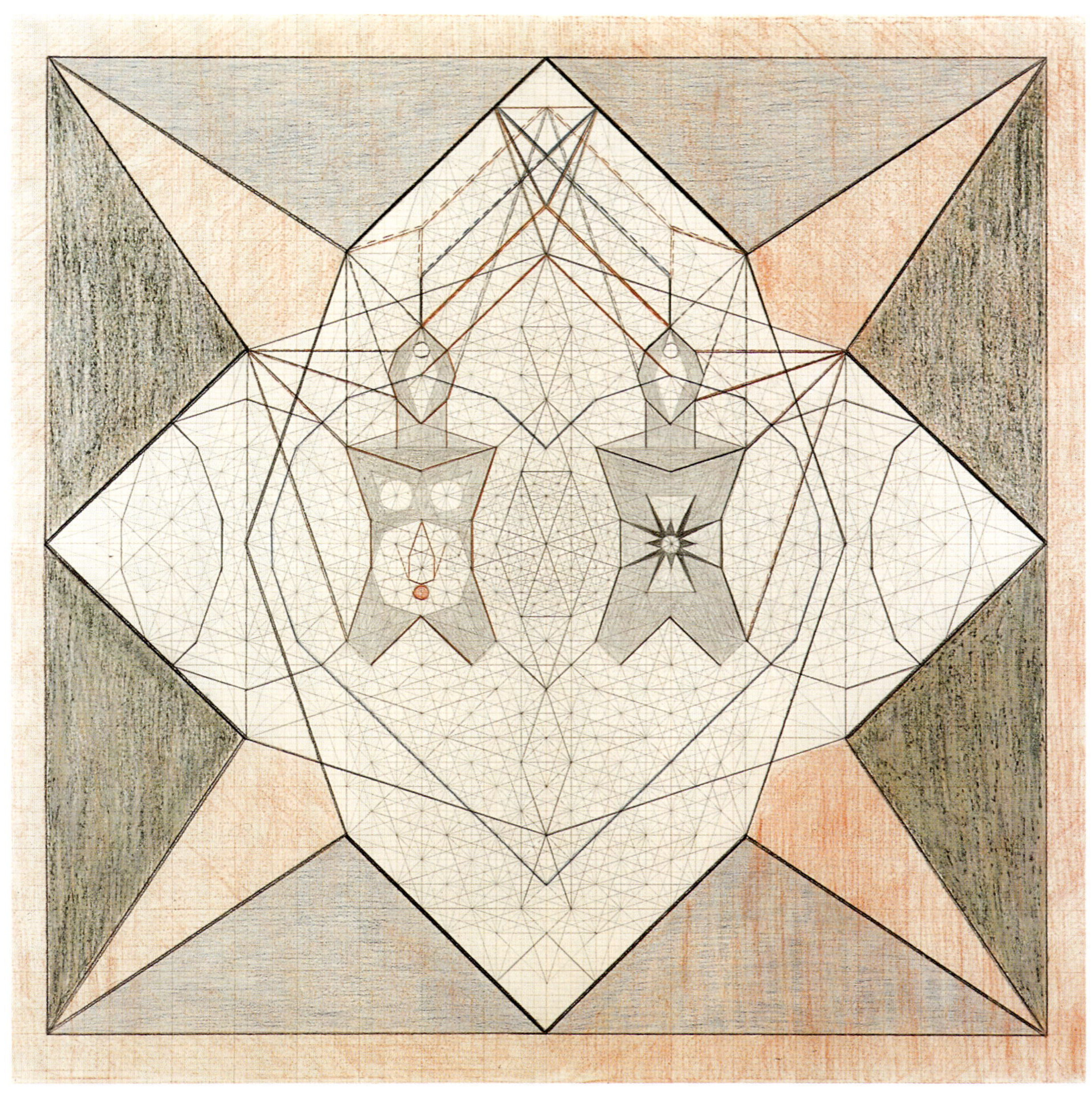

EMMA KUNZ, THE HUMAN COUPLE WITHIN THE COSMOS, 1940, piece no. 086, 35½ x 35½". The woman (see lefthand page, no. 1) with the embryo (2) represents responsibility. She is governed by the sign of the crescent moon (3) and is therefore in a state of ascending evolution. The man (4) with the Maltese cross (5) evolves in the sign of the waning moon (6). Human love and emotional bonds (7) culminate at their intersection (8). The Third Eye (9) represents the spiritual sphere (culminating intersection 10), with two higher spiritual levels above (11, 12). Cosmic integration is symbolized by the twelve astrological houses (I–XII). This picture is a rich repository of Emma Kunz's knowledge; unfortunately only little of this knowledge has survived through oral tradition.

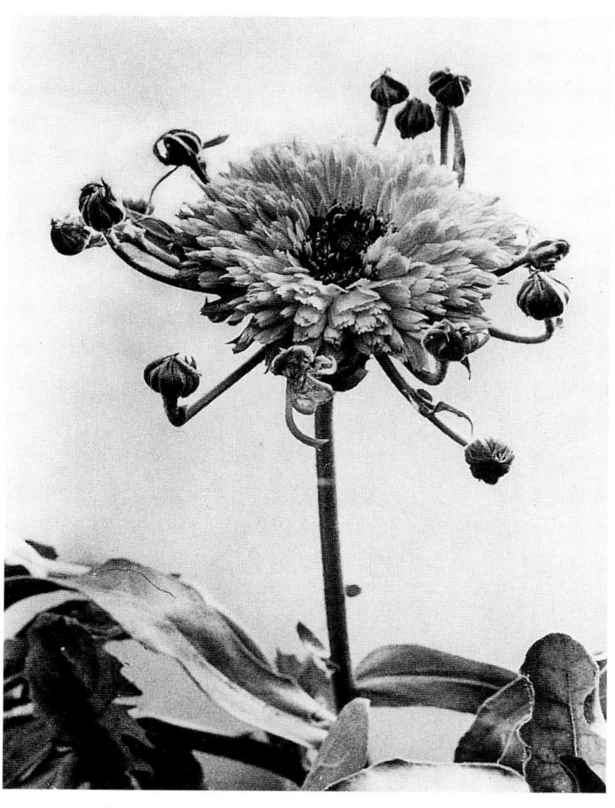

Calendula polarized by Emma Kunz / Polarisierte Ringelblume.

Penta's Parabolas

I can cure your boy.   Emma Kunz

At Emma Kunz's breast, the human child is crystalline and sheltered. All the threads of its life are interwoven to create a radiant being, to infuse devotion, and to achieve enlightenment. Our holy mother from the Canton of Aargau worked miracles and was unlettered. She healed and prophesied in a physician's smock. She was a hermit in her celibate body and all those whose frailties she exorcised fell in love with the Lord's name. She was the source of many a sentimental tremor. But her animistic beauty was not that of André Breton's *Nadja,* the ethereal genius devoted to obscurant moments. Emma Kunz drafted decorative renditions of the world of the soul. But she was not *Hilma af Klint* (1862–1944), the medium who wielded her brush with theosophistical gold and anthroposophistical tempera. Emma Kunz's intentions were beyond artefact. At the core lay the spirit, but not the incarnation through which it works. She predicted J. F. Kennedy's death and, like Cheiron, centaur and healer of Greek mythology, she accepted and absorbed the illnesses of others in her own body, exorcising them on the strength of her empathetic response. That is daunting.

She was born in Brittnau, Switzerland, in 1892. Her father, a poor weaver, drank and took his life; the death of two of her siblings followed. At the age of nineteen, Emma, the village beauty, set out for the New World in pursuit of a pastor's son. Her love knew no bounds, but she loved in vain. Emma did not win over her pastor emigré. Chastened, she returned to the nest in the Canton of Aargau, there becoming the object of ridicule, and nicknamed "Philadelphia" after the site of her unrequited love. Once again she

---

JURI STEINER is an art critic who lives in Zurich. He is not related to Rudolf.

left home, this time taking up factory work in Strengelbach. Between 1923 and 1939 she was employed by the family of artist Jakob Friedrich Welti as bonne and companion. The eclectic artist painted washes of his housekeeping muse. At the age of forty, Emma Kunz acquired faith in her powers, began to work with a pendulum and later with drawings, and adopted the name "Penta," in reference to the Pythagorean symbol of health, the star-shaped pentagram drawn in a single line. After establishing a convent-like institution in Brittnau with her sisters, Penta moved to Waldstatt, Appenzell, where she died in 1963.

She would tack paper, over three feet square, onto a board lying on her living room table, take the pendulum, whose silver and jade bob swung from a chain, and begin to chart the surface of her paper. *Suddenly her attention was arrested, she drew a line in great haste and breathed a sigh of relief. This always happened when a shape became visible to her inner eye.*[1] Thus it was described by Heiny Widmer, Emma Kunz's earliest exegete, on the occasion of the first exhibition of her work at the Aargau Kunsthaus in 1973/74. Building on key lines and key dots, it took Kunz hours, even days, of concentrated effort to create her abstract, geometrical configurations using a compass and, as a ruler, a wooden slat.

Across the squares of the graph paper, interwoven lines form rhombuses, polyhedrons, and hexagons which are symmetrically duplicated or which give way to each other. Each of these shapes, executed in lead or colored pencil, grow out of a straight line—even circles and parabolas. They are, each and every one, lines of vital energy, capillaries of the life-flow.

Emma Kunz called her procedure *A New Method of Drawing*[2] in a self-published booklet of 1953. There she noted the exceedingly cryptic code underlying her guyed images: *The word as transformation (transform), unfolding (unfold); the language of signs as symbols in equals and multiplied; the power of pictures in essence and form as crystal, plant, animal and human…—the choice of two numbers, united and unfolded, determines the manner of form and shape. Therein lies the mystery that is the key to this revelation.*

The circle is fundamental. In her solitary orbit, Emma Kunz instinctively brought forth the *mandala* (Sanskrit for circle), that pancultural primal image,

from the deepest strata of the unconscious, a form found as much in nature, in the building blocks of matter, as in the outgrowths of the human psyche. This symbol has performed its gyrations from the Stone Age cave drawings in Transvaal (South Africa) to C. G. Jung's notebooks. As the commander of a British internment camp in Château-d'Œx between 1916 and 1918, Jung sketched a small circular drawing every morning. *On the basis of the pictures I was able to observe my psychical changes from day to day. Only gradually did I come to comprehend what the mandala actually is: formation—transformation, the eternal sustenance of eternal sense.*[3]

Drawing: what the psychoanalyst pursued in cryptogrammatic investigation of himself was addressed by Emma Kunz with unalloyed altruism. Her works were charts based on the pendulum's movement, used to assist in examining her patients' mental problems and physical weaknesses. Emma Kunz drew because she sensed immanent laws within herself that she could not ignore. The drawings have the character of models and plans which preclude affect. They record basic and efficient harmonic principles "without illustrating a clearcut theory," as Theo Kneubühler observes.[4] The realm of the unknown, she said, cannot be explored with the implements of reason. Only through intuition, vision, harmony with one's own body, precise attention to nature, observation of forms and their changes can contact with this realm be established.[5] Emma Kunz's pictures are, to quote Susan K. Langer's definition of art, "the active termination of a symbolic transformation of experience."[6]

Emma Kunz's drawings must have affected patients the way Jacques Lacan's mirror does a toddler, who, seeing itself for the first time, invents an imaginary picture of its body. In the swaying rhythm of the pendulum, her patients recognized themselves as webs of abstraction, seeing themselves more involved in space and in creation than they had ever dreamed possible.

The attention Emma Kunz has received abandons automated thought and strays through a labyrinth of speculative art theory. Oscillating between the universal and the individual soul, it feels its vertiginous, transcendental way, following a path that remains

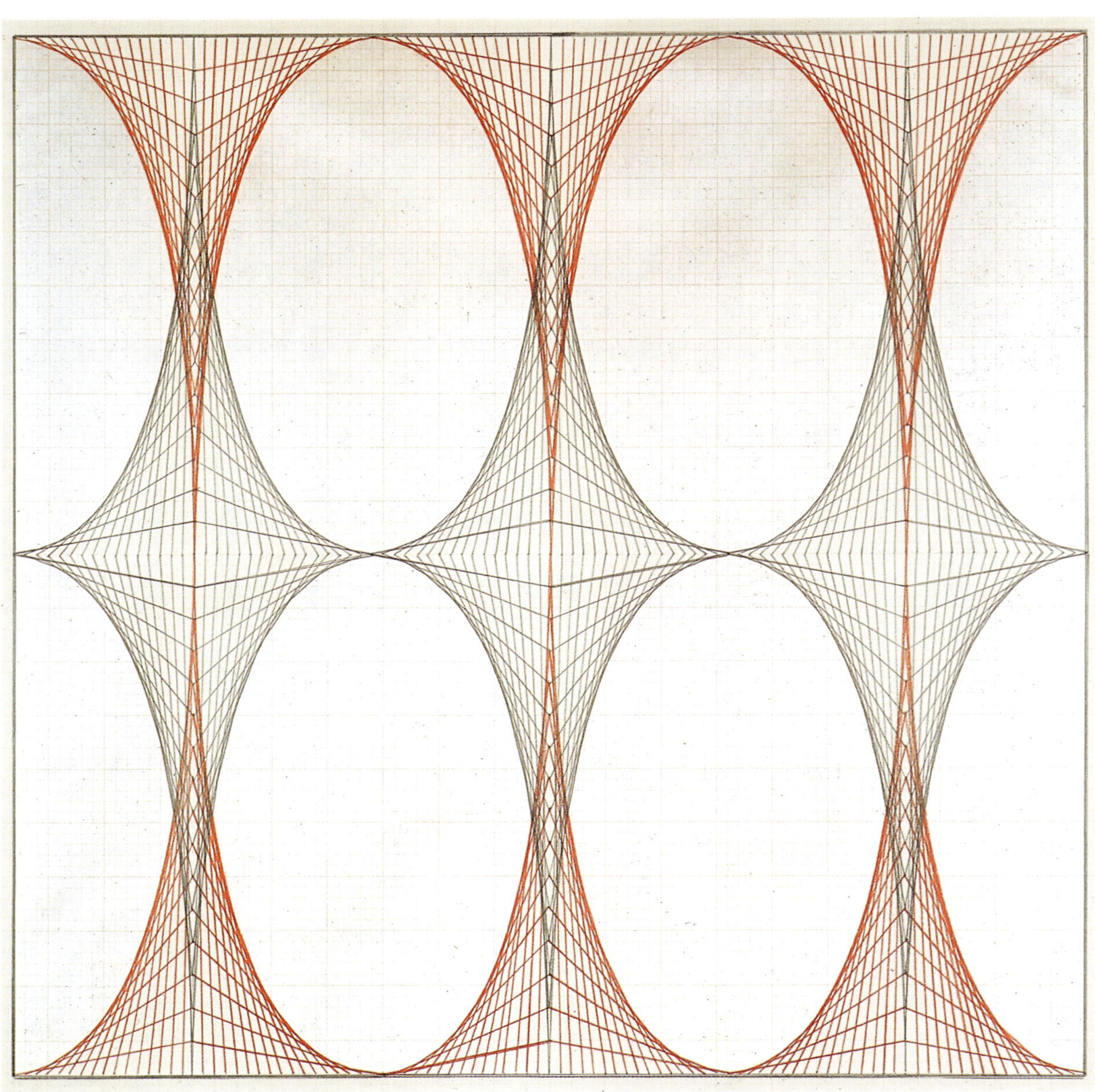

EMMA KUNZ, DREIFALTIGKEIT, Werk Nr. 009, nicht datiert, 101 x 101 cm / TRINITY, piece no. 009, undated, 39¾ x 39¾".

closed to the profane intellect. In the brochure for
"oh! cet écho!," an exhibition devoted to Emma Kunz
in 1992,[7] reference is made to the rhizome postulat-
ed by Deleuze and Guattari. The botanical metaphor
underscores the decentralized diversity so character-
istic of Emma Kunz's universe. *The rhizome is short-
term memory or anti-memory… It is a map. The map is not
defined; it keeps absorbing new changes. It can be drawn on
a wall, envisioned as a work of art or interpreted as a political act or meditation.*[8]

Given the esoteric fog that has settled around this
luminous figure, it is best to stay with the man whose
writings Emma Kunz loved to hear read aloud: "Philippus Aureolus Theophrastus Bombastus Paracelsus
von Hohenheim, the Luther of Medicine and our
greatest Swiss Physician."[9] In the sixteenth century,
Paracelsus promulgated a practical and yet speculative, spiritual and holistic physic, stressing the healing powers of the imagination, which included its
images and signatures. He believed it was possible to
"cast Mount Olympus into the Red Sea or to empty
the ocean on to Mount Etna."[10] Such spiritual feats
make the faithful more equal to God. Emma Kunz
was fairly equal. A believer, her relationship to Christ
seems to have been marked more by empathy than
adoration; on Good Friday she physically shared the
sufferings of the rabbi from Nazareth.

The healing powers of her work attenuate the art-
hermeneutic pros and cons. Her oeuvre neither
begins on paper nor does it stop at the edges. As Paracelsus defined it, the business of healing is the
noblest, highest, and freest of all the arts; Dürer
and Leonardo second his motion. As a healer and
researcher, Emma cultivated a large garden to produce her own supply of herbs for ointments and tinc-
tures. Infirmary medicine was part of the treatment
of St. Vitus' dancers, cataractous theologians, and
entangled fetuses. In 1942 the healer cured a boy of
polio. Today he is the trustee of her estate and more.
He is the living proof of her artistry; he is, in fact, the
work of art liberated by his lady Pygmalion.

Emma Kunz's drawings, as Widmer notes, have
become "art in spite of themselves," to be perceived
intrinsically in canonized, aesthetic terms, because
they are surrounded by artistic solitaires—Klee,
Malevich, Ad Reinhard—and because the mytholo-

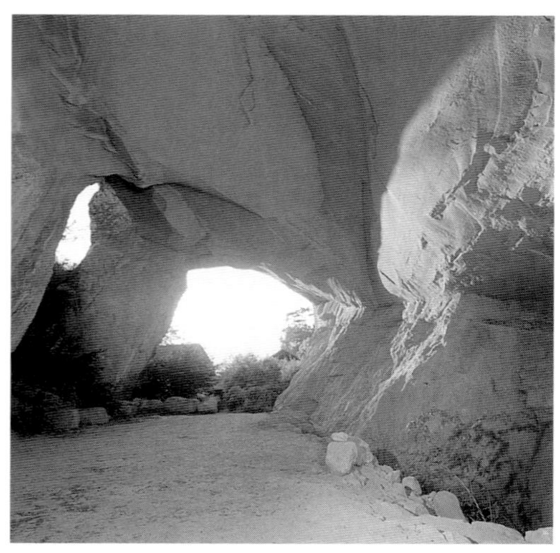

Emma-Kunz-Grotte, Würenlos /
The cave where Emma Kunz found Aion A,
Würenlos, Switzerland.

gies of abstraction and the "cases" of art brut (Adolf
Wölfli, Anton Müller, Louis Soutter, Aloïse Strübin)
have gone down in the history of twentieth century
art. Harald Szeemann, who worked with Widmer
on the 1976 Emma Kunz exhibition at the Musée
d'Art Moderne in Paris, refers to the "naïve construc-
tivists," to the visions of Auguste Herbin (1882–
1960), to the numerical, geometrical investigations
of Alfred Jensen (1903–1981), and to Joseph Beuys'
expanded concept of art. Emma Kunz herself found
only one formal reference: an illustrated newspaper
article by Professor Dr. Ginsburg, director of the
Mathematical Institute at New York's Yeshiva University. She was astonished to find there a picture entitled "The Beauty of the Mathematical Formula" that
duplicated one of her own drawings.

Penta did not lead an eventful life, but she was
a tranquil pole that made the world around her
gyrate, sprout, and grow. Once, in the presence of
a government chemist from St. Gall, she dangled
her pendulum from a spiral rod almost 25 inches
long and, with the pendulum swaying above her
marigolds, she instructed them to produce a certain
number of blossoming offspring. Lo and behold,
the polarized calendula obeyed with the docility of
Tarzan's elephants. Perfectly matter-of-fact and un-

assuming, Emma Kunz classified this miraculous datum as scientific research. In her laboratory, she had scientific equipment—a microscope, a Geiger counter. These she required only for confirmation; they were on call for the skeptics.

The curative visits radiated with ever more hope and cheer after Emma Kunz discovered the healing powers of a rock formation in Würenlos in 1942. There the grotto formed by the Roman quarries emanate strong, positive energies; salubrious vibrations pervade the visitor's entire being. Psychosonic energy is the amniotic fluid of this rocky uterus. We cross the grotto on a vitality path—just as in Lourdes—and following the cliff, we sense swelling "Bovis" values coursing through our bodies, our *chakras* open up, and we find ourselves immersed in the aura of spiritual impulses.

The quarry belongs to the family of the estate trustee. "I can cure your boy. I need a special powder that I will find in the immediate vicinity of your son's home."[11] The child recovered thanks to the "purified, refined, pulverized" Muschelkalk (a European limestone formed from shells) of his forefathers. Known as *Aion A*, it is still available today in pharmacies and drugstores. Emma Kunz recommended that home-builders use only those materials native to the region where they were born and raised. The same principle applied to food. When an ambassador sent by the mystic Sri Aurobindo (1872–1950) journeyed to Brittnau to invite the master Emma Kunz to come

to India, she declined. *All human beings should accept and carry out the tasks assigned to them within their own cultural context, should draw on its spiritual resources and work within its vibrations.*[12]

There are limits even for one who is unbounded. Her place was in Switzerland, Penta said. On an undated, hectographed flyer, a highschool teacher describes her oeuvre as a "special outgrowth of Swiss folk art," criticizing its appropriation by the international art business, for this, he fears, entails a "sellout of the homeland." In an artists' bar in Zurich, the rumor is heard that far, far away from Würenlos the Shah of Persia once expressed an interest in Emma Kunz's oeuvre.

Was it Bazon Brock[13] who questioned the point of showing European avant-garde art in the museums of Asia, at such a great remove from our own civilization? Hasn't a group of "eighty-niners" gathered around Botho Strauss's *Bocksgesang* (stag song)[14] to breath life into the choir that sings of a new, intrinsically Germanic spirituality? We autochthonous children of Helvetia are fortunate, we who successfully rub *Aion A* on our bodies because this is where we come from, we who will never again have to suffer from *tendovaginitis crepitans tibialis*, from the excruciating pains of *epicondylitis* or from insect bites[15] thanks to hip baths and compresses, we who can empathize and identify with Emma Kunz's universal geometry. We are not likely to find salvation in Philadelphia.

(Translation: Catherine Schelbert)

1) Heiny Widmer in: *Emma Kunz*, ex. cat. (Aarau, 1973), p. 11.
2) The full title reads *Neuartige Zeichnungsmethode. Gestaltung und Form als Mass, Rhythmus, Symbol und Wandlung von Zahl und Prinzip.*
3) Aniela Jaffe, *C. G. Jung. Bild und Wort* (Zurich, 1979), p. 78.
4) in: *Emma Kunz, Forscherin, Naturheilpraktikerin, Künstlerin*, edited by Emma-Kunz-Zentrum, Würenlos (Aarau: AT Verlag, 1993), p. 85. Theo Kneubühler is a well known art critic in Switzerland and german speaking Europe.
5) *Emma Kunz, 1892–1963* (Würenlos: Emma-Kunz-Zentrum, 1994), p. 50.
6) Susanne K. Langer, *Philosophy in a New Key. A Study in the Symbolism of Reason, Rite, and Art* (Cambridge: Harvard University Press, 1978³), p. 45.
7) *oh! cet écho!* (Paris: Centre Culturel Suisse, 1992).
8) Gilles Deleuze & Félix Guattari, *Tausend Plateaus* (Berlin, 1992), p. 19.

9) Complete name assembled by Parcelsus's biographer, Dr. Hans Locher, in 1851, quoted from: Pirmin Meier, *Paracelsus. Arzt und Prophet* (Zurich, 1993).
10) Ibid., p. 171.
11) *Emma Kunz, 1892–1963* (Würenlos: Emma-Kunz-Zentrum, 1994), p. 7.
12) Ibid., p. 26.
13) Since the sixties, German publicist and philosopher Bazon Brock (b. 1936) has been propagating a concept of aesthetics that is basically applicable to all of the sciences. This generalist has mastered the practice of mediation like no other (Action Teaching).
14) Botho Strauss (b. 1944), Berlin-based writer of "Anschwellender Bocksgesang," an essay on the failure of left-wing utopias, has become the controversial spokesman of Germany's right-wing intellectuals.
15) Reports on the practical use and application of *Aion A*.

Tony Oursler, born 1957 in New York, lives and works in New York / geboren 1957 in New York, lebt und arbeitet in New York.

Raymond Pettibon, born 1957 in Tucson, Arizona, lives and works in Hermosa Beach near Los Angeles / geboren in Tucson, Arizona, lebt und arbeitet in Hermosa Beach bei Los Angeles.

Thomas Schütte, geboren 1954 in Oldenburg, lebt und arbeitet in Düsseldorf / born 1954 in Oldenburg, lives and works in Dusseldorf, Germany.

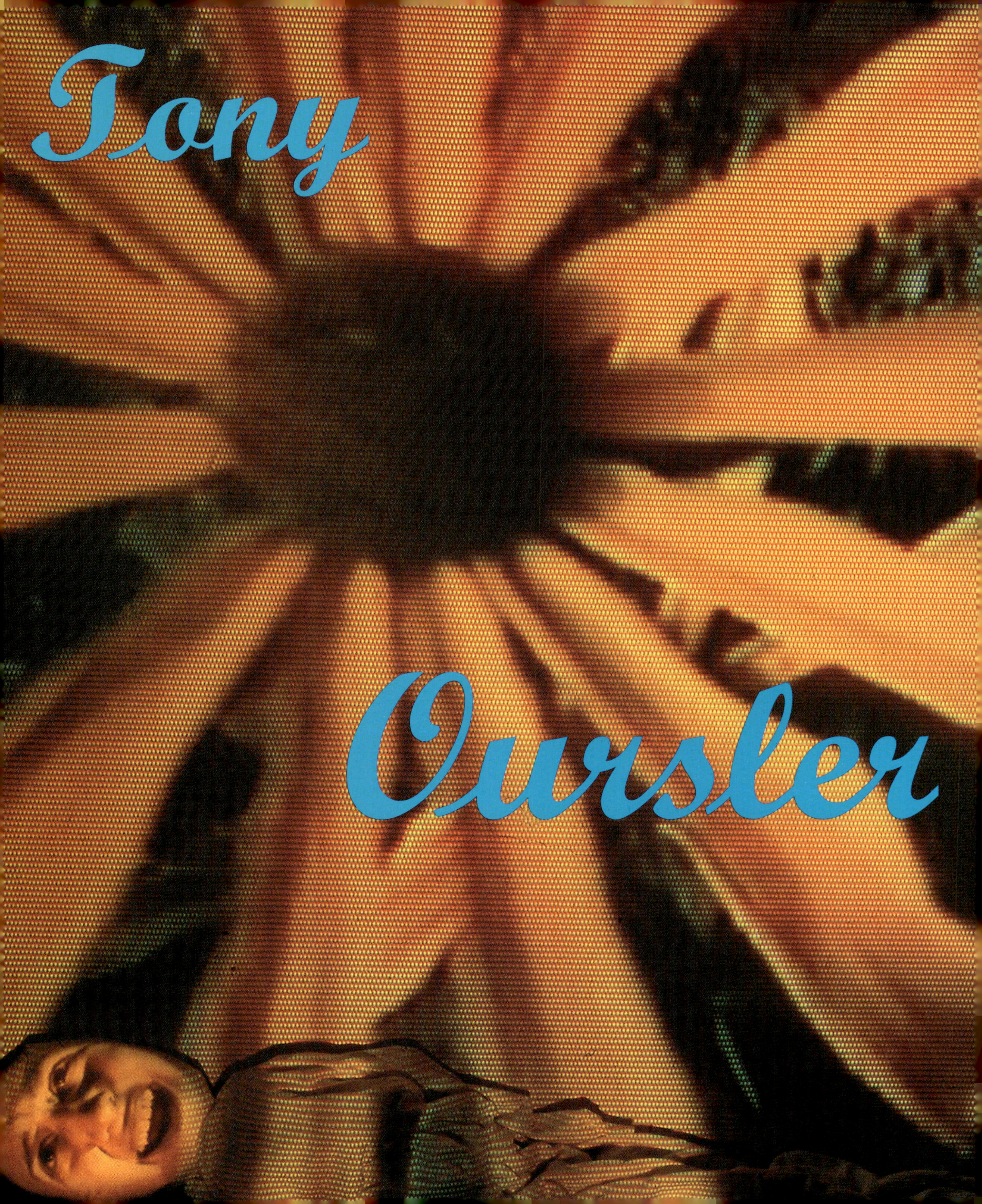

Tony
Oursler

In the Green Room

Tony Oursler and Tracy Leipold*
in Conversation with Louise Neri

Louise Neri: How do you remember the evolution of your work, the practical steps you have taken and the discoveries that these lead to along the way? You started with almost feature-length videos, and that medium slowly transformed into images through your experimenting with simultaneity and fragmentation.

Tony Oursler: I've always been interested in things which are on the verge of falling apart but which still maintain their original quality. It's a constant battle because I have a pretty low boredom threshold. At the beginning, when I started looking at Structuralist films, I just couldn't stand all that repetition.

LN: So, how did this affect your early work?

TO: I only made about one tape a year—such as THE LONER (1980), SPIN OUT (1983), EVOL (1984)—because they were really hard to make and it took a lot of energy and time. When I wanted to make SPIN OUT, for example, I didn't have any money and I didn't have any space. So I had to make all the sets really tiny. I'd fold up my bed, set up the shot, and work. EVOL was like a Busby Berkeley piece—it was shot on a big soundstage in Buffalo, and I hired lots of local teenagers and flew all my friends up there. But for the editing, I was put under extreme time pressure by the producer. In both films, the sound track is extremely layered, obsessive. You can't take it all in in one shot. That was my attempt at breaking down time, to make these things so dense that they would be true to the experience of plugging into someone's mind.

I've always made videotapes along with everything else, and you'd think "Oh, maybe what he really wants to do is make movies or T.V. shows." But, by 1991, I had decided that I didn't want to. The difference between being an artist and being a filmmaker is the ratio of ideas to work. The ideas just aren't in the movies. Of course there are some movies that come close to art, but...

LN: Kubrick probably comes closest to the idea of mainstream filmmaker as artist. He's audacious in his use of time; in *2001: A Space Odyssey*, a scene can run twenty-five minutes without anything really happening. It's very trancelike. Similarly, your work can be apprehended in a split second, but the longer you spend with it the more apparent its formal subtleties and complexities become. Formally and temporally it behaves like painting or sculpture or drawing. It activates the same mechanisms of contemplation in the viewer.

TO: Yes. When I wrote the scripts for some of the first figures, I toyed with how they would function as installations. My first attempts were weird because they were text-heavy, with somewhat linear progressions relating to narrative cinema and its different genres—horror, sci-fi, softcore porn, and so on. I arrived at the next step through this kind of deconstruction of the "screened world" and its rituals and how it all connects to the psyche. I dropped the linear deconstructions to pursue the cataloguing of emotional states.

LN: Why are you drawn to such expressionistic emotions?

TO: Just like some artists like certain colors. This raw stuff is important to me and Tracy's interpretation of it is so amazing. I attenuate these emotions

* *Tracy Leipold is an actress who collaborates regularly with Tony Oursler.*

like musical notes, just to see what happens. They are worked almost to the point where they fall apart. That's how they transcend being a special effect in a movie, or part of a good performer's repertoire, or an insult from someone in the street. When I got Tracy to weep, that was the beginning of it. Emotion passed from being something that you would believe into another realm.

Our culture is obsessed with the whole horror-sex-violence thing. It's a weird form of refinement, like bonsai. We love to watch it, and I'm obsessed by the fact that we love to watch it.

LN: So, how do you develop a concrete expression of fear or neurosis? By steeping yourself in it?

TO: A lot of the later pieces have been written through this new process I've been following. I'll turn on a couple of different T.V. sets and radios all at the same volume and I'll write with that on for hours, channel-surfing continually. A mix of subjects results so that I can't tell whether I'm thinking it or it's just coming in, all these different voices which are really one voice. I hit on this method at the tail-end of my interest in multiple personality disorder (MPD). I had been making doubles, two figures sitting and talking, big figures and little figures interacting in various ways, but I'd always wanted to do a cluster. One of the books I read on MPD was titled *The Flock*. I liked that idea of all these personalities buzzing around in someone's head. That's how the script for FLOCK (1996) got done.

Tracy performed the script using various voices. I took that video footage and edited it, using a looping process to make different-sized faces on the screen at the same time. It was very intuitive. I'd just kind of balance the faces on the screen because they were all coming from one projector. I got very involved in the editing, and how the faces work together like a crowd. I used to go to a restaurant or a bar and record the sound; it sounds incredibly played back. You hear fragments of sentences, but it's just this din, a babble—the stuff of life.

I had to work in reverse for the sculptures, because I had to fit the sculptures to the video. The editing process had defined how many figures there would be and how they would relate to each other. My favorite figure is the tiny one whose head is made up of about twenty-five pixels. That one is something I'd really like to work more on if I could, because it goes back to the idea of things that barely exist.

LN: How did you come to this idea of fitting "templates" of the temporal and the figural together seamlessly?

TO: Figures featured prominently in the earlier videotapes, and then around 1989 the figures leapt out into space. I had found this beautiful book of photographs of New England scarecrows and that did it. I wanted to bypass the entire history of figuration. The veil of video separated these puppets or half-bodies from my having to treat them as sculpture. They lost some of their magic when they came off the screen, because when you looked into the screen, they were created more in your head than anywhere else.

LN: Scarecrows are totems, talismans.

TO: Exactly—this thing is going to save your crops, or scare off the bogey man. It's directly connected to the question of why we have art to begin with, why we have performers. It's important to look at these things in folk culture to work out how figurative problems are solved by people who aren't inculcated with all these aesthetic concerns.

So, I went to thrift stores and bought suits and tried a hundred different ways of manipulating them, to see the range of states they could attain, from suit to human.

They were very Frankensteinian. I was stuffing and sewing figures, but the problem was that the elegance and movement inherent in the suits was convincing, but when I put faces to them, they became too static. So, the first figures had no heads. I made them as surveillance pieces. There were these headless figures in the gallery and one had a lens coming out of its fly like a penis, another was draped over a monitor that was a close-circuit system with camera. They were about power situations; one figure was watching and had the power of the camera, another was seeing itself on the monitor. The blood or energy flowing between these headless figures consisted of surveillance and conduits. I did things like that until I discovered the miniature liquid crystal diode (LCD) projectors.

LN: So you went straight into making the heads through video?

TO: Only after I had tried several other things, like the suits with matching monochrome heads, just shapes with nothing on them. When I finally got into the projectors, the heads started to take over. The first figures I made were anatomically correct but, as the video became more and more important, the heads got bigger and bigger and the bodies became more and more collapsed. This happened really fast. With F/X PLOTTER (1992), for example, you had to look closely to discern the arms and legs; it was a completely deflated suit.

There are some pieces that are less well known where I projected full figures onto parts of another figure, such as BIGGER (HEM) (1994). It was about imagining another self in your stomach, or nipping at your heels. In SYSTEM FOR DRAMATIC FEEDBACK (1994), the dummies had real penises projected onto them, getting erections and then deflating. But I noticed that as soon as you get away from the head, it's much more difficult for people to relate to them.

LN: Without the face, the disembodied limb seems more pornographic; not because it's genital, but because the body is reduced to faceless parts.

TO: Then I wondered what would happen if the bodies vanished completely. So I guess that's how I arrived at SUBMERGED (1996), which does away with the body altogether. When I was working on the eye pieces, I thought that I would be able to get the same emotional effects as before. But I discovered that the eye is a reptilian organ: It's the face—the skin around the eyes, the mouth, the tilt of the head— that is emotive. As soon as the eyes are disembodied and projected onto those spheres they're devoid of emotion. At first it was disturbing, but then I really liked it, because it brought the pieces into a hypna-gogic state. They became just light-measuring organs, with this peristaltic motion.

LN: This idea of progressive disembodiment is fasci-nating in your work. In narrative film, the logic of an emotion depends on the body and its physical and psychological environment, but you remove the body, and with it, its environment and the narrative. How much further can you take this idea before it falls apart?

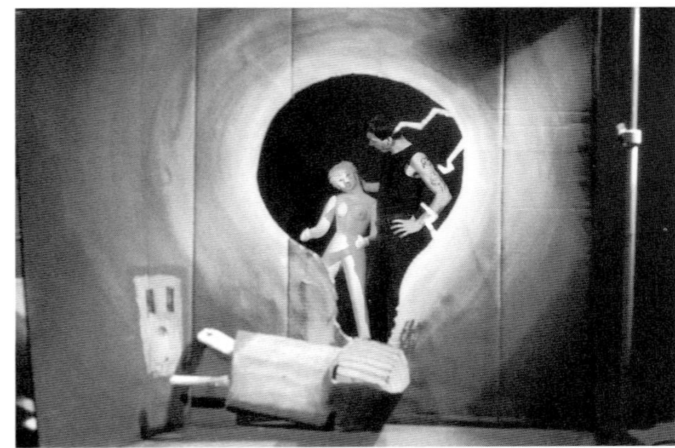

TONY OURSLER, SPHÈRES D'INFLUENCE (LUMIÈRE NOCTURNE), 1985, production still, Centre Pompidou, Paris.

TO: In TALKING LIGHT (1996), Tracy's bodily pres-ence is reduced to a single light source. And now I'm working on a large piece for the San Diego Museum of Contemporary Art, a glass room with a single light source inside, and a soundtrack outside. It will stay on all day and all night.

LN: God, how annoying. Tracy, when Tony directs you, do you know what you're doing?

Tracy Leipold: I don't, usually. If I'm just sort of going along, one step beyond myself, that's when it works.

LN: Are the takes quick?

TL: Generally, yes, they're continuous takes of about ten minutes which peak in the middle; this arc is a natural rhythm for me.

LN: Is this some kind of method acting in which you access stored emotions? It seems that you must have certain formulae, because the form is so evolved, so perfectly balanced.

TL: I warm up, and it builds faster and faster, and then I let it drop; I think that also has to do with the text. More and more, the levels and peaks of the per-formance are dictated by the text and how I interpret it. In the earlier pieces, it was more about how I per-formed the process of an emotion. For the pieces that were made up of different emotions, Tony and

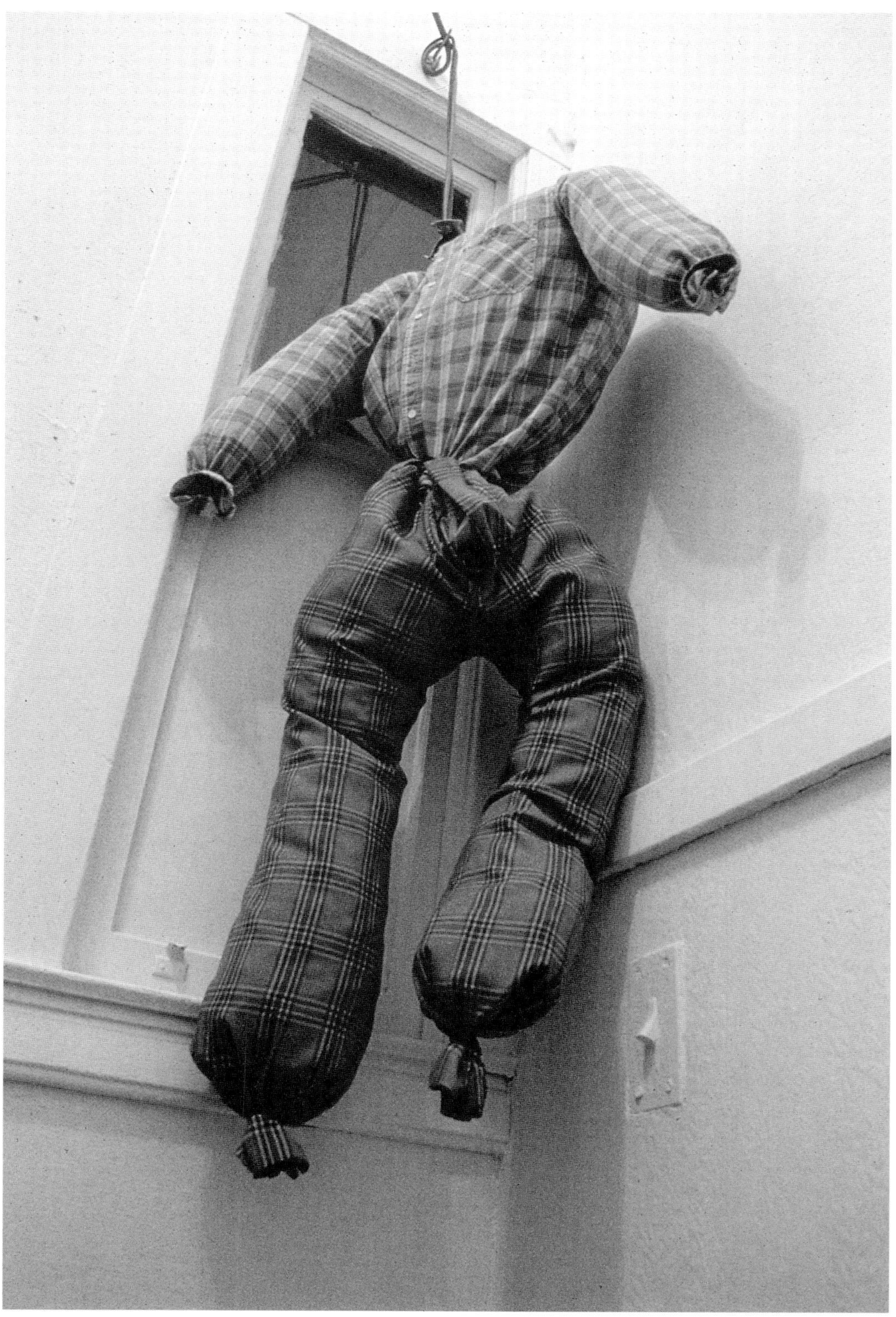

*TONY OURSLER, DUMMY 1, 1991,
detail, cloth, camera, monitor, human scale / Detail, Kleider, Kamera, Monitor, lebensgross.*

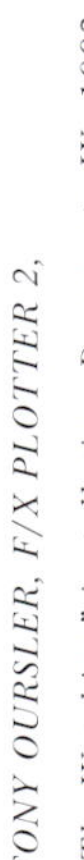

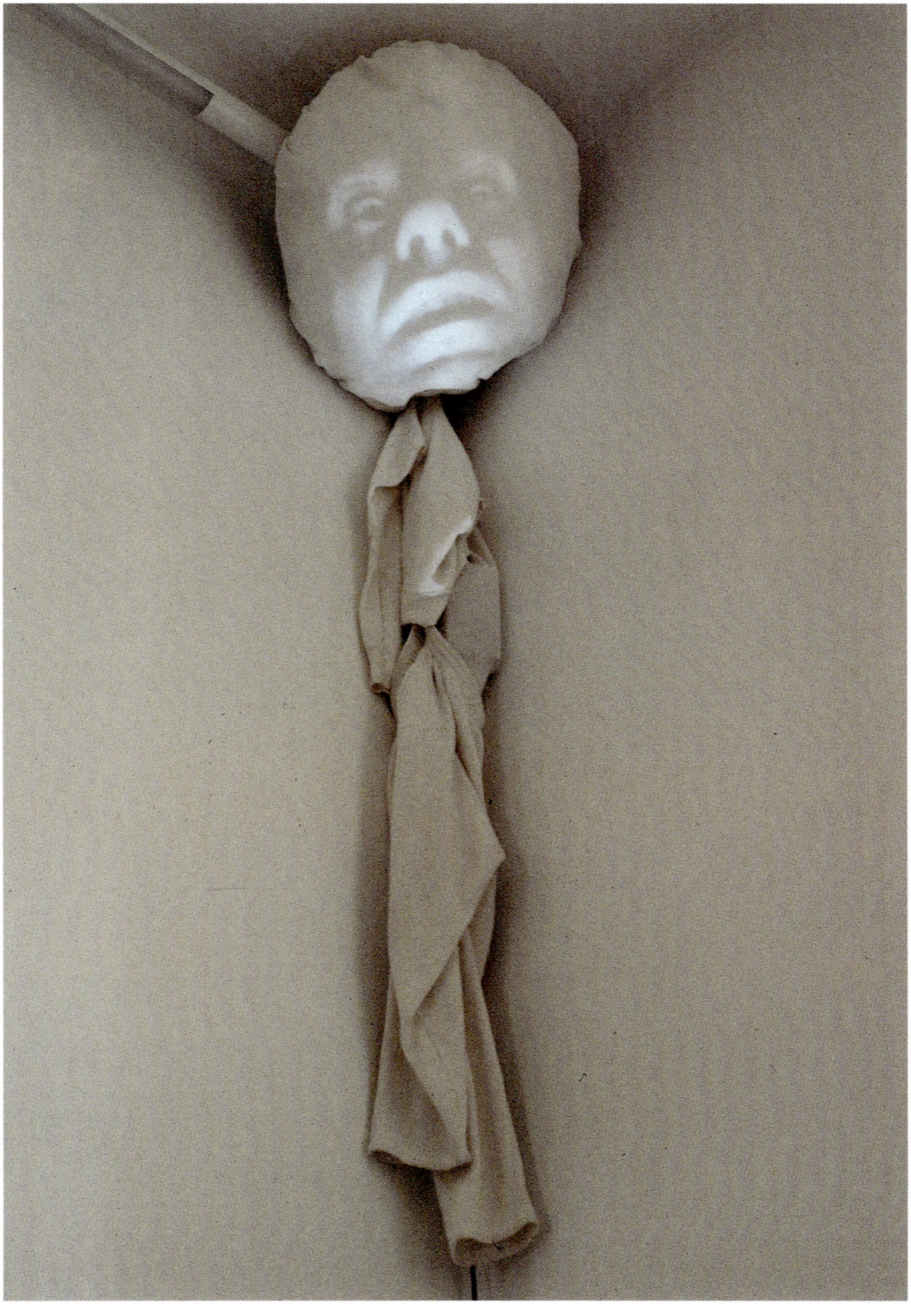

TONY OURSLER, F/X PLOTTER 2,
"The Watching" installation, Documenta IX, 1992.

I talked about how "long" each emotion should be and where the line was between, say, eroticism and anger. During the take I started flipping back and forth between two different emotions and Tony would do this thing with his hand to indicate the moment at which I should make the flip. So he was largely responsible for the dynamic of the take.

LN: Tony, are your decisions intuitive, is there some kind of light meter or framing device in your brain?

TO: As a performer myself, I know that, as well as worrying about the technical stuff, you have to keep in mind exactly where you're going with the performance. Sometimes it's one too many tasks, and to have instant feedback, as I do with Tracy, is another level of control that enables freedom.

LN: And a discipline, having to get it all in the take. Not having second chances, being bound by economy.

TO: That's the difference between installation and cinema. I eventually realized that we had a lot more flexibility than we had originally thought. The camera extends and amplifies time and the presence of time. So people tend to speed their brains up. Cinema implies compression because it's entertainment. Cinema is the compression of the thousands of hours performed by the huge pyramid of participants—director, the screenwriter, the actors, the grips, and so on—into an hour and a half. That's why it's so exciting for us. Whereas my work, since it's not meant to "entertain" or be hypertime, is, in a sense, "inanimate."

LN: Let's say you're working with dramatic "frequencies" rather than dramatic narratives. And intrinsic to your sculptural structure is Tracy's projection of those high-keyed frequencies which become cathartic.

TO: Sometimes I force Tracy to keep doing the same thing.

TL: There are times when the ball starts rolling, it keeps going and going and then it stops.

TO: You arrive at some of those expressions by picturing something horrible happening to you or to someone else, and then you react to it. As you make the sound, hearing yourself do it makes you even more emotional. So there's a feedback process happening inside your body.

TL: I don't know that I ever really try to picture anything from the start, but hearing my own voice makes the pictures happen. When you really hear yourself scream, it seems disembodied.

TO: So you are dissociating! Just as I suspected.

TL: It's all feedback.

LN: The work is filled with equivalences: the visual aspect, the aural aspect, the melding of those two aspects with a third in the process of grafting a temporal, pixellated image onto a solid form. Everything is looped and confounded in this tight web of production. And if you lose one beat, the whole momentum, and thus the whole form, would collapse.

TO: Exactly. It's the bare minimum that's needed to keep it together.

LN: This formal tension is almost immaterial.

TO: I do think of these pieces as being immaterial. When I first made them I was struck with how the figure seemed to have popped its head through into another dimension, and yet somehow simultaneously remained here. We could see the figure, but the figure couldn't see us. It was experiencing certain things, and exposing us to them, but we were blind to what was causing these experiences. That to me is where Tracy's performance comes in. It's a space that no one else can get into, because where it really happens is inside one's own head.

LN: You try to touch it and it dematerializes. Do people ever try and touch your pieces?

TO: Yes.

TL: Yes, they do.

LN: That's what I love about FLOCK: It's so real. Children believe in fairies and want their dolls to talk back. And there they are!

TO: I'd love to make a series of dolls for kids. But the technology required would make them so expensive.

LN: In a few years there will be probably be rear-projection equipment small enough to be hidden inside the heads. But now the projector's presence in the sculpture reenacts your presence as director and cinematographer, the moment of your filming Tracy's performance.

TO: Also, if the projectors were not there, it would move into another level of magic instead of performance. It was something I battled with in the beginning, all this apparatus. But it's like Kabuki theater where there are three or four guys operating a flower or a butterfly or a cloud; at first it's distracting, but eventually you stop taking any notice and the setup becomes invisible. It was like that with the eye pieces. The eye is a mechanism that works like a little theater, or a camera, which are pretty much the same thing—it's just a question of which way the light is going.

LN: You said that what you and Tracy first did together was "sublingual," very emotive and not tightly scripted, and then the scripts got longer and longer. Why did that happen?

TO: When we started working together I didn't like the way the text was coming out, because I was doing the text and Tracy was doing the emoting. So then we started bringing in a layer of random phrases over the mix of emotive texts and sayings. Tracy would say "God dammit," or "Get outta my face!" or start laughing, whipping that stuff into rhythms. One of my favorite ones was a gangster, very sarcastic. I remember seeing these two little kids watching it in Geneva. Tracy was saying, "Fuck off! Ba-da-bing, ba-da-boom!" and they were loving it. Tracy, how did we do those?

TL: You would be listening, and you would think of something and whisper it to me. There would be a few lines, and some sort of emotional process indicated in between.

TO: They were very spontaneous because the mikes we were using were so lo-fi that I could actually just whisper the next line right there. They were about seeing how far you could go without really using language, just a series of lines or phrases punctuated with laughing or growling. They were really important to our development, because—as we were saying about live editing—they were about things that wouldn't generally go together.

LN: How did you and Tracy move from the sublingual idea into exploring multiple characters?

TO: We did a piece called JUDY (1994) where Tracy was projected severally onto an environment of objects, as a mutable character who was broken up and dialoguing with itself. That was where the idea of having one cipher for many different characters began. The scripts that came after that were frag-

mented, so Tracy invented these different voices at my request, starting with the highest voice she could do, and then the lowest voice, which was kind of androgynous. So, whereas before the text had been broken up by, say, a kissing sound or laughter, these texts were broken up by different characters. So there was the high voice, the low voice…

TL: … the slow voice, the urgent voice.

TO: Then I asked you to try to talk with your tongue sticking out, and that became the retarded voice. The glossolalia voice came about at around the same time as the animal voices.

LN: So you are fascinated by channeling or "directing the unconscious," as you call it.

TO: I'm interested that the multiple personality consciousness creates many characters to protect the core identity, attempting to invent and control its own life, rather than just being pulled by Freudian or Jungian strings. It's a model for a new consciousness.

LN: So, you are safely exploring this idea with Tracy in terms of an aesthetic reflection on these hyperbolic, crazy situations. But what about the fact that Tracy claims she doesn't know where these voices come from, that she feels completely ambivalent about seeing all these versions of herself out there?

TO: Tracy, do you know where the glossolalia voice comes from?

TL: There's no way I could ever know. It's just me, it just happens. It's an imitation of something I've heard, my imagining what it would be like, just playing. A lot of these voices that I'm imitating are voices I've heard on T.V.

LN: But have you—as Tony obviously has—researched glossolalia?

TL: There was an event in my childhood at a Baptist church involving my sister. I remember all of a sudden being surrounded by people and she was gone. I looked up and she was in a white robe sitting on the stage, about to be dunked in the water. I couldn't hear anything she was saying, but I could see that her mouth was moving, and people said she was speaking in tongues. I don't think I had ever heard anyone imitate what speaking-in-tongues sounds like or actual documentation of it, only that it sounds garbled. So I guess I channeled my sister.

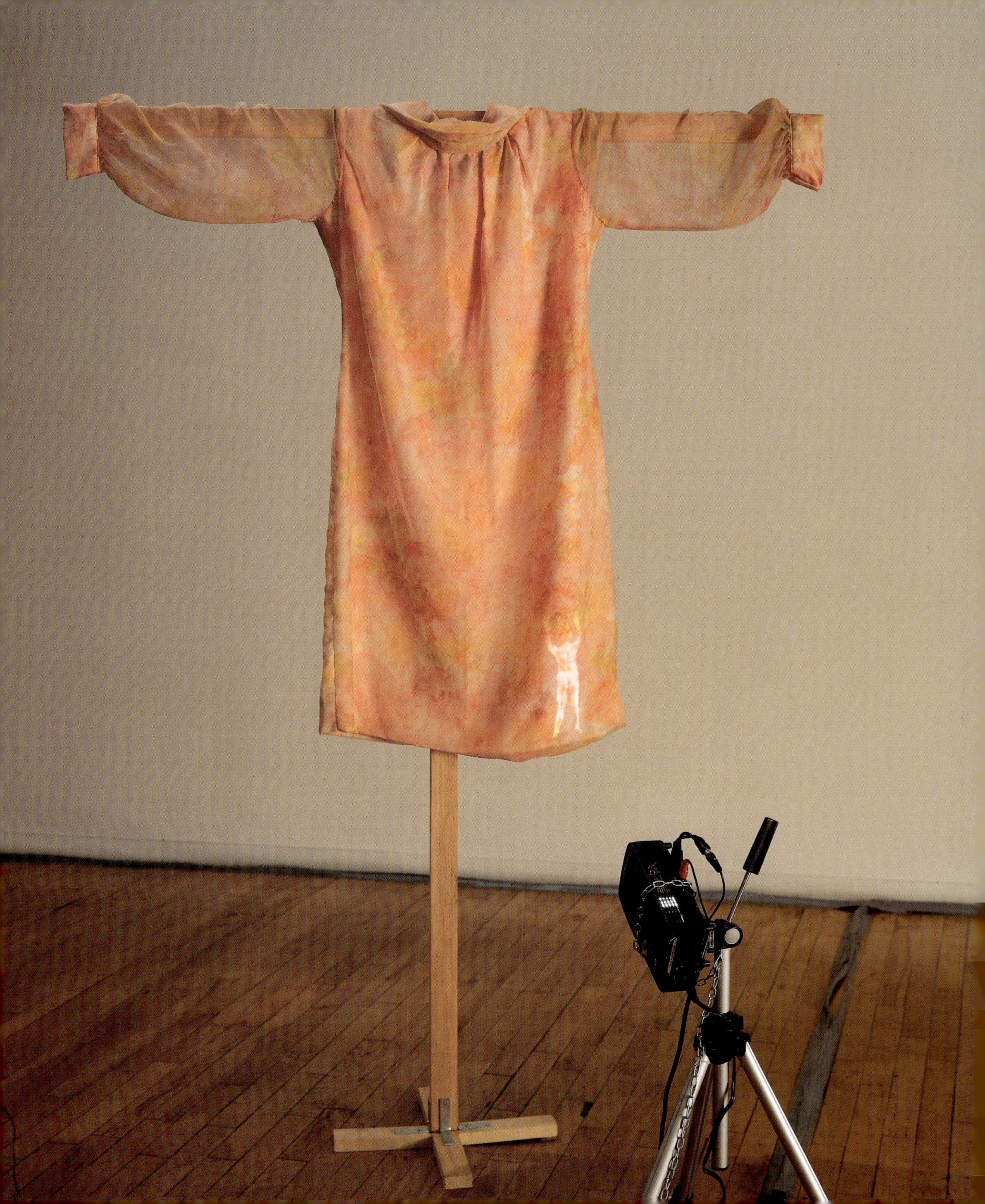

Hinter der Bühne

Tony Oursler und Tracy Leipold*
im Gespräch mit Louise Neri

Louise Neri: Wie sind deine Arbeiten, wie ist dein Werk entstanden? Weisst du noch, welche konkreten Schritte du unternommen hast und zu welchen Entdeckungen sie dich geführt haben? Du hast mit Videos in Spielfilmlänge begonnen, und diese haben sich langsam in Einzelbilder verwandelt durch deine Experimente der Gleichzeitigkeit und der Fragmentierung.

Tony Oursler: Mich interessierten immer die Dinge, die drauf und dran waren auseinanderzufallen, deren ursprüngliche Eigenschaften aber noch vorhanden waren. Es ist ein dauernder Kampf, denn ich langweile mich sehr schnell. Als ich begann, mir strukturalistische Filme anzuschauen, gingen mir die dauernden Wiederholungen schlicht auf die Nerven.

LN: Welchen Einfluss hatte das auf deine frühen Arbeiten?

TO: Ich machte nur etwa ein Video pro Jahr – wie THE LONER (1980), SPIN OUT (1983), EVOL (1984) –, weil es wirklich schwierig war, sie herzustellen, es brauchte sehr viel Zeit und Energie. Ich suchte eine neue Art des Erzählens und der Wahrnehmung, ich wollte eine Anti-Hollywood-Ästhetik entwickeln, die mehr mit dem zu tun hatte, was wir wirklich denken und sehen. Als ich zum Beispiel SPIN OUT machte,

hatte ich kein Geld und viel zu wenig Platz. So musste der Szenenaufbau immer auf kleinstem Raum stattfinden. Ich klappte mein Bett zusammen, bereitete eine Aufnahme vor und begann mit der Arbeit. EVOL war wie ein aufwendiges Show-Szenario: Es wurde in einem grossen Studio in Buffalo aufgenommen, und ich warb vor Ort haufenweise Teenager an und flog alle meine Freunde ein. Aber bei der Montage setzte mich der Produzent unter enormen Zeitdruck. In beiden Filmen ist der Ton äusserst vielschichtig und eindringlich. Man macht das eigentlich nicht alles in einem Durchgang. Ich versuchte Zeit zu sparen, indem ich die Dinge so dicht aufeinander folgen liess, dass es wirkte, als hätte man direkt jemandem das Hirn angezapft.

Ich habe immer Videos gemacht, egal was ich sonst noch tat, deshalb könnte man meinen, dass ich eigentlich am liebsten Filme oder Fernsehshows machen würde, aber dem ist nicht so. 1991 war mir klargeworden, dass ich genau dies **nicht** wollte. Der Unterschied zwischen der Arbeit des Künstlers und jener des Filmemachers liegt in der Distanz von Idee und Werk. Das Denken kommt im Film nicht zum Tragen. Natürlich gibt es Filme, die beinahe Kunst sind, aber...

LN: Kubrick entspricht wahrscheinlich am ehesten der Vorstellung eines erfolgreichen Filmemachers, der zugleich Künstler ist. Er ist kühn im Umgang mit der Zeit; in *2001: A Space Odyssey* gibt es Szenen, die

* *Tracy Leipold ist Schauspielerin und arbeitet regelmässig mit Tony Oursler zusammen.*

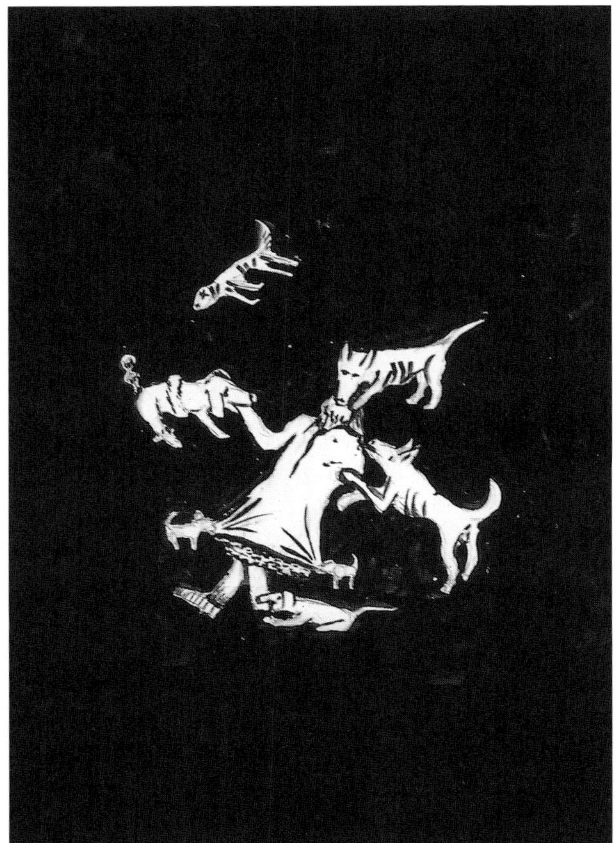

fünfundzwanzig Minuten dauern, ohne dass etwas Nennenswertes passiert. Es ist ein tranceähnlicher Zustand. Genauso kann man eine deiner Arbeiten in einem Sekundenbruchteil erfassen, aber je mehr Zeit man damit zubringt, desto deutlicher wird ihre formale Raffinesse und Komplexität. Hinsichtlich Form und Zeit funktioniert sie ähnlich wie ein Gemälde, eine Skulptur oder eine Zeichnung. Sie setzt beim Betrachter dieselben gedanklichen Mechanismen in Gang.

TO: Ja. Als ich die Skripts für einige meiner ersten Figuren schrieb, spielte ich damit, wie sie als Installationen funktionieren würden. Meine ersten Versuche waren ziemlich seltsam, weil sie zu textlastig ausfielen und quasi eine lineare Fortsetzung des narrativen Films und seiner verschiedenen Genres – Horror, Science-fiction, Softporno usw. – waren. Der nächste Schritt war eine Art von Dekonstruktion der «Welt des Bildschirms und der Filmleinwand» und

ihrer Rituale und psychischen Zusammenhänge. Ich liess die lineare Dekonstruktion fallen zugunsten einer Katalogisierung emotionaler Zustände.

LN: Weshalb fühlst du dich zu so heftigen emotionalen Ausbrüchen hingezogen?

TO: Aus demselben Grund, wie manche Künstler gewisse Farben bevorzugen. Dieses rohe Material ist wichtig für mich, und Tracys Interpretation ist einfach hinreissend. Ich arrangiere diese Gefühle wie Musiknoten, einfach um zu sehen, was passiert. Ich bearbeite sie beinah bis zur Zerstörung. Dadurch können sie zu einem Spezialeffekt im Film oder zum Repertoire-Bestandteil eines guten Schauspielers oder zur Beleidigung eines Passanten werden. Es begann damit, dass ich Tracy zum Weinen brachte. Die Gefühle hörten auf, glaubwürdig zu sein, und erhielten eine neue Dimension.

Unsere Kultur ist ganz besessen vom Thema Horror/Sex/Gewalt. Wir sehen das offenbar gern, und die Tatsache, dass wir das tun, lässt mich nicht los.

LN: Wie erarbeitest du den konkreten Ausdruck einer Angst oder Neurose? Indem du dich selbst in einen solchen Zustand hinein versetzt?

TO: Viele der neueren Arbeiten habe ich auf ganz neue Art geschrieben. Ich mache das seit einiger Zeit so: Ich schalte mehrere Fernseh- und Radioapparate gleichzeitig ein, alle gleich laut, und schreibe dann stundenlang, während ich laufend die Sender wechsle. Daraus ergibt sich ein Themensalat, bei dem ich nicht mehr unterscheiden kann, was ich denke und was von aussen dazugekommen ist, all die verschiedenen Stimmen sind letztlich eine Stimme. Diese Methode ist ein Resultat meiner Beschäftigung mit der multiplen Persönlichkeit. Ich hatte Doppelgängerpaare gemacht, zwei Figuren, die dasassen und redeten, grosse Figuren und kleine, die auf verschiedene Weise miteinander kommunizierten, aber ich

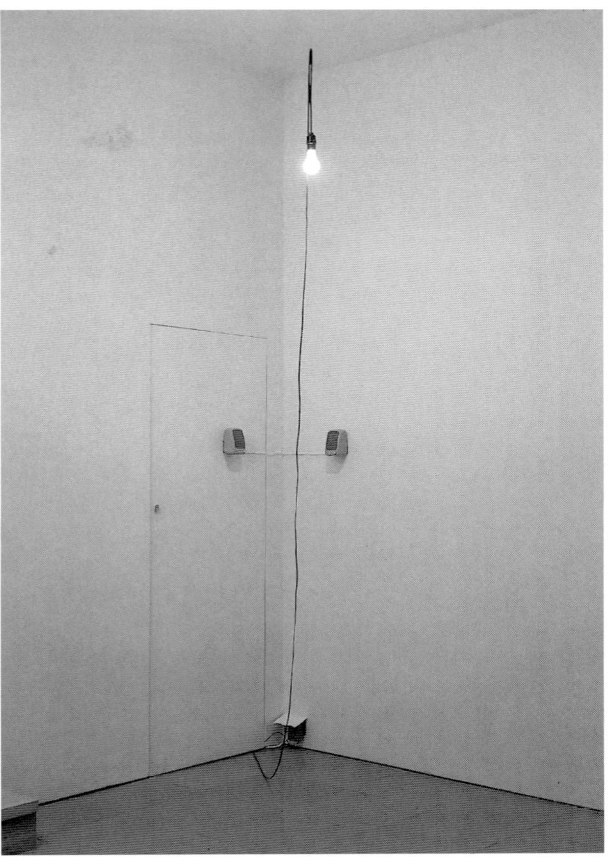

TONY OURSLER, TALKING LIGHT, 1996,
light bulb and cable, speaker system, 138¾ x 27½ x 47¼"
(installation variable) / SPRECHENDES LICHT,
Glühbirne und Kabel, Lautsprecheranlage, 352,5 x 70 x 120 cm
(variable Installation). (PHOTO: STEPHEN WHITE)

hatte schon lange eine Gruppe machen wollen, die als ein Ganzes funktionierte. Eines der Bücher über die multiple Persönlichkeit hiess *The Flock* (Die Herde). Die Vorstellung von all diesen Persönlichkeiten in einem einzigen Kopf gefiel mir. So entstand das Drehbuch zu FLOCK (1996).

Tracy sprach den Text und setzte dabei verschiedene Stimmen ein. Ich nahm dieses Video als Ausgangsprodukt und bearbeitete es, ich verwendete eine Schleifentechnik, die es ermöglichte, verschieden grosse Gesichter gleichzeitig auf den Bildschirm zu projizieren. Das Ganze war sehr intuitiv. Ich richtete einfach die Gesichter irgendwie auf den Schirm aus, weil sie alle vom selben Projektor kamen. Ich war fasziniert von dieser Arbeit und davon, wie die Gesichter zusammen als Horde funktionierten. Ich ging jeweils in ein Restaurant oder eine Bar und zeichnete die Geräusche dort auf; es klingt unglaublich, wenn man das abspielt. Man versteht einzelne Gesprächsfetzen, aber das Ganze ist nur ein Geraune, ein «Rhabarber» – das wahre Leben, halt.

Bei den Skulpturen musste ich den Prozess umkehren, weil ich die Skulpturen dem Video anpassen musste. Durch die Montage war die Zahl der Figuren und ihr Verhältnis zueinander bereits festgelegt. Meine Lieblingsfigur ist die winzige, deren Kopf etwa durch fünfundzwanzig Pixel wiedergegeben wird. Sie ist etwas, was ich, wenn möglich, wirklich gern weiter ausarbeiten würde, denn sie geht zurück auf meine Idee von Dingen, die nur am Rand des Verschwindens existieren.

LN: Wie kamst du darauf, das zeitliche Nacheinander in ein räumliches Nebeneinander überzuführen?

TO: In den frühen Videos spielten die Figuren die Hauptrolle, und erst später, etwa ab 1989, begannen sie den Raum ausserhalb zu erobern. Ich war auf die-

ses wunderschöne Buch mit Photos von amerikanischen Vogelscheuchen gestossen, und das gab den Ausschlag. Ich wollte die ganze Geschichte der bildlichen Gestaltung kurzschliessen. Der Videoschleier legte sich über diese Puppen oder Körperfragmente und verhinderte so, dass ich sie als Skulpturen behandeln musste. Ein bisschen von ihrer Magie ging verloren, als sie den Bildschirm verliessen, denn solange man in den Bildschirm schaute, existierten sie mehr in den Köpfen der Betrachter als irgendwo sonst.

LN: Vogelscheuchen sind Totems, Talismane.

TO: Genau – dieses Ding schützt deine Pflanzen oder verscheucht böse Geister. Es hat ganz direkt mit dem Ursprung der Kunst zu tun und mit dem Ursprung des Schauspiels. Es ist wichtig, diese Elemente der Volkskultur zu beachten, um zu verstehen, wie Leute ohne besondere ästhetische Bildung ihre gestalterischen Probleme gelöst haben.

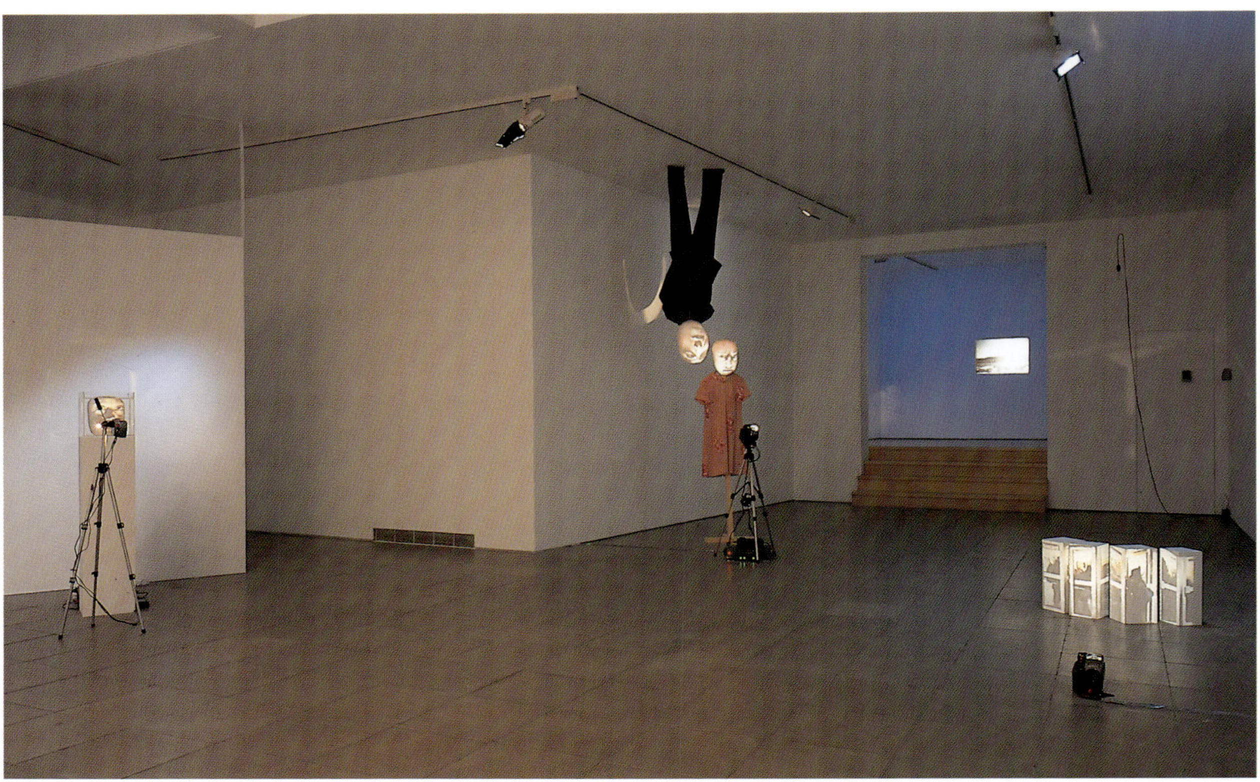

Also ging ich in Brockenhäuser, kaufte Anzüge und versuchte sie auf hundert Arten zu verändern, um ihre Möglichkeiten – vom blossen Anzug bis zur menschlichen Gestalt – zu erforschen. Sie hatten etwas sehr Frankensteinisches. Ich stopfte und nähte, aber das Problem war, dass zwar die Eleganz und Bewegung der Anzüge überzeugte, dass sie aber zu statisch wirkten, sobald ich Gesichter hinzufügte. Deshalb hatten die ersten Figuren keine Köpfe. Es waren Arbeiten zum Thema Überwachung: Die kopflosen Figuren standen in der Galerie, und eine hatte eine Linse, die aus ihrer Hosentür hervorlugte wie ein Penis, eine andere war über einen Monitor gestülpt, der ein geschlossenes System mit Kamera war. Es ging um Machtkonstellationen; eine Figur beobachtete und verfügte über die Kamera, die andere sah sich selbst auf dem Bildschirm. Der Blut- oder Energiestrom zwischen diesen kopflosen Gestalten bestand in der Überwachung und Übertragung. Solche Dinge machte ich, bevor ich die Miniatur-Flüssigkristalldioden-Projektoren entdeckte.

LN: Also machtest du die Köpfe von Anfang an mit Video?

TO: Erst nachdem ich einige andere Dinge ausprobiert hatte, etwa die Anzüge mit dazu passenden monochromen Köpfen, einfach Formen ohne irgendwas drauf. Als ich schliesslich mit den Projektoren umgehen konnte, begannen die Köpfe zu dominieren. Die ersten Figuren waren anatomisch korrekt, aber als das Video immer wichtiger wurde, wurden die Köpfe immer grösser, und die Körper fielen immer mehr in sich zusammen. Das geschah blitzschnell. Bei F/X PLOTTER (1992) etwa musste man sehr genau hinschauen, um die Arme und Bei-ne auszumachen; es war ein ganz leerer, zusammen-gefallener Anzug.

Es gibt einige Arbeiten, die weniger bekannt sind, bei denen ich ganze Figuren auf Teile einer anderen Figur projizierte, etwa BIGGER (HEM) (1994). Es ging darum, sich ein anderes Ich im eigenen Bauch vor-zustellen oder eines, das dich in die Fersen piekst. In SYSTEM FOR DRAMATIC FEEDBACK (1994) wurde ein wirklicher, erigierender und wieder abschlaffender Penis auf die Puppe projiziert. Aber ich stellte fest, dass es den Leuten viel schwerer fällt, eine Bezie-hung zur Puppe herzustellen, sobald es nicht mehr um den Kopf geht.

LN: Das projizierte Glied erscheint hier eher por-nographisch; nicht weil es ein Genital ist, sondern weil der Körper auf gesichtslose Teile reduziert ist.

TO: Ich fragte mich nun, was geschähe, wenn die Körper ganz verschwinden würden. Ich glaube, auf diesem Weg kam ich auf SUBMERGED (1996), das völlig körperlos ist. Als ich an den Sachen mit den Augen arbeitete, dachte ich, ich würde dieselbe emotionale Wirkung erreichen wie vorher. Aber ich entdeckte, dass das Auge ein reptilähnliches Organ ist: Es ist das Gesicht – die Haut um die Augen her-um, der Mund, die Kopfform –, das Gefühle hervor-ruft. Sobald man die Augen isoliert und auf jene Kugeln projiziert, sind sie völlig emotionslos. Zu-nächst war das irritierend, aber dann gefiel es mir sehr, denn es versetzte die Objekte in einen unbewussten Dämmerzustand. Sie wurden zu blos-sen lichtmessenden Organen in rein peristaltischer Bewegung.

LN: Dieser Gedanke der fortschreitenden Ent-körperlichung in deiner Arbeit ist faszinierend. Im Erzählkino ist die Logik des Gefühls vom Körper und seinem psychologischen Umfeld abhängig, du aber entfernst den Körper und mit ihm auch das Umfeld und die Story. Wie weit kannst du das noch treiben, bevor sich alles zersetzt?

TO: In TALKING LIGHT (1996) ist die Präsenz auf eine einzige Lichtquelle reduziert, die via Tonspur gesteuert wird. Und nun arbeite ich an einer grösse-ren Sache für das *San Diego Museum of Contemporary Art,* einem Glasraum mit einer einzigen Lichtquelle darin und einem Tonband ausserhalb. Es wird Tag und Nacht laufen.

LN: O Gott. – Tracy, wenn Tony Regie führt, weisst du, was du tust?

Tracy Leipold: Meistens nicht. Ich mache es einfach irgendwie, immer einen Schritt jenseits meiner selbst, so läuft es jedenfalls, wenn's klappt.

LN: Gehen die Aufnahmen schnell?

TL: Normalerweise ja. Es sind fortlaufende Auf-nahmen von etwa zehn Minuten, deren Höhepunkt jeweils in der Mitte liegt; dieser Bogen ist für mich ein natürlicher Rhythmus.

LN: Ist es eine Art methodischer Schauspielkunst, in der du eingeübte Emotionen durchspielst? Mir scheint, du musst über gewisse Formeln verfügen, sonst wäre die Form nicht so entwickelt, so vollkom-men im Gleichgewicht.

TL: Ich beginne langsam, dann steigert es sich immer mehr, und schliesslich lasse ich es fallen; ich glaube, das hat auch mit dem Text zu tun. Je länger, je mehr werden die Intensität und die Höhepunkte durch den Text und meine Interpretationsweise bestimmt. Bei den Arbeiten, in denen es um ver-schiedene Gefühle ging, besprachen Tony und ich, wie «lang» jedes Gefühl dauern sollte und wo die Grenze liegen sollte, zum Beispiel zwischen eroti-schem und zornigem Erregtsein. Während der Auf-nahme begann ich hin und her zu pendeln zwischen zwei Gefühlen, und Tony gab mir ein Handzeichen, wann ich den Wechsel vollziehen sollte. So lag die Dynamik der Aufnahme weitgehend in seiner Hand.

LN: Tony, sind deine Entscheidungen intuitiv, hast du eine Art Lichtmesser oder Aufbauschema im Kopf?

TO: Da ich selbst Schauspieler bin, weiss ich, dass man neben all dem technischen Zeugs auch das Ziel nie aus den Augen verlieren darf. Manchmal ist das schlicht zu viel verlangt, und ein direktes Feedback, wie Tracy und ich das praktizieren, ist ein weiteres Kontrollwerkzeug, das Freiheit ermöglicht.

LN: Und eine Frage der Disziplin, wenn man alles in einer Aufnahme reinbringen muss. Ohne zweite Chance, aus finanziellen Gründen.

TO: Das ist der Unterschied zwischen der Instal-lation und dem Film. Nach und nach wurde mir klar, dass wir viel flexibler waren, als wir zunächst dachten. Die Kamera dehnt und erweitert die Zeit und die Gegenwart der Zeit. Also neigen die Leute dazu, ihr Denken zu beschleunigen. Kino heisst Verdichtung, weil es unterhalten will. Kino ist eine Verdichtung von Tausenden von Arbeitsstunden einer Menge von Mitwirkenden – Regisseur, Drehbuchautor, Schauspieler, Kulissenschieber usw. – zu anderthalb Stunden. Deshalb ist es so aufregend für die Zuschauer. Dagegen sind meine Arbeiten, da sie nicht unterhalten oder eine Hyperzeit wiedergeben wollen, in gewissem Sinn «unbelebt».

LN: Man könnte sagen, du arbeitest eher mit dramatischen «Frequenzen» als mit dramatischen Begebenheiten. Und zur inneren Struktur deiner Skulpturen gehört Tracys Projektion jener hohen Frequenzen, die eine kathartische Wirkung haben.

TO: Manchmal zwinge ich Tracy dazu, mit demselben immer weiter fortzufahren.

TL: Manchmal, wenn der Ball ins Rollen kommt, rollt und rollt er, und plötzlich ist Schluss.

TO: Manche dieser Ausdrucksformen erreichst du, indem du dir vorstellst, es passiere dir oder jemand anderem etwas Furchtbares, und dann reagierst du darauf. Und wenn du den Ton herauslässt, hörst du ihn selbst, und das steigert dein Gefühl noch mehr. So läuft ein Prozess in deinem Inneren ab.

TL: Ich glaube nicht, dass ich je von Anfang an versucht habe mir etwas vorzustellen, aber wenn ich meine Stimme höre, tauchen die Bilder auf. Wenn man sich selbst schreien hört, ist das nichts Körperliches.

TO: Also spaltest du dich auf! Genau wie ich vermutet habe.

TL: Alles entsteht durch Feedback.

LN: Es gibt überall Entsprechungen in deinem Werk: den visuellen Aspekt, den akustischen Aspekt, die Vermischung dieser beiden mit einem dritten, während ein zeitliches, in Punkte aufgerastetes Bild mit einem festen Körper in Verbindung gebracht wird. Alles ist verschlungen und vermischt in diesem dichten Produktionsnetz. Und wenn du einen Fehler machst, fällt die Konstruktion und damit die ganze Form auseinander.

TO: Genau. Es ist das absolute Minimum, das nötig ist, um die Form zusammenzuhalten.

LN: Diese formale Spannung ist fast immateriell.

TO: Ich halte diese Arbeiten für immateriell. Zunächst war ich betroffen, dass es schien, als hätte die Figur ihren Kopf irgendwie in eine andere Dimension hinüber gestreckt, und trotzdem war sie noch hier. Wir konnten sie sehen, aber sie konnte uns nicht sehen. Sie erlebte gewisse Dinge und setzte uns ihnen aus, aber wir bleiben blind für die Ursache dieser Erlebnisse. Hier kommt für mich Tracys Arbeit herein. Es entsteht ein Raum, in den kein anderer eindringen kann, weil sich alles innerhalb des eigenen Kopfes abspielt.

LN: Wenn man es zu berühren versucht, löst es sich auf. Versuchen die Leute eigentlich deine Arbeiten zu berühren?

TO: Ja.

TL: Ja, natürlich.

LN: Das gefällt mir an FLOCK: Es ist so real. Kinder glauben an Märchen und möchten, dass ihre Puppen sprechen. Und hier tun sie's!

TO: Ich würde gern eine Puppenserie für Kinder machen. Aber wegen der teuren Technologie würde sie unerschwinglich.

LN: In einigen Jahren wird es wahrscheinlich Projektionsapparate geben, die so klein sein werden, dass sie in die Köpfe hineinpassen. Aber heute verkörpert die Gegenwart des Projektors noch deine Präsenz als Regisseur und Filmer und den Akt deiner Aufnahme von Tracys Performance.

TO: Kommt hinzu, dass das Ganze ohne die Projektoren auf einer neuen Ebene des Magischen spielen würde, statt auf der der Performance. Zu Beginn hatte ich damit zu kämpfen, mit diesem ganzen technischen Aufwand. Aber es ist wie im Kabuki-Theater, wo drei oder vier Typen eine Blume, einen Schmetterling oder eine Wolke darstellen; zuerst ist es irritierend, aber allmählich beachtet man sie nicht mehr, und die Konstruktion der Szene wird unsichtbar. So war es mit den Augen-Arbeiten. Das Auge ist ein Mechanismus, der ähnlich funktioniert wie ein kleines Theater oder eine Kamera, was auf dasselbe herauskommt – es ist nur eine Frage der Richtung des Lichtstrahls.

LN: Du hast gesagt, dass das, was Tracy und du zuerst zusammen machten, «vorsprachlich» gewesen sei, sehr gefühlsbezogen und nur lose im Drehbuch angedeutet. Erst im Lauf der Zeit seien die Drehbücher ausführlicher geworden. Warum?

TO: Als Anfang unserer Zusammenarbeit gefiel

mir das Resultat nicht, weil ich den Text schrieb und Tracy das Gefühl beisteuerte. Deshalb begannen wir, beliebige Sätze in das Gemisch der emotionalen Texte und Aussagen einzustreuen. Tracy sagte etwa «God dammit» oder «Get outta my face!», oder sie begann zu lachen und brachte so einen Rhythmus ins Ganze. Eine meiner Lieblingsfiguren war ein total sarkastischer Gangster. Ich erinnere mich an zwei Kinder, die sich das ansahen. Tracy sagte, «Fuck off! ba-da-bing, ba-da-boom!» und die beiden fanden es prima. Tracy, wie haben wir das damals bloss gemacht?

T L : Du hast zugehört, und wenn dir etwas in den Sinn kam, hast du es mir zugeflüstert. Es waren nur wenige Zeilen Text, und dazwischen wurde irgendein emotionaler Prozess angedeutet.

T O : Es war sehr spontan, weil die Mikrophone, die wir hatten, derart mies waren, dass ich dir die nächsten Brocken jeweils wirklich gleich zuflüstern konnte. Es ging darum, was man tun konnte, ohne wirklich Sprache zu gebrauchen, einfach eine Reihe von Ausdrücken, die hin und wieder durch ein Lachen oder Knurren akzentuiert wurden. Das war wirklich wichtig für unsere Entwicklung, denn wie bei der Live-Montage machten wir Dinge, die gewöhnlich nicht zusammengehen.

L N : Wie seid ihr von der Idee des Vorsprachlichen zur Untersuchung der multiplen Persönlichkeit gekommen?

T O : 1994 arbeiteten wir an JUDY. Tracy wurde dabei mehrfach auf ein Environment aus verschiedenen Gegenständen projiziert, als veränderliche Person, die sich aufspaltete und mit sich selbst ein Gespräch führte. Damit war die Idee, eine Gestalt für mehrere verschiedene Personen einzusetzen, geboren. Alle Drehbücher danach bestanden aus Fragmenten, also erfand Tracy auf meine Bitte hin diese verschiedenen Stimmen. Sie begann mit der höchstmöglichen Stimme und fuhr dann mit der tiefsten weiter, die irgendwie androgyn wirkte. Während die Texte vorher durch das Geräusch eines Kusses oder eines Lachers durchbrochen wurden, geschah das jetzt durch die unterschiedlichen Charaktere. Da war also die hohe Stimme, die tiefe Stimme ...

T L : ... die langsame Stimme, die gehetzte Stimme.

T O : Dann bat ich dich zu versuchen, ob du mit her-

ausgestreckter Zunge sprechen kannst, und das ergab die lallende Stimme. Die Glossolalie kam etwa zur gleichen Zeit wie die Tierstimmen.

L N : Dich fasziniert also das Kanalisieren oder «Dirigieren des Unbewussten», wie du es nennst?

T O : Ich finde es interessant, dass das mehrfach gespaltene Bewusstsein mehrere Personen erzeugt, um die zentrale Identität zu sichern, dass es versucht, das eigene Leben zu entwerfen und zu kontrollieren, und nicht an irgendwelchen Freudschen oder Jungschen Marionettenfäden hängt. Es ist ein Modell für ein neues Bewusstsein.

L N : Du untersuchst also diesen Gedanken mit Tracy im sicheren Rahmen einer ästhetischen Reflexion über diese verrückten Extremsituationen. Aber was sagst du dazu, dass Tracy behauptet, sie wisse nicht, woher diese Stimmen kämen, und dass sie sehr zwiespältige Gefühle habe angesichts der verschiedenen Versionen ihrer selbst dort draussen im Raum?

T O : Tracy, weisst du, woher die automatischen Stimmen kommen, oder nicht?

T L : Wie sollte ich das wissen. Ich bin es, es passiert einfach. Es ist eine Nachahmung von etwas, was ich gehört habe, meine Vorstellung davon, wie es sein könnte, einfach ein Spiel. Viele der Stimmen, die ich imitiere, habe ich im Fernsehen gehört.

L N : Aber hast du – wie Tony das offensichtlich getan hat – dich über Glossolalie informiert?

T L : Es gab da ein Ereignis in meiner Kindheit in einer Baptistenkirche. Es ging um meine Schwester. Ich erinnere mich, dass ich plötzlich von Leuten umgeben war, und sie war weg. Ich sah nach oben, und da sass sie, in einem weissen Kleid, im Begriff, ins Wasser getaucht zu werden. Ich konnte nichts von dem hören, was sie sagte, aber ich sah, dass ihre Lippen sich bewegten, und die Leute sagten, sie rede in Zungen. Sie sah etwas seltsam aus. Ich glaube, ich hatte nie eine Imitation des Sprechens in Zungen gehört und auch keine echte Aufzeichnung davon. Ich wusste nur, dass es verzerrt tönt. Also bin ich wohl das Medium meiner Schwester.

(Übersetzung: Wilma Parker)

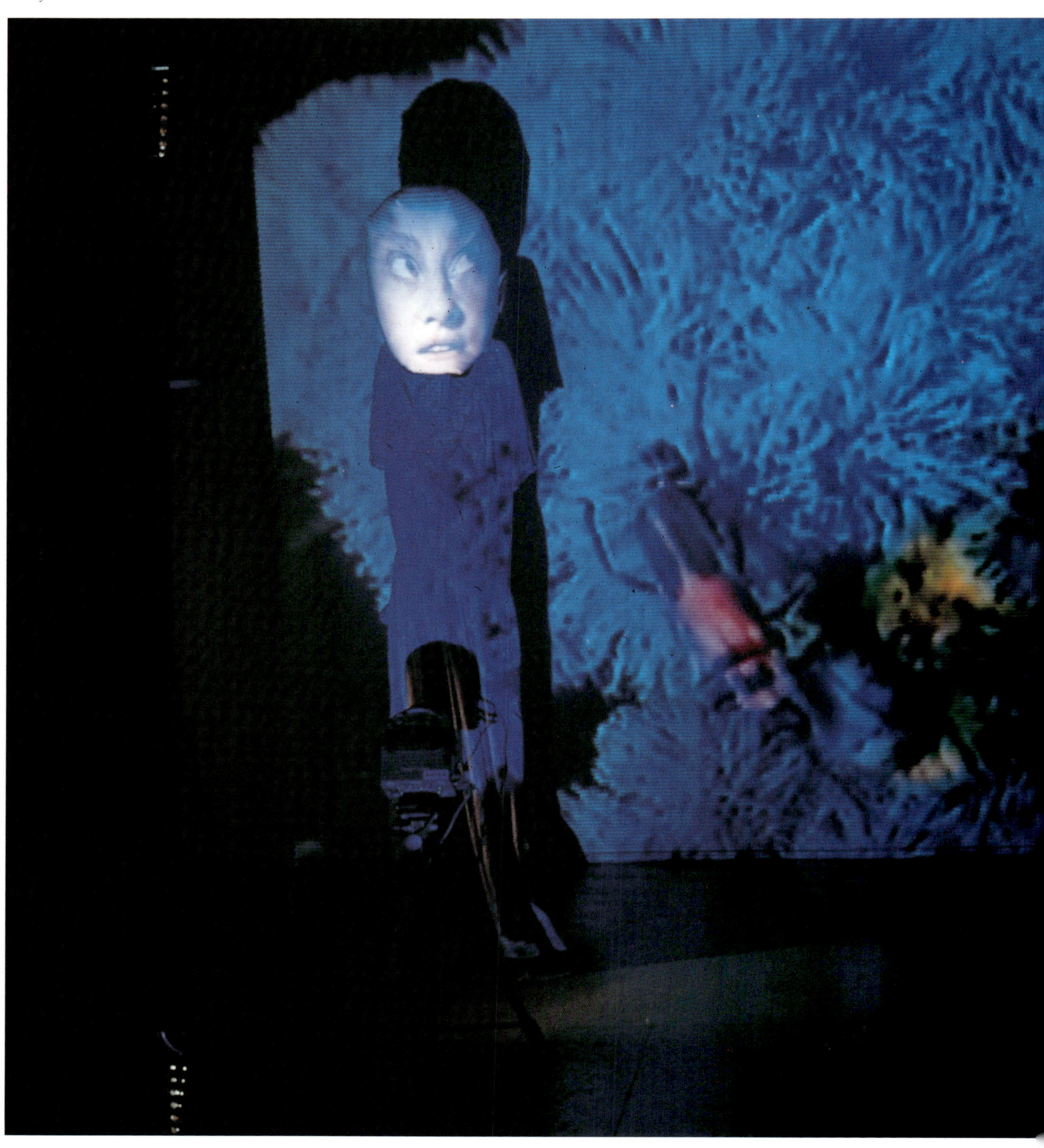

Tony Oursler

TONY OURSLER, SKETCHYBLUE, 1996, 2 videoprojectors, 2 tapes, sound, approx. 96 x 108 x 60", performance by Tracy Leipold /
FLÜCHTIGES BLAU, Videoprojektion mit 2 Projektoren und Ton, ca. 244 x 275 x 152 cm, Performance: Tracy Leipold.

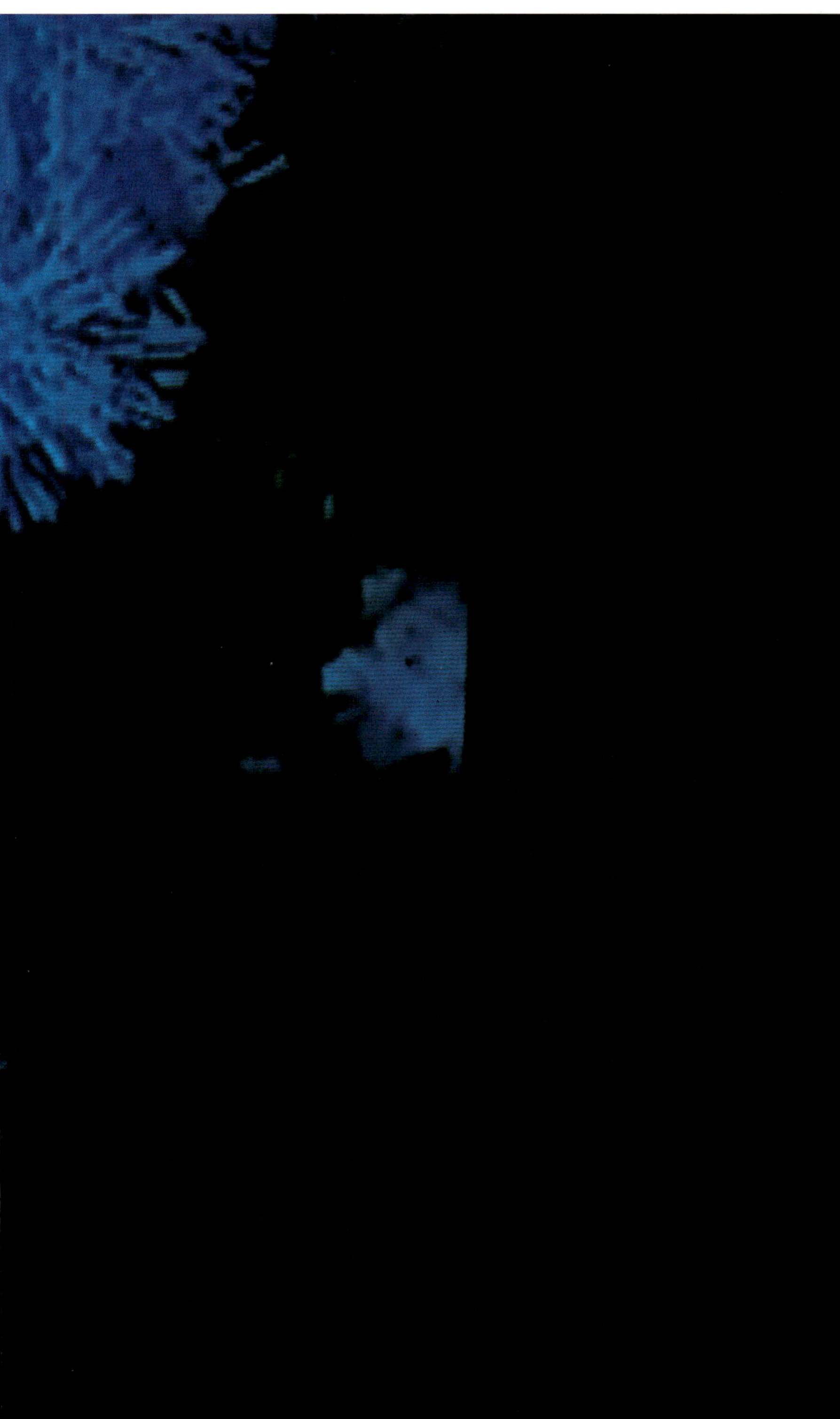

Excerpt from Soundtrack / Textbeispiel aus
SKETCHYBLUE:

HEY. SKETCHY. RED LIGHT. BLUE LIGHT.
I CAN'T TELL THE DIFFERENCE... STOP
(INHALE) SMELL THE FLOWERS. INFOR-
MATION IS SKETCHY. THE SOUND IS
DEAFENING...GRIEF, ANGER, LOSS, OHIO,
TEXAS, UTAH. HOO, HOO, HOO. YOU
KNOW...LIFE IS A JOURNEY...PLUG IN,
GLUG GIN, RIG CHIN, 605GK24, 9:30,
1984...TAKE IT OR LEAVE IT. WHO
CARES? I DO. NO, INFORMATION IS
SKETCHY. MY CLOTHES ARE ON INSIDE
OUT. STOP STEALING MY MEMORIES.
STOP STEALING...MY MEMORIES. I CAN
HEAR THEM BUT I CAN'T UNDER-
STAND WHAT THEY ARE SAYING. WACKO.
WACKO. WACKO. THIS IS NOT HAPPEN-
ING...THIS IS NOT HAPPENING...WHAT
ROLE DID YOU PLAY? DARKER GOOD...
YOU NEVER SAW THIS, IT NEVER HAP-
PENED.
HE. FLÜCHTIG. ROTES LICHT. BLAUES
LICHT. ICH KANN'S NICHT UNTERSCHEI-
DEN . . . HALT (ATME EIN). RIECH MAL,
DIE BLUMEN. DIE INFORMATION IST
FLÜCHTIG. DER TON IST OHRENBETÄU-
BEND . . . KUMMER, WUT, VERLUST, OHIO,
TEXAS, UTAH. HUU, HUU, HUU. WEISST
DU . . . DAS LEBEN IST EINE REISE . . .
STECK DEN STÖPSEL REIN, SCHLUCK GIN,
STRECK DAS KINN. 605GK24, 9 UHR 30,
1984 . . . NIMM, ODER LASS ES BLEIBEN.
WEN KÜMMERT'S? MICH. NEIN, INFORMA-
TION IST FLÜCHTIG. ICH TRAGE MEINE
KLEIDER VERKEHRTHERUM. HÖR AUF,
MIR MEINE ERINNERUNGEN ZU STEHLEN.
HÖR AUF ZU STEHLEN . . . MEINE ERIN-
NERUNGEN. ICH KANN SIE HÖREN, ABER
ICH KANN NICHT VERSTEHEN, WAS
SIE SAGEN. BÄNG. BÄNG. BÄNG. DAS
GESCHIEHT NICHT WIRKLICH . . . DAS
GESCHIEHT NICHT . . . WELCHE ROLLE
HAST DU GESPIELT? DUNKLER GUT . . .
DU HAST DAS NIE GESEHEN, ES IST NIE
GESCHEHEN.

LYNNE COOKE

Tony Oursler:
ALTERS

…Video's real medium is a psychological situation, the very terms of which are to withdraw attention from an external object—an Other—and invest it in the Self, wrote

Rosalind Krauss in a pioneering study of seventies video.[1] Basing her analysis on a series of single-channel videotapes, she argued that the video apparatus functioned as a mirror, and that the works of art it generated served as records of this technologically mediated, narcissistic encounter. Describing that mode of seventies practice as "intrasubjective," David Joselit has identified an alternate yet concurrent mode, based in video installation, which he designates "intersubjective."[2] Citing installations by Dan Graham and Peter Campus, which also incorporated instant feedback, Joselit contends that this second strand of video art was engaged in a psychological self-encounter constructed in and by social space. These two modes of narcissism suggest, he concludes, "the continuum along which video practice has long been charted: On the one hand as a privatized exploration of the self, and on the other as a remapping of the discursive formations of the mass media."[3]

Tony Oursler's recent video projections imbricate these two strands, weaving them together with the tropes of mass-media pop-psychologizing in a reevaluation of the medium's novel capacity for instant feedback. While he, too, attributes metaphorical power to that technological innovation, Oursler dispenses with the technique itself. Though he still keeps the projected image hostage to its source, he relinquishes the monitor, which the two earlier theoretical models had used both as a vehicle and as the literal site of encounter. Replacing the immaterial transmission of the screen with a projection in real space, Oursler not only makes these embodiments incarnate but posits as integral to such self-encounters a disturbing, phantasmic actuality.

Since 1992, Oursler has been employing mannikins—dolls and puppets—onto whose heads he projects faces. Emoting at the least, but more often narrating at length, these figures whine, wail, threaten, complain, and cajole relentlessly, indifferent to the presence—or absence—of anyone else. Prisoners of various predicaments whose physical circumstances are only manifestations or exacerbations of their mental disorders, they heedlessly pour forth their litanies of woe into the darkened gallery spaces. In GET AWAY 2 (1994) the figure lies prone, staring balefully from beneath the corner of a mattress which pins it to the ground; the "alter" of JUDY (1994) cowers underneath a sofa, one side of which has been propped up to create a makeshift shelter. WHITE TRASH/PHOBIC (1993) presents its dual, overlapping psyches as protagonists who engage in an abstract conversation while wedged in opposite

LYNNE COOKE is a writer and is Curator at Dia Center for the Arts, New York City.

corners of a room. Others are crammed into—or alternately, take refuge in—giant empty pill capsules, the possible sources of their delirious ravings.

The term Oursler prefers for these characters, these spectral manifestations, is "effigy." While the word may be a synonym for a sculpted likeness, it also has a more specific meaning, one that catches the dark undertones ever present in his art: "a crude figure often in the form of a stuffed dummy that is tortured or disposed of (often by burning or by hanging) to represent treatment felt to be due to a person who is the object of hatred."[4] From golems to voodoo dolls, effigies thus have manifold affiliates which function similarly as repositories of malevolent projections or repressed desires, cravings, and fantasies.

Staring back at the beams of light illuminating them, Oursler's projected figures seem transfixed by the very sources of their being. The transference of the physiognomy from the depthless screen of the monitor to the discombobulated body of a mannikin enacts metaphorically that externalizing of the self or part-self which characterizes dissociations of the

TONY OURSLER, STONE BLUE, 1995,
video projector and tape, large cloth figure, white plastic chair, performance by Tracy Leipold /
KATZENJAMMER, Videoprojektor und -tape, grosse Stoffpuppe, weisser Plastikstuhl, Performance: Tracy Leipold.

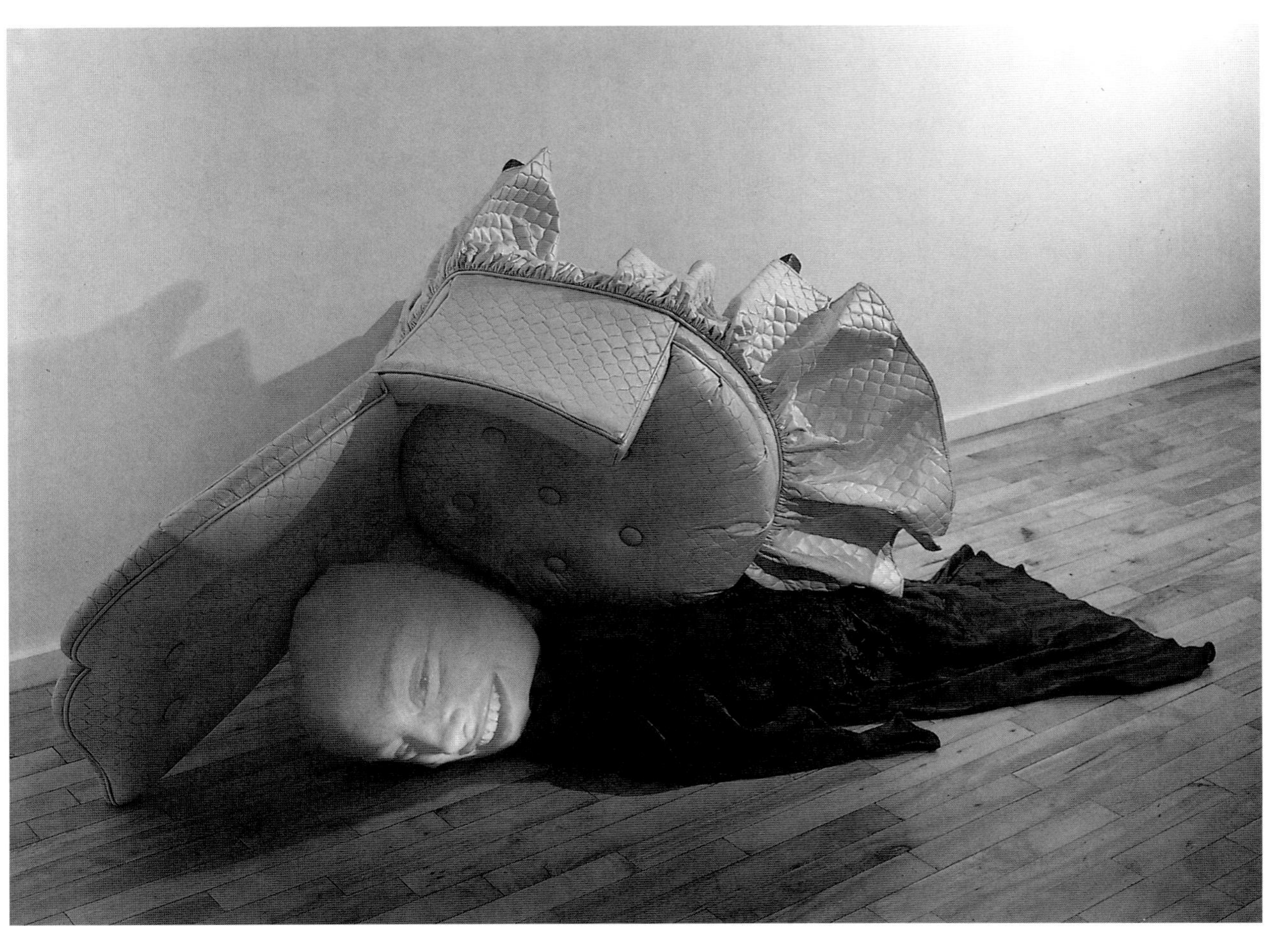

psyche; that is, it mirrors that unconscious defense mechanism in which a set of mental activities is split off from the mainstream of consciousness to function as a separate unit. Irrespective of identifications as hysterical, phobic, obsessive, manic, paranoic, depressive, or psychotic, Oursler's spectral characters exhibit the unidimensional persona of the crazed or possessed. Narcissistically fixated by the glare that animates them, they take on hallucinatory appearances reminiscent of phantoms, poltergeists, grotesques and ghouls—the archetypal protagonists not only of nightmares but of the modern genres of horror and their timeless predecessors, folk tales: all sanctioned collective repositories for the repressed and the suppressed. In addition to supplementing these traditional arenas for figuring psychoses and neuroses, today's mass media welcomes variants in the guise of docudramas and tabloid scoops featuring multiple personality disorders. Oursler's eerie dummies partake equally of all these realms.

Temporarily relinquishing video, over the past few months Oursler has made several works which, while retaining his signature makeshift fabrication, now allude to the rapidly evolving media of computer-based technologies. Reduced to a bare electric bulb paired with a synchronized sound track, this series no longer addresses the psychopathologies of the self but the very basis of identity in any subject. In TALKING LIGHT (1996), for example, a bare lightbulb and a synchronized, forlorn voice burst forth intermittently into the silent darkness of the exhibition space. Divested of all corporeality and condemned to repeating its tedious monologue in an undefined and indefinite space, this disembodied speaker comes one stage closer to annihilation than the talkative, truncated organs found in SUBMERGED (1995–1996) and related works, which are kept "alive" in jars of a formaldehyde-like substance. The possession of a body, and hence the capacity to situate itself physically in space, is a prerequisite not only for being able to take up a position as a subject, but is the very foundation of a coherent identity. In certain psychotic states, notably psychasthenia, subjectivity is no longer anchored in the body, since the body and subject fail to mesh. Such psychotics both lose their perspective on the world and cease to be a

source of perception, for space itself captivates and replaces them. This results, according to theorist Elizabeth Grosz, in the primacy of the subject's own perspective being "replaced by the gaze of another for whom the subject is merely a point in space, not the focal point organizing space."[5]

TALKING LIGHT might be read as a wry reprise of Samuel Beckett's famous protagonist from *Not I,* which also spews its fractured monologue out into a dimensionless world. Like Oursler's, Beckett's sparely embodied subject—nothing but a silhouetted mouth—displaces its identity (in this case from the first to the third person, "she"), and yet its laconic utterances convey an unexpected resilience, a surprising irrepressibility. By contrast, TALKING LIGHT'S wan stutterer, devoid of all forms of dissociation, of all externalizing, lacks not only the possibility of self-encounter but even a self-sustaining, if deprecatory, humor. Split off from its physical body and hence deprived of spatial coordinates, this spark of consciousness, this blip in a limitless and liminal void, offers a sly yet incisive critique of the immaterial subjects deemed unique to cyberspace. The avatars of cyberspace identities extoll the freedoms that stem from the transparency, dispensability and redundancy of the body—mere "meat"—yet for Grosz and other skeptical critics, such conditions both create a radically flawed subject, and are inimical to the task of self-consolidation or self-reconstruction. Indeed, as TALKING LIGHT attests, they closely approximate the symptoms of certain psychoses. If this bleak work is prophetic of his future forays, for Oursler the virtual worlds of electronic and cyberspace are unlikely to prove any more reassuring or reaffirming than the tragicomic universe overrun with phantom representations that is his vision of our everyday, phenomenal world.

1) Rosalind Krauss, "Video: The Aesthetics of Narcissism,"*October* 1 (Spring, 1976), p. 57.
2) David Joselit, "Film and Video Installation in the Biennale of Sydney," unpublished paper, 1996.
3) Ibid.
4) *Webster's Third New International Dictionary,* 1986.
5) Elizabeth Grosz, "Lived Spatiality: Insect Space/Virtual Sex," *Agenda* 26–27 (November/December and January/February, 1992–1993), p. 7.

TONY OURSLER, FLOWERS (UNDERMIND), detail of JUDY, 1994,
video projector and tape, silk flowers, dimensions variable, performance by Tracy Leipold / Videoprojektion auf Seidenblumen, Grösse variabel.

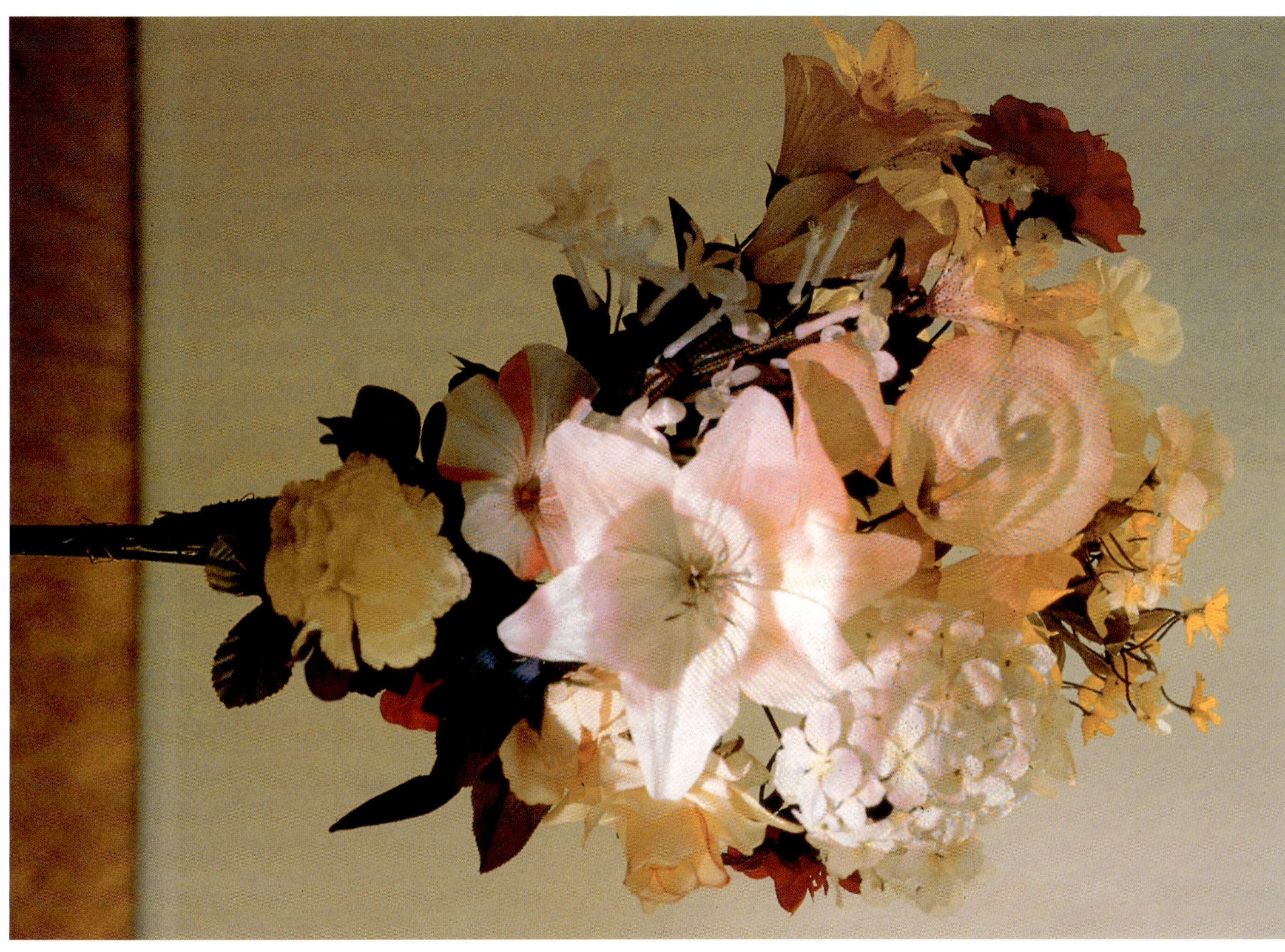

LYNNE COOKE

Tony Ourslers
ALTER EGOS

…Das eigentliche Medium des Video ist eine psychologi-

sche Situation, in der die Aufmerksamkeit vom äusseren

Gegenstand – einem anderen – abgezogen und auf das

Selbst gerichtet wird, schrieb Rosalind Krauss in einer bahnbrechenden Studie über die Videofilme der siebziger Jahre.[1] Ihre Analyse basierte auf einer Reihe von Einkanal-Videos und zeigte, dass der Video-Apparat als eine Art Spiegel dient; die dabei entstehenden Kunstwerke verstand sie als Aufzeichnungen dieser technologisch vermittelten, narzisstischen Begegnung. David Joselit nennt diese Praxis der siebziger Jahre «intrasubjektiv», während er die gleichzeitig entwickelte, auf der Videoinstallation aufbauende Variante als «intersubjektiv» bezeichnet.[2] Er führt Installationen von Dan Graham und Peter Campus an, die ebenfalls mit dem sofortigen Feedback arbeiten, und behauptet, dass diese zweite Form der Videokunst auf die psychologische Begegnung mit sich selbst im und durch den sozialen Raum zielt. Er kommt zu dem Schluss, dass diese zwei Formen von Narzissmus «jenes Kontinuum bilden, in dem die Videopraxis sich lange Zeit entwickelt hat: einerseits als private Erkundung des Selbst und andererseits als Nachvollzug der Diskursformen der Massenmedien.»[3]

LYNNE COOKE ist Autorin und Kuratorin am Dia Center for the Arts, New York.

Tony Ourslers neue Videoprojektionen verknüpfen diese beiden Entwicklungsstränge und verbinden sie mit den Bildformeln der populär-psychologischen Massenmedien zu einer Neueinschätzung der überraschenden Möglichkeiten dieses Mediums, das ein unmittelbares Feedback zu liefern vermag. Während Oursler dieser technologischen Innovation auch metaphorische Kräfte zuschreibt, geht er zugleich aber doch auf Distanz zur Technik selbst. Das projizierte Bild bleibt zwar bei ihm auch unmittelbar an seinen Ursprung gebunden, aber der Monitor, der in den beiden früheren theoretischen Modellen sowohl als Vehikel wie auch im wörtlichen Sinn als Ort der Begegnung gedient hat, ist verschwunden. Oursler ersetzt die immaterielle Bildschirmübertragung durch eine Projektion im realen Raum; solchermassen konkretisiert er die Verkörperung und beschwört zugleich den irritierend phantasmatischen Realismus solcher Selbstbegegnungen.

Seit 1992 arbeitet Oursler mit Puppen und Figuren, auf deren Köpfe er Gesichter projiziert. Diese Figuren mimen Gefühle, noch häufiger aber erzählen sie Geschichten, und dabei jammern, schreien, schimpfen, drohen und beschwatzen sie uns unaufhörlich, egal ob ihnen jemand zuhört oder nicht. Gefangen in den Schranken einer physischen Situation, die lediglich Ausdruck bzw. Verschärfung ihrer geistigen Verwirrtheit ist, erfüllen sie die verdunkelten Galerieräume rücksichtslos mit ihren Klagelitaneien. In GET AWAY 2 (Entkommen 2, 1994) liegt die Figur darnieder und stiert traurig unter der Ecke der Matratze hervor, die sie zu Boden drückt. Das Alter ego in JUDY (1994) kauert unter einem Sofa, dessen eine Seite so aufgebockt ist, dass es einen notdürftigen Unterschlupf bietet. WHITE TRASH/PHOBIC (Weisser Plunder/Phobisch, 1993) präsentiert zwei einander überlagernde Psychen als Protagonisten, die in eine abstrakte Unterhaltung vertieft sind, während sie sich in zwei einander gegenüber liegende Ecken eines Raumes zwängen. Wieder andere sind in riesige leere Pillen-Kapseln, vielleicht der Ursprung ihres Deliriums, gepfercht – oder suchen darin Zuflucht.

Diese Figuren, Manifestationen im Lichtspektrum, nennt Oursler selbst gern «Effigien». Das Wort bezeichnet einerseits das skulpturale Bildnis, andererseits schwingt darin auch eine Redewendung mit, die jene dunkleren Untertöne anklingen lässt, die mit zu seiner Kunst gehören: jemanden *in effigie* hinrichten oder verbrennen heisst, das einer verhassten Person zugedachte Urteil an einer Puppe oder einem Bild symbolisch zu vollstrecken. Vom Golem bis zur Voodoo-Puppe gibt es zahlreiche bekannte Figuren, die als Projektionsfläche für den Hass oder auch für unterdrückte Wünsche, Begierden und Phantasien dienen.

Ourslers Figuren starren zurück in jenes Licht, das sie sichtbar macht, und scheinen so gleichsam von dem Lichtstrahl durchbohrt, dem sie ihr Dasein verdanken. Die Verlagerung der Physiognomie vom eindimensionalen Bildschirm des Monitors auf den zerbeulten Körpersack einer Puppe ist eine Metapher für jene Projektionen des Selbst bzw. eines Teils des Selbst nach aussen, die bei Persönlichkeitsspaltungen auftreten. Sie widerspiegelt den unbewussten Abwehrmechanismus, bei dem bestimmte geistige Aktivitäten sich vom zentralen Bewusstsein abspalten und als eigenständiger Teil weiter funktionieren. Ohne dass sie ausdrücklich als hysterische, phobische, obsessive, manische, paranoide, depressive oder psychotische Charaktere klassifiziert werden, zeigen Ourslers Lichtgeburten die eindimensionale Persönlichkeit von Wahnsinnigen oder Besessenen. Narzisstisch fixiert auf den Strahl, der sie zum Leben erweckt, werden sie zu halluzinatorischen Erscheinungen, die an Phantome, Poltergeister, groteske Figuren und böse Dämonen erinnern; sie alle sind

archetypische Protagonisten nicht nur unserer Alpträume, sondern auch der modernen Horrorgenres und ihrer klassischen Vorläufer, der Volkssagen: kollektiv sanktionierte Deponien für das Unterdrückte und Verdrängte. Die heutigen Massenmedien ergänzen diese traditionellen Arenen der Inszenierung von Psychosen und Neurosen auf ihre Art und stürzen sich in der Maske des dramatischen Dokumentarfilms und der Sensationsreportage gierig auf Persönlichkeitsstörungen aller Art. Bei Ourslers geisterhaften Puppen haben wir es mit all diesen Bereichen zu tun.

In den letzten Monaten hat Oursler zeitweise auf die Arbeit mit Video verzichtet und Arbeiten produziert, die sich – unter Beibehaltung seiner typischen, provisorisch wirkenden Herstellungsweise – mit den Medien einer sich rapide entwickelnden Computertechnologie beschäftigen. Diese Werkreihe beschränkt sich auf eine nackte Glühbirne in Kombination mit einer synchronisierten Tonspur und handelt nicht mehr von der Psychopathologie des Ich, sondern von der Identitätsgrundlage eines jeden Subjekts schlechthin. Bei TALKING LIGHT (Sprechendes Licht, 1996) beispielsweise brechen in regelmässigen Abständen eine nackte Glühbirne und eine laute Synchronstimme in die lichtlose Stille des Ausstellungsraums ein. Aller Körperlichkeit beraubt und zur ständigen Wiederholung eines ausladenden Monologs in einem undefinierten und undefinierbaren Raum verurteilt, ist dieser körperlose Sprecher der Auflösung in nichts noch einen Schritt näher als die redseligen Organstümpfe in SUBMERGED (Eingetaucht, 1995–96) und vergleichbaren Arbeiten, die in Behältern mit einer Formaldehyd-ähnlichen Lösung «am Leben» erhalten werden. Einen Körper zu haben und damit einen physischen Platz im Raum einnehmen zu können ist Voraussetzung, nicht nur um sich selbst als Subjekt zu behaupten, sondern auch um eine zusammenhängende Identität zu entwickeln. Bei bestimmten psychotischen Zuständen, namentlich bei Psychasthenie, ist das Selbstgefühl nicht im Körper verankert, weil der Kontakt zwischen Körper und Subjekt abgebrochen ist. Solche Psychotiker verlieren ihren Blick auf die Welt und können sich selbst nicht mehr als Wahrnehmende begreifen, weil der Raum von ihnen Besitz ergreift

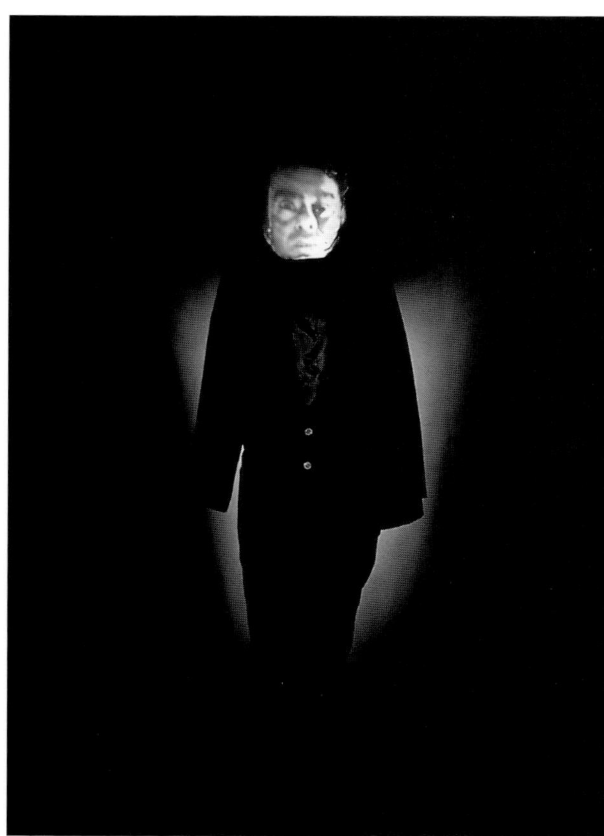

TONY OURSLER, WHITE TRASH, detail from
WHITE TRASH/PHOBIC, 1993, figure, human scale,
video projectors, cloth / WEISSER PLUNDER,
Teil der Installation WEISSER PLUNDER/PHOBISCH,
lebensgrosse menschliche Figur, Videoprojektoren, Stoff.

TONY OURSLER, INSOMNIA, 1996, L.C.D. projector,
videotape, 6 cloth pillows, 6 pillow cases, small figure, 31 x 26 x 17",
performance by Tracy Leipold / SCHLAFLOSIGKEIT,
LCD-Projektor und Videoband, 6 Stoffkissen mit
verschiedenfarbigen Bezügen, kleine Puppe, ca. 79 x 66 x 43 cm,
Performance: Tracy Leipold.

und sie ersetzt. Nach Meinung der Theoretikerin Elizabeth Grosz führt das schliesslich dazu, dass das Subjekt den Primat seiner eigenen Sicht *ersetzt durch den Blick eines anderen, für den das Subjekt lediglich ein Punkt im Raum ist, nicht aber der Mittelpunkt, der den Raum organisiert.*[4]

TALKING LIGHT könnte man als verzerrte Reprise jenes berühmten Protagonisten aus Samuel Becketts *Nicht Ich* verstehen, der seinen zersplitterten Monolog ebenfalls in eine Welt ohne Dimensionen absondert. Wie bei Oursler verlagert Becketts spärlich verkörpertes Subjekt – nichts als ein silhouettenhafter Mund – seine Identität (in diesem Fall von der ersten zur dritten Person: «sie»); doch die lakonischen

Äusserungen verfügen über eine unerwartete Widerstandsfähigkeit, eine erstaunliche Ununterdrückbarkeit. Der gesichtslose Stotterer in TALKING LIGHT, dem selbst die Möglichkeit der Spaltung und Externalisierung genommen ist, kann sich dagegen nicht nur nicht mehr selbst begegnen, sondern es geht ihm auch jeder selbsterhaltende, wenn auch böse Humor ab. Abgetrennt vom physischen Körper und daher seiner räumlichen Koordinaten beraubt, leistet dieser Bewusstseinsfunke, dieses nackte Piepen und Blinken in der endlosen, äussersten Leere, eine listige, aber beissende Kritik des immateriellen Subjekts, das ausschliesslich zur Existenz im Cyberspace verdammt ist. Das Faszinosum der Cyperspace-Persönlichkeit ist die Freiheit, die sie aus der Transparenz, Entbehrlichkeit und Überflüssigkeit des Körpers – blosses «Fleisch» – gewinnt; doch für Grosz und andere Skeptiker erzeugen solche Zustände einerseits ein radikal entstelltes Subjekt und stehen andererseits der Selbstbestätigung und Selbstfindung des Ich entgegen. Wie TALKING LIGHT zeigt, weisen sie eine deutliche Nähe zu gewissen Psychose-Symptomen auf. Und wenn sich in diesem beklemmenden Werk bereits Ourslers künftige Attacken abzeichnen, so wird eines bereits deutlich: Die virtuellen Welten der Elektronik und des Cyberspace werden da kaum ein tröstlicheres oder beruhigenderes Bild abgeben als jenes tragikomische, von Phantomen bevölkerte Universum, das Ourslers visionärer Blick auf unsere heutige, alltägliche Erscheinungswelt zutage gefördert hat. *(Übersetzung: Nansen)*

1) Rosalind Krauss, «Video: The Aesthetics of Narcissism», *October* 1, Frühjahr 1976, S. 57.
2) David Joselit, «Film and Video Installation in the Biennale of Sydney», unveröffentlichtes Arbeitspapier, 1996.
3) Ebenda.
4) Elizabeth Grosz, «Lived Spatiality: Insect Space/Virtual Sex», *Agenda* 26–27, November/Dezember und Januar/Februar 1992–93, S. 7.

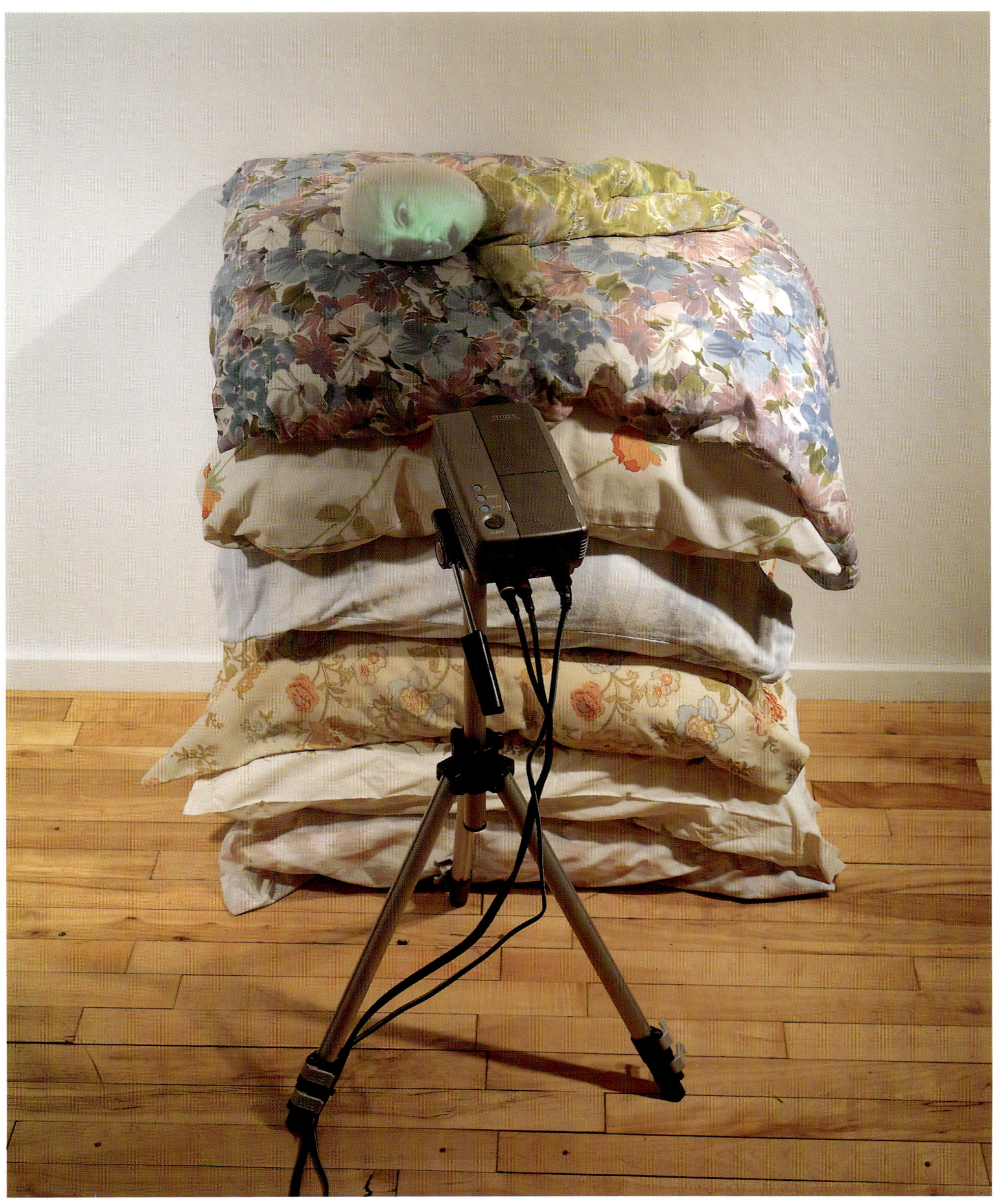

FRANCES RICHARD

Like Water

Deep space, we are told, is a vacuum, soundless and endless—although it has also been supposed to be filled by the music of the spheres. The realm of the divine and the home of aliens, a reality we cannot know outside the mediation of technology, space is a frontier whose finality consists mainly in the collective imagination. Since most of us will never actually go there, space becomes what is inside us, an elastic metaphor for all that is boundless and foreign.

Tony Oursler's sculptures are emissaries from this parallel universe, creatures whose task it is to remind us that the forces controlling things out there are sometimes indistinguishable from the strange predicaments holding sway in here. The ether flows into us whether we want it to or not, and the commercial moving image—like the space through which its satellite transmissions bounce—becomes a matrix we exist in as much as an idea that we create. The banal cacophony of cable culture has been Oursler's most accessible fascination, and his video-animated figures clearly act as totems of the dissociation such culture propagates. What may not be so obvious, initially, is the delicate relationship between this techno-junkie reading of the work and the impact of what Oursler has called his "very active spiritual

mind."[1] The "spiritual" element expresses itself in a reliance on the simple wonderment of motion, an allegiance to the lowest common denominators of human presence: a face, a voice. Although in most cases the verbal portions of his works are scripted, Oursler is not interested in storytelling so much as in extending the energy field of his effigies beyond the visual into the crackling air.

Suspended on invisible strands from the ceiling, or seeming to float across the floor in pools of their own shed light, are thirteen white balls, ranging in size from six to eighteen inches in diameter: On each is projected the full-color, moving image of an eye. Pupils track and stare, lids blink. One cries. Each watcher is different, their blues and browns set in diverse ellipses of glistening sclera, skin, and lash. The semidarkened room is filled with a solar system of huge, staring gods, each seemingly transfixed by the source of its existence—sleek, modestly sized video cameras which stand like pert, inquiring E.T.s directly in front of each bright orb.[2] A fuzzy, ambient din fills the room. If we look closely, we can see floating in each iris—like the gestural dollop of white paint which signifies the gleam of life in the engaging eye of an Old Master portrait—the image of a tiny T.V. screen.

There is a deliberate tension in these cyclops' specularity. Generating and generated by the glow of

FRANCES RICHARD is a writer who lives in New York City.

television, they offer a poised comment on self-hypnosis by cathode ray; the twist is that, until we notice the reflected screens and connect the sound in the room to the shows recorded there, there seems to be no question that these creatures are looking at and murmuring to us. Passing among them as viewers, suddenly self-conscious about the wholeness and mobility of our bodies, the anxiety of surveillance overlaps with a kind of voyeuristic awe—the kind one might feel gazing through a telescope for the first time, or peering through the glass at the fluid, brilliant forms in an aquarium. Then we pause, and try to decipher what the eyes are saying: Their messages turn out to be closed circuits. No revelation is delivered—unless, perhaps, this multichannel whisper is what revelation sounds like.

The one who has been SUBMERGED (1995–96) can only speak in muffled gurgles; s/he or it is underwater and has to hold its breath. This androgynous presence is nothing but a head—and not even fully that, since the back, sides, and top of its cranium are eerily smooth and white, earless and hairless—but enough self has been left intact by the powers that be to allow a clear understanding of trouble. Anxiously eyeing the waterline above, puffing out its cheeks and then squeezing its eyes shut, this drowned unfortunate is stripped back to pure gesture, communicating in a universal language of distress. Unlike the eye pieces, which surround their spectators, engulfing interloping humans in their altered atmosphere, SUBMERGED underlines the separation between viewer and viewed. It's a piteous position, dangerous, uncomfortable, ignominiously and inexplicably public. "Get it out of there!" a small gallery-goer urged her parents. But there was nothing to be done—to release it from its element would destroy it altogether.

Facing the tidy existential one-liner of SUBMERGED is FLOCK (1996), a family of articulated wooden dummies fitted with the now-familiar oversized white heads. There are two large figures, one standing protectively behind, and one sitting down in front, each with an arm extended around an assortment of four little ones. All six heads reflect the outlook of a continuously recorded single face, its features awkwardly too big for the bald lozenges onto which they are projected, but each is caught at a different moment. Their expressions are manic variations on a "let's just make the best of it" smile, the kind of emotional defense mechanism passed osmotically from parent to child. "Read your Bible… fight…fight…fight," one mumbles. "What about the family? What about the family? What about the family?" squeaks another. "What did you expect?" demands the seated figure, the one who, in traditional family-portrait iconography, would be the mother. Their voices are tinny, monomaniacal, hard to hear. It is necessary to stand still and lean into the Flock to understand them clearly, and even then an almost reflexive impatience moves us away before the tape loops have cycled completely through. The result is that we hear only garbled snatches and blurred rantings that, like the atmospheric static of the eye pieces, are more nervous aural scribble than shaped narrative.

The video images fit so exactly on the lumps of these heads, fading imperceptibly into the curves of their white mass, that even the presence of the cameras in front of their pedestals does not destroy the conceit. What is painterly about Oursler is this faith in two-dimensional illusion, in the time-honored practice of applying color to a flat surface so that its modeled shadows read as lifelike representation. The difference, of course, is that these pictures are not solid matter simulating movement, but immaterial flickers simulating tangibility. "Video is like water," Oursler has said, "this completely ethereal form that's been boxed for forty years in a television."[3] Released—or ejected—from the authority of the box, Oursler's video is a labile amusement, a perceptual trick whose satisfying mystery exists in exact proportion to its simplicity.

1) Elizabeth Janus, "A Conversation with Tony Oursler," *Paletten* (March 1995), p. 70.

2) The technological apparatus is very much a part of the visual impact of the pieces, and Oursler obviously foregrounds the utterly symbiotic relationship between camera and image; it is thus interesting to note that, except in installation shots, the machines are cropped out of the frame in the photographic documentation of these works.

3) Michael Ritchie, "Tony Oursler: Technology as an Instinct Amplifier," *Flash Art* (January/February 1996), p. 76.

TONY OURSLER, *all 1996, video projection on fiberglass spheres of 9 or 18" diameter.*
Videoprojektion auf Fiberglaskugeln von 23 bzw. 46 cm Durchmesser.

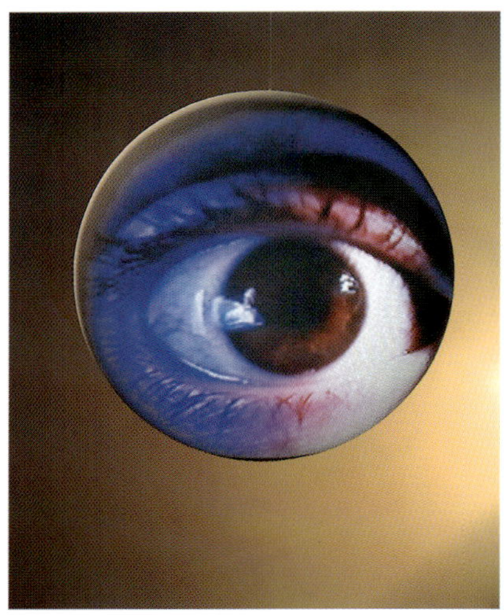

WHO'S / WESSEN

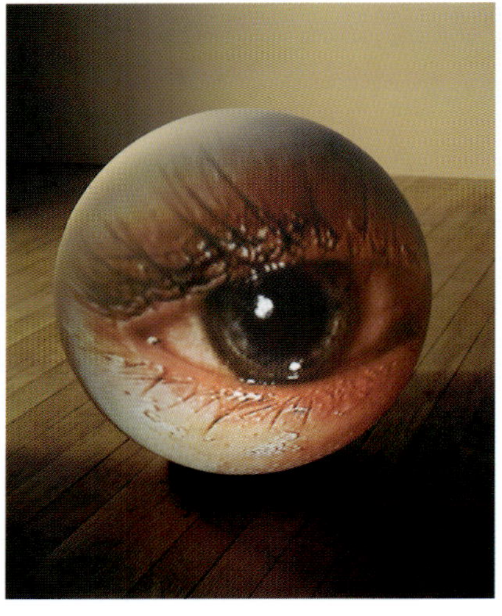

CRYING / WEINEND

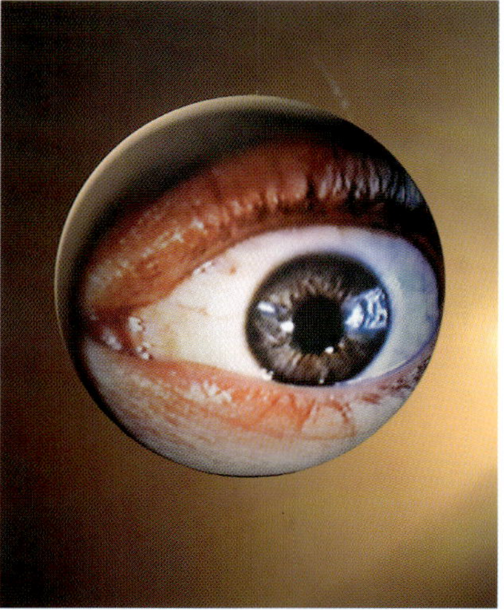

THE THREE FACES OF... / DIE DREI GESICHTER VON...

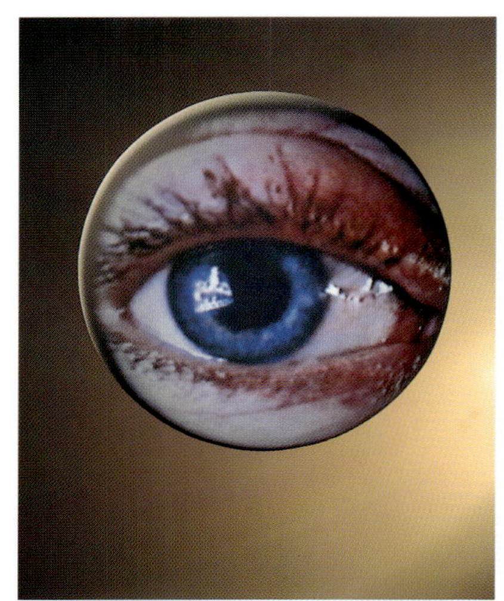

FIRE / FEUER

Performers:

Linda Bennett, Tracy Leipold, Ben Barzune, Constance Dejong, Joe Gibbons, Tia Shin, Noel Williams, Kristin Lucas

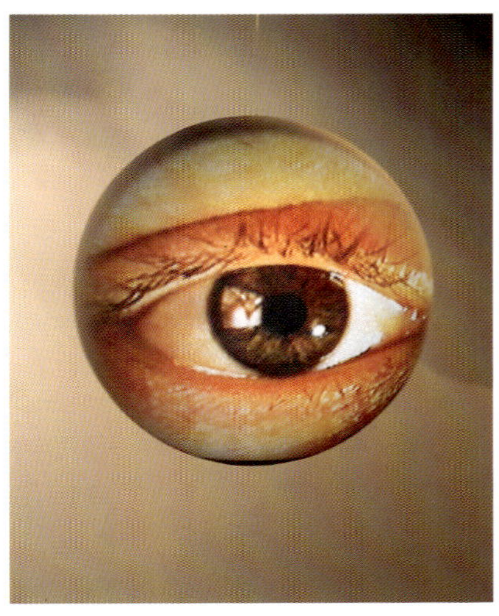

(NO) SKIN / (KEINE) HAUT

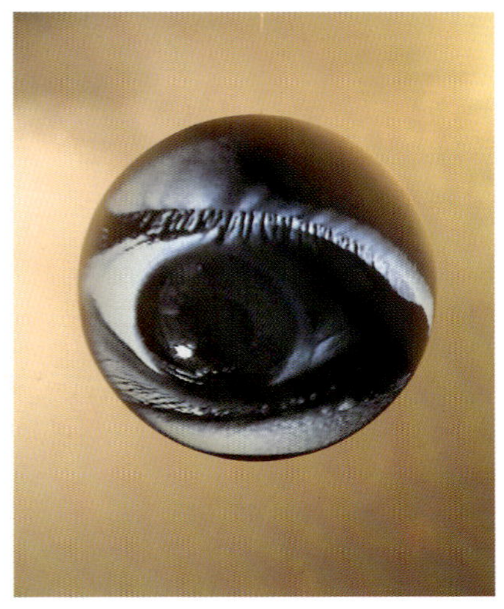

TRAIN / ZUG

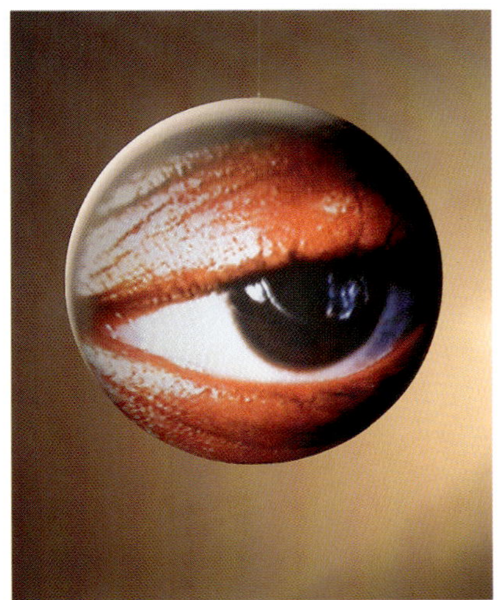

SYBIL & ME / SYBIL & ICH

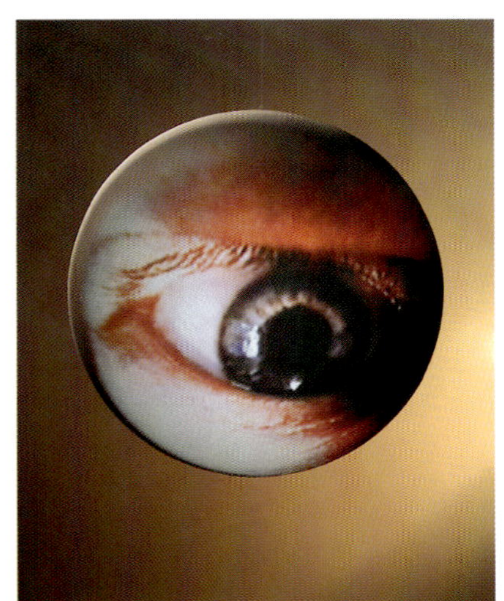

ATARI

FRANCES RICHARD

Wie Wasser

Der Weltraum ist angeblich ein Vakuum – stumm und unendlich, obwohl er mit Klängen von Sphärenmusik erfüllt sein soll. Als Gefilde des Göttlichen und Heimat der Ausserirdischen besitzt das All eine Realität, die wir nur mit Hilfe der Technologie erfahren können. Es stellt eine Grenze dar, deren Endgültigkeit im kollektiven Bewusstsein lebendig ist. Da kaum einer diesen Raum je direkt erlebt, verlagert er sich in unser Inneres und wird zur unendlich dehnbaren Metapher für alles, was fremd und grenzenlos ist.

Tony Ourslers Skulpturen sind Gesandte aus dieser Parallelwelt, Kreaturen, die uns daran erinnern sollen, dass die herrschenden Mächte dort draussen sich manchmal kaum von den seltsamen Zwängen hienieden unterscheiden. Der Äther strömt durch uns hindurch, ob wir es wollen oder nicht, und das kommerzielle bewegte Bild – wie der Raum, durch den die Satellitensignale flitzen – ist genauso ein unsere Existenz bestimmender Faktor wie eine von uns entwickelte Vorstellung. Die banale Kakophonie der verkabelten Kultur macht die am leichtesten verständliche Faszination von Ourslers Arbeiten aus, und seine durch Video animierten Figuren sind offensichtliche Totems einer durch diese Kultur geförderten Schizophrenie. Zunächst weniger augenfällig ist die heikle Beziehung zwischen dem Verständnis seines Werkes als das eines Technofreaks und dem, was Oursler als seine «höchst vergeistigte Seite»[1] bezeichnet. Das «Vergeistigte» drückt sich in seinem Vertrauen auf das einfache Wunder der Bewegung aus und im Festhalten am kleinsten gemeinsamen Nenner menschlicher Gegenwart: Gesicht und Stimme. Obwohl es für den verbalen Teil seiner Arbeiten meist eine Art Drehbuch gibt, will Oursler weniger Geschichten erzählen, als vielmehr das Energiefeld seiner Figuren über das Visuelle hinaus in die knisternde Luft ausdehnen.

An unsichtbaren Bändern hängen dreizehn weisse Ballen mit einem Durchmesser von 20 bis 45 Zentimeter von der Decke, beinah könnte man glauben, sie schwebten in selbsterzeugten Lichtkegeln über dem Boden: Auf jeden wird das farbige, bewegliche Bild eines Auges projiziert. Pupillen wandern oder starren vor sich hin, Lider zucken, ein Auge weint. Jeder dieser Beobachter ist anders, ihre Blau- und Brauntöne sind in unterschiedliche Ellipsen aus schimmernder Sklera, Haut und Wimpern eingebettet. Das Halbdunkel des Raumes birgt ein Sonnensystem riesiger, vor sich hinstarrender Götter, die offenbar völlig hypnotisiert sind von der Quelle ihrer Existenz, schnittigen, kleinen Videokameras, die wie kecke, fragende E.T.s vor jedem schimmernden Augapfel stehen.[2] Ein undefinierbares, allgegenwärtiges Geräusch erfüllt den Raum. Und bei genauerem Hinsehen entdecken wir in jeder Iris einen winzigen Bildschirm, vergleichbar dem entscheidenden weissen Farbtupfer, dem Lebensfünklein in den leuchtenden Augen der Porträts alter Meister.

Es entsteht eine gewollte Spannung im Glitzern dieser Zyklopenaugen. TV-Strahlen erzeugend und von TV-Strahlen erzeugt, sind sie ein treffender Kommentar zur durch Kathodenstrahlen erzeugten Selbsthypnose. Verblüffend ist, dass man nicht daran zweifelt, dass diese Wesen uns anschauen und uns etwas zumurmeln, bis man die reflektierten Bildschirme sieht und das Geräusch im Raum mit den dort aufgezeichneten Shows verbindet. Geht man als

FRANCES RICHARD lebt und schreibt in New York.

TONY OURSLER, SUBMERGED, 1995/1996,
video projection system, wood, plexiglass, ceramic, water, performance: Tracy Leipold, 53 x 11 x 11" plus equipment /
EINGETAUCHT, Videoprojektionsanlage, Holz, Plexiglas, Keramik, Wasser, 134,6 x 28 x 28 cm plus technische Apparate.

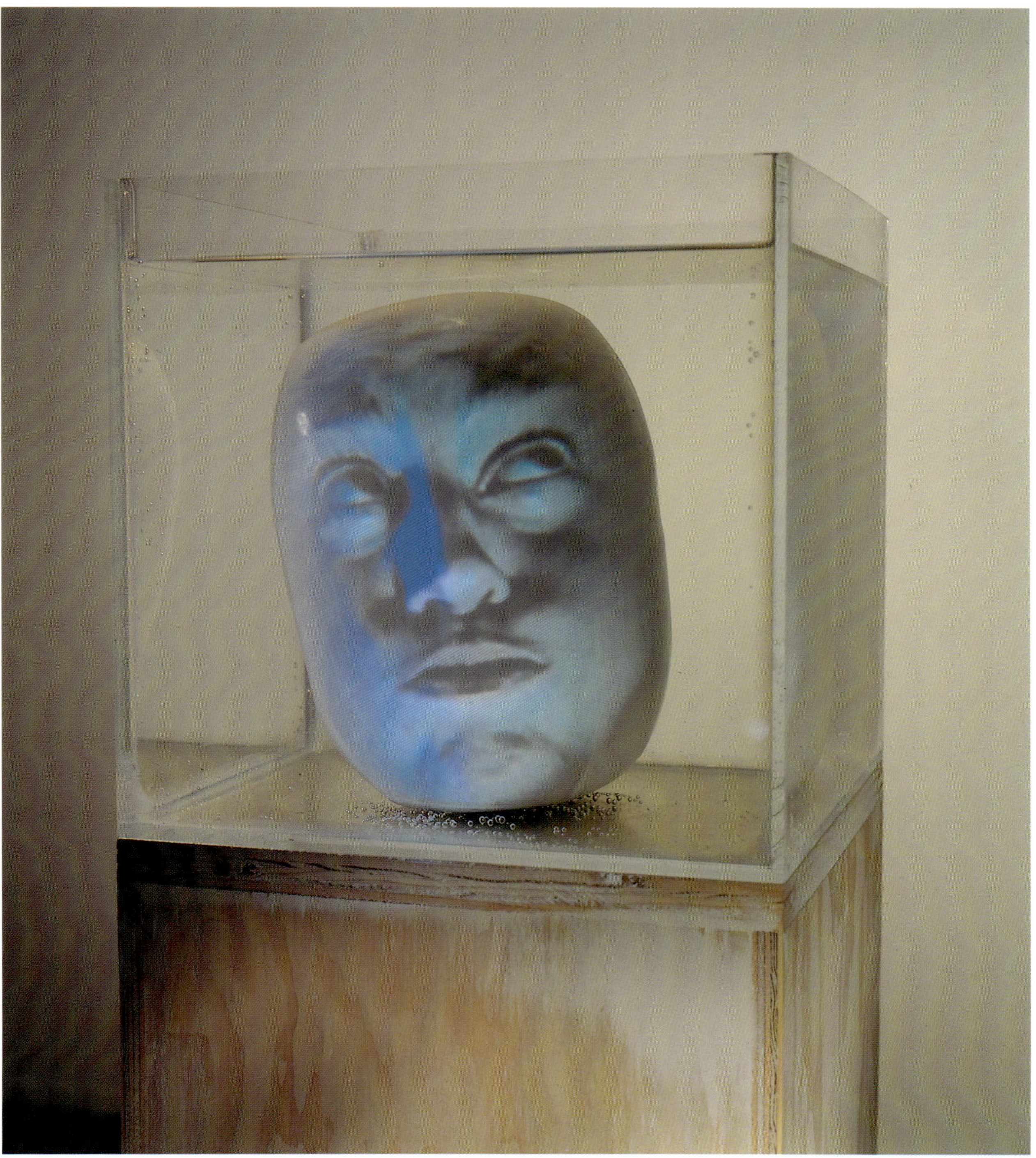

Betrachter, sich seines eigenen Körpers und seiner Bewegungen nun plötzlich bewusst, zwischen ihnen durch, kommt zu dem Unbehagen, überwacht zu werden, eine Art voyeuristisches Staunen hinzu, ähnlich dem, das man empfindet, wenn man zum ersten Mal durch ein Fernrohr blickt oder durch das Glas auf die bewegten, leuchtend bunten Formen in einem Aquarium. Wir halten inne und versuchen zu erraten, was diese Augen sagen. Doch ihre Botschaften erweisen sich als geschlossene Kreise. Die Offenbarung bleibt aus – ausser dass sich dieses Mehrkanal-Geflüster vielleicht wie eine Offenbarung anhört.

Unter Wasser kann man nur gurgelnde Laute von sich geben oder den Atem anhalten. Das androgyne Wesen in SUBMERGED (Eingetaucht, 1995–96) besteht nur aus einem Kopf, und der ist noch nicht einmal vollständig, denn der Hinterkopf, die Seiten und die Schädeldecke sind erschreckend glatt und weiss, ohne Haare und Ohren. Und doch hat die entscheidende Instanz dem Wesen genügend Individualität zugestanden, um seine Situation bedrohlich erscheinen zu lassen. Dieser mitleiderregende Ertrinkende, der angstvoll nach der Wasseroberfläche schielt, die Backen aufbläst und die Augen fest zusammenpresst, ist auf die reine Gebärde reduziert und spricht die universale Sprache der Not. Im Gegensatz zu den oben erwähnten Augen, die die Zuschauer umgeben und dazwischentretende Menschen in ihre befremdende Atmosphäre hineinziehen, betont SUBMERGED den Abstand zwischen Betrachter und Betrachtetem. Es ist eine schreckliche Situation, gefährlich, ungemütlich und auf eine schändliche und unerklärliche Art öffentlich. «Holt es da raus!» bedrängte eine kleine Ausstellungsbesucherin ihre Eltern. Aber was tun? Das Wesen aus seinem Element zu befreien hiesse es ganz zu zerstören.

Dem klaren existentiellen Einzeiler von SUBMERGED steht FLOCK (Herde, 1966) gegenüber, eine Familie sprechender Holzpuppen mit den inzwischen bekannten riesigen, weissen Köpfen. Es sind zwei grosse Figuren, die eine steht schützend hinter der Gruppe, die zweite sitzt vorn, und beide legen je einen Arm um die vier kleinen dazwischen. Alle sechs Gesichter geben die Mimik ein und desselben, über längere Zeit aufgezeichneten Gesichts wieder. Dieses ist schlicht zu gross für die kahlen Beulen, auf

die es projiziert wird. Die daraus resultierenden Mienen könnte man als manische Variationen eines «Machen-wir-das-Beste-draus»-Lächelns bezeichnen, eine Art emotionaler Verteidigungsmechanismus, der osmotisch von den Eltern auf die Kinder übertragen wird. «Lies deine Bibel … kämpfe … kämpfe … kämpfe», murmelt eine Figur. «Was ist mit der Familie? Was ist mit der Familie? Was ist mit der Familie?» fiept eine andere. «Was hast du erwartet?» fragt die sitzende Figur, die im traditionellen Familienbild der Mutter entspräche. Ihre Stimmen klingen blechern, monoman, kaum verständlich. Man muss stehenbleiben und sich den Gesichtern zuwenden, um sie zu verstehen, doch selbst dann treibt uns eine unwillkürliche Ungeduld weiter, bevor das Endlosband einmal durchgelaufen ist. Deshalb hören wir auch nur Redefetzen und unverständliches Geplapper, das analog zur atmosphärischen Starrheit der Augen-Arbeiten eher ein nervöses akustisches Gezischel ist als eine gestaltete Erzählung.

Die Videobilder passen perfekt auf die Kopfstümpfe, sie folgen der Form ihrer weissen Masse, und selbst die Gegenwart der Kameras vor ihren Podesten zerstört nicht die Illusion. Hier entpuppt sich Oursler als Maler, der auf die zweidimensionale Illusion vertraut, auf die bewährte Praxis, Farbe auf eine Fläche aufzutragen, so dass die modellierten Schatten eine lebensechte Wirkung erzeugen. Nur sind seine Bilder nicht aus einem festen Material, das Bewegung vortäuscht, sondern ein unstoffliches Geflimmer, das den Eindruck des Körperlichen vermittelt. «Video ist wie Wasser», meint Oursler, «eine völlig ätherische Form, die fünfzig Jahre lang im Fernseher eingeschlossen war.»[3] Befreit – oder aus der Enge der Kiste entlassen, ist Ourslers Video ein wechselhaftes Vergnügen, ein ständiges Spiel mit der Wahrnehmung, dessen Erfolgsgeheimnis in seiner Einfachheit liegt. *(Übersetzung: Uta Goridis)*

1) Elizabeth Janus, «Ein Gespräch mit Tony Oursler», *Paletten*, Nr. 222, März 1995, S. 70.
2) Die technischen Vorrichtungen sind ein wichtiger Bestandteil der Arbeiten, und Oursler rückt die symbiotische Beziehung zwischen Kamera und Bild deutlich in den Vordergrund. Interessant ist in diesem Zusammenhang, dass, abgesehen von Aufnahmen der Installationen, in der photographischen Dokumentation dieser Arbeiten die Apparate nicht im Bild erscheinen.
3) Michael Ritchie, «Tony Oursler: Technology as an Instinct Amplifier», *Flash Art*, Januar/Februar 1996, S. 76.

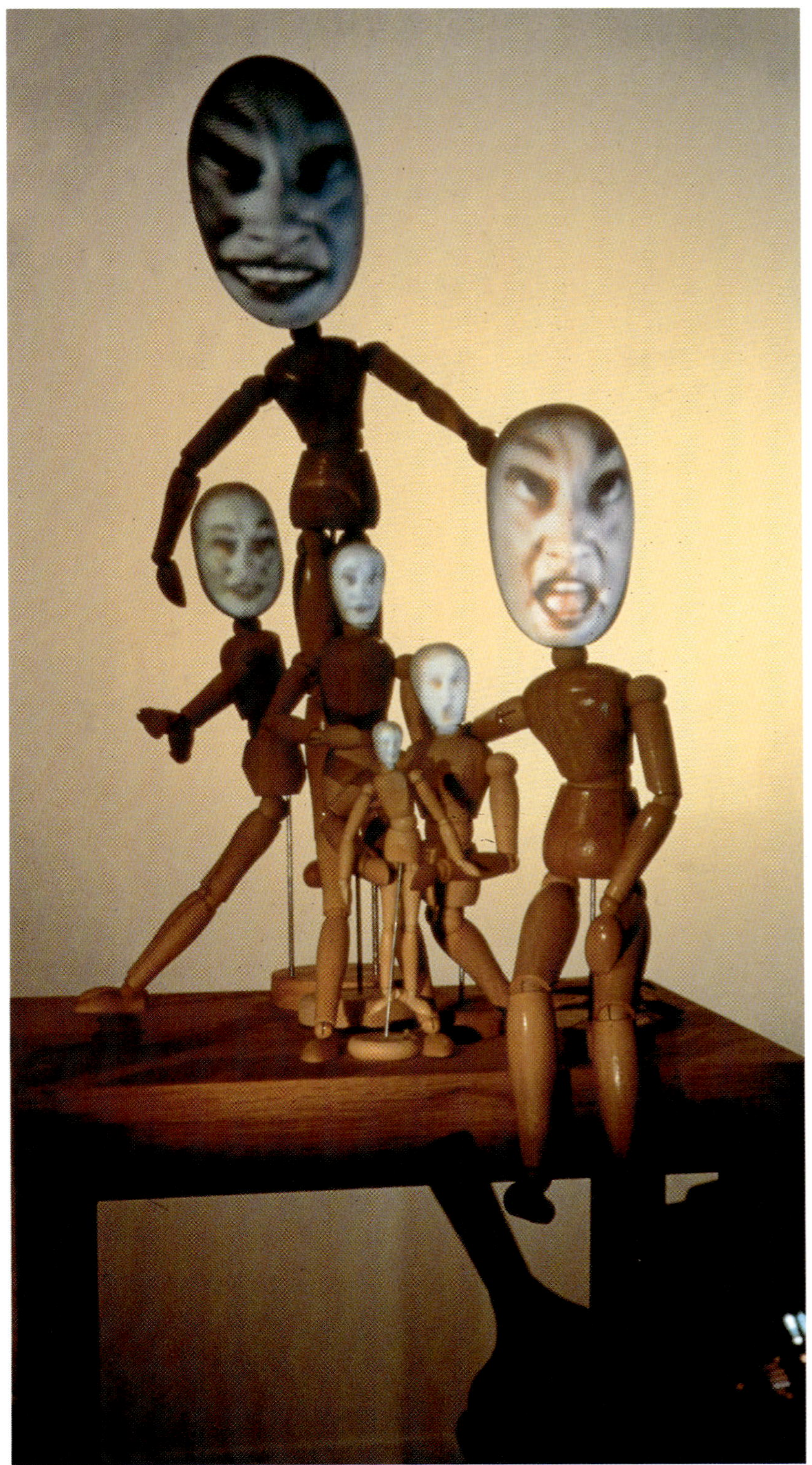

ANYWHERE IN THE COUNTRY AT ANY TIME, ANYONE...PEACE, IT'S ROTTING YOUR BRAIN...MINE, YOURS, MINE, YOURS...WHAT DID YOU EXPECT?...THAT'S NOT FUNNY—IT HURT!...NEW JERSEY, MORE LIQUOR, O.K...ALL MEN ARE SINNERS, NONE IS RIGHTEOUS...FREAKED FREAK FREAKING SPIDER MAN...DID YOU SAY $16.99? YES, I SAID $14.99...NO, YOUR HEAD IS GOING TO EXPLODE!... THE ELECTRONIC FRONTIER, SHOOT THE GUN, DROP THE BOMB, FEED THE PIG...SHADOW, ORAL, LOW, CHANNEL... TIME, THINK...ALL OF A SUDDEN SOMETHING NEW, UNKNOWN, COLD, VOLATILE.

IRGENDWO IM LAND, IRGENDWANN, IRGENDWER... FRIEDEN, ER SCHLÄGT DIR AUFS HIRN... MEIN, DEIN, MEIN, DEIN... WAS HAST DU ERWARTET?... DAS IST NICHT LUSTIG – HAT WEH GETAN!... NEW JERSEY, MEHR SCHNAPS, O.K... ALLE MENSCHEN SIND SÜNDER, KEINER IST GERECHT... ZERLUMPTER FREAK, LAUSIGER SPINNENMANN... HAST DU GESAGT 19 FRANKEN 95? JA, ICH SAGTE 16.95... NEIN, DEIN KOPF WIRD GLEICH EXPLODIEREN!... DIE ELEKTRONISCHE GRENZSICHERUNG, SCHIESS MIT DEM GEWEHR, WIRF DIE BOMBE AB, FÜTTERE DIE SCHWEINE... SCHATTEN, MUND, NIEDRIG, KANAL... ZEIT, DENK... PLÖTZLICH ETWAS NEUES, UNBEKANNTES, KALTES, FLÜCHTIGES.

TONY OURSLER, FLOCK, 1996, video projection system, wood, paint, 64 x 16 x 14" plus equipment / HERDE, Videoprojektion, Holz, Farbe, 163 x 41 x 36 cm.

TONY OURSLER
TALKING LIGHT, 1996

(heavy breathing) AAAAA-CHHHHHH....AAAAA-HHHHHHH.... CHHHHHHH.... ■ AAAAHHHH-HHHHHH..vast areas...vast areas...ultra marine...ultra marine... ■ shadows...shadows...shadows...they move...they balance (thud)...turn up the intensity... ■ turn up the intensity...turn-up-the-intensity...the living energy...golden...golden...notice the alternation...notice the alternation...it is my Objective to pit light against dark...cobalt blue...cobalt blue...the space is broken...the space is broken...unlock the code... ■ CK...UH...O...EH...EE...contrast...color...discipline...HA ha HA HA HA...UNNHH-HHHHH...HHHHH-HHHHH....UNNHHH-HHHH...areas seem to exude different moods...now...now...I can lead you...I can lead you...look at me...Look At Me...Look-at-Me!...Loook at Meeee...give me colors...give me colors...more, more, more, mooore!... ■ details, details, details...the devil is in the details...am I giving off the wrong message?...am I giving...off...the wrong...message...message...AH...EE...MMM...OH...EH...UH...ULP.. ■ blocks...unlock the code...the recorders...one eighth...twelve sixteenths...is it on or off... ■ is...it...on...or...off...on...off...ON...OFFF...think, think, think, think, think, think, think, think, think, think, think, think, think, think, think, think...HHHHHH...UNH-HHHHH... ■ UNH-HHHHH...UNH-HHHH...make me a shadow...make me a shadow...make... ■ me...a...shadow...now...cadmium red...cadmium red...cadmium redddddd... ■ HHHHHCHHHCHH (coughing)...lightlightlightlightlightlight...clear...bold...(coughing) day...night...day...night...my deepest values Serve to separate...violet Is overwhelming...do not use violet...lucky...lucky...lucky...blocks...recognize Your Mistakes...recognize Your achievements...details, details, details...the god is in the details...AH...HHHH...UCH-HHHHH-UUUUCHK...don't...don't...don't turn out the light...don't...I can't stand the darkness...I...can't...stand...the darkness...UCKHHH....yellow...yellow is dangerous...stay away from...yellow...stay close to...stay close to pink...pink is good...ULP...six... ■ fourteen...eight...sixty-five...three...okay...okay...all of the previous steps..have been executed...proceed...don't stay in one place For too long...if you are not going forward, you are going backwards...uh...contrast, oh...contrast...light, shadow, pattern, uh...you cannot see the object, you cannot see the object, you cannot see the object...you cannot see the object...only the light which it reflects...now...I...have...established...the light source. HHaa...HHAAA-HAA!...I have established the light source...day...night... ■ day...night...UHHH-HHHH....OHHH...HHCCHHHH (coughing)...highlights... ■ highlights...more highlights...the Center of the composition Lacks interest...the center...center...the underlying Harmony is in the shapes, unlock the code... ■ AH...OO...LA...HEH...UR...do not read the wrong message..." (transcription from CD, voice of the artist)

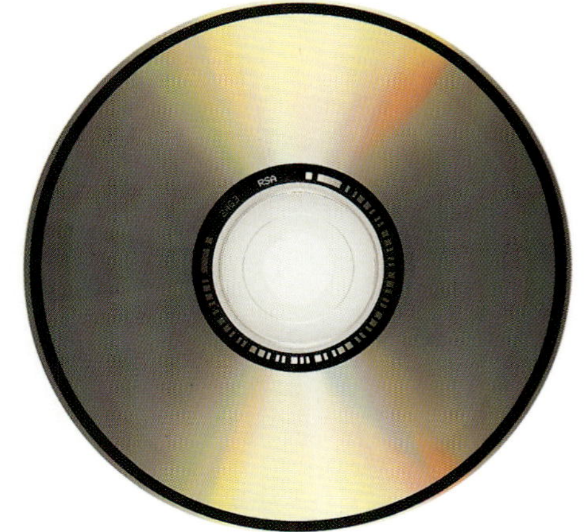

TALKING LIGHT, 1996
**Compact disk with artist's voice, light bulb,
sound organ kit; the light bulb reacts to the
frequency of the voice on the CD.**
Edition: 50/XX

**Compact Disk mit der Stimme des Künstlers,
Glühbirne, Tonverstärker mit Zubehör;
die Glühbirne reagiert auf die Frequenzen der
Stimme auf der CD.**
Auflage: 50/XX

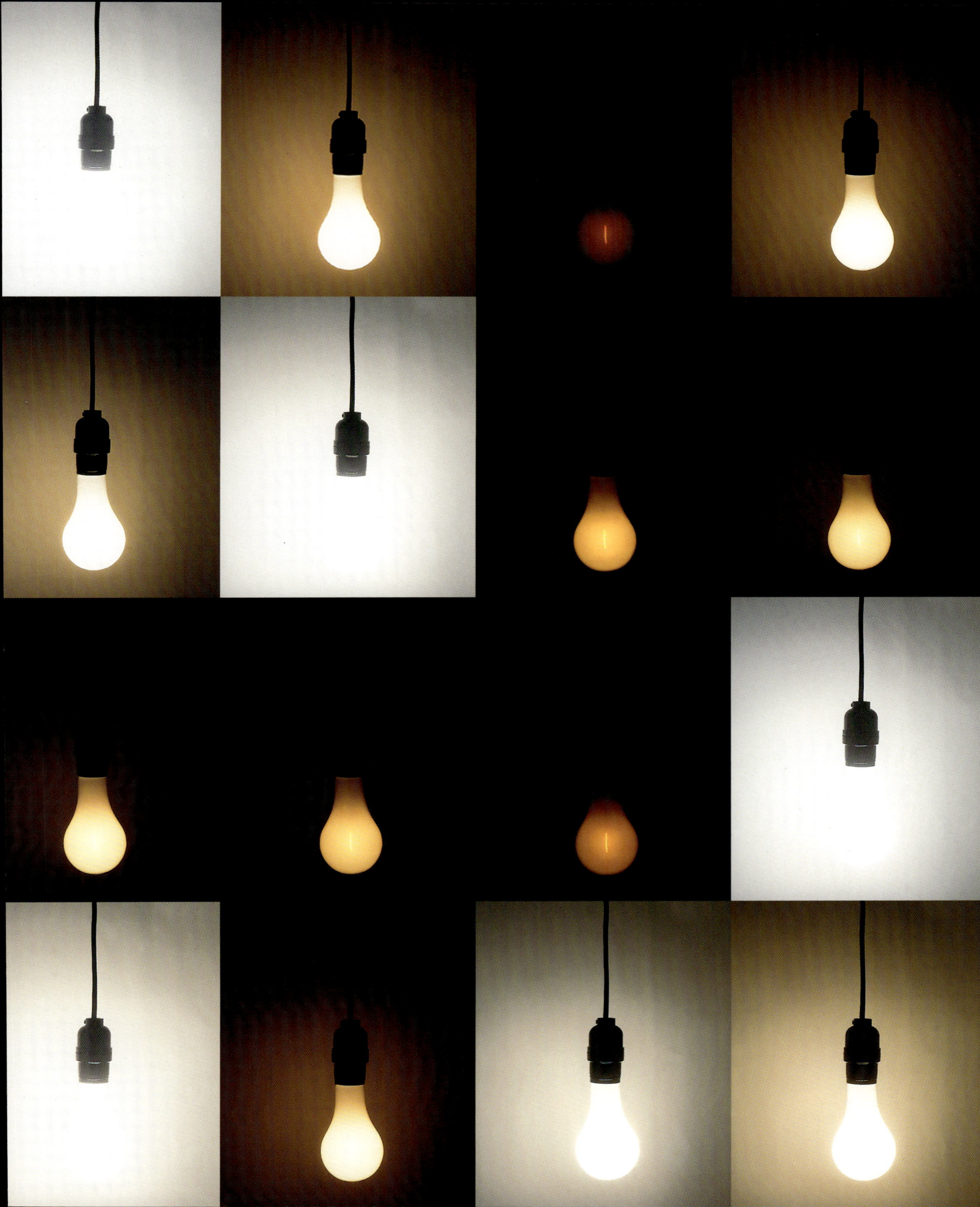

Raymond

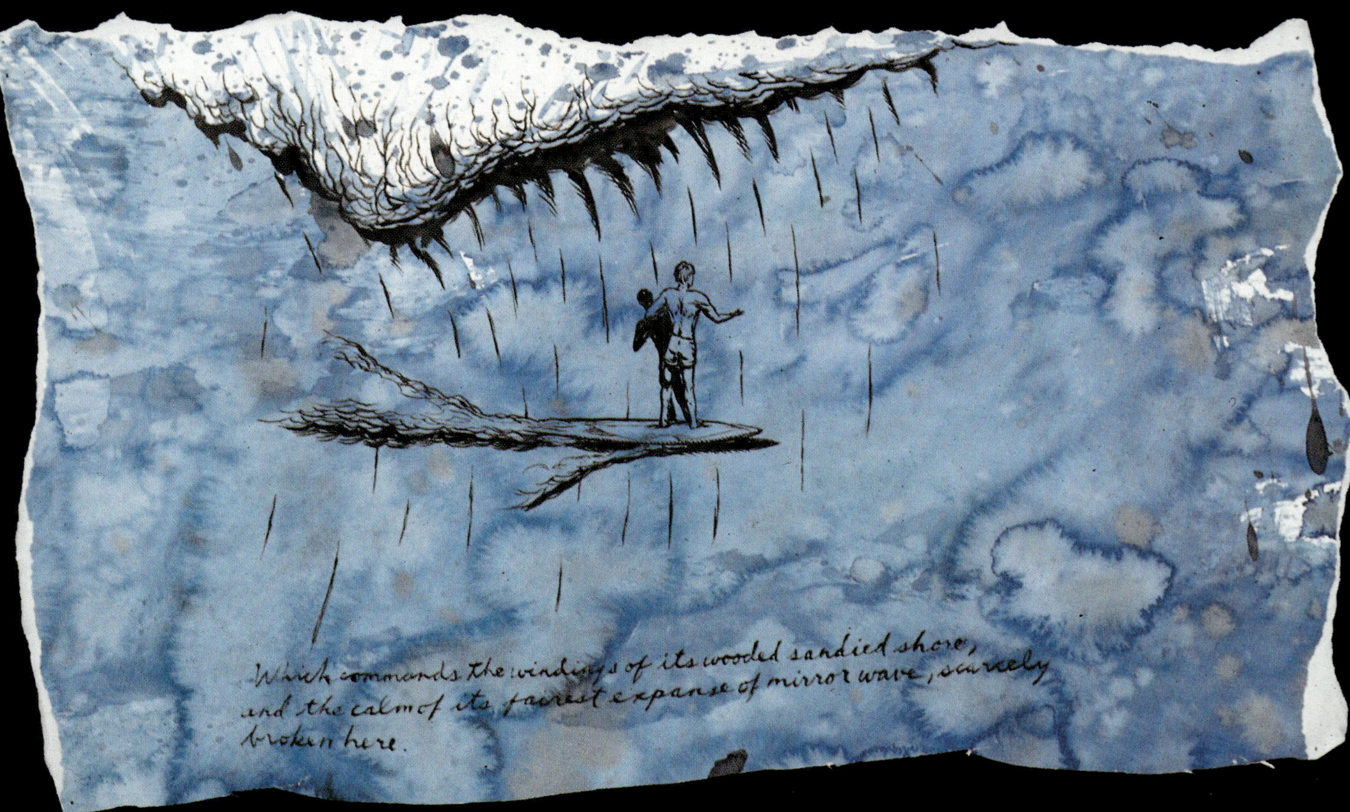

Pettibon

JIM LEWIS

A Conversation with
Raymond Pettibon

We need a new word for the kind of apprehending we bring to bear on a Pettibon drawing; our standard understanding of the eye's saccade and the mind's recreation of meaning just doesn't seem to be sufficient. Indeed, everything we do is opposite from its ordinary nature: We read the images as easily and immediately as if they were words, and let our eyes wander back and forth over the texts, piecing their meaning together the way we do the elements of a cubist painting. And no sooner has one finished than another drawing appears, and another, and another, a thousand Pettibons, each of them broodingly beautiful, subtle and complex, each to be admired for the fragility of its faith, its humor, its erudition. As much as any artist I can think of, Pettibon makes good on the promise of the Twentieth Century: that every scrap of culture counts for something, that the individual bits and pieces of our experience and our history can be reconstituted into some able story of our lives.

JIM LEWIS is a critic and a writer who lives in New York City.

JIM LEWIS: I always wondered what's important to you about the images in your drawings. Why didn't you just become a writer?

RAYMOND PETTIBON: You could ask the same question of a writer: You know, why doesn't he do what I do? I think it's as legitimate a form as any other; I always wondered why it wasn't exploited more often. It's not like the visual part is a crutch or anything. It's true, my primary interest has always been the writing part of it much more then the visual arts, but I don't think it stands by itself as writing: It's not literature, it's art.

JL: Do you think of the drawings as illustration of the text, or the text as commentary on the visuals?

RP: I don't really think of it in those terms at all. Sometimes I kind of play with the whole idea of illumination, as if the text was something that was passed down from God to the lowly monks, who spend the duration of their lives illuminating it. But that's just another way of placing the whole question in a context that makes it senseless. Sometimes I almost wish I could have some kind of contract with the devil, giving away my everyday life, if that would buy me the thousand years I need to really begin to understand the work I'm doing.

JL: Can you give me a sense of the influences on the visual side of your work?

RP: When I started, they were derived from a kind of etching style, of, for instance, Whistler, or Samuel Palmer, or the style of Turner's paintings and his watercolors. Who else? John Sloane or Joseph Pennell, or Hopper. If you look at my earlier work, you can see Goya in it. Those are the kinds of the people who I learned to draw from. But as pure drawing my work didn't really amount to much; it probably still doesn't. The point about, for example, Pennell, is just that as an artist your influences aren't necessarily the people you admire the most, as a whole.

JL: The videos of yours that I've seen—the one about the *Weathermen*, for instance—are so much looser than the drawings, though I understand they're scripted down to the word. What's the relationship between the two media?

RP: In a sense the drawings are kind of like video stills; for a while I used to actually draw them from the video screen, by pausing a tape, usually some movie or something. I think that's how my style arose; it was kind of unintentional on my part, the film noir aspect of it.

I'd make more of my own videos, except that, even the way I do it—without a crew or anything—you still have to involve other people, and it's just a lot of trouble getting everyone on the same page. I'm not trying to be folksy and primitive; often I work in the form I do just for practical reasons. No aesthetic reasons at all. Money, time, talent, skill, the number of assistants I have, those can dictate the form.

JL: How much of the text in your drawings is your own and how much is quotation?

RP: I don't really know. It depends on the period. I remember going a few years at least just writing entirely on my own. But a lot of my work is a combination of both, and a lot of times neither the words nor the drawings are finished for several years. In the last year or so I've been borrowing a lot more, but overall maybe a third is borrowed. It might be more. It's hard to say; because it's not just borrowed, it's changed around sometimes. And I can revert, in my own writing, to the style I'm borrowing from; and

in any one drawing there might be any number of voices.

JL: I've always wondered how much Melville there is in them. You use the same sort of humor, the same very sly sentence structure. And you seem to like a certain exclamatory rhetoric; your people are always blurting out things.

RP: I like Melville a lot, but oddly enough there's very little of him in my work. I use the kind of blurting out that's caught off guard, very fragmentary expressions, rather than something that's fully formed. Shakespeare is another writer that I don't borrow from much, partly because the expressions in his plays are so fully formed. Whereas the writing of Marlowe, for instance, who's from the same period, lends itself a lot easier to what I'm doing. But my primary sources are the great prose writers, like Henry James and Proust and Ruskin and Pater. And Thomas Browne. If you read them you'll come across quite a bit.

JL: These are all writers with a very elaborate syntax.

RP: Right, they're very elaborate, and the sentence structure can elaborate itself into very long paragraphs. But in a fragmentary way. Their work, taken out of context, can mean something completely different, and at the same time it's so beautifully said.

JL: When you read, do you read fitfully, or do you sit down and read books all the way through, and then go back and pull out your favorite passages?

RP: That depends: Lately it's been fitfully. And even if I'm reading something cover to cover, it's very… fitful. I can't think of a better description. Because it's a type of reading that's always looking for something between the lines. And I kind of rewrite as I go. It's as if I bring myself to this universe or something, and… It's hard to explain. But it becomes the world you're living in or thinking in.

JL: What is it about James that appeals to you?

RP: James, especially late in his career, had such a complicated mind. He was writing in a narrative form, but he couldn't for the life of him look at the simplest thing without looking at it from many different views. He always writes out of an inner struggle between the dramatic form and narrative, and this wealth of ideas and information that's imploding in each sentence. If you read his notes, you see what he

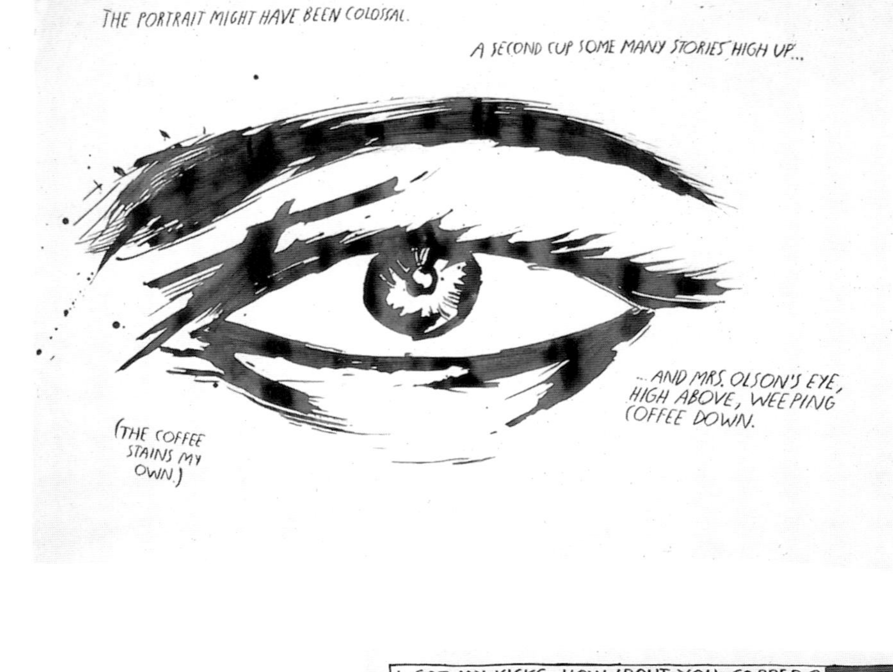

RAYMOND PETTIBON, NO TITLE (THE PORTRAIT), 1992,
pen and ink on paper, 12 x 17" / OHNE TITEL (DAS PORTRÄT),
Feder und Tusche auf Papier, 30,5 x 43,2 cm.

– NO TITLE (I'M SORRY. I'M), 1985, 12 x 9" /
OHNE TITEL (TUT MIR LEID. ICH BIN), 30,5 x 22,9 cm.

– NO TITLE, 1986, 11 x 8,5" / OHNE TITEL, 28 x 21,6 cm.

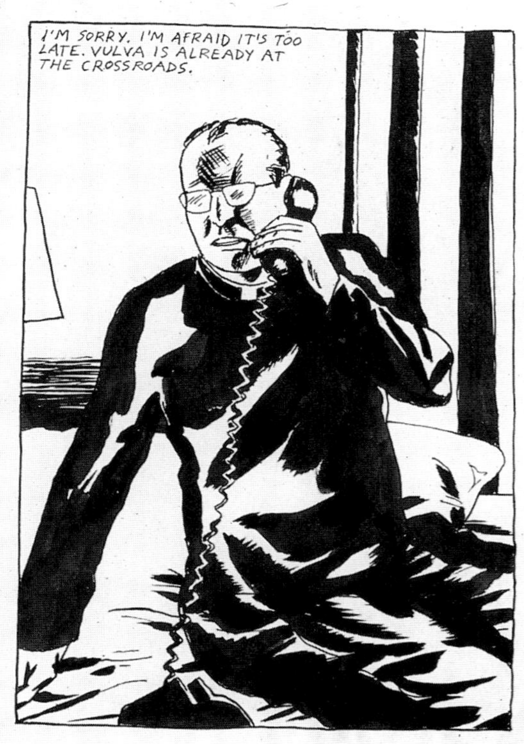

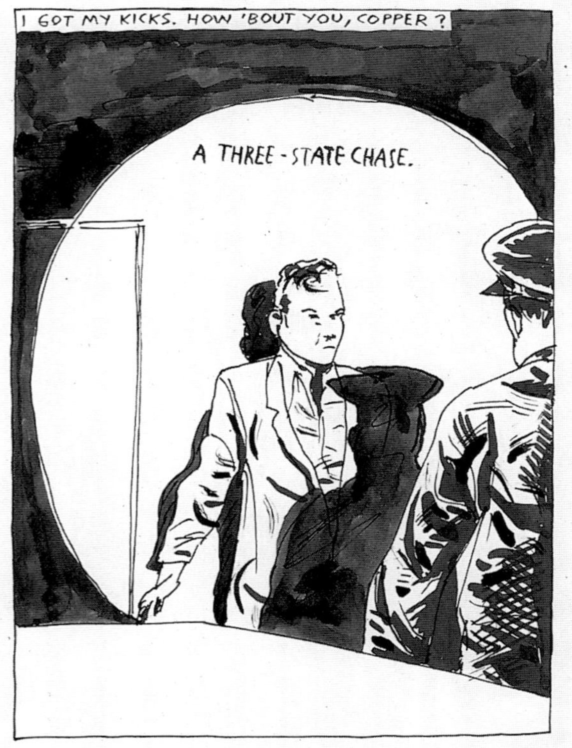

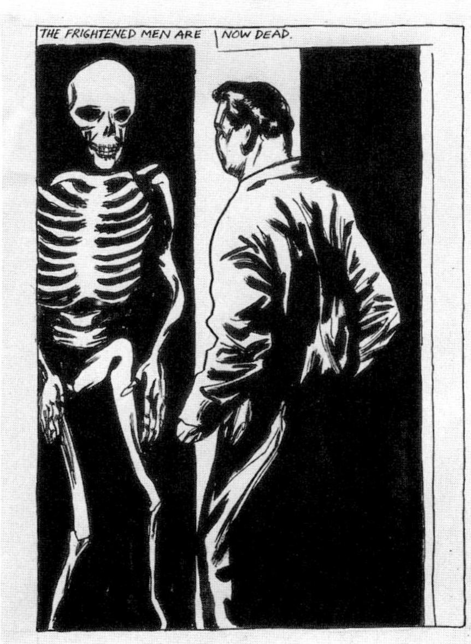

RAYMOND PETTIBON, NO TITLE (THE FRIGHTENED), 1985, pen and ink on paper, 14 x 10½" / OHNE TITEL (DIE ERSCHROK-KENEN), Feder und Tusche auf Papier, 35,6 x 26,7 cm.

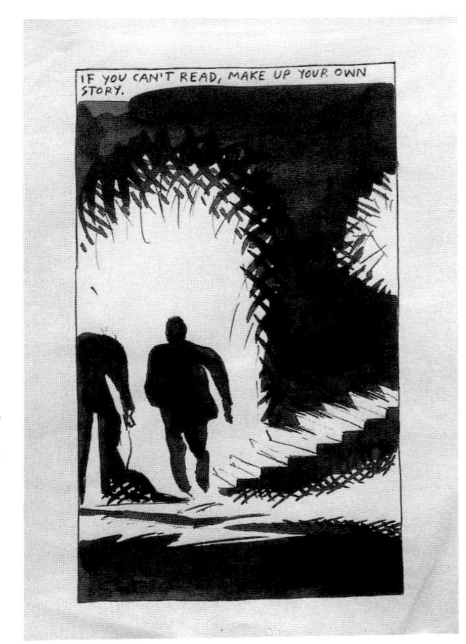

RAYMOND PETTIBON, NO TITLE (IF YOU CAN'T READ, MAKE), 1986, pen and ink on paper, 14 x 11" / OHNE TITEL (WENN DU NICHT LESEN KANNST, ERFINDE), Feder und Tusche auf Papier, 35,6 x 28 cm.

goes through to keep to the narratives he sets up for himself, which start with these very simple ideas. They're kind of pathetic; it's like something you'd hear in a Disney story conference, these moral conundrums, or what-ifs, you know.

I have this funny image of him dictating to his old secretary and just going off on all this stuff, and trying desperately to maintain some kind of narrative, dramatic organization. And for a lot of people not really succeeding, which is why he's so difficult to read; you immediately lose the thread of the narrative, and it seems like he's meandering around in language. But he actually isn't. He's desperately trying to keep control. For the kind of reading I do, it's perfect. To me it's—I don't know if you'd say fun to read—but I guess I would.

JL: Do you find that it mimics thought patterns, or do you like it precisely because it is so mannered?

RP: The criticism of him is that it isn't real, that it's all mannerism, but it does mimic thought patterns. To me that's its appeal. I mean, people have always said that about me, too, that, you know, you don't want to get me started, I can't stick to the facts or the starting point without adding another tangent that I have to go off on. But I think that's a mimicking of the com-

plexity of thought and reality, and the relationship between the two, more than anything else. Whereas, to pretend to tell a simple story and tie everything up at the end is actually wrong, really. It's dishonest.

JL: Your work seems to me to be perfectly contemporary— not so much because you take on, for example, Elvis cults and Ronald Reagan, but because of the means of representation that you use, which is at once fragmentary and ephemeral, and very... lapidary. It's peculiar to find that the syntax and the structure of a Jamesian sentence can be so perfectly applied to a contemporary situation.

RP: Yeah, well that's what's fun about it. There's a sense of humor to it that has really found its audience in the art world. But I'm not a throwback; I think my work is contemporary.

JL: I find it striking that in some sense you're very much an American artist, even very much a California artist, and yet none of your sources in literature seem to be American.

RP: Well, that's not true. Hawthorne. Twain—sometimes he tries too hard to be funny, but sometimes, for some reason, just a phrase can seem really funny to me. I remember when I was young, reading Huck Finn, and this kid says, "Give me chaw tobacker, won't ye?" And for some reason I just thought the

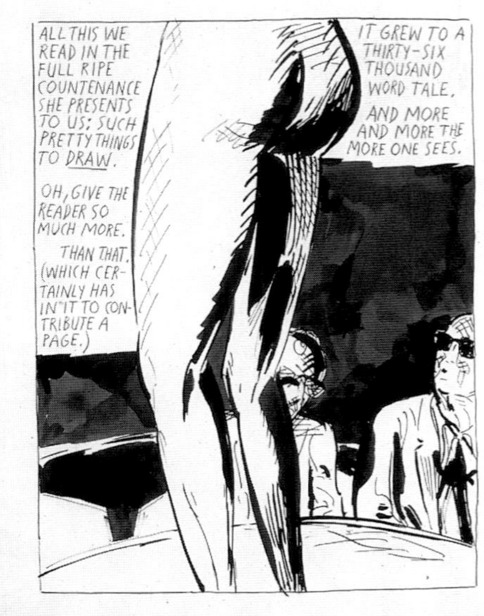

RAYMOND PETTIBON, NO TITLE (ALL THIS WE READ), 1989, pen and ink on paper, 14 x 11" / OHNE TITEL (DAS ALLES LESEN WIR), Feder und Tusche auf Papier, 35,6 x 28 cm.

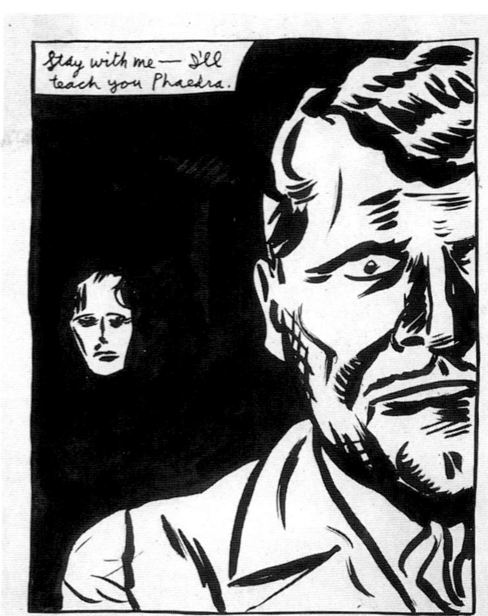

RAYMOND PETTIBON, NO TITLE (STAY WITH ME), 1987, pen and ink on paper, 14 x 11" / OHNE TITEL (BLEIB BEI MIR), Feder und Tusche auf Papier, 35,6 x 28 cm.

image of that, the vernacular, and the context was just so funny. But I guess I do have more of an affinity with a British sense of humor; I think of someone like Pinter, or Anthony Powell, or Evelyn Waugh. As long as you don't take it as far as Monty Python, or British musical-hall comedy. I can be as vulgar as anyone, I guess, but even when I'm writing about Ronald Reagan's asshole or something, I try to have a measure of decorum.

JL: Are cartoons a context in which you're comfortable having your work seen?

RP: No. No. My work comes from a lot of traditions, including those, but I wouldn't say that cartoons or comics are that important. On the other hand, that's not a qualitative judgment; I'm not putting myself above them; I just think they're two different things.

JL: Are you so sure that there are no qualitative judgments to be made, based on a distinction between high and low art?

RP: That's a different question altogether. Is that to say that the best of George Herriman is automatically worse than the worst of Norman Mailer?

JL: No. On the other hand I am a little tired of the whole cultural studies thing. It seems as if the pendulum has swung so far in the opposite direction that it may be

time, people started wondering if maybe, for example, pop music really wasn't capable of expressing a very wide range of emotions, or capturing a very wide range of phenomena.

RP: I've wondered exactly about that myself. Sometimes I blame the times, and ask, what happened? All I can say is that I keep expecting something from people who work in the "lower" arts, because I don't think there's any innate reason why these forms can't encompass the same range of emotion and thought as anything else. But it doesn't seem to have happened, so maybe it's now necessary to say, no, they can't. And at the same time I keep thinking that, well, maybe, it's just that the right people aren't going into it.

And I also have to check myself sometimes, because I tend to apply literary standards to things that either don't need them or shouldn't. Rock and roll, for instance. It's something that doesn't have to translate to paper, to poetry, in the first place. I don't know. I mean, I like rock and roll, too, and I like some of it better than I like some poetry. So, the issue does get muddied up. All I can say is I'm fed up with the discussion and the uses it's put to. Most of the writers I like aren't even read anymore.

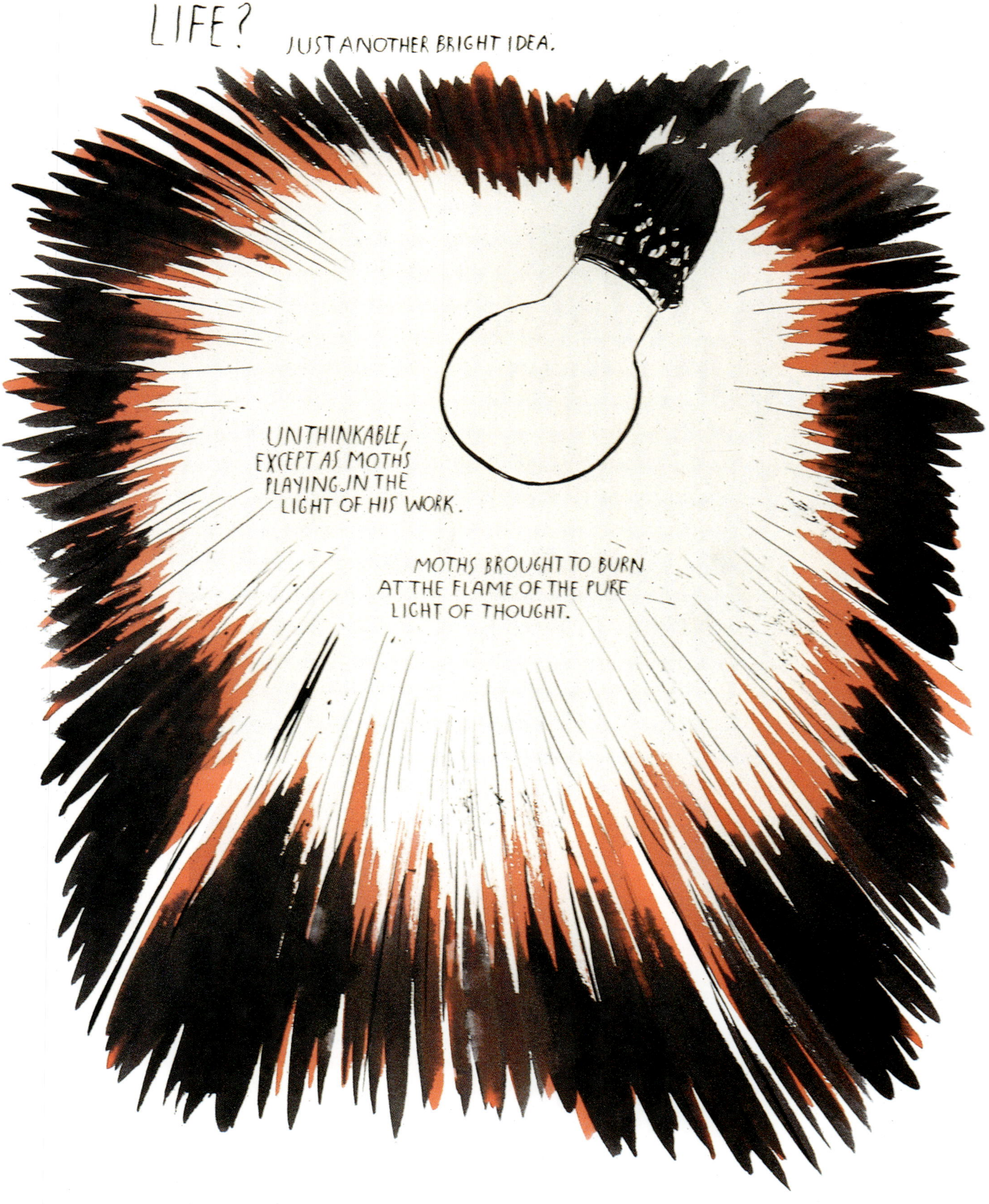

LIFE?
JUST ANOTHER BRIGHT IDEA.
UNTHINKABLE,
EXCEPT AS MOTHS
PLAYING IN THE
LIGHT OF HIS WORK.
MOTHS BROUGHT TO BURN
AT THE FLAME OF THE PURE
LIGHT OF THOUGHT.

JIM LEWIS

Ein Gespräch mit

Raymond Pettibon

Wir brauchen ein neues Wort für die Art, wie wir einer Zeichnung Pettibons zu Leibe rücken: Unser normales Verständnis des Vorganges als registrierendes Bewegen der Augen und Sinnrekonstruktion durch das Hirn erscheint einfach unzulänglich. Tatsächlich ist alles, was wir dabei tun, anders als sonst: Wir nehmen die Bilder so leicht und unmittelbar auf, als wären es Wörter, wir lassen unseren Blick über die Texte schweifen und stückeln ihre Bedeutung zusammen wie Elemente eines kubistischen Bildes. Und kaum sind wir soweit, taucht schon die nächste Zeichnung auf und noch eine und noch eine, tausend Pettibons, jeder einzelne tiefgründig schön, subtil und vielschichtig, jede einzelne Zeichnung bewundernswert ob der Zerbrechlichkeit ihrer Wahrheit, ihres Humors, ihrer Wissensfülle. Wie kaum ein anderer Künstler, der mir in den Sinn kommt, erfüllt Pettibon die Verheissung unseres Jahrhunderts, dass jedes Fetzchen Kultur zu etwas gut ist, und dass sich aus den einzelnen Bruchstücken unserer Erfahrung und Geschichte jederzeit eine brauchbare, unser Dasein reflektierende Erzählung rekonstruieren lässt.

JIM LEWIS ist Kritiker und Schriftsteller und lebt in New York.

JIM LEWIS: Ich habe mich schon immer gefragt, warum dir die Bildelemente in deinen Zeichnungen so wichtig sind. Warum bist du nicht einfach Schriftsteller geworden?

RAYMOND PETTIBON: Das gleiche könntest du einen Schriftsteller fragen. Warum macht er nicht dasselbe wie ich? In meinen Augen ist es eine Ausdrucksform, die so legitim ist wie jede andere; ich habe mich schon immer gefragt, warum man sich ihrer nicht häufiger bedient hat. Das bildliche Element ist ja keine Krücke oder so was. Zugegeben, mein Hauptinteresse galt schon immer mehr dem Geschriebenen als der bildnerischen Seite meines Werkes, aber ich glaube nicht, dass das Geschriebene für sich steht: Es ist keine Literatur, es ist bildende Kunst.

JL: Begreifst du die Zeichnungen als Illustration des Textes oder den Text als Kommentar zu den Bildern?

RP: Eigentlich betrachte ich das Ganze überhaupt nicht unter diesem Gesichtspunkt. Manchmal liebäugle ich ein bisschen mit der Idee der Buchmalerei, so als hätte Gott den Text demütigen Mönchen eingegeben, die sich daraufhin ihr Leben lang seiner Illumination widmeten. Aber das ist nur eine der vielen Möglichkeiten, das Ganze in einen Zusammenhang zu stellen, der es jeden Sinnes beraubt. Manchmal wünsche ich mir fast, ich könnte so was wie einen Pakt mit dem Teufel schliessen und mein Alltagsleben gegen die tausend Jahre abtreten, die ich bräuchte, um das, was ich mache, allmählich wirklich zu verstehen.

JL: Kannst du mir etwas zu den Einflüssen auf den bildlichen Teil deiner Arbeit sagen?

RP: Als ich anfing, war der Ausgangspunkt ein bestimmter Stil der Radierung, Whistler zum Beispiel oder Samuel Palmer, oder auch der Stil der Gemälde und Aquarelle Turners. Wer sonst noch? John Sloane etwa, oder Joseph Pennell. Oder Hopper. Wenn man mein früheres Werk anschaut, ist Goya darin auszumachen. Das sind die Leute, von denen ich zeichnen lernte. Aber rein zeichnerisch gibt mein Werk nicht viel her; wohl auch heute noch nicht. Die Sache mit Pennell zum Beispiel ist einfach die, dass man als Künstler nicht unbedingt von den Leuten am meisten beeinflusst ist, die man am meisten bewundert.

JL: Die Videos von dir, die ich gesehen habe – etwa das über die *Weathermen*[1] –, sind so viel freier als die Zeichnungen, obgleich, wie ich erfahren habe, alles bis zur letzten Silbe vom Drehbuch vorgegeben ist. Wie verhalten sich diese beiden Ausdrucksmittel zueinander?

RP: Die Zeichnungen entsprechen sozusagen einzelnen Videostills: Eine Zeitlang zeichnete ich sie tatsächlich vom Bildschirm ab, indem ich das Band, meist irgendein Spielfilm oder so, anhielt. So hat sich wohl mein Stil herausgeschält: Der *Film-noir*-Effekt ergab sich mehr oder weniger ungewollt.

Ich würde gern mehr eigene Videos machen, nur dass man, selbst wenn man so arbeitet wie ich, also ohne Drehteam oder so, trotzdem andere Leute hinzuziehen muss, und es ist einfach sehr mühsam, all die Leute unter einen Hut zu bringen. Ich will keine populäre und primitive Wirkung erzielen: Oft arbeite ich aus rein praktischen Gründen in einer bestimmten Art, ohne jeden ästhetischen Grund. Geld, Zeit, Talent, Können, die Zahl meiner Mitarbeiter, all das kann die Form diktieren.

JL: Wieviel vom Text in deinen Zeichnungen stammt von dir und wieviel ist Zitat?

RP: Ich weiss es eigentlich nicht. Das ist immer wieder anders. Ich erinnere mich, dass ich zumindest einige Jahre lang alles selbst geschrieben habe. Aber ein Grossteil meines Werkes ist eine Kombination von beidem, und oft bleiben Text und Zeichnungen jahrelang unabgeschlossen. In den letzten ein, zwei Jahren habe ich wesentlich mehr Anleihen gemacht, insgesamt aber ist vielleicht ein Drittel Zitat. Möglicherweise auch mehr. Es lässt sich schwer sagen, weil es sich nicht um reine Zitate handelt: Manchmal findet eine Umarbeitung statt. Ausserdem kommt es vor, dass ich in meiner eigenen Schreibe auf den Stil zurückgreife, bei dem ich Anleihen mache; und in einer Zeichnung kann es eine beliebige Anzahl von Stimmen geben.

JL: Ich habe mich immer gefragt, wieviel von Melville drinsteckt. Du arbeitest mit der gleichen Art von Humor, dem gleichen, raffinierten Satzbau. Und du magst offenbar Ausrufesätze: Deine Figuren platzen immer mit irgend etwas heraus.

RP: Ich schätze Melville sehr, aber seltsamerweise steckt sehr wenig von ihm in meinem Werk. Ich arbeite mit unkontrollierten Äusserungen, die in einem unbedachten Moment fallen: meist Bruchstückhaftes, Unausgefeiltes. Auch Shakespeare ist so ein Autor, von dem ich wenig übernehme, unter anderem auch deshalb, weil seine Sprache so ausgefeilt ist. Wohingegen sich die Art, wie sein Zeitgenosse Marlowe schreibt, wesentlich besser eignet für das, was ich mache. Meine wichtigsten Quellen sind jedoch die grossen Prosaschriftsteller, Henry James und Proust, John Ruskin und Walter Pater. Und Thomas Browne. Wenn man die liest, findet man eine ganze Menge.

JL: Das sind alles Schriftsteller mit einer hochkomplexen Syntax.

RP: Genau, ihre Sprache ist sehr komplex, und einzelne Sätze können sich zu ganzen Absätzen auswachsen. Allerdings in einer bruchstückhaften Art und Weise. Ihre Aussagen können, aus dem Zusammenhang gerissen, eine völlig andere Bedeutung annehmen, und gleichzeitig sind sie wunderschön formuliert.

JL: Wenn du liest, pickst du dann einfach etwas heraus, oder setzt du dich hin, liest ein Buch ganz durch und gehst dann wieder zurück, um dir deine Lieblingsstellen herauszuschreiben?

RP: Das kommt drauf an: Neuerdings picke ich eher einfach etwas heraus. Und sogar wenn ich etwas von Anfang bis Ende lese, ist es eine sehr willkürliche

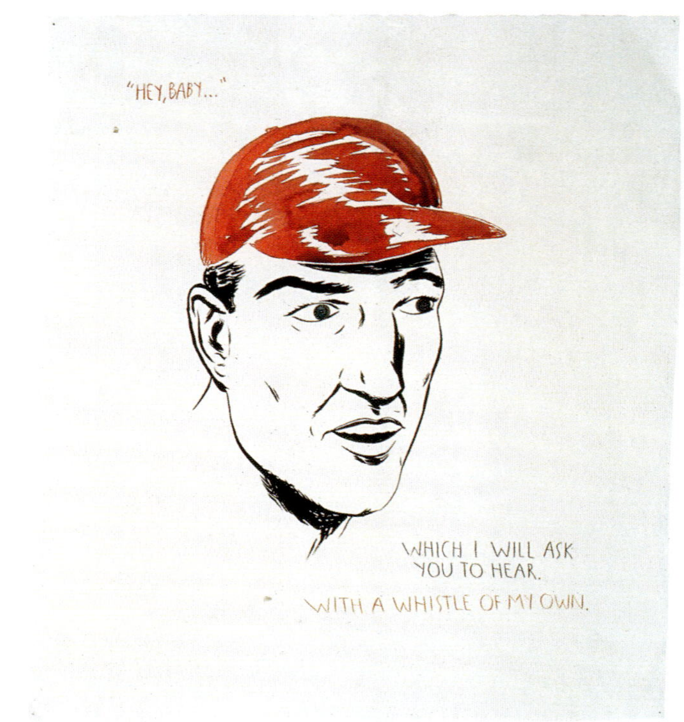

RAYMOND PETTIBON, NO TITLE (HEY BABY...), 1991,
pen and ink on paper, 22 x 18" / OHNE TITEL (HEY BABY...),
Feder und Tusche auf Papier, 55,9 x 45,7 cm.

– NO TITLE, 1992, 22¼ x 16" / OHNE TITEL, 56,5 x 40,6 cm.

– NO TITLE (I KNOW WHEN TO), 1985, 14" x 10¼" /
OHNE TITEL (ICH WEISS, WANN ICH), 35,6 x 26 cm.

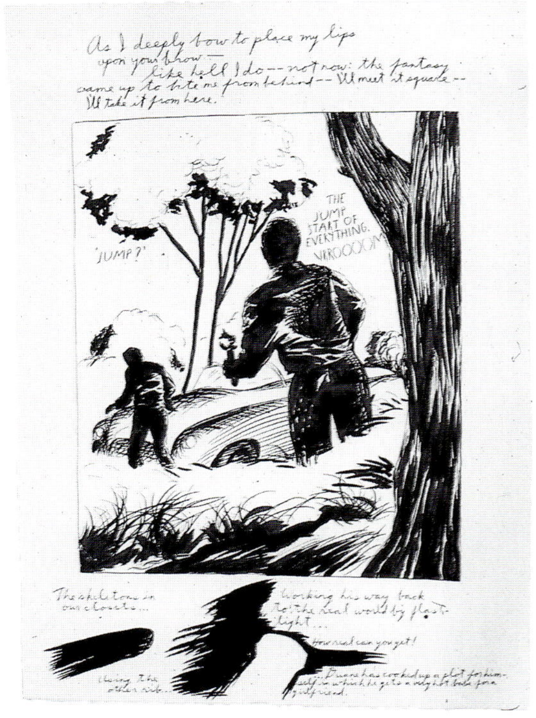

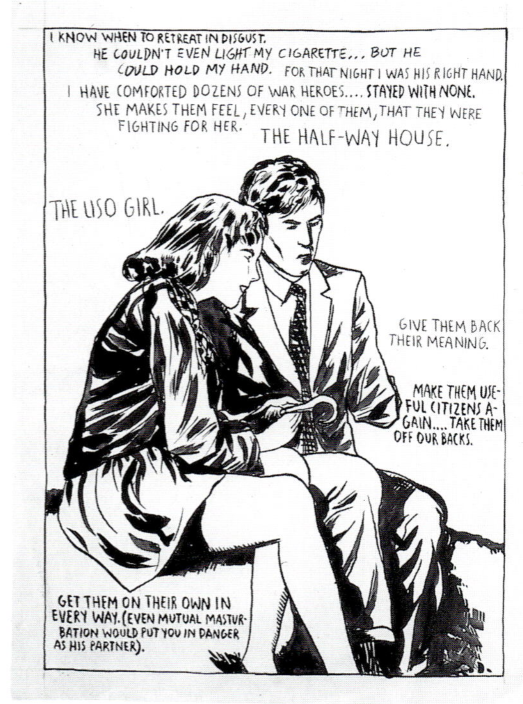

Lektüre. Mir fällt keine passendere Bezeichnung ein. Denn es ist eine Art des Lesens, die stets nach etwas zwischen den Zeilen Ausschau hält. Ausserdem schreibe ich beim Lesen gewissermassen neu. Es ist, als brächte ich mich selbst in die jeweilige Welt ein oder so, und... Es lässt sich schwer erklären. Aber am Ende wird dieser «erlesene» Ort zur Welt, in der man lebt, in der man denkt.

JL: Was gefällt dir an Henry James?

RP: James war, besonders in seinem Spätwerk, ungemein kompliziert in seinem Denken. Er schrieb in Erzählform, aber er konnte nicht umhin, noch das Allereinfachste aus den verschiedensten Blickwinkeln zu betrachten. Er schreibt immer aus einem inneren Kampf zwischen Drama und Erzählung heraus, und dann ist da diese Fülle an Ideen und Einzelheiten in jedem einzelnen Satz. Wenn man seine persönlichen Aufzeichnungen liest, sieht man, was er alles unternimmt, um sich an die Erzählstrukturen zu halten, die er sich selbst vorgibt und die von ganz einfachen Gedanken ausgehen. Diese Aufzeichnungen haben etwas rührend Erbärmliches, wie etwas, das man vielleicht in einer Drehbuchkonferenz bei Disney zu hören bekäme: du weisst schon, von der Sorte «Moralische Zwickmühle» oder «Was-wäre-wenn».

Ich sehe das komische Bild vor mir, wie James, während er seiner alten Sekretärin diktiert, loslegt und den Stoff immer weiter ausspinnt, dabei aber verzweifelt versucht, an irgendeiner Art von narrativer, dramatischer Organisation festzuhalten. Und zwar, nach Auffassung vieler Leute, ohne Erfolg, weshalb er eben so schwer zu lesen ist: Man verliert sofort den Faden der Erzählung, und es ist, als verliere er sich in der Sprache. Aber das stimmt nicht. Er versucht vielmehr verzweifelt die Übersicht zu behalten. Für meine Art zu lesen ist das ideal. Mir macht es Spass, ihn zu lesen.

JL: Erkennst du in seiner Art zu schreiben eine Nachahmung von Denkmustern, oder gefällt dir daran gerade das Manierierte?

RP: Ihm wird vorgeworfen, dass es nicht echt sei, sondern reiner Manierismus, tatsächlich aber ist es eine Nachahmung von Denkmustern. Darin liegt für mich der Reiz. Ich meine, man sagt das auch immer über mich, also, dass ich Gefahr laufe, mich zu ver-

zetteln, dass ich mich nicht an die Fakten oder den Ausgangspunkt halten könne, ohne einen weiteren Nebenstrang ins Spiel zu bringen, auf dem ich dann herumreiten müsse. In meinen Augen geht es dabei aber vor allen Dingen um ein Nachempfinden der Komplexität des Denkens und der Wirklichkeit sowie des Verhältnisses zwischen beiden. Dagegen ist es ein Fehler, so zu tun, als würde man eine einfache Geschichte erzählen, bei der am Ende alles aufgeht. Das ist unehrlich.

JL: Deine Arbeit erscheint mir ganz und gar zeitgemäss – nicht so sehr, weil du dich mit dem Elvis-Kult oder mit Ronald Reagan auseinandersetzt, sondern wegen der Darstellungsmittel, mit denen du arbeitest. Deine Darstellung ist fragmentarisch, ephemer und zugleich überaus... lapidar. Es ist verblüffend zu sehen, wie sehr die Syntax eines Satzes von Henry James der heutigen Situation angemessen sein kann.

RP: Ja, das ist eben das Lustige daran. Es spielt ein Sinn für Humor hinein, der im Bereich der Kunst tatsächlich sein Publikum gefunden hat. Ich bin aber kein Nostalgiker und betrachte mein Werk als zeitgenössisch.

JL: Mir fällt auf, dass du in gewisser Hinsicht ein sehr amerikanischer, ja sogar ein sehr kalifornischer Künstler bist, und doch scheint keine deiner literarischen Quellen amerikanisch zu sein.

RP: Also, das stimmt nicht. Hawthorne, Twain. Bei letzterem ist das Bemühen, witzig zu sein, mitunter zu angestrengt, manchmal aber gibt es eine einzige Wendung, die ich aus irgendeinem Grund zum Totlachen finde. Ich erinnere mich, wie ich als kleiner Junge *Huckleberry Finn* las, und da sagt dieser Knirps, «Give me chaw tobacker, won't ye».[2] Irgendwie wirkten diese Vorstellung, die Mundart und die Umstände auf mich unheimlich komisch. Vermutlich fühle ich mich aber tatsächlich mehr dem britischen Sinn für Humor verbunden; ich denke da an jemanden wie Harold Pinter, Anthony Powell oder Evelyn Waugh. Aber nicht Monty Python oder die britische Varieté-Komik. Ich schätze, ich kann auch ziemlich vulgär sein, aber selbst wenn ich über Ronald Reagans Arschloch schreibe, versuche ich doch ein gewisses Mass an Anstand zu wahren.

JL: Kannst du dich damit anfreunden, wenn man dein Werk in Zusammenhang mit Cartoons sieht?

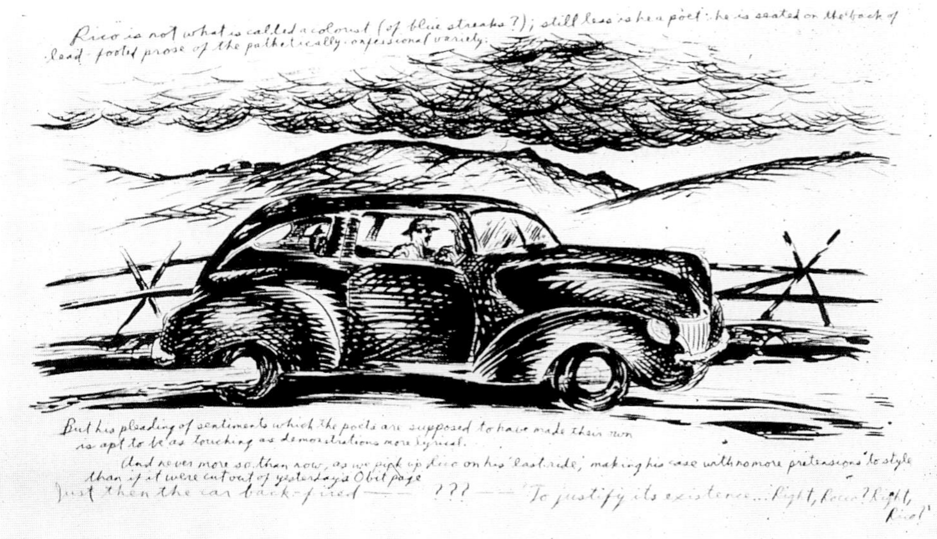

RAYMOND PETTIBON, NO TITLE, 1992, ink on paper 12 x 21" / OHNE TITEL, Tusche auf Papier, 30,5 x 53,3 cm.

RP: Nein. Nein. Mein Werk entspringt den verschiedensten Traditionen, darunter auch denen von Cartoon und Comic, aber ich würde nicht sagen, dass sie eine besonders grosse Rolle spielen. Andererseits ist damit kein wertendes Urteil verbunden: Ich stelle mich nicht darüber, ich glaube nur, dass es sich um zwei Paar Schuhe handelt.

JL: Bist du dir so sicher, dass sich keine Qualitätsurteile auf der Grundlage einer Unterscheidung zwischen E- und U-Kunst treffen lassen?

RP: Das ist eine völlig andere Frage. Soll das heissen, dass das Beste von George Herriman automatisch schlechter ist als das Schlechteste von Norman Mailer?

JL: Nein. Andererseits hängt mir das ganze kulturkritische Getue ein wenig zum Hals heraus. Das Pendel hat meines Erachtens dermassen weit in die entgegengesetzte Richtung ausgeschlagen, dass es vielleicht an der Zeit ist, sich einmal zu fragen, ob zum Beispiel die Popmusik vielleicht wirklich keine besonders grosse Bandbreite von Gefühlen oder Phänomenen auszudrücken oder zu erfassen vermochte.

RP: Eben darüber habe ich mir auch Gedanken gemacht. Manchmal schiebe ich es auf die Zeit und frage mich, was ist passiert? Ich kann nur sagen, dass ich nach wie vor Erwartungen habe an Leute, die im Bereich der U-Kunst tätig sind, weil ich nicht glaube, dass es irgendeinen triftigen Grund gibt, weshalb diese Ausdrucksformen nicht imstande sein sollten, dieselbe Bandbreite des Empfindens und Denkens abzudecken wie irgendwelche anderen. Aber es scheint bisher nicht der Fall zu sein, also muss man jetzt vielleicht sagen, nein, sie sind dazu nicht imstande. Gleichzeitig denke ich immer noch, dass es vielleicht daran liegt, dass da einfach nicht die richtigen Leute einsteigen.

Ausserdem muss ich manchmal mit mir selbst ins Gericht gehen, denn ich neige dazu, literarische Massstäbe an Dinge anzulegen, die das entweder gar nicht nötig haben oder nicht nötig haben sollten. Rock and Roll zum Beispiel. Das ist grundsätzlich nicht etwas, was sich auf Papier, in Dichtung übersetzen lassen muss. Ich weiss nicht. Ich meine, ich mag Rock and Roll ebenso, und manches davon gefällt mir besser als manche Dichtung. Die Sache wird also letztlich doch ziemlich verzwickt. Ich kann nur sagen, dass mir diese Debatte und deren Instrumentalisierung zum Hals heraushängt. Die meisten Schriftsteller, die ich wirklich mag, werden gar nicht mehr gelesen.

(Übersetzung: Magda Moses, Bram Opstelten)

1) Radikale Untergrundbewegung im Amerika der 60er Jahre, die gegen den Vietnamkrieg und für die Bürgerrechte kämpfte.
2) *chaw tobacker:* chewing tobacco = Kautabak.

RAYMOND PETTIBON,
NO TITLE (SMOOTH OF MY), 1992,
11¼ x 8¾" / 28,6 x 22,2 cm.

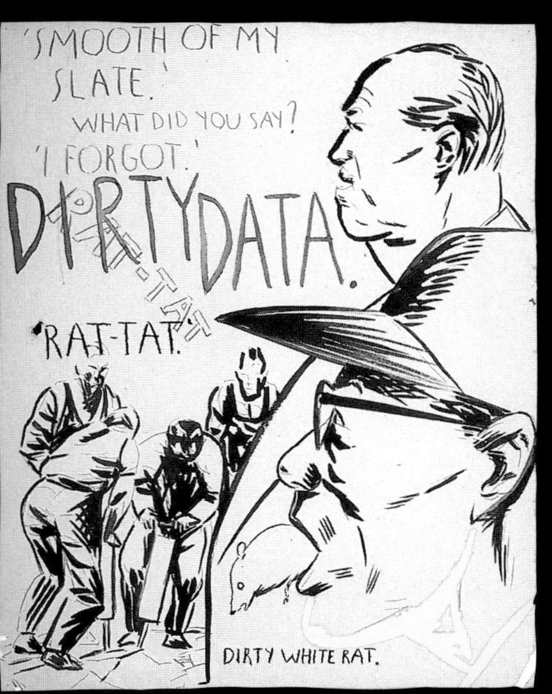
'SMOOTH OF MY
SLATE.'
WHAT DID YOU SAY?
'I FORGOT.'
DIRTY DATA.
RAT-TAT-TAT
'RAT-TAT.'
DIRTY WHITE RAT.

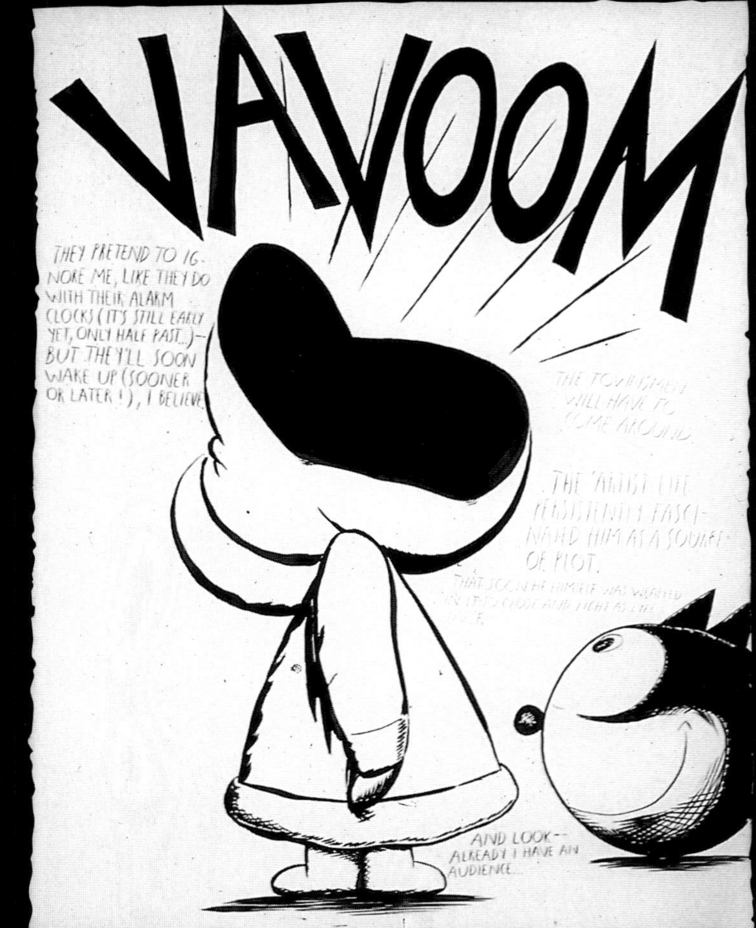
VAVOOM
THEY PRETEND TO IG-
NORE ME, LIKE THEY DO
WITH THEIR ALARM
CLOCKS (ITS STILL EARLY
YET, ONLY HALF PAST...)—
BUT THEY'LL SOON
WAKE UP (SOONER
OR LATER!), I BELIEVE.
THE TOWNSMEN
WILL HAVE TO
COME AROUND.
THE 'ARTIST LIFE'
PERSISTENTLY FASCI-
NATED HIM AS A SOURCE
OF PLOT.
AND LOOK—
ALREADY I HAVE AN
AUDIENCE...

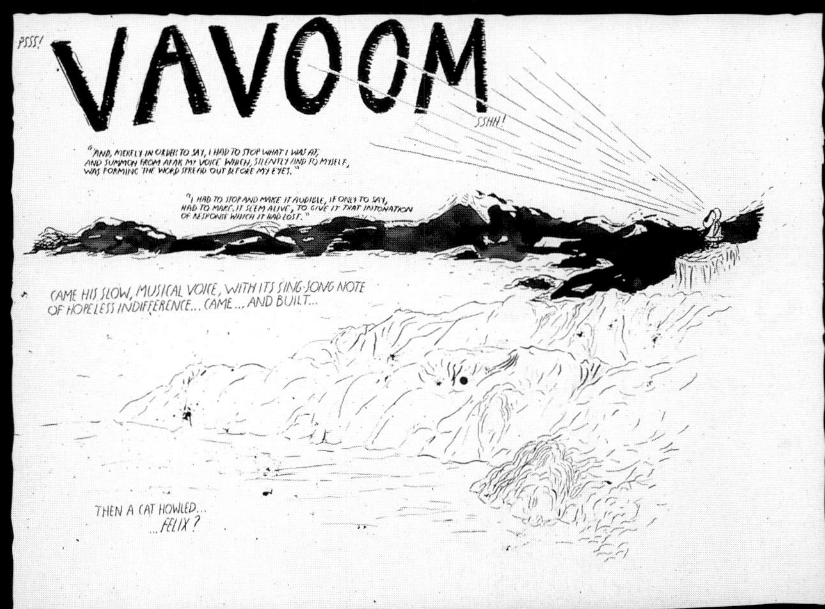
PSSS!
VAVOOM
SSHH!
"AND, MERELY IN ORDER TO SAY, I HAD TO STOP WHAT I WAS AT,
AND SUMMON FROM AFAR MY VOICE WHICH, SILENTLY AND TO MYSELF,
WAS FORMING THE WORD SPREAD OUT BEFORE MY EYES."
"I HAD TO STOP AND MAKE IT AUDIBLE, IF ONLY TO SAY,
HAD TO MAKE IT SEEM ALIVE, TO GIVE IT THAT INTONATION
OF RESPONSE WHICH IT HAD LOST."
CAME HIS SLOW, MUSICAL VOICE, WITH ITS SING-SONG NOTE
OF HOPELESS INDIFFERENCE... CAME... AND BUILT...
THEN A CAT HOWLED...
...FELIX?

RAYMOND PETTIBON, NO TITLE
(WELL? WHY NOT?), 1989,
14 x 11" / 35,6 x 28 cm.

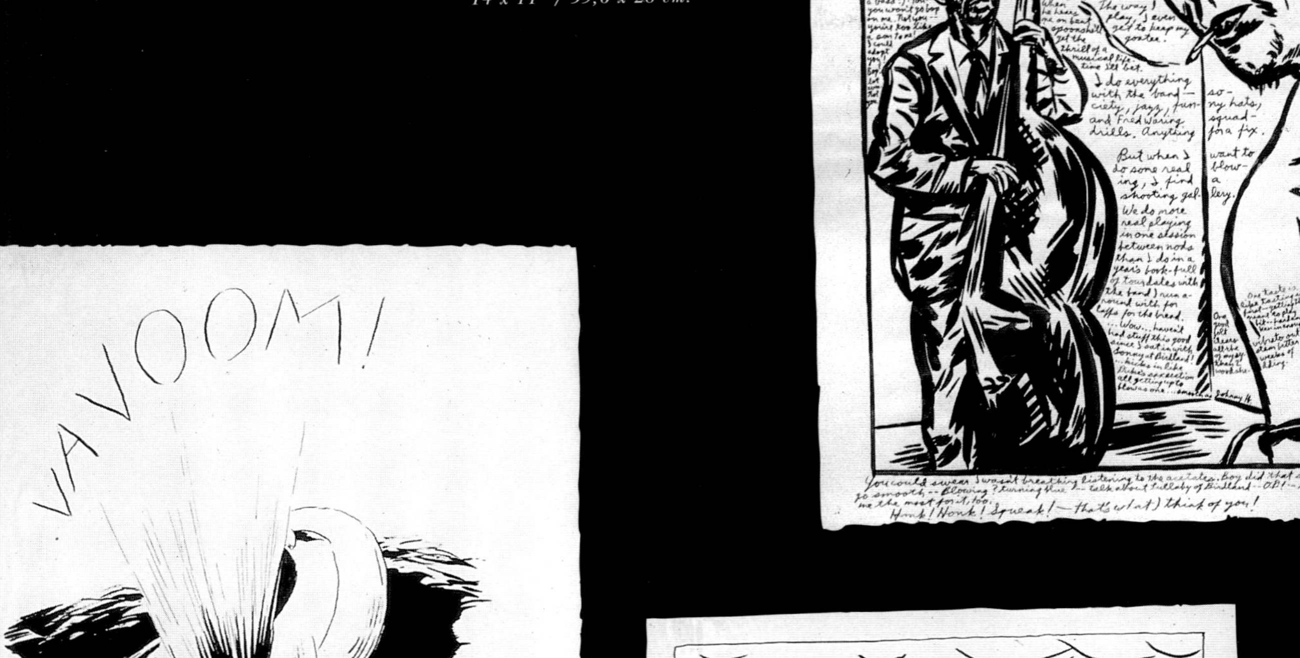

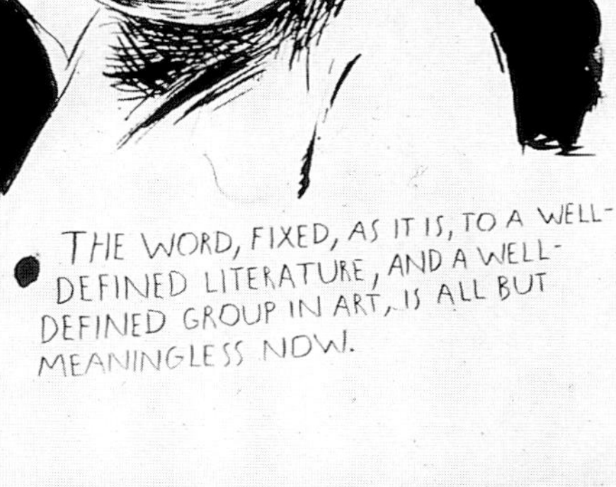

RAYMOND PETTIBON, "Vavoom"-sheets, 1961–1993,
ink on paper, various sizes / «Vavoom»-Blätter, Tusche auf Papier,
verschiedene Grössen.

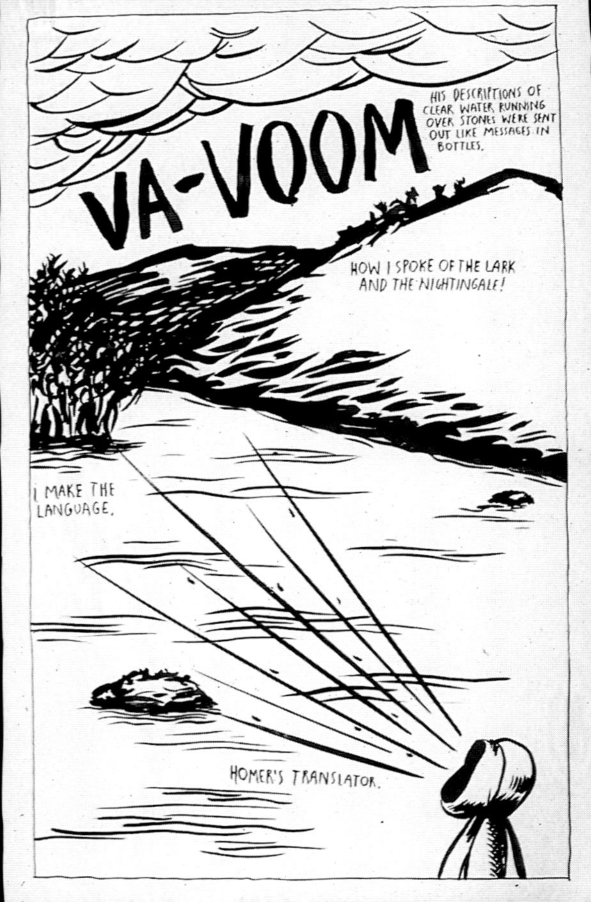

Die Rettung

◆ der Poesie ◆

durch das Bild

BORIS GROYS

Wenn ein Schreiber Werke der bildenden Kunst zu sehen bekommt, in denen auch Texte verwendet werden, ist er quasi automatisch elektrisiert und auf einer viel tieferen Ebene berührt, als wenn es sich um ein «reines» Bild handelt. Das passiert vor allem dann, wenn diese Texte, wie im Falle der Arbeiten von Raymond Pettibon, offensichtlich von ihrer Plazierung in einem Bildkontext profitieren und zusätzliche Dringlichkeit, Eloquenz und Suggestivität gewinnen. Der Schreiber fragt sich dann: Warum bin ich kein Künstler? Warum müssen meine Texte bloss geschrieben und deswegen auch so blass bleiben? Lamentos helfen aber nicht, und dem armen Schreiber bleibt nichts anderes übrig, als darüber nachzudenken, warum und inwieweit der Bildkontext den Texten hilft, sich aus gewissen Sackgassen zu befreien, in denen die heutige Literatur bekanntlerweise steckt.

In der Moderne wollte die Literatur sich genauso vom Narrativen befreien, wie es die Musik und die bildende Kunst gemacht haben. Die Geschichte der modernen Kunst und Musik ist nämlich nichts anderes als die Geschichte ihrer Befreiung von der Herrschaft der Erzählung oder die Geschichte ihres Kampfes gegen die Literatur. Die Literatur hat sich auch diesem Kampf angeschlossen. Daraus wurde nun ein Kampf gegen sich selbst. Der moderne Schriftsteller will die einzelne rhetorische Figur, den einzelnen Satz, das einzelne Wort, den einzelnen Laut aus ihrer Bindung an das Narrative lösen und sie als völlig autonom erstrahlen lassen.

Als Folge dieses Strebens ist die moderne Literatur zerfallen. Es blieb ein nacktes Narrativ, das in der Massenliteratur seinen Platz gefunden hat. Eine solche, von allen literarischen Ansprüchen befreite Erzählung ist aber eigentlich nicht mehr lesbar. Sie mag noch als Vorlage für eine Verfilmung dienen, bei der das fehlende Literarische durch das Visuelle kompensiert wird. Das kinematographische Schattenspiel bringt dieser Erzählung nämlich all das zurück, wessen sie durch den literarischen Zerfall beraubt wurde: Metapher, Bild, Suggestivität, Geheimnis, Reichtum. Auf diese Weise kapituliert die narrative Massenliteratur, die ihre traditionellen, literarischen Vorzüge verloren hat, vor den visuellen

BORIS GROYS ist Philosoph und Dozent an der Staatlichen Hochschule für Gestaltung in Karlsruhe.

Künsten. Noch interessanter ist es aber, dass auch die sogenannte hohe modernistische Literatur zunehmend das gleiche Schicksal erleidet.

Der Verlust des Narrativen ist der hohen Literatur nicht gut bekommen. Gestehen wir es: Modernistische Texte sind langweilig; vor allem deswegen, weil die Befreiung des literarischen Wortes aus seiner Bindung an das Erzählen einer Geschichte den Zugang zum Wort allzu leicht macht. Wenn man die Moderne Literatur liest, kann man nicht mehr nach den einzelnen Wortperlen suchen: unverborgen liegen sie vor dem Leser, wie eine wohlgeordnete Kollektion. Man erkennt sie auf den ersten Blick – und bleibt unberührt. Literatur erfordert nämlich eine gewisse Langsamkeit, Verzögerung, Ermüdung und schmerzende Augen, damit sie die ersehnte Befriedigung bringt. Es darf gar nicht alles sofort begriffen werden. Die lange, komplizierte Erzählung diente früher eben diesem Zweck, das schnelle Begreifen zu verhindern. Indem die Literatur sich aber von der Narrativität befreit hat, ist sie so leicht einsehbar geworden wie ein Bild – und damit im Grunde überflüssig.

Die Zeichnungen von Pettibon können als Arzneimittel gegen diese Krankheit der modernen Literatur interpretiert werden: Das Bild, das die Literatur erkranken liess, soll sie jetzt retten. Das Bild, das Pettibon dafür benützt, ist seinerseits jedoch ein erzählendes Bild. Zumindest suggerieren die Zeichnungen von Pettibon, erzählerisch zu sein. Erstens sind sie – von ihrer eigenen Struktur her betrachtet – narrativ, da sie verschiedene erkennbare Gegenstände miteinander verbinden. Zweitens erinnert ihr Stil an Cartoon und Comic, die beide ebenfalls narrativ sind. Drittens werden in diesen Zeichnungen bestimmte Mythen des amerikanischen Alltags evoziert, so dass sie als Illustrationen zu diesen Mythen gesehen werden können. Viertens tauchen bestimmte Figuren auf mehreren verschiedenen Zeichnungen auf, so dass der Eindruck entsteht, es handle sich um eine lange Geschichte mit immer denselben Helden. Diese Liste der Merkmale des Narrativen könnte man weiterführen. Das Wichtigste ist aber, dass diese Zeichnungen in grossen Mengen vorhanden sind. So entsteht beim Betrachter der Eindruck, er versäume etwas Wesentliches, wenn er nicht alle Zeichnungen

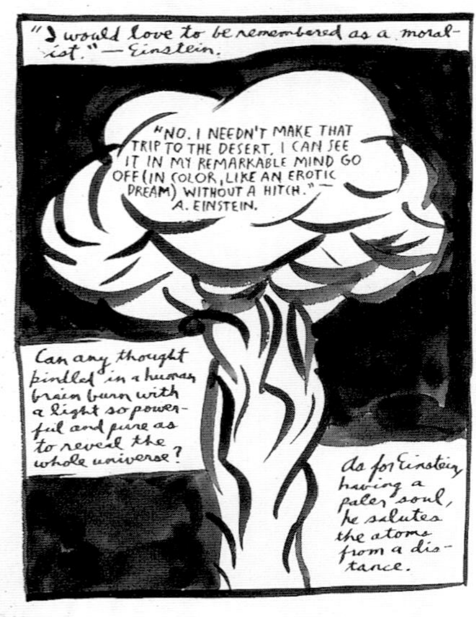

RAYMOND PETTIBON, NO TITLE (I WOULD LOVE), 1988,
pen and ink on paper, 11 x 9¾" / OHNE TITEL
(ICH WÜRDE GERN), Feder und Tusche auf Papier, 28 x 24,8 cm.

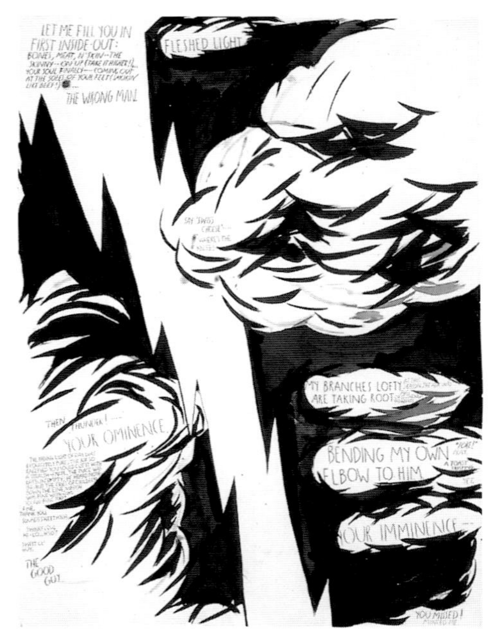

RAYMOND PETTIBON, NO TITLE (LET ME FILL), 1992,
pen and ink on paper, 30 x 22½" / OHNE TITEL (LASS MICH
ZUERST), Feder und Tusche auf Papier, 76,2 x 57 cm.

zu sehen bekommt – ähnlich wie bei einem Leser von *Krieg und Frieden,* der den Roman noch nicht gelesen, sondern erst ein bisschen darin geblättert hat. Unter Androhung der Todesstrafe kann man diesen allerdings dazu bringen, *Krieg und Frieden* ganz zu lesen. Im Falle von Pettibons Zeichnungen ist dies prinzipiell unmöglich, denn sie sind in vielen kleinen Sammlungen zerstreut und teils verschollen, auf jeden Fall nicht an einem Ort und zur gleichen Zeit vollständig vorhanden. Für Zeichnungen von Pettibon gilt also in verstärktem Masse das, was für die traditionelle narrative Literatur konstitutiv ist: Sie machen müde, die Augen tun weh, bis man sie endlich gesehen und entziffert hat, das Wichtigste bleibt ungesehen, der Gesamtüberblick ist unnachholbar verschoben.

Die Texte, die in diese Zeichnungen integriert sind, sehen wie Texte moderner Literatur aus. Es handelt sich um rhetorische Figuren, die «für sich selbst sprechen», die ihre Mehrdeutigkeit, Autonomie und Sprachmagie behaupten, dadurch dass sie von ihrer dienenden Funktion in der traditionellen Erzählung befreit sind. Der Weg zu diesen autonomen Sprachfragmenten ist aber im Kontext von Pettibons Zeichnungen ein steiniger. Die Texte sind in den Zeichnungen integriert und müssen deswegen vom Auge des Lesers zunächst einmal herausgelöst

werden. Oft sind sie in einer Handschrift geschrieben, die ihre Lektüre weiter verkompliziert. Zusätzlich erschwert und verzögert die Plazierung der Texte im Bildkontext die Entzifferung. Man fragt sich, welche Bedeutung es hat, dass sich die Texte an einer bestimmten Stelle der Bildfläche befinden: Vielleicht spielen sie in der Geschichte, die durch das Bild erzählt wird, eine bestimmte Rolle? Vielleicht muss man die ganze Handlung verstehen, damit man ihre Bedeutung versteht, vielleicht muss man sich auch andere Bilder aus einer bestimmten Reihe anschauen, damit endlich alles klar wird? In Pettibons Zeichnungen wird also das fehlende, traditionelle literarische Narrativ durch das erzählerische Bild ersetzt. Wenn das kommerzielle Kino die nackte Erzählung dadurch bereichert und rettet, dass es ihr eine reizvolle visuelle Verpackung verpasst, rettet Pettibon die nichterzählerische, modernistische Prosa dadurch, dass er sie in ein narratives Bild einbettet. So wird in beiden Spielarten der modernen Literatur das abhanden gekommene Narrative durch die visuelle Kunst ersetzt.

Freilich kann die Wirkung der Zeichnungen Pettibons nicht darauf reduziert werden, dass das modernistische Schreiben dadurch wieder interessant wird. Denn diese Zeichnungen schaffen auch einen ästhetischen Mehrwert, indem sie erlauben, das

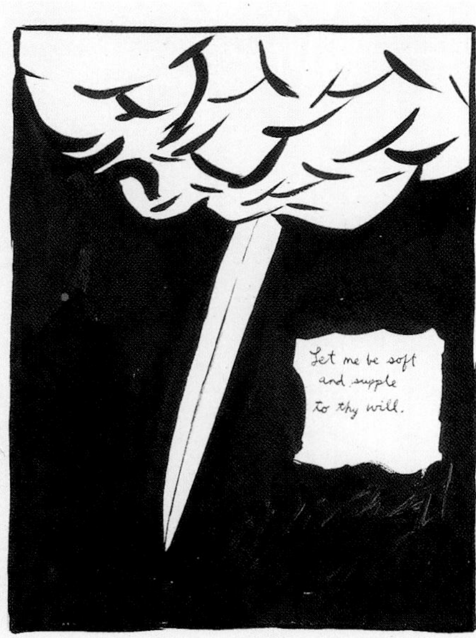

RAYMOND PETTIBON, NO TITLE, 1987,
mixed media on paper, 22¼ x 17½" /
OHNE TITEL, Mischtechnik auf Papier, 56,5 x 44,5 cm.

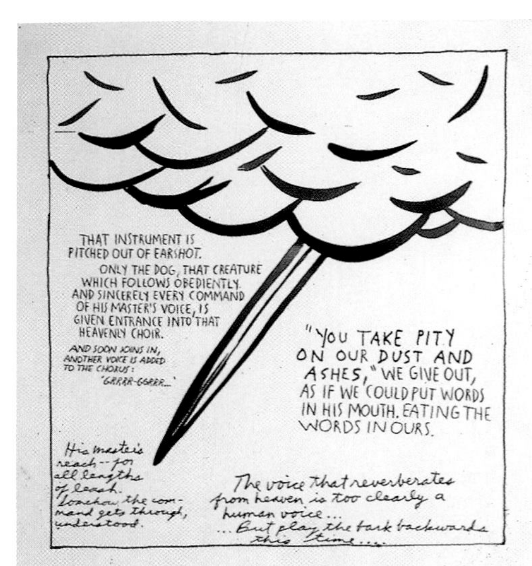

RAYMOND PETTIBON, NO TITLE
(THAT INSTRUMENT IS), 1987, pen and ink on paper,
12 x 11" / OHNE TITEL (DIESES INSTRUMENT IST),
Feder und Tusche auf Papier, 30,5 x 28 cm.

Ready-made-Verfahren auf den Text zu erweitern. Der wichtigste Vorzug der modernen Kunst gegenüber der modernen Literatur besteht nämlich darin, dass das *Ready-made*-Verfahren, das in der Kunst heutzutage dominiert, in der Literatur nicht anwendbar zu sein scheint: Auch literarische Bücher werden nämlich «publiziert», d. h. von Anfang an vervielfältigt, was das direkte Zitieren aus anderen Büchern überflüssig und widersinnig macht. Die literarische Appropriation der Massenliteratur ist schon deshalb unmöglich, weil jede Literatur tendenziell Massenliteratur ist, weil sie von Anfang an auf technische Reproduktion angelegt ist.

Indem Pettibon Texte in Zeichnungen plaziert, die als Einzelwerke konzipiert sind, kann er diese prinzipielle Schwierigkeit überwinden und das ästhetische Potential der «schlechten», kommerziellen Massenliteratur im Rahmen seiner Kunst realisieren. Sicher ist Pettibon nicht der einzige Künstler, der in den letzten Jahrzehnten mit diesem Ziel mit Texten arbeitet. Im Unterschied zu den meisten Künstlern des Konzeptualismus interessiert sich Pettibon aber nicht für die kritische, kunsttheoretische oder soziale Relevanz der von ihm verwendeten Texte, sondern in erster Linie für ihre poetische, melodische und rhetorische Qualität. Das Bild steht hier im Dienste der Poesie, die sich unter den Bedingungen der heutigen Kultur Dinge nicht leisten kann, die sich in der bildenden Kunst längst durchgesetzt haben.

So rettet Pettibon auf der Ebene der hohen Literatur, was mit Hilfe des Bildes dort noch zu retten ist. Aber damit wird nicht etwa ein Sieg der bildenden Kunst über die Literatur erreicht. Denn dadurch, dass der Text auf Pettibons Zeichnungen direkt und sozusagen materiell inmitten der visuellen Welt plaziert wird, bekommt das Wort bei Pettibon eine zusätzliche magische Kraft: Das Wort wird Fleisch. In seinem Interview mit Ulrich Loock[1] spricht Pettibon immer wieder über das Wort Gottes und über das Wort «Vavoom», das Berge zu versetzen vermag; auch darüber, dass die Linien, mit denen die visuelle Welt gezeichnet ist, wie Klammern sind, in denen offensichtlich, wenn auch unausgesprochen, ein Wort – oder soll man sagen, das Wort – stehen soll. Da die Literatur sich infolge des selbstmörderischen Kampfes gegen ihre eigene Narrativität dem Bild annäherte, hat das Bild die Möglichkeit erhalten, poetisch zu werden. Und vielleicht sind die interessantesten Künstler heute diejenigen, die – wie Pettibon – diese Möglichkeit gespürt und in ihrem Werk realisiert haben.

1) In: *Raymond Pettibon*, Katalog der Kunsthalle Bern, 1995.

RAYMOND PETTIBON, NO TITLE (WITH A SHUDDER), 1990, pen and ink on paper, 12³⁄₄ x 12" / OHNE TITEL (MIT EINEM SCHAUDERN), Feder und Tusche auf Papier, 32,4 x 30,5 cm.

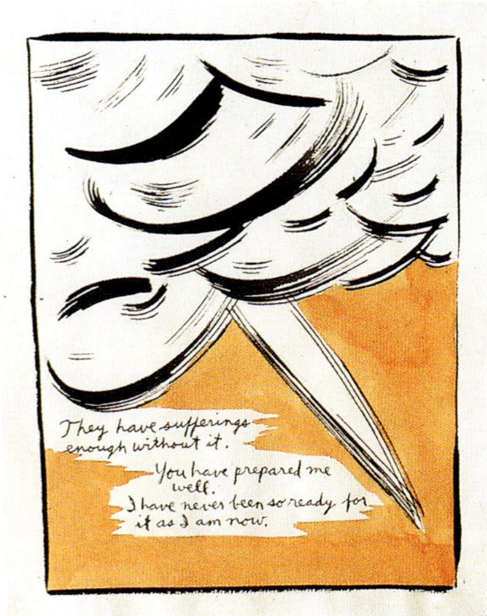

RAYMOND PETTIBON, NO TITLE, 1988, mixed media on paper, 11¼ x 8¾" / OHNE TITEL, Mischtechnik auf Papier, 28,6 x 22,2 cm.

Some faithless shepherd
has made it ache.

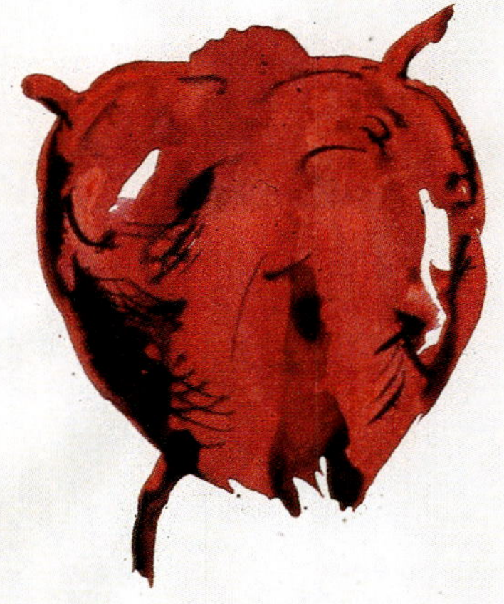

The Drawing Rescues Poetry

BORIS GROYS

When a writer sees a work of visual art in which texts are also used, the experience is automatically electrifying and makes a much greater impact than if it were "only" a picture. This happens above all when—as in the case of Raymond Pettibon—these texts are obviously enhanced through their placement in a pictorial context, there becoming even more urgent, eloquent, and suggestive. Writers begin to ask themselves: Why am I not an artist? Why are my texts condemned to be merely written and therefore so pallid? But there is no point in moaning; the poor writer has no choice but to think about why and to what extent the pictorial context is a way of breaking the impasse that has pulled literature up short.

In modernism, literature—like music and the fine arts—wanted to escape narration. The history of modern art and music is, in fact, nothing but the history of their being liberated from subjugation to the narrative, or the history of their struggle against literature. And literature, by joining the fray, internalized the battle. The modernist author seeks to break the ties between narration and its rhetorical devices, sentences, words, and sounds, treating each of these as single, autonomous elements.

The result: Modern literature has fallen apart. On the one hand, we have the naked narrative that has found a home in pulp fiction. But storytelling stripped of literary ambitions is basically unreadable. At most it can function as the plot of a film in which the visual material compensates for the paucity of the written word. Cinematographic methods flesh out the narrative using all the devices that have fallen by the wayside with the disintegration of modern literature: metaphor, image, suggestion, mystery, richness. Pulp fiction has capitulated, surrendering its traditional literary advantages to the visual arts. Significantly, high modernist literature is suffering the same fate.

The loss of the narrative does not agree with it. One must admit that modernist texts are boring, above all because the liberation of the literary word from its ties to narration has oversimplified access to it. On reading modern literature, it is no longer

BORIS GROYS is a philosopher and lecturer at the Staatliche Hochschule für Gestaltung in Karlsruhe, Germany.

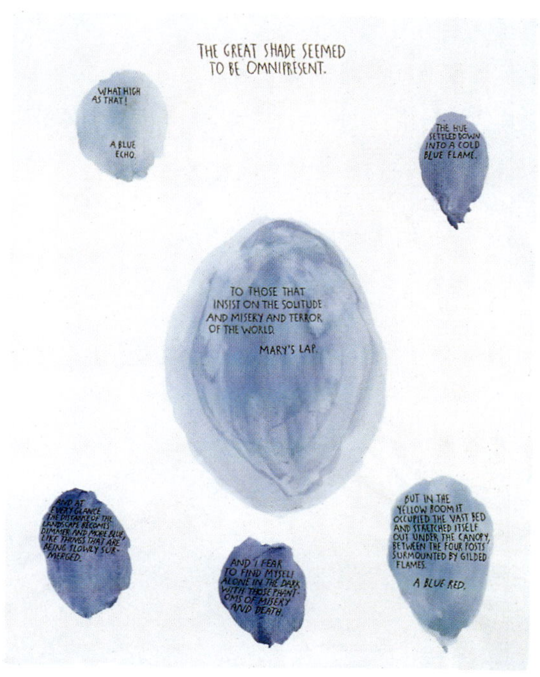

RAYMOND PETTIBON, NO TITLE (THE GREAT SHADE), 1990, mixed media on paper, 22 x 17" / OHNE TITEL (DER GROSSE SCHATTEN), Mischtechnik auf Papier, 55,9 x 43,2 cm.

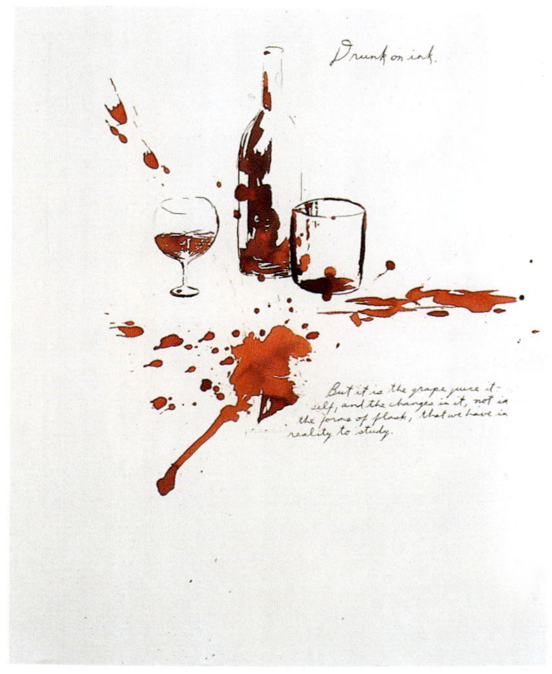

RAYMOND PETTIBON, NO TITLE, 1992, mixed media on paper, 24 x 19¼" / OHNE TITEL, Mischtechnik auf Papier, 61 x 49 cm.

necessary to seek out the single pearls: They are all spread out before us like a well-ordered collection. We can take them in at one glance—and remain unmoved. Literature has to slow us down; it must entail delay, fatigue, pain in the reader's tired eyes for it to provide cherished satisfaction. Not everything should be instantly clear and comprehensible. Long, rambling tales once served this purpose of slowing down understanding. But by doing away with the narrative, literature can be scanned, like a picture—and has, in the process, become superfluous.

Pettibon's drawings might be interpreted as a remedy for this disease of modern literature: The picture that caused literature's illness shall now be its salvation. But the pictures that Pettibon uses to this end are themselves narratives, or imply, at least, that they are telling a story. To begin with, their very structure is narrative, since they combine a variety of recognizable objects. Secondly, they draw on the technique of cartoons and comics, both of which are also narrative genres. Thirdly, by evoking certain myths of everyday life in the United States, the drawings could be seen as illustrations of these myths. Fourthly, certain figures keep cropping up, so that one might be led to believe that Pettibon is spinning a long tale with a given set of protagonists. This list of narrative properties could, of course, be elaborated. Of importance here is the fact that there are great quantities of these drawings, so that viewers feel they have missed something if they have not seen all of them—like skimming through *War and Peace* instead of reading the novel in its entirety. Threatened with the death penalty, one can, of course, be forced to read all of *War and Peace.* Not so in Pettibon's case. His drawings are scattered about in numerous small collections and some are lost, so that it is impossible to see the complete collection at the same time in one place. Certain constitutive elements of traditional narrative literature therefore have an even greater thrust in Pettibon's oeuvre. His drawings are tiring; by the time we have seen and decoded them all, our eyes hurt; the most important things remain unseen; the overall view is irretrievably postponed.

The texts integrated in his drawings look like the texts of modern literature. They are figures of speech that "speak for themselves," that assert their ambiguity, autonomy, and linguistic magic because they have been liberated from the subordinate function traditionally assigned to them by conventional literature. But in Pettibon's drawings, the path to these autonomous linguistic fragments is strewn with rocks. The texts are integrated in the drawings and must be isolated by the reader. They are often "written" in a hand that compounds the difficulties of reading, and their placement in the picture is an additional impediment. One asks oneself what significance is invested in the positioning of the texts: Perhaps they play a particular role in the story told by a given picture; perhaps we can only understand them when we understand the entire plot; perhaps we have to look at other drawings in a particular series to finally understand what it's all about. Pettibon's storytelling drawings make up for the loss of the traditional literary narrative. Whereas commercial cinema facilitates the naked narrative by packaging it in an attractive visual setting, Pettibon rescues plotless modernist prose by placing it in a narrative picture. In both cases, the visual arts make up for the missing half of a modern literature that is split in two.

However, the impact of Pettibon's drawings is not to be reduced to generating renewed interest in modernist writing. They also provide what might be called an aesthetic added-value by applying the readymade procedure to language. The most important advantage of modern art over modern literature lies in the fact that the currently prevalent readymade procedure is evidently inapplicable to literature: Books are "published"; they are reproduced by definition. Literary appropriation of mass writing is in fact impossible because all literature is potentially mass writing, since it is, by definition, made for technical reproduction.

By placing texts in unique, single drawings, Pettibon has found a means of surmounting this intrinsic difficulty and revealing the aesthetic potential of "bad" commercial mass literature within the framework of his art. Pettibon is not the only artist over the past few decades to pursue such ends in incorporating texts in his work; others have also grasped this opportunity—both literally and figuratively. However, in contrast to most conceptual artists, Pettibon is not interested in the critical, art-theoretical or social relevance of his words but primarily in their poetic, melodic, and rhetorical qualities. His pictures serve the interests of poetry, which—given the hegemony of the mechanically-printed word in current culture—cannot afford the appropriations and re-contextualizations which have already become standard practice in art.

Thus with the help of the picture Pettibon rescues whatever there is left to be rescued on the level of high literature. But in the final analysis art has not made a definitive conquest. By placing text directly and materially in the middle of the visual world, as it were, the word in Pettibon's art acquires an additional magic power because it has now become flesh. In an interview with Ulrich Loock,[1] Pettibon repeatedly mentions the Word of God and the word "Vavoom" that can move mountains, and he talks about the lines with which the visual world is drawn. To him, these lines are like parentheses that are obviously though tacitly intended to embrace a word—or rather the Word. Now that literature—in the wake of the murderous campaign to slaughter its narrativity—has come closer to the picture, the picture has been given the chance to become poetic. Perhaps the most interesting artists today are those who, like Pettibon, have sensed this opportunity and exploited it to advantage in their oeuvre.

(Translation: Catherine Schelbert)

1) In *Raymond Pettibon*, ex. cat. (Berne: Kunsthalle, 1995).

HILTON ALS

Untitled

A scientific impossibility but, nevertheless, one writer's wish: to know the exact physical weight of those words which comprise the Writer's lexicon, "favorite" words that express, time and again, what the Writer means to express as he works within the God-given parameters or context of the self.

In posing such a wish, one wonders soon after: What would Raymond Pettibon's words weigh after being totted up, one by one, and put on the scale of semantic curiosity? Those Pettibon words that become sentences which float like some strange yet familiar anxiety in the mind-field of his drawings—what would they weigh? Would the weight be oppressive? "You are only here because you are a writer" is one such Pettibon sentence whose sharp gravity one feels, a gravity that remains quite independent of the drawing proper even as one realizes, yes, yes, the words used in this drawing—as in all Pettibon's work—are part of the distinctly visual narrative he builds on his surfaces.

Nevertheless, being a writer and, therefore, consumed by one's relationship to the world and the self, one feels Pettibon's statement deeply—as deeply as one understands how the Writer is viewed by Japanese cognoscenti, *par exemple:* as a creature who is born to observe, and who is thus the most likely to disappear from society altogether, given his horror in the face of human folly, which is often too repetitive and banal for words.

The great nineteenth-century Brazilian writer Machado de Assis, author of *Epitaph of a Small Winner, Don Casmurro,* and *Philosopher or Dog?* wrote novels comprised of words whose full weight he wanted his audience to know, and he did this by placing these words in the smallest chapters possible—chapters that contained, at times, one or two lines. In *Epitaph,* Chapter 66, "Legs," the narrator writes: *While I was thinking about these people, my legs were carrying me along, street after street, until, to my surprise, I found myself at the door of the Hotel Pharoux... Blessed legs! And yet some people treat you with indifference.* Pettibon places his words—which make big thoughts happen on the page—on the spindly legs of letters, letters which sometimes have little dribbles of ink on their edges. Those dribbles are like the spittle of afterthought, when it becomes clear to the Writer that words alone do not suffice. (For the "real" visual artist, images do not suffice, ever.) He does not treat those legs with indifference, like "some people." We do not know the scientific properties of Machado de Assis's words, or the actual physical weight of Pettibon's words, either; but each are grave and adult and grand, like lines of thought that do not give up.

HILTON ALS is a staff writer for *The New Yorker.* His first book, *The Women,* is forthcoming from Farrar Strauss & Giroux in November 1996.

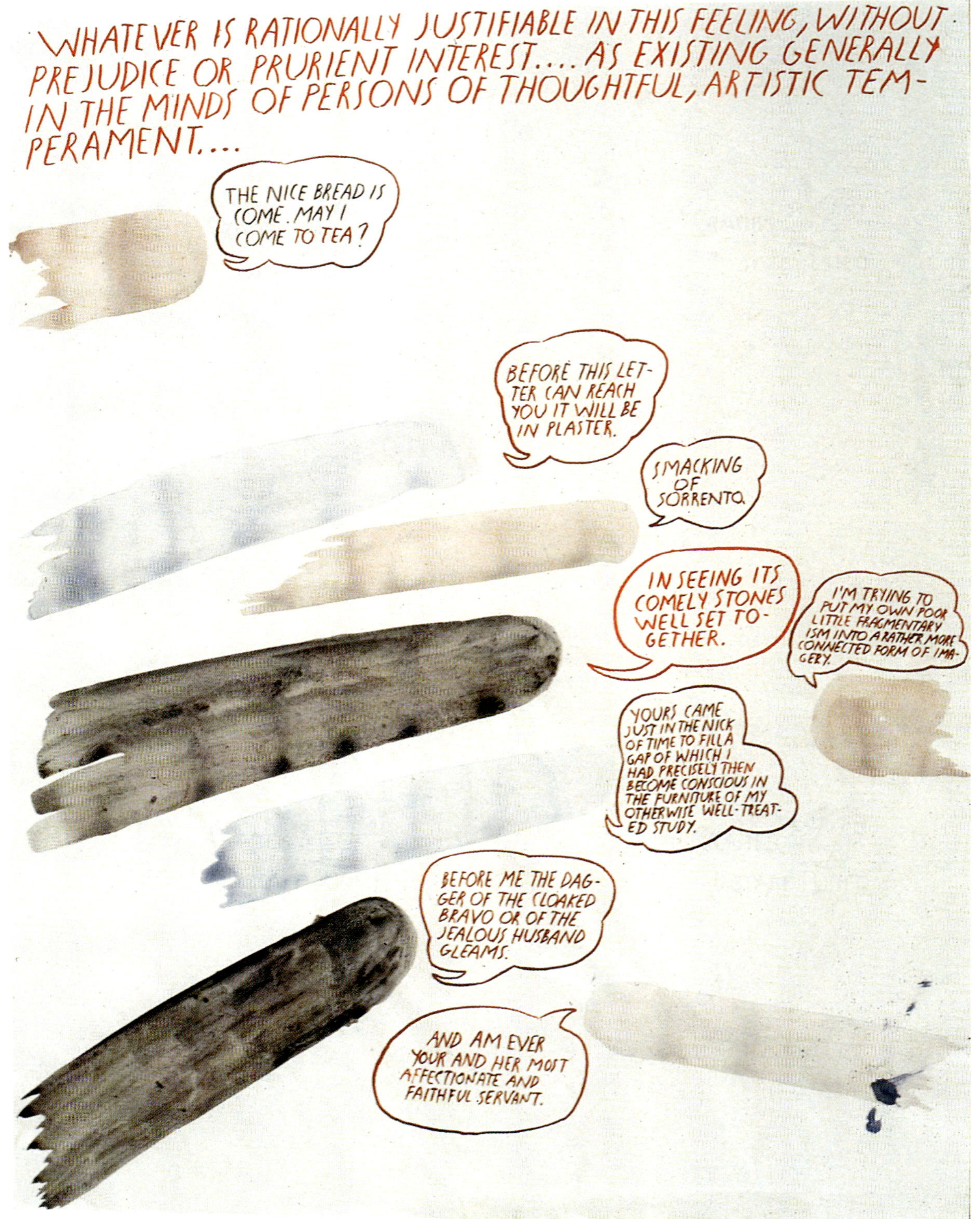
WHATEVER IS RATIONALLY JUSTIFIABLE IN THIS FEELING, WITHOUT PREJUDICE OR PRURIENT INTEREST.... AS EXISTING GENERALLY IN THE MINDS OF PERSONS OF THOUGHTFUL, ARTISTIC TEMPERAMENT....
THE NICE BREAD IS COME. MAY I COME TO TEA?
BEFORE THIS LETTER CAN REACH YOU IT WILL BE IN PLASTER.
SMACKING OF SORRENTO.
IN SEEING ITS COMELY STONES WELL SET TOGETHER.
I'M TRYING TO PUT MY OWN POOR LITTLE FRAGMENTARY ISM INTO A RATHER MORE CONNECTED FORM OF IMAGERY.
YOURS CAME JUST IN THE NICK OF TIME TO FILL A GAP OF WHICH I HAD PRECISELY THEN BECOME CONSCIOUS IN THE FURNITURE OF MY OTHERWISE WELL-TREATED STUDY.
BEFORE ME THE DAGGER OF THE CLOAKED BRAVO OR OF THE JEALOUS HUSBAND GLEAMS.
AND AM EVER YOUR AND HER MOST AFFECTIONATE AND FAITHFUL SERVANT.

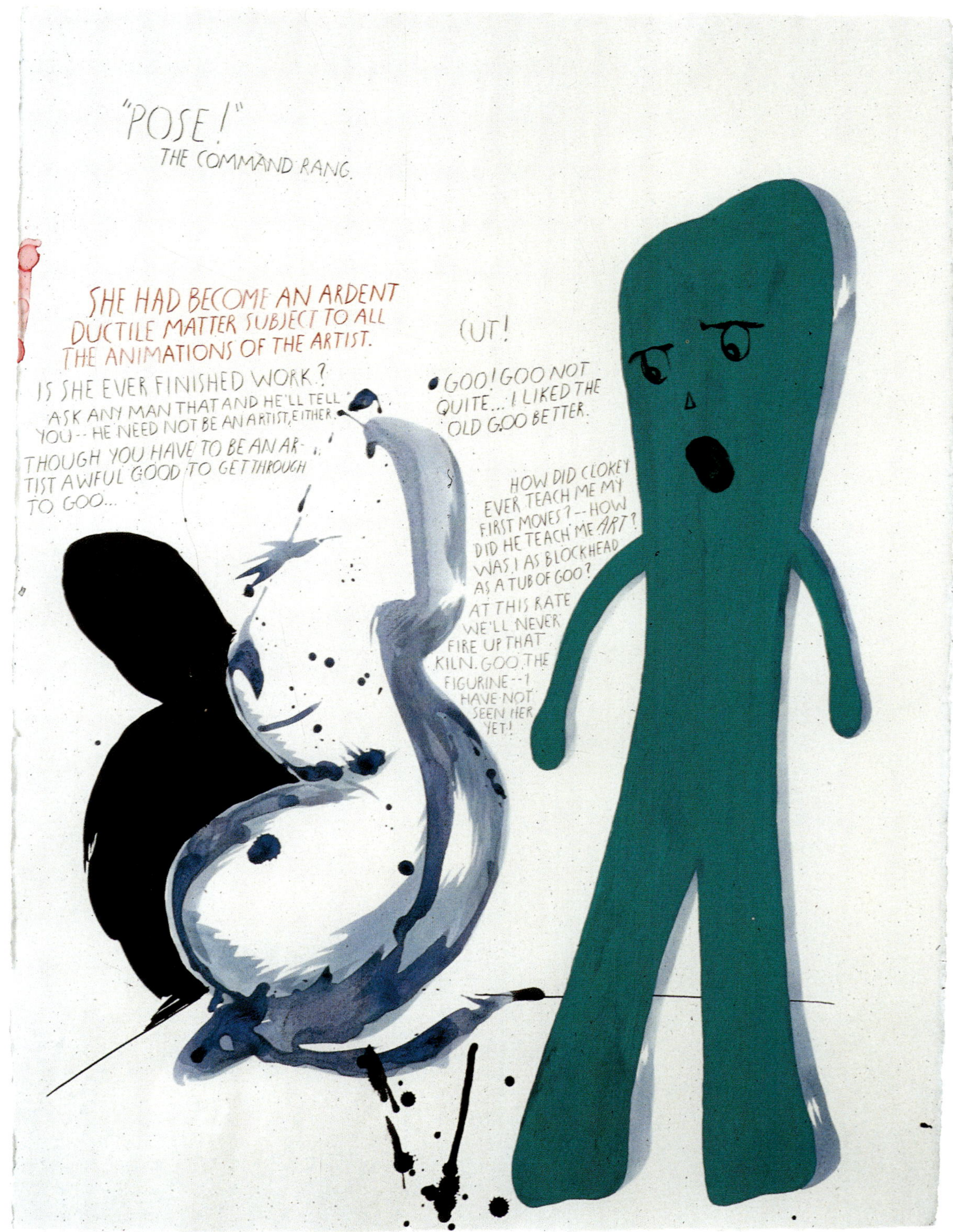
"POSE!"
THE COMMAND RANG.

SHE HAD BECOME AN ARDENT
DUCTILE MATTER SUBJECT TO ALL
THE ANIMATIONS OF THE ARTIST.

IS SHE EVER FINISHED WORK?
ASK ANY MAN THAT AND HE'LL TELL
YOU -- HE NEED NOT BE AN ARTIST, EITHER.
THOUGH YOU HAVE TO BE AN AR-
TIST AWFUL GOOD TO GET THROUGH
TO GOO...

CUT!

GOO! GOO NOT
QUITE... I LIKED THE
OLD GOO BETTER.

HOW DID CLOKEY
EVER TEACH ME MY
FIRST MOVES? -- HOW
DID HE TEACH ME ART?
WAS I AS BLOCKHEAD
AS A TUB OF GOO?
AT THIS RATE
WE'LL NEVER
FIRE UP THAT
KILN. GOO, THE
FIGURINE -- I
HAVE NOT
SEEN HER
YET!

HILTON ALS

Ohne Titel

Es ist ein von der Wissenschaft nicht zu erfüllender, von Schreibenden jedoch gern gehegter Wunsch, das exakte physikalische Gewicht der Wörter zu kennen, die ihren Wortschatz ausmachen, das Gewicht der «Lieblingswörter», die immer wieder von neuem ausdrücken, was der Schreibende sagen will bei seiner Arbeit innerhalb gottgegebener Parameter bzw. aus dem spezifischen Kontext seines Ich heraus.

Angesichts dieses Wunsches mag man sich fragen, was wohl Raymond Pettibons Worte wiegen würden, legte man sie alle zusammen, eines nach dem anderen, auf die Waage der Bedeutungsschwere. Diese Pettibon-Wörter, die zu Sätzen geraten, welche wie eine merkwürdige und doch vertraute Beunruhigung durch den geistigen Raum seiner Zeichnungen wabern – wie schwer wären sie? Wäre ihr Gewicht erdrückend? «Du bist nur da, weil Du schreibst», ist so ein Pettibon-Satz, dessen Schwere man deutlich spürt. Es ist eine von der eigentlichen Zeichnung völlig unabhängige Schwere, obwohl man ganz klar wahrnimmt, dass die Wörter, die in dieser Zeichnung – und überall in seinem Werk – verwendet werden, Teil des eindeutig visuellen Erzählgeflechts sind, das Pettibon auf seinen Blättern entwickelt.

Und doch, wenn man selbst schreibt und deshalb in sein Verhältnis zur Welt und zum eigenen Ich verstrickt ist, trifft einen Pettibons Aussage tief – vielleicht ähnlich tief wie das Bild der japanischen Weisen vom Dichter als einer zum Beobachten bestimmten Kreatur, die sich gerade deshalb meist völlig aus der Gesellschaft zurückziehen wird, entsetzt über das verrückte Gehabe der Menschen, oft so banal und ewig gleich, dass es in Worten kaum zu fassen ist.

Der grosse brasilianische Dichter des neunzehnten Jahrhunderts, Machado de Assis, Autor von *Epitaph of a Small Winner, Dom Casmurro,* und *Philosopher or Dog?,* schrieb Romane mit Worten, deren volles Gewicht er seinem Publikum vermitteln und zumuten wollte. Er tat dies, indem er diese Worte in möglichst kurzen Kapiteln unterbrachte, Kapitel, die manchmal nur ein oder zwei Zeilen umfassten. In *Epitaph,* Kapitel 66, «Füsse», sagt der Erzähler: *Während ich über diese Leute nachdachte, trugen mich meine Füsse weiter, von einer Strasse in die andere, bis ich zu meiner Überraschung beim Eingang des Hotel Pharoux angelangt war... Ihr wunderbaren Füsse! Und doch schenken Euch manche Leute keinerlei Beachtung.*[1] Pettibon stellt seine Worte – die auf dem jeweiligen Blatt entscheidende Gedanken auslösen – auf die wackligen Füsse von Buchstaben, die manchmal an den Enden in kleine Tintenfäden ausfransen. Es sind dies gleichsam Zitterspuren eines gedanklichen Zögerns, als realisierte der Schreibende, dass Worte allein nicht zu bestehen vermögen (wie für den «eigentlichen» visuellen Künstler die Bilder allein nie zu bestehen vermögen). Pettibon schenkt diesen Füssen, anders als «manche Leute», aber sehr wohl Beachtung. Zwar kennen wir weder die naturwissenschaftlichen Daten der Wörter von Machado de Assis noch das physische Gewicht der Wörter Pettibons, aber alle beide haben sie Gewicht, Reife und Grösse, und sie gleichen Gedankensträngen, die weder abreissen noch nachgeben.

(*Übersetzung: Susanne Schmidt*)

HILTON ALS schreibt als festangestellter Mitarbeiter für *The New Yorker.* Sein erstes Buch, *The Women,* erscheint im November 1996 bei Farrar Strauss & Giroux.

1) Von den genannten Werken ist zur Zeit lediglich *Dom Casmurro* in deutscher Übersetzung greifbar (Bibliothek Suhrkamp). Das Zitat aus *Epitaph* wurde von der Redaktion aus dem Englischen übersetzt.

RALPH RUGOFF

Surfing with Raymond Nobody Rides for Free

Beginning with his dauntingly fabulous exhibitions during the late 1980s and early 90s, Raymond Pettibon has invented a new medium. Although on the surface his materials of paper and ink could not be more traditional, and his mixing of pictures and words conjure precedents from the comic strip to Blake, Pettibon presents his work in a significantly novel way, cluttering walls with hundreds of drawings of varying sizes, bombarding the viewer with far more to read and look at than could ever be absorbed. As if mimicking the ceaseless maelstrom of our mass-media landscape, these shows engulf you in a whirlpool of words and images; yet unlike the media, they generate unexpected layers of meaning, black humor, and barbed lyricism, while surfing across a seemingly haphazard cross section of cultural history.

Though composed of individual drawings, a wall-to-wall display by Pettibon functions like a single work, a discordant symphony where leitmotifs repeat themselves in unpredictable rhythms. Amid the multitude of pictures and scrawled texts, half a dozen major themes may gradually emerge, weaving across the walls. While an exhibition never lapses into randomness, it never totally resolves itself, either; instead, it teases you along cresting waves of delirium, and just when you feel utterly overwhelmed and about to drown, a half-formed riptide or partially delineated current spins you to the next drawing, towards a new thematic connection.

This kind of installation is a labyrinth. There is no real sense of escape in a Pettibon show, because you're continually confronted by the work of reading and rereading, deciphering and searching. You can take on as much or as little as you like, of course; but in the end, nobody rides for free. Pettibon enlists you, Dear Reader, in the pleasures of his endless spidery activity, and the web in which you find yourself is astonishingly far-reaching. Ingeniously plundering everything within reach of his eclectic sensibility, Pettibon seamlessly slips in references from Ruskin to Felix the Cat, from baseball trivia to Henry James, from Charles Manson to Gumby and Ad Reinhard—sometimes all in a single work. Probing dark subcultural pools, cosmic assholes, and

RALPH RUGOFF is the author of *Circus Americanus* (Verso) and *Through the Eye of the Needle,* a monograph on microminiature sculptor Hagap Sandaljian (Museum of Jurassic Technology Press). He is the curator of the exhibition "Scene of the Crime," which will open at the Armand Hammer Museum in Los Angeles in 1997.

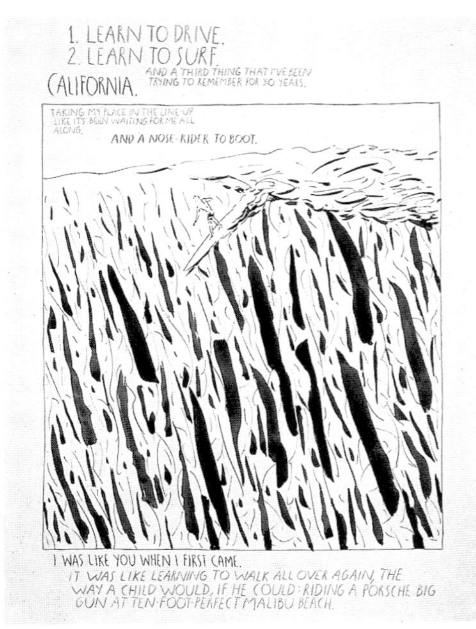

RAYMOND PETTIBON, NO TITLE, 1990, ink on paper, 22 x 17" / OHNE TITEL, Tusche auf Papier, 55,9 x 43,2 cm.

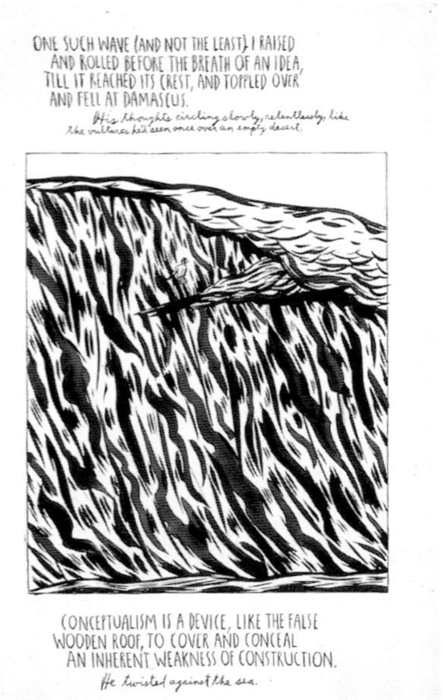

RAYMOND PETTIBON, NO TITLE (ONE SUCH WAVE), 1990, pen and ink on paper, 23 x 14" / OHNE TITEL (EINE DIESER WELLEN), Feder und Tusche auf Papier, 58,4 x 35,6 cm.

nightmarish conflations of history (in one drawing, William Kennedy Smith rapes a girl on the grassy knoll), the artist's erratic pen leaves a wake of churning cartoon thought-bubbles.

In a Pettibon installation, as brilliant as certain individual pieces might be, one is inevitably reminded that it's not the pearls that make the necklace, but the thread. In the fugitive associations between sentences, phrases, and images, Pettibon's art traces the contingent motions of thought itself, the unrepeatable ride across waves of meaning impossible to anchor. This same propulsive diffusion characterizes not only Pettibon's large-scale installations, but also his single works. A medley of dark quips, philosophical queries, acerbic asides, and literary quotes may swirl around a given image, not illustrating so much as reframing it. If certain visual motifs recur in the oeuvre—fires, trains, clocks, surfers, Gumby, hearts, and mushroom clouds—it's because Pettibon's work is a lesson in context. Even the barest icon, a sparsely sketched lightbulb, takes on endless resonance when coupled with his shrewdly evocative texts.

Pettibon's drawing style is often characterized as illustrational or generic, which is odd considering how idiosyncratic and psychologically charged it is. What distinguishes it is less any particular technique than the artist's conception of imagery: Pettibon's pictures are simple enough to seem immediately accessible, yet on closer inspection they often remain curiously elusive. They seem to be less representations, per se, than metaphoric emblems, black boxes of displaced meaning. Even Pettibon's self-portraits are essentially metaphorical images—instead of providing insights into their creator, they tell us about the fiction of the artist, the gulf separating representation and subject, author and reader. It is precisely into this gap that Pettibon's art plunges, extending an offer to play, rather than merely to "communicate." Indeed, Pettibon doesn't communicate with the reader, he communicates with the inexpressible; hence the sense of loss and absence that haunts his art as a whole.

Unlike his pictures, Pettibon's words address us in a motley array of styles, drastically shifting tone, grammatical structure, and tense, gliding from first to second to third person as his pen travels across a page. Quieting this multiphrenic din, his words, whether borrowed or original, are all forged in the same handwriting, an obsessive scrawl that suggests jottings from a private notebook, the record perhaps of a mind assailed by its own inner chorus, but nevertheless the record, at least apparently, of a single mind.

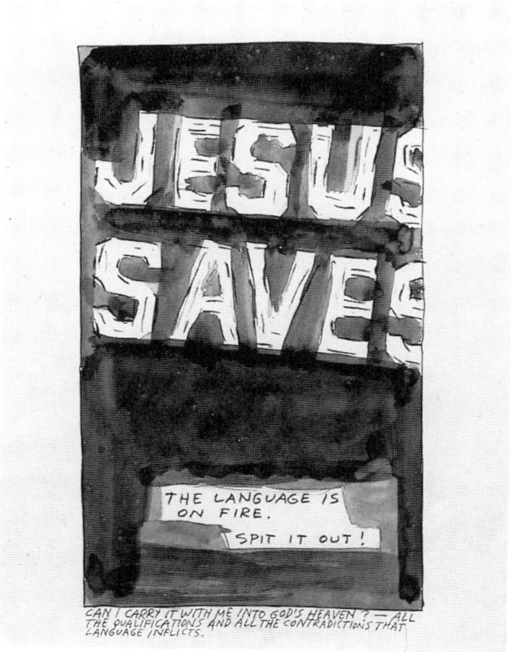

RAYMOND PETTIBON, NO TITLE (JESUS SAVES), 1986,
pen and ink on paper, 14 x 10½" / OHNE TITEL (JESUS ERLÖST),
Feder und Tusche auf Papier, 35,6 x 26,7 cm.

RAYMOND PETTIBON, NO TITLE, 1991,
ink on paper, 30¼ x 22½" /
OHNE TITEL, Tusche auf Papier, 76,8 x 57,2 cm.

Pettibon elaborates on this faux intimacy with his penchant for addressing his "Dear Reader," evoking a bond of trust as well as our own fictitious role as innocent viewer. But the contract of good faith that allows us to inhabit the secure structures of traditional eighteenth- and nineteenth-century literature is difficult to maintain with so splintered a voice; and besides the reader is rarely treated genteelly: a slight snarl, a hint of nastiness, implications of less cordial relations sometimes creep into Pettibon's direct appeals. In a 1992 self-portrait, a first person text warns that the artist cannot be trusted because the voices he repeats belong neither to his muse nor to the man himself.

By wryly calling attention to the conventions of our respective roles, Pettibon prompts us to step back and re-imagine the rules of our communication, to see the border between producer and consumer as infinitely flexible. Given his own repositioning of purloined texts, reading, especially rereading, starts to seem like an art form itself, an act of creative inter-

pretation where even a single word—like "Vavoom!", the sublimely inarticulate call that dwarfs its very speaker in Pettibon's drawings—is capable of promiscuously shifting nuance and connotation with every changed context.

In *The Tragic Muse,* Henry James observes that there are two "affections"—that which "isolates and simplifies its object" and that which "seeks communication and contacts for it." Pettibon's generous art clearly embodies the latter affection: In derailing trains of conventional thought, his work consistently forges contacts where none before existed. It moves us towards the open sea and away from the fixed shore. Indeed, consistency represents a kind of death in Pettibon's aesthetic, a conceptual rigor mortis; the price of growth, on the other hand, is uncertainty and a rigorous resistance to our habitual modes of interpretation. In this way, Pettibon qualifies as a moral visionary—not a bluenose, certainly, but an artist whose freedom of style seems to guarantee the purity of his credo.

RALPH RUGOFF

Wellenreiten mit Raymond – kein Spaziergang

Mit seinen geradezu überwältigend erfolgreichen Ausstellungen in den späten 80er und 90er Jahren hat Raymond Pettibon ein neues Medium geschaffen. Auch wenn seine Materialien – Papier und Tinte – auf den ersten Blick traditioneller nicht sein könnten und seine Kombination von Wort und Bild an zahlreiche Vorgänger, vom Comic strip bis zu William Blake, denken lässt, präsentiert Pettibon seine Arbeit auf eine völlig neue Art. Indem er die Wände mit Hunderten von Bildern verschiedener Grösse förmlich zukleistert, bombardiert er die Betrachter mit einer Masse von Texten und Bildern, die sie nie und nimmer vollständig zu rezipieren vermögen. Als ahmten sie die uferlose Reizüberflutung durch die

Massenmedien nach, ziehen uns diese Ausstellungen in einen Strudel der Worte und Bilder; aber anders als die Massenmedien erschliessen sie unerwartete Bedeutungsschichten voll schwarzen Humors und beissender Poesie, während sie einen scheinbar zufälligen Querschnitt durch die Kulturgeschichte offenlegen.

Obwohl die raumfüllenden Arbeiten Pettibons aus vielen einzelnen Zeichnungen bestehen, funktionieren sie als ein Ganzes, als dissonante Symphonie, in der die Leitmotive in unregelmässigen Abständen wiederkehren. Innerhalb der Fülle von Bildern und hingekritzelten Texten mögen sich dabei nach und nach ein halbes Dutzend zentrale Themen herauskristallisieren, die sich über ganze Wände hinziehen. Die Präsentation gleitet nie ins Willkürliche ab, aber sie ist auch niemals völlig zu entschlüsseln; statt dessen lotst und lockt sie den Betrachter den sich kräuselnden Brechern des Deliriums entlang, und just wenn man sich endlich überwältigt glaubt und drauf und dran ist unterzugehen, gerät man in den Sog

RALPH RUGOFF ist der Autor von *Circus Americanus* und *Through the Eye of the Needle,* einer Monographie über den Microminiatur-Bildhauer Hagap Sandaljian (Museum of Jurassic Technology Press). Er ist Kurator der Ausstellung «Scene of the Crime», die 1997 im Armand Hammer Museum in Los Angeles eröffnet wird.

einer anderen Strömung und driftet ab zur nächsten Zeichnung und zu einer anderen thematischen Verknüpfung.

Pettibons Installationen sind eigentliche Labyrinthe. Für die Besucher der Ausstellungen gibt es kein Entkommen und keinen Ausweg: Ununterbrochen ist man mit der Arbeit des Lesens und Wiederlesens konfrontiert, man entziffert und rätselt. Dabei kann man sich natürlich so viel oder so wenig anstrengen, wie man will; nur geschenkt wird einem nichts. Pettibon verstrickt dich, lieber Leser, liebe Leserin, in die Freuden seiner endlosen spinnenähnlichen Aktivität, und das Netz, in dem du dich wiederfindest, hat erstaunliche Ausmasse. In einem geschickten Raubzug auf alles in Reichweite seiner eklektischen Sensibilität flicht Pettibon übergangslos Anspielungen auf alles mögliche mit ein, von Ruskin[1] bis Felix the Cat, von Baseballtrivialitäten bis Henry James, von Charles Manson bis Gumby[2] und Ad Reinhard – manchmal alles in einer einzigen Arbeit. Der sprunghafte Stift des Künstlers durchmisst dabei dunkle subkulturelle Tümpel, kosmische Arschlöcher und alptraumhafte Verdichtungen zeitgeschichtlicher Ereignisse (in einer Zeichnung vergewaltigt William Kennedy Smith ein Mädchen auf einer kleinen Graskuppe, «on the grassy knoll» – ein Ort, der mit den Ermittlungen über den Mord an John F. Kennedy verknüpft ist) und erzeugt eine Bugwelle aufschäumender Comic-Denkblasen.

Wie brillant auch manche der einzelnen Zeichnungen sein mögen, eine Pettibon-Installation macht einem unweigerlich klar, dass es nicht die Perlen sind, die das Halsband ausmachen, sondern die Schnur. In den flüchtigen Assoziationen zwischen den Sätzen, Wendungen und Bildern spürt Pettibons Kunst die zufälligen Bewegungen des Denkens selbst auf, den nicht wiederholbaren Ritt auf den Wellen der Bedeutungen, die nirgends festzumachen sind. Diese nach vorn und in die Weite gerichtete Bewegung kennzeichnet nicht nur Pettibons grosse Installationen, sondern auch seine Einzelwerke. Um ein einziges Bild kann ein Gemisch aus dunklen Wortspielen, philosophischen Fragen, bitterbösen Zwischenbemerkungen und literarischen Zitaten schwirren, die die Zeichnung weniger erläutern, als vielmehr in einen neuen Bezugsrahmen stellen. Wenn einzelne

visuelle Motive innerhalb des Werks öfter wiederkehren – Feuer, Züge, Uhren, Surfer, Gumby, Herzen und Atompilze –, so deshalb, weil Pettibons Werk uns eine Lektion in Sachen Kontext erteilt. Noch sein kümmerlichstes Requisit, eine knapp skizzierte nackte Glühbirne, weckt endlose Resonanzen durch die Verbindung mit raffiniert alles mögliche heraufbeschwörenden Texten.

Pettibons Zeichnungsstil wird oft als illustratorisch oder leicht verständlich charakterisiert, was merkwürdig anmutet, wenn man bedenkt, mit welcher Sensibilität er arbeitet und wie psychologisch durchdacht alles ist. Was diesen Stil auszeichnet, ist nicht eine bestimmte Technik, sondern Pettibons Bildsprache: Seine Bilder sind einfach genug, um unmittelbar zugänglich zu erscheinen, doch bei näherem Hinsehen bleiben sie oft merkwürdig unergründlich. Sie scheinen weniger eigentliche Darstellungen von etwas zu sein als vielmehr metaphorische Symbole, *black boxes* voll entwurzelter Bedeutungen. Sogar Pettibons Selbstporträts sind im wesentlichen metaphorisch: Statt uns ihren Urheber zu präsentieren, erzählen sie von der Fiktion des Künstlers, von der Kluft zwischen Darstellung und Gegenstand, zwischen Autor und Leser. Es ist genau diese Kluft, in die sich Pettibons Kunst stürzt, indem sie uns das Angebot macht mitzuspielen, statt bloss zu «kommunizieren». Tatsächlich kommuniziert Pettibon nicht mit dem Leser, sondern mit dem Unaussprechlichen; daher rührt auch das Gefühl von Verlust und Leere, das seine Kunst vermittelt.

Anders als seine Bilder wenden sich Pettibons Worte in einem wilden Stilgemisch an uns. Da gibt es drastische Wechsel in der Tonlage, in der Satzgrammatik und der Zeitenfolge; von der ersten geht's zur zweiten und zur dritten Person, während die Feder über das Papier gleitet. Es hat eine beruhigende Wirkung auf dieses laute Stimmengewirr, dass Pettibons Worte, egal ob geborgt oder original, alle in derselben Handschrift erscheinen; sie wirkt wie ein Tagebuchgekritzel und lässt uns an persönliche Notizen denken oder an die Aufzeichnungen eines Geistes, der von einem Chor innerer Stimmen heimgesucht wird, aber es sind immer noch, so scheint es wenigstens, die Aufzeichnungen eines Einzelnen.

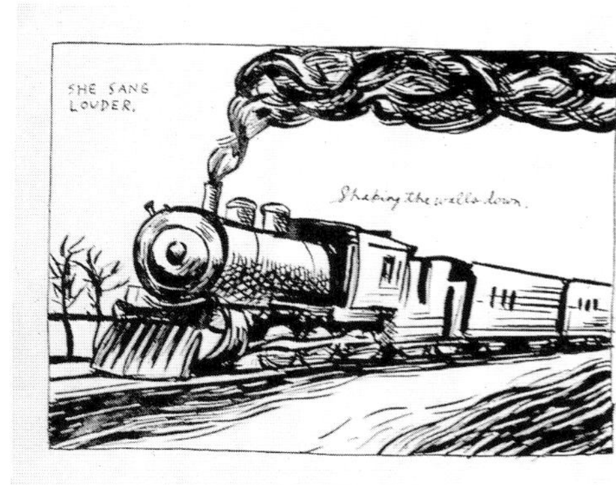

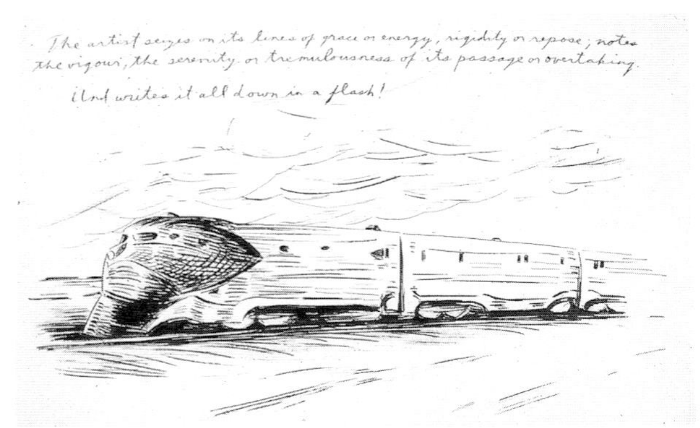

RAYMOND PETTIBON, NO TITLE (SHE SANG LOUDER), 1986,
pen and ink on paper, 11 x 14" / OHNE TITEL
(SIE SANG LAUTER), Feder und Tusche auf Papier, 28 x 35,6 cm.

RAYMOND PETTIBON, NO TITLE, 1992,
ink on paper, 11 x 17" /
OHNE TITEL, Tusche auf Papier, 28 x 43,2 cm.

Pettibon steigert diesen Eindruck des Intimen noch, indem er sein Gegenüber mit Vorliebe direkt mit «lieber Leser» anredet und dadurch eine Vertrauensbeziehung herstellt, die uns zugleich in die fiktive Rolle eines unschuldigen Betrachters versetzt. Aber der Vertrag gegenseitigen Vertrauens, der es uns erlaubt, uns in den sicheren Erzählstrukturen der Literatur des 18. und 19. Jahrhunderts zu bewegen, ist für eine derart brüchige Stimme schwer einzuhalten; im übrigen wird der Leser gar nicht etwa besonders höflich behandelt: Ein grimmiger Unterton, eine Prise Bosheit als Hinweise auf ein weniger freundliches Verhältnis schleichen sich des öfteren in Pettibons direkte Anreden ein. In einem Selbstporträt von 1992 warnt ein in der ersten Person gehaltener Text davor, dem Autor zu trauen, da die Stimmen, die er wiedergebe, weder die seinen seien noch diejenigen seiner Muse.

Dadurch, dass er uns in seiner trockenen Art auf die Konventionen unserer jeweiligen Rolle aufmerksam macht, bringt er uns dazu, Abstand zu nehmen, uns der Regeln unserer Kommunikation bewusst zu werden und zu erkennen, dass die Grenzen zwischen Produzent und Konsument unendlich dehnbar sind. Sein Umgang mit fremden, entlehnten Texten lässt das Lesen und vor allem das Wiederlesen beinah als eine neue, eigene Kunstform erscheinen, als einen Akt schöpferischer Interpretation, wo selbst ein einzelnes Wort imstande ist, Bedeutungsnuancen und Konnotationen, je nach Kontext, beliebig zu wechseln – wie etwa «Vavoom!», der sublim unartikulierte Ausruf, der den jeweiligen Sprecher in Pettibons Zeichnungen winzig erscheinen lässt.

In *The Tragic Muse* bemerkt Henry James, es gebe zwei «Haltungen» – eine, die «ihr Objekt isoliert und vereinfacht darstellt», und eine andere, die «das Gespräch sucht und dafür Kontakte knüpft».[3] Pettibons grosszügige Kunst ist ein klares Beispiel für die zweite Haltung: Indem es die Schienen konventionellen Denkens verlässt, schafft sein Werk fortwährend Kontakte, wo vorher keine waren. Es führt uns auf das offene Meer, weg vom Festland. Tatsächlich stehen Sicherheit und Beständigkeit in Pettibons Ästhetik für eine Art Tod, eine geistige Todesstarre; der Preis des Wachstums andrerseits ist die Unsicherheit und ein strikter Widerstand gegen alle bestehenden Interpretationsgewohnheiten. Pettibon entpuppt sich so als ein visionärer Moralist – sicher kein Puritaner, aber ein Künstler, dessen Ungebundenheit in Sachen Stil für die Reinheit und Unbestechlichkeit seines Credos spricht.

(Übersetzung: Susanne Schmidt)

1) John Ruskin, 1819–1900, britischer Schriftsteller und Kunstkritiker, der vor allem jene Gemälde für gross hielt, die dem Betrachter eine grosse Idee vermittelten.
2) Felix the Cat und Gumby: Amerikanische Comicfiguren für Kinder.
3) Übersetzung des Zitats durch die Redaktion.

Raymond Pettibon Reads Henry James

THYRZA NICHOLS GOODEVE

I HAVE AN INTERIOR THAT I NEVER KNEW OF.
EVERYTHING PASSES INTO IT NOW. I DON'T KNOW WHAT HAPPENS THERE.
Rainer Maria Rilke, *The Notebooks of Malte Laurids Brigge*

Eyes blinking into focus in response to the bright California sun outside, the crowd entered the cool interior of the Berkeley Art Museum to hear Raymond Pettibon give a talk. Shuffling across the entrance, we gravitated into an informal gallery space on the ground floor. At the front of the room was a long table covered with books, pencils, and stacks of paper; behind it was an empty chair. The wall to the right was covered with Pettibon's drawings. People sat down cross-legged on the floor near the table, or milled about looking at the exhibition; expressions passed from face to face, rhythmically attuned to the drawings on view—a smile here, a frown there, a whispered conversation exchanged. The room, as it filled, took on the air of a high school gymnasium packed with expectant bodies.

It was unclear what kind of event we were gathered for as Pettibon sat down at the table and began to address the audience. He gave no overture or formal introduction, nor did he seem compelled to command the space. He was merely up there amidst his books, sifting through pages, randomly verbalizing quotes in what seemed to be a state of total self-absorption. Backpacks rustled, shoes squeaked as feet shifted restlessly against the floor, hands fiddled with the hems of pants. Pettibon— lodged at the desk, head lowered, eyes and hands flitting over the pages of his book—read aloud from what sounded like Henry James. He continued on like this, interrupting himself every so often. Although we were there—indeed we were his audience for the afternoon—it was as if we did not exist for him. He was merely reading, alone, although he gave

THYRZA NICHOLS GOODEVE is a writer who lives in New York City.

the impression of being more like a sculptor carving a block of wood than a reader extracting units of meaning.

Something about his lack of public consciousness recast the mood in the room. The rustling stopped, the atmosphere seemed to dim although the lights remained bright. It was as though we had been thrust into a softly lit, private chamber, a log fire roaring, he with his book, reading aloud—in effect, our awareness was being conducted by the motion of his mind across the text. He was reading, not for sense, but as a way of creating a sculptural form, where interiority was no longer contained within one person but enveloped many. The division between speaker and listener, public and private, creation and display collapsed. We were inserted—sentence by sentence—among the images and texts of his drawings, drawn into this reader's interior process.

"Basically what I do is just find a sentence and put it down and then draw whatever comes to mind," he said as he jotted down quotes on the cardboard stacked before him. "The drawing may relate to it, or may not—it really isn't about fitting the two together. It's just my way of working inside the text." He passed out a handful of the inscribed sheets to the crowd and told those of us who took them to draw in the space left open. We were all on our own time and in our own peculiar internal states, listening to him as he continued to read; he served not as our guide or inspiration, but as our atmosphere. Some sat with eyes closed, others just watched and listened. Some of us drew. Like hushed and diligent toddlers working at our individual tablets, we were caught somewhere between absentminded doodling and the intense concentration of assertive strokes.

RAYMOND PETTIBON, installation view, Kunsthalle Berne, Switzerland, 1995 / Ausstellung in der Kunsthalle Bern, 1995. (PHOTO: ROLAND AELLIG)

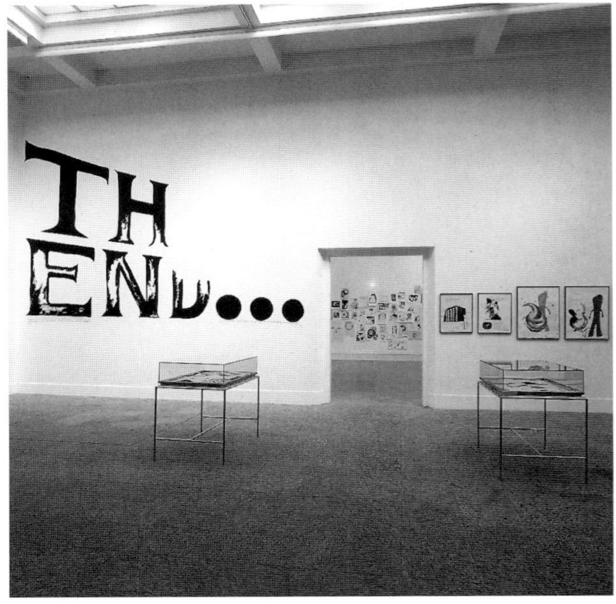

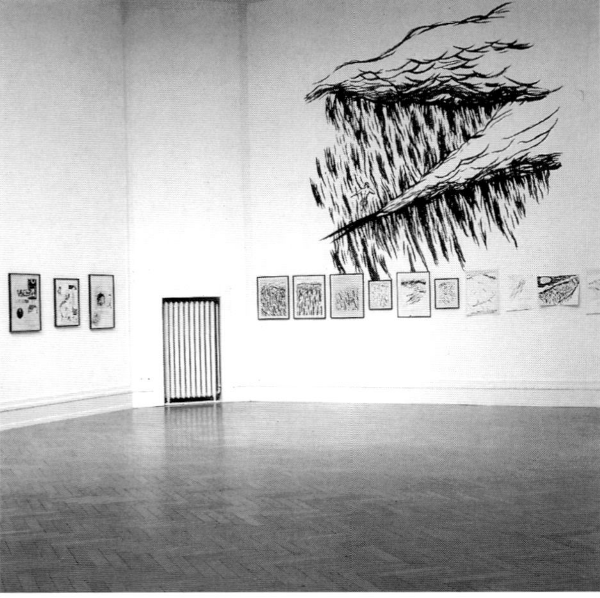

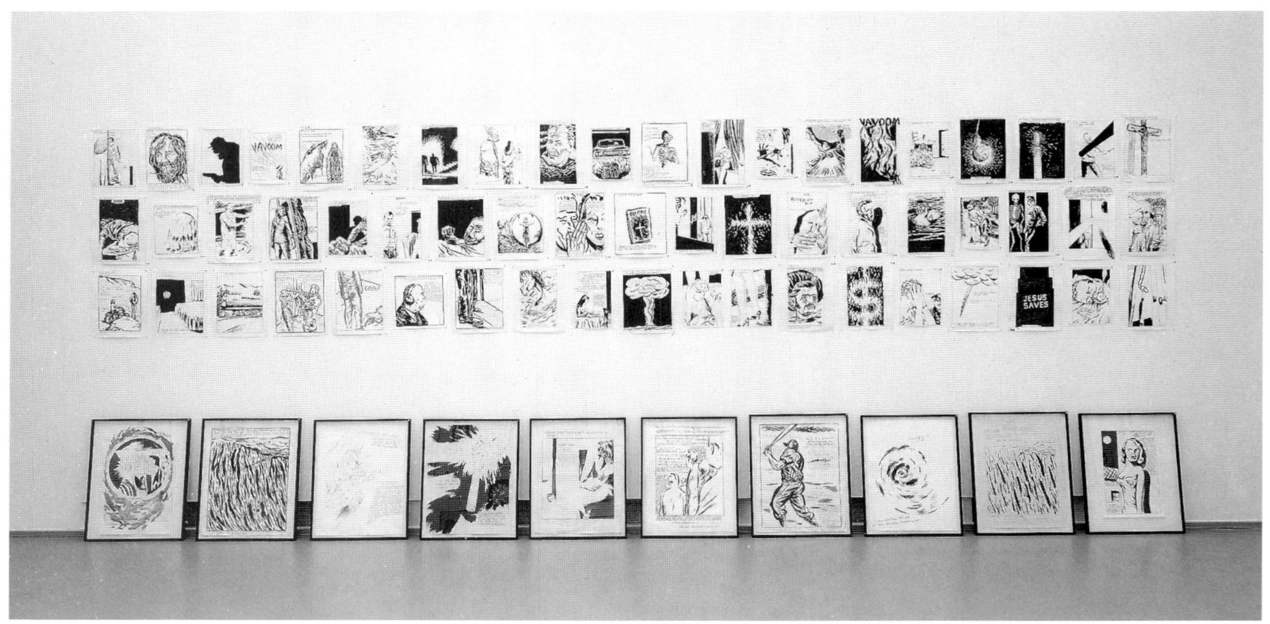

RAYMOND PETTIBON,
installation view /
Ausstellung 14/16 Verneuil,
Marc Blondeau, Paris 1995.

There was little sense of waiting for a conclusion—the process Pettibon had set up had no such rise or fall to it. In fact, I can't remember
how the session ended. All I do know is that eventually it did, and Pettibon told those of us who had made drawings to pin them on the wall
among his if we liked. Oddly, some asked for his signature on the bottom
of their sheets, suggesting that, although many different hands had been
at work, Pettibon was ultimately the author of them all.

I don't know what happened to the drawings left on the wall with
Pettibon's. I took mine home, held onto it for a few months and eventually threw it away. It didn't make sense to keep it as a fetish, because
Pettibon's presentation hadn't been about producing some lasting interpretation to hang on my wall. In fact, he'd made a point to stress that
"text and image don't have to relate." The event had been about cultivat-
ing something much less tangible than a finished product. It was about
capturing an inner flicker or movement and refashioning it into a visible, encompassing architecture. Reading has long been associated with
the production—and visualization—of interiority; a performed process
through which everything passes, and yet, as Rilke reminds us, we never
quite know what happens there. What was extraordinary about the day
we gathered to hear Pettibon speak was how each of us had become wit-
ness to, and participant in, an art wrought from the "never quite known"
which we had produced—alone and together. Interiority was what was
produced that day. It was our material, a substance belonging neither to
Raymond Pettibon, nor to Henry James, nor to us.

Raymond Pettibon liest Henry James

THYRZA NICHOLS GOODEVE

ICH HABE EIN INNERES, VON DEM ICH NICHT WUSSTE.
ALLES GEHT JETZT DORTHIN. ICH WEISS NICHT, WAS DORT GESCHIEHT.
Rainer Maria Rilke, *Die Aufzeichnungen des Malte Laurids Brigge*

Nach dem grellen Licht der kalifornischen Sonne draussen blinzelnd um Klarheit des Blicks bemüht, betrat die Menge das kühle Innere des *Berkeley Art Museum,* um einer Lesung von Raymond Pettibon beizuwohnen. Uns durch den Eingangsbereich schiebend, strebten wir einem schlichten Ausstellungsraum im Erdgeschoss zu. An der Stirnseite des Raums stand ein langer Tisch voller Bücher, Bleistifte und Papierstapel; dahinter stand ein leerer Stuhl. Die Wand zur Rechten war mit Zeichnungen Pettibons tapeziert. Leute setzten sich im Schneidersitz in der Nähe des Tisches auf den Boden oder liefen herum und sahen sich die Ausstellung an; in schönem rhythmischem Einklang mit den ausgestellten Zeichnungen liefen Veränderungen der Mimik – hier ein Lächeln, dort ein Stirnrunzeln, im Flüsterton ausgetauschte Sätze – von einem Gesicht zum nächsten. Als er sich allmählich füllte, wirkte der Raum wie eine mit erwartungsvollen Körpern vollgepfropfte High-School-Turnhalle.

Es war nicht klar, zu welcher Art von Veranstaltung wir uns eingefunden hatten, als sich Pettibon an den Tisch setzte und das Wort an das Publikum richtete. Er verzichtete auf eine Vorrede oder förmliche Einleitung und schien auch keinen Drang zu verspüren, den Raum zu «bespielen». Er sass einfach da oben inmitten seiner Bücher, blätterte sie durch und rezitierte in einem Zustand scheinbar völliger Selbstvergessenheit aufs Geratewohl Passagen. Rucksäcke raschelten, Schuhe

THYRZA NICHOLS GOODEVE lebt und schreibt in New York City.

quietschten, während rastlose Füsse auf dem Boden scharrten, Hände fingerten an Hosensäumen herum. Pettibon, der sich am Tisch niedergelassen hatte, den Kopf gesenkt, Augen und Hände über die Seiten seines Buches gleiten lassend, las laut etwas vor, das sich wie Henry James anhörte. So fuhr er, mit gelegentlichen Unterbrechungen, fort. Obgleich wir da waren – wir waren ja sein Publikum an diesem Nachmittag –, war es, als existierten wir für ihn gar nicht. Er las nur, alleine, wobei er allerdings eher einem Bildhauer glich, der einen Holzblock bearbeitet, als einem Leser, der nach sinnbehafteten Fragmenten sucht.

Etwas an diesem fehlenden Öffentlichkeitsbewusstsein liess die Stimmung im Raum umschlagen. Das Rascheln verstummte, der Raum schien sich zu verdunkeln, obwohl die Lampen nach wie vor hell leuchteten. Es war, als wären wir in ein Privatgemach hineinkatapultiert worden, bei gedämpftem Licht und einem knisternden Kaminfeuer, Pettibon mit lauter Stimme aus seinem Buch lesend – tatsächlich orientierte sich unser Bewusstsein unwillkürlich an der Bewegung seines Geistes quer durch den Text. Er las nicht um des Sinngehaltes willen, sondern das Lesen diente ihm dazu, ein skulpturales Gebilde zu schaffen, bei dem Innerlichkeit nicht länger innerhalb einer Einzelperson angesiedelt war, sondern viele mit einschloss. Die Schranken zwischen Sprecher und Zuhörer, zwischen öffentlich und privat, zwischen Darbietung und schöpferischem Akt brachen in sich zusammen. Wir wurden – Satz für Satz – in die Bild- und Textwelt seiner Zeichnungen hineinversetzt, hineingezogen in den Denkprozess dieses Lesenden.

Was ich im Grunde mache, ist, dass ich einfach auf einen Satz stosse, den niederschreibe und dann zeichne, was mir gerade in den Sinn kommt, sagte er, während er Zitate auf die Blätter vor sich schrieb. *Die Zeichnung kann sich auf das Geschriebene beziehen oder auch nicht – es geht eigentlich nicht darum, dass die beiden zusammenpassen. Es ist einfach meine Art, im Innern des Textes zu arbeiten.* Er verteilte eine Handvoll der beschriebenen Blätter an die Zuhörer und trug denen, die sie entgegennahmen, auf, die leer gebliebene Fläche mit einer Zeichnung auszufüllen. Jeder von uns war für sich und in seiner spezifischen Geistesverfassung gefangen; wir lauschten ihm, während er weiterlas, wobei er uns nicht als Führer oder Inspiration diente, sondern als etwas, das uns atmosphärisch umfing. Manche sassen da mit geschlossenen Augen, andere warteten einfach und hörten zu. Einige von uns zeichneten. Wie verstummte, fleissige Erstklässler über unsere Täfelchen gebeugt, bewegten wir uns irgendwo zwischen gedankenlosem Gekritzel und der intensiven Konzentration resoluter Striche.

Von der Erwartung eines Endes der Veranstaltung war kaum etwas zu spüren – dem Prozess, den Pettibon in Gang gesetzt hatte, fehlte ein solches An- und Ausklingen. Ich kann mich tatsächlich nicht entsinnen, wie die Sitzung ausging. Ich weiss nur, dass sie irgendwann zu Ende war und dass Pettibon zu uns sagte, wenn wir wollten, könnten wir unsere Zeichnungen zwischen seine an die Wand heften. Kurioserweise baten ihn einige um seine Signatur unter ihre Zeichnung, suggerierend, dass, obgleich viele Hände am Werk gewesen waren, letztlich alles das Werk Pettibons war.

Ich weiss nicht, was mit den Zeichnungen geschah, die an der Wand neben denen von Pettibon zurückblieben. Ich nahm meine mit nach Hause, hob sie einige Monate lang auf und warf sie schliesslich weg. Es hatte keinen Sinn, sie wie einen Fetisch aufzubewahren, denn bei Pettibons Veranstaltung war es ja nicht darum gegangen, irgendeine gültige zeichnerische Interpretation des betreffenden Textes hervorzubringen und an die Wand zu hängen. Tatsächlich hatte er nachdrücklich darauf bestanden, dass «Text und Bild sich nicht aufeinander beziehen müssen». Bei der Veranstaltung war es um das Erzeugen von etwas gegangen, das weit weniger greifbar war als ein fertiges Produkt; es war darum gegangen, ein inneres Flackern, eine innere Regung zu erfassen und diese in ein sichtbares, umfassendes Gebilde umzusetzen. Mit dem Lesen wird seit langem schon die Schaffung – und Visualisierung – eines Innenlebens verbunden: Ein Vorgang, im Zuge dessen alles nach innen dringt, und doch wissen wir, wie Rilke uns in Erinnerung ruft, nie so richtig, was sich dort wirklich abspielt. Das Besondere an dem Tag, an dem wir zusammenkamen, um Pettibon zuzuhören, war die Art und Weise, wie jeder einzelne von uns zum Zeugen und Mitwirkenden einer Kunst geworden war, welche einem «Inneren, von dem wir nicht wussten», abgerungen wurde und die wir – jeder für sich und alle gemeinsam – zutage gefördert hatten. Was dabei entstanden war, war Innerlichkeit. Sie war unser Material, ein Stoff, der weder Raymond Pettibon noch Henry James, noch uns gehört.

(Übersetzung: Magda Moses, Bram Opstelten)

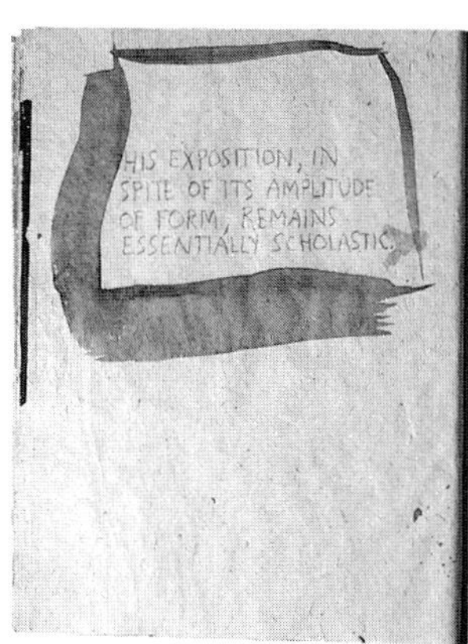
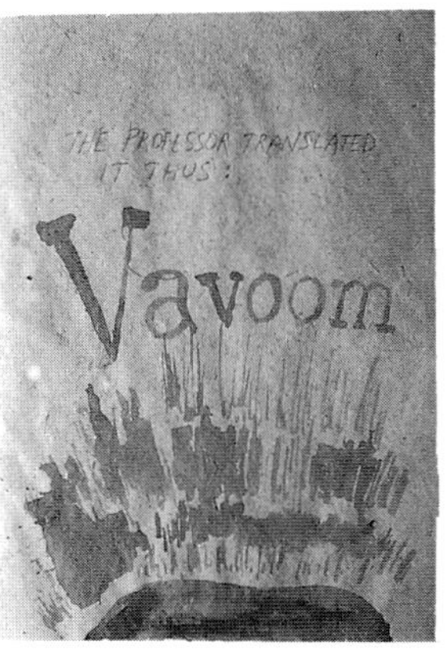

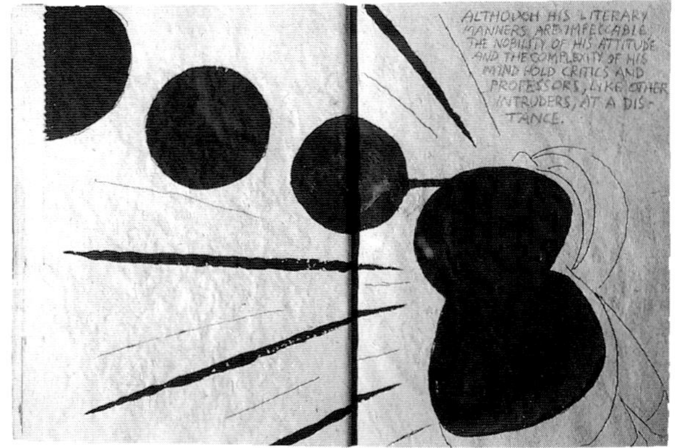

RAYMOND PETTIBON, SPEAKS VOLUMES, 1995, unique artist book, mixed media, 138 pages, details, 9¼ x 6¾" each / SPRICHT BÄNDE, Künstlerbuch, Unikat, Mischtechnik, 138 Seiten, Doppelseiten, je 23,5 x 17,2 cm.

RAYMOND PETTIBON

UNTITLED (JUSTLY FELT AND BRILLIANTLY SAID), 1996
Silkscreen, hand-written texts by the artist which vary in each edition,
pressed flower, printed by Lorenz Boegli, Zurich, on Arches 120 g,
approx. $9^5/_8$ x $7^5/_8$", a 10-part foldout, full length $9^5/_8$ x $76^3/_4$".
Edition: 60/XX, signed and numbered

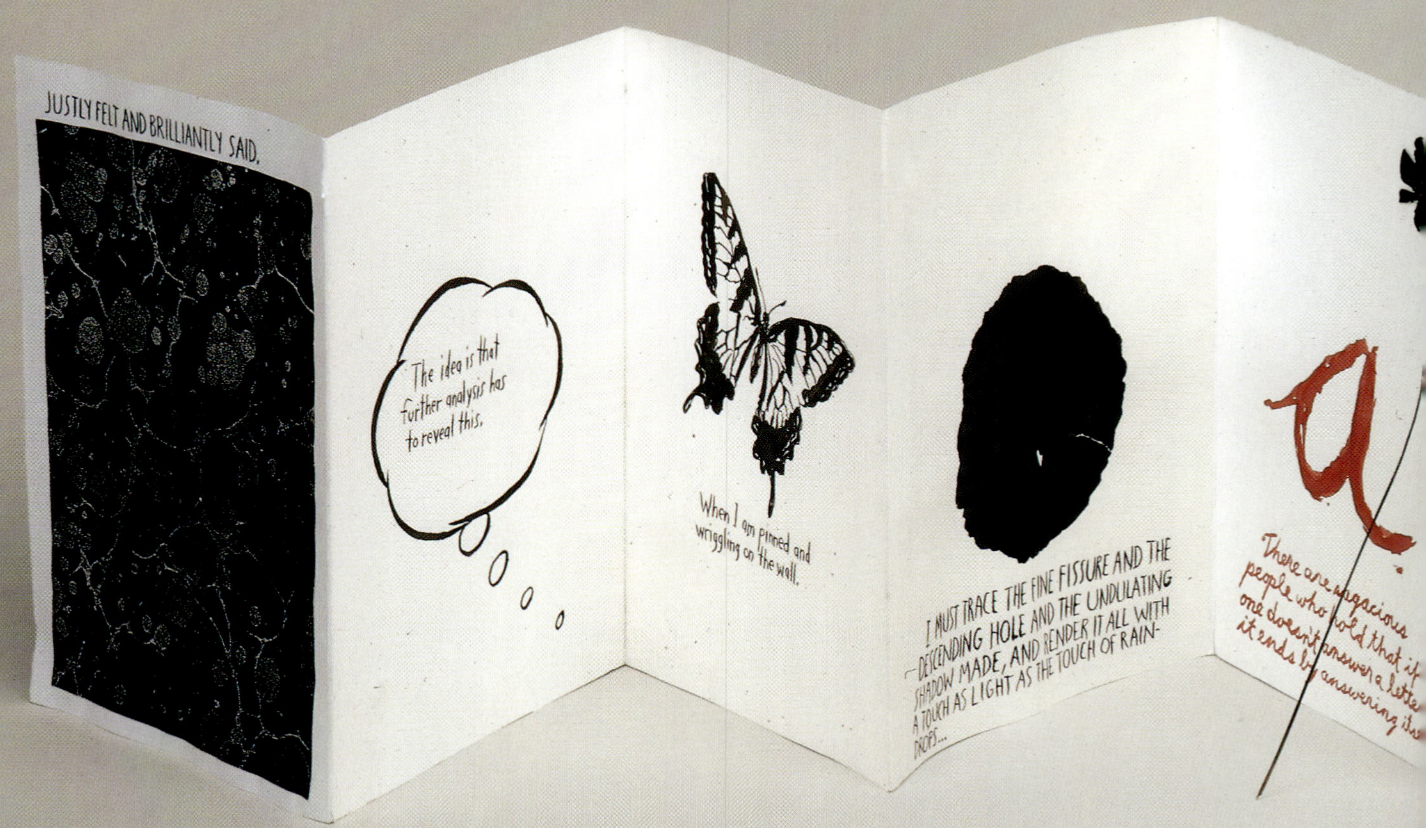

**OHNE TITEL (JUSTLY FELT AND BRILLIANTLY SAID /
RICHTIG EMPFUNDEN UND BRILLANT FORMULIERT), 1996**
Siebdruck, mit handgeschriebenen Texten des Künstlers,
die von Edition zu Edition variieren, gepresste Blume, gedruckt
im Atelier für Siebdruck Lorenz Boegli, Zürich, auf Arches 120 g,
ca. 24,5 x 195 cm (10teiliges Leporello gefalzt auf 24,5 x 19,5 cm).
Auflage: 60/XX, signiert und numeriert

(PHOTO: MANCIA/BODMER)

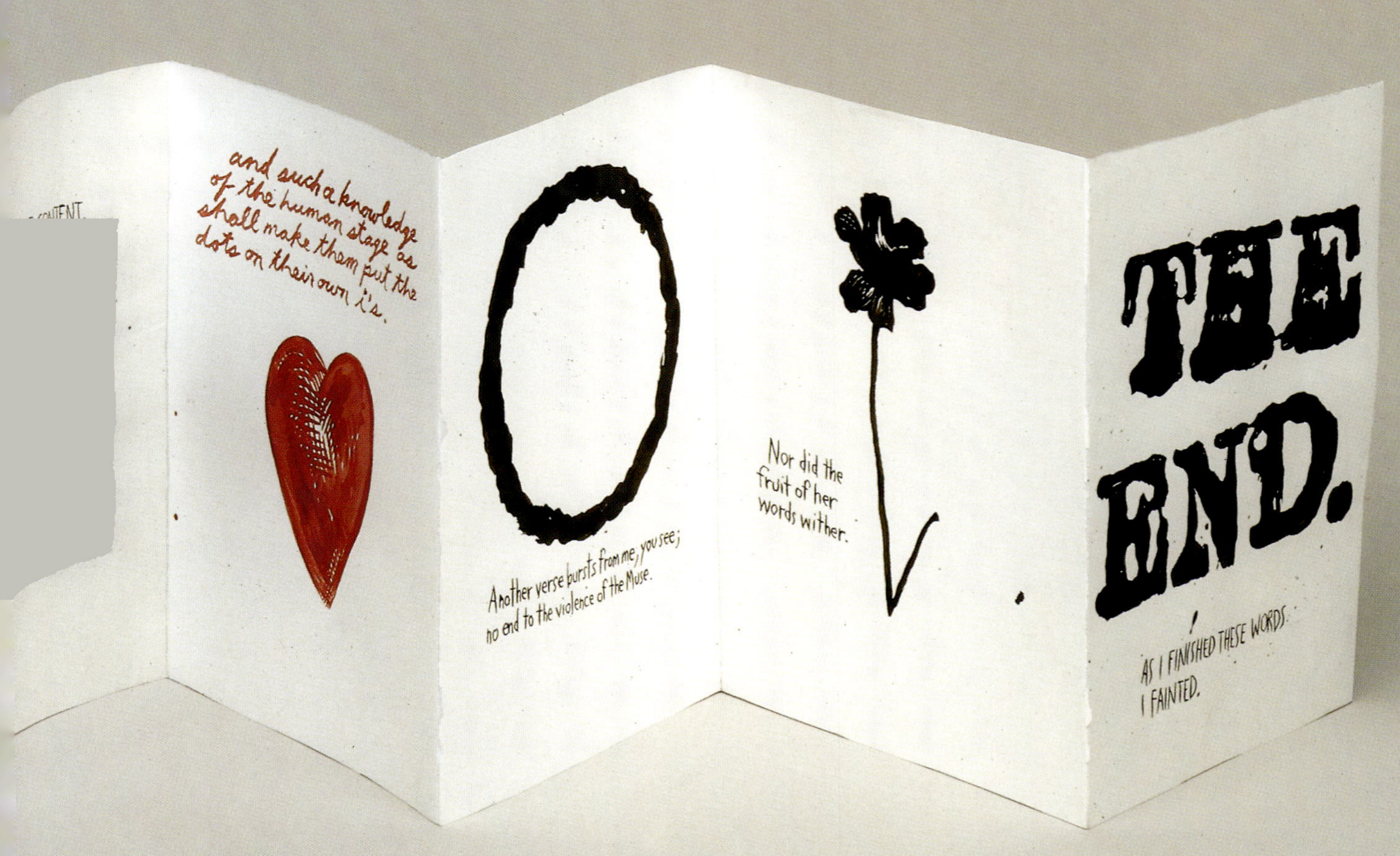
CONTENT.
and such a knowledge
of the human stage as
shall make them put the
dots on their own i's.
Another verse bursts from me, you see;
no end to the violence of the Muse.
Nor did the
fruit of her
words wither.
THE
END.
AS I FINISHED THESE WORDS,
I FAINTED.

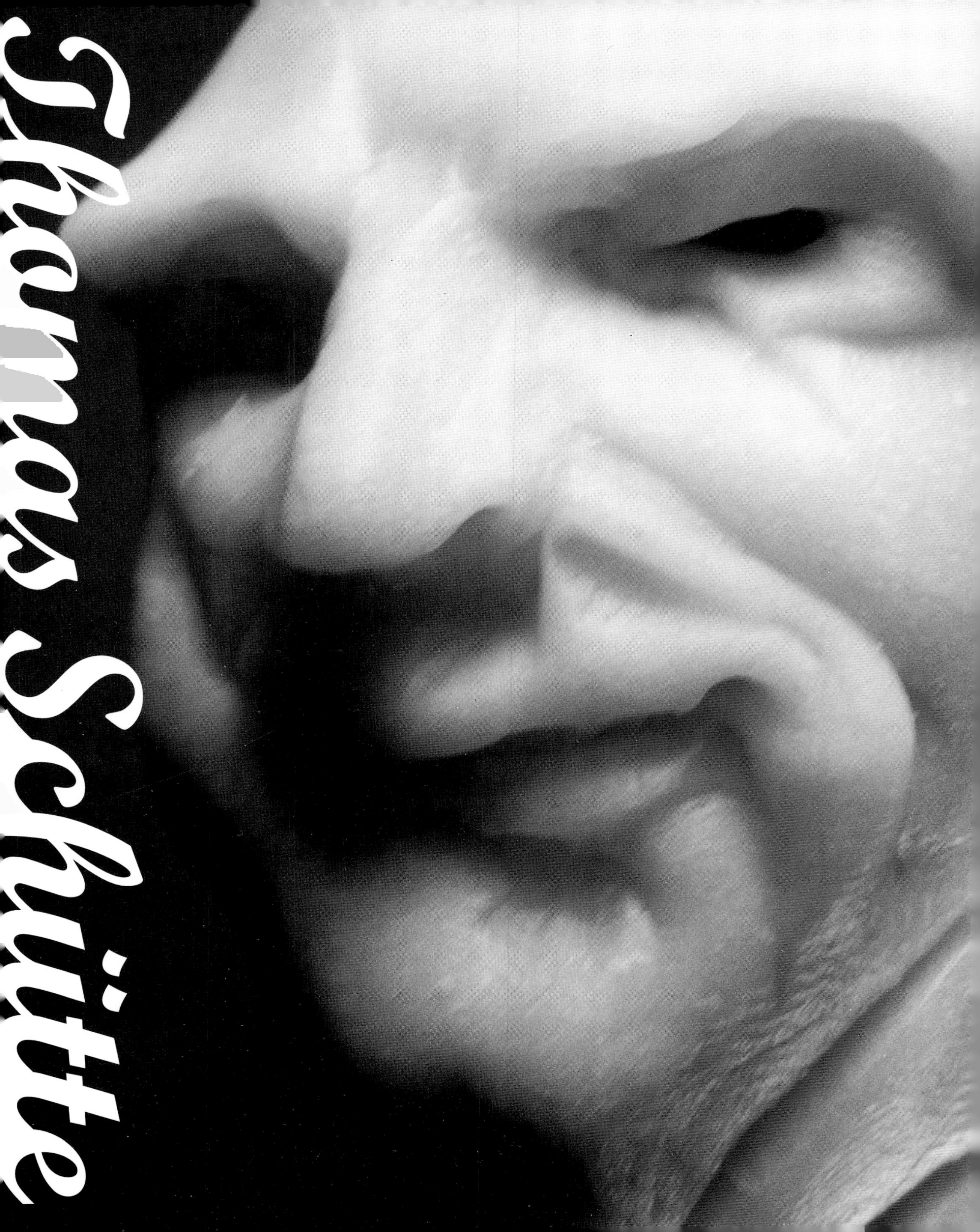
Thomas Schütte

ADRIAN SEARLE

THOMAS SCHÜTTE

Figures and faces, you said, faces and figures. You rang me as I was making my way along the street to work. I stopped to take your call, catching my reflection in a shop window, amongst the dummies and the new season's clothes. Atget photographed just such a scene, mannequins in the window, people passing by; but that was Paris before the war, a different street, different windows, another time of year.

Here is my text for Thomas. I have spent a long time looking at the images, remembering works I have seen, reminding myself of Thomas himself. Thomas in his glasses, Thomas quiet, Thomas smoking, Thomas laughing. Thomas sitting apart from the others. The way he stands. I hardly know him, although we have found ourselves, once or twice, in the same cities, in the same bar, at the same dinners, at another man's table. Faces and figures, Thomas's friends. Sometimes, I think, he makes them up.

But there are some of them in the reunion photo. There's Frank, and behind him Gustav, Alfred, Udo, then Wilhelm and Ehrhard. Ehrhard, the yellow one, there! That must be Dieter, in green. Heinz. Anton, that's Anton. Serious Anton. Paul, fat Paul, and Erwin, Erwin with the blue head. Glen. The others I forget.

Tied in their soft wrappings, a handkerchief, a scarf, a bit of old toweling, new friends and old. On their stilts. Working at their grudges. In the unchanging moment of the photograph you imagine they will always be together like this. My friend's friends and my enemy's enemies. My enemy's enemy, my friend. United enemies, that's how it is between friends.

ADRIAN SEARLE is an artist, writer, and curator who lives in London. He is art critic at *The Guardian*.

Those heads, those faces, we want to meet them at our own level, as equals, just as we greet the strangers that we meet. Standing together on the same podium, crossing the same square, raising the same flag, walking hand in hand towards a tower, huddled together in the bunker. You can't judge by appearances. But you can, oh yes, you can.

Those passersby, who come and go in the glare of the afternoon, the sun wedged in the jamb of the street between the buildings, flaring into view and then eclipsed. A man runs past you, and just along the street lies the assassinated politician, just out of the cinema with his wife, still light, late light, long summer evening, the man running into the dark underpass beneath the precinct, the shortcut, just as you emerge blinking into the daylight. Then a car slewing away into the traffic. What film was it that they had gone to see that day in Stockholm, like an ordinary couple?

Then there were those two fellows hurtling down towards Via Laietana away from the guy lying on the pavement, the blood on the stones and the three women standing around him. Blood and shadows on the stones, an ordinary man. And you only just off the bus, first time in the city, what a first impression. And there I am in the supermarket, upset by the sight of a woman slapping a child. *Get out from under my feet,* she said. The trash in her trolley, an incident in a bright aisle amongst the happy colours, the background music, the shiny cellophane. The kid, when he recovers from his tears, will probably end up a rocket scientist, Nobel Prize, first flight to Venus, time travel. If they had time travel, we'd have heard about it by now.

On the street, bumping into a man as he rounds the corner, him hurrying, both of us head down—he

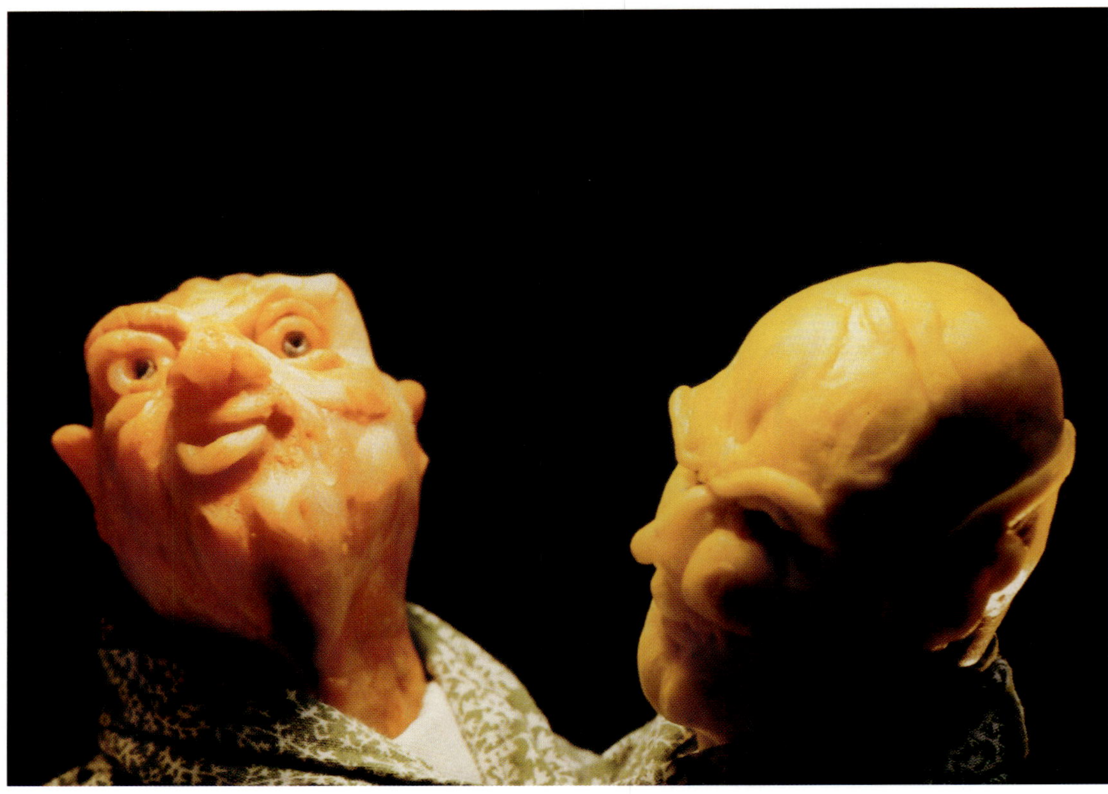

dropped his bag of groceries as we met full on. *I'm sorry,* I said, stooping down to catch a lemon as it rolled toward the gutter. *I'm sorry,* and he glared back at me, *You will be.* Even now I can't turn from the alley into the market where the butcher used to be without thinking of him, that moment and that voice of his. Is this what we mean by time travel? I stand before the window, and close my eyes against the day.

Golems, gremlins, and trolls; the painted and masked protagonists in Noh plays; shoppers in their heavy coats; science-fiction humanoids after long hours in make up, with painted prosthetic head extensions, latex ears, and extruded chins. Model train-set dioramas with little plastic figurines that you paint yourself; brown trousers, a blue dress, a white head scarf. Waving to the trains, carrying luggage, scurrying along the platform.

The alien is made in our own image, not least because we have nothing else to go on. *Life,* I read today. *Life on another planet would likely be based on the same chemical structures as our own—carbon compounds, liquid water, and so on. This does not mean, however, that anything resembling a horse would roam on anything resembling grassy plains. But there could well be two- or four-legged creatures, with eyes at the top of the body adapted to the wavelengths of light emitted by the planet's star, and it might have as food some plant-like surface growth that built its own tissue by some local version of photosynthesis...* Surface growth, local versions. The underlying principles remain the same, the details going to show that the universe has only a little imagination, a limited repertoire. The spaceships from fifties movies look like the fifties. The future belongs, as always, to its age.

On this other planet, will they have professors and mechanics, ballroom-dancing instructors, travelling salesmen staying in cheap hotels, lone round-the-

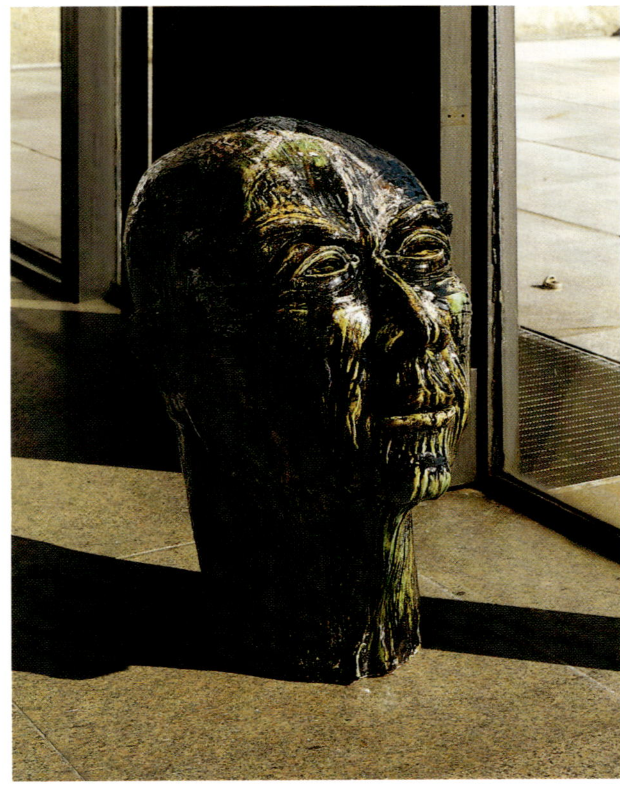

THOMAS SCHÜTTE,
UNITED ENEMIES, 1994. Detail.

THOMAS SCHÜTTE, GROSSER KOPF,
1993, glasierte Keramik, Württembergischer
Kunstverein, Stuttgart, 1994.
(PHOTO: NIC TENWIGGENHORN)

world yachtsmen, painters in their studios, boxers on the mat, analysts with their couches, madwomen locked away for inexplicable crimes? Will there be chiropodists, Thursday mornings, socks drying on a radiator, melon sliced on a plate? The smell of wood shavings, ripe cherries, mug shots, the quiet of three a.m., movie monsters, bedtime stories for the children, loneliness? We can't count on the humanity of the aliens. Imagine their molten anger and stupefying dumbness, their boredom. Moving at a different speed to us, in slow time, their bodies extruding slowly into gestures that last for a hundred years. A mouth that takes a human lifetime to open against the immense pull of gravity in the unaltering light. A fist blurring into a punch that we will never see land.

They're all at my feet, down around my ankles, doing their stuff. Hefting bales, piling things up in corners and along the wainscot. Going about their business. One has built a palisade, another gives a speech. Purposeful, cooperative, though to us dull and repetitive, lives they lead. Their quicksilver bodies gleam with Art Deco newness, softened shrapnel molded into Michelin men, a dream of the future that began in the past. Like us and not like us, as close to us, and as distant, as the saints in their niches, the statues on their plinths. Hercules and Achilles, St. Sebastian and St. Agatha, Scott of the Antarctic, Bismarck, Nelson Mandela, Alain Colas, the Greyfriars' Bobby, Mother Theresa, Barbie and Ken, Darth Vader, the Masters of the Universe, Terminator T-2000. On plinths, on parapets, on top of columns, open to the weather and the birdshit, the graffiti and the coming insurrections. All the effort to have put them there might have been wasted. But it is all a matter of scale and time, of one thing coming after another. The passing of an age, the memorials to a moment.

ADRIAN SEARLE

THOMAS SCHÜTTE

Figuren und Gesichter, sagst du, Gesichter und Figuren. Du riefst mich an, als ich auf dem Weg zur Arbeit war. Ich blieb stehen, um deinen Anruf entgegenzunehmen, und sah mein Spiegelbild in einem Schaufenster zwischen den Modellpuppen und der neuen Mode der Saison. Atget hat solch eine Szene photographiert: Schaufensterpuppen und in der Fensterscheibe die Reflexe der Passanten; aber das war Paris vor dem Krieg, eine andere Strasse, ein anderes Fenster, eine andere Jahreszeit.

Hier ist mein Text für Thomas. Ich habe die Bilder lange betrachtet, mich an Arbeiten erinnert, die ich gesehen habe, und an Thomas gedacht. Thomas mit Brille, Thomas ganz still, Thomas rauchend, Thomas abseits von den anderen sitzend. Seine Art zu stehen. Ich kenne ihn kaum, wenngleich wir uns gelegentlich in irgendeiner Stadt, einer Bar, bei einem Essen begegnet sind oder zufällig am selben Tisch sassen. Gesichter und Figuren, Thomas' Freunde. Ich glaube, manchmal erfindet er sie.

Aber einige von ihnen sind auf dem Gruppenphoto. Da ist Frank und hinter ihm Gustav, Alfred, Udo, dann Wilhelm und Ehrhard, der Gelbe da! Das muss Dieter sein, in Grün. Heinz. Anton, das ist Anton. Der ernsthafte Anton. Paul, der dicke Paul, und Erwin, Erwin mit dem blauen Kopf. Glen. Die anderen habe ich vergessen.

Eingewickelt in ihre weichen Hüllen, ein Taschentuch, ein Schal, ein Stück altes Frotteetuch, neue und alte Freunde. Auf ihren Stelzen. Grollend. Auf dem zum Unveränderlichen erstarrten Photo sieht es aus, als wären sie immer so zusammen. Die Freun-

de meines Freundes und die Feinde meines Feindes. Der Feind meines Feindes, ein Freund. Vereinigte Feinde, so ist das unter Freunden.

Diese Köpfe, diese Gesichter, wir wollen ihnen auf unserem eigenen Niveau begegnen, von gleich zu gleich, so wie wir im Vorbeigehen Fremde grüssen. Zusammen auf demselben Podium stehen, denselben Platz überqueren, dieselbe Flagge hissen, Hand in Hand auf einen Turm zugehen, zusammengepfercht im Bunker sitzen. Man kann nicht nach dem Aussehen urteilen. Und doch kann man es, o ja, man kann.

Diese Passanten, die im grellen Nachmittagslicht kommen und gehen, in den sonnigen Lichtstreifen zwischen den Häusern leuchten sie auf und verschwinden wieder. Ein Mann läuft an dir vorbei, und am Strassenrand liegt der ermordete Politiker, der gerade mit seiner Frau das Kino verlassen hat; noch ist es hell, ein spätes Licht, ein langer Sommerabend, der Mann läuft in die dunkle Unterführung unter dem Platz, eine Abkürzung, gerade als du herauskommst und ins Tageslicht blinzelst. Dann schwenkt ein Auto in den Verkehrsfluss ein und verschwindet. Welchen Film hatten sie sich doch gleich an diesem Tag in Stockholm angesehen, wie ein ganz normales Paar?

Dann waren da diese zwei Typen, die in Richtung Via Laietana rannten, weg von dem Menschen, der auf dem Bürgersteig lag, weg vom Blut auf den Pflastersteinen und von den drei Frauen, die um ihn herumstanden. Blut und Schatten auf dem Pflaster, ein gewöhnlich sterblicher Mann. Und du bist gerade aus dem Bus gestiegen, zum erstenmal in der Stadt, was für ein erster Eindruck! Und da bin ich im Supermarkt, aufgeregt über den Anblick einer Frau, die ihr Kind ohrfeigt. *Steh mir nicht vor den Füssen*

ADRIAN SEARLE ist Künstler, Kritiker und Ausstellungsmacher. Er lebt in London und ist Kunstkritiker der Zeitung *The Guardian*.

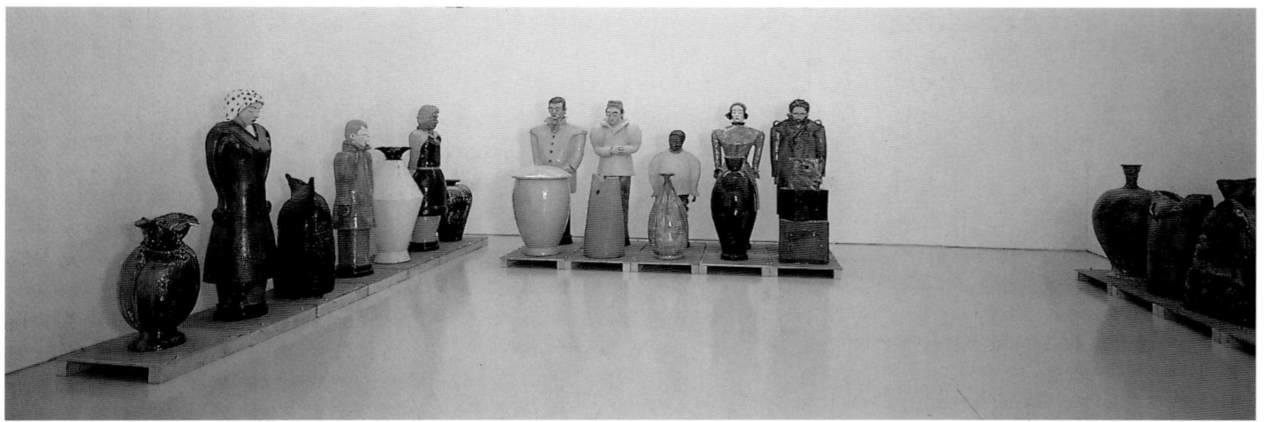

rum, sagt sie. Der Plunder in ihrem Einkaufswagen, ein Blickfang in einem hellen Gang zwischen all den fröhlichen Farben, die Musik im Hintergrund, das glitzernde Zellophan. Aus dem kleinen Jungen wird, wenn er zu weinen aufgehört hat, bestimmt einmal ein Raumfahrtspezialist, Nobelpreis, erster Flug zur Venus, Zeitreise. Wenn Zeitreisen möglich wären, müssten wir eigentlich längst davon gehört haben.

Auf der Strasse stosse ich mit einem Mann zusammen, der gerade in grosser Eile um die Ecke biegt, wir beide mit gesenktem Kopf – er liess seine Einkaufstasche fallen beim Zusammenprall. *Tut mir leid,* sagte ich und bückte mich nach einer Zitrone, die gerade in den Rinnstein rollte. *Tut mir leid,* und er erwiderte meinen Blick grollend, *das soll es auch.* Bis heute kann ich nicht von der Strasse auf jenen Markt abbiegen, wo früher die Metzgerei war, ohne an ihn zu denken, an diesen Augenblick und an seine Stimme. Nennt man das eine Zeitreise? Ich stehe vor dem Fenster und verschliesse meine Augen vor dem Tag.

Golems, Kobolde und Unholde; die geschminkten und maskierten Protagonisten aus No-Theaterstücken; Einkaufende in ihren schweren Mänteln, Science-fiction-Humanoide nach stundenlanger Maskenbildnerei, mit bemalten künstlichen Kopf-Erweiterungen, Gummiohren und vorstehendem Kinn. Modelleisenbahn-Dioramen mit kleinen selbstbemalten Plastikfiguren; braune Hose, blaues Kleid,

weisses Kopftuch. Den Zügen nachwinkend, Gepäck tragend, den Bahnsteig entlang eilend.

Die Ausserirdischen schaffen wir nach unserem eigenen Bild. Woran sonst sollten wir uns halten? *Das Leben,* las ich heute, *das Leben auf einem anderen Planeten wiese wahrscheinlich dieselben chemischen Strukturen auf wie bei uns – Kohlenstoffverbindungen, Wasser und so weiter. Das heisst aber nicht, dass etwas, das aussähe wie ein Pferd, auch auf so etwas wie einer grünen Wiese herumliefe. Aber es könnte sehr wohl zwei- oder vierbeinige Kreaturen geben mit Augen am oberen Körperende, ausgerichtet auf die Wellenlänge des Lichts, das die Sonne des betreffenden Planeten aussenden würde; als Nahrung könnte ihnen ein pflanzenähnlicher Oberflächenbewuchs dienen, der durch eine lokale Version der Photosynthese entstünde...* Oberflächenbewuchs, lokale Version. Es sind immer dieselben Grundprinzipien, wobei die Details zeigen, dass das Universum wenig Phantasie zur Verfügung hat, ein begrenztes Repertoire. Die Raumschiffe aus den Filmen der 50er Jahre sehen wie Raumschiffe aus den 50ern aus. Die Zukunft bleibt hier wie überall an die Gegenwart gebunden.

Wird es auf diesem anderen Planeten Professoren und Mechaniker geben, Tanzlehrer, Handelsreisende, die in billigen Hotels absteigen, einsame Weltumsegler, Maler in ihren Ateliers, Boxer im Ring, Analytiker und ihre Couchen, verrückte Weiber, die wegen unerklärlicher Verbrechen eingesperrt werden? Wird es Fusspfleger und Donnerstagvormittage geben, Socken, die zum Trocknen auf dem Heizkörper liegen, Melonenschnitze auf einem Teller? Den Geruch von Holzspänen, reife Kirschen, Verbrecherphotos, die Stille um drei Uhr früh, Filmmonster, Gutenachtgeschichten für Kinder und Einsamkeit? Wir können uns nicht auf die Menschlichkeit der Ausserirdischen verlassen. Man stelle sich ihre weissglühende Wut vor, ihre bestürzende Sprachlosigkeit, ihre Langeweile. Wie sie sich mit einer völlig anderen Geschwindigkeit bewegen, in Zeitlupe, wobei sich ihre Körper in Gebärden ergehen, die hundert Jahre dauern. Ein Mund, der ein ganzes Menschenleben braucht, um sich gegen die immense Schwerkraft im niemals wechselnden Licht allmählich zu öffnen. Eine Faust, die zu einem Schlag ausholt, den wir nicht mehr erleben werden.

Sie sind alle zu meinen Füssen, um meine Knöchel herum, und tun irgendwas. Sie heben Bündel hoch, stapeln Sachen in den Ecken und entlang der Täfelung. Sie gehen ihrem Geschäft nach. Der eine hat einen Zaun errichtet, der andere hält eine Rede. Das Leben, das sie führen, ist zielbewusst, kooperativ, doch in unseren Augen stumpfsinnig und immer gleich. Ihre quecksilbrigen Körper schimmern im Glanz ihrer *Art Deco*-Neuheit, eingeschmolzene Geschosse, die zu Michelin-Männern umgegossen wurden, ein Traum von der Zukunft, der gestern begann. Wie wir und doch nicht wie wir, so nah und so fern von uns wie Heilige in ihren Nischen oder Statuen auf ihren Sockeln. Herkules und Achill, der heilige Sebastian und die heilige Agathe, der vom Südpol besessene Scott, Bismarck, Nelson Mandela, Alain Colas, Greyfriars Bobby,[1] Mutter Theresa, Barbie und Ken, Darth Vader, die Herrscher des Universums, Terminator T-2000. Auf Sockeln, Säulen und Brüstungen, Wind, Wetter und Vogelscheisse ebenso ausgesetzt wie Graffiti-Sprayern und künftigen Revolutionen. Vielleicht war die ganze Mühe, die es kostete, sie aufzustellen, umsonst. Aber es ist immer eine Frage der Verhältnisse und der Zeit, des Aufeinanderfolgens der Dinge. Das Vergehen eines Zeitalters in zahllosen Denkmalen für den Augenblick.

(Übersetzung: Nansen)

1) Im englischen Sprachraum allgemein bekanntes Monument für den treuen Bobby, einen Scotchterrier, der vierzehn Tage lang am Grab seines Herrn trauerte, und zwar auf dem *Greyfriars Kirkyard* in Edinburgh.

THOMAS SCHÜTTE, GROSSER RESPEKT, 1994, Stahl und Bronze, Durchmesser 480 cm / steel and bronze, 15' 9" diameter; DEKA FAHNEN 1989/90, Stoff, je 200 x 330 cm, Installation Württembergischer Kunstverein Stuttgart, 1994 / cloth, 6' 6¾" x 4' 3¼" each. (PHOTO: NIC TENWIGGENHORN)

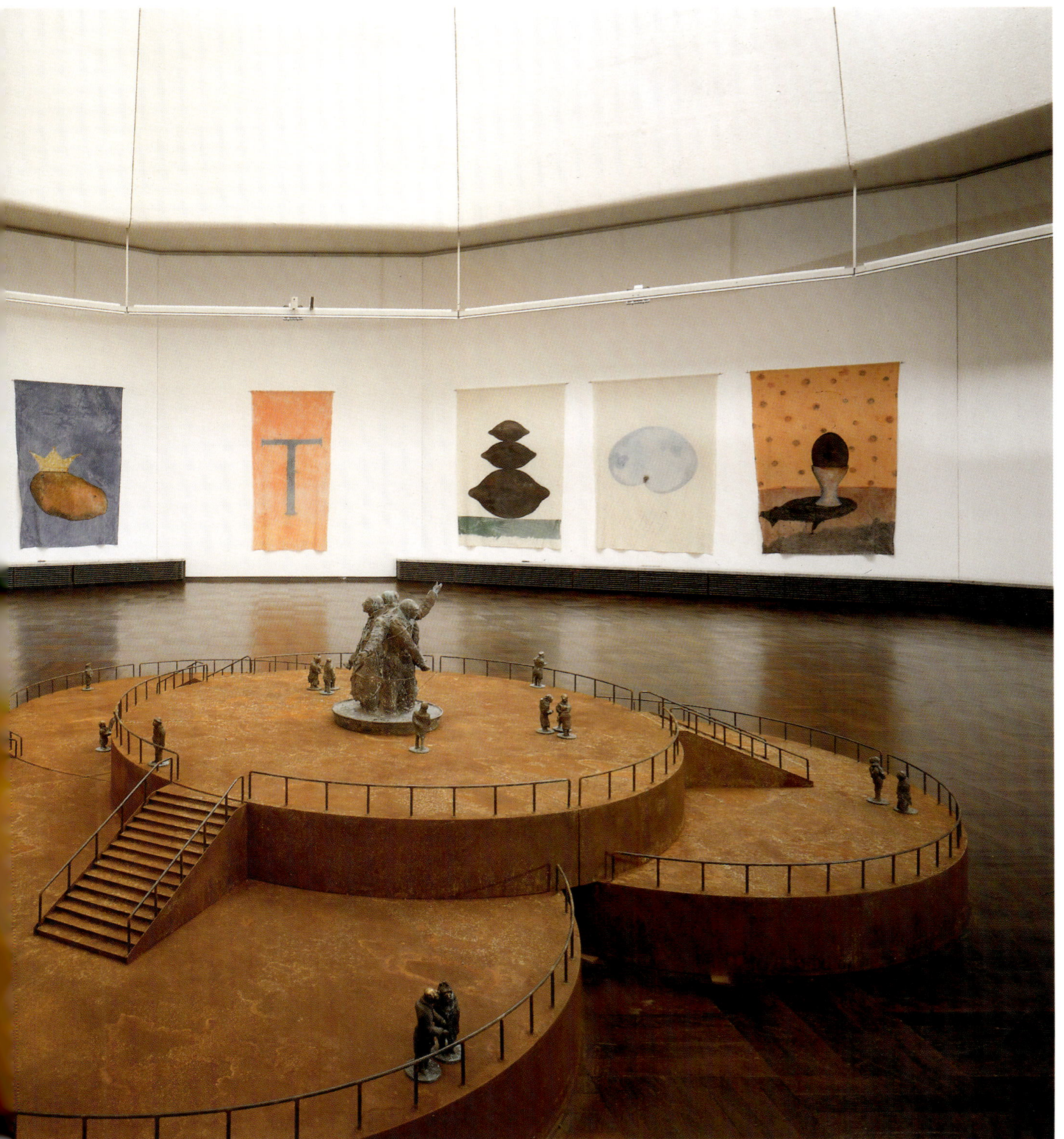

BARTOMEU MARI

DER TRANSPARENTE RAUM

Thomas Schüttes Werk hat eine seltene Qualität: Es ist zeitgenössisch, ohne modernistisch zu sein. Es ist subjektiv, aber seine Subjektivität ist frei von Egoismus. Es verfügt über Gewandtheit im Ausdruck und über eine programmatische Strenge, was bald versteckt ist, bald offen zutage liegt. Schüttes Anliegen ist die Darstellung der *Conditio humana* hier und heute. Was mich daran fasziniert, ist die Tatsache, dass er weder an utopischen noch an apokalyptischen Zukunftsbildern interessiert ist und dass er auch nicht in ein goldenes Zeitalter in einer imaginären Vergangenheit entschlüpft. Schütte ist ein Realist: Er stellt dar, was er sieht, und arbeitet mit Materialien, die direkt mit seiner Sicht der Dinge zu tun haben, Mittel, die ihren Grund im Inhaltlichen des Bildes haben. Bleibt die Frage: Welches Bild ist das konstruierte, und wie unabhängig ist es von der Natur?

Seit 1983 schafft Schütte Bilder, die mindestens drei oder vier Dimensionen beanspruchen. Als Bildhauer benützt er oft das Vokabular des Architekten, um zu zeigen, dass die Kunst es auch mit dem Gebrauch und dem Eingreifen in den Raum der allgemeinen Kommunikation und Erfahrung zu tun hat, mit dem kollektiven Schaffen von Bildern. Wenn er die Darstellungsfunktion des architektonischen Modells wieder in die Skulptur einführt – samt den damit verbundenen Spielen mit der Relativität, die mit der Phantasie, den Dimensionen, Grössenverhältnissen und der Definition des Raumes zusammenhängen –, so rückt Schütte einerseits den Begriff des Idealen in der Architektur wieder in unseren

BARTOMEU MARI ist Direktor des Witte de With Center for Contemporary Art in Rotterdam.

Blick sowie deren Fähigkeit, sich ins Ersehnte auszudehnen, andrerseits aber auch die missglückten Realisierungen der architektonischen Utopien dieses Jahrhunderts. Eine Utopie ist ein Werturteil, das auf der Ablehnung des Gegenwärtigen beruht. Die zeitliche Dimension – unabhängig vom statischen Zustand des Gegenstandes – muss deshalb eingeführt werden als ein unausweichliches Kommen und Gehen zwischen dem Jetzt und seinen Grenzen.

1983 begann Schütte mit einer Reihe von Skulpturen, die aus drei Hauptelementen bestanden: einer horizontalen Ebene auf vier senkrechten Stützen und darauf eine gebäudeähnliche Konstruktion. Die Vertrautheit des Bildes ist irritierend, weil nichts wirklich vertraut ist: Die Farben sind ungewohnt, die Symmetrie ist nicht einheitlich, und die Teile des Gebäudes scheinen manchmal nicht die richtige Grösse zu haben. Die verwendeten Elemente (Wände, Türen, Fenster, Dächer usw.) sind zunächst so überdimensioniert und detailgenau, dass sie an die unmögliche Kombination von Rationalität und Klassizismus der Architektur in den ersten Jahrzehnten dieses Jahrhunderts erinnern.

Die frühen Modelle arbeiten mit der Symmetrie der Fassade und dem Fehlen jeden erkennbaren Stils. Die zeitgenössische Architektur treibt die Idee des «Stils» auf die Spitze (man erinnere sich an die heroischen 20er Jahre, wo der Stil zum Markenzeichen wurde ...) und identifiziert das produzierende Subjekt (den Künstler) mit dem produzierten Objekt (dem Projekt), insofern als dieses Träger einer neuen Ausdrucksform ist. Schütte dagegen verwirft jeden Stil, um sein Augenmerk auf das Seltsame, Unheimliche der konstruierten Räume zu richten.

Eine direkte Bezugnahme auf das Urbane ist selten in dieser Werkreihe. Die «Gebäude» sind isoliert, losgelöst von jedem städtebaulichen oder historischen Kontext. Die Plazierung auf Stützen erlaubt es dem Betrachter nicht, ein Verhältnis zu irgendeinem Raum ausserhalb des Werkes selbst herzustellen. Seine Charakteristiken laden jedoch dazu ein, nach solchen Bindegliedern zu suchen, die ein von der westlichen Kultur geprägtes Denken uns nahelegt.

Die Entwicklung dieser systematischen und darstellerischen Beständigkeit zeigt sich besonders in zwei Installationen: BASEMENTS (Untergeschosse, 1993) besteht aus vier Skulpturen, deren Material in gleicher Weise bearbeitet wurde, um einen unfertigen Zustand anzudeuten, Holzspäne und Materialreste vom Verkleben der verschiedenen Elemente blieben deutlich sichtbar. Aber die horizontalen Ebenen dieser Arbeiten tragen keine Gebäudeteile. Statt dessen gehen die Bauwerke in die Tiefe. Jede Arbeit enthält mehrere Treppen, deren Aneinanderreihung einer Logik folgt, die aber alle in ihr eigenes Inneres und ins Leere führen. Die fehlende Ausrich-

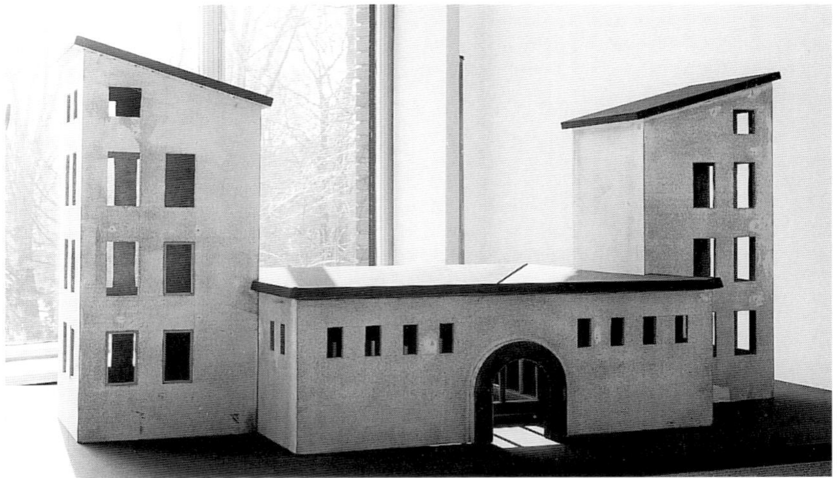

*THOMAS SCHÜTTE, HAUS FÜR
ZWEI FREUNDE, 1983, Holz / wood.
(PHOTO: THOMAS SCHÜTTE)*

Aber was geschieht mit der Architektur ohne die städtebauliche Entwicklung? Wie können wir an Gebäude glauben, ohne sie uns im Umfeld einer Stadt vorzustellen? Ist Schüttes Verwendung der Sprache der Architektur eine Art Kritik der Tätigkeit jener, die Räume planen und entwerfen? Man ist schliesslich versucht zu fragen, wo denn der «urbane» Bezugspunkt der Kunst zu finden sei. Antwort: in ihr selbst. Und Schütte macht das konkret deutlich, wenn er als Ort für seine Werke den öffentlichen Raum wählt, sei der nun städtisch oder nicht. Alltagsbilder und deren Aufblähen zu unerwarteter Grösse und Proportion kommen häufig vor. Und hier liegt wohl der Grund für die kontinuierliche Gegenwart des Architektonischen in seinem Werk.

tung auf ein Ziel und die scheinbare Sinnlosigkeit der in der Oberfläche ausgesparten Gänge und Räume vermitteln den Eindruck der Negierung des Gebäudes. Ein Gebäude zu verneinen, indem man den Sinn des Raumes verkehrt, führt aber auch das Thema der verrückten Architektur ein. Die Autonomie des Raumes ersetzt die Autonomie des Gebäudes, und dieser Un-Ort, wo die Fluchtpunkte der Treppen zusammenfallen, ist der unbekannte Ort, den jeder Korridor und jeder Durchgang ankündigt, wenn er um eine Ecke führt oder in einer Biegung verschwindet. Diese Un-Orte entsprechen auch den logischen Ungereimtheiten, welche die Spiele der Architektur manchmal erzeugen und die es in jedem Gebäude und in jeder Stadt geben sollte, Ungereimtheiten von jener Art, die auch Piranesi in seinen Zeichnungen und Plänen umtrieben.

Schüttes jüngste Installation in der Marian Goodman Gallery in New York besteht aus vier Tischen. Die horizontale Oberfläche zeigt Pläne, die direkt auf das aufgerauhte Holz gezeichnet sind. Das Gebäude ruht so in seinen eigenen Spuren. Die Zeichnungen geben den Lebensraum des Künstlers selbst wieder, sein Atelier, die Konrad Fischer Galerie, in der die meisten seiner Einzelausstellungen stattfanden, und das Museum Haus Esters in Krefeld, der Ort seiner ersten Museumsausstellung. Die autobiographischen Bezüge wechseln zwischen der privaten, der beruflichen und der öffentlichen Dimension seiner Arbeit. Wiederum ist es die öffentliche Dimension der Skulptur, die mich hier interessiert: die Suche nach einer Bildsprache, in der Realismus und Abstraktion nicht länger zum unabdingbaren Vokabular des Künstlers gehören. Das Wiedererkennen und die Interpretation sind natürliche, sozusagen biologische Funktionen des Verstandes, der in den Objekten seiner Erfahrung unermüdlich nach sich selbst sucht und dabei darum ringt, eben diese Erfahrung auch mitzuteilen.

(Übersetzung aus dem Englischen: Susanne Schmidt)

THOMAS SCHÜTTE, 3 HÄUSER, 1989.
Collection Anton Herbert, Gent.
(PHOTO: PHILIPPE DE GOBERT)

THOMAS SCHÜTTE, BASEMENTS II,
1993, detail, wood, 40⅛ x 59 x 80⅝" /
Holz, 102 x 150 x 205 cm.
(PHOTO: TOM POWEL)

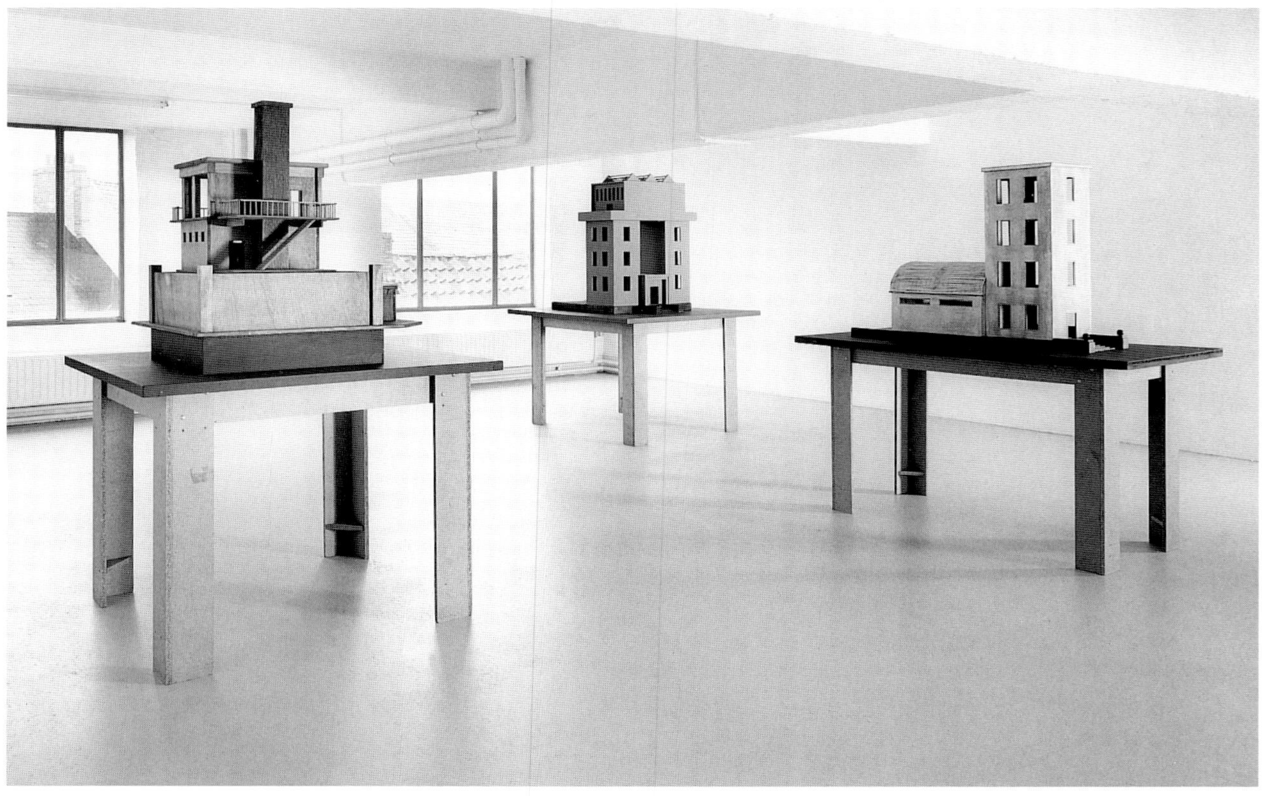

BARTOMEU MARI

A PUBLIC
FOR THE SPACE

Thomas Schütte's oeuvre possesses a rare quality: It is contemporary without being modernist. It possesses subjectivity, but a subjectivity devoid of egoism. It possesses versatility of expression along with the rigor of a program it sometimes hides and sometimes reveals. Schütte's concern is the representation of the human condition as it is right now. But what fascinates me is the fact that he is not interested in either a utopian or a catastrophic future, or why he doesn't drift into golden ages located in some imaginary past. Schütte is a realist: He represents what he sees using materials directly linked to that vision, materials anchored in the literalness of the image. The question remains: Which image is the constructed one, and how independent can it be from the natural sphere?

Since 1983, Schütte has been building images that occupy at least three or four dimensions. He is a sculptor who often uses the vocabulary of architects to declare that intention implies using and intervening in the space of common communication and experience, of collective image-making. When he reintroduces into sculpture the representative function of the architectural maquette, with its plays on relativity all connected to imagination, dimension, scale, and the definition of space, Schütte recovers on one hand the notion of the ideal in architecture and its ability to extend itself through desire, and on the other the failed reality of the architectural utopias of this century. A utopia is a value judgement based on negating the present. The temporal dimen-

sion—separate from the stasis of the object—must be introduced in this way: an inexorable coming and going between the present moment and its frontiers.

In 1983, Schütte began a series of sculptures made up of three main components: a horizontal base raised up on four members perpendicular to the base and the ground, above which rises a construction that resembles a building. The familiarity of the image is perturbing because this familiarity is

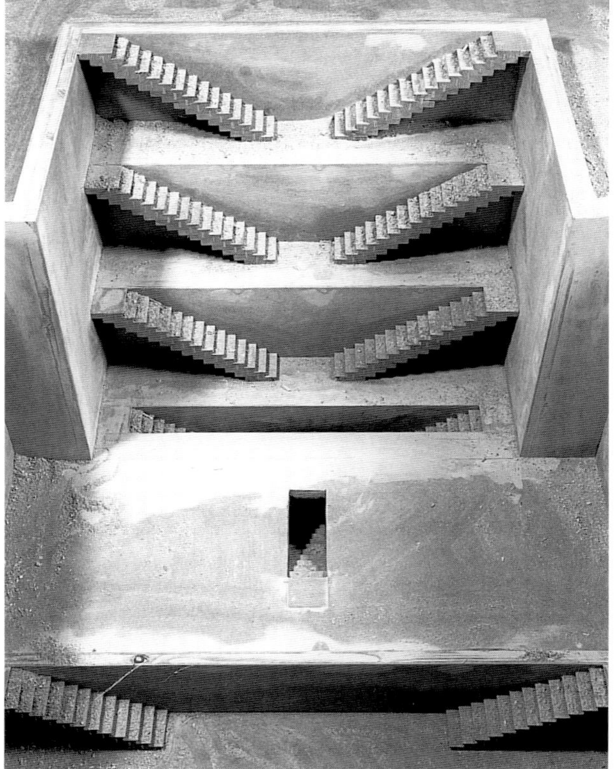

BARTOMEU MARI is Director of Witte de With Center for Contemporary Art in Rotterdam.

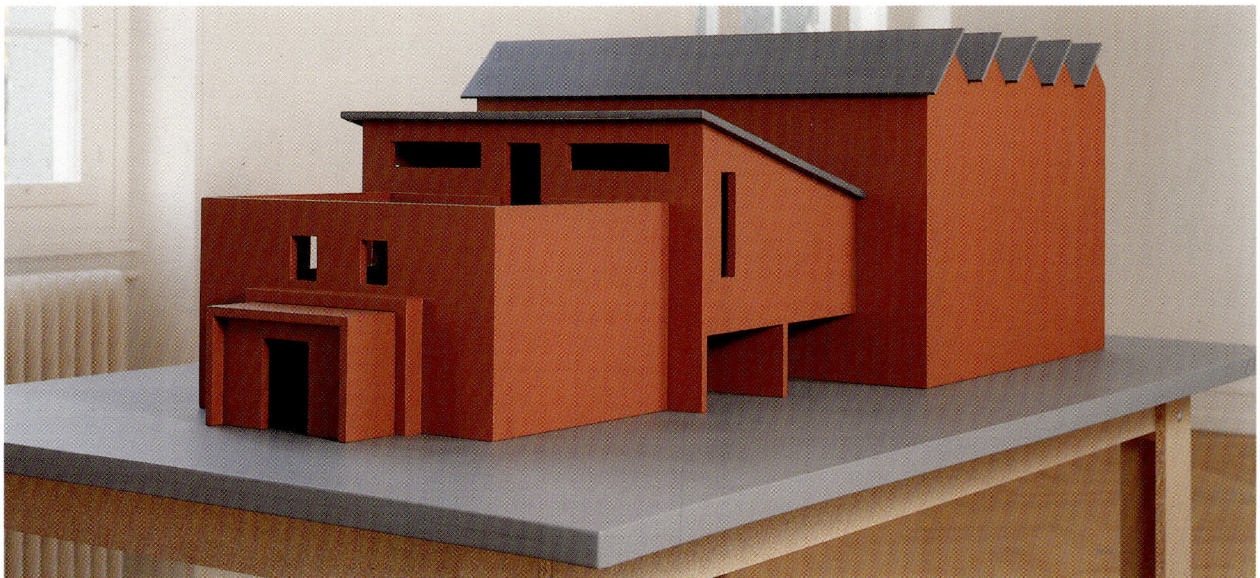

not genuine: the colors do not correspond to what we are used to, the symmetry is not uniform, and the elements that go into the building appear, at times, out of scale. The forms used (walls, doors, windows, roofs, and so on) are first combined with an architectonic oversizedness and detailing that remind us of the impossible combination of rationality and classicism that dominated the architecture of the first decades of our century.

The first models are based on the symmetry of facade and the absence of any recognizable style. Contemporary architectural production exacerbates the idea of "style" (remember that during the heroic twenties, style acquired the status of slogan…) and identifies the producing subject (the artist) with the object produced (the project), insofar as it is a figure of new expression. Schütte, however, rejects all style in order to direct his intention toward the "uncanny" in the constructed spaces.

Direct reference to the urban is rare in this series of works. The "buildings" are isolated, disconnected from any urban or historical context. Their position on the support does not allow us to see any relationship to any space other than that of the work itself. Its characteristics, however, invite us to seek those links which the action Western culture exercises on all imagination proposes as something natural. But

THOMAS SCHÜTTE, E.L.S.A., 1989,
painted wood / Holz bemalt, Installation Kunsthalle Bern, 1990.
(PHOTO: ROLAND AELLIG)

what would happen to architecture without urban development? How can we believe in buildings without making them exist within the context of a city? Is Schütte's appropriation of the language of architects some kind of critique of the activity of those who conceive space? One feels tempted to conclude in this way: Where, then, is the "urban" referent in art located? In itself. And Schütte clearly renders it material when he chooses the terrain of public space, urban or not, for the construction of his works. The language of quotidian imagery and its explosion into unexpected scales and proportions are frequent. This is probably the source of the constancy of the architectural in his work.

This systematic and representative constancy evolves toward the present moment through two particular installations that temporarily finish it. BASEMENTS (1993) comprises four sculptures whose material has been treated in a uniform manner to suggest an unfinished state, with wood-shavings and remnants of the caulking of the seams of the different levels left clearly visible. But the horizontal planes of the works do not support the body of any building. Instead the constructions take place in depth. Each work contains a number of staircases whose concatenation follows a logic but which descend toward their own interior, to nowhere. Absence of finality and apparent uselessness of the courses and spaces excavated in the surface appear as negative impressions of the construction. To deny the building by inverting the meaning of space introduces as well the theme of the architectural "folly." Autonomy of space replaces the autonomy of the building, and that "non-place" toward which the finality of the stairways converges is that unknown place which all corridors, all hallways announce when they turn a corner or disappear at a bend. They are also those mental incongruities that the play of architecture sometimes creates, and which any building and any city should contain, the kind that disturbed Piranesi in his drawings and plans.

Thomas Schütte's installation at the Marian Goodman Gallery in New York earlier this year included four tables. Here, the horizontal surface reveals plans drawn directly on the sanded wood. The building rests in its own traces. The drawings correspond to the artist's own living space, his study, the Konrad Fischer Gallery where most of the artist's solo exhibitions took place, and the Museum Haus Esters in Krefeld, the site of his first museum show. The autobiographical references oscillate between the private, the professional, and the public dimension of his work. Again, it is this public dimension of sculpture that interests me here: the search of a system of images where realism and abstraction are no longer part of the necessary vocabulary of the artist. Recognition and interpretation are natural, virtually biological functions carried out by understanding, which searches continuously for itself in the objects it experiences while searching for the possibility of communicating that experience.

(Translation from the Spanish: Alfred MacAdam)

THOMAS SCHÜTTE, BIG BUILDING, 1989, wood / Holz,
Stedelijk Van Abbemuseum, Eindhoven, 1990. (PHOTO: PETER COX)

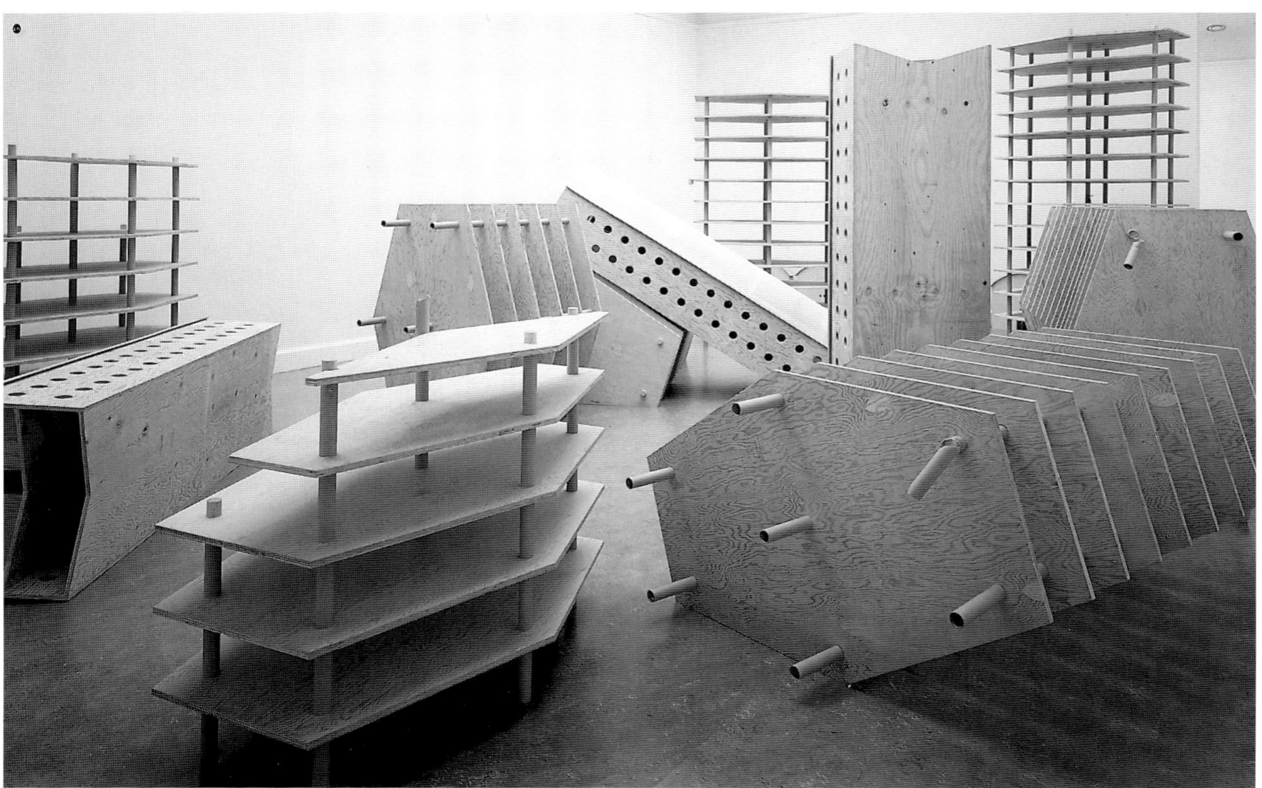

HANS RUDOLF REUST

Lilien-Lügen

Nach einem längeren, zweifellos brillanten Vortrag wurde der Referentin im Museum ein Blumenstrauss überreicht. Die Köpfe der Tulpen hingen schwer. Blumen lügen nicht. Frisch glänzten an den Saalwänden noch immer die Blumenstücke der alten Meister, Spuren jener ungezählten künstlerischen Konfrontationen mit dem stets aktuellen, stets uneinholbaren, fragilen Zauber der Natur.

Die Kunstwissenschaft dürfte das Thema für sich abschliessen, sobald die Käfer auf sämtlichen Stillleben gezählt sind: memento mori. Blumen, so scheint es, sind dem Gewicht ihrer Motivgeschichte erlegen. Sie bringen allein noch rhetorische Blüten hervor, um die vakante Stelle des Motivs in der Malerei zu schmücken. Mit dem Zweifel an der Repräsentation hat auch die Lilie in der Kunst ihre Unschuld verloren. Das Gespräch über Bäume, das nach Bertolt Brecht ein Schweigen über so viele Untaten einschliesst, wurde immer auch durch die Blume geführt.

Im Alltag sind Blumen schmuck, immerzu. Sie sagen, so kommuniziert es die Werbung, das Unaussprechliche und überbrücken Verlegenheiten im Moment der Trauer. Blumen sind selten allein. Jedes Paar bildet schon ein «Arrangement»: komponierte Natur mit dem Reiz höchster Künstlichkeit. Wo aber könnte der Entwurf eines Blumenstücks heute ansetzen, wenn schon die Floristin beim Gencode beginnt?

Filmische Sequenz in fünf Stills: Eine Architektur tropischer Stengel und Blüten, ausladend, prall und schroff zugleich, bizarr verschachtelt, leuchtet übermässig aus schwarzem Grund. Vor allem dieses Rot, wie aus einer Verletzung. *Drehung und Blickwechsel:* Einblenden der Pflanzen als Leerstellen im Grund einer Darstellung, die sich in den feinen Linien der raschen Vorzeichnung ankündigt. *Drehung und Blickwechsel:* Der weisse Grund behauptet sich und nimmt die lineare Struktur der Blumen in sich auf. Mehrfach überlagerte Formen, eine leicht sich verschiebende Farbigkeit von Strichen gehen ineinander über, durchdringen sich. Schnitt-Blumen. Das Arrangement wird zum filigranen Netz von Andeutungen, in dem das Sehen sich verfängt. *Drehung und Blickwechsel:* Scharf konturiertes Aufblitzen von Weiss und Gelb, Grau, Grün und Rot aus heiterem Himmel. *Drehung und Blickwechsel:* Und schliesslich die Trübung. Eine lautlose Implosion der Darstellung in verfliessende Farben. Der Stillstand im Fluss.

Jenseits von freiem Dekor und Bravourstücken der Repräsentation, im Vakuum zwischen überladener Symbolik und Blumen als einem Ready-made reiner Unterhaltung beginnt Thomas Schütte seine zeichnerische Arbeit am Modell. Immer von neuem. Blatt für Blatt. Gerade weil die Blumen inzwischen alles und nichts mehr bedeuten können, werden sie in einer seltsamen Nähe zum Nullzeichen wieder sichtbar. Ohne programmatische Vorentscheidungen schaut er hin. Unter einer Voraussetzung: Reflexion auf die eigene Praxis begleitet die zeichnende Hand beim Sehen und schaltet sich mitunter auch in Worten dazwischen: «Können Lilien lügen?»[1] – Diese Frage kann nur ein Aquarell einwerfen, das nicht länger über seinen prekären Status lügt. Jedem Blatt folgt ein nächstes, das die vorausgehende Identifi-

HANS RUDOLF REUST ist Kunstkritiker und lebt in Bern.

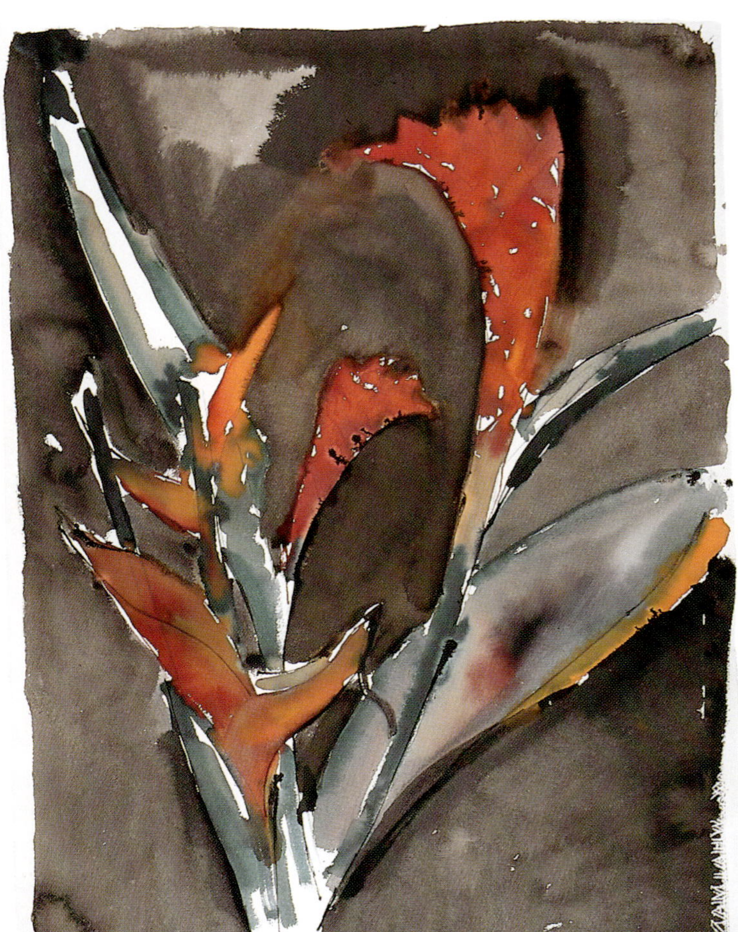

kation des Gegenstandes wieder aufbricht. Schüttes Blumen werfen Schatten, die Schatten zeichnen Blumen: Und wo lag das Modell? Bleibt schliesslich ein intrigierendes Moment des Zweifels selbst an der allgegenwärtigen Dekonstruktion in Zeichnung und Malerei. Wie, wenn eine Rose, die eine Rose, die eine Rose ist, durch die Erinnerung an ihren Duft doch plötzlich und flüchtig präsent wäre?

Im Frühsommer die Fahrt durch den weiten Süden eines nordischen Landes: Tannendunkel, unterbrochen von Birkenstämmen mit viel frischem Grün, schwarz und ruhig spiegelnde Wasserflächen dazwischen, rohe Felsen in rötlichem Braun, und jede gelbe Blume ein Eclat. Eine Differenz, die punktuell noch den Unterschied schafft.

1) In: THOMAS SCHÜTTE, OHNE TITEL (5.1.1995), Gouache und Tinte auf Papier, 32,5 x 25 cm.

THOMAS SCHÜTTE, BLUMEN II, 1996,
Aquarell, 56 x 76 cm / watercolors, 22 x 30".

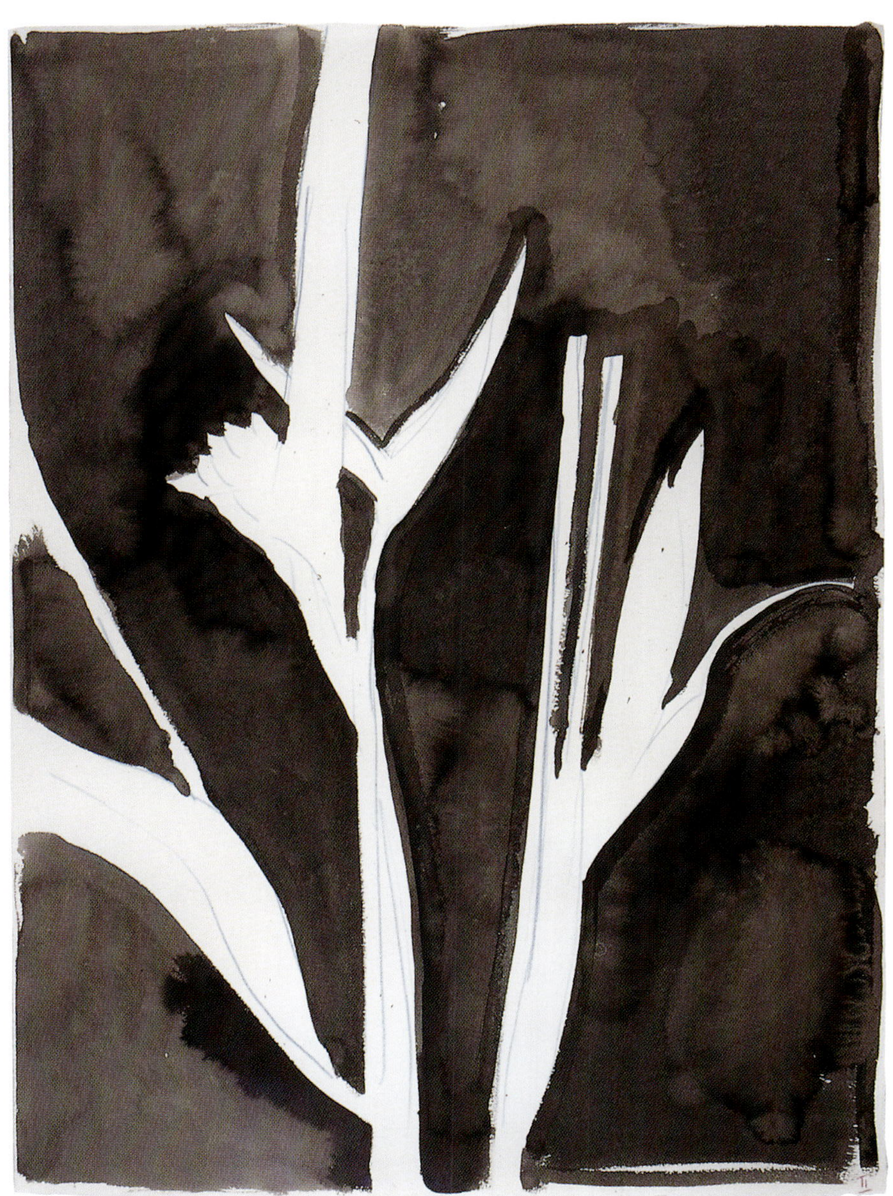

THOMAS SCHÜTTE, BLUMEN III, 1996,
Aquarell, 56 x 76 cm / watercolors, 22 x 30".

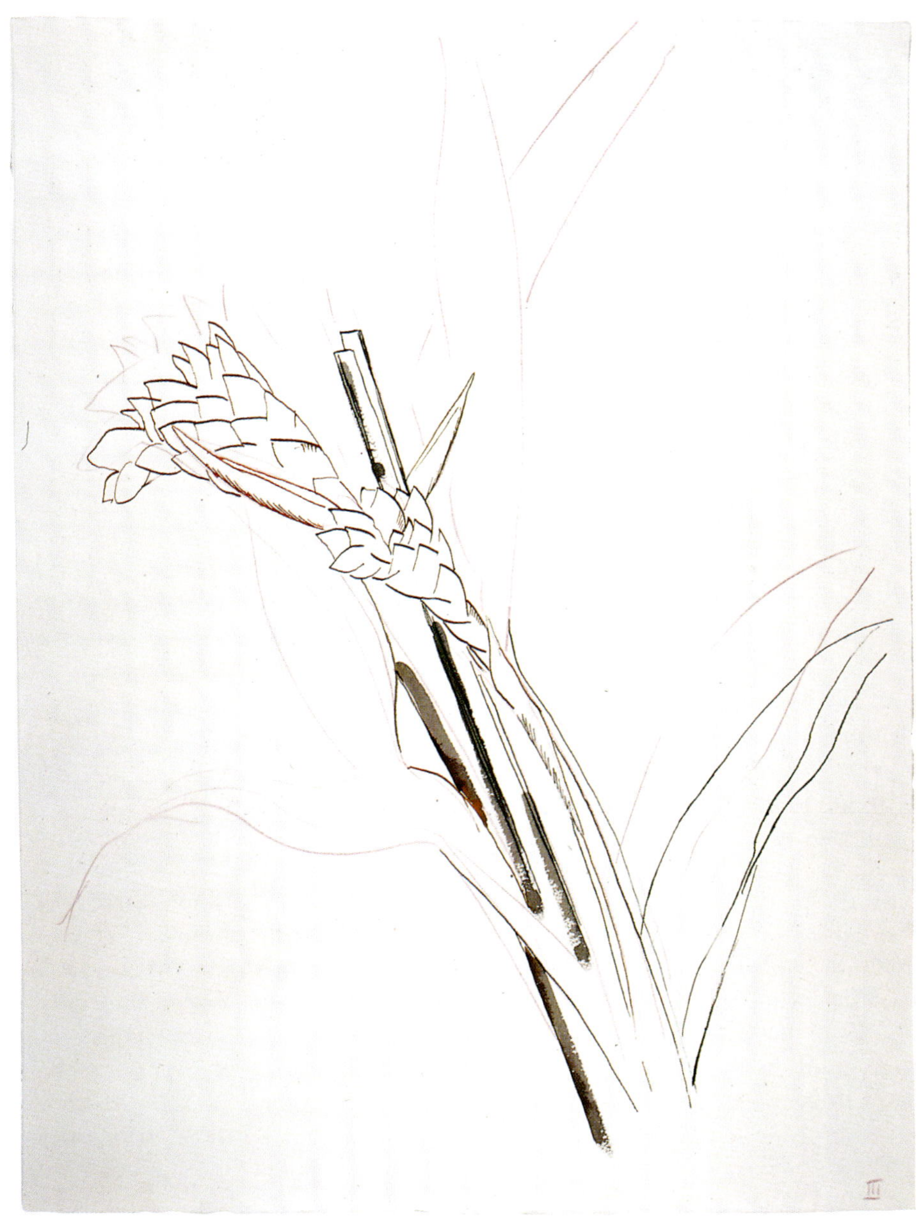

HANS RUDOLF REUST

Lily Lies

After giving a lengthy, undoubtedly brilliant paper, the speaker in the museum was handed a bouquet of flowers. The tulips' heads were drooping. Flowers don't lie. On the walls of the lecture hall, the flower pieces of the old masters still radiated their pristine glory, tokens of untold artistic confrontations with the fragile magic of nature, whose immediacy is forever beyond reach.

The issue will finally come to rest when artistic scholarship has counted every single beetle in a still life: memento mori. Flowers, it seems, have succumbed to the weight of their history as a motif. Only flowers of speech have survived to fill the vacancy left behind by the motif's desertion of painting. Loss of faith in representation has also robbed the lily of its innocence. And a bloom lies over conversations about trees, which according to Bertolt Brecht include silence in the face of so many atrocities.

Flowers are invariable embellishments of daily life. We know from advertising that they express the ineffable and bridge confusion in moments of mourning. Flowers are rarely alone. Two suffice to make an "arrangement," the composition of nature with the appeal of utmost artificiality. But where to begin in designing a flower piece today, when florists are already starting with genetic codes?

Film sequence in five stills: an architecture of stems

and blossoms, profuse, both lavish and abrupt, crazily intertwined, inordinately luminous against a black ground. *Rotation and a new angle:* Plants as spaces reserved in the background of a representation, barely visible in the delicate lines of the cartoon. *Rotation and a new angle:* The white ground prevails and absorbs the linear structure of the flowers. Several layers of superimposed shapes, lines twisting and turning in gently shifting colors. Cut flowers. The arrangement becomes a filigree network of meanings, in which seeing is entangled. *Rotation and a new angle:* Sharply contoured flashes of white and yellow, gray, green and red—out of the blue. *Rotation and a new angle:* And finally the bloom. The representation silently imploding in running colors. Standstill in flux.

Beyond autarchic decoration and bravura pieces of representation, in the vacuum between overcharged symbolism and flowers as a ready-made of pure entertainment, Thomas Schütte's draftsmanship begins with the model. Starting from scratch each time. Sheet after sheet. Precisely because flowers have come to mean everything and nothing, their visibility paradoxically increases the closer they come to the zero point. His gaze does not follow programmatic assumptions. He works with only one given: reflection on his own practice guides the drawing hand while seeing and occasionally intervenes with words: "Do lilies lie?"[1] This question can only be posed by a watercolor that has left off lying about its precarious status. Each sheet is followed by another that subverts the identification of the

---

HANS RUDOLF REUST is an art critic who lives in Berne (Switzerland).

THOMAS SCHÜTTE, BLUMEN IV, 1996,
Aquarell, 56 x 76 cm / watercolors, 22 x 30".

THOMAS SCHÜTTE, BLUMEN V, 1996,
Aquarell, 56 x 76 cm / watercolors, 22 x 30".

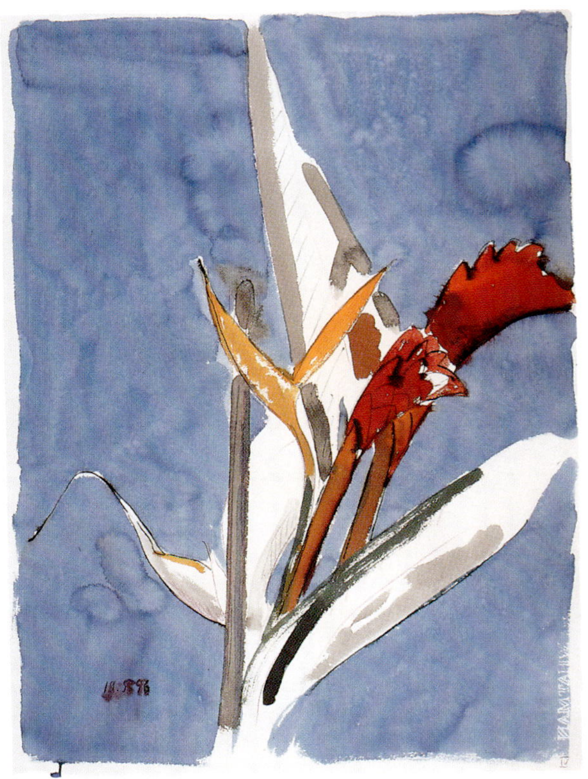

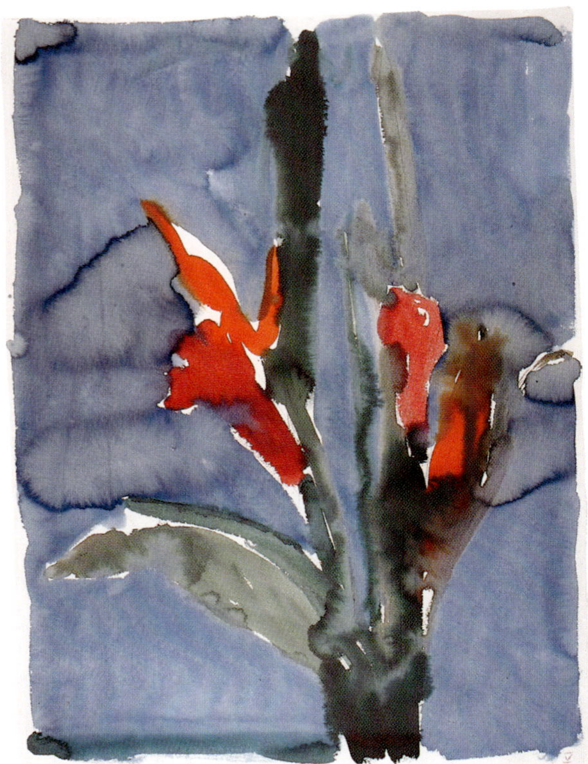

subject matter that went before. Schütte's flowers cast shadows, the shadows draw flowers: And where did the model lie? What remains is a machinating moment of skepticism even towards the omnipresent deconstruction of drawing and painting. What happens when the presence of a rose that is a rose that is a rose is suddenly and fleetingly felt through the memory of its scent?

Driving in early summer through the southern expanses of a northern country: dark woods of pine broken by beech trees full of the freshest green, black and serenely mirroring waters in between, raw reddish brown cliffs, and every single yellow flower an éclat. A nuance that still makes a periodical difference.

(Translation: Catherine Schelbert)

1) In: THOMAS SCHÜTTE, UNTITLED (5.1.1995), gouache and ink on paper, 32,5 x 25 cm / 12¾ x 9⅞".

NEVILLE WAKEFIELD

LOST AT SEA

The conceptual pleasures of open ocean navigation lie in the formalization of informal relationships elsewhere held with the unknown. Whether defined as a process, a method of determining a position, or a voyage, navigation without the aid of geostationary satellites and digital fixes relies on the production of error for exactitude. Using the Greenwich meridian as both temporal and physical fixed point, celestial navigation seeks to establish latitude and longitude as relational vectors read and measured as the angular distance of a celestial body or point from the ecliptic (the sun's apparent path amongst the stars). From the sight of the heavens and the movement of astrological bodies a non-site is produced on the chart—a position read as a calculus lamination of visual record and conceptual process. Integral to this equation is an erratic component known as a dead reckoning track. A fictitious line, the D. R. track is the speculative hypothesis of forward motion based on the collation of variables; of the displacement and lateral resistance of the hull, the effects of wind, tide, current, and so on. Thus fiction, in navigation as in art, becomes the measure of reality, deviance the measure of accuracy. Continually testing hypotheses, the sailor, like the artist, enacts Rilke's prophecy that *what happens is so far ahead of what we think, of our intentions, that we can never catch up with it or ever really come to know its true appearance.*[1]

In March 1968, spurred by the media publicity surrounding Francis Chichester's record-breaking one-stop circumnavigation, the London *Sunday Times* magazine upped the ante by announcing the creation of the Golden Globe, a trophy dedicated to the first sailor to circumnavigate the world alone, without stopping. If Chichester's achievement provided the model for the competitive monadism of round-the-world racing, his yacht, the Gypsy Moth, enshrined in Greenwich, had become its monument, rekindling the embers of maritime pride with the romantic oxygen of unwitnessed and solitary heroics. For Donald Crowhurst, one of eight Golden Globe contestants, Chichester's vessel was a galling reminder of everything his trimaran Teighnmouth Electron was not. Having barely made it through the sea trials before leaving British shores on October 31st, he wrote in his diary: "I am going because I would have no peace if I stayed. I'm very disappointed in the boat. It's not right, I'm not prepared."

After six weeks of tacking against the attritious winds of disappointment, the character and navigational procedure of the journey dramatically changed. Somewhere off the Cape Verde Islands in the grip of hubris and paranoia, Crowhurst abandoned the practice of dead reckoning and astro-correction in favor of exact positioning and astro-reckoning. The stars, no longer the nature against which the hypothesis of culture and position were tested, were enlisted as props in a navigational universe from which error had been abolished. For the following thirty weeks, Crowhurst's Byzantine calculations allowed him to post positions from around the world while he languished in doldrums both literal and metaphorical: a mid-Atlantic world of his own. By the

NEVILLE WAKEFIELD is a writer who lives in New York City.

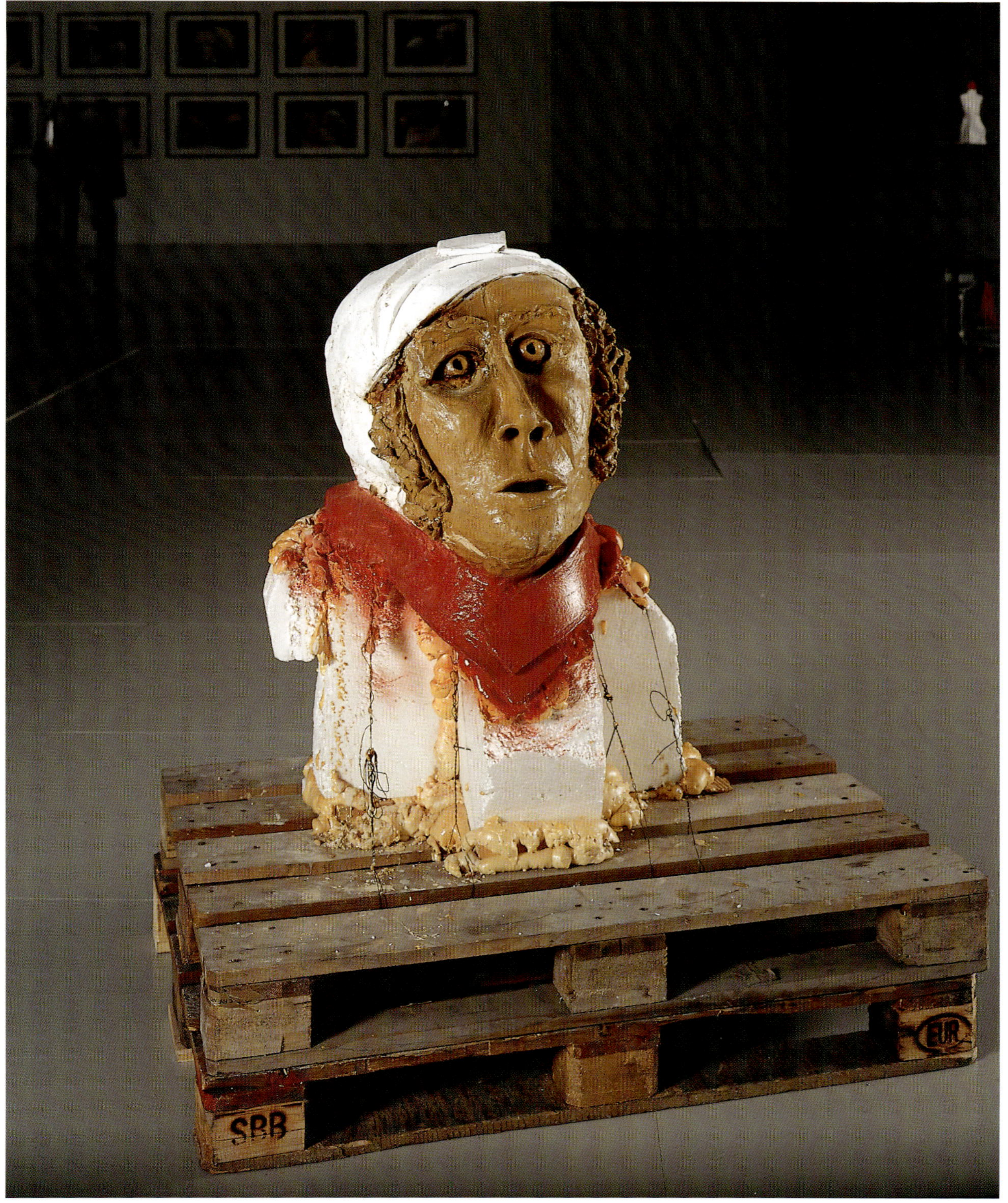

THOMAS SCHÜTTE, ALAIN COLAS, 1989,
wood, clay, styrofoam, installation Württembergischer Kunstverein, Stuttgart, 1994 / Holz, Lehm, Spritzschaumstoff. (PHOTO: NIC TENWIGGENHORN)

end of June the following year, Crowhurst had, according to his log entries, lost all track of time and place. Unable to maintain the deceit, he jumped overboard clutching the single chronometer that continued to mark time. Like Ahab's whale, Crowhurst's Golden Globe became a trophy not of return but of its impossibility: *God help thee, old man,* narrates Melville, *thy thoughts have created; and he whose intense thinking thus makes him a Prometheus; a vulture feeds upon that heart for ever; that vulture the very creature he creates.*[2]

Roughly a decade later, on November 16th, 1978, the lone yachtsman Alain Colas transmitted his daily, routine message from aboard the trimaran Manureva. Leading the Guadalupian leg of the single-handed Route du Rhum race, he reported his situation as being just south of the Azores. Colas belonged to a new breed of competitive sailors for whom the rites of ocean passage—the rigors of navigational and existential uncertainty—had become forces of which the race itself was merely a charismatic public celebration. Familiar with the perils of the oceans and the corrosive effects of months of self-enforced solitary confinement, Colas had broken records throughout the seventies. In 1973 he had taken on the challenge of the "Cape-Horners," beating a time set by the tea-clipper Cutty Sark which had stood since the nineteenth century. The following year, a single-handed one-stop circumnavigation of the globe lopped fifty-seven days off the existing record set by Chichester. But the November 16th message from the Manureva, signing off with a customary "All's well aboard," was followed by silence—a silence that marked both the end and apotheosis of the Corinthian ideal of passage and return.

The official monument to the deceased sailor was funded by the A.M.A.C. (Association pour le Monument Alain Colas), a commemorative foundation based in France. The literature accompanying the fund-raising effort is liberally strewn with images of a windswept seaman staring towards unknown horizons, his eyes slits, his brows furrowed with the Gallic fortitude and presence of mind that had in the past served so well in the struggle against adversity. Like the tri-hull in which he met his end, his face is flanked on either side by vast sideburns, hairy outrig-

gers of his lean virility. Partially lapping one such image, the eulogy reads: "A man of challenges, effort, fellowship and adventure, Alain Colas could not be allowed to disappear from the collective memory." Countering the evanescence of man and memory, the A.M.A.C. proposed the construction of a four-masted schooner. Seventy-two meters in length, it would be the largest sailing boat ever steered by a single man. An oceangoing monument befitting "one of the greatest navigators of the twentieth century," it would substitute for the erratic art of sailing the technologies of conquest and survival.

The proposal for another monument, ALAIN COLAS, MONUMENT FOR A SAILOR LOST AT SEA (1989) by Thomas Schütte, is pure bathos. Stripped of immortalizing rhetoric, it barely floats within the space of public tribute, its materials too makeshift, its relationship to the outside world too under-determined, its coordinates without bearing or compass. The head and torso of a man is easily recognizable as that of Colas even though the eyes that once squinted into uncharted futures now pop with the proximity of present revelation. Crudely injected with expanded foam (of the sort that may ultimately have failed to save his life), the torso sits on a pallet, like a cargo of human flotsam, Gericault's raft remade for the lone sailor, the mariner monad of the late twentieth century. The jury-rigged figure, stayed to its unstable base by wire halyards, is both sculpture and shipwreck: position lost and lost position. Just as the material of the body brings to mind the stuff of buoyancy aids and life jackets, so the pallet's multiple suggestions unfold across the fable of Colas's probable demise. While the exact nature of his fate still remains unknown, the sculpture itself, mounted on its container-pedestal, suggests perhaps the irony of the navigator mown down by an uncalculated force while immersed in the delicate negotiation of error and position—the unreported victim of a cargo vessel's "unmanned watch." No distress signals were transmitted other than those of a crude sculptural effigy—navigation's Mayday.

1) In: *Requiem for Wolf Graf von Kalckreuth,* Paris, 1908.
2) Herman Melville, *Moby Dick,* End of Chapter 44.

NEVILLE WAKEFIELD

VERSCHOLLEN

Zu den geistigen Genüssen der Navigation auf hoher See gehört es, dass unsere andernorts unausgesprochenen Beziehungen zum Unbekannten deutlich zum Ausdruck kommen. Ob man unter Navigation einen Prozess, eine Methode der Positionsbestimmung oder einfach eine Schiffsreise versteht, der Navigator, der ohne die Hilfe von geostationären Satelliten und Bordcomputer arbeitet, schliesst mögliche Irrtümer und Abweichungen bei seiner Berechnung der exakten Position mit ein. Die Astronavigation benützt den Greenwich-Meridian als zeitlichen und örtlichen Fixpunkt und versucht Längen- und Breitengrad als aufeinander bezogene Vektoren zu bestimmen, die als Winkelabstand eines Himmelskörpers oder Punktes von der Ekliptik (Ebene der Sonnenbahn) abgelesen und gemessen werden können. Aus dem Bild des Himmels und der Bewegung der Himmelskörper wird ein Nicht-Ort auf der Karte konstruiert – eine Position, die als differentiale Annäherung von sichtbarem Befund und theoretischer Analyse zu verstehen ist. Integraler Bestandteil dieser Gleichung ist eine fehlerbehaftete Komponente, bekannt als abgelenkter Kurs. Als fiktive Linie ist der abgelenkte Kurs die spekulative Hypothese der Vorwärtsbewegung, die auf dem Zusammenwirken von verschiedenen Variablen beruht: Ortsveränderung und seitlicher Widerstand des Schiffsrumpfs, Windeinwirkungen, Gezeiten, Strömungen und so weiter. So wird die Fiktion in der Seefahrt wie in der Kunst zum Massstab der Wirklichkeit, die Abweichung zum Mass der Genauigkeit. Indem er fortlaufend Hypo-

thesen prüft, erfüllt der Seefahrer wie der Künstler Rilkes Prophezeiung:

> *Das was geschieht, hat einen solchen Vorsprung*
> *vor unserem Meinen, dass wirs niemals einholn*
> *und nie erfahren, wie es wirklich aussah.*[1]

Im März 1968, angeregt durch den Medienrummel um Francis Chichesters alle Rekorde brechende Weltumsegelung mit nur einem Zwischenhalt, steckte die Londoner *Sunday Times* die Latte sogleich höher, indem sie die Schaffung des *Golden Globe* ankündigte. Diese Trophäe sollte derjenige erhalten, der als erster allein und ohne Zwischenhalt um die Welt segelte. Wenn Chichesters Leistung zum Modellfall für das darauffolgende, wettbewerbsmässige, einsame Um-die-Welt-Segeln wurde, so geriet seine Yacht, die *Gypsy Moth,* die in Greenwich ausgestellt wurde, zu einem Monument dieser Segelkunst, das die schwachen Gluten des alten Seefahrerstolzes durch den romantischen Hauch eines unerhörten und einsamen Heldentums von neuem zu entfachen vermochte. Für Donald Crowhurst, einer der acht *Golden-Globe*-Anwärter, war Chichesters Schiff ein schmerzlicher Hinweis auf alles, was sein Trimaran, die *Teighnmouth Electron,* nicht war. Nachdem er, noch vor dem Verlassen der britischen Küste, den verschiedensten Widrigkeiten nur mit Ach und Krach zu trotzen vermochte, schrieb er am 31. Oktober in sein Tagebuch: «Ich gehe nur, weil es mir keine Ruhe liesse, wenn ich hier bliebe. Ich bin sehr enttäuscht von dem Schiff. Es ist nicht in Ordnung, ich bin nicht wirklich gerüstet.»

NEVILLE WAKEFIELD lebt und schreibt in New York.

Nach sechswöchigem Ringen mit den bösen Winden der Enttäuschung, trat eine dramatische Veränderung in der Art und den Navigationsmethoden der Reise ein: Irgendwo in der Nähe der Kapverdischen Inseln, hin und her gerissen zwischen Hybris und Paranoia, gab Crowhurst die Methode der Berechnung des abgelenkten Kurses mit Korrektur anhand der Sterne auf zugunsten der exakten Positionierung mittels Astronavigation. Die Sterne galten nicht länger als das Naturphänomen, anhand dessen die Hypothesen von Kultur und Position zu überprüfen waren, sondern wurden zum tragenden Element eines navigatorischen Universums, aus dem Irrtum und Abweichung verbannt waren. Für die folgenden 30 Wochen erlaubten seine ausgefeilten Berechnungen Crowhurst alle Positionen rund um die Welt festzuhalten, während er in seiner eigenen Welt mitten im Atlantik verschiedene tatsächliche und metaphorische Flauten durchlitt. Ende Juni des folgenden Jahres hatte Crowhurst laut seinen Logbucheinträgen jedes Gefühl und jeden Anhaltspunkt für Raum und Zeit verloren. Als er sich dies eingestehen musste, sprang er über Bord, in der Hand die einzige Uhr, die noch die Tageszeit anzeigte. Wie Ahabs Wal wurde der *Golden Globe* für Crowhurst nicht zu einer Trophäe der Rückkehr, sondern zu einem Symbol der Unmöglichkeit dieser Rückkehr: *Gott steh dir bei, alter Ahab,* schreibt Melville, *dein Streben hat ein Geschöpf in dir selber erschaffen; und wer durch Dichten und Denken zum Prometheus wird, dessen Herz zerfleischt ein Geier allezeit; der Geier, das selbsterschaffene Geschöpf.*[2]

Rund zehn Jahre später, am 16. November 1978, übermittelte der einsame Segler Alain Colas seine tägliche Routinemeldung von seinem Trimaran *Manureva*. Als Leader der Guadeloupe-Etappe des Einmannwettbewerbs der *Route du Rhum,* hatte er seine Position als «knapp südlich der Azoren» angegeben. Colas gehörte zu einer neuen Generation von Wettkampfseglern, welche die Riten der Ozeanüberquerung – die Extreme navigatorischer und existentieller Verunsicherung – als die eigentliche Herausforderung begriffen, der das Rennen selbst lediglich die glanzvollen öffentlichen Weihen verlieh. Vertraut mit den Gefahren des Meeres und mit der zermürbenden Wirkung der monatelangen selbstauferlegten Einzelhaft, hatte Colas in den 70er Jahren zahlreiche Rekorde gebrochen. 1973 hatte er sich am Kap-Horn-Rennen beteiligt und schlug den Rekord des Teeklippers *Cutty Sark,* der seit dem 19. Jahrhundert ungeschlagen geblieben war. Im folgenden Jahr unterbot er bei einer Einmann-Weltumsegelung mit nur einem Zwischenhalt den bestehenden Rekord von Chichester um 57 Tage. Aber in der Meldung vom 16. November 1978 von der *Manureva* folgte nach dem üblichen «Alles in Ordnung an Bord» nur noch Schweigen – ein Schweigen, das für das Ende und die Apotheose des Korinthischen Ideals von Ausfahrt und Rückkehr stand.

Die offizielle Gedenkstätte für den verschollenen Segler wurde von der AMAC (Association pour le Monument Alain Colas) finanziert, einer Gedenkstiftung mit Sitz in Frankreich. Die Schriften, welche bei den Anstrengungen der Stiftung zur Beschaffung finanzieller Mittel eingesetzt wurden, waren voll mit Bildern eines von Wind und Wetter gezeichneten Seemannes, der den Blick auf unbekannte Horizonte richtet, die Augen zu Schlitzen verengt, die Brauen zusammengezogen mit der Tapferkeit und Geistesgegenwart eines Galliers, welche ihm in der Vergangenheit so gute Dienste im Kampf gegen alle Widerwärtigkeiten geleistet hatten. Wie das Schiff mit den drei Rümpfen, auf dem er den Tod fand, ist sein Gesicht von langen Koteletten flankiert, haarige Ausleger seiner schlaksigen Männlichkeit. Teilweise über eine solche Abbildung verlaufend, lautet der Nachruf: «Ein Mann der Herausforderungen, der Anstrengung, der Kameradschaft und der Abenteuer, darf Alain Colas nicht aus unserem kollektiven Gedächtnis verschwinden.» Gegen die Flüchtigkeit von Mensch und Gedächtnis schlug die AMAC den Bau eines viermastigen Schoners vor. 72 Meter lang, wäre es das grösste Segelschiff, das je von einem einzigen Mann gesteuert wurde. Ein hochseetaugliches Monument, passend für «einen der grössten Seefahrer des zwanzigsten Jahrhunderts», würde es an die Stelle der für Irrtümer anfälligen Kunst des Segelns die Technologie des Eroberns und Überlebens setzen.

Der Vorschlag für ein anderes Monument, ALAIN COLAS, MONUMENT FÜR EINEN VERSCHOLLENEN SEEMANN (1989) von Thomas Schütte, ist das pure

Gegenteil jeder pathetischen Beschwörung. Bar jeder Unsterblichkeitsrhetorik, ist es kaum fähig, sich im Raum der öffentlichen Aufmerksamkeit über Wasser zu halten, zu beliebig das Material, aus dem es gefertigt ist, zu unbestimmt sein Verhältnis zur Aussenwelt, sein Ort ohne Bezug oder Ausrichtung. Kopf und Torso eines Mannes sind gut als jene von Colas erkennbar, obwohl die Augen, die einst zusammengekniffen den Horizont erforschten, nun weit aufgerissen sind vor dem gegenwärtig Offenbaren. Auf krude Weise mit Spritzschaum gefüllt (dasselbe Material, das es zuletzt vielleicht nicht schaffte, sein Leben zu retten), sitzt der Torso auf einer hölzernen Palette, wie eine Sendung menschlichen Treibguts, eine Nachbildung von Gericaults Floss für den einsamen Segler, die Seefahrer-Monade des späten zwanzigsten Jahrhunderts. Die notdürftig zusammengeschusterte Figur, die auf ihrem wackligen Fundament mit Drahtleinen festgehalten wird, ist Skulptur und Schiffbruch in einem: ohne Position und auf verlorenem Posten. Wenn das Material des Körpers an jenes von Schwimmhilfen und Schwimmwesten erinnert, so regt die Fracht-Palette zu vielfältigen Spekulationen über Colas' vermutliches Ende an. Während uns sein tatsächliches Schicksal verborgen bleibt, weist die Skulptur auf ihrem Container-Sockel vielleicht auf die Ironie im Schicksal des Seemannes hin, der durch eine unerwartete Gewalt vernichtet wird, während er in ein minutiöses Abwägen von Abweichung und Position vertieft ist – ein nie gemeldetes Opfer des Autopiloten eines anonymen Frachters. Keinerlei Notsignale wurden empfangen ausser denen einer kruden Skulptur – ein *Mayday* der Navigation selbst.[3]   *(Übersetzung: Susanne Schmidt)*

1) In: *Requiem für Wolf Graf von Kalckreuth*, Paris 1908.
2) Herman Melville, *Moby Dick*, Kapitel 44; deutsche Übersetzung von Fritz Güttinger, Manesse Verlag, Zürich 1944, S. 345.
3) Mayday: internationales Notsignal, von frz. «m'aidez».

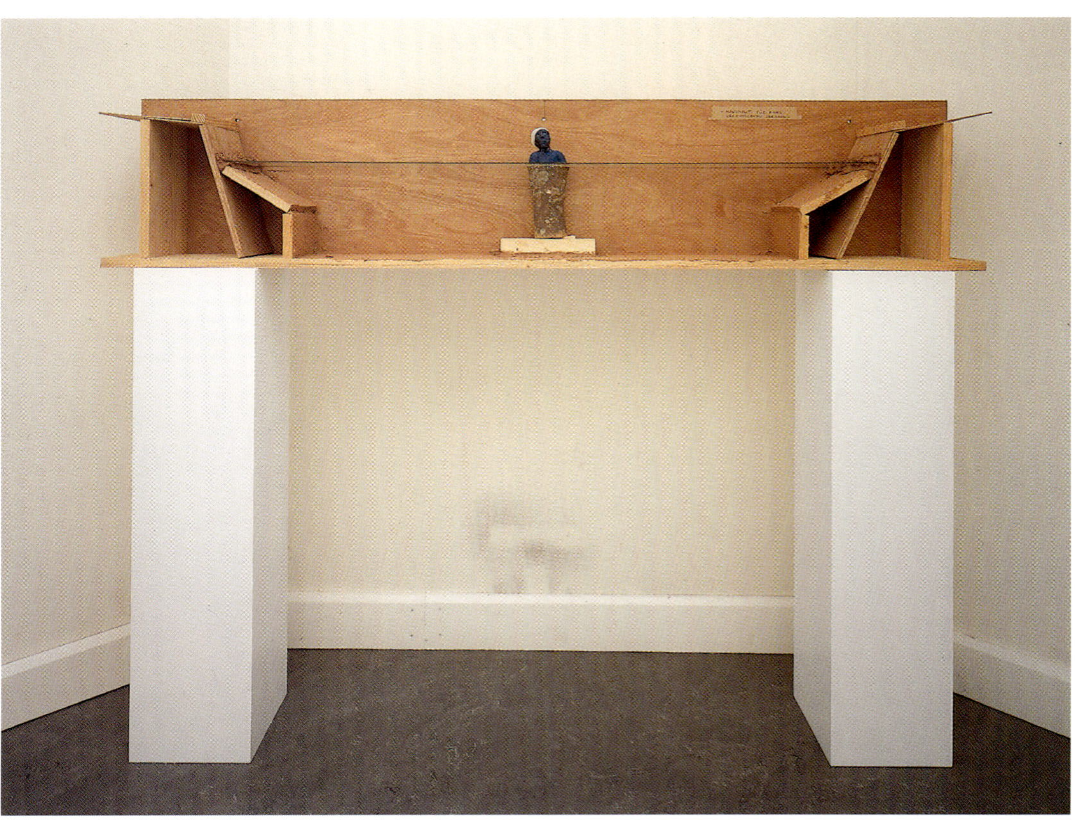

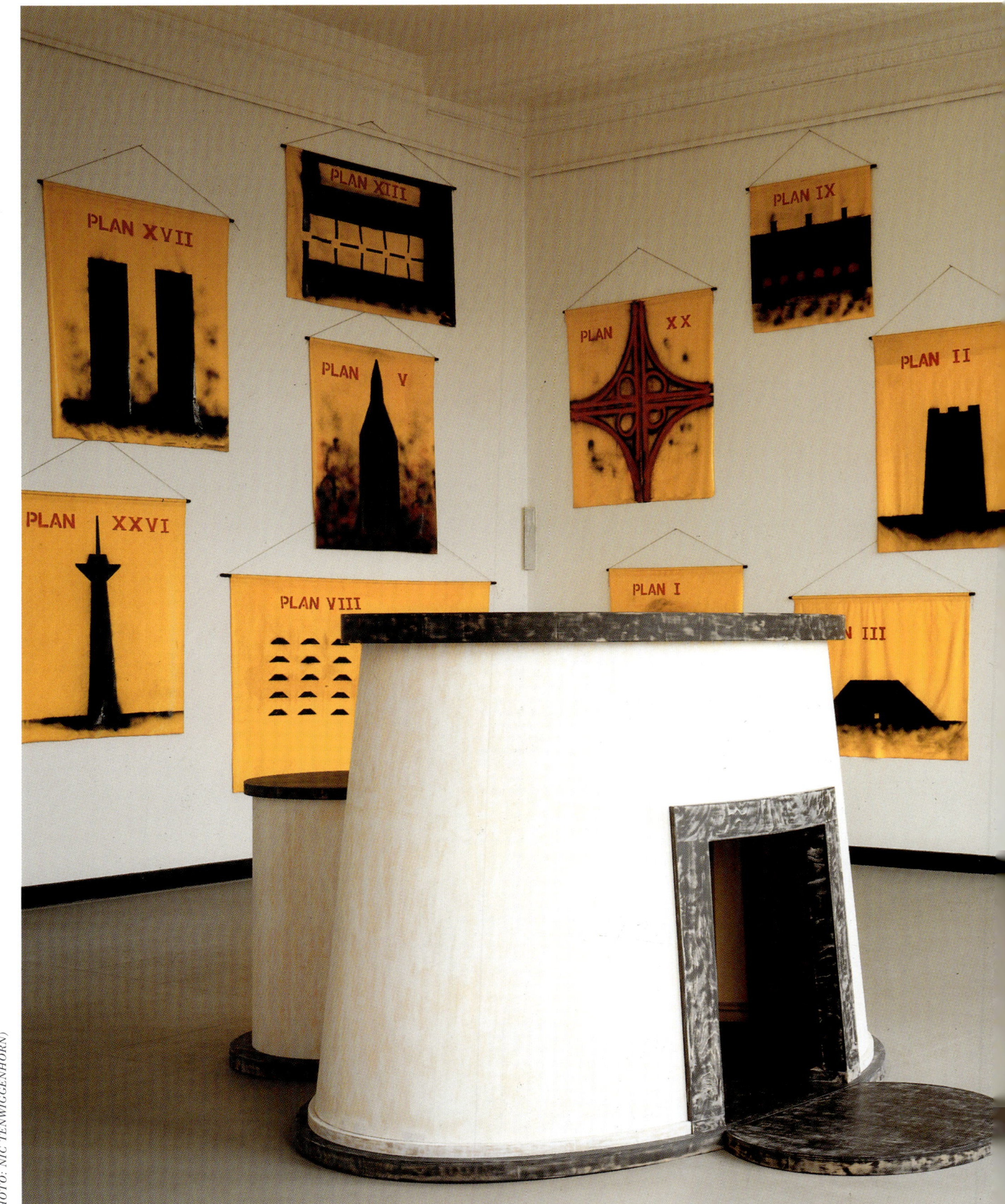

THOMAS SCHÜTTE, PLAN I–XXX, 1981, Lack auf Wachstuch / varnish paint on wax cloth; EIS, Modell für Documenta 8, 1987–91, Kunsthalle Hamburg, 1992 / model for documenta 8.

(PHOTO: NIC TENWIGGENHORN)

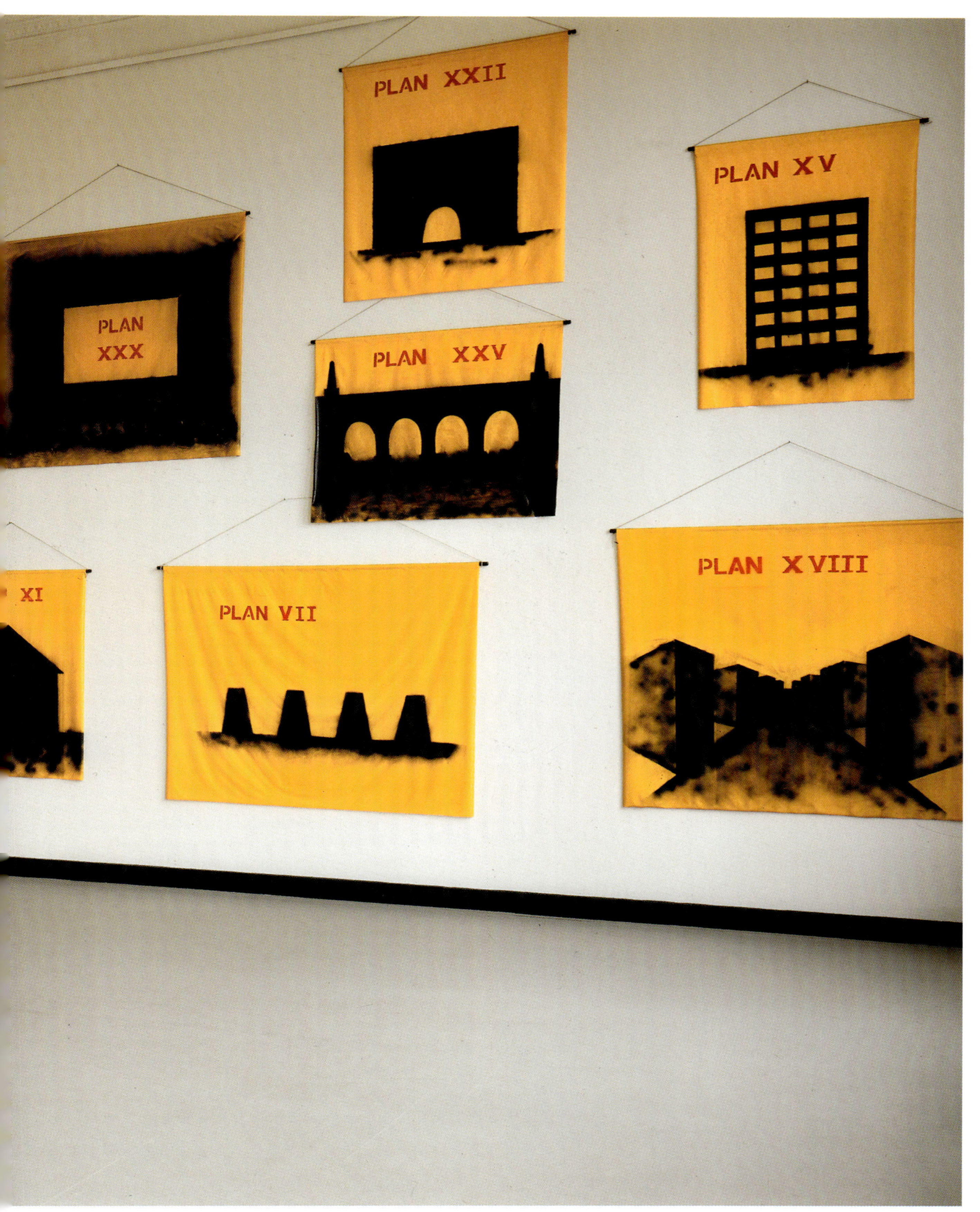

PLAN XXII
PLAN XV
PLAN XXX
PLAN XXV
PLAN XVIII
XI
PLAN VII

Thomas Schütte

Installationen

ULRICH LOOCK

1986 hatte Thomas Schütte eine denkwürdige Ausstellung in der Galerie von Rüdiger Schöttle in München. Noch einmal wurde sein MODELL FÜR EIN MUSEUM (1982) gezeigt. Mit dieser mittelgrossen Skulptur hatte er im Raum der (fiktiven, architektonischen) Brauchbarkeit die formale Einfachheit wieder aufgenommen, mit der das *Minimal* die Geschichte der Formensprachen zu einem entropischen Stillstand hatte bringen wollen. Zugleich war das Modell ein Reflex der hybriden Entwürfe der Revolutionsarchitektur, die damals unter dem Obertitel einer *architecture parlante* ziemlich viel diskutiert wurden. Auf Staffeleien standen neben dem Modell zwei Tafeln mit Zeichnungen, welche die Funktion des Museums erkennen liessen: Es wäre der Ort, wo, von den Künstlern selbst eingeliefert, die Werke umstandslos und ohne weitere Verzögerung verfeuert würden.

In einem zweiten Raum, der Modellpräsentation benachbart, hatte Schütte eine Installation gemacht. Er hatte also jene Form gewählt, die im Zusammenhang mit Versuchen populär geworden war, den Objekt- und Warencharakter des Kunstwerkes abzuschaffen. Idealerweise erzeugt die Installation eine Umgebung; der «Betrachter» des «Werkes» findet sich eingetaucht in eine Situation: vom Gegenüber zum Darinnen. Schüttes Arbeit trägt den Titel SCHROTT: an die Wand gezeichnet, so hoch wie der Raum, also gross, schematisch ein Brennofen, zwei weitere in Umrissen, und im Raum verteilt drei Gestelle mit zusammengerollten (aufgegebenen) Zeichnungen.

Das Medium der Installation ist bei Schütte allerdings nur in dem Masse wirkungsvoll, in dem es alle situationistische Utopie der Kunst zur Erstarrung bringt, sie gerade noch als betrauerte Erinnerung

bewahrt. Einerseits ist die räumliche Situation – imprägniert von Unzugänglichkeit und Funktionsuntüchtigkeit – nicht weniger fiktional als das Modell. Was sie andererseits erwarten lässt, wäre nicht der Übergang der Kunst in eine Situation realer Brauchbarkeit, sondern Brauchbarkeit würde in realer Vernichtung der Kunst resultieren. Mit einer solchen Installation betreibt Schütte die subversive Affirmation neo-avantgardistischer Prätentionen, an die Geschichte der frühen Moderne anzuknüpfen.

Zu diesem Komplex von Arbeiten gehört auch das Modell einer Bühne mit hineingesetzten Kontaktabzügen der Reproduktionen eigener Zeichnungen. Viel stärker situativ orientiert sind andererseits Stücke, die scheinbar das Feld der Dekoration besetzen, etwa GIRLANDEN (1979/80), die mit ironischer Referenz auf das institutionskritische Paradigma der 60er und 70er Jahre das Arbeitszimmer eines Ausstellungskurators rahmen. Später macht Schütte gelegentlich wieder Installationen, z.B. werden 1989 THE LAUNDRY und MOHR'S LIFE an verschiedenen Orten eingerichtet. Diese Arbeiten sind in höherem Masse erzählerisch als die früheren. Auch kehrt der zuvor ausgeschlossene Körper zurück, allerdings in der Form von puppenartigen Stellvertreterfiguren für dargestellte Personen. Tücher mit verschiedenen Schriftzügen, teilweise bezogen auf die Welt der Kunst, nach dem Durchlauf durch die Waschmaschine auf die Leine gehängt, nehmen den Platz der im Museum verbrannten Bilder ein. Wasser ersetzt das Feuer. Wenn eine solche Installation freundlicher aussieht als die früheren, ist das gewiss Ausdruck erhöhter Selbstsicherheit des Künstlers, aber auch ein weiterer heikler Schritt der scheinbaren Erfüllung imaginierter Wünsche des Publikums.

Um noch einmal auf die Ausstellung bei Schöttle zurückzukommen: Zumindest in Deutschland, beim Werk eines Künstlers dieser Generation, können sol-

ULRICH LOOCK ist Direktor der Kunsthalle Bern.

che Arbeiten nicht gesehen werden, ohne dass sich die Bilder der Öfen von Auschwitz darüberlegen. Die Beziehung des Mediums Installation zur Avantgarde vom Beginn des Jahrhunderts – man denke etwa an Lissitzkys Verständnis seiner Proun-Bilder als «Umsteigestation zur Architektur» – ist aufgerufen im Horizont einer Utopie, die nach der Verbrennung der Menschen nur mehr zugänglich ist in Form ihrer Negativität. Umgekehrt bewahrt die Installation im Bild einer negativen Utopie der Kunst die Erinnerung an die Todeslager der Nazis. Was nicht darstellbar ist, tritt durch Evokation hervor. Die Bedeutung dieser Dimension der deutschen Geschichte für Schüttes Arbeit wird etwa bestätigt durch den Tisch zum Gedenken an die Hamburger Widerstandskämpfer, TISCH (1984), eine Skulptur im öffentlichen Raum; durch die Arbeit WO IST HITLERS GRAB? (1991) oder Schüttes kürzliche Mitarbeit bei der Einrichtung des Museums im ehemaligen Konzentrationslager Neuengamme bei Hamburg, RAUM DES GEDENKENS (1995).

Aus persönlicher Erinnerung, anekdotisch: Schon als Student und später immer wieder hat Thomas Schütte vom Massstab der Brauchbarkeit für (seine) Kunst gesprochen. Gegen Anfang seiner Studienzeit bereits hat er in geduldiger Arbeit Tapetenbahnen gemalt, sogar – mehr oder weniger ernsthaft – nach einem Hersteller gesucht, der seine Entwürfe für die Massenproduktion übernehmen würde. Interessanterweise hat er nicht etwa versucht, auf eigene Kosten oder im Zusammenhang einer Ausstellung Tapeten drucken zu lassen. Auf den ersten Blick nun könnte es scheinen, als sei es mit der Errichtung eines Eispavillons auf dem Gelände der «Documenta 8» (1987) endlich gelungen, das Feld der rein symbolischen Produktionen zu verlassen. Doch unverkennbar zeigt sich Schütte auch hier noch auf die Negativität avantgardistischer Utopie verpflichtet. Der ursprüngliche Entwurf für EIS besteht aus einem umgedrehten Farbeimer, und das Kriterium der Brauchbarkeit wird in einer Art bitterer, verzweifelter Fröhlichkeit nur gewürdigt: Ein kleiner Konsumtempel von geradezu ärmlicher Schlichtheit hat für es einzustehen. So bleibt lediglich zu wiederholen, dass die Harmlosigkeit dieser Assimilation an Installationen der Freizeitindustrie nichts als die

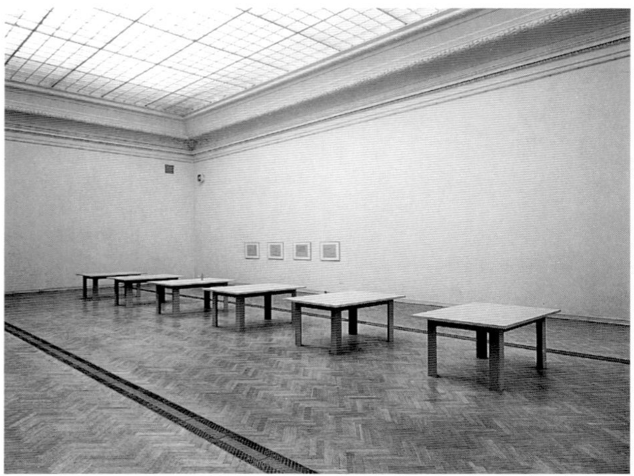

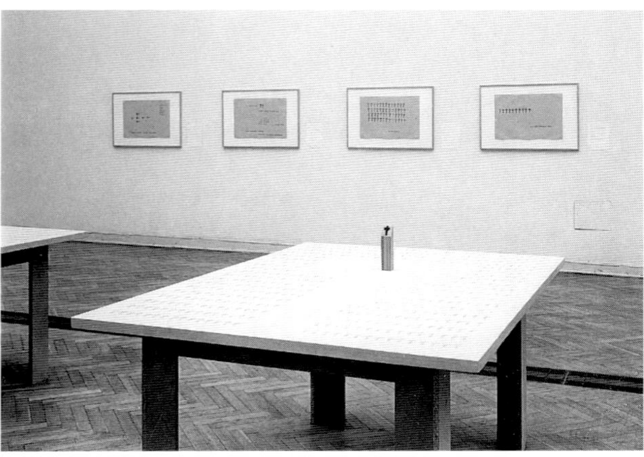

Inversion des Schreckens ist, der das MODELL FÜR EIN MUSEUM durchtränkt. EIS hat keine eigene Dimension, die ausgeführte Architektur ist nichts als eine Vergrösserung der Verkleinerung.

Diese Sicht sollte einen klareren Blick auch auf eine Arbeit im öffentlichen Raum, die kontroverse KIRSCHENSÄULE von 1987 in Münster, erlauben. Die Übererfüllung supponierter Publikumswünsche dürfte in der Tat eine subtilere und auf die Dauer vielleicht sogar effizientere Form des Widerstandes gegen die Konsumansprüche an die Kunst sein als die anerkannten Brachialgesten der Inkommensurabilität.

Installations

ULRICH LOOCK

In 1986 Thomas Schütte mounted a memorable exhibition in Rüdiger Schöttle's gallery in Munich, again showing his MODELL FÜR EIN MUSEUM (Model for a Museum, 1982). This medium-sized sculpture represents a return—in the context of (fictional, architectural) utility—to the formal simplicity with which minimalism once tried to bring the history of form to an entropic standstill. It was also a knee-jerk reaction to the hybrid designs of the late eighteenth century architecture of the Revolution, much discussed at the time under the heading of *architecture parlante*. Drawings placed on two easels next to the model revealed the function of the museum as a site where the works, delivered by the artists themselves, are to be efficiently and unceremoniously incinerated.

In a second, adjacent room, Schütte had put up an installation: that is, he had elected to use the form that had become popular with attempts to subvert the commodity and object character of the work of art. Ideally, an installation creates an environment, "viewers" of the "work" find themselves immersed in a situation: from "out there" to "in here." This work is entitled SCHROTT (Detritus): a diagram of a large oven covers the wall from floor to ceiling; two other ovens are drawn in outline; and three racks of rolled-up drawings (rejects) are placed in the room.

The mode of the installation in Schütte's oeuvre is, however, effective only inasmuch as it freezes the situationist utopia in art, which just barely survives as a mourned memory. On one hand, the spatial situation, imbued with inaccessibility and inoperative functionality, is no less fictional than the model. On the other hand, it cannot translate art into a situation of real utility because utility would result in the real extermination of art. Schütte's installation sub-

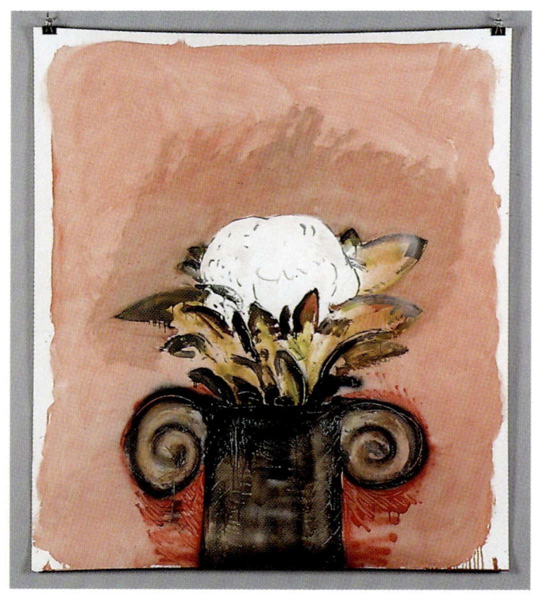

THOMAS SCHÜTTE, BLUMENKOHL, 1986,
Lack auf Papier, 110 x 130 cm /
varnish paint on paper, 43⅜ x 51⅛"

versively affirms the neo-avantgarde ambition of following up the history of early modernism.

Included in this complex of works, for example, is the model of a stage to which contact prints of the artist's own drawings have been affixed. The situational orientation is more apparent in pieces like the GIRLANDEN (Garlands, 1979/80), draped around a curator's office in ironic reference to the fashionable institutional critique of the sixties and seventies. Schütte occasionally made installations later on as well, such as THE LAUNDRY and MOHR'S LIFE, exhibited in several venues in 1989. These works are more narrative than earlier ones, and the previously excluded body makes a comeback as well, albeit in the form of puppet-like surrogates. Banners with a variety of inscriptions, some of which refer to the world of art, look as if they had been washed and hung up to dry: substitutes for the pictures burned in the earlier

---

ULRICH LOOCK is director of the Kunsthalle Berne.

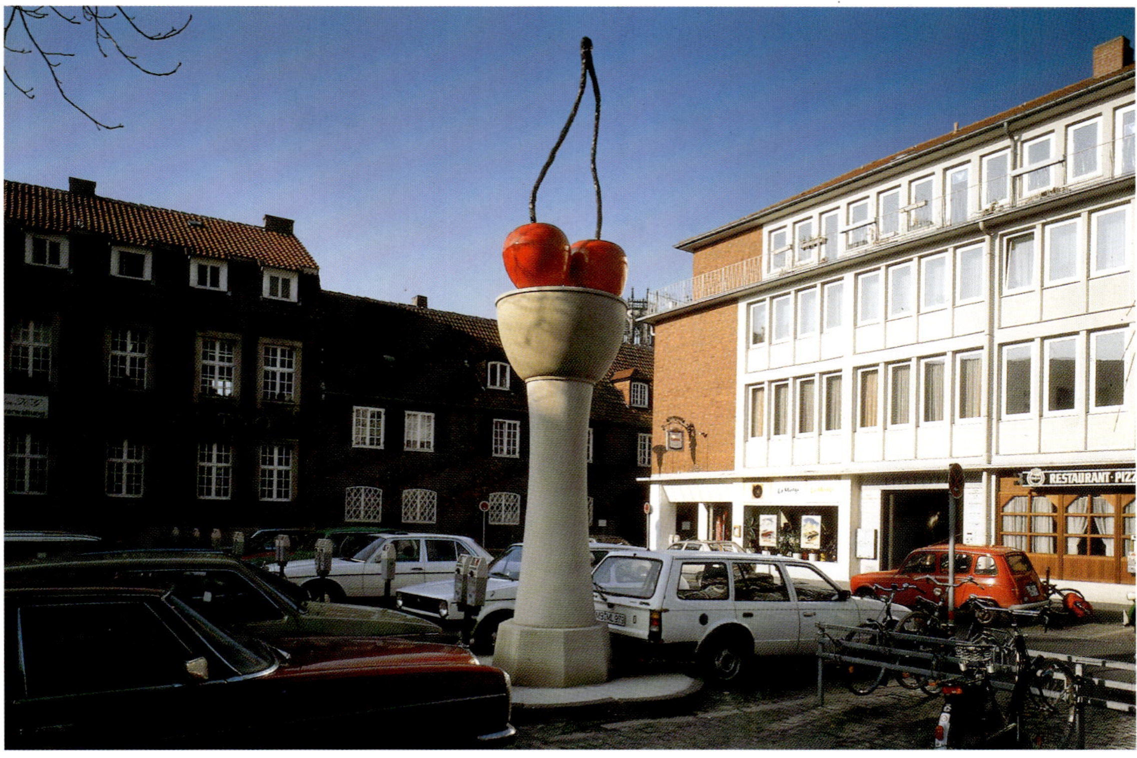

THOMAS SCHÜTTE, KIRSCHENSÄULE, 1987,
Sandstein und Aluminium, ca. 4 m hoch, Skulpturprojekte Münster /
sandstone and aluminum, ca 13' high.

museum model. Here, water takes the place of fire. This installation looks friendlier than earlier ones, not only because of the artist's own growing confidence but also because it takes another tongue-in-cheek step towards filling the imaginary wishes of the public.

But to return to the exhibition at the Schöttle gallery: It is impossible, at least in Germany, to look at such works by an artist of this generation without seeing the ovens in Auschwitz superimposed upon them. In the wake of human incineration, the utopian evocation of the relationship between the medium of the installation and the avant-garde at the beginning of the century—for instance, El Lissitzky's interpretation of his PROUN pictures as a "way station to architecture"—can be accessed only in its negative form. Conversely, the idea of art as a negative utopia in the installation preserves the memory of Nazi extermination camps. Schütte's preoccupation with this aspect of German history is reinforced by such works as his outdoor sculpture TISCH (Table, 1984) commemorating Hamburg's resistance fighters, WO IST HITLERS GRAB? (Where Is Hitler's Grave?, 1991), and his recent RAUM DES GEDENKENS (Memorial Space, 1995) created for a new museum in the former Neuengamme concentration camp near Hamburg.

Already as a student and repeatedly in later phases of his work, Schütte spoke about (his) art's measure of utility. When he first started studying, he painstakingly painted strips of wallpaper, even making a more or less serious effort to find a manufacturer to mass-produce his designs. Interestingly enough, he did not try to print the wallpaper at his own expense or have it printed in conjunction with an exhibition. When he put up an ice-cream kiosk at

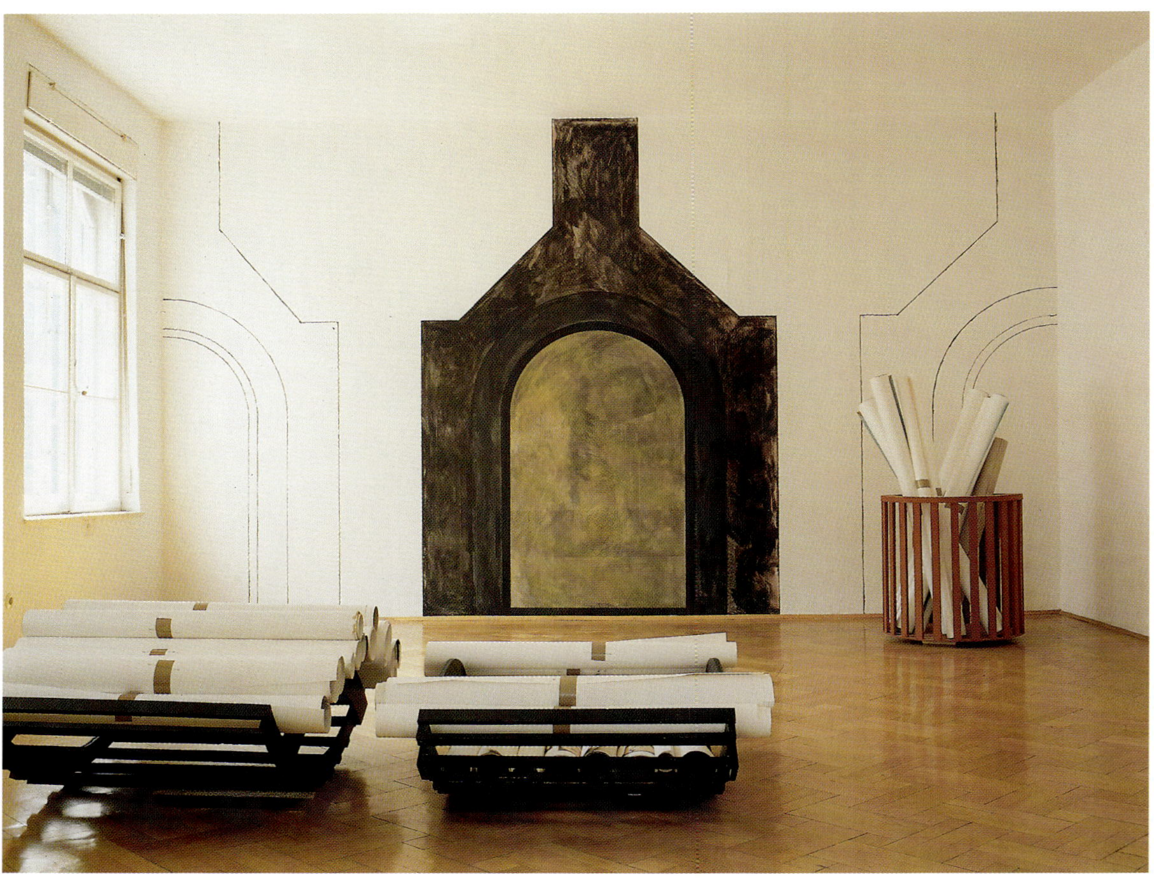

documenta 8 (1987), it seemed at first that he had finally succeeded in abandoning the field of pure symbolic production. But here, once again, Schütte unequivocally demonstrates his allegiance to the negativity of avant-garde utopias. The original design for EIS (Ice) consists of an overturned paint-bucket; the criterion of utility is honored in bitter and desperate gaiety: a small temple to consumption erected in the protected space of the art exhibition, whose architecture has the look of a hobby gardener's toolshed. One can only reiterate that this installation's harmless assimilation of the recreation industry is nothing but an inversion of the horror that permeates MODELL FÜR EIN MUSEUM. EIS has no dimensions of its own; the executed architecture is nothing but the enlargement of diminution. This point of view should allow a clearer view of another work in public space, the controversial KIRSCHENSÄULE (Cherry Column), erected as part of "Skulpturprojekte Münster" in 1987. The overkill of invented consumer wishes may actually turn out to be a more subtle and, in the long run, more efficient form of counteracting the commodification of art than the brute-force gestures of generally accepted incommensurability.

(Translation: Catherine Schelbert)

ELIZABETH JANUS

DIE UNSCHULDIGEN

Hinter den meisten wirklich grossen und kreativen Errungenschaften in Wissenschaft, Philosophie, Literatur und Kunst steht ein fundamentales Interesse für das Wesen der menschlichen Existenz und die Bedingungen menschlichen Verhaltens. Die Faszination dieser Grundfragen war und ist die Triebfeder aller Denkenden, die versuchen, die Geheimnisse des menschlichen Charakters und seiner Beweggründe und damit die zentralen Fragen jeder humanwissenschaftlichen Disziplin zu ergründen. Auch Thomas Schüttes Werk fügt sich nahtlos in diese Tradition ein, denn Ursprung und Gegenstand seiner Arbeit ist die *Conditio humana* in ihren alltäglichsten und fundamentalen Erscheinungsformen. In Schüttes frühen Zeichnungen, architektonischen Modellen und Installationen war der Mensch oft nur indirekt präsent: in den Anspielungen auf öffentliche und private, für Menschen bestimmte Räume. Wenn dennoch menschliche Gestalten auftauchten, so gewöhnlich in Form von abstrahierten Darstellungen anonymer Zuschauer, etwa als puppenartige Schablonen im MODELL K (1981–82) und in den beiden Versionen von LAUFBAHN (1987), als roh geformte, innerhalb einer umfassenderen Werkanlage auftretende Figuren in der MANN IM MATSCH-Serie (ab 1982), als grosse von ihren Körpern getrennte Tonköpfe in MANN UND FRAU (1986) oder in den VIER SCHWESTERN IM BAD (1989).

Im Lauf der Jahre trat der Mensch jedoch immer deutlicher in den Vordergrund, und in seinen Zeichnungen und Aquarellen, in den Entwürfen für Denkmäler, in den Skulpturen und schliesslich den Photographien ist zu beobachten, wie Schütte seine Figuren nach und nach aus der Anonymität herausholt. Er tut dies, indem er sie zu Repräsentanten bestimmter Individuen macht, etwa des Künstlers als solchen, in MOHR'S LIFE (1988), des verschollenen Seemanns, in ALAIN COLAS (1989), oder indem er Typen mit spezifischen, wiedererkennbaren Gesichtszügen und anderen menschlichen Attributen schafft, wie in den grossformatigen Tonfiguren DIE FREMDEN (1992), die an der Documenta IX in Kassel auf einem Portikus aufgereiht waren. In dieses Umfeld gehören auch einige Photoserien, die immer die gleiche Gruppe kleiner Figuren mit individuell und ausdrucksstark modellierten Köpfen aus Fimo-Modelliermasse zeigen. Dazu gehören ALTE FREUNDE (1992), «Porträts» in leuchtenden Farben, deren jedes einen eigenen Namen hat; VEREINIGTE FEINDE (1993), ebenfalls in Farbe, vereint zwei kontrastierende Gesichter, und schliesslich das jüngste und kühlste dieser Reihe, INNOCENTI (1995), eine Gruppe von einunddreissig Photographien einzelner weisser Köpfe vor einem schwarzen Hintergrund. Als ginge es um eine Lektion in Charakterkunde, zeigt hier jedes Gesicht andere Züge – gefurchte Stirn, riesige Nase, Hängebacken und weit aufgerissene Augen –, eine Parade der Persönlichkeiten und Gemütszustände.

Eine derart systematische Untersuchung individueller Erscheinungsformen erinnert uns an die Physiognomisten und ihre Überzeugung, dass das Gesicht, das jahrhundertelang als Ort der Vereinigung von Körper und Seele galt, ein Spiegel des Charakters und seiner Beweggründe sei. Man denke etwa an die Versuche Johann Kaspar Lavaters, des Begründers der Physiognomielehre, die Gesichtszüge in Kategorien einzuteilen, die spezifischen sittlichen und

ELIZABETH JANUS ist Kunstkritikerin und lebt in Genf.

geistigen Neigungen entsprechen sollten; oder auch an die Versuche von Psychologen und Kriminologen, mit Hilfe der Photographie eine Verbindung zwischen Physiognomie und asozialem Verhalten herzustellen. Schüttes Gesichter lassen allerdings weniger auf ein wissenschaftliches Interesse schliessen als vielmehr auf den persönlichen Wunsch, anhand des sichtbarsten Zeichens der Differenz die unendliche Vielfalt des Menschlichen darzustellen. Das tritt am deutlichsten in den INNOCENTI zutage, weil dies die bisher nüchternste und strengste Darstellung dieser Art ist. Jedes Gesicht ist in klaren, erhabenen Formen modelliert und aus extremer Nähe photographiert, oft aus verblüffenden Blickwinkeln und mit starken Lichtkontrasten. Die daraus resultierenden schattigen Konturen betonen die ohnehin überzeichneten Züge jedes Gesichtes noch mehr und lassen es, ähnlich wie die Karikatur, zugleich unwirklich und gespenstisch vertraut erscheinen.

Der Titel INNOCENTI (Die Unschuldigen) weckt naheliegende biblische Assoziationen. Er kann aber auch einfach solche meinen, die sich moralisch und rechtlich nichts haben zuschulden kommen lassen, oder die Naivität schlechthin, die aber wiederum ein gewinnender Charakterzug sein kann oder, weniger schmeichelhaft, eine Form von Ignoranz und Dummheit. Es wäre jedoch irreführend oder doch zumindest eine arge Einschränkung, diese Photographien in erster Linie hinsichtlich ihrer religiösen oder moralischen Bedeutung zu befragen. Vielmehr ist diese Bandbreite von Gesichtsausdrücken in einem einzigen Bild und im Namen der Unschuld ein eindrücklicher Hinweis darauf, dass Unschuld ein Urzustand ist, der erhalten bleiben oder verlorengehen kann. Betrachtet man sie im Kontext von Schüttes Werk, das oft die Situation des Menschen angesichts unerbittlicher, grösserer Mächte thematisiert, so könnten diese Gesichter auch solche von «rechtmässigen» Übeltätern sein, deren Wille zur Macht sie jeder Verantwortung gegenüber Abhängigen enthebt. Eine ähnliche, ebenso pragmatische wie philosophische Behandlung dieses Themas findet man in den Büchern von Herman Melville, der seine Aufmerksamkeit schon früh den Abgründen und Widersprüchen der menschlichen Existenz widmete. Insbesondere fühlt man sich an *Billy Budd*,

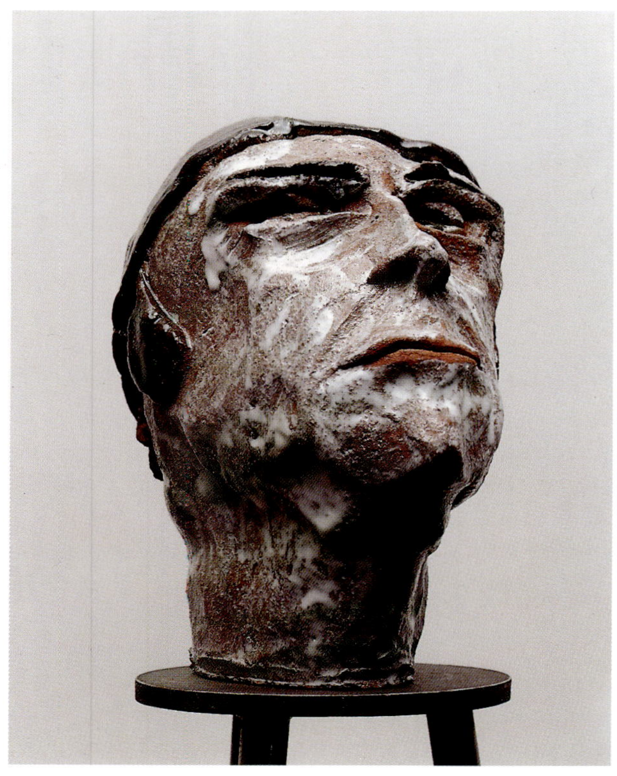

THOMAS SCHÜTTE, DER KAPITÄN, 1993, *glazed ceramics, Collection* *Carré d'art, Nîmes / glazed ceramics.* (PHOTOS: NIC TENWIGGENHORN)

seine klassische Erzählung über den Verlust der Unschuld erinnert, in der moralische Integrität und ein guter Charakter den Helden weder vor den chaotischen Kräften des Bösen noch vor Willkür und Ungerechtigkeit zu bewahren vermögen.

Die Art, wie die INNOCENTI präsentiert werden, ist – wie könnte es auch anders sein – von Schüttes Auffassung des Raums bestimmt. Diese ist einerseits die des Architekten, der sich mit der Funktion und dem Handeln des Menschen im Raum befasst, andrerseits jene des Bildhauers, der untersucht, wie ein Gegenstand im Raum wirkt. Korrekt installiert – und für Schütte ist die Installation seiner Arbeiten ebenso wichtig wie ihre Fabrikation –, hängen alle einunddreissig Photographien hoch oben, an den Wänden eines einzigen Raumes. Diese Anordnung in einer fortlaufenden linearen Reihe, die sich über die

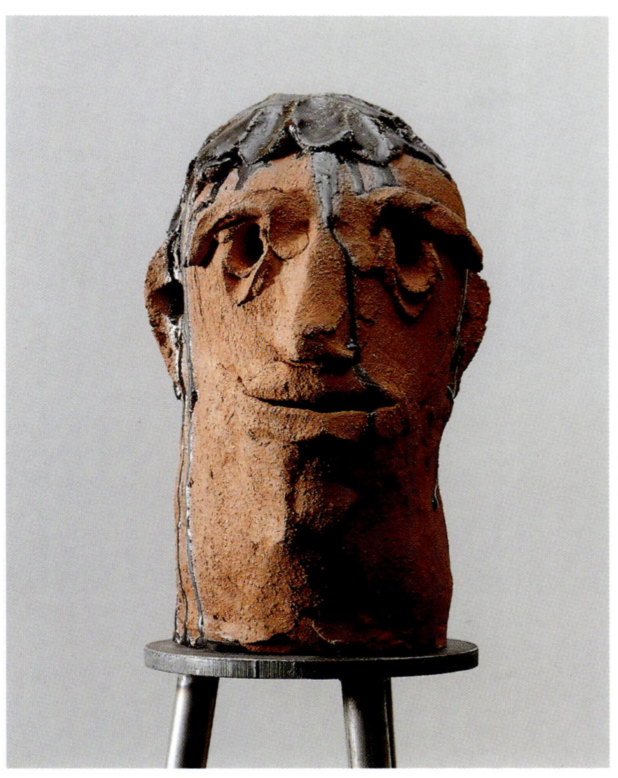

THOMAS SCHÜTTE, BORIS, 1993,
glasierte Keramik, 33 x 21 x 23 cm /
glazed ceramics, 13 x 8¼ x 9".

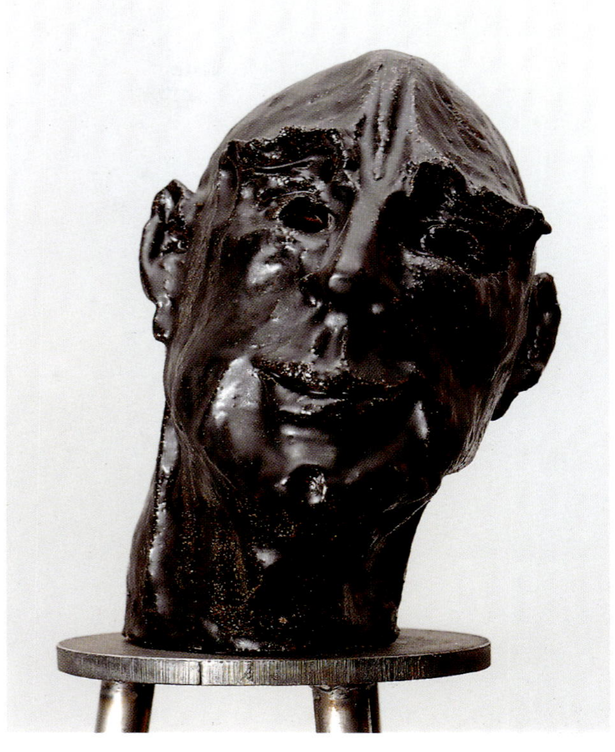

OHNE TITEL, 1993,
glasierte Keramik, 24 x 19 x 24 cm /
glazed ceramics, 9½ x 7½ x 9½".

oberen Wandhälften des Raumes hinzieht, zwingt den Betrachter, nach oben zu schauen, und gibt ihm so eher das Gefühl, eine zweidimensionale Entsprechung zu den Reliefskulpturen eines architektonischen Frieses vor sich zu haben als eine Serie von Einzelporträts.

Im Mittelalter gaben die Bildhauer ihre klassischen Vorbilder auf und entwickelten eine Bildsprache, die ihnen den Ausdruck von tiefen religiösen Ideen in einer neuen, dekorativen Weise erlaubte. Die daraus entstandene Form des Erzählens von Geschichten in Bildern, die eine stärkere Ausarbeitung der Gebärden und Stellungen der Heiligen wie der Sterblichen, der Dämonen und anderer mythologischer Tiere mit sich brachte, wurde zum leicht verständlichen und damit auch zum wirkungsvollsten Mittel, jene moralischen Imperative zu transportie-

ren, die sie ursprünglich inspiriert hatten. Mit zeitgenössischen Mitteln erneuert Schütte dieses alte Verfahren. Er befreit es von allen religiösen, inhaltlichen oder didaktischen Intentionen, nicht um uns Respekt oder Furcht einzuflössen, sondern um die Frage zu stellen, ob unser Wunsch, zwischen Gut und Böse – und in der Folge zwischen Schuld und Unschuld – zu unterscheiden, nicht im Grunde der nichtige Versuch sei, zwei Seiten ein und derselben Medaille als Gegensätze zu betrachten. Diese Ungewissheit spiegelt sich in den Gesichtern der INNOCENTI: Es sind Gesichter von solchen, die gelebt haben, die weder jung noch a priori unschuldig sind, Gesichter, die ihre je eigenen Geschichten erzählen, an denen wir aber kollektiv teilhaben.

(Übersetzung: Susanne Schmidt)

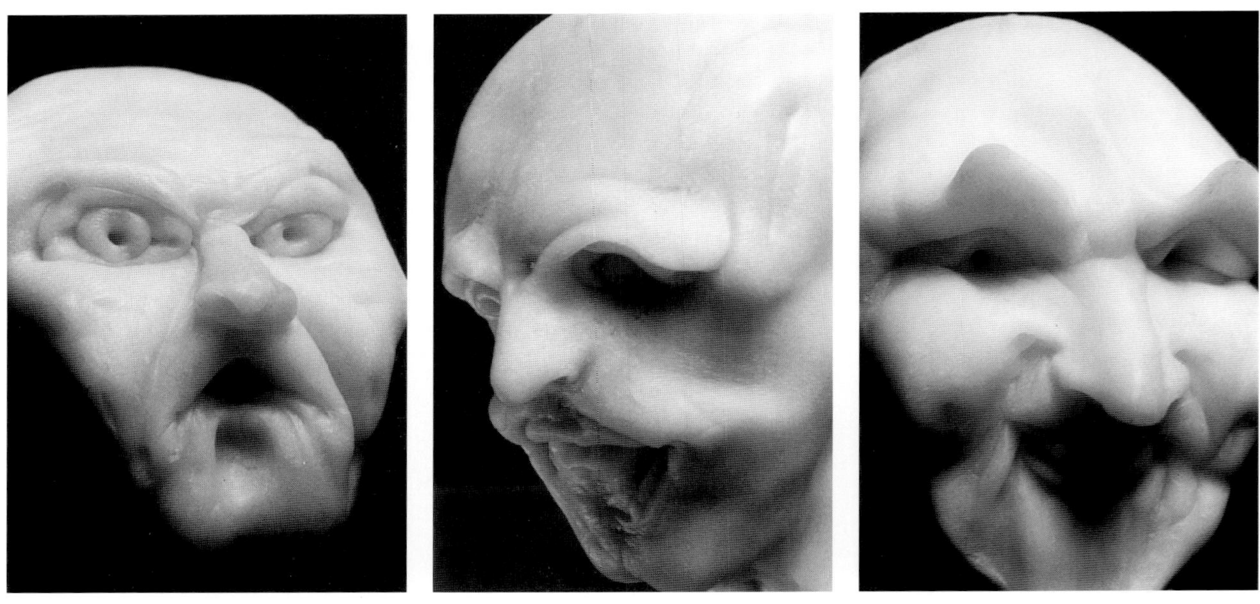

THOMAS SCHÜTTE, INNOCENTI, 1994,
Photoserie schwarzweiss / photo series, edition of 3.

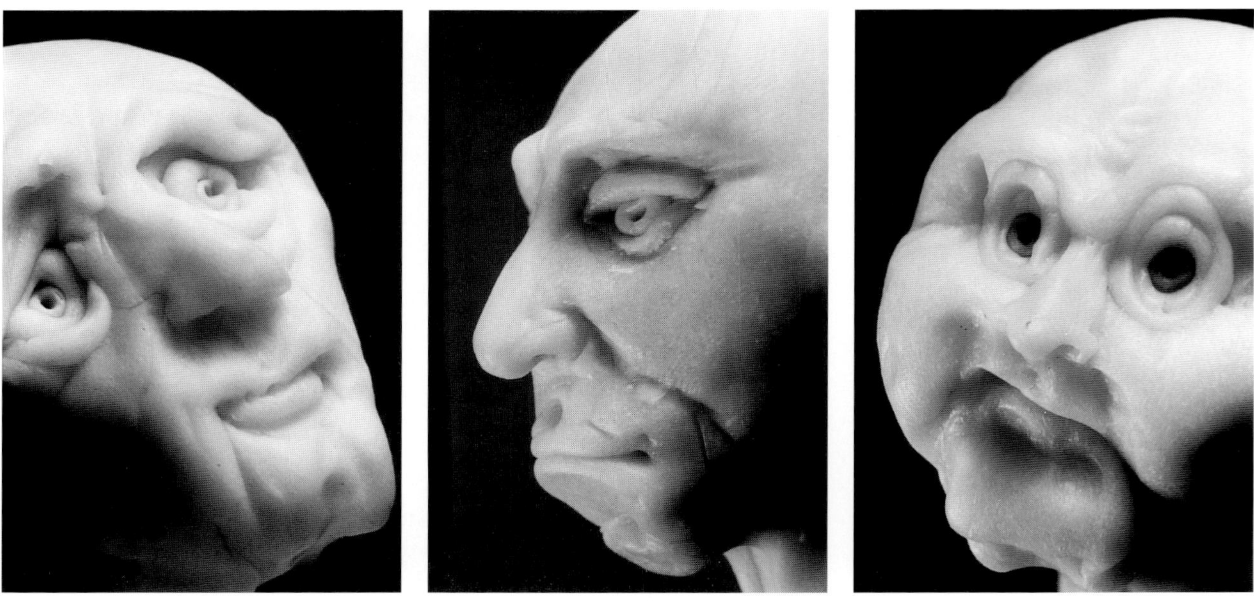

SCHÜTTE'S INNOCENTS

ELIZABETH JANUS

Behind many of the greatest and most creative advances in science, philosophy, literature, and art is a basic curiosity about the substance of human existence and the conditions that affect human behavior. This fascination has driven thinkers to try and unlock the mysteries that form a person's character and motivate his or her actions and are thus central to the preoccupations of every humanistic discipline. With little hesitation, Thomas Schütte places himself within this long tradition, taking on the human condition at its most ordinary and its most profound, as both source and subject. In his earliest drawings, architectural models, and installations, a human presence was often only alluded to through the evocation of the public and private spaces that we inhabit. Figures, when they appeared, typically were abstracted representations of anonymous spectators, as in the doll-like cutouts found in MODELL K (Model K, 1981–82) and the two versions of LAUF-BAHN (Career, 1987); crudely modeled figurines incorporated into larger structures, such as those found in the MANN IM MATSCH (Man in Muck) series beginning in 1982; or large clay heads severed from their bodies, such as MANN UND FRAU (Man and Woman, 1986), or VIER SCHWESTERN IM BAD (Four Sisters in the Tub, 1989).

Over the years, however, this human presence has become increasingly obvious and in Schütte's drawings, watercolors, models for monuments, sculptures, and most recently, photographs, one sees him gradually pulling his figures out of their anonymity. This is done by making them stand-ins for particular individuals, such as the quintessential artist in his studio (MOHR'S LIFE, 1988) and the lost sailor

(ALAIN COLAS, 1989), or by creating recognizable types with specific facial features and other human attributes, as in the large-scale clay figures of DIE FREMDEN (Strangers, 1992) that were ranged on the portico of a building in Kassel at Documenta IX. Within the context of this latter category also fall several series of photographs featuring the same group of small figures with heads modeled from a clay-like material called Fimo into a variety of expressive states. Among them are OLD FRIENDS (1992), brightly colored "portraits," each of which has been given a person's name; UNITED ENEMIES (1993), which are also in color and pair two contrasting faces; and the latest and most sober, INNOCENTI (1995), a group of thirty-one photographs of individual white heads set against a black background. Like a taxonomy of characters, all these faces have different features—furrowed brows, protruding noses, sagging jowls, and wide-open eyes—that represent an array of personalities as well as states of mind.

Such a systematic examination of individual countenances brings to mind the belief of physiognomists that the face, which for centuries was thought to be the site where body meets soul, could reveal a person's character as well as his motivations. One thinks, for example, of the attempts by Johann Kaspar Lavater, the founder of physiognomics, to divide facial traits into categories corresponding to specific moral and intellectual inclinations; or the early use of photography by psychologists and criminologists to find a link between physiognomy and antisocial behavior. In Schütte's faces, however, there is little evidence of any scientific interest, but rather a very personal wish to use the most visible indication of difference to represent the infinite variety of the human race. This is clearest in INNOCENTI, in that it

ELIZABETH JANUS is a writer who lives in Geneva.

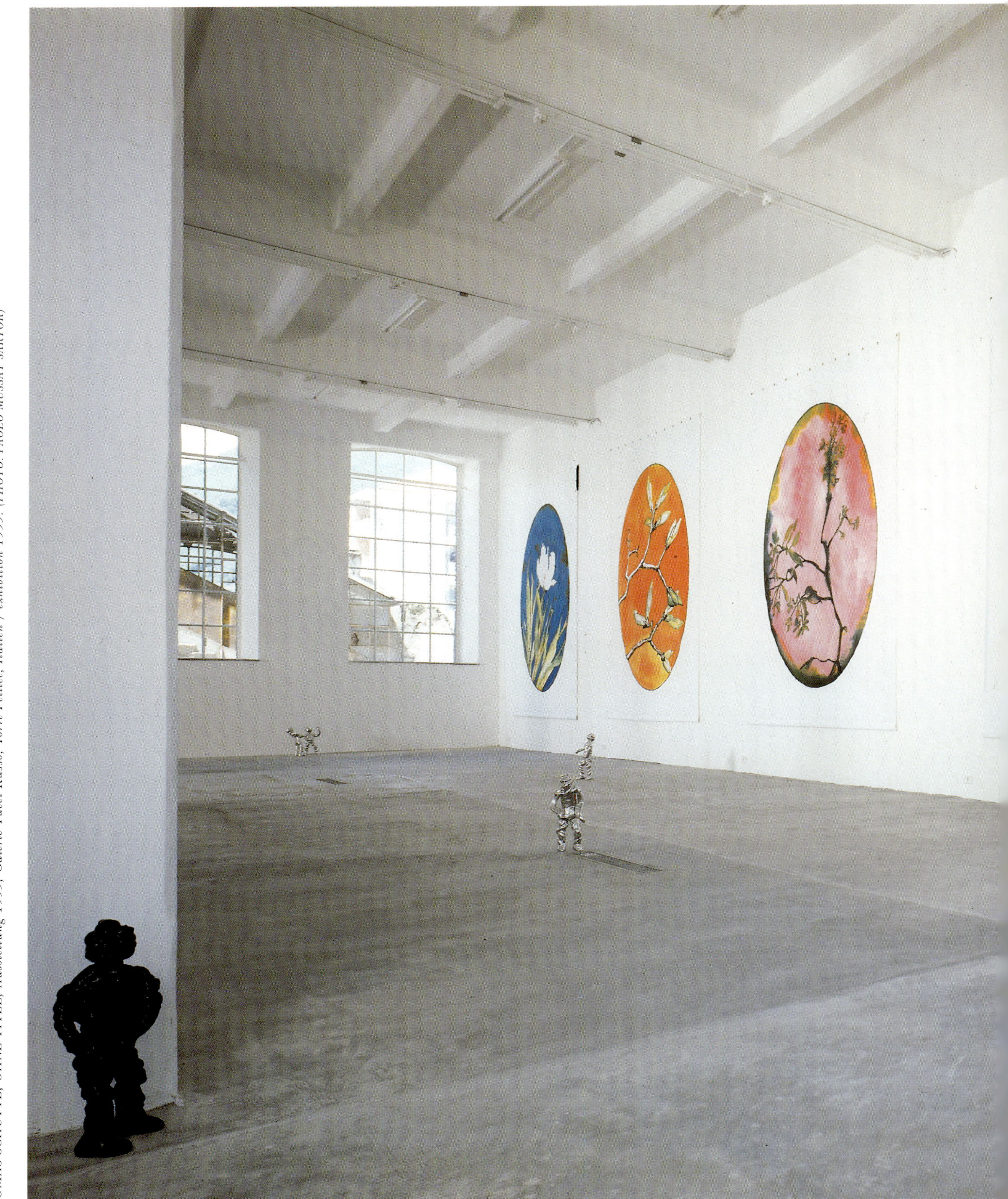

THOMAS SCHÜTTE, OHNE TITEL, Ausstellung 1995, Galerie Tucci Russo, Torre Pellice, Italien / exhibition 1995. (PHOTO: PAOLO MUSSAT SARTOR)

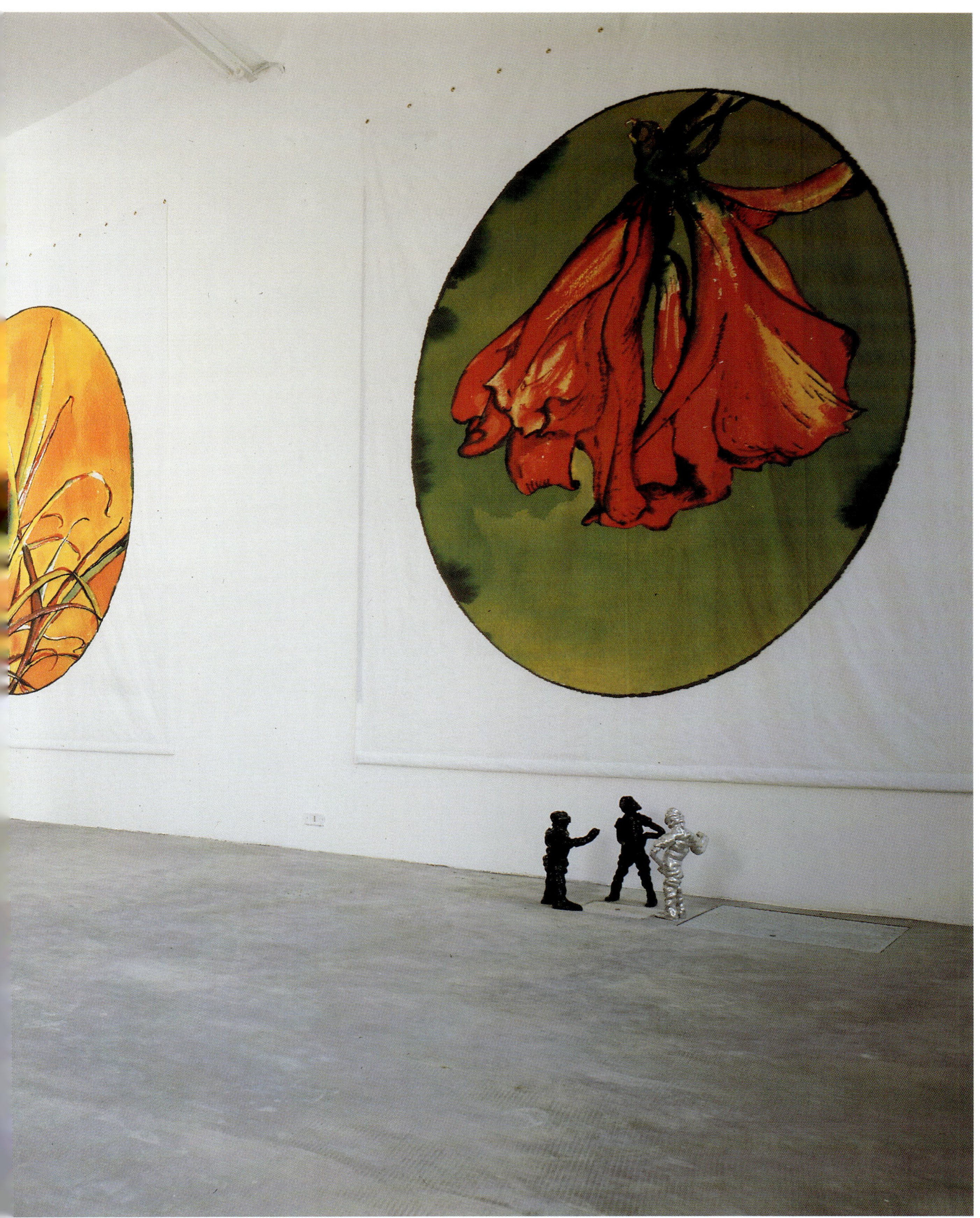

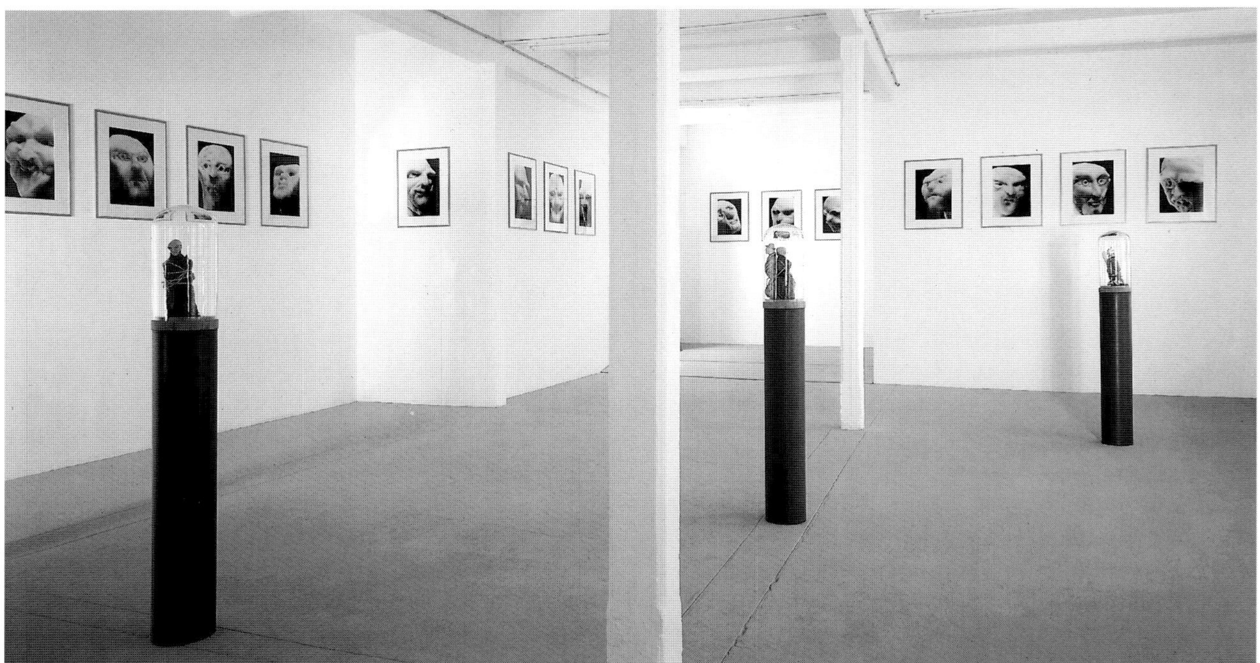

THOMAS SCHÜTTE, INNOCENTI and UNITED ENEMIES,
installation view, Galerie Tucci Russo, Torre Pellice, Italy, 1995.
(PHOTO: PAOLO MUSSAT SARTOR)

is the most austere presentation yet, with each face modeled in sharp relief and then photographed in extreme close-up, often at odd angles, and lit to create sharp chiaroscuro. These resulting shadowy contours emphasize each face's exaggerated features and, as in caricatures, make them at the same time unreal and eerily familiar.

The title INNOCENTI invites obvious biblical associations but also can refer to those who are free from moral or legal wrong, as well as to a simple naïveté that can be either an endearing simplicity or a less complimentary ignorance or stupidity. It would, however, be misleading—or at least limiting—to see these photographs as having primarily spiritual or moral connotations. In fact, this range of facial expressions all grouped together in the name of innocence is a poignant reminder that innocence is a primal state that can be maintained or can be lost. It also suggests, taken in the context of Schütte's oeuvre, which frequently alludes to man's position as subject to the inexorable forces of corporate power,

that these faces might be those of "justified" sinners whose will to power absolves them from all responsibility towards those whom they control. Such an approach to the subject, as pragmatic as it is philosophical, can be found in the literature of Herman Melville, an earlier student of humanity's complexities and contradictions. One is reminded especially of his classic tale about the loss of innocence, *Billy Budd,* in which the protagonist's moral purity and inherent goodness cannot protect him from the indiscriminate forces of evil nor from random injustice.

As always, Schütte's interest in space, which is partly an architect's vision of how people function and interact in it and partly a sculptor's concern about how objects are seen in it, dictates the way the INNOCENTI are presented. When properly installed— and for Schütte the installation of his works is as important as their fabrication—all thirty-one photographs hang high on the walls of a single room. This placement, in a continuous, linear sequence that wraps around the upper reaches of the room, forces the viewer's gaze upward, creating the sensation of viewing two-dimensional equivalents of the relief sculptures from architectural friezes rather than individual portraits.

In the Middle Ages, sculptors abandoned classical models and developed a pictorial language that permitted the expression of profound spiritual ideas within a new decorative idiom. The resulting form of visual storytelling, which emphasized the gestures and poses of holy figures, mere mortals, gargoyles and other mythical beasts alike, became the most accessible and thus the most powerful means of expressing the moral imperatives that inspired it. In contemporary terms, Schütte updates this old device, severing it from all devotional, narrative, or didactic intentions, not to inspire awe or fear but to ask whether our desire to distinguish the differences between good and evil—and the ensuing human responses of guilt and innocence—are not, in fact, futile attempts to set in opposition two faces of the same coin. This uncertainty is reflected in the faces of the INNOCENTI, which are faces of those who have lived, who are neither young nor necessarily innocent, and from whose features one discerns the histories that are uniquely theirs, but also collectively ours.

EDITION FOR PARKETT

THOMAS SCHÜTTE

OLGA'S WALLPAPER, 1996 (1977)
Lithographie vom Stein, 5farbig,
gedruckt von Felix Bauer, Köln,
auf Indisches Handbütten, 250 g,
ca. 102 x 68,5 cm
Auflage: 60/XX, signiert und numeriert

OLGA'S WALLPAPER, 1996 (1977)
Lithograph, stone-pulled, 5 colors,
printed by Felix Bauer, Köln,
on handmade Indian Vellum, 250 g,
$40^{1}/_{8}$ x 27"
Edition of 60/XX, signed and numbered

OLGA'S WALLPAPER, Ausschnitt im Massstab 1:1 / detail in original size.

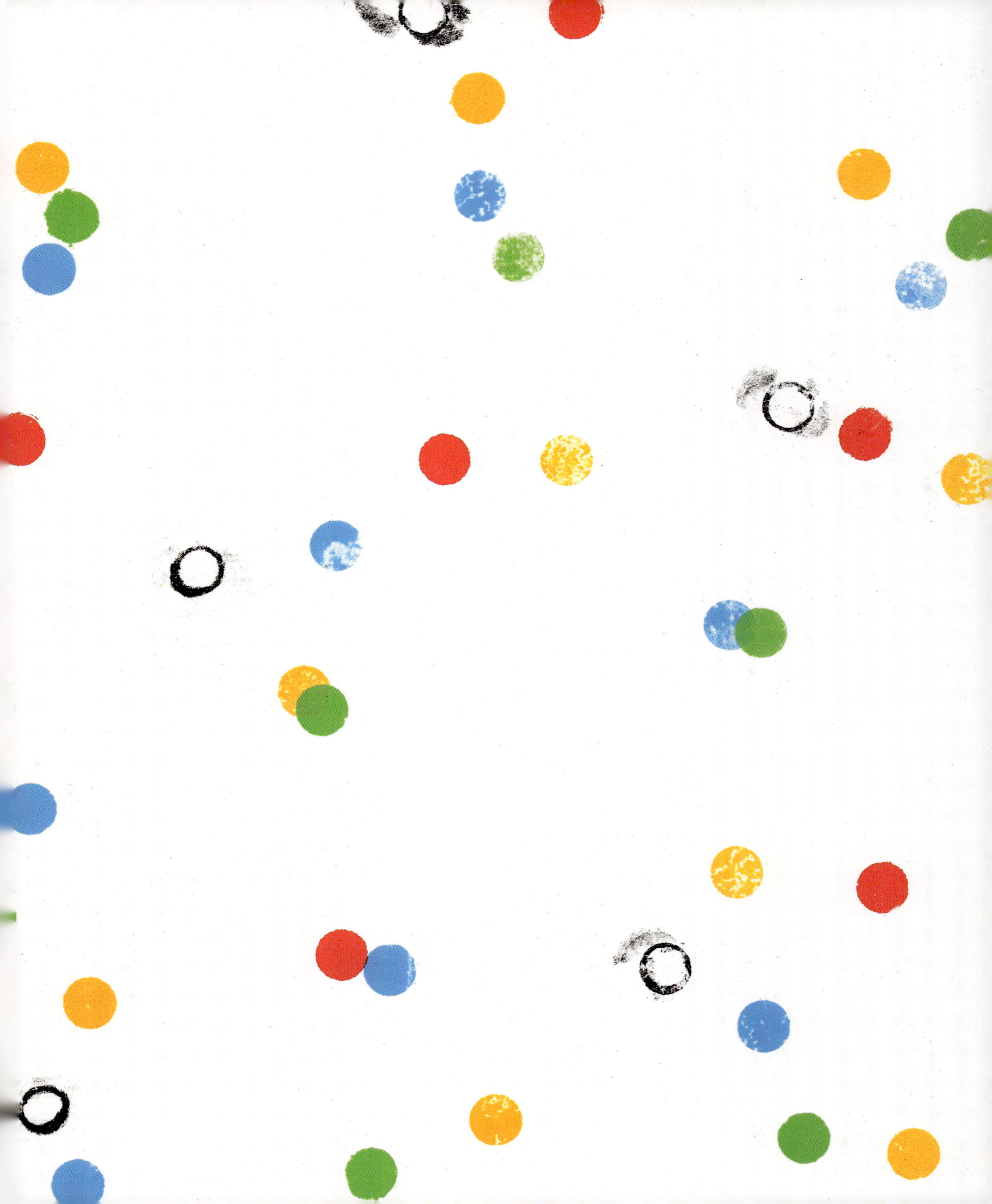

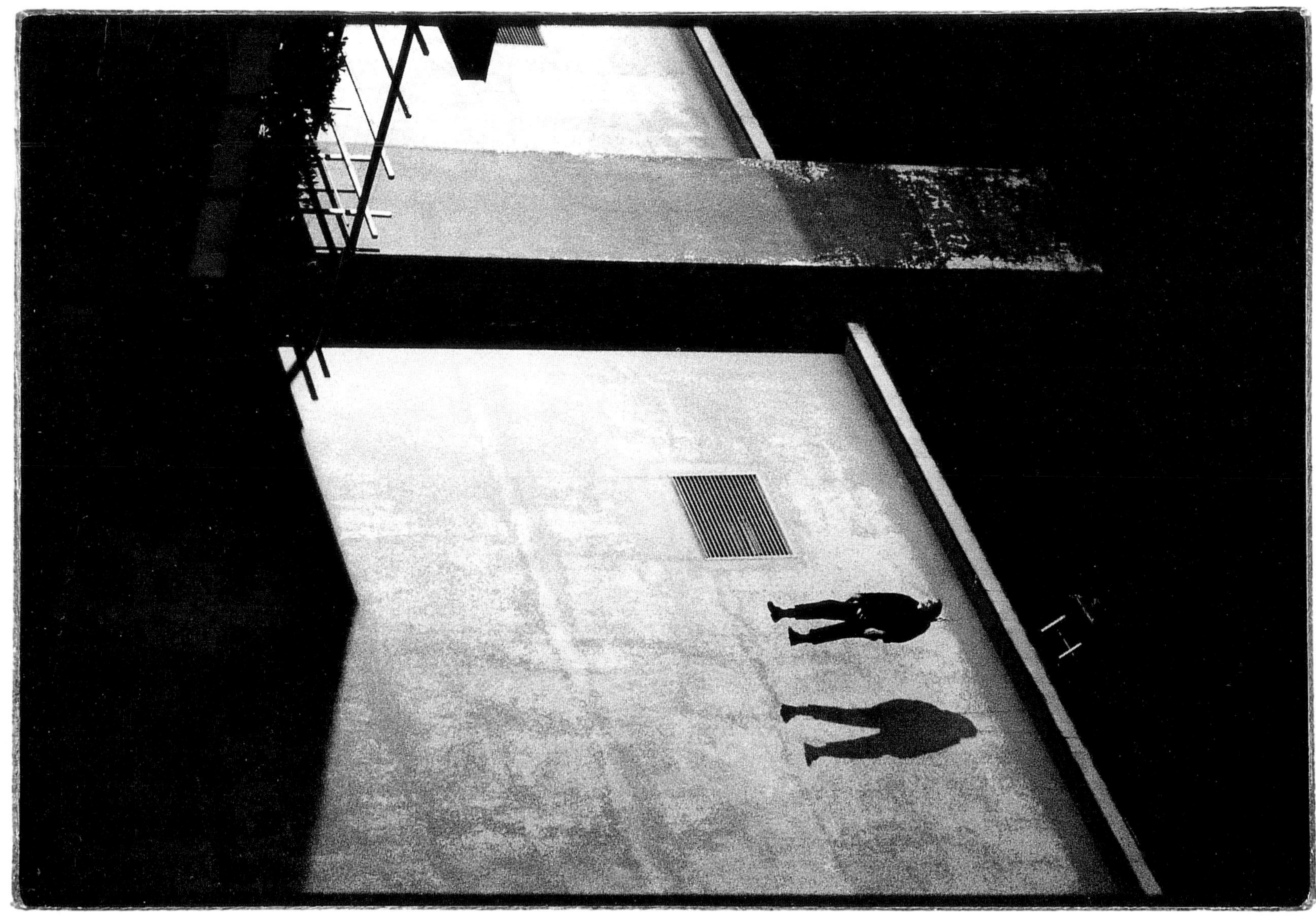

CHRISTOPH RÜTIMANN, HÄNGEN AM MUSEUM, 1994, Performance, Kunstmuseum Luzern / HANGING FROM THE MUSEUM. (PHOTO: MAYA JÖRG)

Jonglieren mit der Gravitation

MAX WECHSLER

ZUR KUNST VON CHRISTOPH RÜTIMANN

Um Christoph Rütimanns Schaffen generalisierend zu charakterisieren, ist bei der Ausdrucksform der Performance anzusetzen, die in seinem Werk schon immer eine zentrale Stellung eingenommen hat. Dies um so mehr, als das weite Spektrum ihrer Erscheinungsformen auch ganz unmittelbar manifestiert, dass dieses Œuvre von hybrid mehrdeutiger Natur ist und auf der Ebene der eingesetzten Materialien und Medien – von Tusche bis Video, von der Installation bis zur Malerei – ein Unternehmen in den unterschiedlichsten Disziplinen darstellt. Die Auseinandersetzung mit Rütimanns Arbeit ist darum immer ein Wechselbad, stehen doch die unterschiedlichsten Elemente formaler und inhaltlicher Natur auf abenteuerliche Weise mehr oder weniger gleichwertig nebeneinander. Es ist dabei selbstverständlich nicht von Ungenauigkeit die Rede, im Gegenteil, es geht um einen grundsätzlichen Versuch, sich verbindlich mit Unsicherheiten zu beschäftigen – sich dem Fall hinzugeben, ohne abzustürzen.

DAS SPIEL EINIGER DORNEN IN WACHS (EINE AUFZEICHNUNG) (1988) illustriert die angesprochene Doppelbödigkeit sehr trefflich: Da sitzt der Künstler in dem durch ein grosses Schaufenster einsehbaren Raum der Galerie auf einem Stuhl, vor ihm steht ein Sockel und darauf ein Kaktus. Über dem Kaktus hängt ein Mikrophon von der Decke, das jene Geräusche registriert, die entstehen, wenn der Künstler eingeschwärzte wachsbeschichtete Papierblätter an den Stacheln des Kaktus bearbeitet. Blatt um Blatt kratzt er feinnervige weisse Zeichnungen in das weiche Schwarz, welche sich am Ende der Performance an der Wand zu einer Ausstellung reihen werden. Das ist jedoch nur ein Aspekt, denn durch den Akt des Zeichnens bringt er die Pflanze zum Klingen und entlockt ihr überraschende Rhythmen und Klänge, eine eigentliche Musik, die gleichwertig neben den Zeichnungen den Raum erfüllt. In diesem poetischen Akt durchdringen sich die Zeichnung und der Klang in wechselseitiger Bedingtheit ganz selbstverständlich: Die Musik produziert im Prozess ihres Entstehens ihre eigene Partitur, und in der Zeit der zeichnerischen Geste, des Sehens und des Hörens fügen sich die Sinnfragmente zu einem ganzheitlichen, wenn auch nicht ebenmässigen Wahrnehmungs-Gewebe. Wenn wir später ein so entstandenes Blatt als autonome Zeichnung betrachten, so verweisen die entstandenen Linien und Schraffuren als konkrete Spuren der Musik immer auch auf den Handlungscharakter des Blattes. Wie der Abzug einer Radierung auf die konkrete Wirklichkeit der Druckplatte, so referiert diese Zeichnung auf das gleichzeitige Konzert des Zeichnens und die zeichnerische Fixierung eines Konzerts.

MAX WECHSLER ist Kunstkritiker und Dozent an der Schule für Gestaltung in Luzern.

Ganz anders ESPRIT D'ESCALIER (1991), eine Arbeit, die er als Beitrag zu einem Duchamp-Symposion in Amsterdam formulierte. Hier handelt es sich um eine Art von *tableau vivant*, in welchem sich in der «Vitrine» eines verglasten Ausstellungsraums der nackte Künstler kopfüber wie ein «gestürzter Engel» auf einem Treppenstück liegend präsentierte, flankiert von einer gewaltigen Pflugschar. Eine feine Hommage an Marcel Duchamp, vor allem aber auch eine Reflexion der künstlerischen Arbeit und der Existenz des Künstlers. Eine Thematik, die Rütimann drei Jahre später noch einmal zum Gegenstand einer Performance machen sollte, in HÄNGEN AM MUSEUM (1994), noch zugespitzter, aber nicht weniger konzentriert und verhalten: In einer kalten Dezembernacht liess er sich – an Gurten über dem Abgrund hängend – von einem selbstkonstruierten Kranfahrzeug knapp unter dem Dachgesims in einer unendlich langsamen Bewegung um das Kunst-

lichen Sinne experimentell motivierten Neugier und Entdeckungslust in Hinsicht auf die spezifischen Eigenschaften von Materialien und die Ordnungsprinzipien von Systemen. So wird die Erarbeitung des Werks bei Rütimann immer zu einer abenteuerlichen Auseinandersetzung mit dem Verhalten von Materialien und mit der Wirkung von Gegenständen unter den jeweils gesetzten speziellen Bedingungen. Das hat im Bereich des Inhaltlichen wie des Materiellen einen schon fast wissenschaftlichen Anstrich, bleibt aber immer im Bereich der Theorie und der Praxis des täglichen Lebens. Vorherrschend ist die Ernsthaftigkeit des Spiels mit Referenz auf die praktische Philosophie des Lebens. Auch die in den einzelnen Werkkomplexen zuweilen thematisierten idealen (seit den Zeiten der Quantenphysik auch nicht mehr ganz schlüssigen) Systeme der Naturwissenschaften oder der Kunst stehen immer in Spannung zu den Unwägbarkeiten des Alltags. So

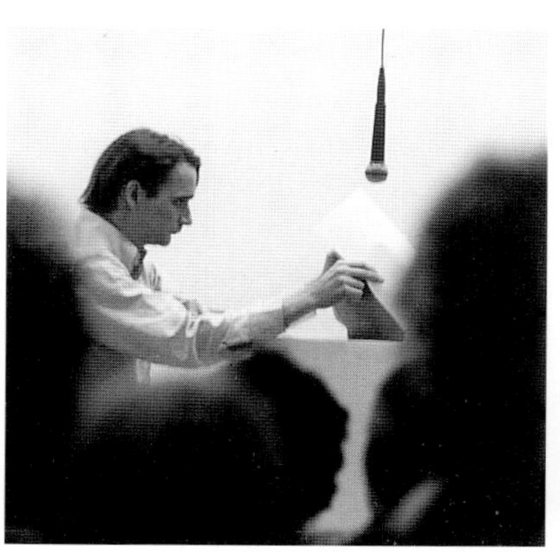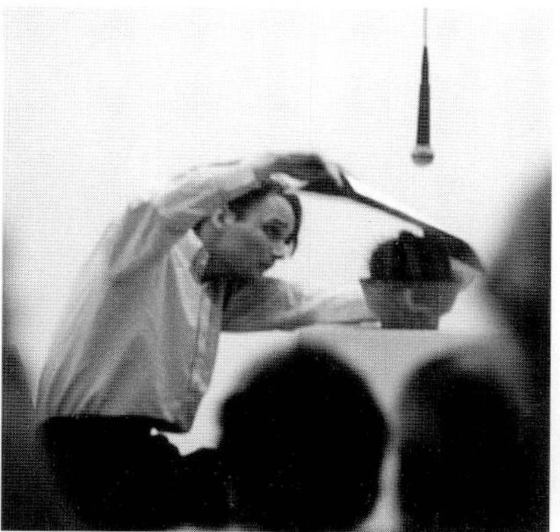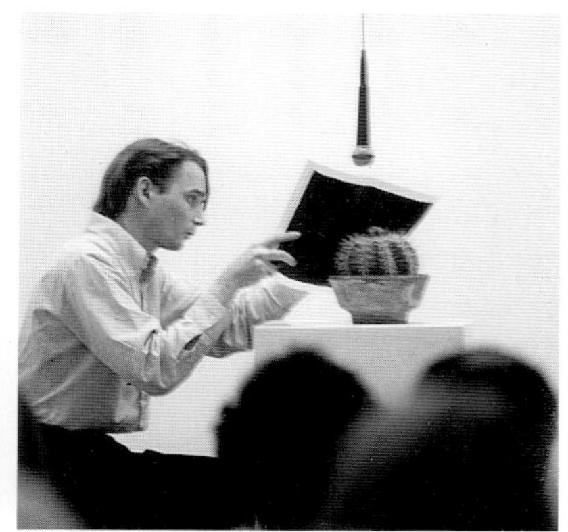

museum Luzern fahren; um dieses dem Abbruch geweihte Haus, *nota bene*, in dem so viele, inzwischen legendäre und für die Entwicklung der Kunst der letzten dreissig Jahre entscheidende Ereignisse und Ausstellungen stattgefunden haben. Unabhängig von den in ihnen angelegten Komplexen der Bedeutung, sollen diese Performances in unserem Kontext vor allem beispielhaft für den hohen Grad an Selbstentäusserung und Radikalität in Rütimanns Schaffen stehen.

Die Qualität der Offenheit im Werk dieses Künstlers entspringt einer ungebrochenen, im eigent-

CHRISTOPH RÜTIMANN, DAS SPIEL EINIGER DORNEN IN WACHS, 1988, Installation und Performance mit Kaktus, Mikrophon und Zeichnung auf schwarzgefärbtem, wachsbeschichtetem Papier, Galerie Apropos, Luzern / THE PLAY OF A FEW SPINES IN WAX, installation and performance with cactus, microphone and sheets of paper coated with a layer of blackened wax. (PHOTOS: MARKUS STEINEGGER)

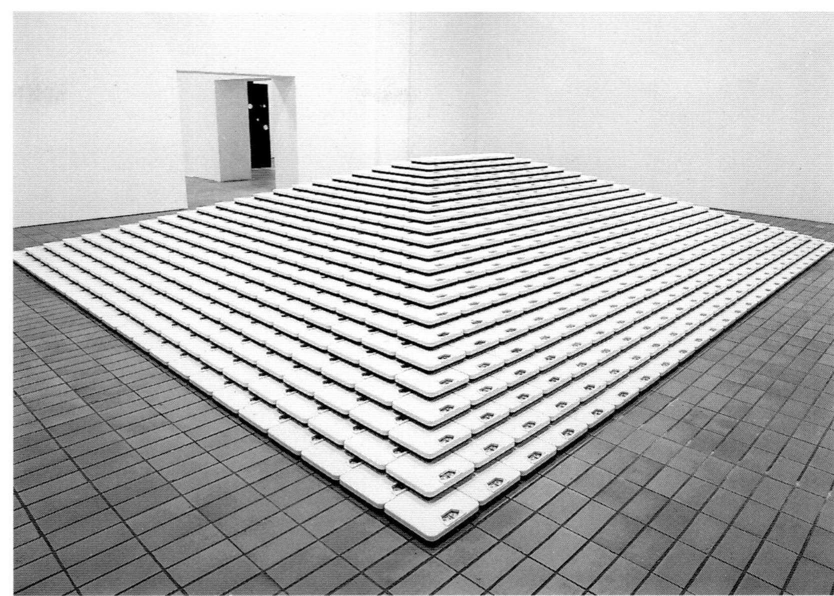

arbeitet Rütimann immer souverän gegen den Strich und setzt die dabei entstehenden Reibungsverluste ganz selbstverständlich in Produktionsenergie um: Er verfolgt sein Ziel nach der Methode von *trial and error*, geht auf die bei der Arbeit auftretenden Attraktionen ein und kommt so über verschwenderische, nicht selten ins Masslose tendierende Abschweifungen immer wieder zu Formulierungen, die am Anfang des Arbeitsprozesses in dieser Art nicht abzusehen waren. Anders gesagt, Rütimann ist nicht nur ein grosser Liebhaber von Chaostheorien, sondern auch ein Besessener des Zufalls.

Die grundsätzliche Dynamik dieses Schaffens lässt sich sehr schön am stets wachsenden Korpus der Tuschezeichnungen ablesen. Es sind Blätter, auf denen das Phänomen der Bewegung im eigentlichen Sinne zur Darstellung kommt. Allerdings nicht als konventioneller Bildgegenstand, sondern als Ausfluss des zeichnerischen Aktes selbst, wobei dieser durch die Verwendung eines ganzen Spektrums von herkömmlichen, selbstkonstruierten und gefundenen Zeicheninstrumenten unmissverständlich Aufzeichnungscharakter hat. Diese Art von Zeichnung ist zwar ein Bild, zeigt jedoch in erster Linie die Spuren ihrer Entstehung in einem «aktionistischen» Sinne, so dass die Lineaturen und die Verdichtungen, die Stellen höchster Dramatik und der Entspannung wiederum im Sinne einer Partitur zu lesen sind – oder, weniger missverständlich, im Sinne einer Kartographie. In beiden Fällen ist eine über die eigentliche Zeichnung hinausweisende Dimension angesprochen, die den Betrachtern eine aktive Mitarbeit oder Interpretation abverlangt. Lesen muss sein. Auf den Künstler bezogen, tendiert diese Art von Zeichnung unausweichlich nach Ausdehnung – zuerst im Format, dann in andere Medien und schliesslich in den realen Raum.

Früher pflegte Rütimann den Wirkungsbereich der Zeichnung häufig dahingehend zu erweitern, dass er sie konkret als Partitur interpretierte und mit einem bizarren Instrumentarium als Klang realisierte. Daneben gab es aber immer auch die Einbindung oder Ausweitung der Zeichnung in den Raum, indem er sie in installative Situationen integrierte und schliesslich indem er die Zeichnung recht eigentlich materialisierte – 1991, zum Beispiel, in Form von riesigen Kunstharzplatten, die nun selbst direkt raumkonstituierende Elemente bildeten.

Doch seit 1987 begegnen wir der Zeichnung in unterschiedlichen Kontexten vor allem auch in der speziellen Form der GROSSEN LINIE: Es ist dies eine in einem Zug über viele Blätter gezogene Gerade. Ihre «klassische» Fassung schuf Rütimann 1989 für seine Ausstellung in der Shedhalle Zürich, wo sie sich mit einer Gesamtlänge von 46,69 Metern auf Augenhöhe den Wänden entlang zog, gebrochen und rhythmisiert durch die notwendige Stückelung in 72 einzeln gerahmte Blätter, wodurch nicht zuletzt ihre Ungerichtetheit unterstrichen wurde. Die Länge ergab sich aus der gegebenen Raumsituation, liess sich aber auch als Anspielung auf Mitchell Feigenbaums Chaoskonstante lesen und eröffnete so den Zugang zu einem Denkhintergrund. Die Linie dehnte sich wie ein Horizont, wie eine äussere Begrenzung über den Ausstellungsraum aus und markierte die Ränder der Sichtbarkeit, während durch diese Assoziation eines Horizonts der Raum sich gleichzeitig auf eine umfassendere Raumvorstellung hin öffnete. Das andere Element der Ausstellung bildete die hier erstmals präsentierte ENDLOSE LINIE, eine in sich geschlossene Kurve aus Stahlrohr, die gleichzeitig den Raumkörper eines Würfels und einer Kugel umschreibt. Hier also eine Skulptur, die als Zeichnung im Raum aufzufassen, dort eine Zeichnung, die auch räumlich zu verstehen war.

Der zeichnerische und skulpturale Charakter der «Linie» und die in ihr angelegte Tendenz nach massloser Ausdehnung erlauben es nur bedingt, diesen Komplex als geschlossenes Werk zu interpretieren. Die «Linie» muss sich in jeder Installation neu formulieren und ihre auf den Raum bezogene Gestalt finden. So wird sie zu einem sich stets ausweitenden Thema, das gleichzeitig als Material und Instrument künftiger Arbeiten funktioniert, so dass jede Ausstellungssituation zu einer Herausforderung wird, die Fragestellung zu radikalisieren und neue Aspekte aufzuzeigen, nicht zuletzt natürlich, um die bisher formulierten Positionen zu relativieren. So dringt die zeichnerische «Linie» in gewaltige Folianten ein, manifestiert sich in Form von bedruckten Papierstapeln als Block oder erscheint als Videodirektübertragung auf einem Monitor, während die skulpturale «Linie» vor allem in architektonischen Kontexten weiter untersucht wird. Hier ist vor allem das Projekt KRAFTSTRASSE 35 (1992) zu nennen, in dessen Verlauf Rütimann die «Linie» in ihrer Kurvenform in einer leerstehenden viergeschossigen Villa installier-

te. Mit Computeranimation waren zuerst die ideale und statisch tragbare Lage der Figur innerhalb der Architektur, dann die zu durchstossenden Punkte zu bestimmen, bevor die Stahlrohre schliesslich zu einer irrwitzigen Konstellation montiert werden konnten. In die Realität der Architektur integriert, wurde die Geschlossenheit der «Linie» gebrochen und in Teilansichten aufgelöst, so dass ihre Wahrnehmung in einen Prozess der Imagination verwandelt wurde.

In jüngster Zeit sind wir der GROSSEN LINIE oft im Zusammenhang mit dem seit 1991 auftretenden Werkkomplex der «Schiefen Ebenen» begegnet, wo sie plötzlich auch als eine Art von Richtschnur funktionierte. Die «schiefe Ebene» erscheint meistens als Eckstück und ist in ihrer skulpturalen Masslichkeit immer auf den gegebenen Raum bezogen. Auf den ersten Blick erscheint sie wie ein weites, abgehobenes Feld der Anschauung, das auf herrliche Weise das Licht moduliert, es in einem fast malerischen Sinne in den Raum einfliessen oder abstrahlen lässt, dann wirkt sie aber auch als visueller Angriff auf die übliche, «rechtwinklige» Wahrnehmung des Raumes, indem sie diesen aus dem Gleichgewicht bringt. Man denke etwa an die imposant hochgezogene schiefe Ebene der INSTALLATION MIT SCHIEFER EBENE UND MALEREI in der Barockkirche San Staë in Venedig, anlässlich der Biennale 1993, oder an die riesige weite Schiefe der INSTALLATION MIT SCHIEFER EBENE UND WAAGENVORHANG (1993) in der Unermesslichkeit des Hauptraums im Musée d'art contemporain in Bordeaux. Das waren souveräne Eingriffe in bestehende Räume von ausgeprägtem Eigencharakter; skulpturale Werke, die in ihrer Abgeklärtheit auf den ersten Blick wie eine Form von Minimal Art wirkten. Doch das Raumerlebnis selbst vermittelt den Eindruck, hier werde nicht nur ein Werk als solches gezeigt, sondern vielmehr ein Raum ausgehebelt und dadurch ein Prozess unmittelbarer Erfahrungen in Gang gesetzt – ein Schwindel der Gefühle und der Gedanken, eine latente Verwirrung. Die in Bordeaux am einen Ende der schiefen Ebene vertikal verspannten Waagenketten verdeutlichen zudem, dass hinter allem auch ein physikalisches Gedankenspiel steckt, insofern als die schiefe Ebene die Wirkung und vor allem die Wahrnehmung der mechanischen

Kräfte verändert. Die dabei thematisierte Gravitation als elementare Kraft, als eine Gerichtetheit, die unsere Weltwirklichkeit und unser tägliches Leben sehr nachdrücklich bestimmt, erscheint mehr oder weniger offenkundig als ein Leitmotiv in Rütimanns Schaffen, selbstverständlich nicht als Vorwand zur Illustration, sondern als Denkmodell und Feld der Praxis. Das Korpus der schiefen Ebenen steht darum auch in enger Nachbarschaft zu seinen weitverzweigten Arbeiten mit «Waagen», denn schliesslich kann eine Briefwaage, so hat er uns 1991 gezeigt, auf einer schiefen Ebene auch ohne sichtbare Belastung 50 GRAMM FÜR EINEN KUNSTVEREIN anzeigen.

Mit Waagen arbeiten heisst messen und impliziert Präzision. So ist die Waage auch das ideale Gerät, um die Relativität der Genauigkeit aufzuzeigen. Gemessen wird die unsichtbare Kraft, mit der die Schwere der Dinge auf die unmittelbare Umgebung einwirkt. Also geht es hier jenseits aller Metaphorik um das Gewicht der Welt. Das zeigt sich besonders schön in den Waagen-Skulpturen, in denen einerseits das Wesen der Skulptur selbst reflektiert und gleichzeitig

die Funktion des Wägens in paradoxer Weise auf den Kopf gestellt wird. Es ist klar, dass Waagen eine denkbar schlechte statische Qualität haben, aber man muss es gesehen haben. Die ihnen notwendig eigene Empfindlichkeit macht sie zu «Schwimmkörpern», die zum Beispiel dem Aufbau einer Pyramide von Waagen sehr schnell Grenzen setzen. Rütimanns WAAGEN-PYRAMIDEN sind darum – gegen den Anschein – ziemlich schwebende Unterfangen. Das lässt mich an die Malerei denken, die für ihn wesentlich in der Organisation von Farbe auf einer Fläche oder im Raum besteht. In früheren Jahren floss dieses malerische Anliegen vielleicht am deutlichsten in seine Photographie ein. In den letzten Jahren erscheint es vor allem in Form von grossen und schweren, monochromen Hinterglasmalereien, wie zum Beispiel in den mächtigen Glasplatten der Installation in Venedig, die trotz ihrer skulpturalen Präsenz die Farbe schier schwerelos als reine Wirkung ins Spiel bringen. Sehr unmittelbar – und doch reflektiert.

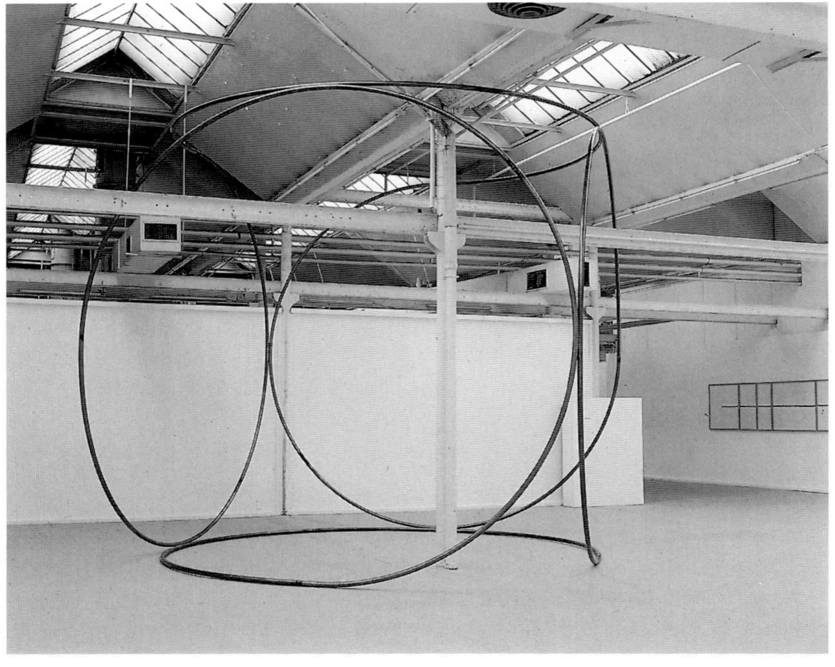

CHRISTOPH RÜTIMANN,
DIE ENDLOSE LINIE, 1989,
im Hintergrund rechts
DIE GROSSE LINIE, 46,69 m,
Shedhalle Zürich /
ENDLESS LINE and
(on the background wall)
BIG LINE, 153.18'.
(PHOTO: WERNER GRAF)

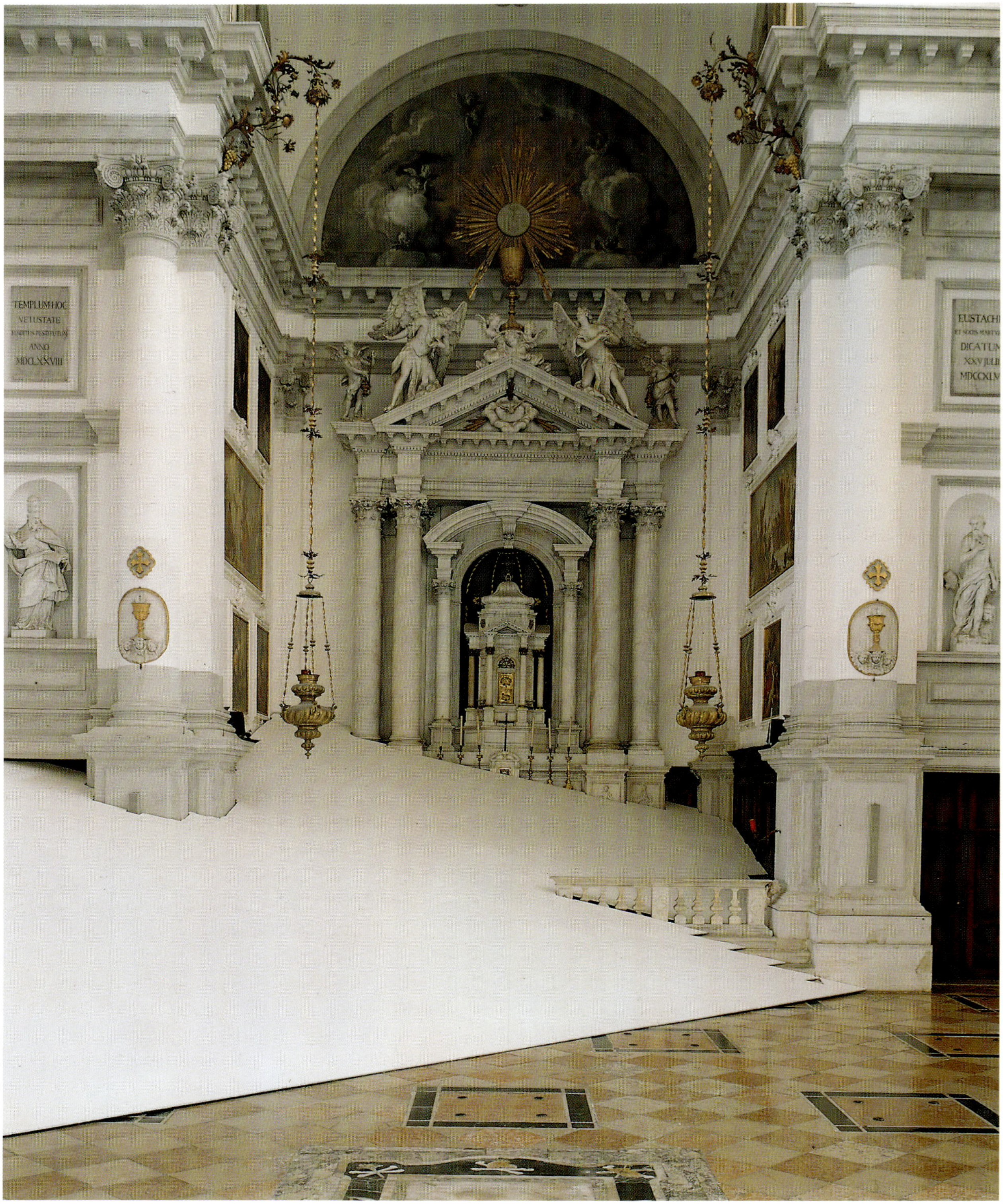

CHRISTOPH RÜTIMANN, SCHIEFE EBENE, San Staë, Biennale Venedig, 1993 / SLANTED PLANE, San Staë, Venice Biennial 1993. (PHOTO: GIACOMELLI)

Juggling with Gravity

MAX WECHSLER

ON THE ART OF CHRISTOPH RÜTIMANN

A study of Christoph Rütimann's art must begin with the performance, a form of expression that has always been central to his artistic approach. It is an ideal vehicle for the hybrid, ambiguous nature of an oeuvre that embraces a wide range of disciplines, materials, and media—from pen and ink to video, from the installation to the painting. Feelings run hot and cold when faced with works that incorporate the most unlikely elements of form and content on a more or less equal and equally daring basis. But it certainly does not follow that the work is imprecise. On the contrary, Rütimann challenges uncertainty; he surrenders to the fall without crashing.

THE PLAY OF A FEW SPINES IN WAX (A RECORDING) (1988) strikingly illustrates the double-bottomed ambiguity of the artist's approach. He was seen, through the large picture window of the gallery, sitting on a chair with a cactus placed on a stand in front of him. A microphone suspended from the ceiling above the cactus registered the sounds made when pieces of paper, coated with a layer of blackened wax, were scratched by the spines. In this way, Rütimann created sheet upon sheet of spidery white drawings on the soft black surface, which then filled the walls of the gallery, ultimately producing an exhibition. This was only one aspect of the perform-ance, however, for in the act of drawing he enticed startling rhythms and sounds out of the cactus, filling the space with aural equivalents to the drawings. The mutual contingency of drawing and sound in this poetic act was perfectly natural—the music in the making produced its own score, and the duration of drawing, watching, and listening conjoined to form a holistically interwoven web of perception. When the results are subsequently viewed as autonomous drawings, their lines and hatching, that is, the concrete traces of the music made by damaging the dark surface, still testify to the active origins of the work. Just as the print of an engraving refers to the concrete reality of the copperplate, Rütimann's drawing refers to the simultaneous concert of drawing and the drafted record of a concert.

ESPRIT D'ESCALIER (1991) is entirely different. Presented at a Duchamp Symposium in Amsterdam, this *tableau vivant* consisted of a glassed off exhibition space showing the naked artist lying upside down on truncated stairs, like a "fallen angel," and flanked by a mighty plowshare. A striking homage to Marcel Duchamp, but above all a reflection on artistic endeavor and the life of the artist. These concerns found even more pointed, but no less controlled and concentrated expression in a performance three years later: HANGING FROM THE MUSEUM (1994). On a cold December evening, Rütimann had himself suspended over a five-story abyss from a moving

MAX WECHSLER is an art critic and lecturer at the School of Art and Design in Lucerne.

crane of his own design that he had installed on top of the flat-roofed art museum in Lucerne. The crane transported him with excruciating slowness around the circumference of the museum, or more specifically around a building facing demolition that has hosted untold, now legendary exhibitions and events of far-reaching influence on artistic developments over the past thirty years. Apart from the complex of meaning inherent in these performances, they here serve to illustrate the extreme renunciation and radicalism of Rütimann's oeuvre.

The quality of openness that marks his work springs from an unbroken, experimentally motivated curiosity, coupled with a delight in exploring the specific properties of materials and the ordering principles that govern systems. Rütimann's projects always entail a daring investigation of how materials behave and how things react under the special conditions to which he subjects them. The result in terms of both content and materials has a near-scientific touch to it although the artist consistently adheres to the theory

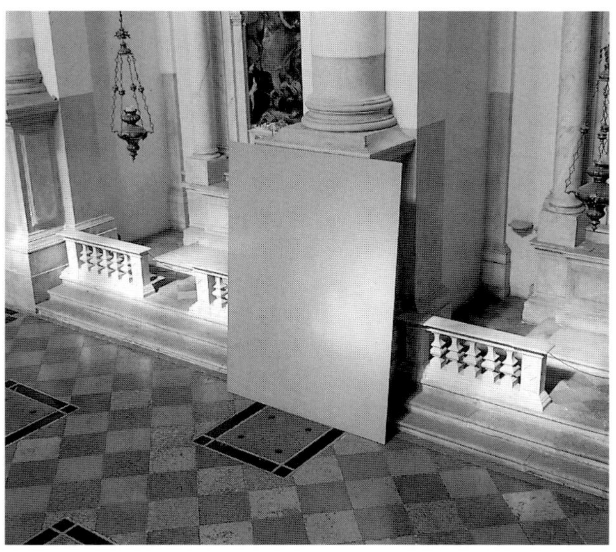

CHRISTOPH RÜTIMANN, HINTERGLASMALEREI, Teil der INSTALLATION MIT SCHIEFER EBENE UND MALEREI, San Staë, Biennale 1993, Venedig, 250 x 320 cm / GLASS PAINTING, part of the INSTALLATION WITH SLANTED PLANE AND GLASS PAINTINGS, San Staë, Venice Biennial 1993, 8' 2⅜" x 10' 6". (PHOTO: GIACOMELLI)

and practice of everyday life. The earnestness of the game dominates in conjunction with a practical philosophy of life. Thus certain groups of work pit the imponderables of everyday life against the ideal systems (of debatable cogency anyway since the rise of quantum theory) of the natural sciences or of art. Rütimann works against the grain with consummate skill and quite naturally converts the losses caused by the resulting friction into the energy of production: that is, he pursues his goals by trial and error; he succumbs to attractions that emerge during the work process, often leading to extravagant detours and entirely unanticipated formulations. To put it differently, Rütimann is not only a great lover of chaos theory but also obsessed with chance.

A growing body of pen-and-ink drawings aptly illustrates the basic dynamic of this oeuvre. The drawings represent the phenomenon of motion incarnate; motion is not treated as conventional subject matter but flows out of the very act of drawing, whereby the use of a wide spectrum of traditional, self-made, and found tools unmistakably points to the act of keeping records. Although the works produced by this mode of drawing are indeed pictures, their primary impact lies in showing the "aktionist" traces of their making, so that linear and dense areas, regions of intense drama and relaxation may again be read as a kind of score or, to be more precise, as cartography. In both cases a dimension is addressed that reaches beyond the drawing itself and exacts the viewer's active collaboration or interpretation. Nothing is unless it is read. In terms of the artist, this kind of drawing inevitably gravitates toward extension—first in format, then into other media, and finally into real space.

Rütimann used to extend the effect of his drawings by literally reading them as scores and "playing" them with a bizarre instrumentarium. In addition he would involve or expand the drawings in space by incorporating them in installations or actually materializing them—in 1991, for instance, in the form of gigantic polyester panels that became constitutive elements of the space. Since 1987, however, we encounter the drawing in a variety of contexts, especially in the form of the BIG LINE: an uninterrupted straight line drawn across a number of pages. The "classical" version, created in 1989 for the Zurich Shedhalle, stretched along the wall at eye level for a length of 153.18 feet, broken and articulated by the necessary subdivision into 72 individually framed sheets of paper. This actually served to underscore the undirected orientation of the line. Although defined by the givens of the space, the length may also be interpreted as alluding to Mitchell Feigenbaum's chaos constant, thereby providing access to theoretical underpinnings. Spread out like a horizon, like an external boundary beyond the exhibition space, the line marked the edges of visibility, while at the same time opening the space itself to a more comprehensive idea of space per se through the associative idea of a horizon. The other element in the exhibition was the ENDLESS LINE, a configuration made of steel tubing that circumscribes a sphere within an imaginary cube in space. The latter is a sculpture that functions like a drawing in space; the former a drawing that has acquired volume.

The drawn and sculpted character of the "line" and its implications of immeasurable extension counteract the notion of a work that is complete and self-contained. The "line" must be reformulated and its shape adapted to the respective space in each new installation. It becomes a steadily expanding issue that operates both as the material and the instrument of future works, so that each successive exhibition provokes a more radical approach and the representation of new aspects—naturally undermining previous positions. Thus the drawn "line" penetrates weighty tomes, takes the shape of stacks of printed notepaper, or appears as a direct video presentation, while the sculptural "line" has been explored primarily in architectural contexts. Noteworthy in this respect is the artist's 1992 project, KRAFTSTRASSE 35. Rütimann installed the "line" in an uninhabited four-story residence. With the help of computer animation, he determined the statically ideal position of the configuration and the points where holes had to be drilled in order to insert the phantasmagoric shape. Integrated into the reality of the building, the uninterrupted flow of the line was broken down into partial views so that the perception of the whole was transmuted into a feat of the imagination.

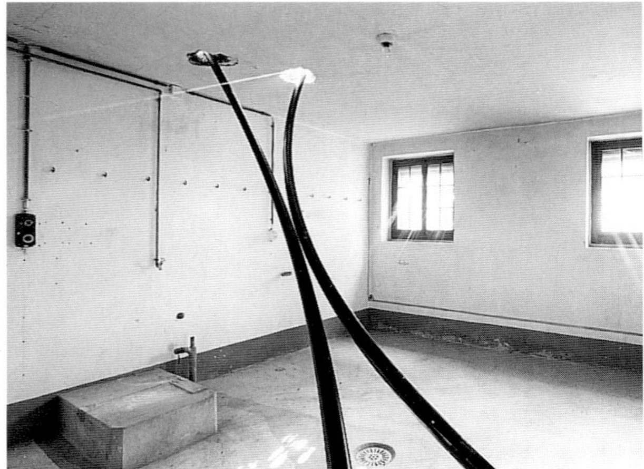

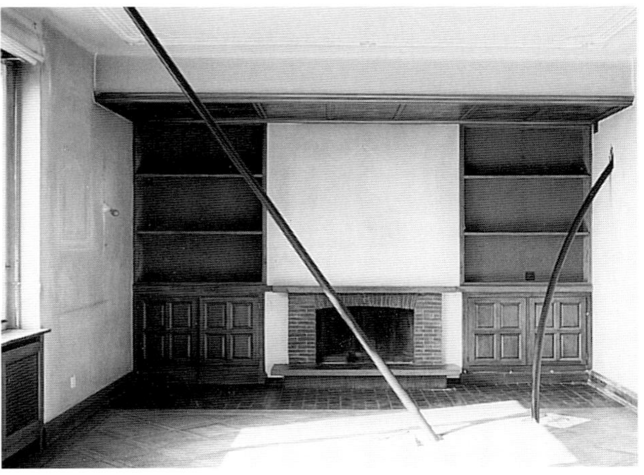

CHRISTOPH RÜTIMANN, KRAFTSTRASSE 35, 1992,
Installation mit endloser Linie durch 22 Zimmer, Stahlrohr /
installation with endless line leading through 22 rooms, tubular steel.
(PHOTO: CHRISTOPH RÜTIMANN, GALERIE MAI 36, ZÜRICH)

More recently the BIG LINE has frequently cropped up in connection with the "slanted planes," which made their first appearance in 1991. Suddenly it began functioning as a kind of guideline. The "slanted planes" are usually corner pieces whose sculptural mass responds to the parameters of the given space. At first sight they look like broad, detached fields of perception that exquisitely modulate the lighting, allowing it to flow into the space or bounce off it with almost painterly effect. But they also visually assault the conventionally right-angled perception of a space by throwing it off kilter.

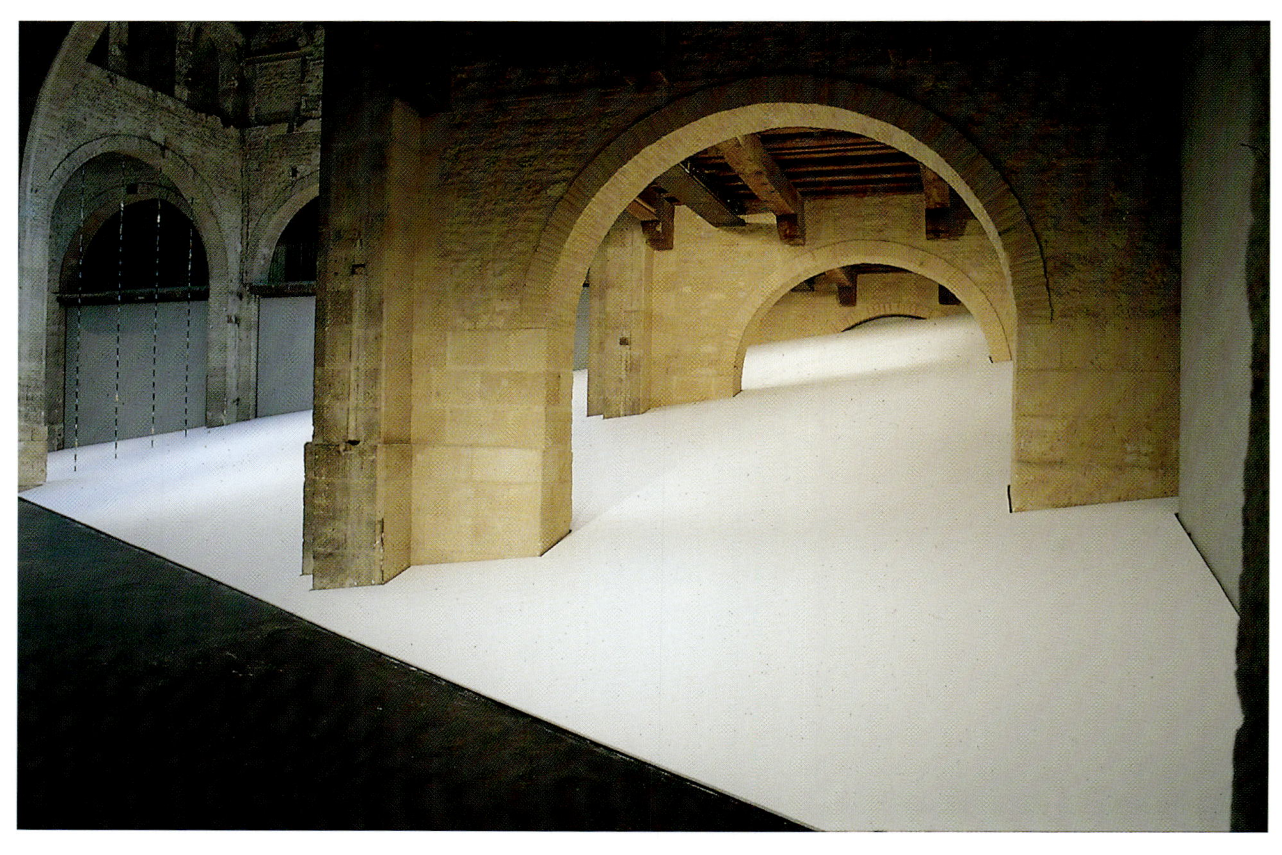

CHRISTOPH RÜTIMANN, INSTALLATION MIT SCHIEFER EBENE UND WAAGENVORHANG, 1993,
CAPC Musée d'art contemporain, Bordeaux /
INSTALLATION WITH SLANTED PLANE AND CURTAIN OF SCALES.
(PHOTO: CHRISTOPH RÜTIMANN)

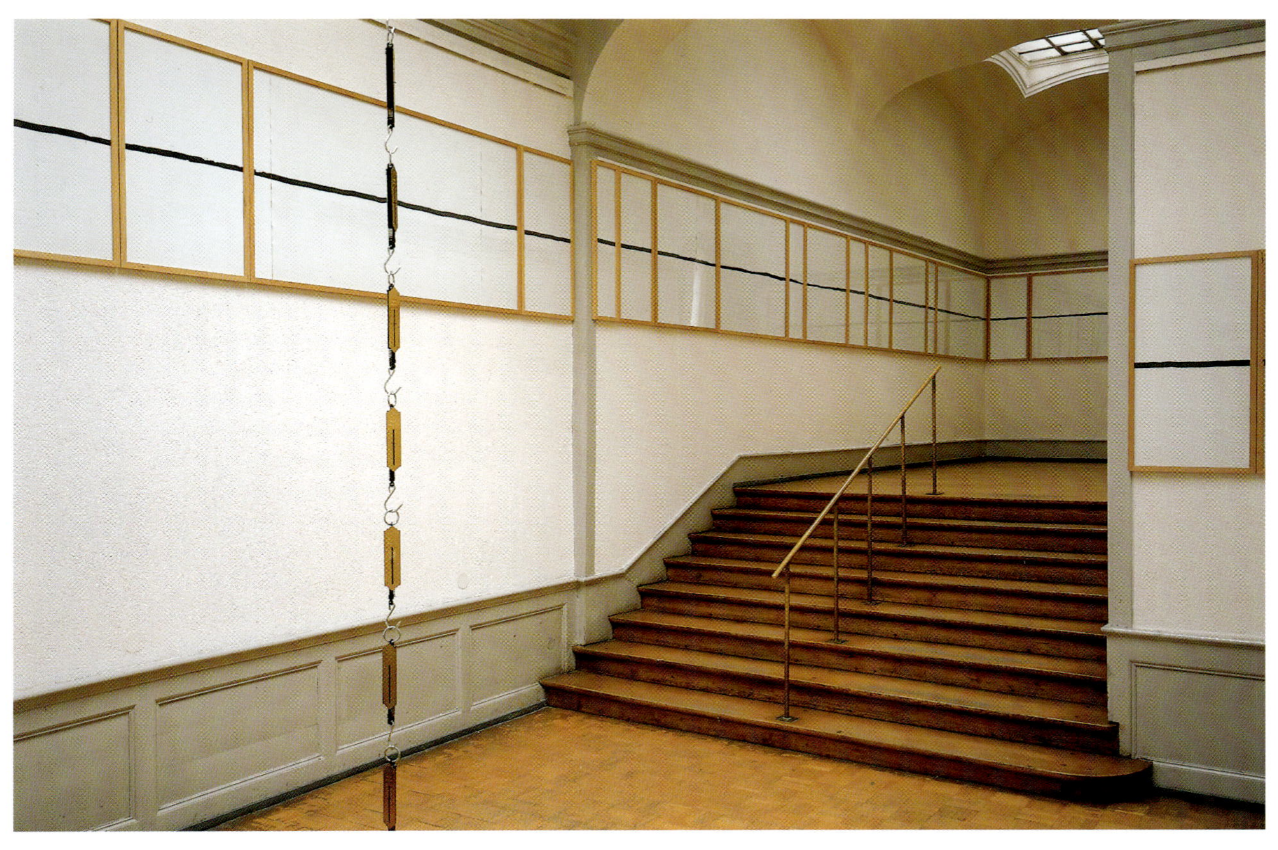

CHRISTOPH RÜTIMANN, INSTALLATION MIT GROSSER LINIE UND WAAGENKETTE, 1990,
Badischer Kunstverein, Karlsruhe /
INSTALLATION WITH BIG LINE AND CHAIN OF SCALES.
(PHOTO: CHRISTOPH RÜTIMANN)

Impressive examples are the monumental, vertically oriented INSTALLATION WITH SLANTED PLANE AND GLASS PAINTINGS in the Baroque Church of San Staë in Venice (Biennial 1993) and the vast expanse of the "inclination" of the INSTALLATION WITH SLANTED PLANE AND CURTAIN OF SCALES (1993) in the huge main hall of the Musée d'art contemporain in Bordeaux. They were superb interventions in spaces with a distinctive character of their own—sculptural works of a rarefied purity that might strike one as a form of minimalism. On second sight, the space itself conveyed the impression that we are not merely being shown a work as such but that a space has been levered, thereby setting off a process of immediate

A KUNSTVEREIN (1991) when placed on a slanted surface.

Scales weigh things and imply precision; they are eminently suited to demonstrating the relativity of accuracy. When we use them, we measure the invisible force exerted by the gravity of things on their immediate environment. We are confronted here with the weight of the world—quite apart from any metaphorical implications. This is beautifully demonstrated in the "balance" sculptures that reflect the essence of sculpture on one hand, while paradoxically wreaking havoc with the function of weighing. Obviously scales have conspicuously poor static properties, but we must see it to believe it.

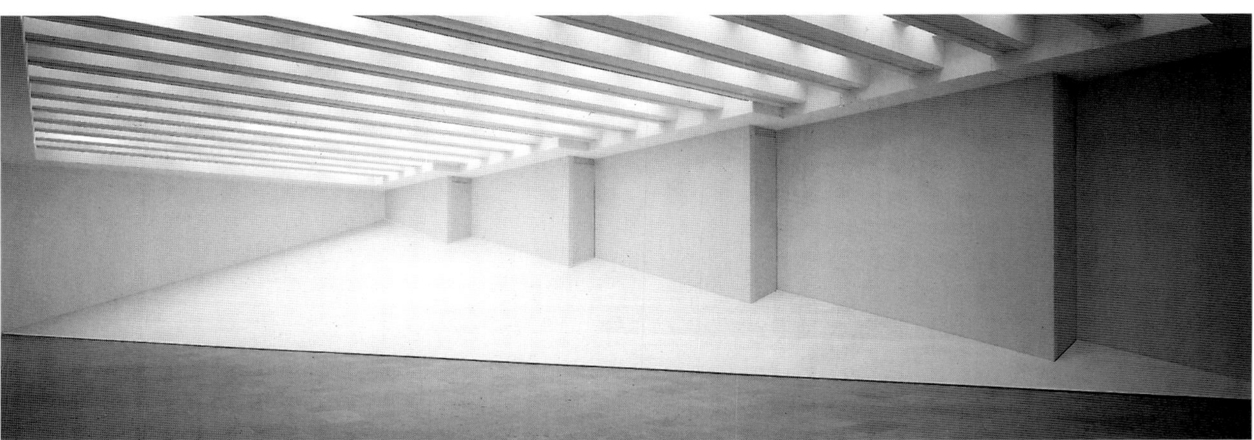

CHRISTOPH RÜTIMANN, SCHIEFE EBENE, 1995, Westfälischer Kunstverein, Münster / SLANTED PLANE. (PHOTO: THOMAS WREDE)

experiences—a vertigo of sensations and thoughts, a latent confusion. Vertically taut chains of scales near one end of the "plane" in Bordeaux reinforced the compelling impression that the artist is toying with the laws of physics since the inclined plane changed the effect and above all our perception of mechanical forces. In fact, gravity as an elementary force, as a vector that incisively conditions our reality and our daily lives, appears as a leitmotif with varying degrees of intensity throughout Rütimann's oeuvre, though obviously not as an excuse for illustration but as a theoretical model and a field of practice. The body of "slanted planes" is thus intimately associated with the artist's ongoing range of works based on "scales." He has, for instance, demonstrated that a letter-balance with nothing on it will read 50 GRAMS FOR

Their necessary sensitivity turns them into "floating bodies" which has its limitations when trying, for instance, to construct a pyramid of scales. Contrary to appearances, Rütimann's PYRAMIDS OF SCALES are therefore rather precarious undertakings. I am reminded of painting, which consists for this artist largely of organizing color on surfaces or in space. In earlier work these painterly concerns were most clearly expressed in photography. In recent years, they take the shape of large and heavy monochrome "paintings behind glass," like the mighty panes of glass in Venice, which bring color into play almost weightlessly, as pure effect, despite their sculptural presence. Extremely visceral—and yet carefully weighed.

(Translation: Catherine Schelbert)

WATERMELON WOMAN: THE FAE RICHARDS PHOTO ARCHIVE

CAST

Fae Richards	Lisa Marie Bronson
Martha Page	Alexandra Juhasz
Oscar	Keylan Bradley
Reba	L. M. Doria Roberts
Josie/Willa Clarke	Fawn McGee
Black Gay man at Party	Jody Benjamin
Fred DeShields	Robert Reid-Pharr
Cassandra Brooke/VanClyde wife	Sara Vogt
Catherine VanClyde	Nora Breen
Bobbi/dyke at HotSpot	Valerie Manenti
Eleanor VanClyde	Anna Blume
Guest	Linda Salerno
Zola Hamilton	Edith Dunye
Hambone Jones	Reggae Griffin
J. Liberty Wells	K. Brent Hill
NAACP/actor in Black Guns	Kenrick Cato
NAACP	Darrell Moore
White actress in Jersey Girls	Carolyn Shapiro
Unidentified friend	Jacqui Bishop
June Walker	Cheryl Clarke
Sandra Vincent	Kristina Deutsch
Black dyke on roof	Cathy McKinley
Black dyke on roof 2	Cheryl Dunye
Woman at opening/woman in audience	Eve Oishi

CREW

Co-Producers	Cheryl Dunye and Zoe Leonard
Executive Producer	Alexandra Juhasz
Co-Directors	Cheryl Dunye and Zoe Leonard
Photographer	Zoe Leonard
Photo Assistant	Kimberly Peirce
Wardrobe	Alison Froling, Sara Vogt
Make-up/Hair	Luciana Moreira, Lily Marnell
Grip	Claudine Benoit, Chris Daniels
Props	Julia Zay, Zoe Bissell
Set	Zoe Bissell, Lily Marnell
Production Coordinator	Petra Janopaul, Shu Hung
Production Assistant	Charlene Gilbert
On-set Still Photography	Amy Steiner, Valery Casey
	Erica Freudenstein
Darkroom	Zoe Leonard, Vivian Selbo, Ann Ruark
	Jack Louth, Elaine Portier, Amy Steiner
	Diana Morrow, Liss Platt, Elizabeth Griggs

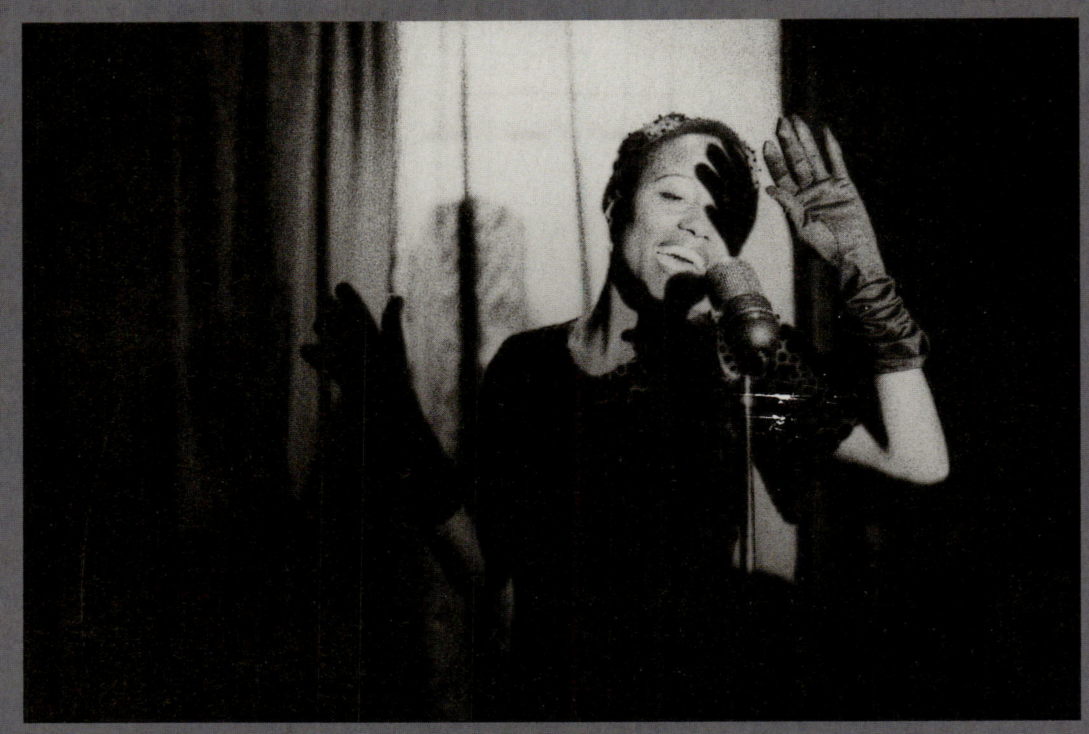

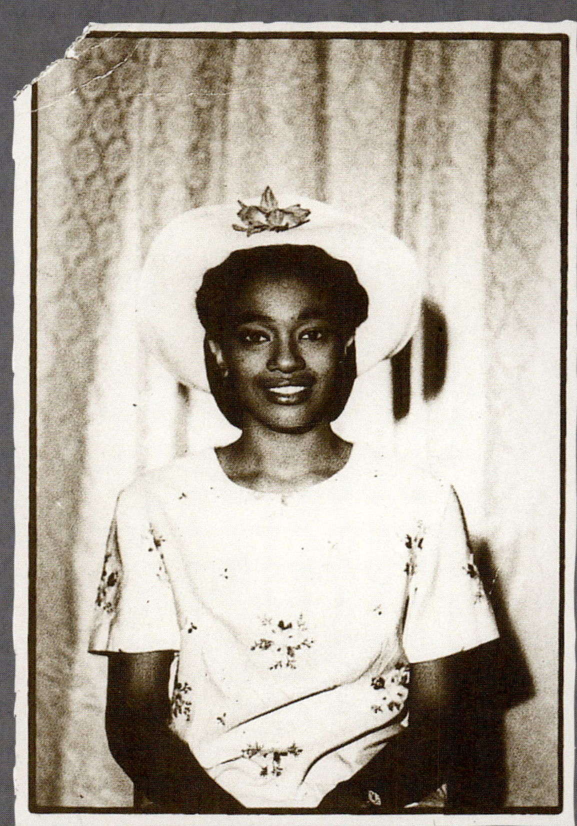

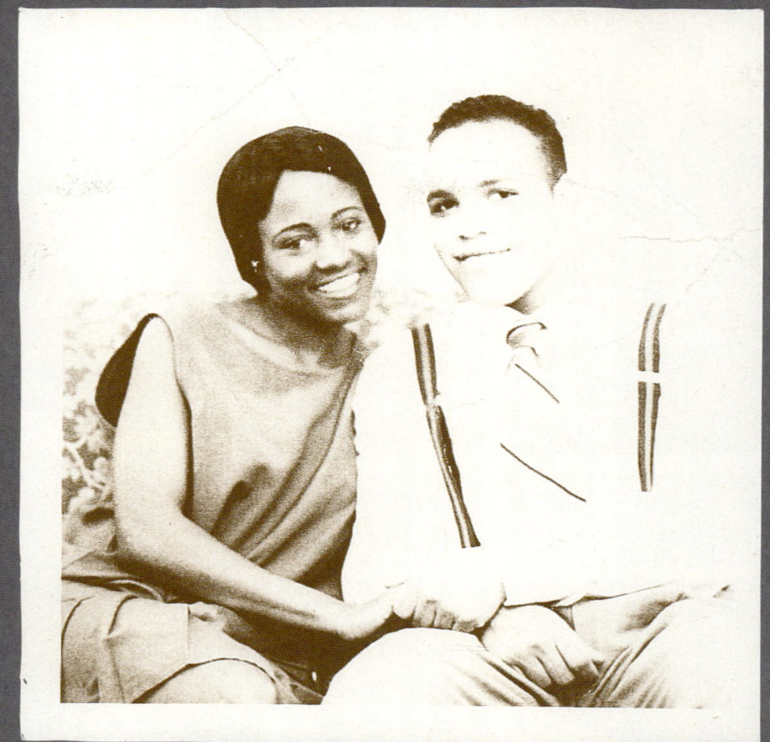

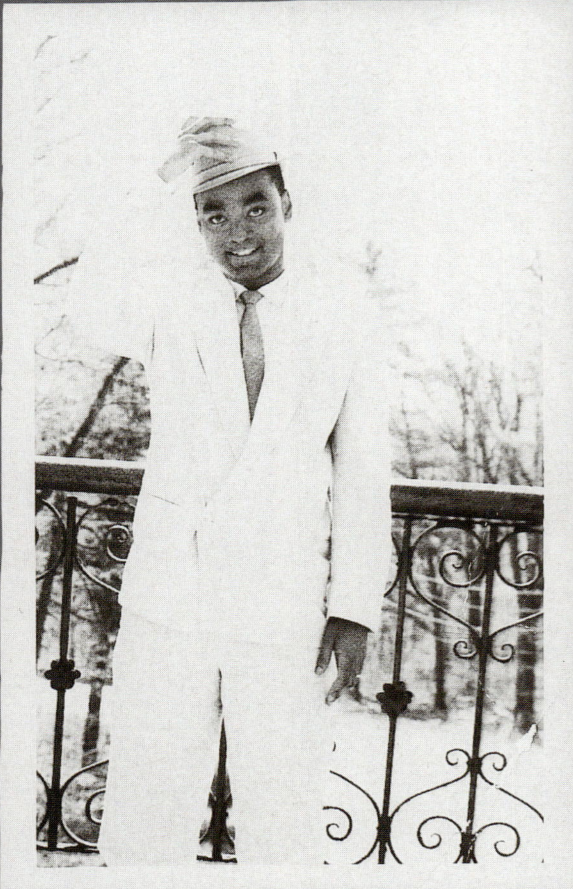

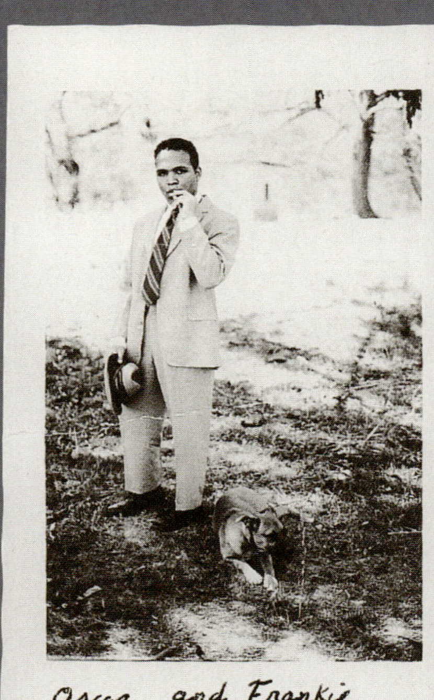

Oscar and Frankie

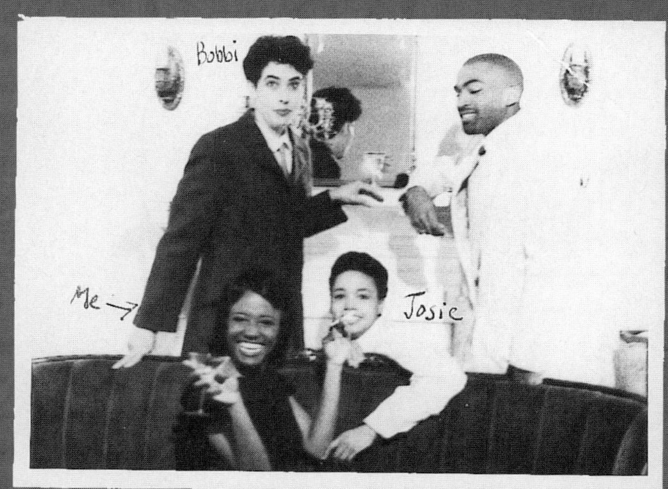
Bobbi
Me→
Josie

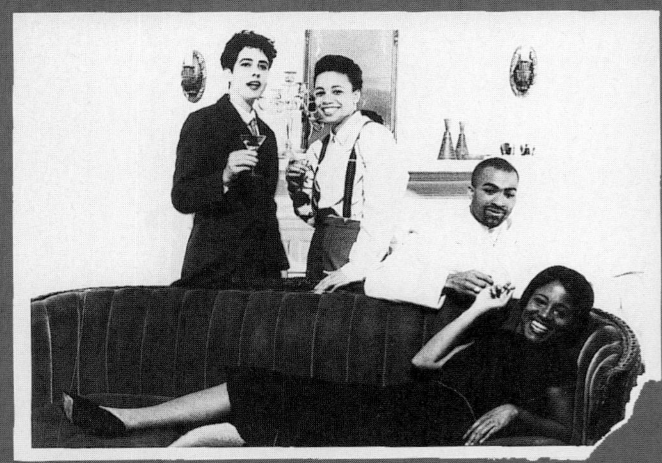

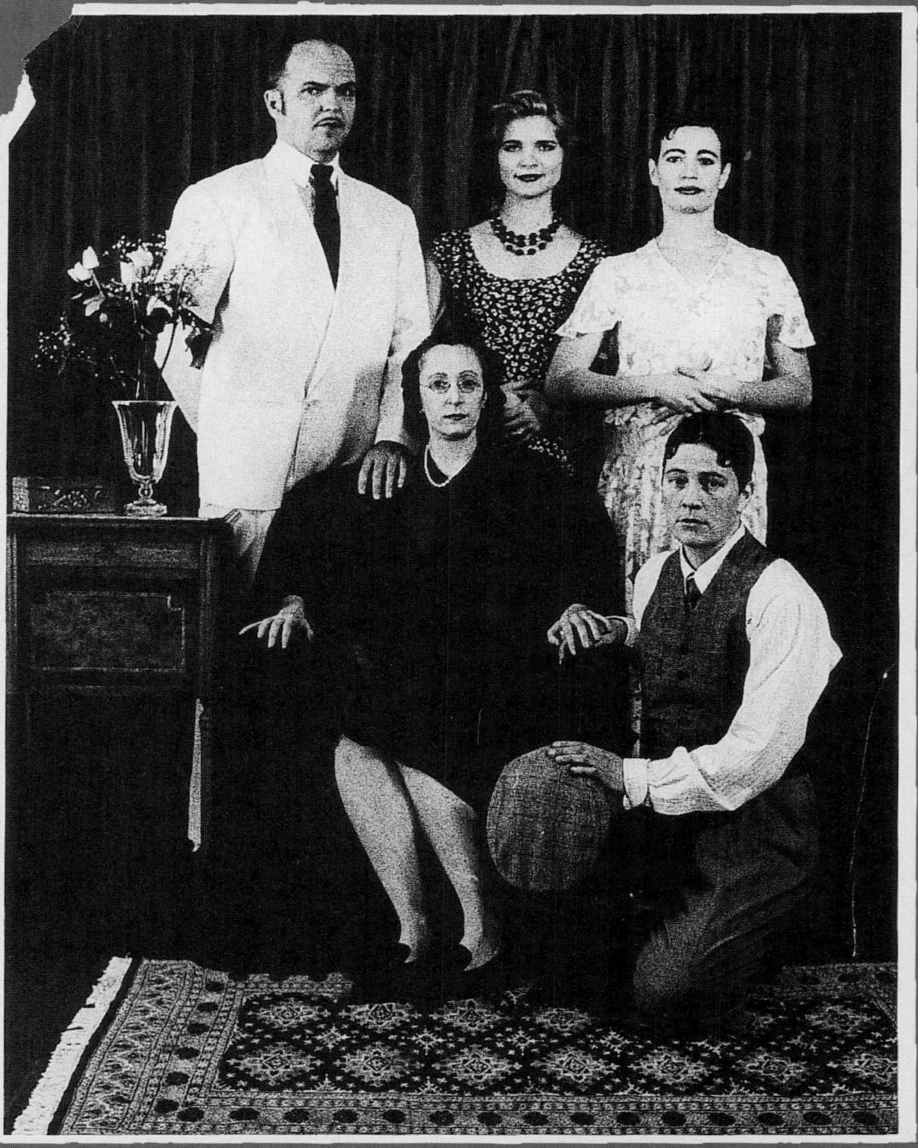

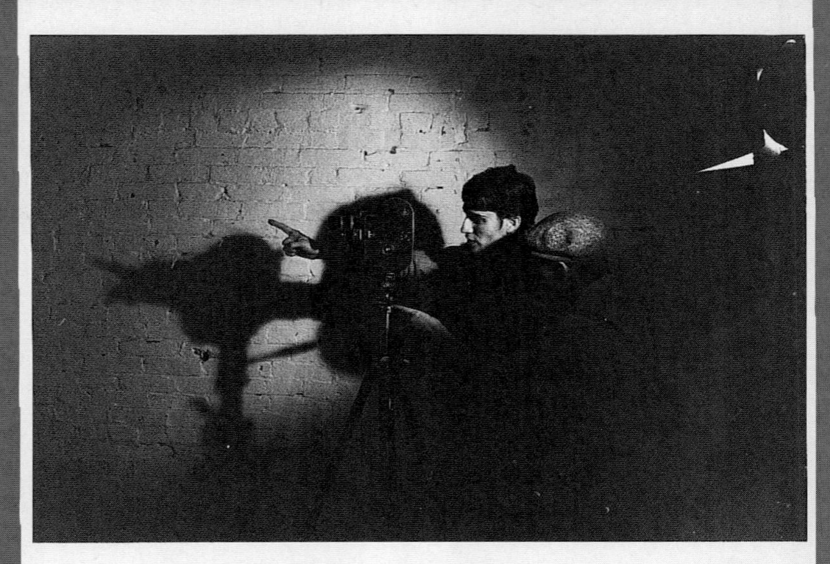

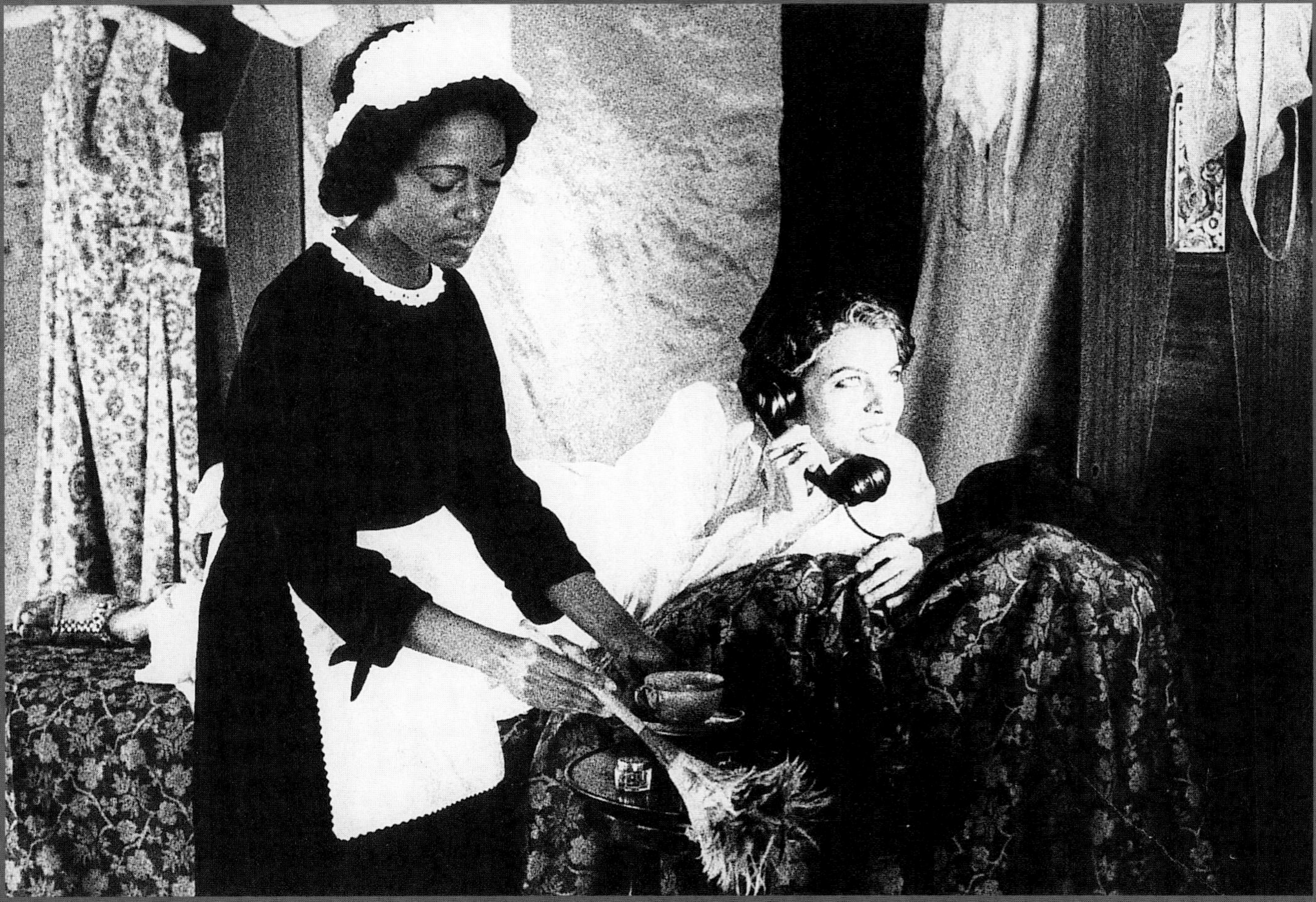

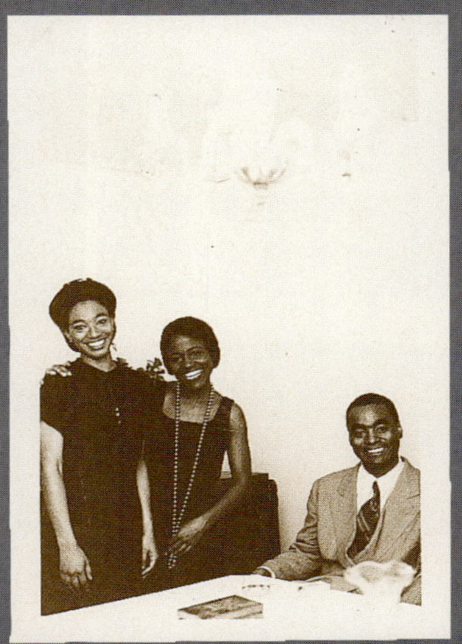

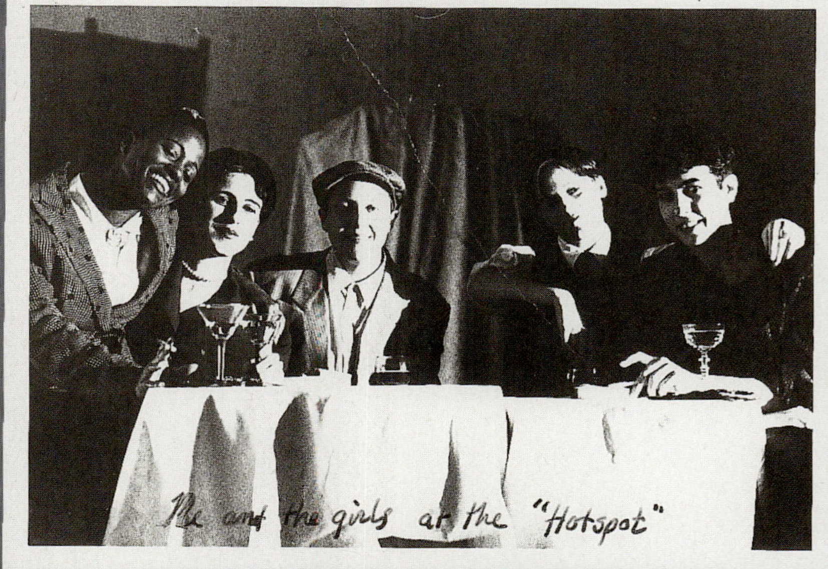
Me and the girls at the "Hotspot"

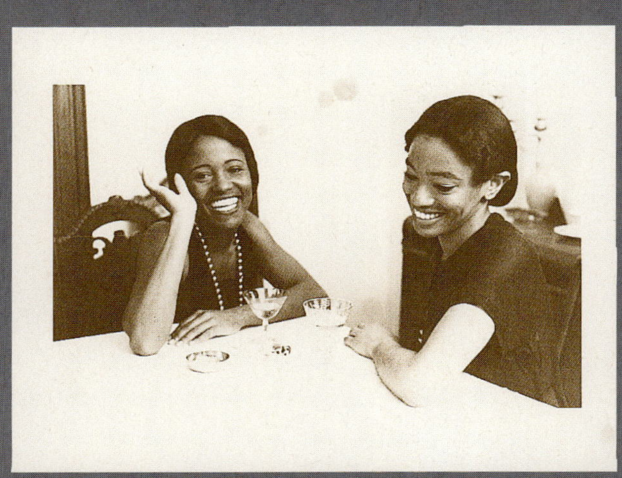

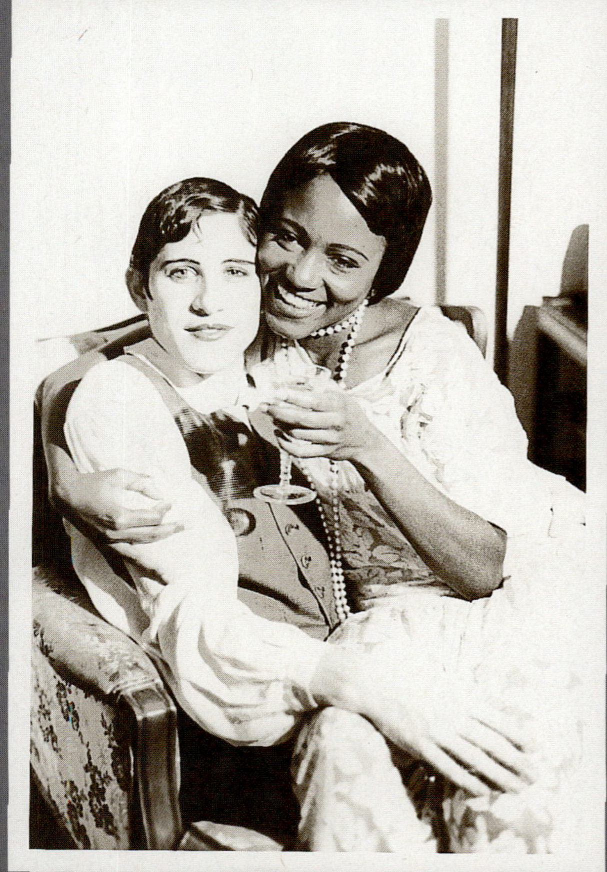

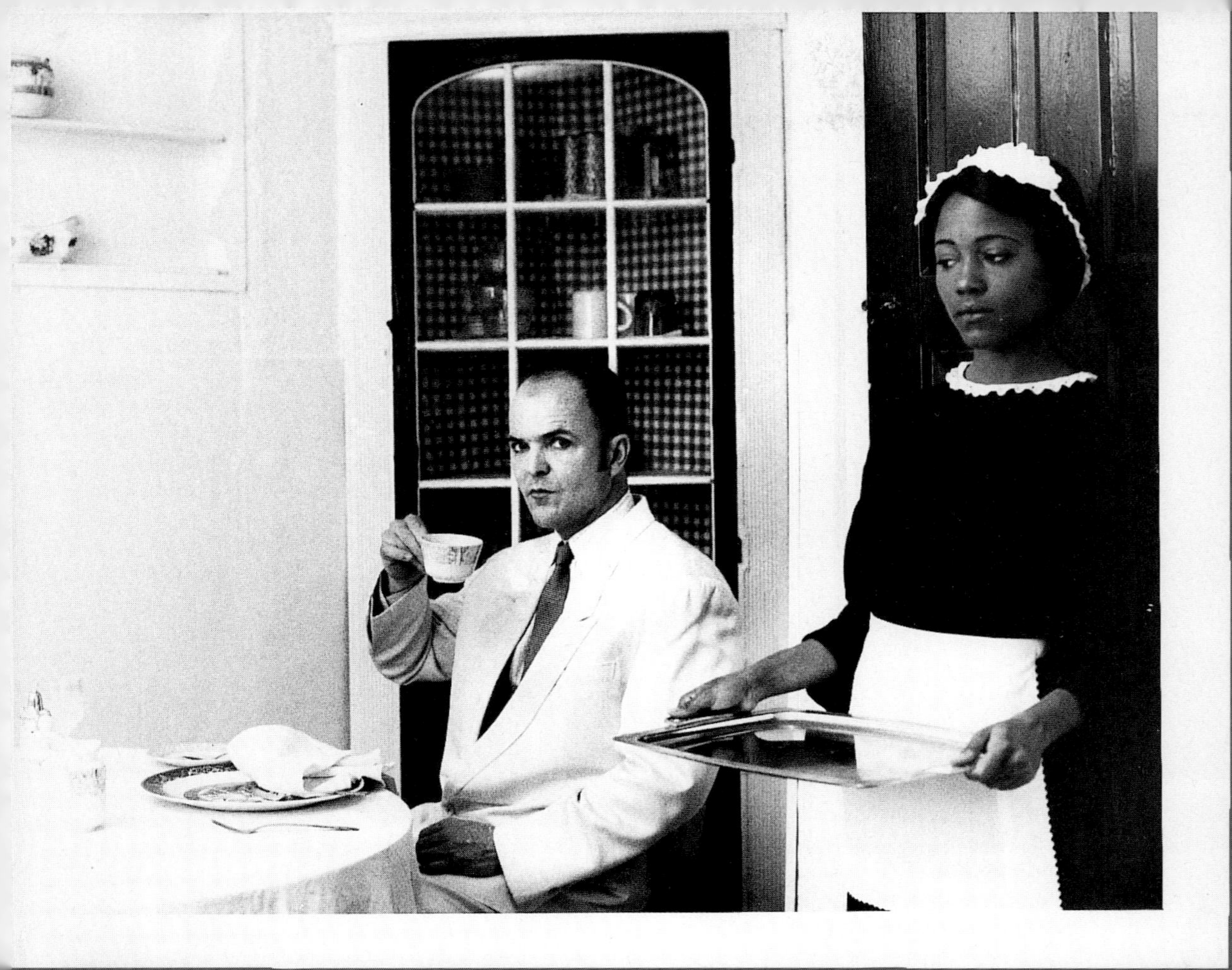

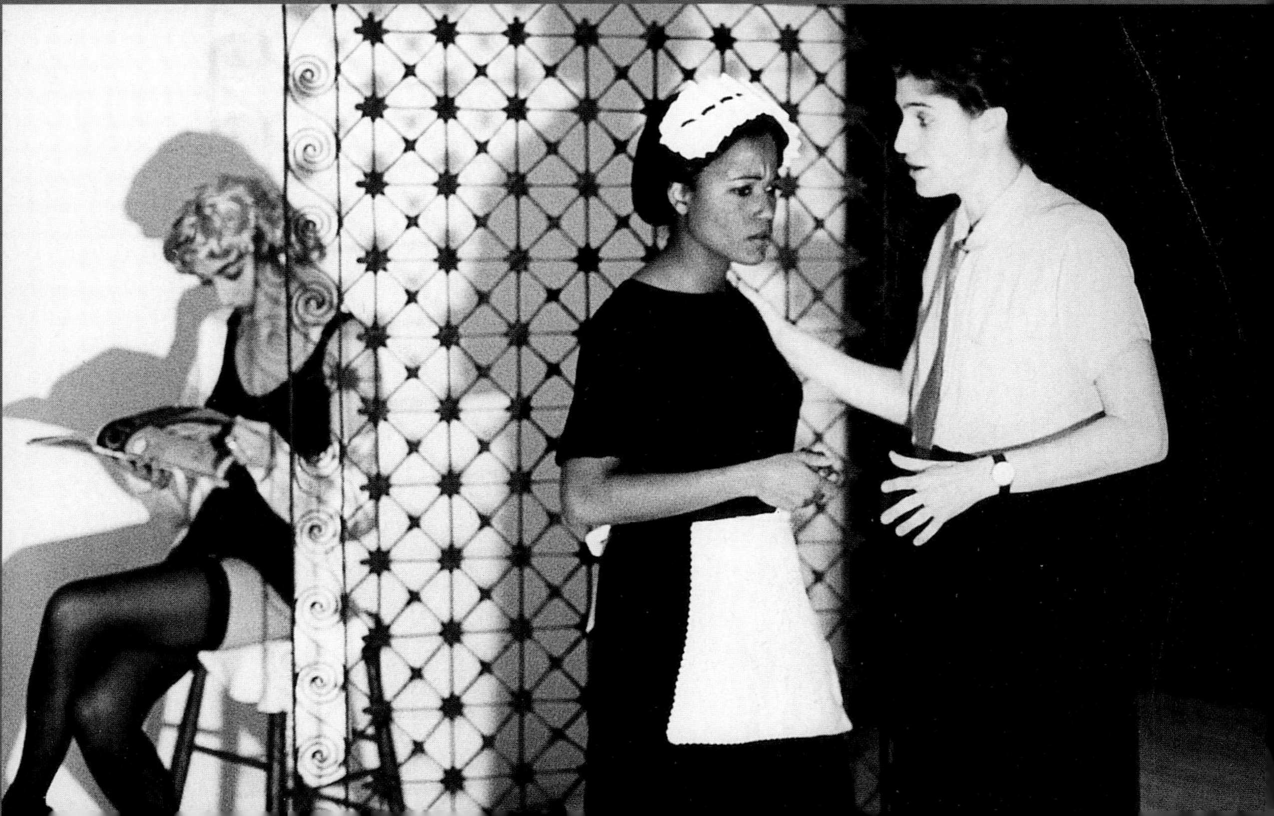

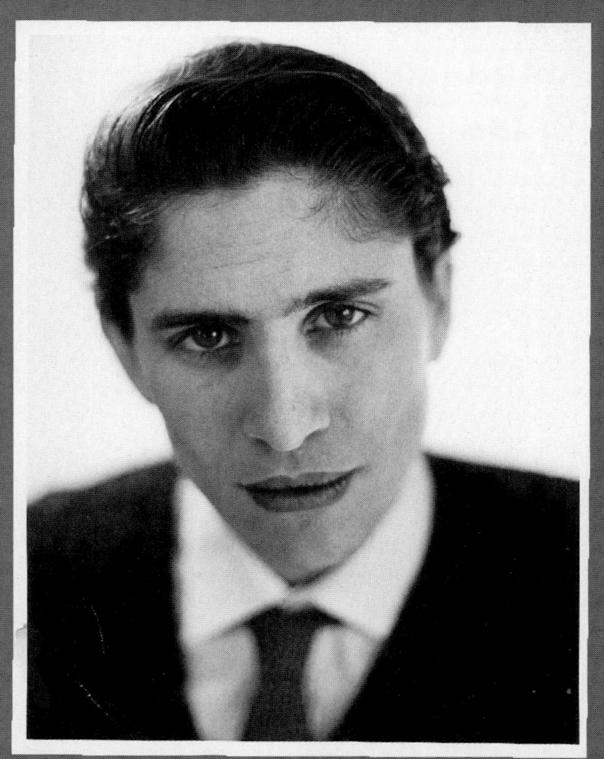
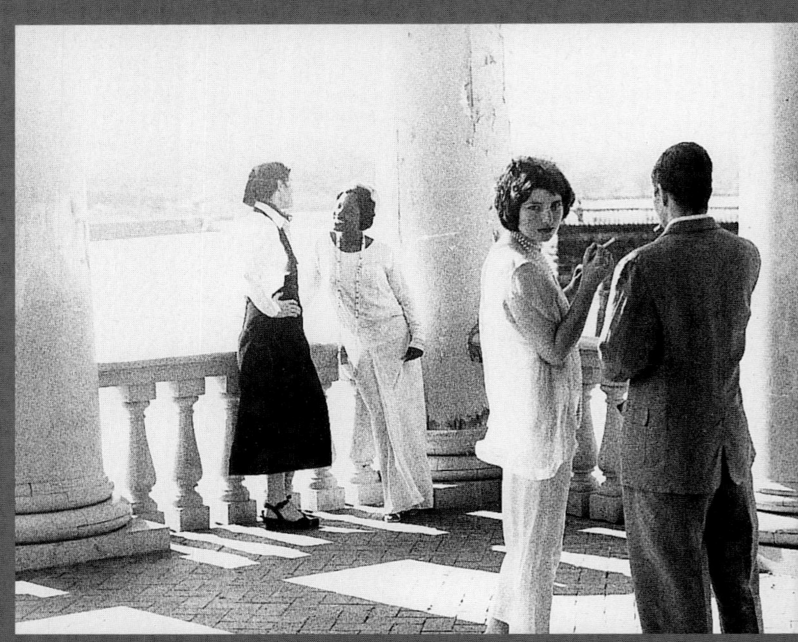

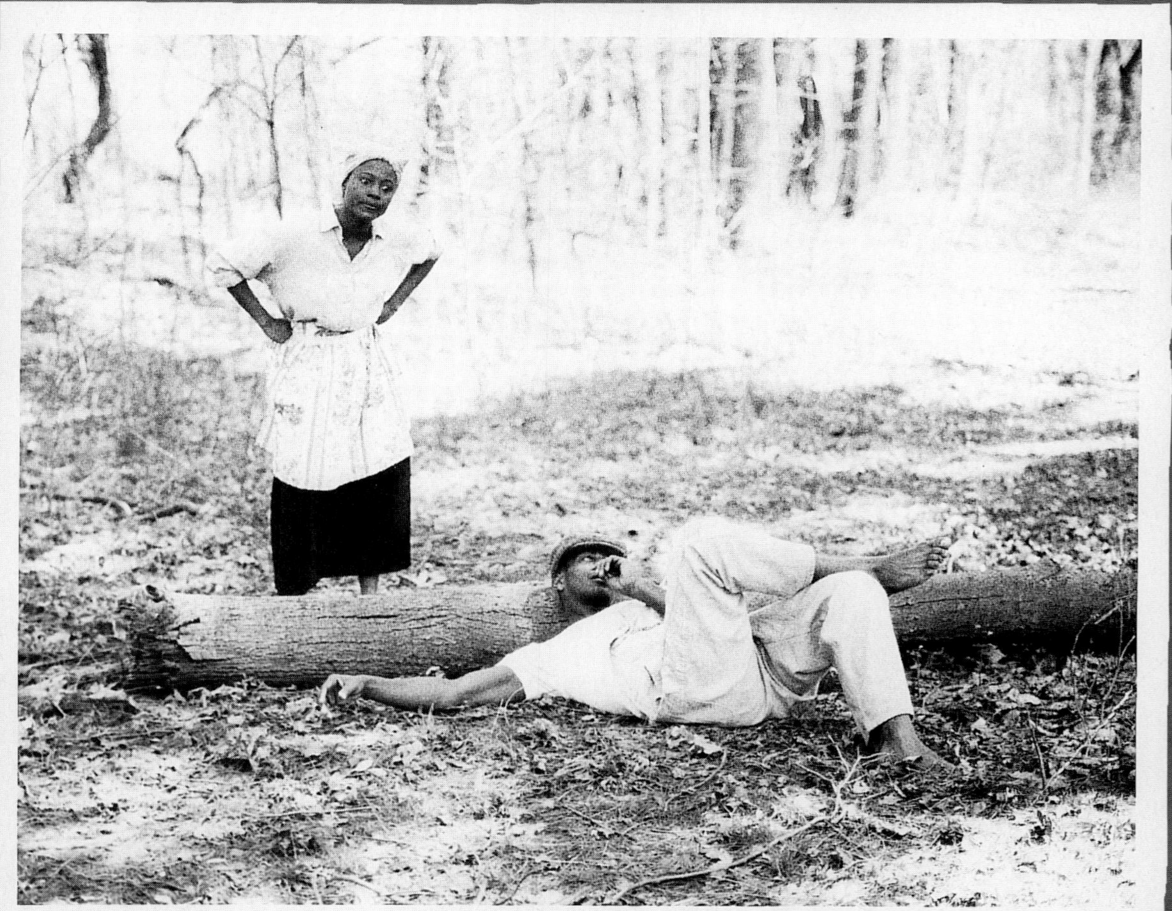

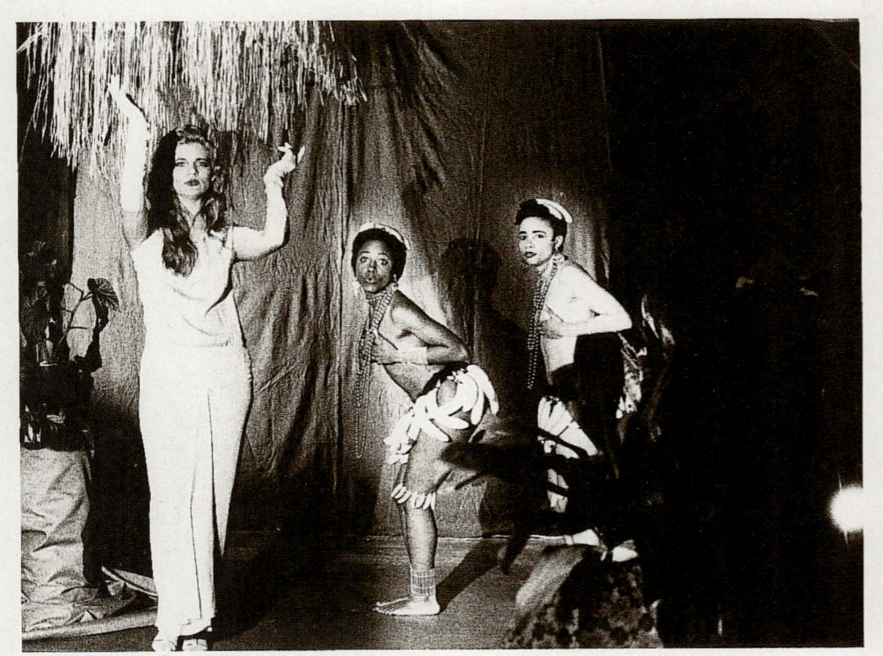

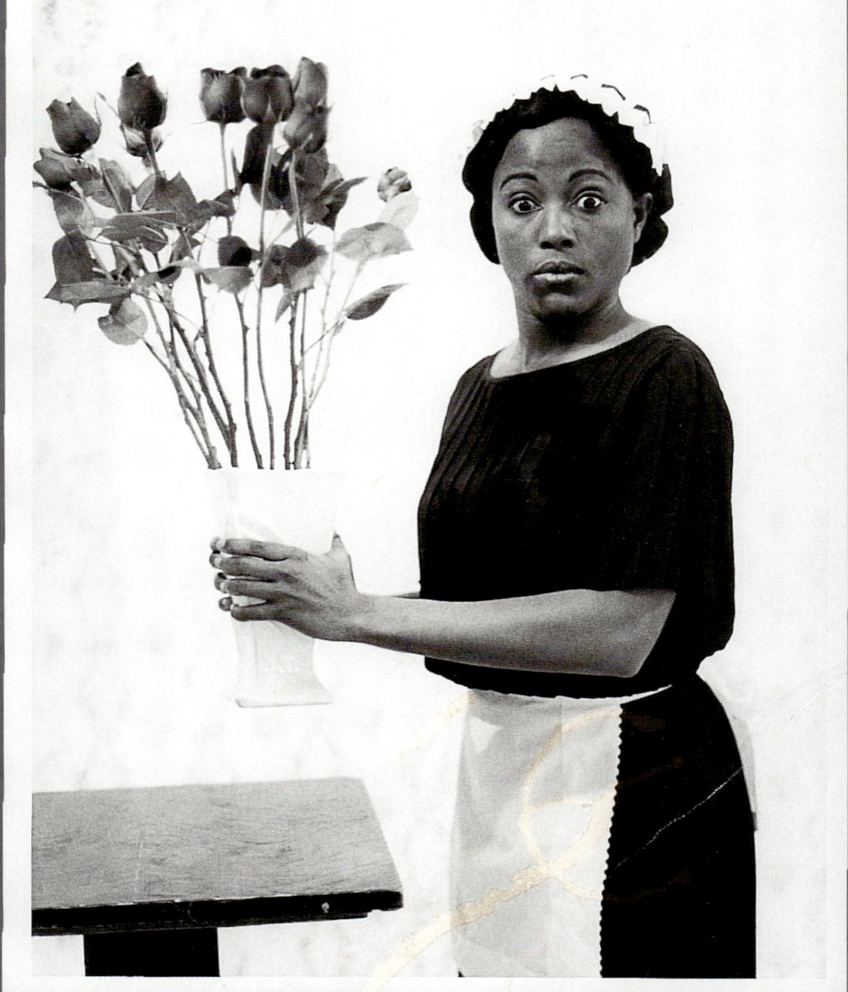

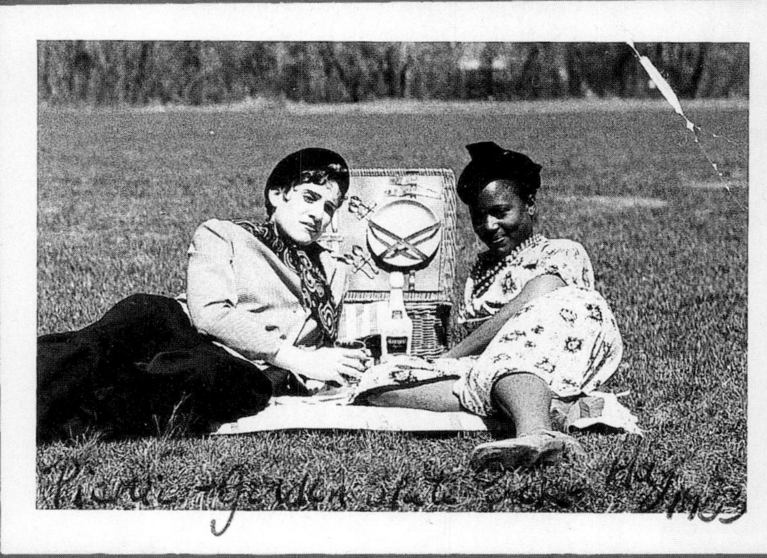
Picnic - Garden State Park 1933

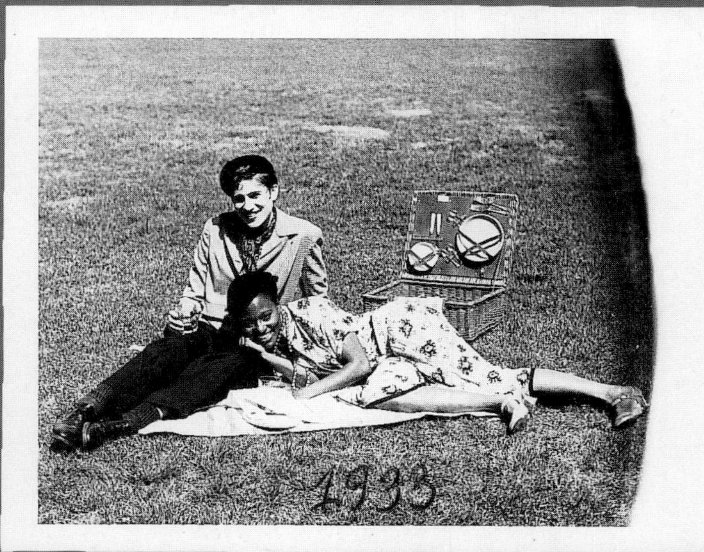
1933

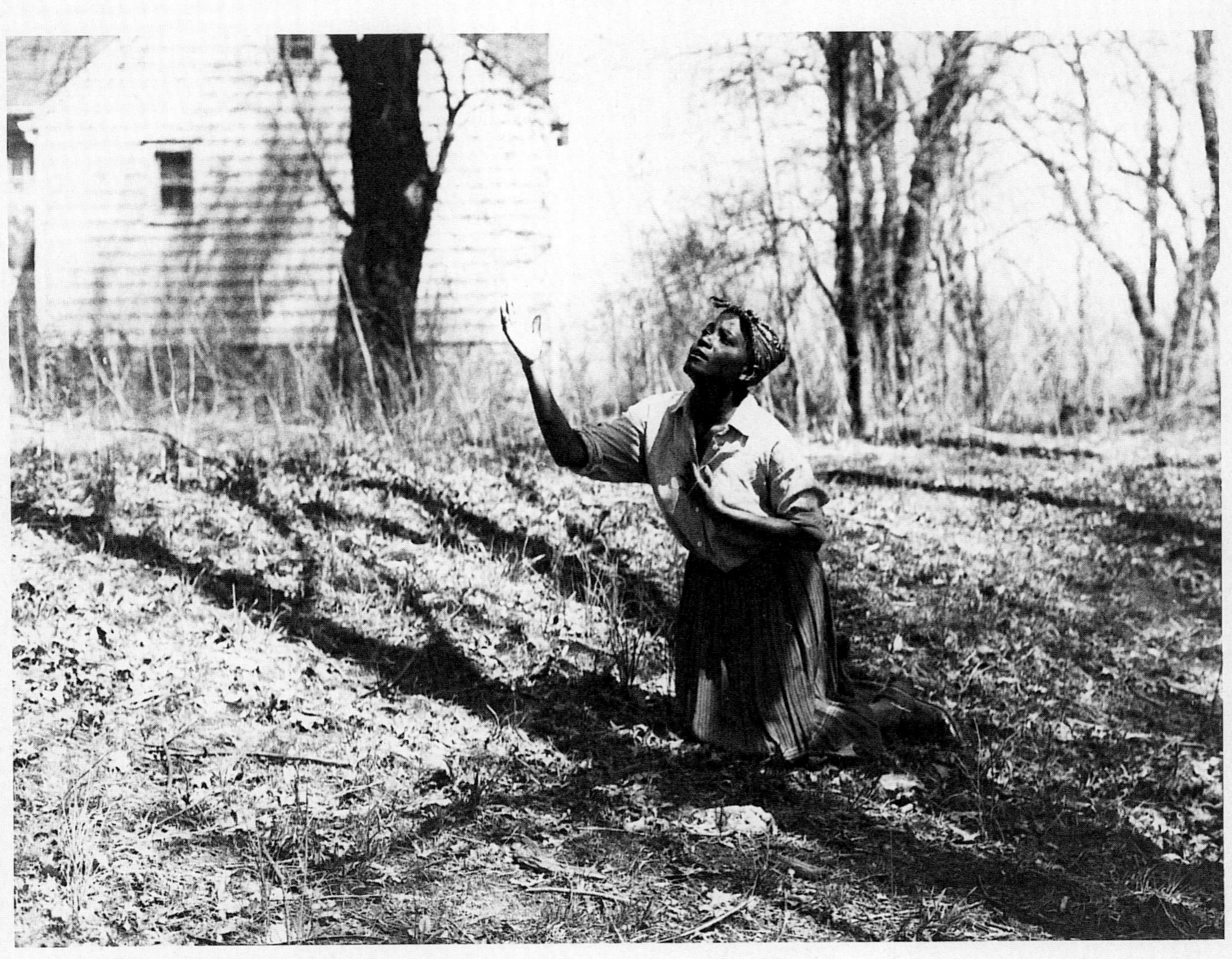

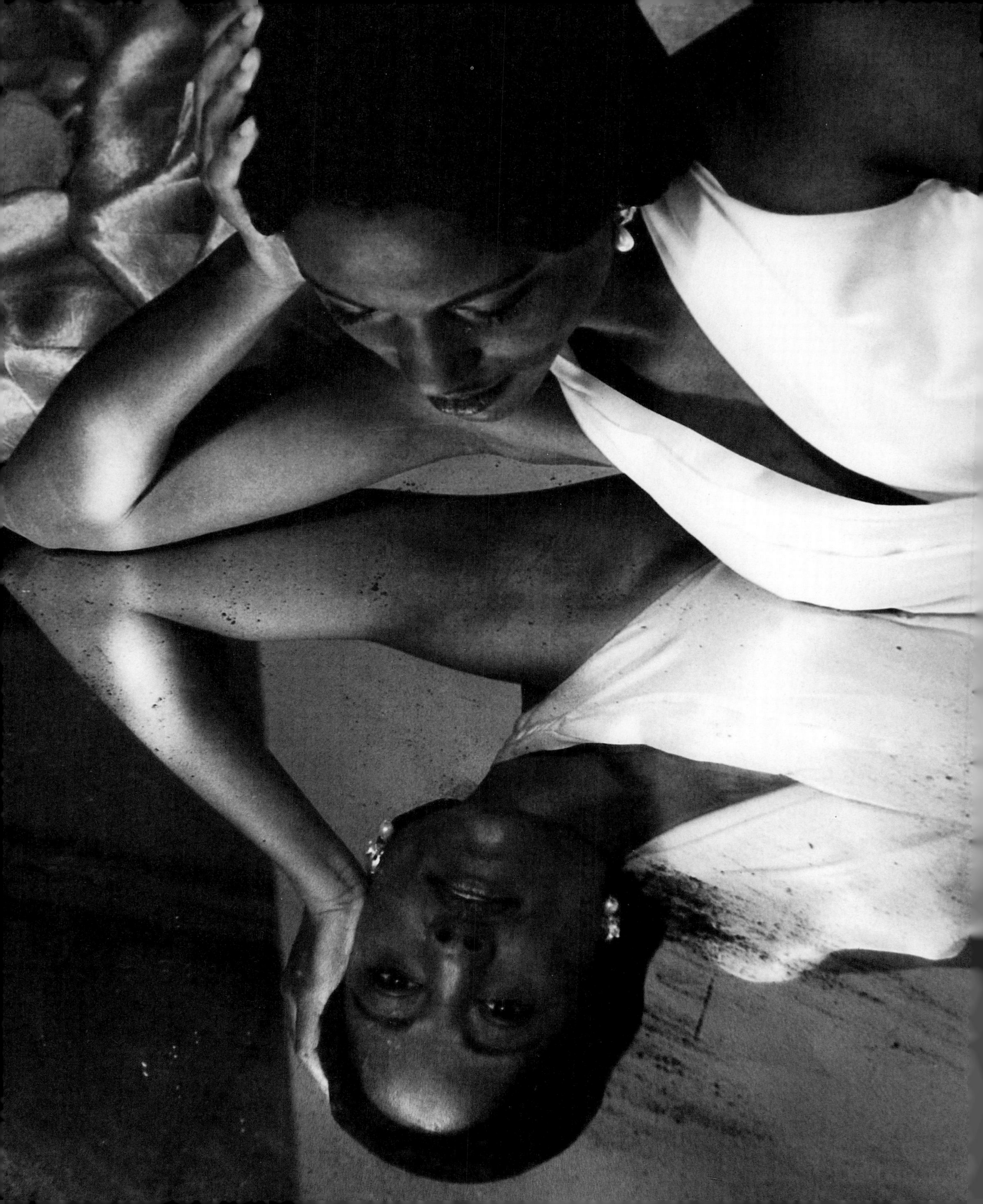

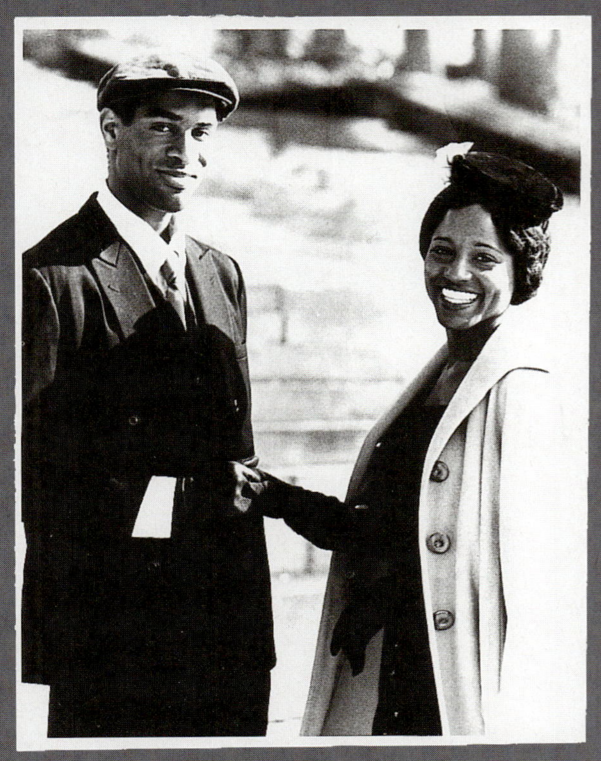

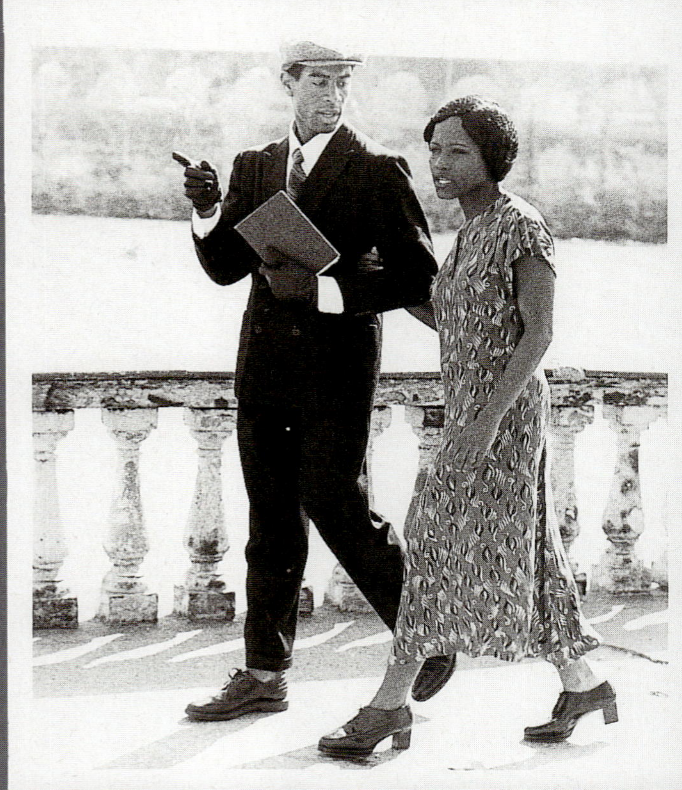

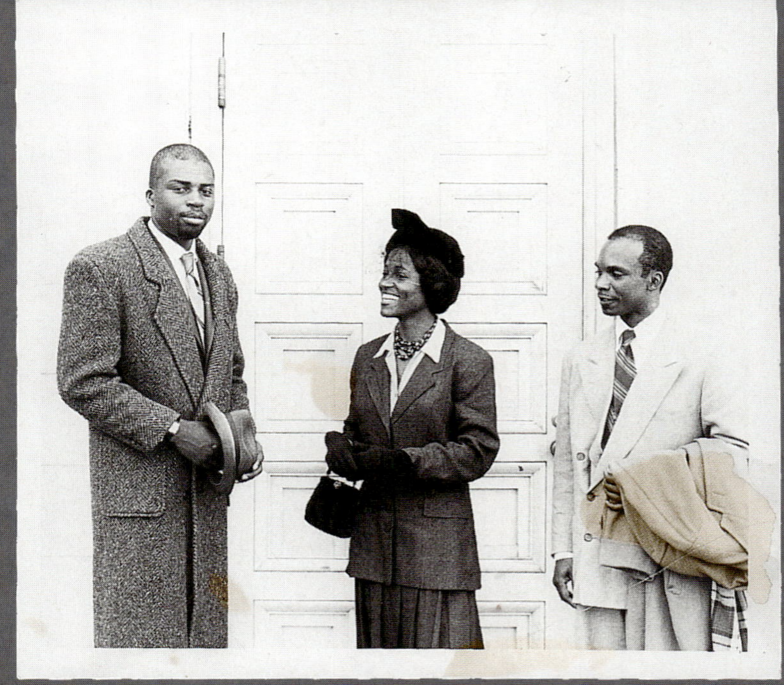

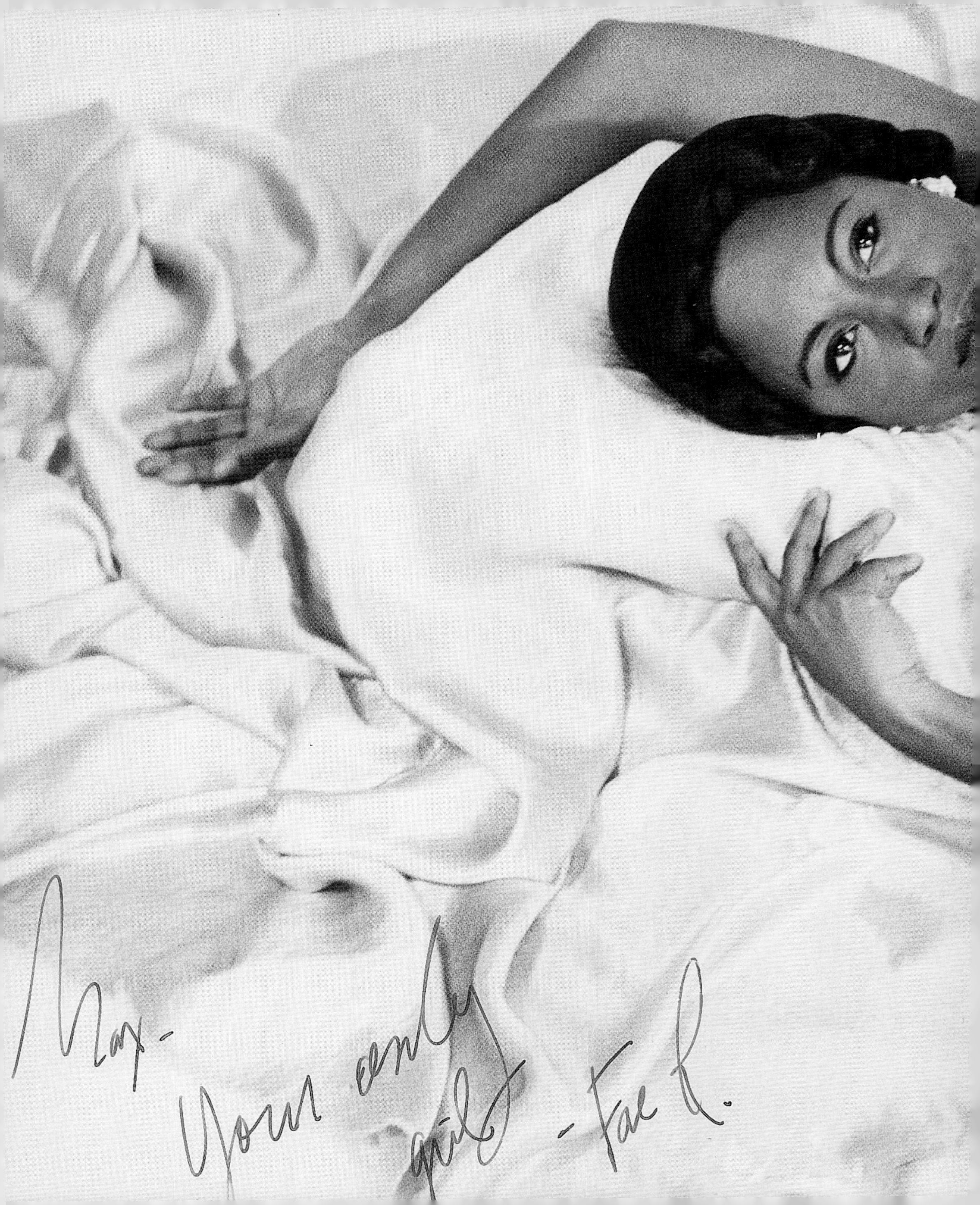

Max-
Your only
girl -Fae R.

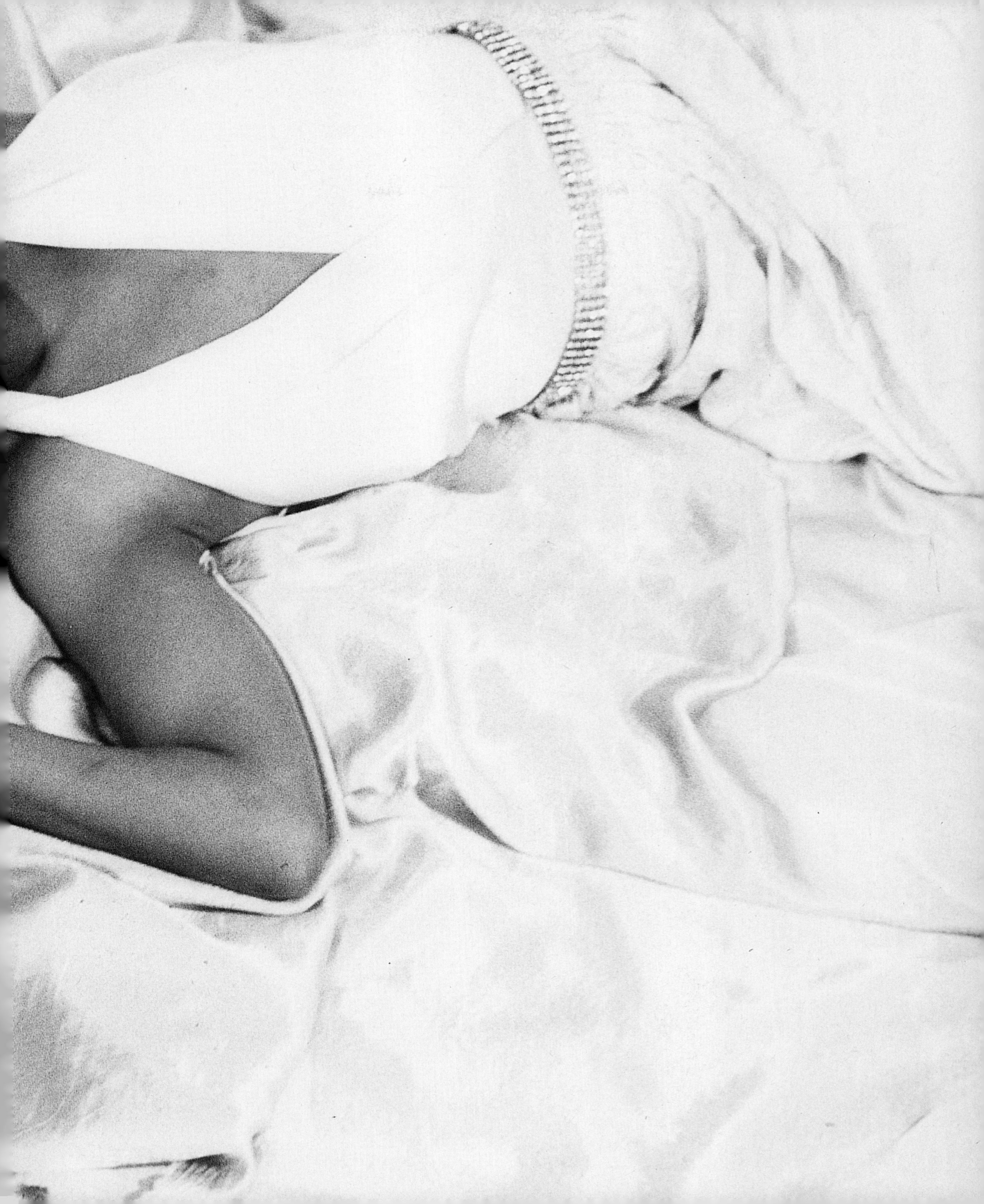

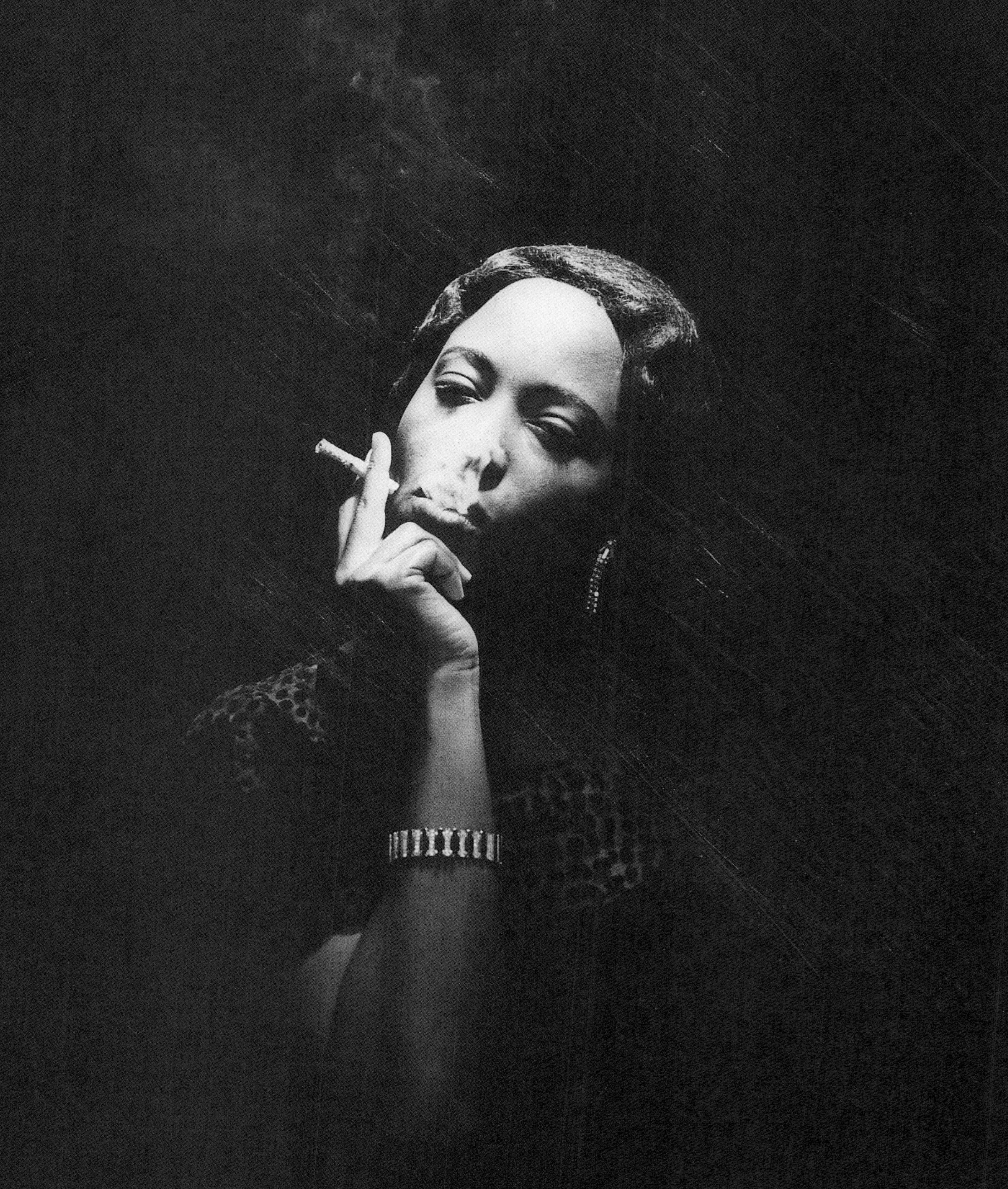

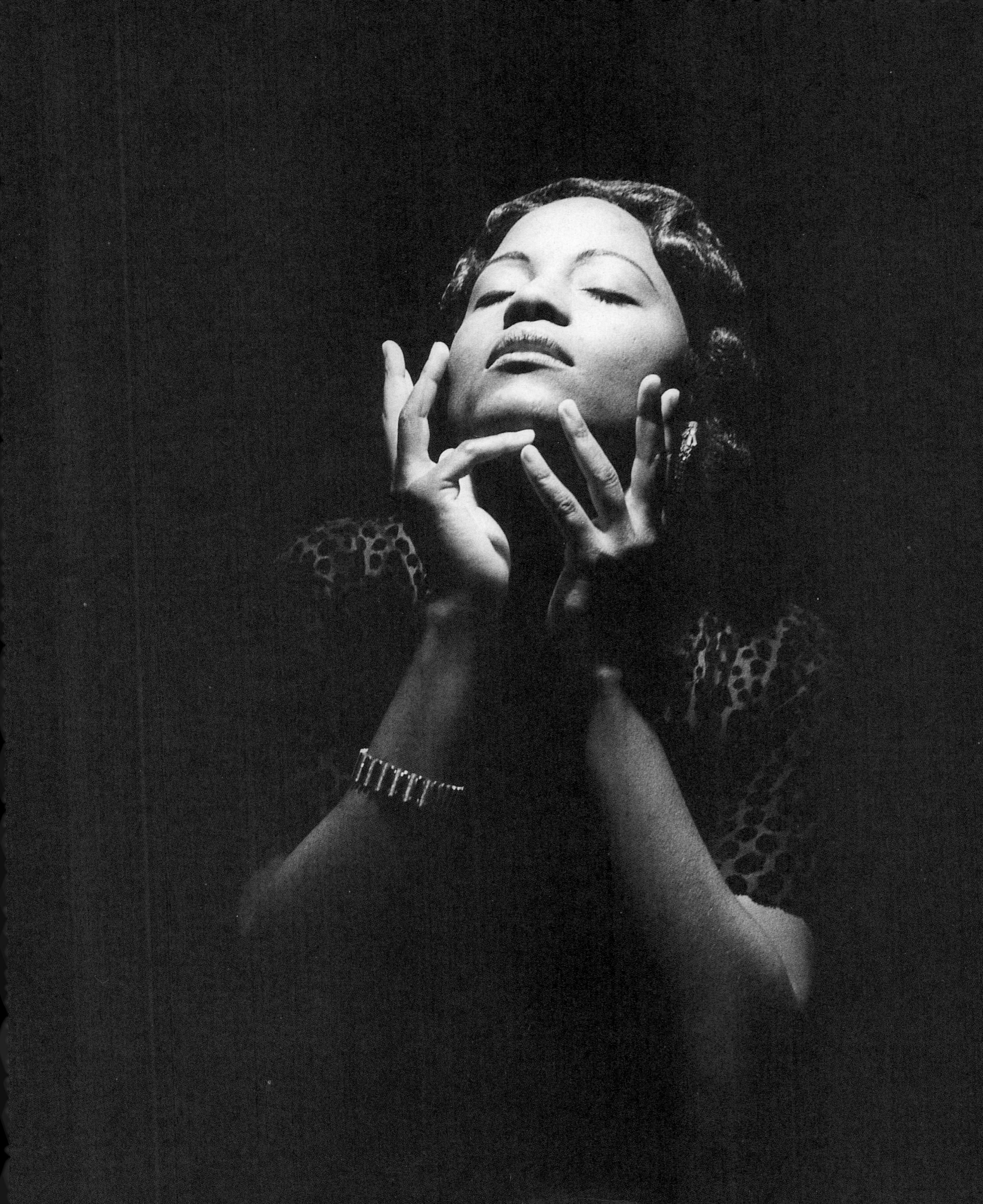

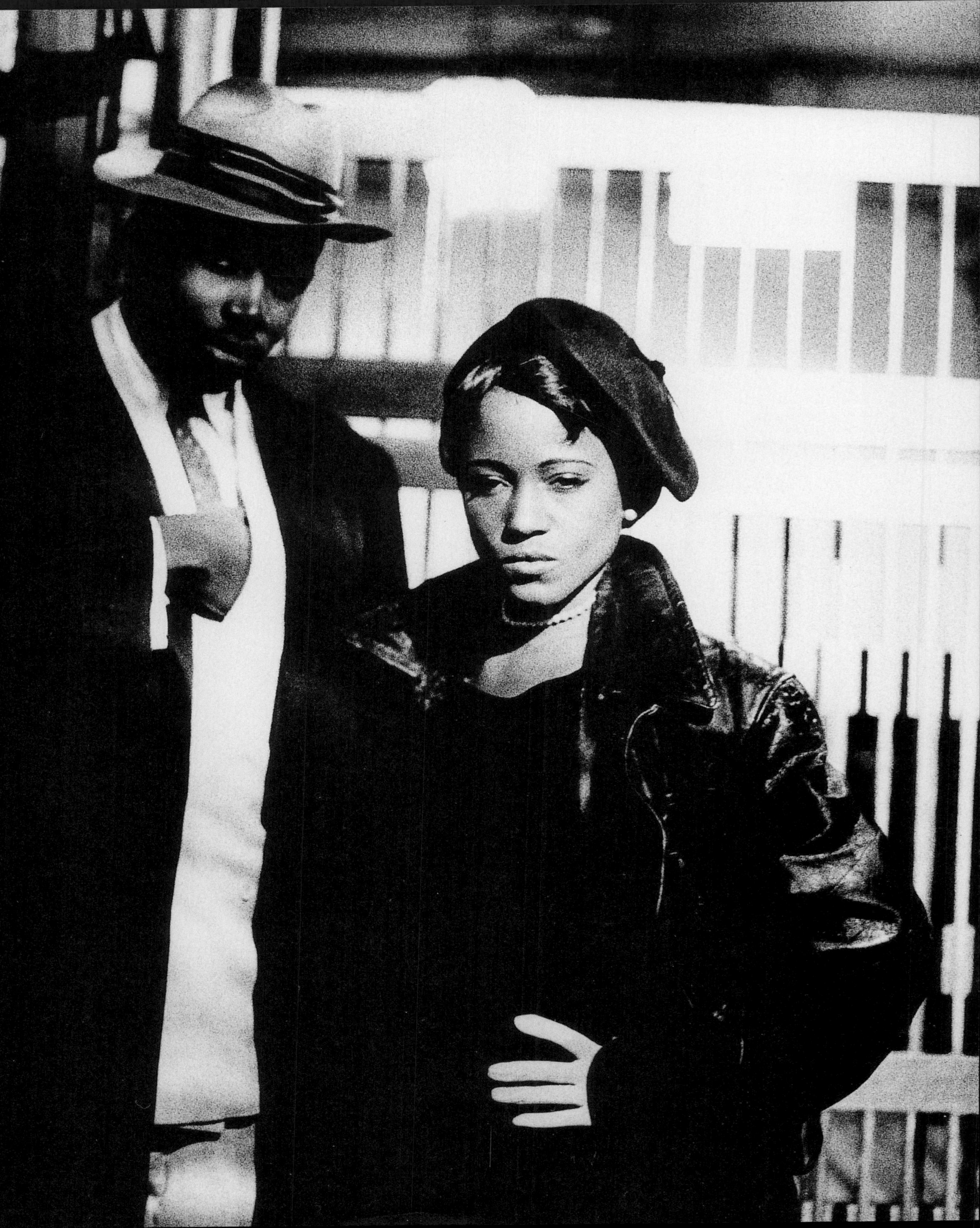

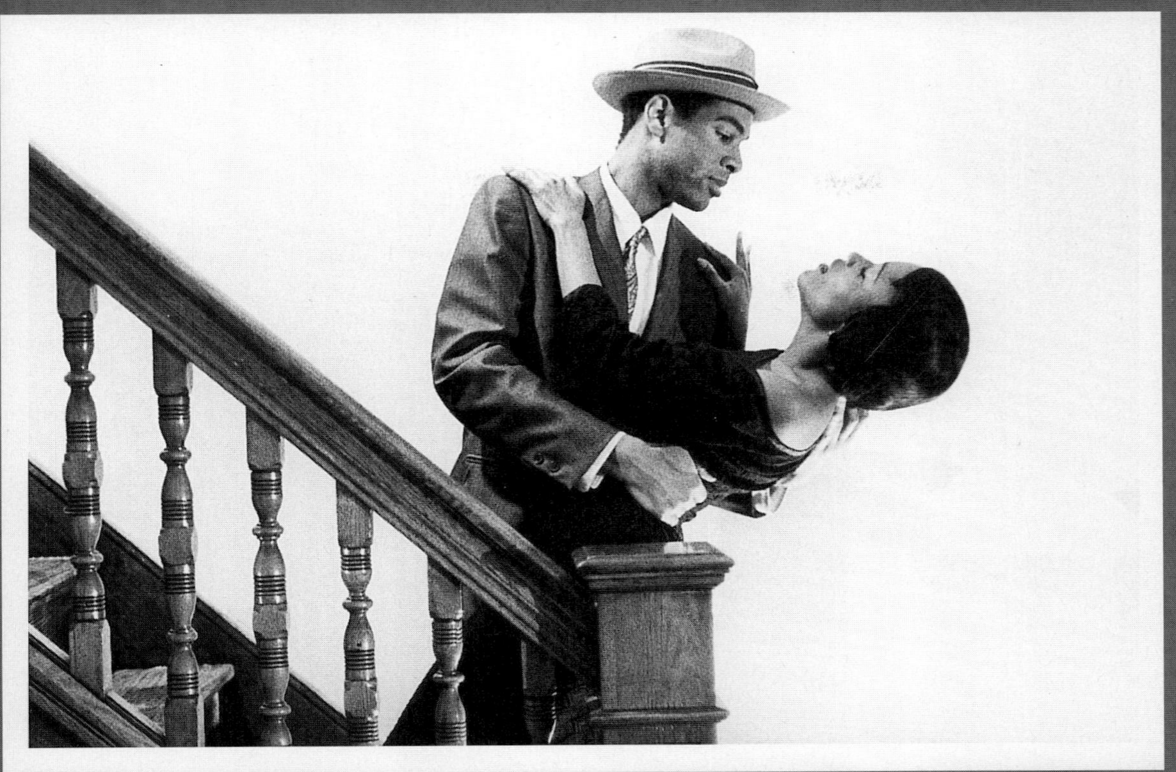

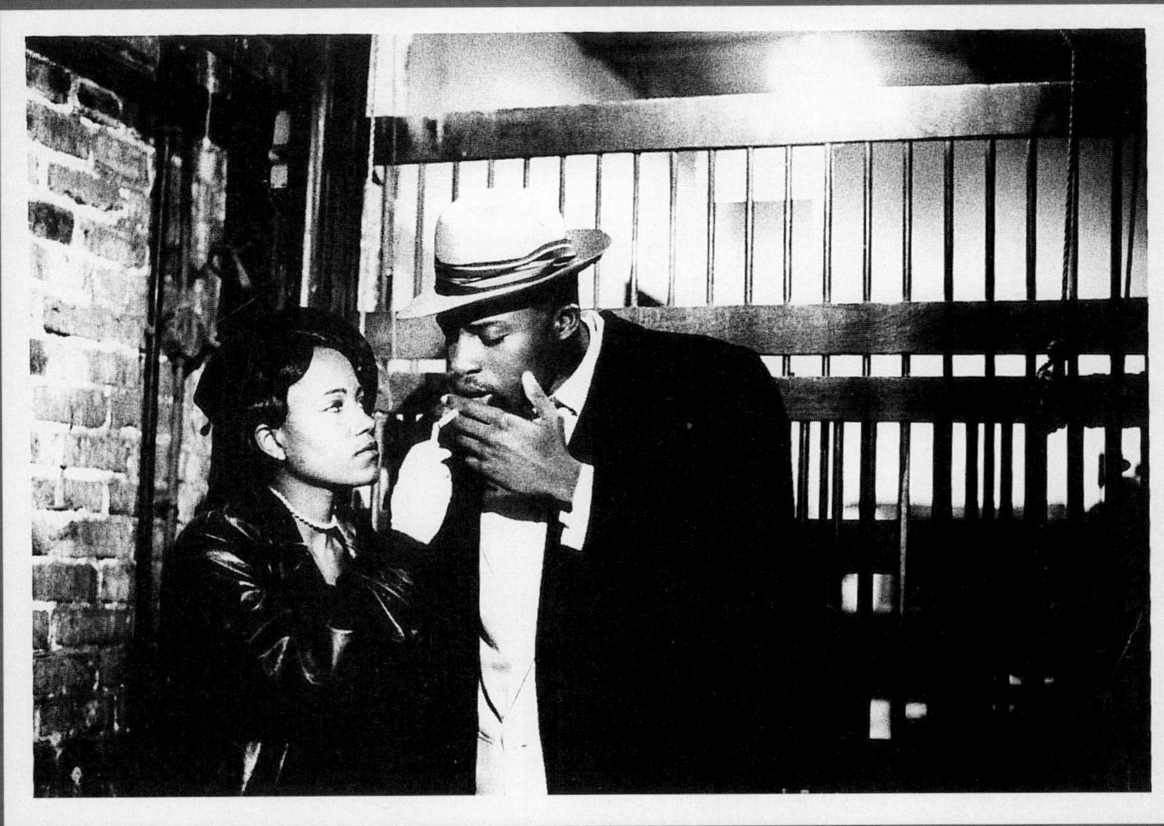

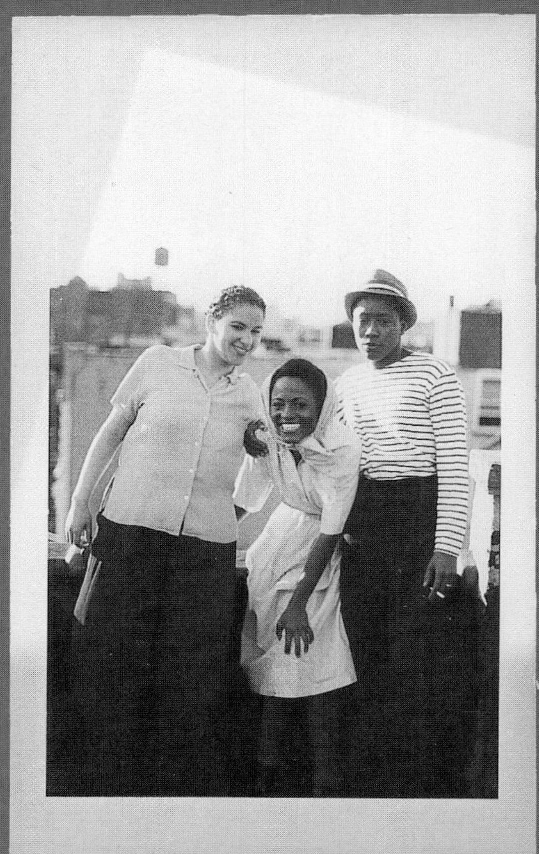

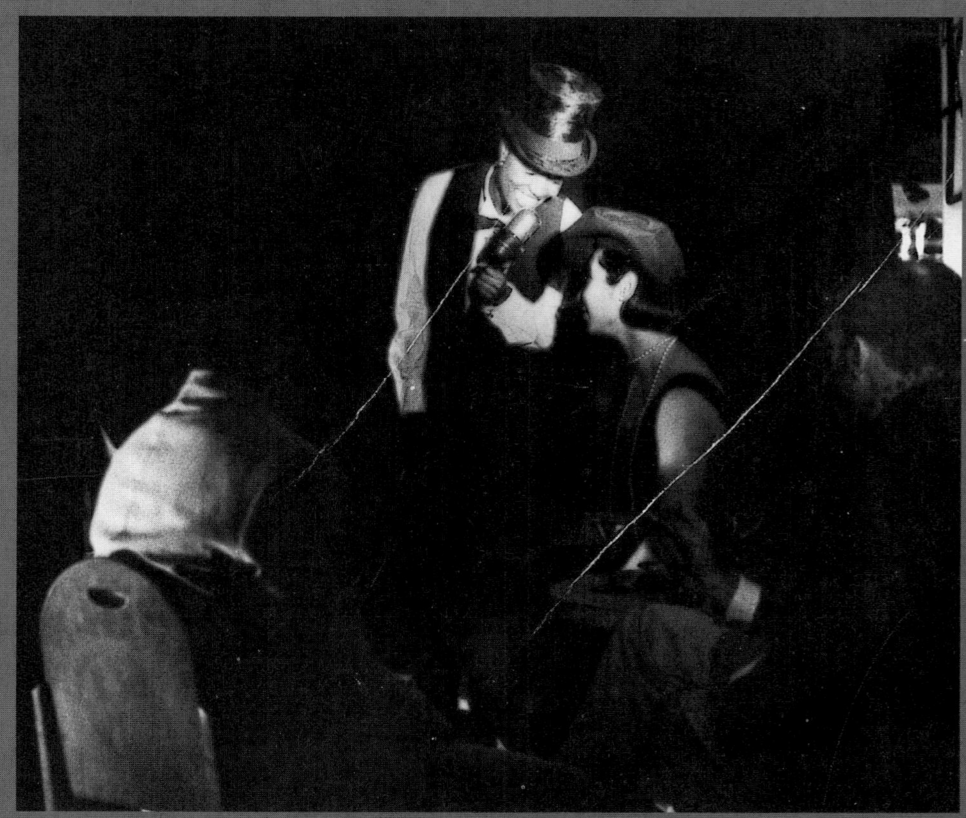

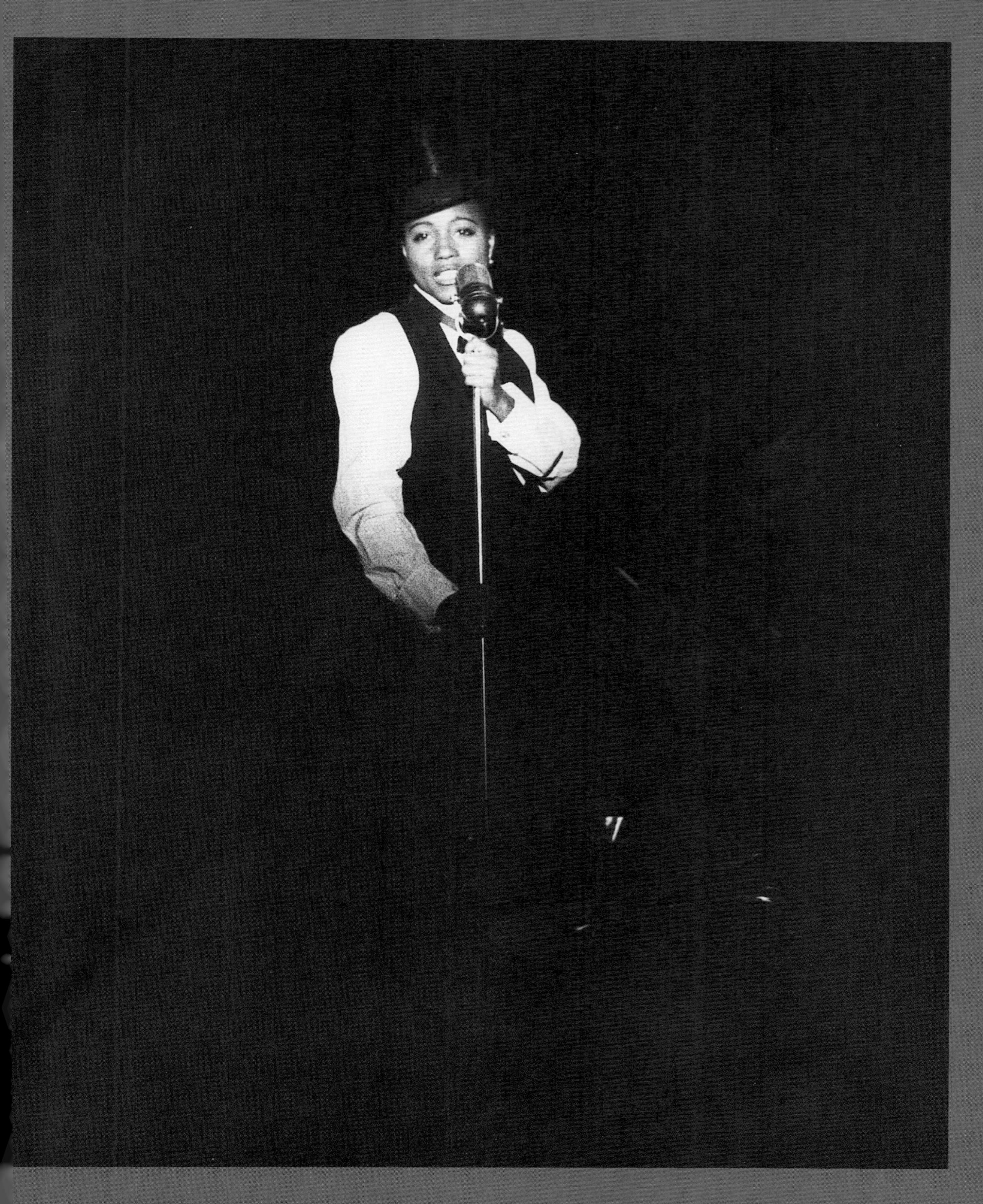

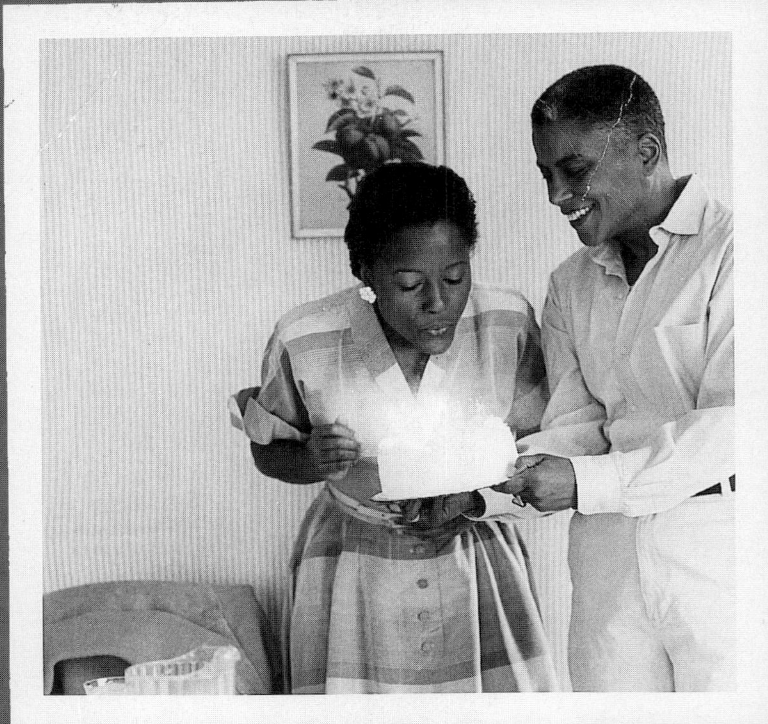
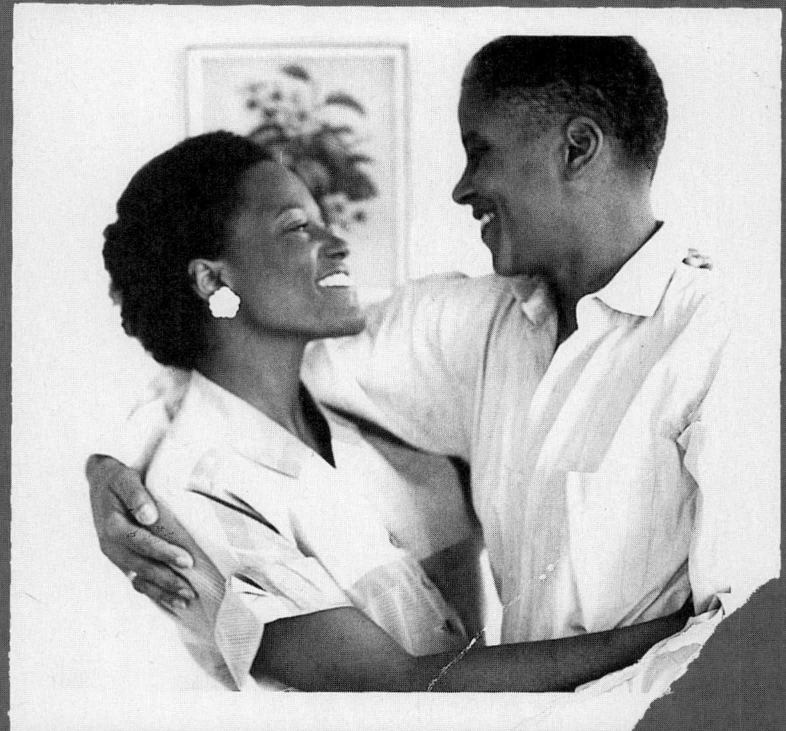
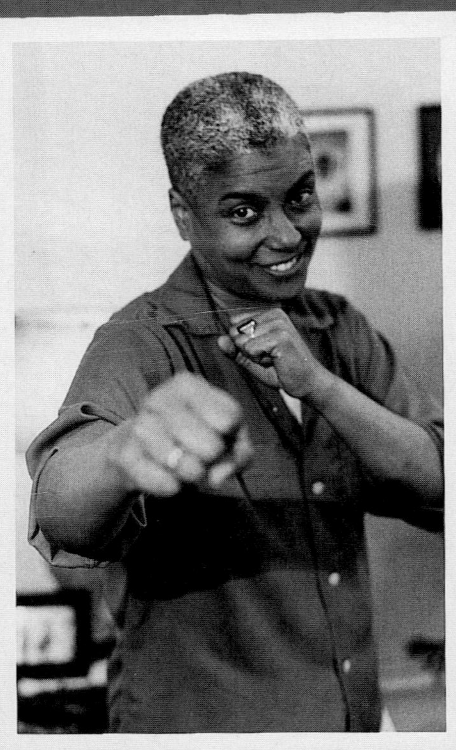

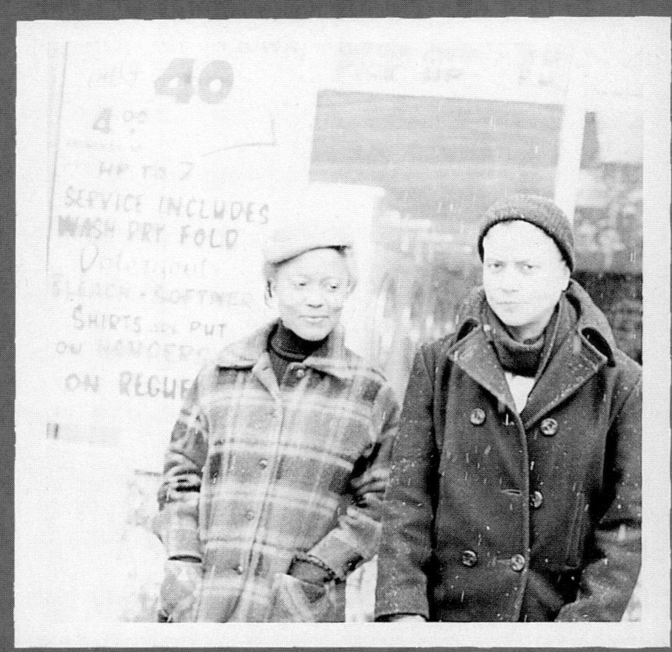
40
4⁰⁰
UP TO 7
SERVICE INCLUDES
WASH DRY FOLD
Detergent
BLEACH + SOFTNER
SHIRTS ... PUT
ON HANGERS
ON REGUE

Watermelon Woman
The Fae Richards Photo Archive

This archive of 82 photographs was created for use in the film
"The Watermelon Woman" directed by Cheryl Dunye. The archive became a
collaboration between Cheryl Dunye and Zoe Leonard. Because the
character Fae Richards is fictional, her story was realized by staging
public and private events from her life and photographing them. The
photos chronicle her early years in Philadelphia, her career in Hollywood, her affair with the director Martha Page, and her later return to
Philadelphia, where she worked for several years in all-Black "race
films." Her nightclub and cabaret performances are also documented. The
pictures of her later years provide evidence of her long relationship
with her lover, June Walker, with whom she lived until she died, at age
sixty-five, in 1973.

Watermelon Woman
Das Fae Richards-Photoarchiv

Diese Sammlung von insgesamt 82 Photos entstand für den Film "The
Watermelon Woman", bei dem Cheryl Dunye Regie führte. Das Archiv entwickelte sich zu einer eigentlichen Zusammenarbeit von Cheryl Dunye und
Zoe Leonard. Die Lebensgeschichte der fiktiven Person Fae Richards
wurde rekonstruiert, indem Ereignisse aus ihrem Leben inszeniert
und photographiert wurden. Die Photos zeigen ihre frühen Jahre in
Philadelphia, ihre Karriere in Hollywood, ihre Liebesaffäre mit der
Regisseurin Martha Page und danach ihre Rückkehr nach Philadelphia, wo
sie einige Jahre lang ausschliesslich "Schwarze Filme" drehte. Auch
ihre Nachtclub- und Kabarettauftritte sind dokumentiert. Die Bilder
aus den späteren Jahren sind ein Zeugnis ihrer langjährigen Liebes-
beziehung zu June Walker, mit der sie bis zu ihrem Tod, 1973, im Alter
von 65 Jahren, zusammenlebte.

Loitering with Intent
DIANE ARBUS AT THE MOVIES

SUSAN MORGAN

In John Schlesinger's 1969 Times Square odyssey *Midnight Cowboy,* Joe Buck, an aspiring hustler, unprofitably trawls West 42nd Street. Evicted from his hotel room and armed only with his Western fringed jacket (buckskin, no doubt) and a transistor radio, Buck strides with stagnant determination across the midtown territory. It's a scene out of a fable: Winter is approaching and the unprepared wanderer is lost in a menacing forest. The agitated landscape of Buck's Times Square is recorded as an assaultive stream of harsh lights, loud noises, and sensational movie posters. Amidst this onslaught of images and sound, there's a glimpse of a dreary black-and-white

SUSAN MORGAN is a contributing writer to *Elle* and *Mirabella,* and is the author of *Portraits: Edward Weston* (Aperture). She lives in Los Angeles.

marquee announcing "Hubert's Museum"; it's just another of the street's faithless enticements, a promise of a basement freak show and flea circus housed beneath an ordinary pinball parlor.

When Hubert's Museum closed down for good in 1965, Hubert habituée Diane Arbus carried away most of the 8 x 10 inch lobby photographs of the museum's featured "stars"—Alberto/Alberta, half male/half female; Lady Olga, the bearded woman; Sealo, the seal boy with flippers for arms; and Professor LeRoy Heckler, a second-generation ringmaster to a flea circus, among others. For Arbus, as an artist, the seemingly tawdry wasteland of Times Square was the source of her sentimental education.

By 1956, Arbus had abandoned a fifteen-year career in fashion photography. She began to study with Lisette

Model, a photographer well-known for her unsentimental studies of (what she called) "extremes": People who were massively overweight, very elderly, outrageously rich, or shockingly poor. Model regarded the camera as a way of asking questions and advised her students to wander the city streets, only photographing when a subject hit them "in the pit of the stomach."

Arbus traversed Times Square. When sixties art world catalyst Emile de Antonio introduced her to a revival-house screening of Tod Browning's 1932 cult classic *Freaks,* she returned to watch the film again and again. Arbus soon discovered that many of the freaks worked locally on the dime museum circuit, at Hubert's and the Coney Island boardwalk. Among them was Lady Olga, who in a 1940 *New Yorker* profile informed the writer Joseph Mitchell that freak society could

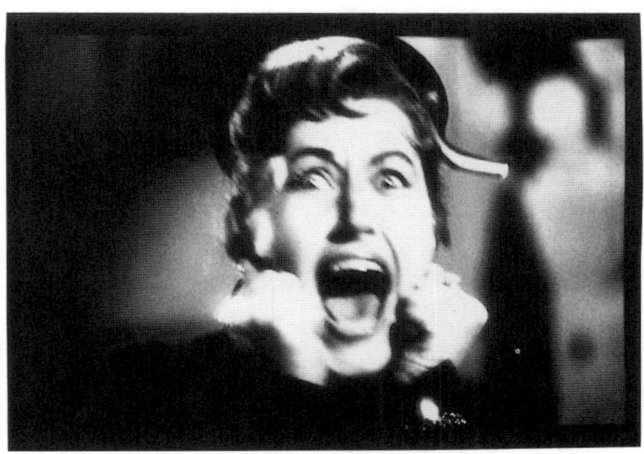

be broken down into three distinct classes: "born freaks, made freaks, and two-timers." Two-timers—has-been celebrities and ex-convicts—were considered the lowest echelon; born freaks like herself were the aristocrats of the sideshow world.

In 1960, after reading a collection of Mitchell's work, Arbus telephoned the writer at his office. They spoke for hours, tracking their shared interests—Kafka, James Joyce, freaks, and eccentrics. Mitchell warned Arbus against romanticizing freaks, insisting that she not worship them as a secret society but acknowledge the banality of their desires as well. Although Arbus continued to telephone Mitchell over a period of seven years, they never met in person. Mitchell admitted to once having noticed Arbus as she took photographs at an East Village nightclub and Arbus revealed that she had spotted Mitchell having lunch at a bar. Their relationship, existing entirely in the ether of telephone conversations, seems to mirror the very nature of her photographs—a fierce curiosity suspended in a non-corporeal reality, pure attentiveness presented without context.

Last year, a previously unexhibited cache of Arbus photographs was shown at Robert Miller Gallery in New York. These extraordinary but unknown works, dating from 1956 through 1958, all focused on the movies. Arbus, who had been raised in the upper middle class of New York's merchant society, observed her native city as a stranger might. She documented the decaying, baroque lobbies of fading picture palaces and captured the dreamless gapes of mesmerized audiences. Arbus photographed the climactic movie scenes: the long-anticipated kiss between the conniving mill boss and the simple-minded child bride in director Elia Kazan's film *Baby Doll;* the horrified screams and bloody corpses so central to any number of urban tabloid thrillers—*New Orleans after Dark, New York Confidential, The Foxiest Girl in Paris.* These still photographs of moving pictures, contrived dramatic moments composed of nothing more than light and celluloid, are as profound and shadowy as memory. Arbus found, in the anonymous and arousing darkness of the movie theater, her own detached but intrusively intimate way of seeing. She surrendered to her capacity to be enthralled.

As Susan Sontag has observed in her harsh appreciation of Arbus's work, "In the world colonized by Arbus, subjects are always revealing themselves. There is no decisive moment." Like a devoted moviegoer, Arbus was fascinated and persistent, confident that something was meant to happen; a revelation would ultimately occur. When she caught the shocked expression of a mother gazing at her own grotesquely overgrown child, Arbus had been photographing this particular family for

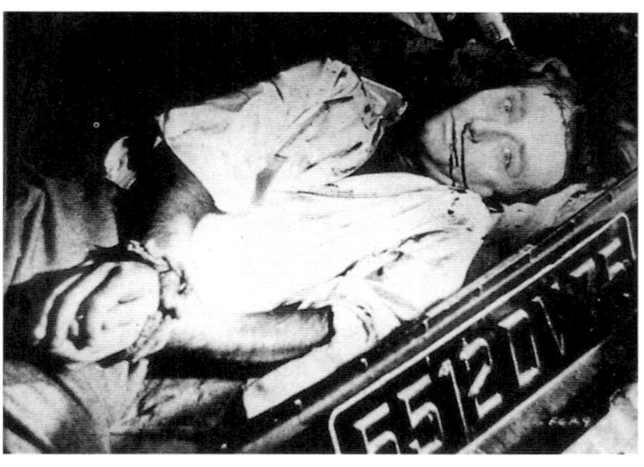

*DIANE ARBUS, A CORPSE, 1958, from / aus «The Foxiest Girl in Paris»,
gelatin-silver print, 11 x 14" / 27,9 x 35,6 cm.*

eight years. The resultant well-known image, A JEWISH GIANT AT HOME WITH HIS PARENTS IN THE BRONX (1970), echoes the tell-tale drama displayed in her earlier photographs of lurid movie posters and cinematic climaxes.

In the darkness of the movie theater, the atmosphere is spectral; the screen is animated by flickering light and the audience, the living world, is cast in shadow. Arbus finds a wry gothic humor in her movie subjects. When her camera stares unflinchingly at bloody hands and gouged eyeballs, she taps into an essential gothic impulse, a desire to shake up the complacency of the smug, familiar, bourgeois world. In Arbus's later photographs, the genteel world continues to surround her startling posers. If one removes her portrait subjects—the madly grimacing boy clutching a toy hand grenade in his clawlike fist, the awkwardly costumed inmates of mental institutions—from the pictures, all that remains is a blurry landscape. Place your hand over the figures in these photographs and a Photo-Secessionist scene emerges: soft patterns of lacy tree branches and dappled light. Arbus's subjects require no setting; they leap out of the mists and darkness. When a version of Arbus's famous identical twins appears in Stanley Kubrick's *The Shining*, they are neatly transported, with all of their sinister charm intact. It's the power of a baby's game of peekaboo infused with the frisson of a peep show.

In Arbus's movie photographs, *Baby Doll*—a sultry Southern drama written by the master weaver of twisted sexual tales, Tennessee Williams—replays several times. When *Baby Doll* opened in 1956, it created a scandal. Condemned by the Catholic Legion of Decency, Williams's story is a hard-times drama about insinuation and manipulation. The film's air of moral depravity is generally decorative—nothing more than a few empty liquor bottles and a beautiful young woman who lazes about in a wrought-iron crib—but the story does cut through to the nasty heart of human behavior, disdaining polite notions of Southern gentility and the sanctity of marriage. In one of Arbus's BABY DOLL photographs, there is an overpowering close-up of Carroll Baker's face. The frame of the movie screen has vanished and no shadows appear at the edges. Baker's Baby Doll, a pale, blurry phantasm, dominates the real space of Arbus's print. In the foreground, there is a dark figure of a man in profile. Like a cutout target in a shooting gallery, he passes obliviously between the viewer and the radiant screen.

At the movies, the audience has only to watch. The moving images aspire to overwhelm. In that easeful darkness, the audience cannot stare too long. As she haunted Times Square, Arbus found her way into her life's work.

Herumlungern mit Methode:
DIANE ARBUS IM KINO

SUSAN MORGAN

In *Midnight Cowboy,* John Schlesingers Times-Square-Odyssee aus dem Jahr 1969, klappert Joe Buck, ein angehender Stricher, erfolglos die 42. Strasse nach Freiern ab. Nur mit einer Cowboy-Fransenjacke (aus Wildleder natürlich) und einem Transistorradio ausgerüstet, macht Buck, der sein Hotelzimmer räumen musste, einen halbherzigen Rundgang durch das Stadtzentrum. Die Szene könnte aus einem Märchen stammen: Der Winter steht vor der Tür, und der unvorbereitete Wanderer hat sich in dem bedrohlichen Dickicht eines Waldes verirrt. Die lebhafte Gegend des Times Square wird als ein aggressiver Strom von grellen Lichtern, ohrenbetäubendem Lärm und schrillen Kinoreklamen dargestellt.

SUSAN MORGAN schreibt regelmässig für *Elle* und *Mirabella*. Sie ist Autorin des Bandes *Portraits: Edward Weston* (Aperture) und lebt in Los Angeles.

Bei diesem Angriff auf Auge und Ohr taucht kurz ein tristes, schwarzweisses Schild mit der Aufschrift *Hubert's Museum* auf. Auch dies ist nur eine weitere der fragwürdigen Verlockungen dieser Strasse: Es verspricht eine Freakshow im Erdgeschoss und einen Flohzirkus im Untergeschoss einer ganz gewöhnlichen Flipperhalle.

Als *Hubert's Museum* 1965 endgültig dichtmachte, nahm Diane Arbus, als langjähriger Stammgast, den grössten Teil der im Eingang des Museums aufgehängten 20 x 24-cm-Porträts von den «Stars» des Museums an sich, darunter auch das von Alberto/Alberta, halb Mann/halb Frau; von Lady Olga, der Frau mit Bart; von Sealo, dem Seelöwen-Jungen mit Flossen anstelle der Arme, und von Professor LeRoy Heckler, Flohzirkusdirektor der zweiten Generation. Das ziemlich heruntergekommen wirkende Niemandsland um den Times Square war für die

Künstlerin Diane Arbus der Ort ihrer *éducation sentimentale.*

1956 hatte Arbus ihre fünfzehnjährige Karriere als Modephotographin aufgegeben. Ihre neue Lehrmeisterin, Lisette Model, eine Photographin, war durch ihre unsentimentalen Bilder von «Extremen» bekannt geworden: Sie photographierte Menschen, die entweder enorm dick, uralt, steinreich oder bettelarm waren. Für Model war die Kamera dazu da, Fragen zu stellen, und sie empfahl ihren Schülern, mit der Kamera durch die Stadt zu streifen und nur dann abzudrücken, wenn das Motiv ihnen einen Stich in die Magengrube versetzte.

Arbus' Territorium war der Times Square. Einmal begleitete sie Emile de Antonio, den Mann, der der Kunst der 60er Jahre wichtige Denkanstösse gab, in ein Programmkino für Filmklassiker, wo *Freaks* von Tod Browning gezeigt wurde, ein Kultfilm aus dem Jahr 1932, der sie so beeindruckte, dass sie ihn mehrmals anschaute. Arbus entdeckte, dass viele der Protagonisten in den Billig-Panoptiken der Stadt auftraten, in *Hubert's* und in den Shows der Strandpromenade von Coney Island. Unter ihnen war Lady Olga, die in einer 1940 erschienenen *New Yorker*-Kurzbiographie ihrem Interviewer Joseph Mitchell erklärte, dass die Freak-Gesellschaft sich in drei Klassen einteilen lasse: die als Freak Geborenen, die zu Freaks Gemachten und die «two timers». Die «two timers», ehemalige Zelebritäten und Zuchthäusler, rangierten ganz unten in der Hierarchie, während die – wie Lady Olga – als Freaks Geborenen die Elite der *Side Shows* darstellten.

Nachdem Arbus 1960 einen Band mit Mitchells Arbeiten gelesen hatte, rief sie den Schriftsteller an. Das Gespräch dauerte Stunden, da alle gemeinsamen Interessen abgeklopft werden mussten: Kafka, James Joyce, Freaks und Exzentriker. Mitchell warnte Arbus vor einer allzu verklärenden Sicht der Freaks; sie sollte diese Leute nicht wie einen Geheimorden verehren, sondern auch die Banalität ihrer Sehnsüchte erkennen. Obwohl Arbus in den folgenden sieben Jahren noch öfter mit Mitchell telefonierte, sind die beiden sich nie begegnet. Mitchell gab zwar zu, Arbus einmal im East Village gesichtet zu haben, als sie Photos in einem Nachtklub machte, und Arbus verriet, Mitchell beim Mittagessen in einer Bar entdeckt zu haben. Ihre ausschliesslich im Äther der Telephongespräche existierende Beziehung scheint das Wesen ihrer Photographien widerzuspiegeln – eine unbezähmbare, in einer körperlosen Welt frei flottierende Neugier, Aufmerksamkeit pur, ohne Kontext.

Letztes Jahr wurden in der Robert Miller Gallery in New York bislang unentdeckte Arbeiten von Arbus gezeigt. Diese aussergewöhnlichen, noch nie ausgestellten Bilder aus den Jahren 1956–58 drehen sich ausschliesslich um den Film. Arbus, die aus einer reichen New Yorker Kaufmannsfamilie stammte, betrachtete ihre Heimatstadt mit den Augen einer Fremden. Sie lichtete die verfallenden, prunkvollen Foyers schäbig gewordener Filmpaläste ab und bannte die traumlosen, weit aufgerissenen Augen hypnotisierter Zuschauer ins Bild. Arbus photographierte die filmischen Höhepunkte: den langerwarteten Kuss zwischen dem intriganten Fabrikbesitzer und der naiven Kindbraut in Elia Kazans Film *Baby Doll;* die grässlichen Schreie und bluti-

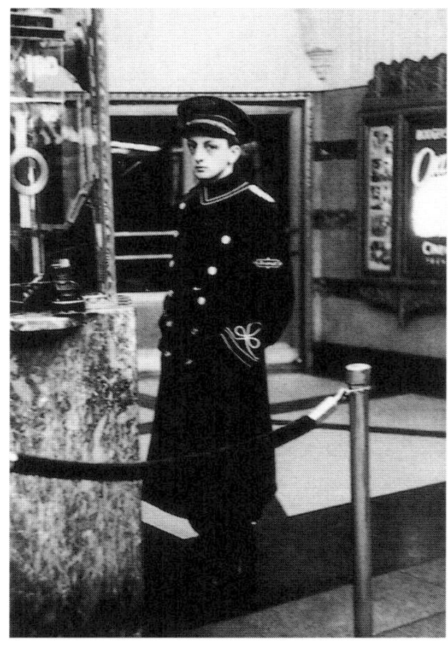

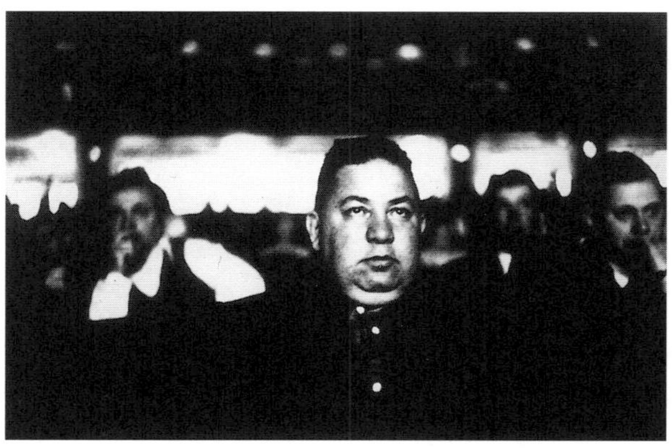

DIANE ARBUS, MOVIE THEATER USHER STANDING BY THE BOX OFFICE, NEW YORK CITY, ca. 1956, gelatine-silver print, 14 x 11" / PLATZANWEISER NEBEN DER KINOKASSE STEHEND, 35,6 x 27,9 cm.

DIANE ARBUS, MAN IN THE AUDIENCE, NEW YORK CITY, 1957, gelatin-silver print, 11 x 14" / MANN IM KINO, 27,9 x 35,6 cm.

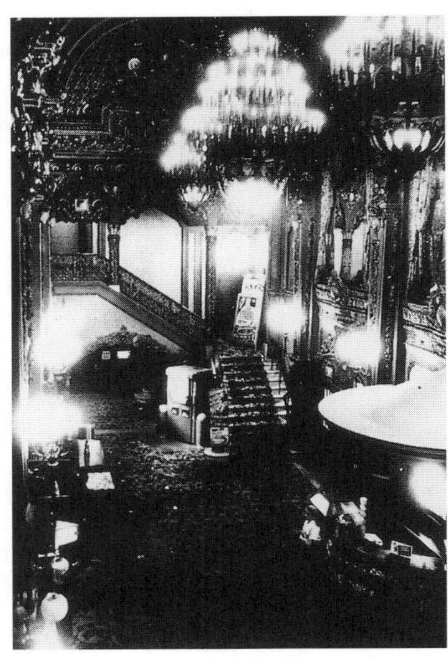

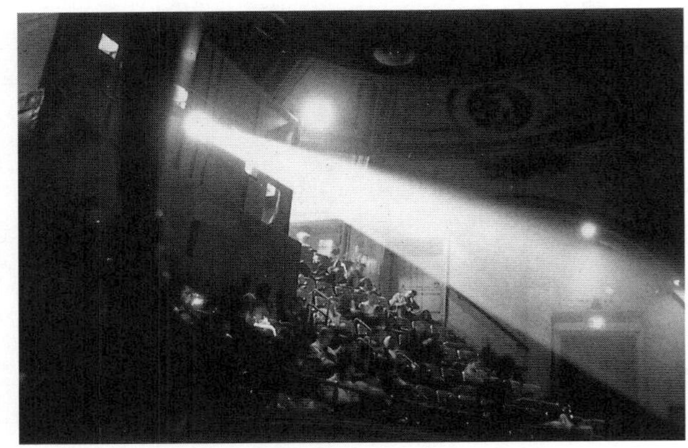

gen Leichen, die zum Repertoire billiger Grossstadtthriller gehörten – *New Orleans after Dark; New York Confidential; The Foxiest Girl in Paris.* Diese Standphotos von bewegten Bildern, von forciert dramatischen Momenten, die nur aus Licht und Zelluloid bestanden, sind so tief und unergründlich wie die Erinnerung. In der Anonymität und dem Dunkel des Kinos fand Arbus zu ihrer eigenen, distanzierten und zugleich schonungslos durchdringenden Sehweise. Sie gab sich ganz ihrer Fähigkeit hin, sich überwältigen zu lassen.

Wie Susan Sontag in ihrer herben Würdigung von Arbus' Œuvre bemerkte: «In der von Arbus kolonialisierten Welt offenbart sich das Subjekt immer selbst. Es gibt keine entscheidenden, enthüllenden Momente ausserhalb.»

Als leidenschaftliche Kinogängerin war Arbus ebenso gefesselt wie hartnäckig; sie vertraute darauf, dass etwas passieren würde, dass sich schliesslich etwas offenbaren würde. Als sie den schokkierten Ausdruck einer Mutter festhielt, die auf ihr grotesk in die Höhe geschossenes Kind blickte, hatte Arbus diese eine Familie bereits während acht Jahren photographiert. In dem daraus entstandenen berühmten Bild A JEWISH GIANT AT HOME WITH HIS PARENTS IN THE BRONX (Ein jüdischer Riese zu Hause bei seinen Eltern in der Bronx, 1970) schwingt die Dramatik ihrer frühen Photographien von grellen Kinoplakaten und Filmhöhepunkten mit.

Im Dunkel des Kinos herrscht eine gespenstische Atmosphäre: Die Leinwand wird durch flimmerndes Licht belebt, und das Publikum, die Welt der Lebenden verschwindet im Dunkeln. Arbus entdeckt in ihren Filmsujets einen trockenen, dem Schauerlichen verpflichteten Humor. Wenn ihre Kamera unerschrocken bluttriefende Hände und ausgestochene Augen fixiert, trifft sie einen zentralen Nerv des Horrorgenres: den Wunsch, die Selbstgefälligkeit einer satten, bürgerlichen Welt zu erschüttern. Diese geordnete Bürgerwelt gibt auch den Hintergrund für die schockierenden Motive ihrer späteren Bilder ab. Wenn man die porträtierten Personen – den wild grimassierenden Jungen mit der Handgranate in der klauenartigen Faust, die grotesk gekleideten Insassen einer Irrenanstalt – aus dem Bild

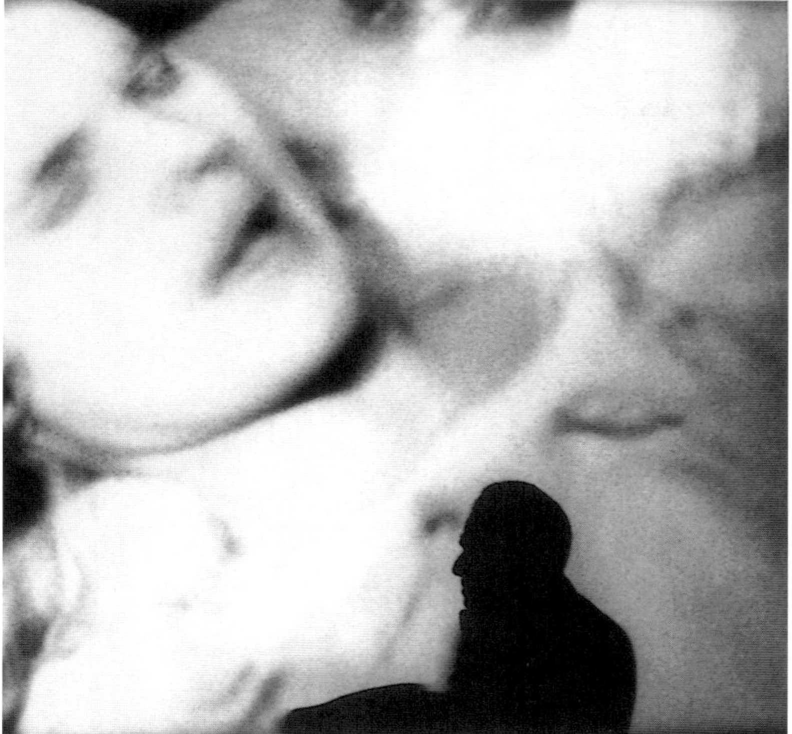

DIANE ARBUS, CARROLL BAKER ON SCREEN in "Baby Doll," 1956,
gelatine-silver print, 14 x 11" /
CARROLL BAKER AUF DER KINOLEINWAND, in «Baby Doll», 35, 6 x 27, 9 cm.

nimmt, bleibt nur eine verschwommene Landschaft. Deckt man die Figuren auf diesen Photos mit der Hand ab, so verwandeln diese sich in Bilder eines Photo-Sezessionisten: hübsche Ornamente aus verschlungenen Ästen, gesprenkeltes Licht. Arbus' Motive brauchen kein Setting; sie stechen aus dem Nebel und aus dem Dunkel hervor. Als in Stanley Kubriks Film *The Shining* Arbus' berühmtes Bild von den identischen Zwillingen erscheint, verlieren diese durch den Transfer nichts von ihrem sinistren Charme. Es ist das Unwiderstehliche eines kindlichen «Guck-guck-wo-bin-Ich», vermischt mit dem Kitzel einer Peepshow.

In Arbus' Filmphotos taucht *Baby Doll*, ein schwüles Südstaatendrama von Tennessee Williams, dem Meister der verqueren Leidenschaften, immer wieder auf. Als *Baby Doll* 1956 Premiere hatte, gab es einen Skandal. Die von den katholischen Sittenwächtern verurteilte Geschichte, die Williams erzählt, ist ein Drama der Verleumdungen und üblen Machenschaften in harten Zeiten. Die moralische Verkommenheit, die im Film gezeigt wird, ist eher dekorativ – nichts weiter als ein paar leere Schnapsflaschen und eine schöne junge Frau, die sich in einem Messingbett räkelt –, doch die Geschichte legt die ganze Gemeinheit menschlicher Verhaltensweisen bloss und entmystifiziert so noble Begriffe wie die Hochherzigkeit des Südens und die Unantastbarkeit der Ehe. Auf einem BABY DOLL-Photo von Arbus sieht man Carroll Bakers Gesicht in einer überwältigenden Grossaufnahme. Der Rahmen der Leinwand ist verschwunden, und an den Rändern erscheinen keine Schatten. Bakers Baby Doll, ein blasses, verschwommenes Phantom, beherrscht den realen Raum von Arbus' Bild. Im Vordergrund sieht man den dunklen Umriss eines Mannes im Profil. Wie eine Schiessbudenfigur schiebt er sich zwischen den Betrachter und die helle Leinwand.

Im Kino muss das Publikum nur zuschauen. Die bewegten Bilder wollen überwältigen. In jenem behaglichen Dunkel kann das Publikum aber nicht beliebig lange auf ein Bild starren. Es sind diese Erfahrungen am Times Square, die für das Lebenswerk von Diane Arbus wegweisend waren.

(Übersetzung: Uta Goridis)

CUMULUS

From America

IN EVERY EDITION OF PARKETT, TWO CUMULUS CLOUDS, ONE FROM AMERICA, THE OTHER FROM EUROPE, FLOAT OUT TO AN INTERESTED PUBLIC. THEY CONVEY INDIVIDUAL OPINIONS, ASSESSMENTS, AND MEMORABLE ENCOUNTERS—AS ENTIRELY PERSONAL PRESENTATIONS OF PROFESSIONAL ISSUES.

OUR CONTRIBUTORS TO THIS ISSUE ARE NANCY PRINCENTHAL, A WRITER AND ART CRITIC WHO LIVES IN NEW YORK, AND LIONEL BOVIER AND CHRISTOPHE CHERIX, TWO ART CRITICS FROM GENEVA.

NOW YOU SEE IT, NOW YOU DON'T
THE MAGIC MAGIC BOOK

NANCY PRINCENTHAL

Compare illusion and deception, and you will arrive at something very close to a minimum threshold for visual art. If there is one accusation more threatening than any other to the entire art-making enterprise, it is the knowing perpetration of deceit. There are, to be sure, qualifications, as for optical tricks: Fooling the eye is, after all, stock-in-trade to centuries of realism, and contributes not a little to several varieties of abstraction as well. Nor is it a question of fakes, or forgeries; the anathema on deceit remains despite a vigorous and extended assault by post-modern theorists on the authority of the original. The problem is, rather, with the kind of dishonesty—of con artistry—in which practitioners try to make the audience believe something they know to be false, or, conversely, hide what is true.

Another way of describing this concealment is as an exercise in bad faith, and if the term seems the most damaging, it is also most suggestive. With it, the full circle of associations is drawn between art and belief. Along its circumference lie religion and magic, once considered a form of apostasy ("the black arts"), sleight of hand, deviant intellectual and physical feats, and the willing suspension of skepticism. And, rotating freely among these positions, *The Magic Magic Book.* Conceived by Whitney Museum librarian May Castleberry, it is the fourteenth title in her "Artists and Writers" series, which has produced consistently stimulating collaborations between the likes of George Condo and William Burroughs, Barbara Kruger and Stephen King, Vija Celmins and Czeslaw Milosz. *The Magic Magic Book* (1995) is a particular tour de force, a sumptuous example of what the author of its introduction, world-renowned magician Ricky Jay, calls the "oldest manufactured conjuring prop." In these volumes images seem to appear and vanish at the displayer's will, a sleight achieved with the use of a system of tabs; along the lines of big dictionaries with thumb-holds for every letter, magic books are designed so that holding each tab in turn makes groups of pages move as one, hiding images in between. In some early versions of this trick, which has been in use for over five hundred years, tissue-thin paper allows the conjurer to turn the pages by blowing on them (hence an alternative name, "blow books"); in the hands of a practiced performer, the pages would seem to move by themselves, each time revealing a different series of pictures.

The magic book Castleberry organized begins with Jay's richly illustrated and altogether fascinating explanatory text, which deftly reveals some secrets while maintaining others; it constitutes the first of two volumes. The second is the magic book proper, with contributions by six artists. Most were given one tab position (i.e., one four-page sequence) on one side of the book, which can be turned upside down to read from back to front. Philip Taaffe's photoengravings from linocuts, each different, send daisy-shaped pinwheels spinning across the page in layered shades of green, orange and black. Taaffe is the only artist to have worked both sides of the book, having created a full eight spreads (with what

are his first editioned prints). From one cover, the pinwheels become progressively bigger and disorderly from one spread to the next; from the other cover, the progression is reversed. Vija Celmins's four-page sequence repeats, twice to a spread, a bright black-and-white wood engraving of a closely rippled sea. Both Celmins's and Taaffe's sequences are, in a deliberately conventional but deeply engrossing way, hypnotic (and though both hint at illusory animation, the images in a magic book are meant to be seen as static; they are not fanned quickly like flip-books). Taking a different perspective on the vocabulary of historical popular entertainment, Jane Hammond created lively collages of imagery found in historical blow books, much of it silhouetted in black; there are harlequins and bunnies, ribbons and combs, and other accessories of childhood and/or circuses.

William Wegman's doleful canine capers here take the form of two dogs striking poses with simple white cubes as props. (The Cristal Raster process in which they are reproduced gives them a suede-soft glow with a magic all its own.) The Weimaraners shadow each

other, one standing and one lying down, or they line up tail-to-nose, or, to greatest comic effect, they partly hide behind the boxes to create, together, the impression of a very long dog, or a headless one. If Wegman makes a (partial) disappearing act into an irresistibly corny joke, Glenn Ligon sharpens it into the shape of a political tool. Ligon's contribution is a repeated stenciled passage from Ralph Ellison's *Invisible Man*, over which is superimposed a degraded xerox of a man who may be black, taken from the earliest known American magic book. Not just the metaphor of invisibility, but the secondary images Ellison used are eerily pertinent. "I am invisible, understand, simply because people refuse to see me," he wrote. "Like the bodiless heads you sometimes see in circus sideshows, it is as though I have been surrounded by mirrors of hard, distorting glass."

Proceeding from the other cover, there are, in addition to Taaffe's pinwheels, borrowed historical images (devils spitting fire from ears and anus, a pair of harlequins disporting in two different poses); an "alphabetical folly" designed by Patrick Reagh, who set the

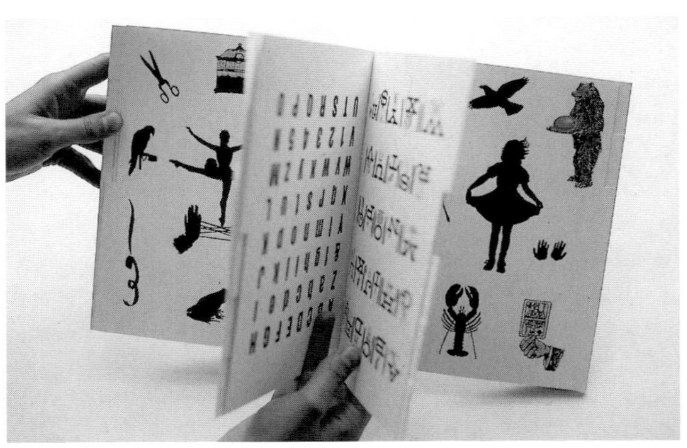

book's letterpress text; and instructions for operating the book, in four languages. The last sequence of pages, in both directions, is blank.

In his prologue, Jay cites a story by Borges about a salesman for a Bible with disappearing images. But the thrust of Borges's writing concerns textuality itself—its immateriality and manifold undecidability, which are of a piece with its immortality. In magic books, on the other hand, it is the conventions of thoroughly material (and materially vulnerable) graven images that are in question, specifically as they appear in bound books. Or rather, these are the conventions that must be securely in place for the illusion to work. The magic book has only an incidental kinship to elaborately structured bookworks built around accordion folds and gatefolds, cutouts and pop-up elements, whether historical or contemporary (as in the recent work of Scott McCarney, Clifton Meador, Margot Lovejoy, or Carol Barton). As with any magician's prop, the magic book is convincing in proportion to its seeming ordinariness. So the thematic continuity between image and effect in Taaffe's optical tricks and Celmins's mesmerizing surfaces, Hammond's dancing silhouettes and Wegman's trained animal act, are to the magic book something like a highwire stunt, putting its success in danger to heighten the pleasure taken in its achievement.

So, the drum rolls. It is preceded by a flourish of precariously stacked cards, drawn by Justen Ladda across the front of the publication's slipcase. And does the magic work? Well, almost. But even for a dexterous and patient reader, the creamy, thick pages of this opulent publication tend to defeat the illusion, by turning too stiffly. Of course, the instructions bound right into it work against it, too, by giving up the game if advertantly revealed. But it's more than that. The images—because they are art, hence irremediably self-conscious?—simply don't disappear on cue. They freeze in plain sight. The oldest trick in the magician's bag is put into our hands, and falters.

Or, looked at another way, has its ultimate triumph: The deception remains intact, since our trouble controlling it only increases our respect for its cunning, and for the deftness of those performers who can keep it alive. Like the midway barker he once was, Jay announces in his prologue, "the most elaborate blow book ever assembled is almost certainly the companion volume to the book you are reading." Step right up, ladies and gentlemen! he might as well say. Try your luck! Test your skill!

The Magic Magic Book can be read, that is, as an essay on power, and in particular the power of illusion. In what plays as a broad burlesque of the intimacy between seer and seen, touch and sight ("vision is palpation with the look") that Merleau-Ponty described in *The Visible and the Invisible, The Magic Magic Book* makes the manual operation of the instrument of deception as important as its visual contents. Viewers become performers and artists are shunted to an eccentric but still critical position somewhere between illustrator and fabulist, while substantial control is exercised by an agent of illusion here known as editor.

Then there is, too, the text's author. In addition to being an acclaimed performer and, recently, consultant to Hollywood screenwriters and directors, Jay is a committed bibliophile, an avid collector of books relating to magic, and an active historian of the field. In *Learned Pigs and Fireproof Women,* he describes four centuries of performances that are as entertaining as they are incredible. While Jay provides extensive notes about source material, there are, not surprisingly, very few revelations of trade secrets (a 1993 profile of Jay in *The New Yorker* stressed his "rigid opposition to public revelations of the techniques of magic"). What is surprising is Jay's evident fascination with genius and abnormality, and, especially, the frailty of the distinction between them. He gives numerous accounts of performers with seemingly impossible capacities for remembering and discerning ("mind reading"), and not a few examples of the same capabilities in trained animals (e.g., the "learned pigs" of the book's title). He describes entertainers who use their bodies to perform prodigious mental feats, as in writing ten different letters simultaneously with chalk tied to each of their fingers. Ray implies that all these acts reflect disciplined practice but doesn't rule out native ability nor even, altogether, the occult.

This ambiguity is, of course, at the heart of audience response to magic. We want magicians to have special, even freakish, powers (that is, we want to be fooled), but we like the realm of their operation to be tightly limited. We want artists, on the other hand, to be like us, but more so, and to tell us things about our world with unflinching candor. That, anyway, is the tidy way to categorize art and magic. It is the strength of *The Magic Magic Book* to mess up these distinctions, to have us question the neat opposition between skillful illusionism and frank deception.

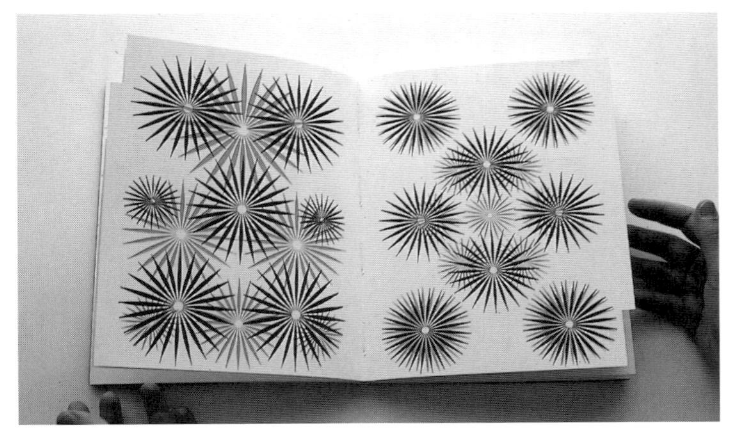

THE MAGIC MAGIC BOOK: Contribution of / Beitrag von Philip Taaffe.

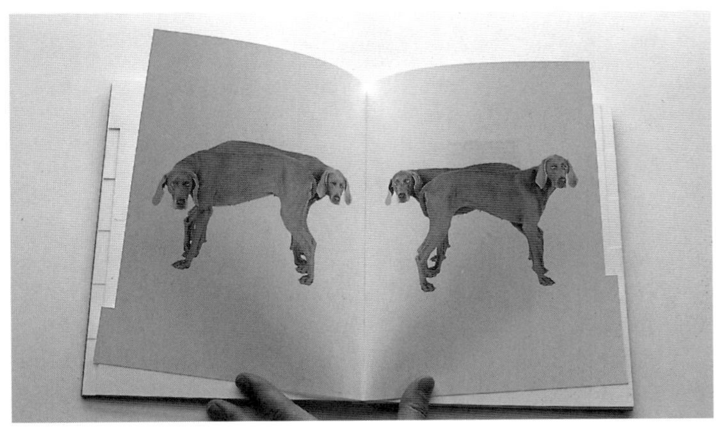

THE MAGIC MAGIC BOOK: Contribution of / Beitrag von William Wegman.

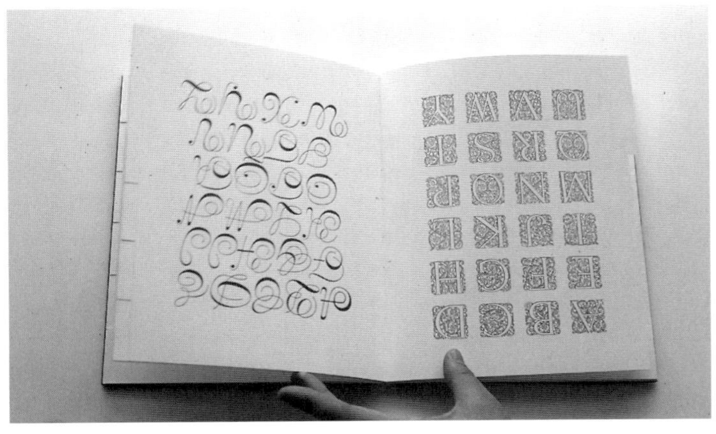

THE MAGIC MAGIC BOOK: historical "blow book" images / historische «Pustebuch»-Bilder.

MAL SIEHT MAN ES, MAL SIEHT MAN'S NICHT

THE MAGIC MAGIC BOOK

NANCY PRINCENTHAL

Vergleicht man Illusion und Täuschung miteinander, so stösst man auf eine Art Mindestkriterium für die bildende Kunst. Der schlimmste und gefährlichste Vorwurf, den man dem ganzen Kunstbetrieb machen kann, ist jener der bewussten Täuschung. Natürlich muss man auch bei den optischen Tricks zu unterscheiden wissen; schliesslich gehört die Irreführung des Auges seit Jahrhunderten zum Handwerkszeug des Realismus und spielt auch in zahlreichen Formen der Abstraktion eine nicht unwesentliche Rolle. Es geht hier auch nicht um die Frage der Imitation oder Fälschung. Ungeachtet eines ebenso nachdrücklichen wie umfassend geführten Angriffs der postmodernen Theoretiker auf die Autorität des Originals ist diese Art der Täuschung nach wie vor verpönt. Das Problem liegt vielmehr in der spezifischen Unaufrichtigkeit, mit der gewisse Scharlatane dem Publikum bewusst etwas Falsches vorgaukeln oder umgekehrt etwas Wahres vorenthalten.

Man könnte eine solche Unterschlagung auch als einen Akt des bösen Willens bezeichnen. Und wie hart dieser Ausdruck auch wirkt, so ergiebig ist er. Er weckt eine Fülle von Assoziationen rund um Kunst und Glauben, als da wären: Religion und Magie – letztere einst als eine Form religiöser Verirrung betrachtet, daher der Name «Schwarze Kunst» –, allerlei Taschenspielertricks, abnorme intellektuelle und körperliche Fähigkeiten sowie der bereitwillige Verzicht auf eine skeptische Haltung. Und frei schwebend zwischen all diesen Positionen, *The Magic Magic Book (Das magische Zauberbuch).* Das ist der 14. Band in der Reihe «Artists and Writers», die May Castleberry, Bibliothekarin am Whitney Museum, konzipierte und die immer wieder anregende Kollaborationen, etwa zwischen George Condo und William Burroughs, Barbara Kruger und Stephen King sowie Vija Celmins und Czeslan Milosz, hervorbrachte. *The Magic Magic Book* (1995) ist ein ganz besonderes Prachtstück, ein aufwendiges Beispiel dafür, was der berühmte Magier Ricky Jay in der Einleitung «die älteste Zauber-Requisite der Welt» nennt. In diesen Büchern scheinen die Bilder nach dem Willen des Magiers aufzutauchen und wieder zu verschwinden, ein Zaubertrick, der mit Hilfe eines Systems von Indexmulden zustande kommt. Wie die grossen Lexika mit Daumenregister, wo für jeden Buchstaben eine Daumenmulde reserviert ist, sind die Zauberbücher so angelegt, dass durch den Griff in eine Mulde eine bestimmte Anzahl Seiten wie eine einzige umschlägt und die Bilder dazwischen unsichtbar bleiben. Bei älteren Varianten dieses Tricks, der seit 500 Jahren praktiziert wird, sind die Seiten so dünn, dass der Zauberer sie durch Blasen umblättern kann (sie heissen deshalb auch «Pustebücher»). In den Händen eines geübten Zauberers blättern sich die Seiten wie von selbst um und zeigen jedesmal eine andere Bilderfolge.

Das von Castleberry zusammengestellte Zauberbuch beginnt mit Jays reich bebilderten und überaus faszinierenden Erläuterungen, die geschickt einige Geheimnisse lüften, andere dagegen nicht. Dies ist der erste von zwei Bänden, der zweite ist das eigentliche Zauberbuch mit Beiträgen von sechs Künstlern. Jeder erhielt (in der Regel) je eine Indexmulde, das heisst vier aufeinanderfolgende Seiten, auf einer Seite des Buches, das sich auch um 180 Grad drehen und von hinten nach vorne lesen lässt. In Philip Taaffes jeweils unterschiedlichen Autotypien nach Linolschnitten drehen sich kleine gänseblümchenförmige Windräder in grünen, orangen und schwarzen Schattierungen über die Seiten. Als einziger Künstler hat Taaffe beide Buchseiten in Anspruch genommen, so dass sich sein (übrigens erster) Auflagendruck über acht Seiten erstreckt. Je nachdem, ob man das Buch von vorn oder hinten durchblättert, werden die Windräder immer grösser und unbändiger bzw. kleiner. Einen immer gleichen, brillanten schwarzweissen Holzschnitt, der eine kabbelige Meeresoberfläche zeigt, verteilt Vija Celmins über vier Seiten, zwei davon auf jeder Doppelseite. Die Bildfolgen von Celmins und von Taaffe wirken beide auf bewusst konventionelle, aber eindrückliche Weise hypnotisch. (Aber auch wenn beide hier mit der Illusion der Animation spielen, sind die Bilder in einem Zauberbuch

doch dazu bestimmt, statisch betrachtet zu werden; sie sind nicht dazu gedacht, wie im Daumenkino schnell am Auge vorbeizufliegen.) Jane Hammond entwickelte einen eigenen Blick auf das Vokabular historisch-volkstümlicher Unterhaltung und schuf rasante Collagen aus Bildmaterial, das sie in historischen «Pustebüchern» gefunden hat. Als schwarze Silhouetten begegnen uns Harlekine und Hasen, Bänder, Kämme und andere Kindheits- und/ oder Zirkusaccessoires.

William Wegmans traurige Hundekapriolen bescheren uns diesmal zwei Hunde, die mit einfachen weissen Würfeln posieren. (Die Kristallraster-Entwicklung verleiht ihnen ein samtenes Leuchten von eigenartigem Zauber.) Die Weimaraner wirken wie ihr gegenseitiges Schattenbild; der eine liegt, der andere steht, oder sie stehen – Nase an Schwanz – hintereinander, oder – was am komischsten aussieht – sie verstecken sich teilweise hinter den Würfeln, um zusammen den Eindruck zu erwecken, es handle sich um einen besonders langen oder kopflosen Hund. Während Wegman das (teilweise) Verschwinden zum unwiderstehlich blöden Witz macht, schmiedet Glenn Ligon daraus ein scharfes politisches Werkzeug. Er hat über eine immer wiederkehrende, mit Schablone übertragene Passage aus Ralph Ellisons *The Invisible Man* eine abgeschwächte Photokopie von einem – wahrscheinlich schwarzen – Mann gelegt, die aus dem ältesten bekannten amerikanischen Zauberbuch stammt. Nicht nur die Metapher der Unsichtbarkeit, sondern auch die Sekundärformen, mit denen Ellison arbeitet, ergeben einen verblüffenden Beitrag zum Thema. «Sehen Sie, ich bin unsichtbar, weil die Leute mich nicht sehen wollen»,

schrieb er. «Wie bei den körperlosen Köpfen, die man manchmal in Zirkus-Shows sieht, ist es auch hier, als wäre ich von Zerrspiegeln umgeben.»

Blättert man das Buch von der anderen Seite durch, stösst man neben Taaffes Windmühlen auf entlehnte historische Bilder, etwa Teufel, die aus Ohren und Anus Feuer speien, oder Harlekine, die sich in unterschiedlichen Posen vergnügen – eine «alphabetische Narretei», die Patrick Reagh entworfen hat, der auch für den Bleisatz verantwortlich zeichnet –, und auf eine viersprachige Anleitung zum Umgang mit dem Buch. Die letzten beiden Seiten sind jeweils leer.

In seinem Vorwort zitiert Jay eine Geschichte von Borges über einen Händler für Bibeln mit verschwindenden Bildern. Borges zielt aber auf den Text als solchen – auf seine Immaterialität und Mehrdeutigkeit, die unmittelbar mit seinem absoluten Geltungsanspruch einhergehen. Die Zauberbücher dagegen spielen mit den Konventionen der durchaus materiellen (und dadurch auch verletzlichen) Radierungen und Stiche, wie sie in gebundenen Büchern verwendet werden. Das heisst, diese Konventionen sind die Voraussetzung dafür, dass die Illusion überhaupt wirken kann. Es besteht eine lediglich zufällige Verwandtschaft zwischen dem magischen Buch und komplizierten Buchgestaltungen, seien diese nun historisch oder zeitgenössisch, mit Leporello, Torfalz, Stanzung und/oder dreidimensionalen Elementen (wie etwa die jüngsten Arbeiten von Scott McCarney, Clifton Meador, Margot Lovejoy oder Carol Barton). Wie alle Zauber-Requisiten ist auch das Zauberbuch um so überzeugender, je unauffälliger es wirkt. So ist die thematische Verbin-

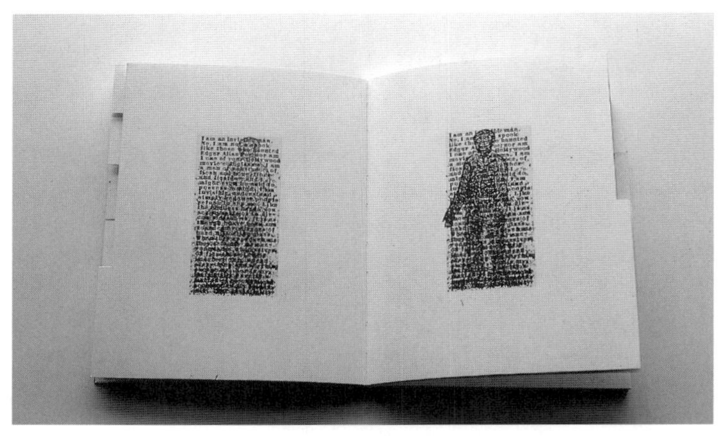

THE MAGIC MAGIC BOOK: Beitrag von / contribution of Glenn Ligon.

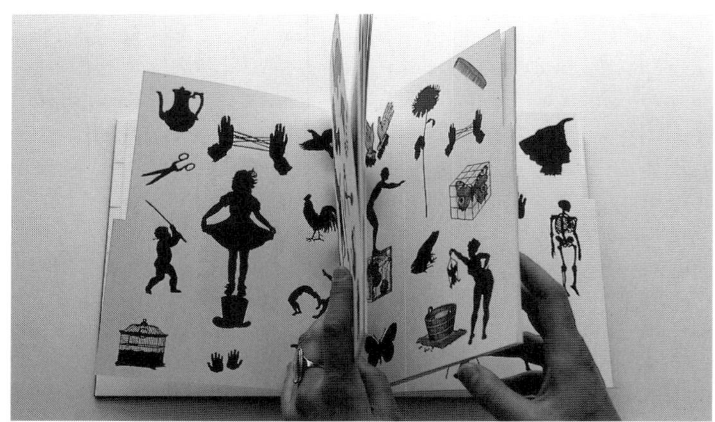

THE MAGIC MAGIC BOOK: Beitrag von / contribution of Jane Hammond.

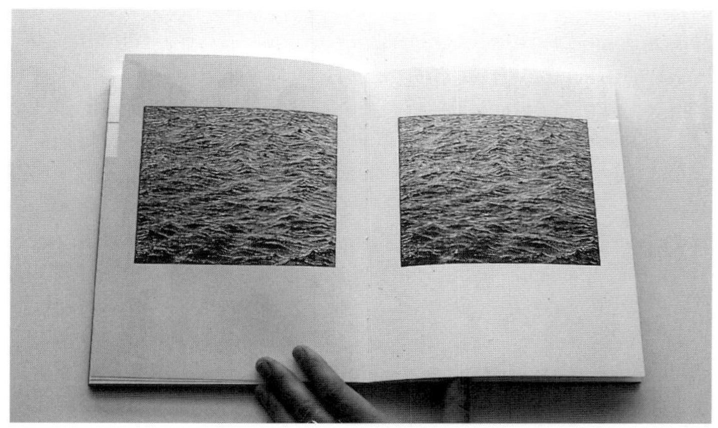

THE MAGIC MAGIC BOOK: Beitrag von / contribution of Vija Celmins.

dung zwischen Bild und Effekt bei Taaffes optischen Tricks ebenso wie bei Celmins hypnotisierenden Oberflächen, bei Hammonds tanzenden Silhouetten wie bei Wegmans Dressurnummer ein Drahtseilakt, der den Erfolg zu gefährden scheint, nur um schliesslich die Lust am Gelingen noch zu steigern.

Die Glückstrommel dreht sich. Zuvor winkt noch ein Bündel zweifelhaft gemischter Karten, die Justen Ladda auf der Vorderseite des Schubers verteilt hat. Und funktioniert der Zauber nun? Na ja, sagen wir fast. Aber selbst einem noch so geschickten und geduldigen Leser können die cremefarbenen, stabilen Seiten dieser oppulenten Publikation die Illusion leicht rauben, weil sie zu steif sind beim Umblättern. Natürlich wirken auch die mit eingebundenen Anweisungen störend, da sie das Spiel bei aufmerksamer Beschäftigung damit auffliegen lassen. Aber es kommt noch schlimmer: Die Bilder – vielleicht weil sie Kunstwerke sind und sich deshalb ihrer selbst unweigerlich bewusst? – verschwinden einfach nicht auf Kommando. Sie sind und bleiben deutlich sichtbar. Man gibt uns den ältesten Trick aus der Zauberkiste in die Hand – und er funktioniert nicht.

Andersherum betrachtet, feiert er seinen grössten Triumph: die ursprüngliche Illusion bleibt unangetastet, denn unsere angestrengten Versuche, den Trick in den Griff zu bekommen, vergrössern nur den Respekt vor seiner Raffinesse und der Gewandtheit derer, die ihn beherrschen. Wie der Marktschreier, der er einmal war, verkündet Jay in seinem Vorwort: «Das ausgeklügeltste Pustebuch, das es jemals gab, ist mit ziemlicher Sicherheit der Begleitband zu diesem Buch.» Aufgepasst,

meine Damen und Herren! Er könnte genausogut sagen: Versuchen Sie Ihr Glück! Testen Sie Ihre Geschicklichkeit!

Man kann *The Magic Magic Book* als Abhandlung über die Macht, insbesondere über die Macht der Illusion, lesen. Als umfassende Persiflage auf die enge Beziehung zwischen Betrachter und Betrachtetem, zwischen Berührung und Anblick («Sehen ist Begreifen mit Hilfe des Blicks»), wie sie Merleau-Ponty in seinem Buch *Das Sichtbare und das Unsichtbare* beschrieben hat, misst *The Magic Magic Book* dem manuellen Umgang mit dem Instrument der Täuschung ebensoviel Gewicht bei wie dem visuellen Inhalt. Die Betrachter werden zu Zauberkünstlern, und den Künstlern wird eine exzentrische, wenn auch durchaus kritische Rolle, irgendwo zwischen Illustrator und Schwindler, zugewiesen, während die eigentliche Kontrolle beim Vermittler der Illusion liegt, hier also beim Herausgeber.

Dann ist da natürlich noch der Verfasser des Textes. Jay ist nicht nur ein gefeierter Illusionist und Zauberkünstler, sondern neuerdings auch Berater von Drehbuchautoren und Regisseuren in Hollywood. Darüber hinaus ist er leidenschaftlich bibliophil und sammelt mit Begeisterung Bücher, die mit Magie zu tun haben, und betätigt sich ausserdem als Historiker auf diesem Gebiet. In *Learned Pigs and Fireproof Women* (Gebildete Schweine und feuerfeste Frauen) beschreibt er 400 Jahre einer ebenso unterhaltsamen wie unglaublichen Geschichte der Zauberkunst. Jay erteilt zwar ausführlich Auskunft über das Quellenmaterial; von seinen Berufsgeheimnissen gibt er dagegen verständlicherweise wenig preis. (In einem Porträt, das *The New Yorker*

1993 von ihm brachte, betonte Jay seine «tiefe Abneigung gegen die öffentliche Preisgabe von Zaubertechniken».) Überraschend ist hingegen seine unverhüllte Faszination durch Genialität und Abnormalität und vor allem durch die hauchdünne Grenze zwischen beiden. Er nennt zahlreiche Beispiele von Zauberern mit scheinbar unmöglichen, telepathischen Gedächtnis- und Erkenntnisfähigkeiten sowie eine ganze Reihe von Beispielen derselben Fähigkeiten bei dressierten Tieren (das sind die «gebildeten Schweine» aus dem Buchtitel). Er beschreibt Entertainer, die mit ihrem Körper erstaunliche geistige Leistungen vollbringen, beispielsweise mit an den Fingern befestigten Kreidestücken zehn verschiedene Buchstaben gleichzeitig schreiben. Jay betont, dass all diese Fähigkeiten von grösster Trainingsdisziplin zeugen, schliesst aber angeborene Talente und selbst Okkultes nicht aus.

Dieses Zwiespältige ist natürlich ein wesentlicher Teil der Faszination, welche die Magie auf das Publikum ausübt. Wir wünschen uns Zauberer mit besonderen, durchaus auch abnormen Kräften (das heisst, wir wollen getäuscht werden), aber ihr Handlungsspielraum soll klar begrenzt sein. Andererseits sollen die Künstler so sein wie wir, aber in ausgeprägterer Form, und sie sollen uns ungeschminkte Wahrheiten über unsere Welt mitteilen. Das ist jedenfalls die übliche Unterscheidung zwischen Kunst und Magie. Es ist das Verdienst von *The Magic Magic Book*, diese klare Unterscheidung zu verwischen und uns dahin zu führen, dass wir den scharfen Gegensatz zwischen raffiniertem Illusionismus und unverhohlener Täuschung in Frage stellen.

(Übersetzung: Nansen)

CUMULUS

Aus Europa

IN JEDER AUSGABE VON PARKETT PEILT EINE CUMULUS-WOLKE AUS AMERIKA UND EINE AUS EUROPA DIE INTERESSIERTEN KUNSTFREUNDE AN. SIE TRÄGT PERSÖNLICHE RÜCKBLICKE, BEURTEILUNGEN UND DENKWÜRDIGE BEGEGNUNGEN MIT SICH – ALS JEWEILS GANZ EIGENE DARSTELLUNG EINER BERUFSMÄSSIGEN AUSEINANDERSETZUNG.

IN DIESEM HEFT ÄUSSERN SICH DIE KUNSTKRITIKER LIONEL BOVIER UND CHRISTOPHE CHERIX AUS GENF SOWIE DIE KRITIKERIN NANCY PRINCENTHAL AUS NEW YORK.

EIN GEDANKENAUSTAUSCH

LIONEL BOVIER UND CHRISTOPHE CHERIX

Die Situation in Genf und im weiteren Umkreis dieser Stadt zeichnet sich zur Zeit durch eine beachtliche Anzahl Ausstellungen von Künstlerinnen aus, deren Arbeit ganz allgemein die Kritik zur Aufdeckung eines feministischen Standpunktes anregt. So die Werke von Sylvie Fleury und Pipilotti Rist, über die Christoph Doswald schreibt, sie würden mit unterschiedlichen Methoden das «Frausein im Postfeminismus» thematisieren.[1] Den beiden Künstlerinnen ist gegenwärtig in Genf im *MAMCO (Musée d'art moderne et contemporain)* beziehungsweise im *Centre d'art contemporain* je eine Ausstellung gewidmet. Durch ein zufälliges zeitliches Zu-sammentreffen können ihre Werke mit jenen von Gillian Wearing in der *Usine, Le Consortium* in Dijon, von Rosemarie Trockel im *Centre genevois de gravure contemporaine* in Genf, von Leni Hoffmann, Vanessa Beecroft und Julia Scher im *Fri-Art* in Fribourg verglichen werden. Diese (Fast-)Gleichzeitigkeit bietet uns die Gelegenheit, in einer Betrachtung der Werke der beiden Künstlerinnen die Erheblichkeit der feministischen Dimension zu überprüfen.

Nichts ist einfacher, als in den Installationen von Sylvie Fleury ein polemisches Engagement gegenüber einer heroischen Tradition der abstrakten Malerei auszumachen, wenn sie ein Paar Schuhe aus der «Mondrian-Kollektion» des Schuhdesigners Patrick Cox auf Pseudo-Bilder von Pollock, Richter, Albers oder Buren, die als Sockel dienen, setzt. Aus diesem Akt der Umkehr könnte man eine Revanche für die typisch männliche Fähigkeit, das Werk vor dem Betrachter aufzupflanzen, herauslesen; und folglich hier die Metapher eines Tretens-an-Ort des Image der heroischen und einschüchternden Kunst-Figuren unserer Zeit erkennen. Das bedeutete allerdings, dem Zusammenstoss zweier heterogener Systeme, Kunst und Mode – dessen Wert vor allem im Zusammenwirken dieser beiden Gebiete liegt –,

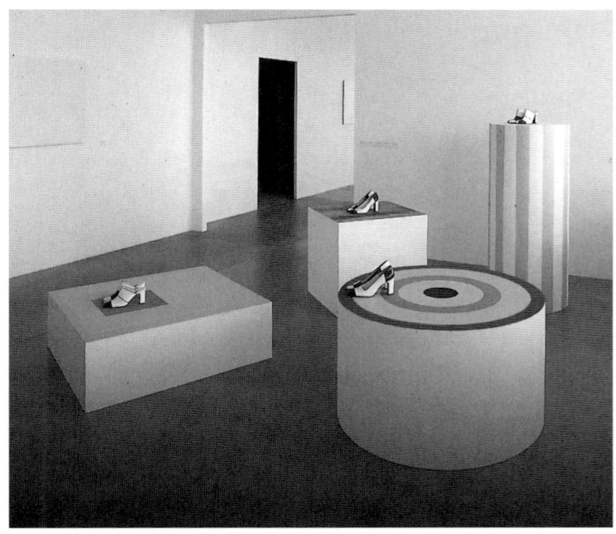

SYLVIE FLEURY, PIET, JOSEPH & PATRICK, 1996;
PIET, GERHARD & PATRICK, 1996; PIET, KENNETH &
PATRICK, 1996; PIET, DANIEL & PATRICK, 1996.
Installation Musée d'art moderne et contemporain, Genève.
(PHOTO: I. KALKKINEN)

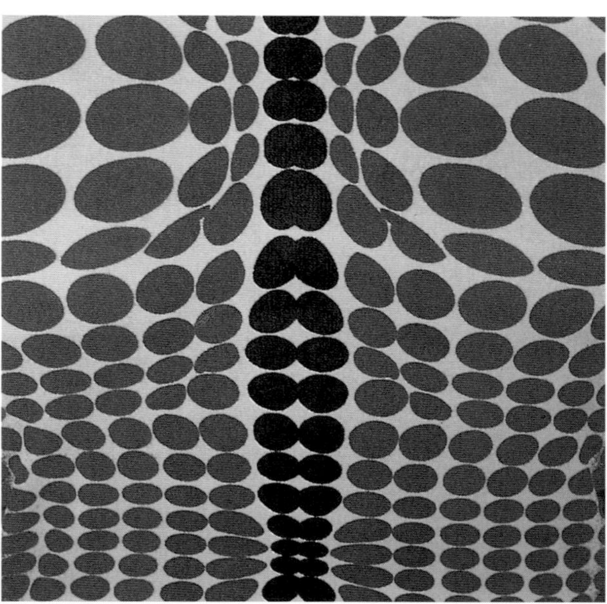

SYLVIE FLEURY, Bild aus der Photoserie /
picture from the photo series VICTOR ET JEAN-PAUL, 1995.

eine übertriebene Tragweite zu verleihen. Anders gesagt: Es ist Mondrian, durch einen spezifischen Kreislauf der Wiederverwertung historischer Formen in die Sprache der Kleidung übersetzt, der hier auf das Bezugssystem einer bestimmten abstrakten Malerei prallt. Die als Sockel benützte Malerei wird somit bereits wie ein ausgedientes Stereotyp behandelt und eignet sich dafür, in das «système de la mode» (Roland Barthes) geworfen zu werden… Zudem kann man sich fragen, ob es in Sylvie Fleurys Photoserie VICTOR UND JEAN-PAUL – ein Gewebe mit geometrischen Motiven, das, um einen optischen Effekt zu erzielen, zerdehnt ist – wichtiger ist, den Druck auf dem Stoff als Kollektion von Jean-Paul Gaultier mit einer Referenz an Vasarely zu erkennen oder zu bemerken, dass es eine weibliche Brust ist, die die optische Täuschung hervorruft.

Schon vor Jahren bemängelte Rosalind Krauss an den mythifizierenden, feministischen Interpretationen der Photographien von Cindy Sherman: «Indem sie ständig Shermans Werk als mythisch liest, will heissen dem Beispiel der Sicht des Mannes folgt – ‹Schauen Sie! Die Frau wird im Strahl des Blicks zum Fetisch erhoben› –, verpasst es die feministische Kritik festzustellen, dass Shermans Kunst den Schleier fallen lässt.»[2] Krauss beanstandete zudem, dass durch die viel zu grosse Aufmerksamkeit für das Narrative der Figuren, in deren Rolle Sherman jeweils schlüpft (in ihren Arbeiten der 80er Jahre), die formale Recherche (Ausschnitt, Blickwinkel usw.) und der Einsatz filmischer Mittel, die in ihrem Verfahren die eigentlichen Sinnstifter sind, unbeachtet bleiben.

Unter diesem Gesichtspunkt müsste Pipilotti Rists Ausstellung «Shooting Divas» eine Neu-Überprüfung ihrer Arbeit einleiten, nicht mehr aus der Perspektive, dass sie «einen via Pop auf eine seltsame Reise (…) in die verborgensten Regionen der weiblichen Psyche führt»,[3] sondern dass hier ein spezifisches Produktionssystem (Video) offengelegt ist, bei dem der Arbeitsvorgang die ästhetische Beurteilung ausschliesst. Durch das Umfunktionieren des Ausstellungsraums zu einem Drehort für zehn Videoclips zu zwei von ihr und Andreas Guggisberg geschriebenen Songs fordert Rist den Besucher auf, in ihr Studio einzudringen, wo die verschiedenen Elemente (vom Dekor zum Esstisch über die Garderobe und die Coiffeuse) vor allem eine funktionelle Aufgabe erfüllen. Dieser Pragmatismus in der Benützung des Raumes und der Ausstellungssituation bringt uns dazu, Pipilotti Rists Eingriff im *Musée d'art et d'histoire*, 1995 in Genf, neu zu überdenken. Die Performance, die sie damals organisiert hatte, als sie eine junge Frau aufforderte, einen Striptease in der artfremden Institution und in ihrem Bühnenbild vor Publikum durchzuführen, entstand wohl weniger in der Absicht, die Besucher mit einer gewissen «spektakulären» Ausbeutung der Frau zu konfrontieren oder eine zeitgenössische Form des akademischen Aktes live vorzuführen, als vielmehr mit dem Vorsatz, die Gelegenheit für eine doppelte Verfilmung zu schaffen – einmal durch die Kameramänner des öffentlichen Fernsehens und einmal durch die Künstlerin selbst – und diese Aufnahmen dann für die Realisation eines Videoclips zu benützen. Genau in dieser Überlagerung von Stereotypen – jener, die an die professionelle Bildproduktion der Medien gebunden sind, und jener einer Tätigkeit, die einem überholten Frauenbild entspricht – liegt der kritische Einsatz einer solchen Arbeit begründet. So möchte man vergleichsweise behaupten, dass Pipilotti Rist in ihrer neuen

Installation SHOOTING DIVAS, selbst wenn die agierenden Frauen Theatergruppen angehören, buchstäblich das Versprechen Warhols, «eine Viertelstunde Berühmtheit für jedermann», einlöst und in die Tat umsetzt. Gleich weit entfernt von *Karaoke* wie von der kommerziellen Videoclip-Produktion, symbolisiert die Ausstellung die Stärke des Integrationsvermögens und der Wiederverwertbarkeit der audiovisuellen Medien. Wie in den Photographien von Cindy Sherman, die Rosalind Krauss mit den Erfahrungen von Kuleshov (1917) vergleicht[4] – der, durch einen beim Schnitt erzeugten, parallelen Aufbau die Bilder mit mehr oder weniger Gefühl auflud, so dass der Betrachter nicht umhin konnte, in das stets gleiche Gesicht eines Schauspielers immer neue Emotionen hineinzulesen, ohne dabei um die bedeutungsverändernde Wirkung des Filmschnitts zu wissen –, so ist es auch in den Videos von Pipilotti Rist die Technik der Aufnahme, die den Sinn steuert.

Im Licht dieser Neubetrachtung der Werke von Pipilotti Rist und Sylvie Fleury scheint es, dass man – bei einer wieder aufgegriffenen feministischen Interpretation, die einst auch auf die Arbeiten von Valie Export, Adrian Piper oder Lynda Benglis angewandt wurde – dazu neigt, die spezifische Funktionsweise ihrer Arbeiten zu vertuschen. Die Distanz der Wiedererwägung des historischen Engagements der Frau auf dem Gebiet der Kunst schiebt sich also zwischen die angeblich feministischen Standpunkte der beiden Künstlerinnen und die erwähnten Werke. Dieselbe Distanz trennt sicherlich auch die «stacks» von Felix Gonzalez-Torres von den elementaren Formen der 60er Jahre. Und aus

derselben Entfernung nährt sich im Grunde auch die Ausstellung «Do it» von Hans-Ulrich Obrist im Ausstellungsraum Forde in Genf: Es kommt dort nicht so sehr darauf an, ob dieses oder jenes Werk von Ilya Kabakov oder Mike Kelley vorhanden ist, das sowieso, wie Lawrence Weiner meint, zu einem Drittel von Dritten (etwa vom jeweiligen Ausstellungsmacher) realisiert wurde, als vielmehr auf seine mehrfache Aktualisierung, bei welcher die subjektive Interpretation in der Fabrikationsart und der spezifischen Anlage der Arbeiten offengelegt wird. Nun waren in den 60er Jahren solche Prozesse, in denen das Werk der Versprachlichung überlassen wurde, immer von einem politischen Engagement getragen, das die Systeme der Kommerzialisierung und Institutionalisierung unterwandern wollte. Weder die Ausstellung «Do it» noch die Installationen von Sylvie Fleury oder Pipilotti Rist verkörpern letztlich die Lesarten, die sie nahezulegen scheinen: Der Rückgriff auf Stereotype (des Frauenbildes in der Kunst und in den Medien sowie der konzeptuellen Anwendungsarten oder Verbreitungsprinzipien) erscheint hier vielmehr wie eine Befreiung sowohl auf der sozialen wie auf der formalen Ebene.

(Übersetzung aus dem Französischen:
Jakobett)

1) Christoph Doswald, «Die Enge – der Diskurs – die Kunst in der Schweiz», in *Neue Bildende Kunst* 3, Juni 1996, S. 22.
2) Rosalind Krauss, «Cindy Sherman's Gravity: A Critical Fable», in *Artforum*, September 1993, S. 206.
3) Elizabeth Janus, «Pipilotti Rist», in *Artforum*, Sommer 1996, S. 100.
4) Rosalind Krauss, op. cit.

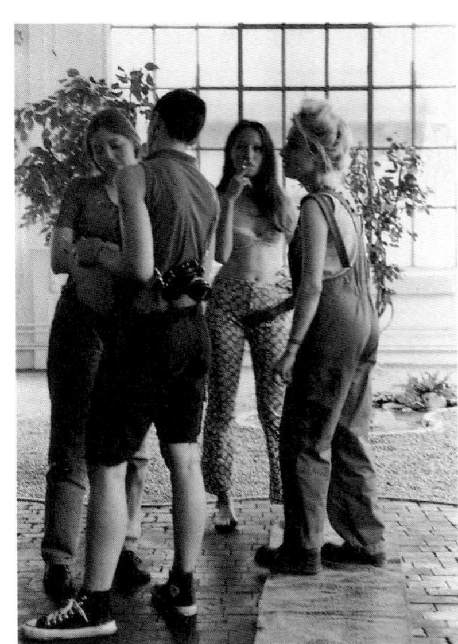

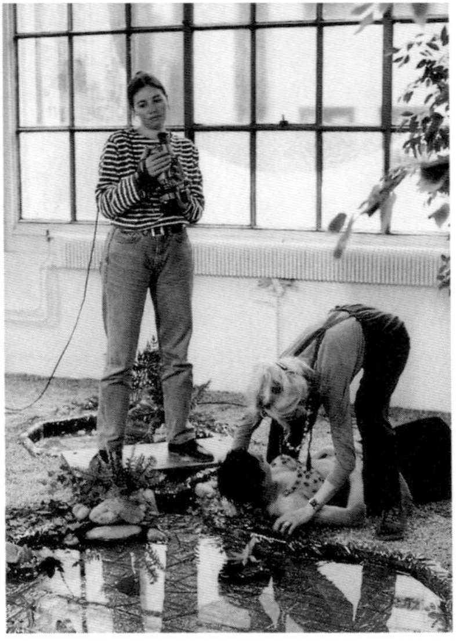

A CONVERSATION

LIONEL BOVIER & CHRISTOPHE CHERIX

The situation in the Geneva area is currently marked by a significant number of exhibitions involving artists whose works generally prompt a feminist reading. The works of Sylvie Fleury and Pipilotti Rist—exhibited respectively at the *MAMCO, Musée d'art moderne et contemporain,* and the *Centre d'art contemporain,* Geneva, and which, as Christoph Doswald has written, "take different approaches in dealing with postfeminist womanhood"[1]—coincide with the recent productions of Gillian Wearing (*Usine, Le Consortium,* Dijon), Rosemarie Trockel (*Centre genevois de gravure contemporaine,* Geneva), and Leni Hoffmann, Vanessa Beecroft, and Julia Scher (*Fri-Art,* Fribourg). Thus this (quasi) simultaneity invites us to reconsider the feminist dimension in our evaluation of these works.

In Sylvie Fleury's installations at *MAMCO,* which superimpose a pair of "Mondrian" shoes by designer Patrick Cox on pseudopaintings by Pollock, Richter, Albers or Buren, it would be easy to identify a polemical stance toward the heroic tradition in abstract painting—to see this upsetting of the frontality and verticality of the picture plane as an obvious subversion of the typically masculine impulse to prop the work up in front of the viewer, and thus as a metaphorical trampling of the leading art figures of our time. But that would be making too much of what is, after all, only a way of playing with the conflagration between the two heterogeneous systems of art and fashion, mainly validated by the reverberations it elicits. In other words, what we have is Mondrian retranslated into the clothing codes of a specific circuit of recycled historical forms and crumpled up on the network of references of a certain kind of abstract painting. And the painting which serves as the base and is already treated as a stereotype, in turn is liable to be absorbed into the "fashion system" (Roland Barthes). Similarly, in the series of Fleury's photographs that show a plot of geometric motifs stretched out for optical effect and bearing such titles as VICTOR AND JEAN-PAUL, is it more important to identify the Jean-Paul Gaultier printed fabric with Vasarely or to note that it's a feminine bust that is creating the visual disturbance here?

A few years ago Rosalind Krauss took aim at the mythifying feminist readings ascribed to Cindy Sherman's photographs: "In constantly reading

Sherman's work mythically, which is to say, as an example of how the Male Gaze works—'You see! There is the woman fetishized in the beam of the gaze'—feminist criticism fails to notice that Sherman's art drops the veil."[2] Krauss thus pointed out that the surfeit of "novelistic" attention given to the characters Sherman slips in and out of (in her eighties work) tends to obscure the formal research (framing, point of view, and so on) and the investment of cinematic codes that are the true meaning-producing elements of Sherman's approach.

Within this same perspective, the exhibition of Pipilotti Rist's SHOOTING DIVAS at the *Centre d'art contemporain* prompts a re-examination of (her) efforts, no longer in terms of an oeuvre that "takes us on a curious journey via pop (...) into the furthest regions of the female psyche,"[3] but in terms of a specific system of production (video) the use of which annuls aesthetic judgements. Transforming the exhibition space into a production site for video-clips shot around two songs whose lyrics are written by her and Andreas Guggisberg, the artist invites the audience to enter a studio whose various components—decor, kitchen table, coatrack—are, first and foremost, functional. Rist's pragmatic use of an exhibition space and situation should compel us to reconsider her intervention at the *Musée d'art et d'histoire*, Geneva, in 1995. Indeed, the purpose of the performance she organized there, where she invited a young woman to execute a striptease on a stage set up inside the venerable building, was perhaps not so much to confront spectators with a certain form of "spectacular" exploitation of women or to present a contemporary, "live" ver-sion of the academic nude, but to create an occasion for a double filming—by the TV cameramen and by herself—and to use these images in the realization of a video-clip. And it is in the overlapping of the stereotypes associated with the professional production of images for the media with those of an activity associated with a retrograde conception of femininity that the critical stakes of such a work lie. By comparison, one would like to claim that with SHOOTING DIVAS, even though the characters represented are women of a theatre troupe, Rist in a sense makes Warhol's promise of "fifteen minutes of fame for everyone" a literal reality. Equidistant from *karaoke* and commercial video production, her exhibition symbolizes the power of integration and cooperation of the audiovisual media. Like Sherman's photographs—which Rosalind Krauss compares to Kuleshov's experiments (1917)[4] in which a parallel montage presented more or less emotionally charged images against the unchanging face of an actor to which the spectator could not help but assign ever-changing emotions, thereby ignoring the semantic power of cinematic montage—the shots in Pipilotti Rist's videos are the means that carry the meaning.

In the light of this reconsideration of the works of Pipilotti Rist and Sylvie Fleury, it would seem that a reading which reproduces the feminist interpretation that one could assign to the works of such artists as Valie Export, Adrian Piper or Lynda Benglis, would tend to obscure the particular modes of operation of these two artists. The feminist points of view that they are presumed to embody and the works in question are thus separated by a requestioning of the historic engage-ment vis-à-vis the position of women in the artistic domain. The same distance, in short, no doubt separates Felix Gonzalez-Torres' "stacks" from the elementary forms of the 1960s. And it is this same distance that sustains, in essence, the current "Do It" show of Hans-Ulrich Obrist (*Forde, espace d'art contemporain*, Geneva): It matters less that a piece by Ilya Kabakov or Mike Kelley may, according to Lawrence Weiner's formula, be assembled by a third party (the exhibition's organizers, in this case) than that it have multiple realizations, highlighting the role of subjective interpretation in the creation and disposition of such work. Of course, in the 1960s, such procedures of delegation and transfer of linguistic entitlement were necessarily accompanied by a political engagement aimed at delegitimizing the system of commercialization and institutionalization. In the end, neither the "Do It" show nor the installations of Sylvie Fleury or Pipilotti Rist reproduce the interpretative schemas they seem to invoke: The use of stereotypes (the image of women in art and the media, conceptual directions for use, and distribution principles) here appears to be a kind of disengagement, both on the social and formal levels.

(Translated from the French by
Stephen Sartarelli)

1) Christoph Doswald, "Die Enge – der Diskurs – die Kunst in der Schweiz," in *Neue Bildende Kunst* 3, June 1996, p. 22.
2) Rosalind Krauss, "Cindy Sherman's Gravity: A Critical Fable," in *Artforum*, September 1993, p. 203.
3) Elizabeth Janus, "Pipilotti Rist," in *Artforum*, Summer 1996, p. 100.
4) Rosalind Krauss, op. cit.

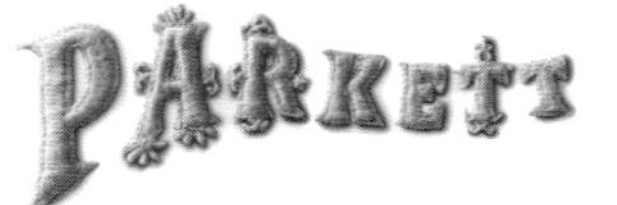

The PARKETT Series is created in collaboration with artists, who contribute an original work available exclusively to the subscribers in the form of a signed limited SPECIAL EDITION. The available works are also reproduced in each PARKETT issue.

Each SPECIAL EDITION is available by order from any one of our offices in New York or Zurich. Just fill in the details below and send this card to the office nearest you. Once your order has been processed, you will be issued with an invoice and your personal edition number. Upon receipt of payment, you will receive the SPECIAL EDITION. (Please note that supply is subject to availability. PARKETT does not assume responsibility for any delays in production of SPECIAL EDITIONS. Postage is not included.)

■ As a subscriber to PARKETT, I would like to order the following Special Edition(s), signed and numbered by the artist.

PARKETT No.	ARTIST	NAME:
PARKETT No.	ARTIST	ADDRESS:
PARKETT No.	ARTIST	CITY:
PARKETT No.	ARTIST	STATE/ZIP:
PARKETT No.	ARTIST	COUNTRY:
PARKETT No.	ARTIST	PHONE:

■ I have indicated my way of payment on the reverse side of this form.

Send this form to the PARKETT office nearest you:

PARKETT PUBLISHERS   155 AV. OF THE AMERICAS   NEW YORK, NY 10013   PHONE (212) 673-2660   FAX (212) 271-0704

PARKETT VERLAG   QUELLENSTRASSE 27   CH-8005 ZÜRICH   TELEFON +41-1-271 81 40   FAX +41-1-272 43 01

PARKETT VERLAG   TANNENWALDALLEE 17   D-61348 BAD HOMBURG   FAX 06172-937 444

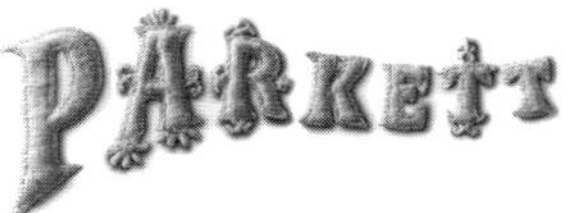

KÜNSTLEREDITIONEN FÜR PARKETT-ABONNENTEN   47

Die PARKETT-Buchreihe entsteht in Zusammenarbeit mit Künstlern, die eigens für die Abonnenten einen Originalbeitrag in Form einer limitierten und signierten EDITION gestalten. Diese Editionen sind auch in der Zeitschrift abgebildet und können mit dieser Bestellkarte in jedem unserer Büros in Zürich, Frankfurt oder New York bestellt werden. Sie erhalten dann Ihre persönliche Editionsnummer und eine Rechnung. Sobald wir Ihre Zahlung erhalten haben, schicken wir Ihnen Ihre Edition(en). (Lieferung nur solange vorrätig. PARKETT übernimmt keine Verantwortung für allfällige Verzögerungen bei der Herstellung der Vorzugsausgaben. Versandkosten zuzüglich.)

■ Ich bin PARKETT-Abonnent(in) und bestelle folgende EDITION(EN), numeriert und vom Künstler signiert:

PARKETT Nr.	KÜNSTLER/IN	NAME:
PARKETT Nr.	KÜNSTLER/IN	STRASSE:
PARKETT Nr.	KÜNSTLER/IN	PLZ/STADT:
PARKETT Nr.	KÜNSTLER/IN	LAND:
PARKETT Nr.	KÜNSTLER/IN	TEL.:

■ Meine Zahlungsweise habe ich auf der Rückseite angegeben.

Schicken Sie diese Bestellkarte an das PARKETT-Büro in Ihrer Nähe:

PARKETT VERLAG   QUELLENSTRASSE 27   CH-8005 ZÜRICH   TELEFON +41-1-271 81 40   FAX +41-1-272 43 01

PARKETT VERLAG   TANNENWALDALLEE 17   D-61348 BAD HOMBURG   FAX 06172-937 444

PARKETT PUBLISHERS   155 AV. OF THE AMERICAS   NEW YORK, NY 10013   PHONE (212) 673-2660   FAX (212) 271-0704

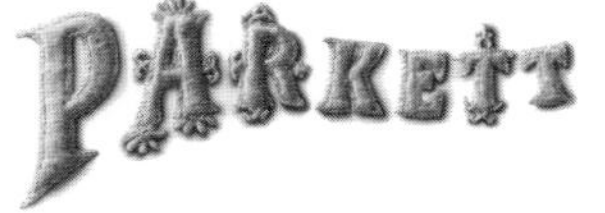

SUBSCRIBE, COMPLETE OR SEND A GIFT SUBSCRIPTION TO THE BEST BOOK SERIES ON CONTEMPORARY ARTISTS

■ I subscribe to the PARKETT series
  ■ for 1 year (3 issues) at US$ 75 (USA/Canada), SFr. 115.– (Europe), SFr. 130.– (Rest of the world; by air mail: SFr. 210.–)
  ■ for 2 years (6 issues) at US$ 135 (USA/Canada), SFr. 205.– (Europe), SFr. 240.– (Rest of the world; air mail: SFr. 395.–)
  ■ for 1 year (3 issues) at a 20% student discount (US$ 60 for USA/ Canada, SFr. 91.– for Europe). A copy of my student ID is enclosed.

■ Send a gift subscription in my name
  ■ for 1 year (3 issues) at US$ 75 (USA/Canada), SFr. 115.– (Europe), SFr. 130.– (Rest of the world; by air mail: SFr. 210.–)
  ■ for 2 years (6 issues) at US$ 135 (USA/Canada), SFr. 205.– (Europe), SFr. 240.– (Rest of the world; air mail: SFr. 395.–)
  A gift card in my name will be sent to the recipient.
Postage included. All prices subject to change.

■ I wish to complete my PARKETT collection and order the following issue no(s):
____
at SFr. 39.– each (up to no. 43: SFr. 30.–), postage not included. Within the USA & Canada $ 29.00 (up to no. 43: $ 19.50), add postage: $ 5 (USA), $ 10 (Canada). (Sold out: No. 1–10, 27, 29–31, 35)

■ I wish to order the catalog raisonné of all PARKETT Artists' Editions from 1984–95 (SILENT & VIOLENT, 183 pages of which 144 in color, text by Susan Tallman, short artists' biographies) for Sfr. 49.– (USA: $ 39.00), excl. postage.

■ I wish to order _________ copies of the set of 36 postcards featuring PARKETT Artists' Editions for Sfr. 19.– (USA: $ 16.00) per set, excl. postage.

NAME:

ADDRESS:

CITY:

STATE/ZIP:

COUNTRY:

TEL.:   FAX:

GIFT RECIPIENT:

ADDRESS:

CITY:

STATE/ZIP :

COUNTRY:

■ Charge my Visa Card   ■ Mastercard   ■ AMEX
Card No. |_|_|_|_|_|_|_|_|_|_|_|_|_|_|_|_| Expiration date _______
■ Payment enclosed (US check or money order)

DATE _______________________

SIGNATURE _______________________

Send this form to the PARKETT office nearest you:

PARKETT PUBLISHERS 155 AV. OF THE AMERICAS NEW YORK, NY 10013 PHONE (212) 673-2660 FAX (212) 271-0704

PARKETT VERLAG QUELLENSTRASSE 27 CH-8005 ZÜRICH TELEFON +41-1-271 81 40 FAX +41-1-272 43 01

PARKETT VERLAG TANNENWALDALLEE 17 D-61348 BAD HOMBURG FAX 06172-937 444

47

ABONNIEREN, VERVOLLSTÄNDIGEN ODER VERSCHENKEN SIE DIE UMFASSENDSTE BUCHREIHE ÜBER GEGENWARTSKÜNSTLER

■ Ich abonniere die PARKETT-Reihe
  ■ für 1 Jahr (3 Ausgaben) zu:
  DM 122,– (BRD), SFr. 98.– (Schweiz), SFr. 115.– (übriges Europa).
  ■ für 2 Jahre (6 Ausgaben) zu:
  DM 222,– (BRD), SFr. 176.– (Schweiz), SFr. 205.– (übriges Europa).
  ■ für 1 Jahr (3 Ausgaben) mit 20% Studentenermässigung
  (BRD: DM 97,–/Schweiz: SFr. 78.–/Europa: SFr. 91.–).
  Eine Kopie meines Studentenausweises lege ich bei.

■ Ich verschenke ein PARKETT-Abonnement
  ■ für 1 Jahr (3 Ausgaben) zu:
  DM 122,– (BRD), SFr. 98.– (Schweiz), SFr. 115.– (übriges Europa).
  ■ für 2 Jahre (6 Ausgaben) zu:
  DM 222,– (BRD), SFr. 176.– (Schweiz), SFr. 205.– (übriges Europa).
  Das Geschenk-Abo mit einer Geschenkkarte wird in meinem Namen versandt.
Preise einschliesslich Versandkosten. Preisänderungen vorbehalten.

■ Ich möchte meine PARKETT-Sammlung vervollständigen und bestelle die folgende(n) noch erhältliche(n) Ausgabe(n) Nr. ________________________________
________________ zu je DM 45,–/SFr. 39.– (bis Nr. 43: DM 35,–/SFr. 30.–), zzgl. Versandkosten (vergriffen: Nr. 1–10, 27, 29–31, 35)

■ Ich bestelle das Werkverzeichnis der PARKETT-Künstlereditionen von 1984–95 (SILENT & VIOLENT, 183 S., davon 144 farbig, Text von Susan Tallman, Kurzbiographien der Künstler) für DM 60,–/Sfr. 49.– zzgl. Versandkosten.

■ Ich bestelle______Ex. des Postkarten-Sets mit 36 PARKETT-Künstlereditionen zum Preis von DM 23,–/SFr. 19.– pro Set, zzgl. Versandkosten.

NAME:

STRASSE:

PLZ/STADT:

LAND:

TEL.:   FAX:

BESCHENKTE(R):

STRASSE:

PLZ/STADT:

LAND:

■ Ich zahle mit Visa   ■ Eurocard/Mastercard   ■ Amex
Karten Nr. |_|_|_|_|_|_|_|_|_|_|_|_|_|_|_|_| Gültig bis _______
■ Mein Scheck über SFr./DM _______________ liegt bei.

DATUM _______________________

UNTERSCHRIFT _______________________

Schicken Sie diese Bestellkarte an das PARKETT-Büro in Ihrer Nähe:

PARKETT VERLAG QUELLENSTRASSE 27 CH-8005 ZÜRICH TELEFON +41-1-271 81 40 FAX +41-1-272 43 01

PARKETT VERLAG TANNENWALDALLEE 17 D-61348 BAD HOMBURG FAX 06172-937 444

PARKETT PUBLISHERS 155 AV. OF THE AMERICAS NEW YORK, NY 10013 PHONE (212) 673-2660 FAX (212) 271-0704

**Erinnern Sie sich an die kleine Katze
in PARKETT Nr. 46?**

Das Photo entstand an der Biennale 1995 in Venedig, im Schweizer Pavillon, wo die Katzenfreunde Fischli/Weiss ausstellten.

Herr *O.S.* in Tokio tippte auf das Guggenheim Museum New York. Das ist allein entschuldbar durch die geographische Entfernung. Wäre er kürzlich in New York gewesen, müsste ihm aufgefallen sein, dass der Platz dort wesentlich knapper bemessen ist....
Es ist auch nicht das Tierspital in Kalkutta, wie *Schwester Ingrid* in Santa Fè, vermutete.

Der 1. Preis (1 Ex. *Silent & Violent*) geht damit ungefochten an Frau *Ines Wejgaard* in Meggen, Schweiz. Ihre Antwort lautete:
«Ob in Venedig, New York oder Zürich, jeden Abend nach Museumsschluss wagt diese Katze einen Sprung – einen Katzensprung – aus dem Fischli/Weiss-Video, wo sie als Star und Publikumsliebling posiert, um mal in aller Ruhe ihre Milch zu schlürfen.»

**Do you recall the cat pictured in
PARKETT no. 46?**

The photograph was taken in front of the Swiss Pavilion at the Venice Biennial last year, where cat lovers Fischli/Weiss had installed their multi-video presentation.

Mr *O.S.* from Tokyo suggested the Guggenheim Museum, an excusable assumption given the distance involved. But, of course, anyone who has been to N.Y. recently will have noticed that space is at a premium there.
An honorable mention goes to *Sister Ingrid* from Santa Fè, who thought it was the animal hospital in Calcutta.

We are proud to announce the winner of the first prize (a copy of *Silent & Violent*): Mrs. *Ines Wejgaard* in Meggen, Switzerland. Her answer reads, "Whether in Venice, New York or Zurich, every evening after the museum closes, this cat plucks up the courage to jump out of her role as the idolized star in a Fischli/Weiss video, and takes a catnap far from the madding crowd."

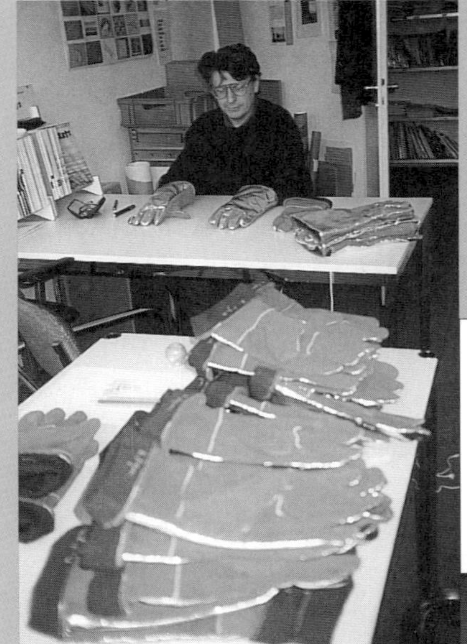

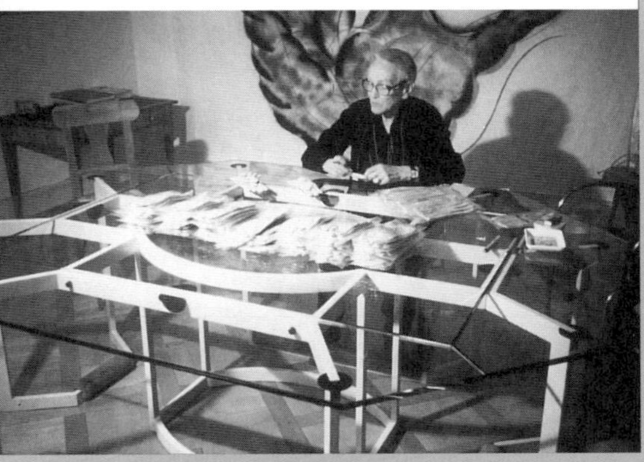

Garderobe

'gär-,drōb

That delightful feeling of "déjà vu" ...
The signing of gloves at PARKETT:
Meret Oppenheim in 1985, Roman Signer in 1996.

Eines dieser seltsamen Déjà-vu-Erlebnisse ...
Das Signieren von Handschuhen bei PARKETT:
Meret Oppenheim, 1985, Roman Signer, 1996.

**5. Videokunst-Förderpreis
Bremen 1996**

Prämiert werden herausragende Videokunst-Konzepte, wobei es sich um ein Videokunstband oder eine Installation handeln kann. Teilnahmeberechtigt sind Videokünstlerinnen und -künstler aus Deutschland und Bremer bzw. Bremerhavener Partnerstädten.
Es gibt einen 1. und 2. sowie einen Förderpreis. Preisgeldsumme DM 16 000. Bewerbungsunterlagen wie immer beim Filmbüro Bremen, Wallerzentrum, Heerstrasse 46, D-28217 Bremen.
Einsendeschluss für Bewerbungen: 10.10.1996.

**Alfried Krupp von Bohlen und Halbach Stiftung:
Stipendium für Museumspraxis und Fotografie**

Das Stipendium ist mit DM 20 000 dotiert und wird für die Dauer eines Jahres für ein konkretes Projekt vergeben.
Ausgewiesene Bewerberinnen und Bewerber mit Studienabschluss und deutscher Staatsbürgerschaft (oder seit drei Jahren in Deutschland wohnhaft) können die Bewerbungsunterlagen schriftlich anfordern bei:
Prof. Dr. Herta Wolf, Geschichte und Theorie der Fotografie, Universität GH Essen, FB 4, D-45117 Essen.
Einsendeschluss für Bewerbungen: 31.10.1996.

COMPLETE YOUR PARKETT LIBRARY

VERVOLLSTÄNDIGEN SIE
IHRE PARKETT-BIBLIOTHEK

TONY OURSLER
RAYMOND PETTIBON
THOMAS SCHÜTTE
COOKE, RICHARD, NERI,
LEWIS, GROYS, ALS, RUGOFF,
GOODEVE, SEARLE, MARI, REUST,
WAKEFIELD, LOOCK, JANUS
INSERT: **ZOE LEONARD & CHERYL DUNYE**
JURI STEINER: **EMMA KUNZ**
MAX WECHSLER: **CHRISTOPH RÜTIMANN**
SUSAN MORGAN: **DIANE ARBUS**
CUMULUS: PRINCENTHAL, BOVIER/CHERIX

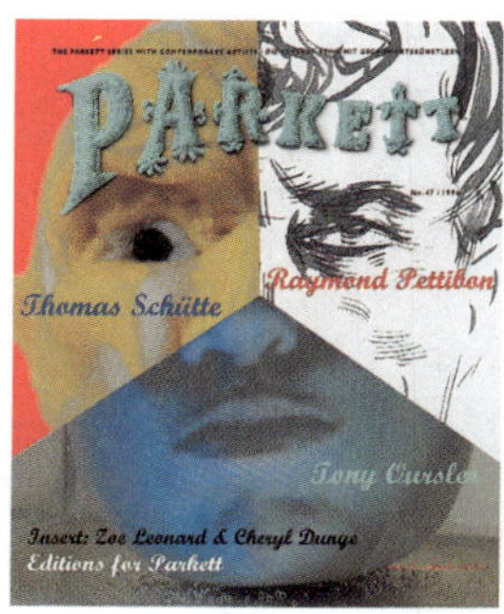

No. 47 - ISBN 3-907509-97-8

RICHARD ARTSCHWAGER
CADY NOLAND
HIROSHI SUGIMOTO
DEITCHER, SCHAFFNER, FORSTER, MUNIZ
ARMSTRONG, RELYEA, BOGDAN, GOODEVE
NICKAS, BRYSON, RUGOFF, DENSON
INSERT: **JOHN M ARMLEDER**
ROLAND WÄSPE: **ERWIN WURM**
DANIEL BIRNBAUM: **ÖYVIND FAHLSTRÖM**
LES INFOS DU PARADIS: ROBERT FLECK
CUMULUS: MILLER, VETTESE
BALKON: MARTIN HELLER

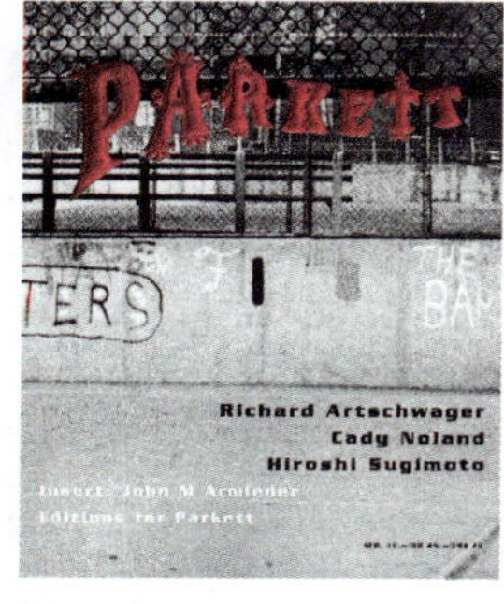

No. 46 - ISBN 3-907509-96-X

MATTHEW BARNEY
SARAH LUCAS
ROMAN SIGNER
BRYSON, ONFRAY, SEWARD, GOODEVE,
SALTZ, VAN ADRICHEM, SCHORR, FREEDMAN,
JOUANNAIS, BITTERLI, DOSWALD,
VIEWING, WECHSLER, DELAND
INSERT: **ELLIOTT PUCKETTE**
HEIDI GILPIN: **WILLIAM FORSYTHE**
ROBYN McKENZIE: **GEOFF LOWE**
MICHAEL TARANTINO: **CHANTAL AKERMAN**
CUMULUS: McEVILLEY, WAKEFIELD

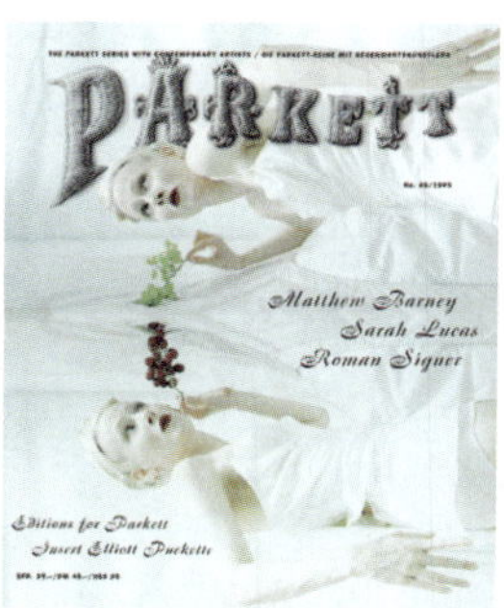

No. 45 - ISBN 3-907509-95-1

VIJA CELMINS
ANDREAS GURSKY
RIRKRIT TIRAVANIJA
PRINCENTHAL, LEWIS, SILVERTHORNE
SHIFF, CRIQUI, BURCKHARDT, WAKEFIELD
SCHORR, MELO, GILLICK, FLOOD, STEINER
INSERT: **HANS DANUSER**
LES INFOS: LIAM GILLICK & DOUGLAS GORDO
LYNNE COOKE, DAVID DEITCHER
DANIEL KURJAKOVIC: **MARIE JOSÉ BURKI**
NAN GOLDIN: **PETER HUJAR**
NOEMI SMOLIK: **ANDREAS SLOMINSKI**
JASON SIMON: **MARK DION**
LUK LAMBRECHT: **MARK LUYTEN**

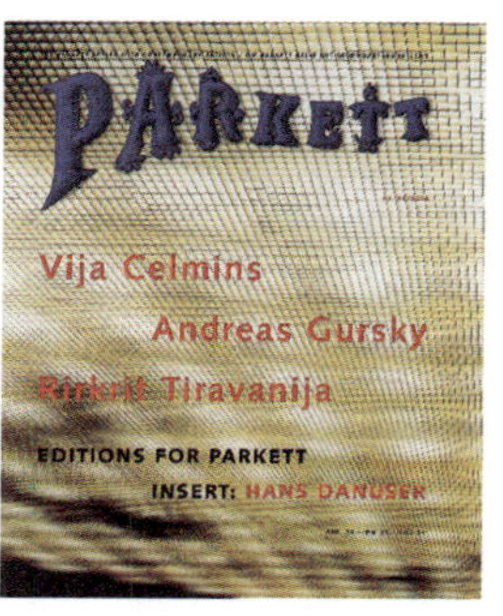

No. 44 - ISBN 3-907509-94-3

JUAN MUÑOZ
SUSAN ROTHENBERG
LYNNE COOKE, ALEXANDRE MELO
JAMES LINGWOOD, GAVIN BRYARS
ROBERT CREELEY, INGRID SCHAFFNER
JEAN-CHRISTOPHE AMMANN
MARK STEVENS, JOAN SIMON
INSERT: **ROBERT SMITHSON**
NEVILLE WAKEFIELD
MICHELLE NICOL: **CARSTEN HÖLLER**
HANS-ULRICH OBRIST: **FABRICE HYBERT**

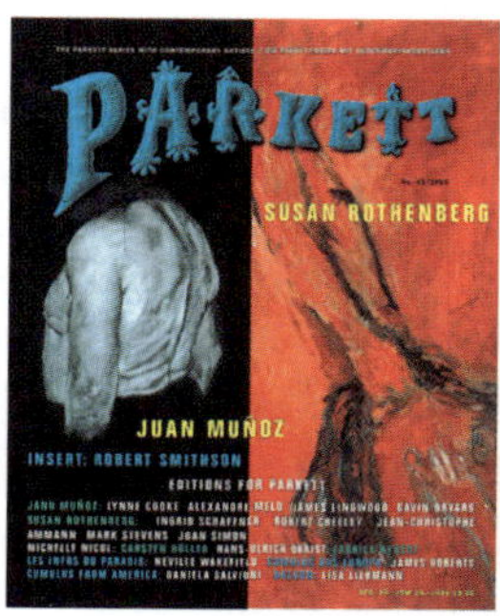

No. 43 - ISBN 3-907509-93-5

LAWRENCE WEINER
RACHEL WHITEREAD
BROOKS ADAMS, FRANCES RICHARD
DIETER SCHWARZ, DANIELA SALVIONI
ED LEFFINGWELL, LANE RELYEA
NEVILLE WAKEFIELD, RUDOLF SCHMITZ
TREVOR FAIRBROTHER, SIMON WATNEY
INSERT: **NAN GOLDIN**
VINCE LEO: **ROBERT FRANK**
CLAUDE RITSCHARD: **MARKUS RAETZ**

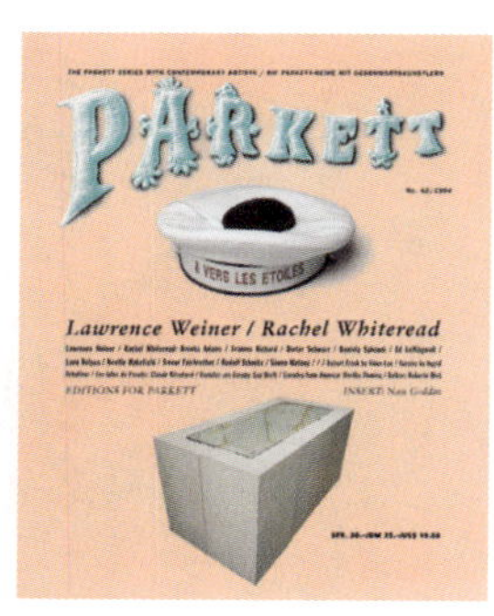

No. 42 - ISBN 3-907509-92-7

FRANCESCO CLEMENTE
GÜNTHER FÖRG
PETER FISCHLI / DAVID WEISS
DAMIEN HIRST
JENNY HOLZER
REBECCA HORN
SIGMAR POLKE
HOLLAND COTTER, BORIS GROYS
MAX WECHSLER, DAVID RIMANELLI
JOAN SIMON, GORDON BURN
GILBERT LASCAULT, WERNER SPIES
BICE CURIGER, JEFF PERRONE
G. ROGER DENSON, VIK MUNIZ
DAVE HICKEY

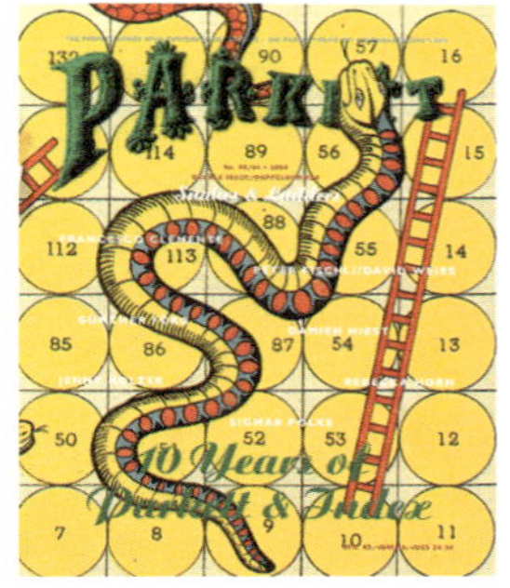

No. 40/41 - ISBN 3-907509-90-0

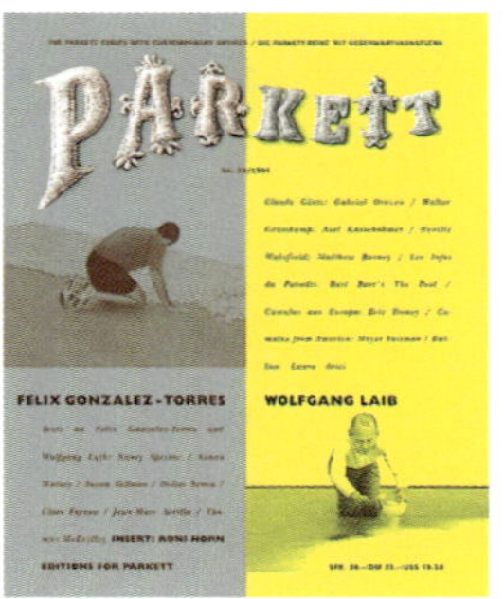

No. 39 - ISBN 3-907509-89-7

FELIX GONZALEZ-TORRES
WOLFGANG LAIB
NANCY SPECTOR, SIMON WATNEY,
SUSAN TALLMAN, DIDIER SEMIN,
CLARE FARROW, JEAN-MARC AVRILLA,
THOMAS McEVILLEY
CLAUDE GINTZ: GABRIEL OROZCO
WALTER GRASSKAMP: AXEL KASSEBÖHMER
NEVILLE WAKEFIELD: MATTHEW BARNEY
INSERT: RONI HORN
LES INFOS DU PARADIS: BURT BARR
CUMULUS: MEYER VAISMAN

ROSS BLECKNER
MARLENE DUMAS
EDMUND WHITE, SIMON WATNEY
JOSE LUIS BREA, MARINA WARNER
ANNA TILROE, INGRID SCHAFFNER
ULRICH LOOCK
INSERT: RUDI MOLACEK
HARTMUT BÖHME
MAX WECHSLER: ADRIAN SCHIESS
DORIS VON DRATHEN:
RACHEL WHITEREAD

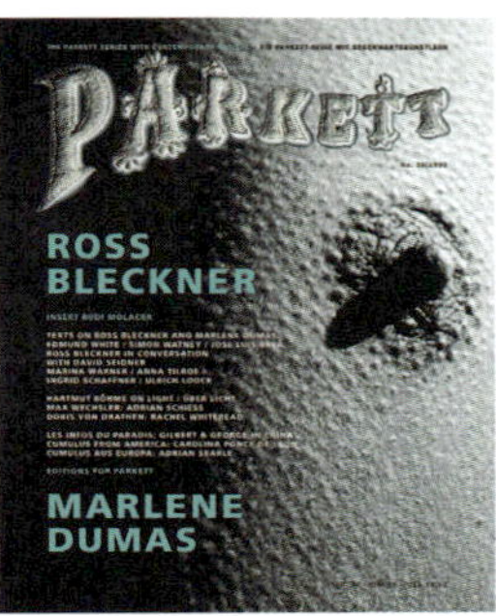

No. 38 - ISBN 3-907509-88-9

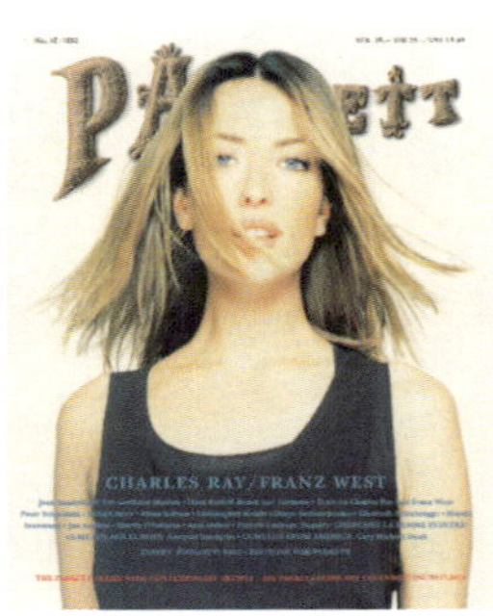

No. 37 - ISBN 3-907509-87-0

CHARLES RAY
FRANZ WEST
KLAUS KERTESS, CHRISTOPHER KNIGHT
PETER SCHJELDAHL, ROBERT STORR
JAN AVGIKOS, AXEL HUBER
MARTIN PRINZHORN, ELISABETH
SCHLEBRÜGGE, HARALD SZEEMANN,
DENYS ZACHAROPOULOS
INSERT: PIPILOTTI RIST
JEAN BAUDRILLARD
HANS RUDOLF REUST: LUC TUYMANS
PARKETT INQUIRY:
CHERCHEZ LA FEMME PEINTRE !

STEPHAN BALKENHOL
SOPHIE CALLE
NEAL BENEZRA, VIK MUNIZ, MAX KATZ
JEAN-CHRISTOPHE AMMANN
LUC SANTE, JOSEPH GRIGELY
PATRICK FREY, ROBERT BECK
INSERT: RICHMOND BURTON
URSULA PANHANS-BÜHLER: EVA HESSE
DOUGLAS BLAU: JON KESSLER
KIRBY GOOKIN: LIZ LARNER
LÁSZLÓ FÖLDÉNYI:
RUDOLF SCHWARZKOGLER

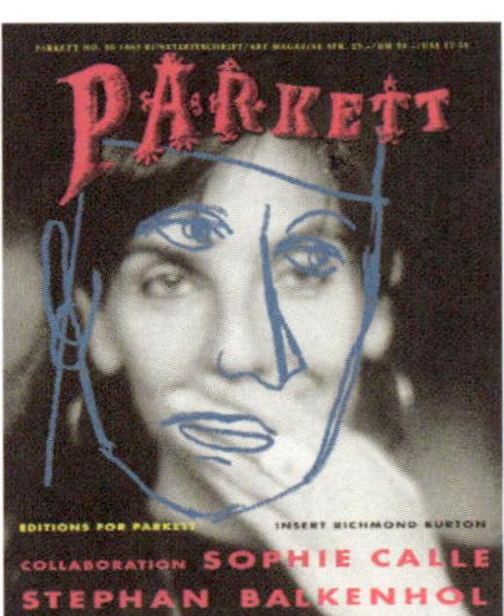

No. 36 - ISBN 3-907509-86-2

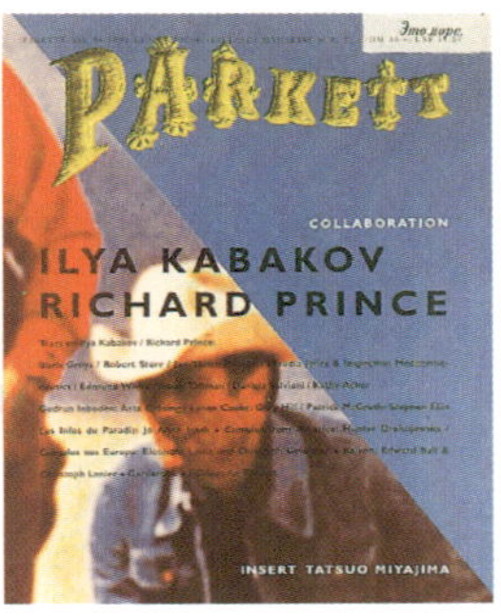

No. 34 - ISBN 3-907509-84-6

ILYA KABAKOV
RICHARD PRINCE
BORIS GROYS, ROBERT STORR
JAN THORN-PRIKKER
CLAUDIA JOLLES, EDMUND WHITE
SUSAN TALLMAN, DANIELA
SALVIONI, KATHY ACKER
INSERT: TATSUO MIYAJIMA
GUDRUN INBODEN: ASTA GRÖTING
LYNNE COOKE: GARY HILL
PATRICK McGRATH: STEPHEN ELLIS

ROSEMARIE TROCKEL
CHRISTOPHER WOOL
VERONIQUE BACCHETTA,
BARRETT WATTEN,
ANNE WAGNER, JIM LEWIS,
GREIL MARCUS, JEFF PERRONE,
DIEDRICH DIEDERICHSEN
INSERT: ADRIAN SCHIESS
MARINA WARNER: PENIS PLENTY
G. ROGER DENSON:
DENNIS OPPENHEIM
CAMIEL VAN WINKEL

PARKETT

WOOL

TROCKEL

33

No. 33 - ISBN 3-907509-83-3

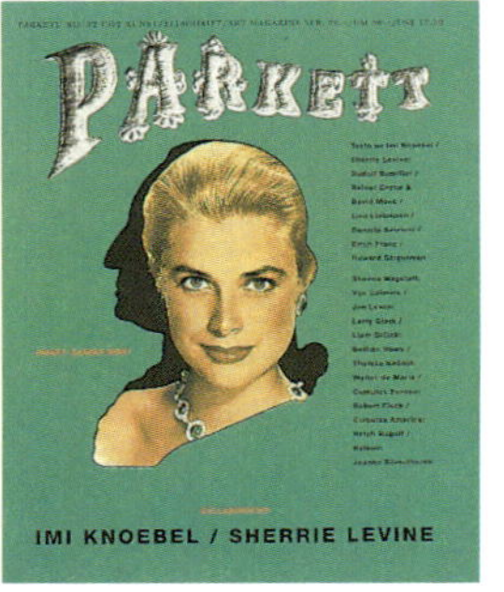

No. 32 - ISBN 3-907509-82-X

IMI KNOEBEL
SHERRIE LEVINE
RUDOLF BUMILLER
RAINER CRONE / DAVID MOOS
LISA LIEBMANN, DANIELA SALVIONI
ERICH FRANZ, HOWARD SINGERMANN
INSERT: DAMIEN HIRST
SHEENA WAGSTAFF: VIJA CELMINS
JIM LEWIS: LARRY CLARK
LIAM GILLICK: BETHAN HUWS
THOMAS KELLEIN: WALTER DE MARIA

FRANZ GERTSCH
THOMAS RUFF
HELMUT FRIEDEL, ULRICH LOOCK
I. MICHAEL DANOFF, AMEI WALLACH
RAINER MICHAEL MASON
MARC FREIDUS, JÖRG JOHNEN
TREVOR FAIRBROTHER/NORMAN BRYSON
INSERT: **LIZ LARNER**
JAMES LEWIS: **RICHARD PRINCE**
DAVID HICKEY:
THE INVISIBLE DRAGON/
DER UNSICHTBARE DRACHEN
PAUL TAYLOR: **JAMES ROSENQUIST**

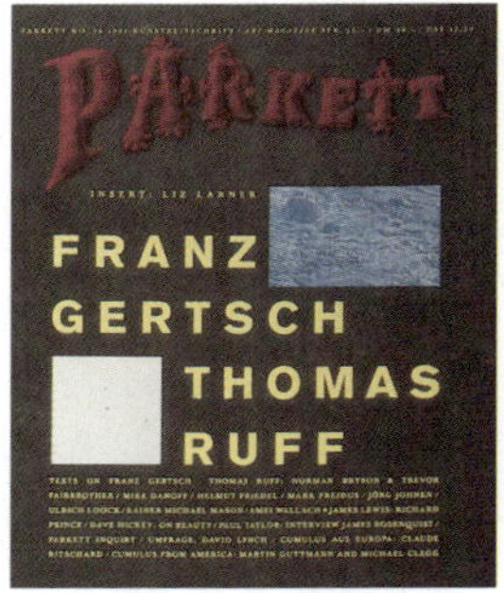

No. 28 - ISBN 3-907509-78-1

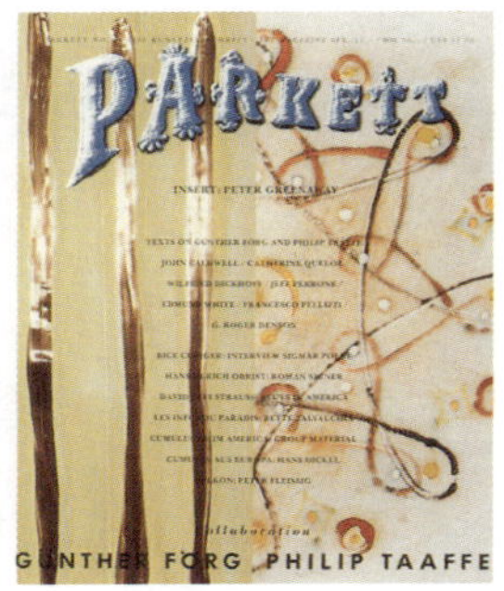

No. 26 - ISBN 3-907509-76-5

GÜNTHER FÖRG
PHILIP TAAFFE
JOHN CALDWELL, CATHERINE QUELOZ
WILFRIED DICKHOFF
JEFF PERRONE, EDMUND WHITE
FRANCESCO PELLIZZI
G. ROGER DENSON
INSERT: **PETER GREENAWAY**
BICE CURIGER: **SIGMAR POLKE**
HANS-ULRICH OBRIST:
ROMAN SIGNER
DAVID LEVI STRAUSS:
JOSEPH BEUYS

KATHARINA FRITSCH
JAMES TURRELL
GARY GARRELS
JULIAN HEYNEN, DAN CAMERON,
JEAN-CHRISTOPHE AMMANN,
DAVE HICKEY, RICHARD FLOOD &
CARL STIGLIANO, TED CASTLE
INSERT: **BEAT STREULI**
PATRICK FREY:
JEAN-FRÉDÉRIC SCHNYDER
DIETER SCHWARZ: **JAMES COLEMAN**
LYNNE COOKE:
RICHARD HAMILTON

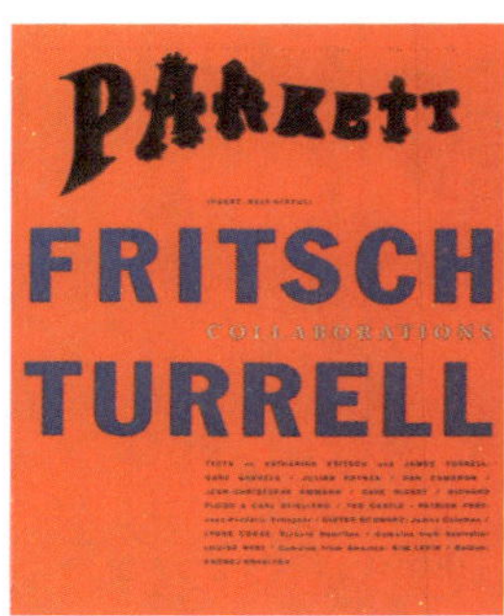

No. 25 - ISBN 3-907509-75-7

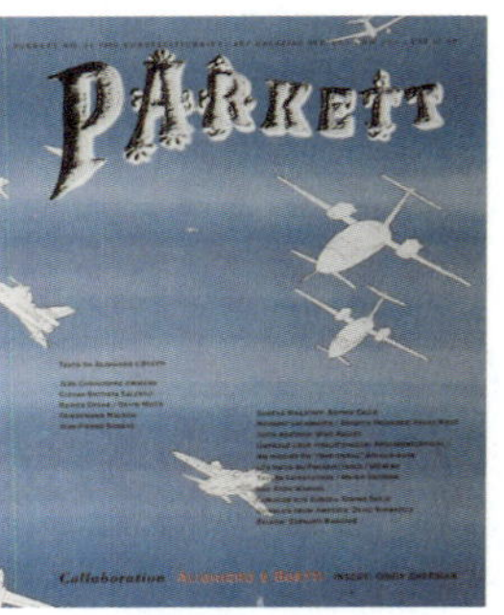

No. 24 - ISBN 3-907509-74-9

ALIGHIERO E BOETTI
JEAN-CHRISTOPHE AMMANN
GIOVAN BATTISTA SALERNO
RAINER CRONE & DAVID MOOS
FRIEDEMANN MALSCH
JEAN-PIERRE BORDAZ
ALAIN CUEFF
INSERT: **CINDY SHERMAN**
SHEENA WAGSTAFF:
SOPHIE CALLE
HERBERT LACHMEYER/
BRIGITTE FELDERER: **FRANZ WEST**
JUTTA KOETHER: **MIKE KELLEY**

RICHARD ARTSCHWAGER
ARTHUR C. DANTO, GEORG KOHLER,
MARIO A. ORLANDO, JOYCE
CAROL OATES, WERNER OECHSLIN,
ALAN LIGHTMAN, PATRICK
McGRATH, DANIEL SOUTIF,
LASZLO F. FÖLDENYI, JEAN STROUSE
INSERT: **DAVID BYRNE**
RENATE PUVOGEL: **ANDRÉ THOMKINS**
ULRICH LOOCK: **THOMAS STRUTH**
NANCY SPECTOR: **MEREDITH MONK**

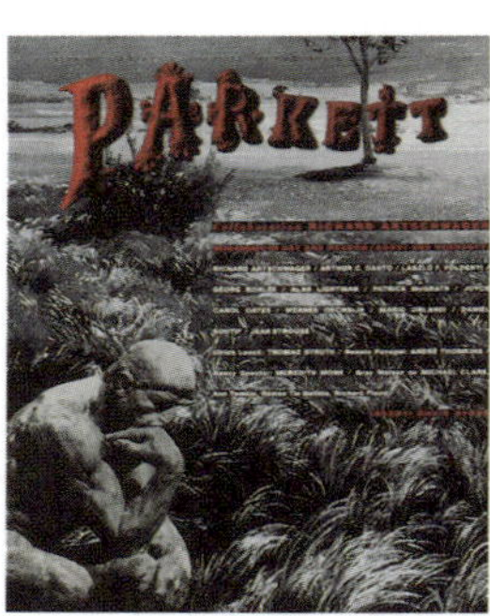

No. 23 - ISBN 3-907509-73-0

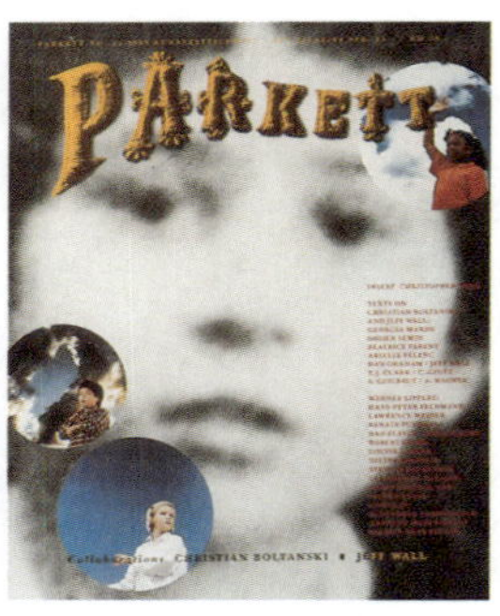

No. 22 - ISBN 3-907509-72-2

CHRISTIAN BOLTANSKI
JEFF WALL
DIDIER SEMIN, GEORGIA MARSH
BÉATRICE PARENT, DAN GRAHAM
JEFF WALL, ARIELLE PÉLENC
INSERT: **CHRISTOPHER WOOL**
DIETER KOEPPLIN:
STEPHAN BALKENHOL
RENATE PUVOGEL:
DAN FLAVIN, DONALD JUDD
WERNER LIPPERT: **VARIOUS SMALL**
FIRES IN THE GUTENBERG GALAXY

ALEX KATZ
JOHN RUSSELL, BROOKS ADAMS,
DAVID RIMANELLI, FRANCESCO
CLEMENTE, MICHAEL KRÜGER,
RICHARD FLOOD, PATRICK FREY,
CARL STIGLIANO, BICE CURIGER,
GLENN O'BRIEN
INSERT: **WILLIAM WEGMAN**
LISA LIEBMAN: **ROBERT GOBER**
JACQUELINE BURCKHARDT:
GIULIO ROMANO

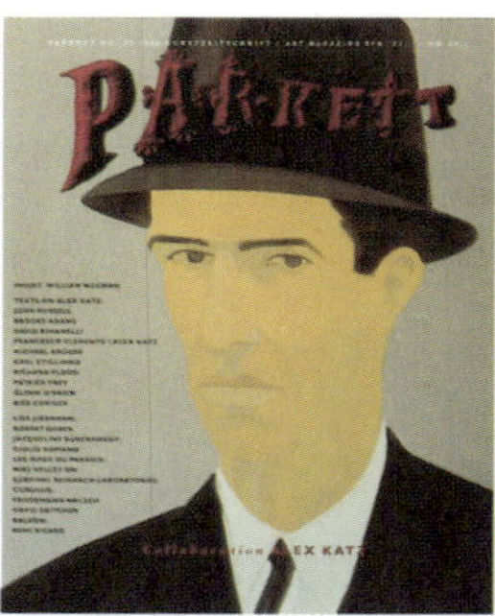

No. 21 - ISBN 3-907509-71-4

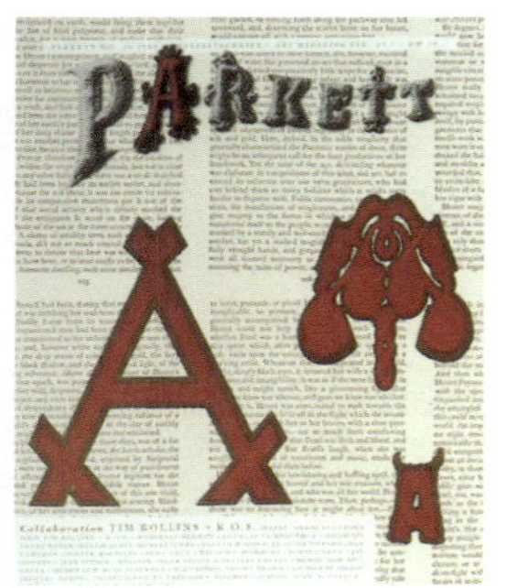

No. 20 - ISBN 3-907509-70-6

TIM ROLLINS + K.O.S.
MARSHALL BERMAN
TREVOR FAIRBROTHER
STATEMENTS, DIALOGUE 5
INSERT: **ANDREAS GURSKY**
MICHAEL NASH: **BILL VIOLA**
STEPHEN ELLIS: **ROSS BLECKNER**
KLAUS KERTESS: **TRISHA BROWN**

JEFF KOONS
MARTIN KIPPENBERGER
KLAUS KERTESS, BURKE & HARE,
JEAN-CHRISTOPHE AMMANN,
GLENN O'BRIEN, DIEDRICH
DIEDERICHSEN, PATRICK FREY,
MARTIN PRINZHORN/BICE CURIGER
INSERT: **ANSELM STALDER**
ANNEMARIE HÜRLIMANN: **BARBARA
BLOOM,** HANNA HUMELTENBERG:
THOMAS RUFF, FELIX-PHILIPP
INGOLD: **RÉMY ZAUGG,** JAN-THORN
PRIKKER: **GERHARD RICHTER**

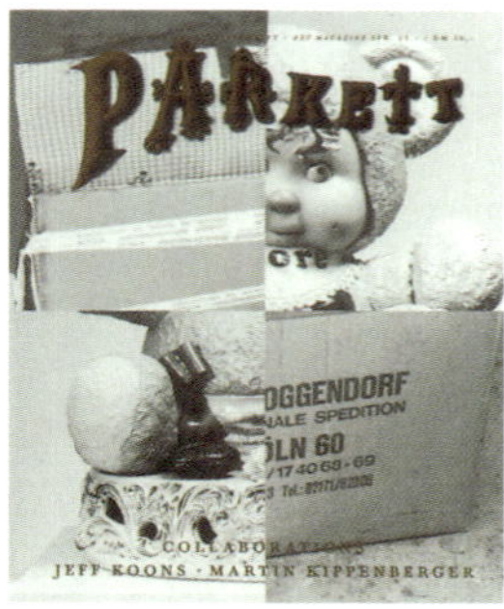

No. 19 - ISBN 3-907509-69-2

EDWARD RUSCHA
DAVE HICKEY, DENNIS HOPPER
ALAIN CUEFF, JOHN MILLER
CHRISTOPHER KNIGHT
INSERT: **BOYD WEBB**
JAN THORN-PRIKKER: **WOLS**
LYNNE COOKE: **TONY CRAGG**
BROOKE ADAMS: **JULIAN SCHNABEL**
DER KÜNSTLER ALS EXEM-
PLARISCH LEIDENDER?
EINE UMFRAGE / THE ARTIST AS A
MODEL SUFFERER? AN INQUIRY

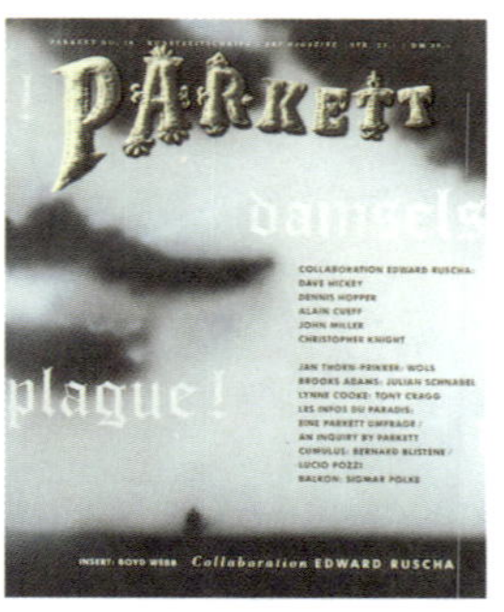

No. 18 - ISBN 3-907509-68-4

PETER FISCHLI/
DAVID WEISS
PATRICK FREY, GERMANO CELANT,
KAREN MARTA, BERNHARD
JOHANNES BLUME, JEANNE SILVER-
THORNE, SIDRA STICH
INSERT: **LOUISE BOURGEOIS**
MAX WECHSLER: **IMI KNOEBEL**
PAUL GROOT: **MATT MULLICAN**
KATHY HALBREICH:
WOOSTER GROUP

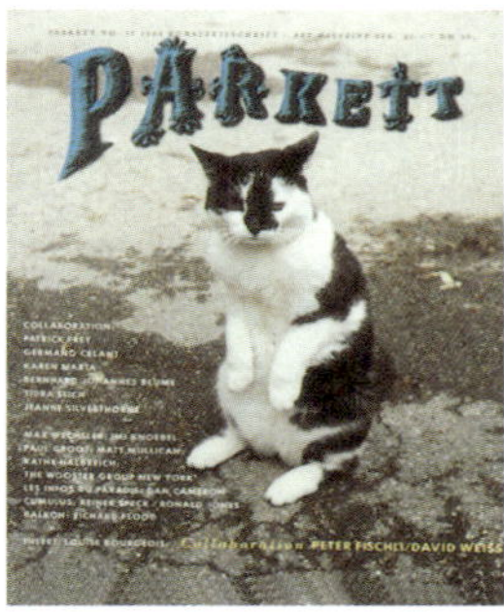

No. 17 - ISBN 3-907509-67-6

MARIO MERZ
MARLIS GRÜTERICH, JEANNE
SILVERTHORNE, DEMOSTHENES
DAVVETAS, HARALD SZEEMANN,
DENYS ZACHAROPOULOS
INSERT: **GENERAL IDEA**
MAX KOZLOFF: **GILLES PERESS**
FRIEDEMANN MALSCH:
GEORG HEROLD
BRUNELLA ANTOMARINI:
FRANCESCA WOODMAN

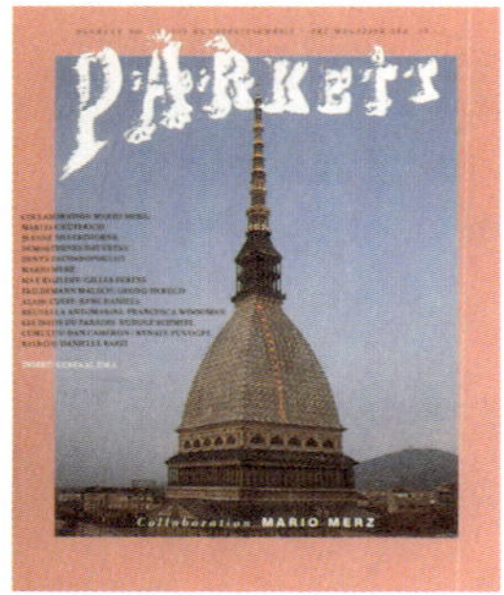

No. 15 - ISBN 3-907509-65-X

GILBERT & GEORGE
DUNCAN FALLOWELL, MARIO
CODOGNATO, JEREMY COOPER,
DEMOSTHENES DAVVETAS,
WOLF JAHN
INSERT: **ROSEMARIE TROCKEL**
ROBERT STORR: **NANCY SPERO**
HAIM STEINBACH: **MANIFESTO**
JÖRG ZUTTER: **THOMAS HUBER**

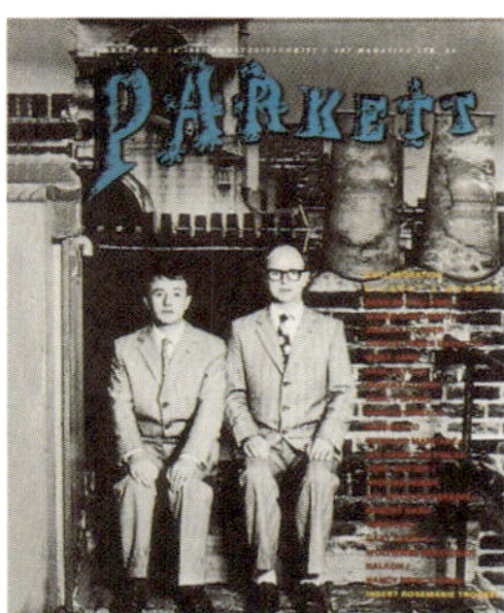

No. 14 - ISBN 3-907509-64-1

REBECCA HORN
BICE CURIGER, DEMOSTHENES
DAVVETAS, MARTIN MOSEBACH,
DANIEL SOUTIF
INSERT: **SIGMAR POLKE**
ALAIN CUEFF:
ALIGHIERO E BOETTI
JEAN-PIERRE BORDAZ:
JENNY HOLZER
JUTTA KOETHER:
KATHARINA FRITSCH

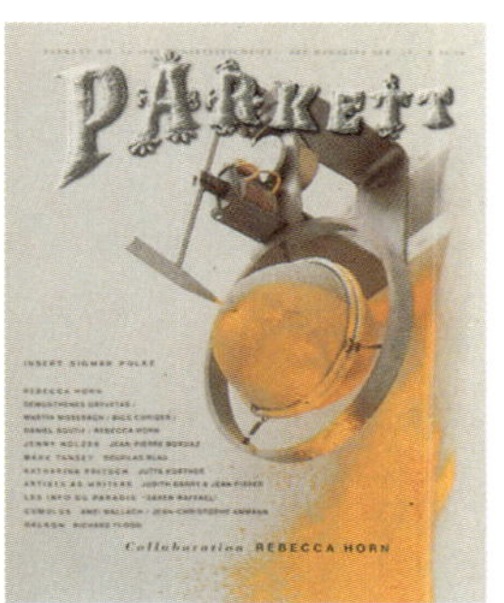

No. 13 - ISBN 3-907509-63-3

ANDY WARHOL
STUART MORGAN, GLENN O'BRIEN,
REMO GUIDIERI, ROBERT BECKER
INSERT: **GÜNTER FÖRG**
LYNNE COOKE: **BILL WOODROW**
AMINE HAASE:
JÜRGEN PARTENHEIMER
PATRICK FREY: **REINHARD MUCHA**

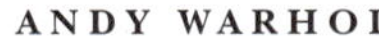
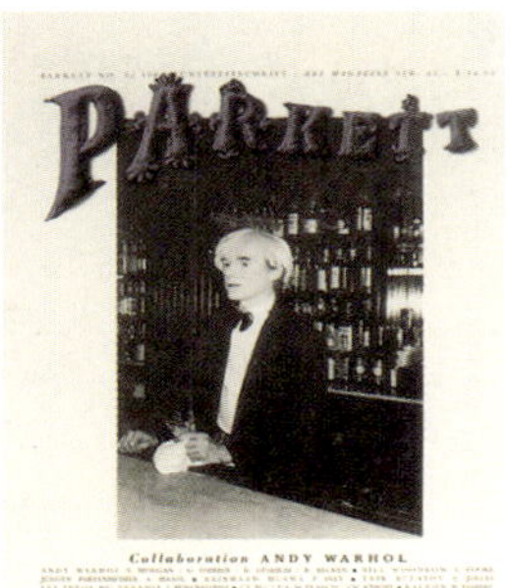

No. 12 - ISBN 3-907509-62-5

GEORG BASELITZ
REMO GUIDIERI, DIETER
KOEPPLIN, ERIC DARRAGON,
RAINER MICHAEL MASON, FRANZ
MEYER, JOHN CALDWELL
INSERT: **BARBARA KRUGER**
GRAY WATSON: **DEREK JARMAN**
CAROL SQUIERS:
PHOTO OPPORTUNITY
ROSETTA BROOKS:
TROY BRAUNTUCH

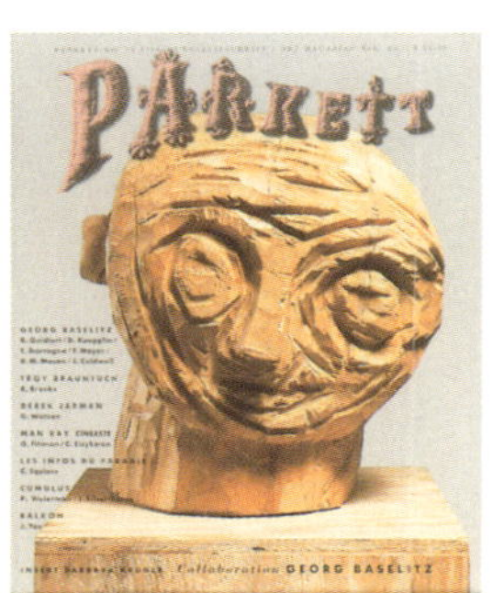

No. 11 - ISBN 3-907509-61-7

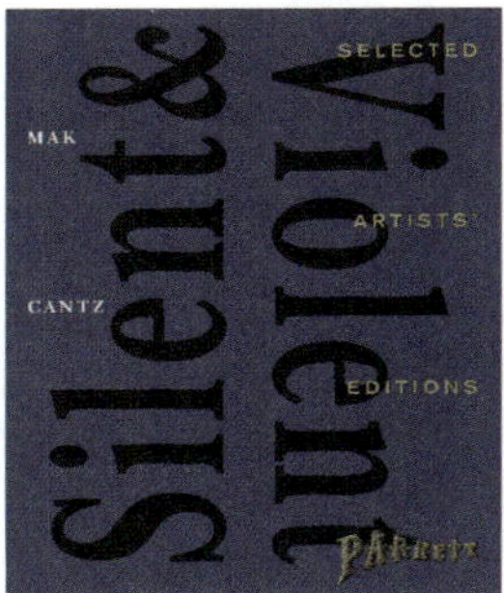

SILENT & VIOLENT
CATALOG RAISONNÉ OF ALL PARKETT ARTISTS' EDITIONS
from No. 1–44, 183 pages, 144 in color
text by Susan Tallmann, short biographies of all artists

WERKVERZEICHNIS ALLER PARKETT-KÜNSTLER-EDITIONEN
von Nr. 1–44, 183 Seiten, davon 144 in Farbe
Text von Susan Tallmann, Kurzbiographien der Künstler

ISBN 3-89322-796-3 (engl.), ISBN 3-89322-787-3 (dt.)

PARKETT-POSTCARD SET
featuring 36 artists' editions made for Parkett

PARKETT-POSTKARTEN-SET
mit 36 Editionen, die von Künstlern für
Parkett geschaffen wurden.

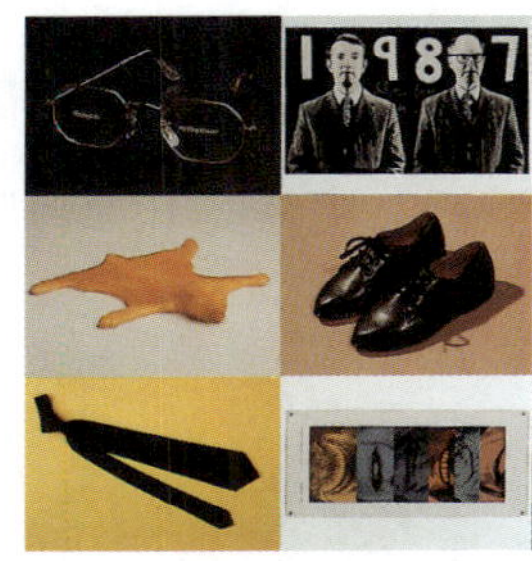

EDITIONS FOR PARKETT

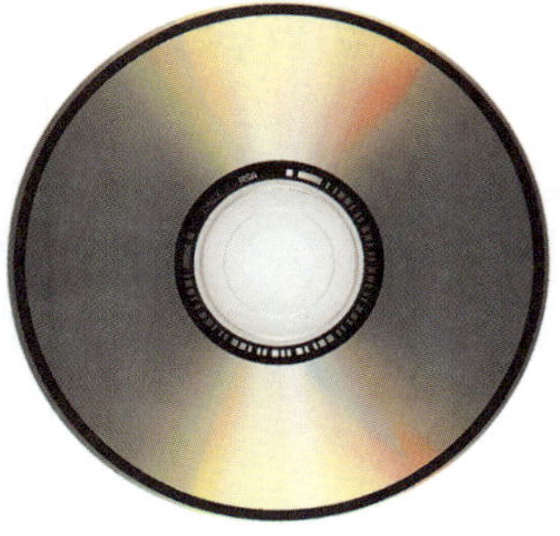

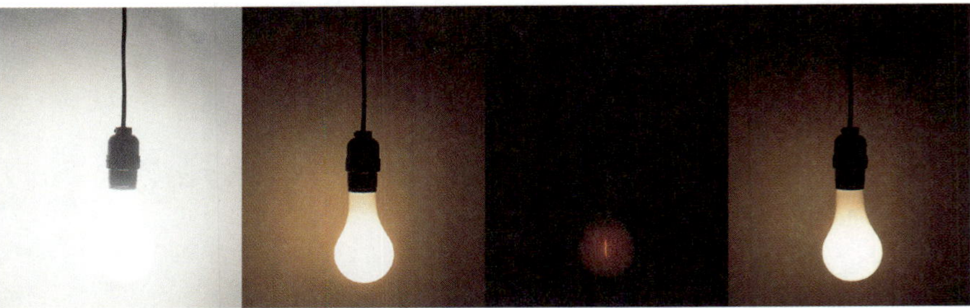

PARKETT 47

TONY OURSLER
TALKING LIGHT, 1996

CD of original script written and performed by the artist (running time approx. 15 minutes), standard 40 watt light bulb, sound organ kit (the light bulb reacts to the frequency of the voice on the CD); installation manual.
Ed. 50/XX, approx. **US$ 850**

TALKING LIGHT, 1996

CD mit der Stimme des Künstlers (Dauer ca. 15 Minuten), 40-Watt-Glühbirne, Tonverstärker mit Zubehör (die Glühbirne reagiert auf die Frequenzen der Stimme auf CD); Installationsanleitung.
Ed. 50/XX, ca. **sFr. 1000.–**

PARKETT 47

RAYMOND PETTIBON
**UNTITLED
(JUSTLY FELT AND BRILLIANTLY SAID), 1996**

Silkscreen, hand-written texts by the artist which vary in each edition, pressed flower, printed by Lorenz Boegli, Zurich, on Arches 120 g, approx. 9⅝ x 7⅝", a 10-part foldout, full length 9⅝ x 76¾".
Edition: 60/XX, signed and numbered, **US$ 750**

**OHNE TITEL
(JUSTLY FELT AND BRILLIANTLY SAID / RICHTIG EMPFUNDEN UND BRILLANT FORMULIERT), 1996**

Siebdruck, mit handgeschriebenen Texten des Künstlers, die von Edition zu Edition variieren, gepresste Blume, gedruckt im Atelier für Siebdruck Lorenz Boegli, Zürich, auf Arches 120 g, ca. 24,5 x 195 cm
(als 10teiliges Leporello gefalzt auf 24,5 x 19,5 cm).
Auflage: 60/XX, signiert und numeriert, **sFr. 850.–**

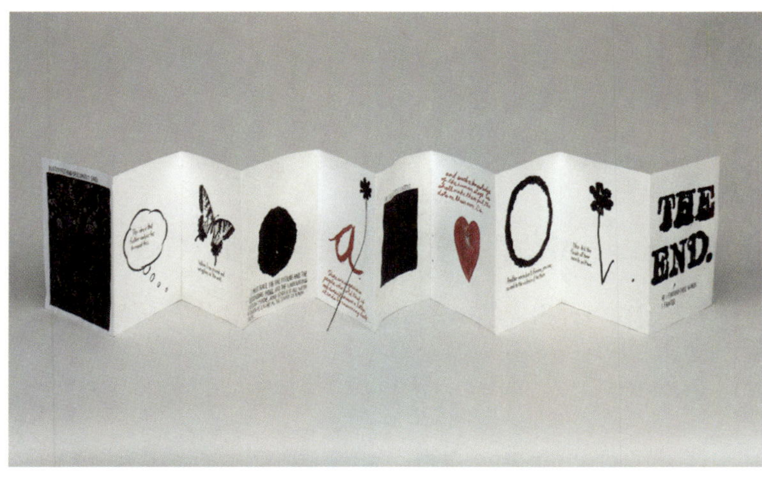

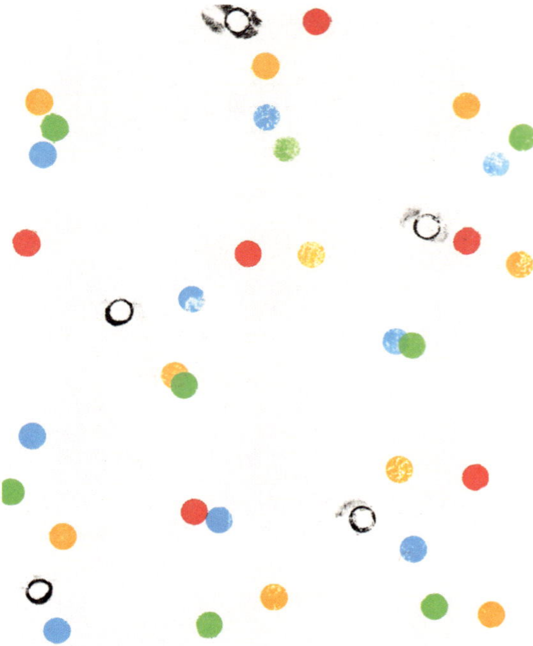

PARKETT 47

THOMAS SCHÜTTE
OLGA'S WALLPAPER, 1996 (1977)
Lithographie vom Stein, 5-farbig, gedruckt von Felix Bauer, Köln,
auf Indisches Handbütten, 250 g, ca. 102 x 68,5 cm
Ed. 60/XX, signiert und numeriert, **sFr. 850.–**

OLGA'S WALLPAPER, 1996 (1977)
Lithograph, stone-pulled, 5 colors, printed by Felix Bauer, Cologne,
on handmade Indian Vellum, 250 g, approx. $40^{1}/_{8}$ x 27"
Ed. 60/XX, signed and numbered, **US$ 750**

For all other available artists' editions please consult the enclosed brochure.

Informationen und Abbildungen zu den übrigen erhältlichen Künstlereditionen
finden Sie in der beiliegenden Broschüre.

AUSKUNFT UND ABONNEMENTS / *INFORMATION AND SUBSCRIPTIONS:*

PARKETT VERLAG AG, QUELLENSTRASSE 27, CH-8005 ZÜRICH, TEL. 01/271 81 40, FAX 272 43 01; TANNENWALDALLEE 17, D-61348 BAD HOMBURG, FAX 06172/937 444

PARKETT, 155 AVENUE OF THE AMERICAS, 2ND FLOOR, NEW YORK, N.Y. 10013, PHONE (212) 673-2660, FAX 271-0704

SCHWEIZ

VERTRIEB
B + I BUCH UND INFORMATION AG
OBFELDERSTR. 35
8910 AFFOLTERN A. A.

BASEL
BUCHHANDLUNG STAMPA, SPALENBERG 2
BÜCHERSTAND STAMPA, KUNSTHALLE BASEL
W. JAEGGI AG, FREIESTR. 32

BERN
HANS HUBER AG, MARKTGASSE 59
BUCHHANDLUNG SCHERZ, MARKTGASSE 25
BUCHHANDLUNG STAUFFACHER, NEUENGASSE 25
BUCHHANDLUNG STAUFFACHER
IM KUNSTMUSEUM BERN, HODLERSTR.12

GENÈVE
LIBRAIRIE DESCOMBES, 6, RUE DU VIEUX-COLLÈGE
LIBRAIRIE PAYOT, 5, RUE DE CHANTEPOULET
LIBRAIRIE WEBER, 13, RUE DE MONTHOUX

LAUSANNE
LIBRAIRE BERNARD LETU,
MUSÉE D'ART CONTEMPORAIN
LIBRAIRIE PAYOT, 1, RUE DE BOURG

SCHAFFHAUSEN
BÜCHER-FASS, WEBERGASSE 13

ST. GALLEN
BUCHHANDLUNG COMEDIA, KATHARINENGASSE 20

ZÜRICH
BUCHHANDLUNG ZUM ELSÄSSER, LIMMATQUAI 18
BUCHHANDLUNG CALLIGRAMME, HÄRINGSTR. 4
SCALO BOOKS & LOOKS, WEINBERGSTRASSE 22 A
HEINIMANN & CO, KIRCHGASSE 17
BUCHHANDLUNG HOWEG, WAFFENPLATZSTR. 1
BUCHHANDLUNG AM KUNSTHAUS AG, RÄMISTR. 45
BUCHHANDLUNG KRAUTHAMMER, OBERE ZÄUNE 24
KUNSTKIOSK, LIMMATQUAI 31/HELMHAUS
ORELL FÜSSLI, FÜSSLISTR. 4
SEC 52, JOSEFSTR. 52

DEUTSCHLAND

VERTRIEB
GWP VERLAGSAUSLIEFERUNG
BEIENRODER HAUPTSTR. 3
38154 KÖNIGSLUTTER

BERLIN
BÜCHERBOGEN, AM SAVIGNYPLATZ
GALERIE 2000, KNESEBECKSTR. 56–58
WASMUTH GmbH & CO., HORDENBERGSTR. 9A
WERNER GmbH, EHRENBERGSTR. 29

BONN
CARL KAYSER, POSTSTR. 16
GALERIE PUDELKO, HEINRICH-VON-KLEIST-STR.

BREMEN
ANTIQUARIAT, BEIM STEINERNEN KREUZ 1
JOHS. STORM, LANGENSTR. 10
KUNSTBUCH, SPITZENKIEL 16/17
B. SIEBRECHT, PANORAMA, VOR DEM STEINTOR 136
KUNST UND BUCH,
AM NEUEN MUSEUM, WESERBURG, TEERHOF 20

BREMERHAVEN
KABINETT FÜR AKTUELLE KUNST, KARLSBURG 4

DÜSSELDORF
M. + R. FRICKE, POSTSTR. 3
WALTHER KÖNIG, HEINRICH-HEINE-ALLEE 15
MÜLLER & TILLMANNS, NEUSTR. 38

FRANKFURT
HUGENDUBEL, STEINWEG 12
KARL MARX BUCHHANDLUNG, JORDANSTR. 11
PETER NAACHER, SCHWEIZERSTR. 57
SCHUMANN & COBET, BÖRSENSTR. 2–4
WALTHER KÖNIG, DOMSTR. 6

HAMBURG
H. VON DER HÖH, GROSSE BLEICHEN 21
SAUTTER UND LACKMANN
ADMIRALITÄTSSTRASSE 71/72
PPS, FELDSTR./ HOCHHAUS

HANNOVER
BUCHHANDLUNG IM SPRENGELMUSEUM
KURT-SCHWITTERS-PLATZ

HEIDELBERG
KUNSTHANDLUNG W. WELKER, HAUPTSTR. 106

KARLSRUHE
KUNSTBUCHHANDLUNG JUST, WALDSTR. 85

KIEL
GALERIE + EDITION KOCH, HOLSTENTÖRNPASSAGE

KÖLN
WALTHER KÖNIG, EHRENSTR. 4

MÜNCHEN
ILKA KÖNIG, AM KOSTTOR 1
H. GOLZ, TÜRKENSTR. 54
L. WERNER, RESIDENZSTR. 18
INT. BAHNHOFSBUCHHANDLUNG, BAHNHOFSPLATZ 2
MAX SUSSMANN GmbH, ARNULFSTR. 1/II
BASIS ANTIQUARIAT, ADALBERTSTR. 43

MÜNSTER
HEINRICH POERTGEN
HERDERSCHE BUCHHANDLUNG, HÖLTENWEG 51

NÜRNBERG
HEINRICH HUGENDUBEL, LUDWIGSPLATZ 1

OSNABRÜCK
H. TH. WENNER GmbH, GROSSE-STR. 69

REUTLINGEN
FETZER BUCH, WEINGÄRTNERSTR. 7

SAARBRÜCKEN
BOCK & SEIP, FUTTERSTR. 2

STUTTGART
WENDELIN NIEDLICH, SCHMALESTR. 9
GALERIE VALENTIEN, KÖNIGSBAU

TÜBINGEN
HUGO FRICK, NAUKLERSTR. 7

ULM
BUCHHANDLUNG UND GALERIE HOLM
HAFENBAD 11

ÖSTERREICH

VERTRIEB
LECHNER + SOHN, HEIZWERKSTRASSE 10, 1232 WIEN

GRAZ
BUCHHANDLUNG GALERIE
VERLAG DROSCHL, BISCHOFPLATZ 1

INNSBRUCK
PARNASS, SPECKBACHERSTR. 21

WAGNERSCHE UNIVERSITÄTSBUCHHANDLUNG
MUSEUMSTR. 4

LINZ
ALEX STELZER, HAUPTPLATZ 17

WIEN
JUDITH ORTNER, SONNENFELSGASSE 8
SHAKESPEARE & COMPANY
BOOKSELLERS, STEINGASSE 2

HOLLAND

DISTRIBUTION
IDEA BOOKS, NIEUWE HERENGRACHT 11
1011 RK AMSTERDAM

AMSTERDAM
ART BOOK, PRINSENGRACHT 645
ATHENAEUM NIEUWSCENTRUM, SPUI 14–16
MENEER KEES, PC HOOFSTRAAT 64-66
NIJHOF & LEE, STAALSTRAAT 13 A
PREMSELA, VAN BAERLESTRAAT 78
VERBEELDING, UTRECHTSESTRAAT 40

ARNHEM
HIJMAN, GROTE OORD 15
ARNHEMS GEMEENTEMUSEUM, UTRECHTSEWEG 87

BREDA
VAN KEMENADE & HOLLAERS, GINNEKENWEG 330

DORDRECHT
BENGEL, VOORSTRAAT 283

EINDHOVEN
MOTTA BERGSTRAAT 35
VAN ABBEMUSEUM, BILDERDIJKLAAN 10

ENSCHEDE
BROEKHUIS, MARKTSTRAAT 12

GRONINGEN
SCHOLTENS/WRISTERS, GULDENSTRAAT 20

HENGELO
BROEKHUIS, ENSCHEDESTRAAT 19

LEIDEN
GINSBERG, BREESTRAAT 127

MAASTRICHT
TRIBUNE, KAPOENSTRAAT 8
VELDEKE, KLEINE STAAT 14

ROTTERDAM
DONNER, LIJNBAAN 150
VAN GENNEP, OUDE BINNENWEG 131B

THE HAGUE
ULYSSES, DENNEWEG 108

TILBURG
DE PONT STICHTING, WILHELMINAPARK 1

UTRECHT
CENTRAAL MUSEUM, AGNIETENSTRAAT 1

BELGIQUE

ANTWERPEN
BRAMANTE, KOEPORTBRUG 4
F.N.A.C. GROENPLAATS
LANDSCHAP, WIJNGAARDSTRAAT 12
STANDAARD, HUIDEVETTERSTRAAT 57

BRUXELLES
PEINTURE FRAÎCHE, 10 RUE DU TABELLION
POST-SCRIPTUM, 37 RUE DES ÉPERONNIERS
TROPISMES, GALERIE DES PRINCES 11

GENT
COPYRIGHT JAKOBIJNENSTRAAT 8
INTELLECT, KALANDESTRAAT 1
KORTRIJK
THEORIA, ONZE LIEVE VROUWESTRAAT 22

E S P A Ñ A
BARCELONA
NOA NOA, CENTRE CULTURAL DE LA FUNDACIÒ
CAIXA, PASSEIG DE SANT JOAN, 108
NOA NOA LIBRES D'ART
CENTRE D'ART STA. MONICA
RAMBLA STA. MONICA 7
MADRID
LIBROS ARGENSOLA, DOCTOR MATA, 1
CENTRO REINA SOFIA, STA. ISABEL 52

F R A N C E
AIX-EN-PROVENCE
LIBRAIRIE VENTS DU SUD, 7, RUE MARÉCHAL FOCH
BORDEAUX
LIBRAIRIE DU MUSÉE CAPC, ENTREPÔT LAINÉ
LIBRAIRIE MOLLAT, 9–15, VITAL CARLES
LYON
LIBRAIRIE LE RÉVERBÈRE, 4, RUE NEUVE
PARIS
LA HUNE, 170 BLVD ST-GERMAIN
«FLAMMARION 4», CENTRE GEORGES POMPIDOU
PLATEAU BEAUBOURG
LIBRAIRIE DU MUSEE D'ART MODERNE
9, RUE FERRIÈRE
GALERIE NATIONALE DU JEU DE PAUME
PLACE DE LA CONCORDE
TOULOUSE
LIBRAIRIE OMBRES BLANCHES, 50, RUE GAMBETTA

I S R A E L
TEL AVIV
BOOKWORM, 30 BASEL ST.

I T A L I A
MILANO
A&M BOOKSTORE, VIA PLINIO 15
MILANO LIBRI, VIA G. VERDI 2
MODENA
LOGOS IMPEX
VIA CURTATONA, 5/F, 41010 SAN DAMASO/MODENA
ROMA
FELTRINELLI, VIA DEL BABUINO 41
GALLERIA PRIMO PIANO, VIA PANISPERNA 203

P O R T U G A L
LISBOA
COMICOS ESPAÇO INTER-MEDIA
RUA TENENTE RAUL CASCAIS 1B

S V E R I G E
STOCKHOLM
BOK & BILD, KULTURHUSET, SERGELSTORG 3
NORDENFLYCHTSVÄGEN 70

G R E A T   B R I T A I N
DISTRIBUTOR
CENTRAL BOOKS, 99, WALLIS RD. LONDON E9 5LN
LONDON
HAYWARD GALLERY BOOKSHOP, SOUTH BANK
ICA BOOKSHOP, NASH HOUSE
12, CARLTON HOUSE TERRACE
LIBERTY, BOOK DEPT., 210 REGENT STREET

U S A
DISTRIBUTOR
D. A. P. (DISTRIBUTED ART PUBLISHERS)
636 BROADWAY, RM 1208 NEW YORK, NY 10012

ANN ARBOR, MI
MAIN STREET NEWS, 220 S. MAIN
AUSTIN, TX
BOOK PEOPLE, 603 N. LAMAR
BERKELEY, CA
CODY'S BOOKS, 2454 TELEGRAPH AVENUE
UNIVERSITY ART MUSEUM, 2625 DURANT AVENUE
BOSTON, MA
MIT PRESS BOOKSTORE, 292 MAIN STREET,
CAMBRIDGE, MA 02142
TRIDENT BOOKSELLERS, 338 NEWBURY STREET
BUFFALO, NY
TALKING LEAVES, 3158 MAIN STREET
CHICAGO, IL
THE ART INSTITUTE OF CHICAGO,
104 EAST CHICAGO AVENUE
MUSEUM OF CONTEMPORARY ART
220 EAST CHICAGO AVENUE
COLUMBUS, OH
WEXNER CENTER, 30 W. 15TH AVENUE
DALLAS, TX
MCKINNEY AVENUE CONTEMPORY
3120 MCKINNEY AVENUE
HOUSTON, TX
BRAZOS BOOK STORE, 2421 BISSONNET
CONTEMPORARY ARTS MUSEUM SHOP
5216 MONTROSE AVENUE
MENIL COLLECTION BOOKSTORE, 1520 SUL ROSS
KANSAS CITY, MO
WHISTLER'S BOOKS, 427 WESTPORT ROAD
LOS ANGELES
BOOKSOUP, 8818 SUNSET BOULEVARD
MUSEUM OF CONTEMPORARY ART, 250 S. GRAND
UCLA/ARMAND HAMMER MUSEUM OF ART
10899 WILSHIRE BOULEVARD
MIAMI, FL
BOOKS & BOOKS, 296 ARAGON AVENUE,
CORAL GABLES, FL 33134
MOCA MUSEUM SHOP, 770 N.E. 125TH STREET
NORTH MIAMI, FL 33161
MINNEAPOLIS
WALKER ART CENTER, VINELAND PLACE
NEW YORK
BOOKS AND COMPANY, 939 MADISON AVENUE
GUGGENHEIM MUSEUM, 575 BROADWAY
RIZZOLI BOOKSTORES, 300 PARK AVENUE SOUTH
SAINT MARKS BOOKSHOP, 31 THIRD AVENUE
OAKLAND, CA
DIESEL, A BOOKSTORE, 5433 COLLEGE AVENUE
OMAHA, NE
JOSELYN ART MUSEUM, 2200 DODGE STREET
PHILADELPHIA, PA
WATERSTONE'S BOOKSELLERS, 2191 HORNIG ROAD
PITTSBURGH, PA
CARNEGIE INSTITUTE, 4400 FORBES AVENUE
PORTLAND, OR
POWELL'S BOOKS, 7 NW 9TH STREET
PROVIDENCE, NY
ACCIDENT OR DESIGN, 128 N. MAIN STREET
RHODE ISLAND SCHOOL OF DESIGN
30 N. MAIN STREET
SAN FRANCISCO, CA
CITY LIGHTS BOOKSHOP, 261 COLUMBUS AVENUE

JACK HANLEY GALLERY, 41 GRANT AVENUE
MUSEUMBOOKS SFMOMA, 151 3RD ST., 1ST FLOOR
ST. LOUIS, MO
LEFT BANK BOOKS, 399 NORTH EUCLID
SANTA MONICA, CA
ARCANA, 1229 3RD ST. PROMENADE
MIDNIGHT SPECIAL BOOKSTORE
1318 3RD ST. PROMENADE
SEATTLE, WA
UNIVERSITY BOOK STORE
4326 UNIVERSITY AVENUE
WASHINGTON, D.C.
FRANZ BADER BOOKSTORE, 1911 "I" STREET, NW
NATIONAL GALLERY OF ART
6TH & CONSTITUTION AVENUE, NW

C A N A D A
CALGARY
TREPANIER BAER GALLERY, 999 8TH STREET
MONTREAL
ARTEXTE, 3575 ST. LAURENT
TORONTO
ART METROPOLE, 788 KING STREET WEST
ART GALLERY OF ONTARIO, BOOKSTORE
317 DUNDAS ST. WEST
EDWARDS BOOKS & ART, 356 QUEEN ST. WEST
DAVID MIRVISH BOOKS ON ART, 596 MARKHAM ST.
VANCOUVER
ART GALLERY STORE, 750 HORNBY ST.

A U S T R A L I A
DISTRIBUTORS
MANIC EX-POSEUR, WORLD TRADE CENTER
MELBOURNE 3005
THE ARTS BOOKSHOP, 1067 HIGH STREET
ARMADALE, VICTORIA 3143
VICTORIA
HARTWIGS BOOKSHOP
245 BRUNSWICK STR., VICTORIA 3182

N E W   Z E A L A N D
DISTRIBUTOR
PROPAGANDA, 44 COLLEGE HILL, AUCKLAND

H O N G   K O N G
PUBLISHERS MARKETING LTD.
TUNG ON BUILDING, 171, PRINCE EDWARD ROAD
KOWLOON
TAI YIP ART BOOK CENTRE
HONG KONG MUSEUM OF ART
TSIM SHA TSUI, KOWLOON

J A P A N
TOKIO
EUROPA ART GmbH, KAMIOGI 4-16-4, SUGINAMI-KU
ON SUNDAYS, 3-7-6 JUNGUMAE, SHIBUYA-KU
AOYAMA BOOKCENTER, ROPPONGI STORE
MINATO-KU
HAKUO TRADING COMPANY
KOJIMACHI SHINE BLD., 8F, CHIYODA-KU
SANSEIDO BOOKSTORE, 7-11-8 KOHAKU, ADACHI-KU
MY BOOK SERVICE, AOI BLD. 5-8, SARUGAKU-CHO

E X H I B I T I O N S

ZÜRICH

THOMAS AMMANN FINE ART	Restelbergstrasse 97 P.O. Box 922 8044 Zürich Tel. 01 252 90 52	**IMPRESSIONISTS & 20TH CENTURY MASTERS** by appointment only	
ARS FUTURA	Bleicherweg 45 8002 Zürich Tel. 01 201 88 10	**ELLEN CANTOR** **MAURIZIO CATTELAN** **ART COLOGNE '96, HALLE 5.1/A 17** **STEFAN BANZ**	2.8.–7.11.96 20.9.–2.11.96 10.11.–17.11.96 22.11.–28.12.96
BRANDSTETTER & WYSS	Limmatstrasse 270 8005 Zürich Tel. 01 440 40 18	**ANDREA ALTENEDER** **STEPHEN WILLATS** **BARBARA MÜHLEFLUH**	24.8.–28.9.96 5.10.–16.11.96 23.11.–JAN. 97
PETER KILCHMANN	Limmatstrasse 270 8005 Zürich Tel. 01 440 39 31	**JONATHAN HAMMER** **STEFAN ALTENBURGER** **JOHN COPLANS**	24.8.–28.9.96 5.10.–9.11.96 16.11.–21.12.96
MAI 36 GALERIE	Rämistrasse 37 8001 Zürich Tel. 01 261 68 80	**ANDREAS KNOBLOCH** **«WORRINGER HOF»** **STEPHAN BALKENHOL**	 6.9.–5.10.96 11.10.–23.11.96
MARK MÜLLER	Gessnerallee 36 8001 Zürich Tel. 01 211 81 55	**JÜRG STÄUBLE – SKULPTUREN** **IM KABINETT: GRUPPE OTTO** **DOMINIQUE LÄMMLI & RENÉE LEVI** **INT. KUNSTMARKT BERLIN** **JOACHIM BANDAU – SKULPTUREN** **DUANE ZALOUDEK – MALEREI**	 28.8.–28.9.96 5.10.–16.11.96 31.10.–4.11.96 23.11.–31.12.96
M.O.B BELLEVUE Contemporary furniture and objects	Waldmannstrasse 8 8001 Zürich Tel. 01 261 88 04	**NATANEL GLUSKA «A CHAIR IS A PLACE»** **«WIR ERLEUCHTEN ZÜRICH»** **KERZENSTÄNDER-AUSSTELLUNG**	21.9.–26.10.96 22.11.–24.12.96

Öffnungszeiten: Do 17–20 Uhr, Sa 10–16 Uhr und nach Vereinbarung

E X H I B I T I O N S

SCHWEIZERISCHES	Museumstrasse 2	«minimal tradition – **MAX BILL UND DIE**	
LANDESMUSEUM	8023 Zürich	‹**EINFACHE**› **ARCHITEKTUR**»	5.9.–13.10.96
	Tel. 01 218 65 11	Öffnungszeiten: Di–So 10–17 Uhr	
SEMINA RERUM	Cäcilienstrasse 3	**ERIK STEFFENSEN**	
IRÈNE PREISWERK	8032 Zürich	«**SHORT CUTS**»	11.9.–2.11.96
	Tel. 01 251 26 39		
BOB VAN ORSOUW	Limmatstrasse 270	**RINEKE DIJKSTRA**	24.8.–28.9.96
	8005 Zürich	**ALAN UGLOW**	5.10.–16.11.96
	Tel. 01 273 11 00	**THOMAS STALDER**	23.11.–JAN. 97
ANNEMARIE VERNA	Neptunstrasse 42	**FRED SANDBACK**	
	8032 Zürich	**INSTALLATIONS AND DRAWINGS**	12.9.–26.10.96
	Tel. 01 262 38 20	**ROBERT MANGOLD**	
		NEW PAINTINGS	31.10.–21.12.96
JAMILEH WEBER	Waldmannstrasse 6	**CATHERINE LEE**	
	8001 Zürich	«**DAEMONS & VALENTINES**»	18.8.–21.9.96
	Tel. 01 252 10 66	**ROBERT RAUSCHENBERG**	
		«**ANAGRAMS**»	4.10.–16.11.96
		CHRISTIAN HERDEG	
		«**LICHTSKULPTUREN**»	23.11.–21.12.96

BERN

GALERIE	Junkerngasse 39	**GÄSTE / GUESTS 2: HANS RUDOLF REUST ZEIGT**	
ERIKA + OTTO	3011 Bern	**WERKE VON THOMAS SCHÜTTE**	13.9.–19.10.96
FRIEDRICH	Tel. 031 311 78 03	**AL TAYLOR**	25.10.–29.11.96
		GÄSTE / GUESTS 3: KONRAD BITTERLI ZEIGT	
		MATTHEW Mc CASLIN	**DEZEMBER 96**

GENÈVE

DANIEL VARENNE	8, rue Toepffer	**PAINTINGS AND DRAWINGS**	
	1206 Genève	**19TH AND 20TH CENTURY**	
	Tel. 022 789 16 75		

OPENING EXHIBITION

CARL ANDRE

EARLY WORKS

12 OCTOBER – 24 NOVEMBER

PAULA COOPER

534 WEST 21 STREET NEW YORK 10011
TEL 212 255 1105 FAX 212 255 5156

JOSEPH CORNELL

Boxes Collages Films

SCULPTURE

Arp	Judd
Artschwager	Kelly
Baselitz	LeWitt
Bill	Merz
Bourgeois	Miró
Broodthaers	Moore
Calder	Nauman
Chamberlain	Oldenburg
Chillida	Paik
Flavin	Picasso
Fontana	Richter
Giacometti	Roth
Gober	Rückriem
González	Tinguely

GALERIE HAUSER & WIRTH

Limmatstrasse 270 CH-8005 Zurich Tel +41 1 446 80 50 Fax +41 1 446 80 55 Gallery hours: Tu – Fr 12 – 18 h Sa 11 – 16 h

Raymond Pettibon

is represented by

Regen Projects

629 N. Almont Drive, LA. CA. 90069
Tel. 310 276 5424   Fax 310 276 7430

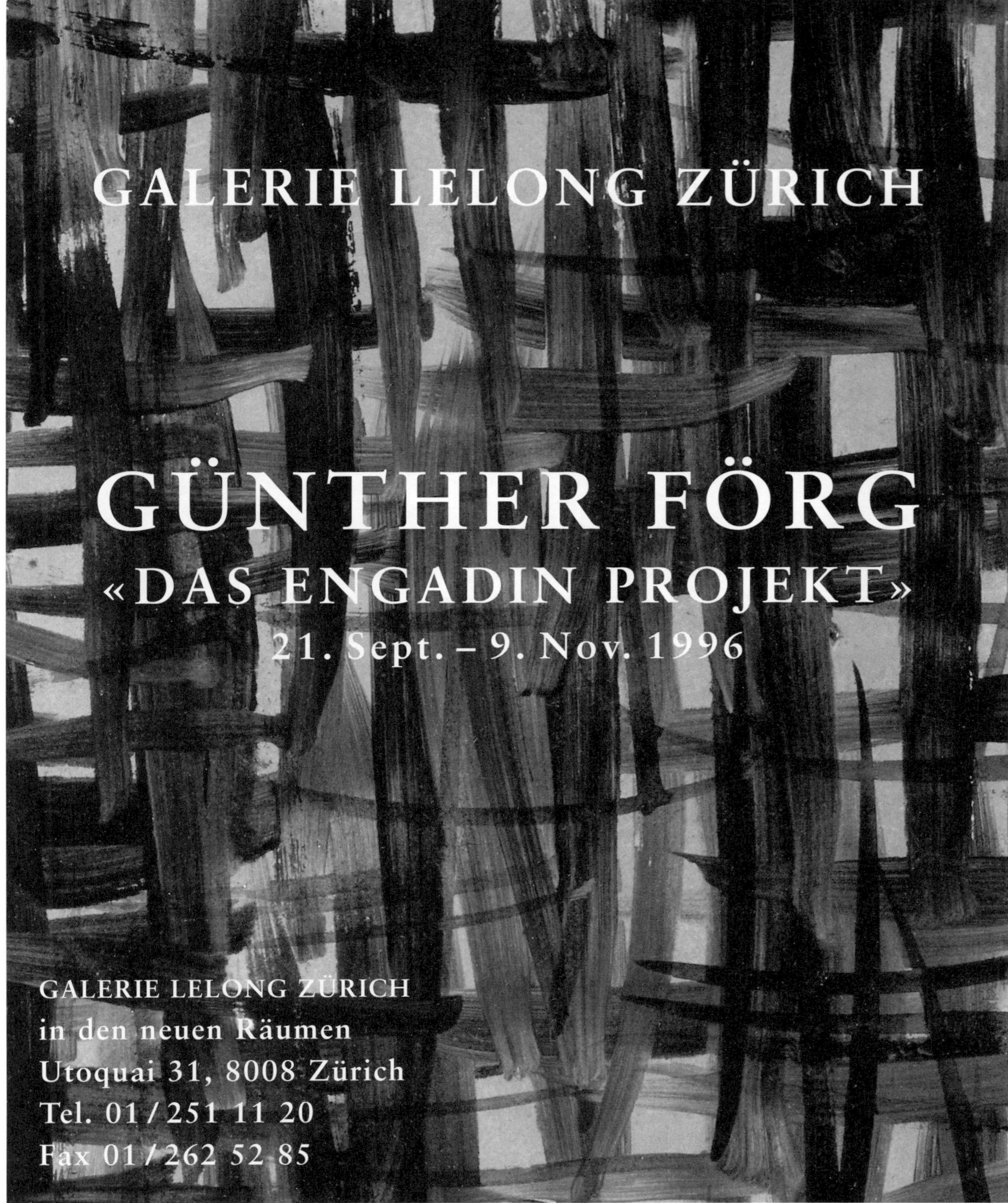
GALERIE LELONG ZÜRICH

GÜNTHER FÖRG
«DAS ENGADIN PROJEKT»
21. Sept. – 9. Nov. 1996

GALERIE LELONG ZÜRICH
in den neuen Räumen
Utoquai 31, 8008 Zürich
Tel. 01 / 251 11 20
Fax 01 / 262 52 85

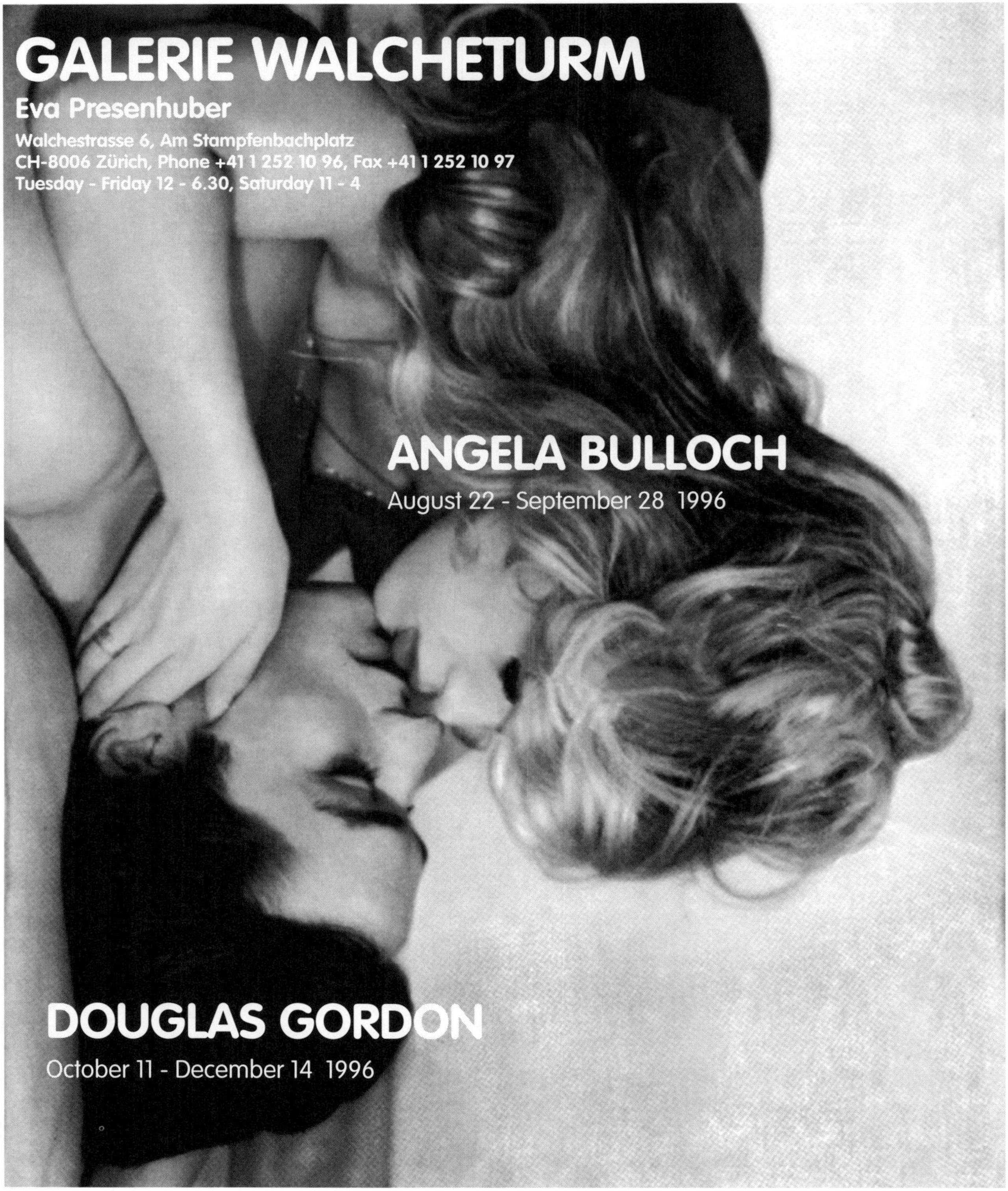

GALERIE WALCHETURM
Eva Presenhuber
Walchestrasse 6, Am Stampfenbachplatz
CH-8006 Zürich, Phone +41 1 252 10 96, Fax +41 1 252 10 97
Tuesday - Friday 12 - 6.30, Saturday 11 - 4
ANGELA BULLOCH
August 22 - September 28 1996
DOUGLAS GORDON
October 11 - December 14 1996

James Casebere

Gaylen Gerber

12th September – 12th October

LISSON GALLERY

52–54 Bell Street London NW1 • Tel: 0171 724 2739 Fax: 0171 724 7124

JEAN BERNIER
51 MARASLI STR., GR–106 76 ATHENS, GREECE
TEL. 723 56 57   FAX: 722 61 89

TAKIS & STELLA KAVALLIERATOS

SEPTEMBER 1996

PIA STADTBÄUMER

NOVEMBER 1996

TONY OURSLER

DECEMBER 1996

Patrick Faigenbaum

7 September – 5 October 1996

BARBARA GLADSTONE

99 Greene Street New York 10012
Telephone 212.431.3334
Telefax 212.966.9310

NEW ADDRESS: NOVEMBER

515 West 24th Street New York 10011
Telephone 212.206.9300
Telefax 212.206.9301

MITSUO MIURA

October - November

JAVIER VALLHONRAT

November - January

DAN FLAVIN

January - March

GABRIEL OROZCO

SEPTEMBER 10 – OCTOBER 12

GERHARD RICHTER

OCTOBER 18 – NOVEMBER 30

MARIAN GOODMAN GALLERY

24 WEST 57TH STREET   NEW YORK, NY 10019   TEL 212 977-7160

FAX 212 581-5187   E-MAIL: MGOODGAL@AOL.COM

Martha Fleming & Lyne Lapointe

September 12 — October 19

Liz Magor

October 24 — November 30

Robin Collyer

December 5 — January 18

Sandra Meigs

January 23 — March 1

Susan Schelle

March 6 — April 12

Shirley Wiitasalo

April 17 — May 24

Magdalen Celestino

May 29 — July 5

Susan Hobbs

Susan Hobbs Gallery Inc.
137 Tecumseth Street
Toronto, Canada M6J 2H2
Telephone 416 504 3699
Facsimile 416 504 8064

Hours:
Thursday – Saturday
1:00 p.m. – 5:00 p.m.
or by appointment

MAI 36 GALERIE

New Location:
Rämistrasse 37, 8001 Zürich

ANDREA KNOBLOCH

September 6 – October 5, 1996

STEPHAN BALKENHOL

October 11 – November 23

Rämistrasse 37, CH-8024 Zürich, Tel. 01 261 68 80, Fax 261 68 81

S.L. Simpson Gallery

September

Judith Schwarz

main + upper gallery

October

Uta Barth

main gallery

Michael Snow

upper gallery

November

David Clarkson

main gallery

Steven Shearer

upper gallery

515 Queen Street West, Toronto Canada   Tel 416 504 3738 Fax 416 504 7979

CENTRO GALEGO
DE ARTE
CONTEMPORÁNEA

ANA MENDIETA
July / October 96

PEREJAUME
October / November 96

ARNULF RAINER
October 96 / January 97

MEDARDO ROSSO
October 96 / January 97

ANXEL HUETE
December 96 / January 97

PERMANENT COLLECTION
Deposit of the ARCO Foundation Collection

Rúa Valle Inclán, s/n

15704 Santiago de Compostela

SPAIN

Tel. + 34 (81) 546629

Fax + 34 (81) 546605/25

Gäste / guests 2

Hans Rudolf Reust zeigt
Werke von

Thomas Schütte

Blumen mit Luise

13. September – 19. Oktober 1996

GALERIE ERIKA + OTTO FRIEDRICH
Junkerngasse 39 CH-3011 Bern
Tel 031 311 78 03 Fax 312 13 45

SEAN KELLY

43 MERCER STREET
NEW YORK NY 10013
TELEPHONE 212 343-2405
FAX 212 343-2604

Pieter Laurens Mol

Sean Kelly New York

September 20 - November 9 1996

Pieter Laurens Mol

Project Room

Museum of Modern Art New York

September 19 - November 12 1996

Christine Borland

November 15 1996 - January 4 1997

RICHTER

POLKE

RAINER

KUNSTHALLE BADEN-BADEN

14. SEPTEMBER–3. NOVEMBER 1996

Lichtentaler Allee 8a, 76530 Baden-Baden, T.: (0 72 21) 2 32 50, Fax: (0 72 21) 3 85 90,
geöffnet Di. bis So. 11–18 Uhr, Mi. 11–20 Uhr

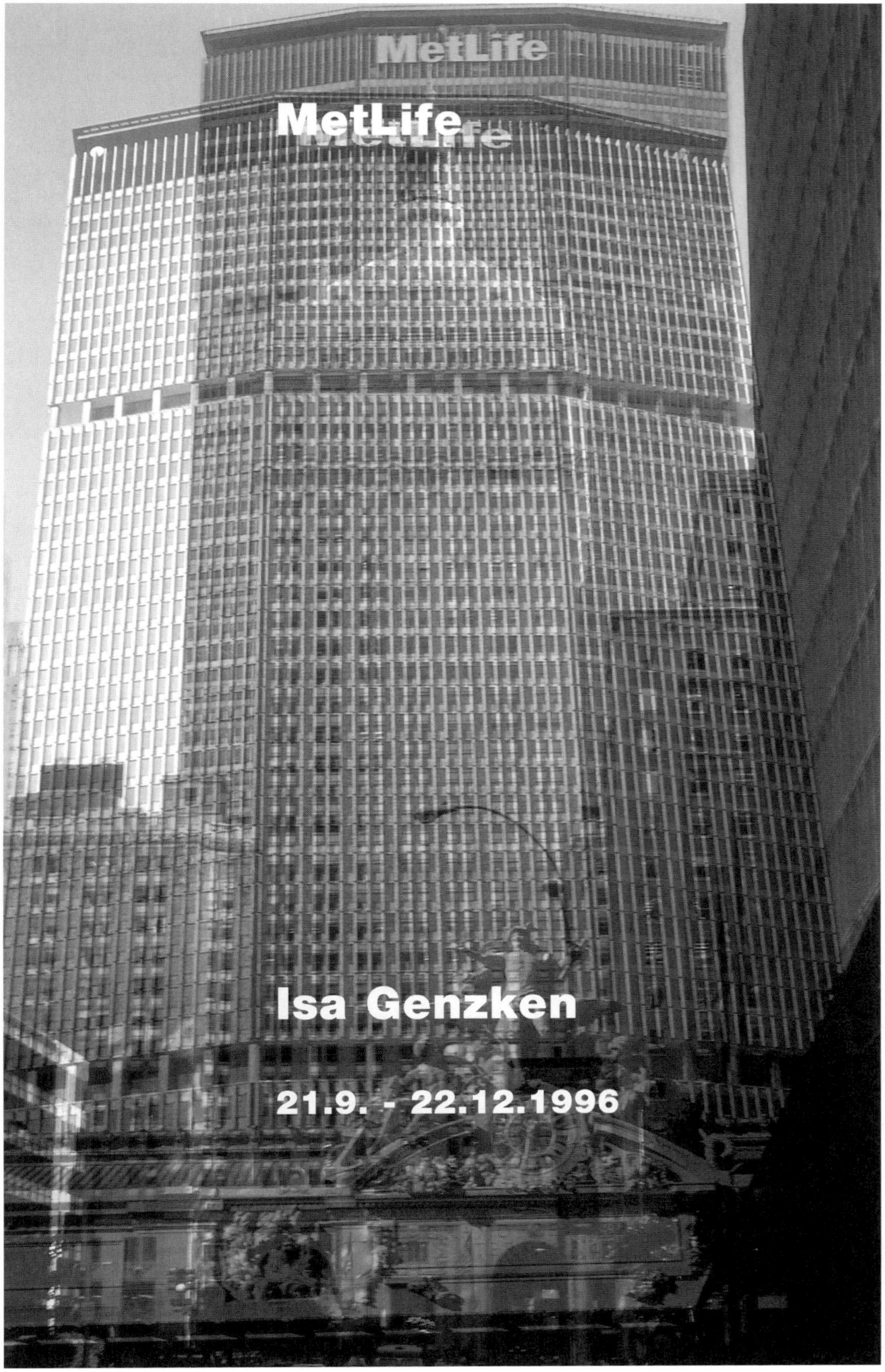

EA-Generali Foundation
Wiedner Hauptstraße 15, A-1040 Wien
Telefon (+43 1) 504 98 80, Telefax (+43 1) 504 98 83
e-mail: office@eagf.co.at
http://www.ping.at/users/aw/ea-generali.foundation
Katalog erhältlich

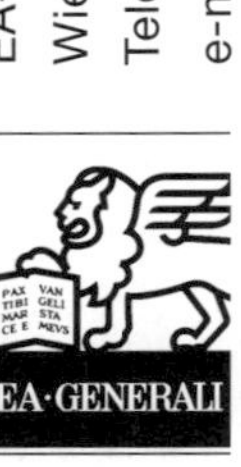

EA·GENERALI

FOUNDATION

Jake Berthot and Harvey Quaytman
Works on Paper September 5-October 1, 1996

Philip Guston
Late Paintings October 5-November 9, 1996

Susana Solano
New Sculpture November 15-December 1996

McKee Gallery

745 Fifth Avenue New York 10151 Tel 212.688.5951 Fax 212.752.5638

Galerien im Löwenbräu, Limmatstrasse 270, 8005 Zürich

Brandstetter & Wyss tel 01 440 40 18, fax 01 440 40 19 e-mail: brandstetter@access.ch di–fr 12–18, sa 11–16 uhr		
	Andrea Alteneder	24. August–28. September
	Stephen Willats	5. Oktober–16. November
	Barbara Mühlefluh	23. November–Januar 1997

Peter Kilchmann tel 01 440 39 31, fax 01 440 39 32 e-mail: kilchmann@access.ch di–fr 12–18, sa 12–16 uhr		
	Jonathan Hammer	24. August bis 28. September
	Stefan Altenburger	5. Oktober–9. November
	John Coplans	16. November–21. Dezember

Bob van Orsouw tel 01 273 11 00, fax 01 273 11 02 di–fr 12–18, sa 11–16 uhr		
	Rineke Dijkstra	24. August–28. September
	Alan Uglow	5. Oktober–16. November
	Thomas Stalder	23. November–Januar 1997

KUNST- UND AUSSTELLUNGSHALLE
DER BUNDESREPUBLIK DEUTSCHLAND

MEDIENKUNSTRAUM
BILL SEAMAN – PASSAGEN KOMBINATIONEN
MAN MANÖVRIERT DREHUNGEN AUF DER ZUNGENSPITZE

6. SEPTEMBER BIS 3. NOVEMBER 1996

53113 BONN · MUSEUMSMEILE · FRIEDRICH-EBERT-ALLEE 4
TELEFON (49)228/9171-200 · HTTP://WWW.KAH-BONN.DE
GEÖFFNET DIENSTAGS BIS SONNTAGS 10 BIS 19 UHR

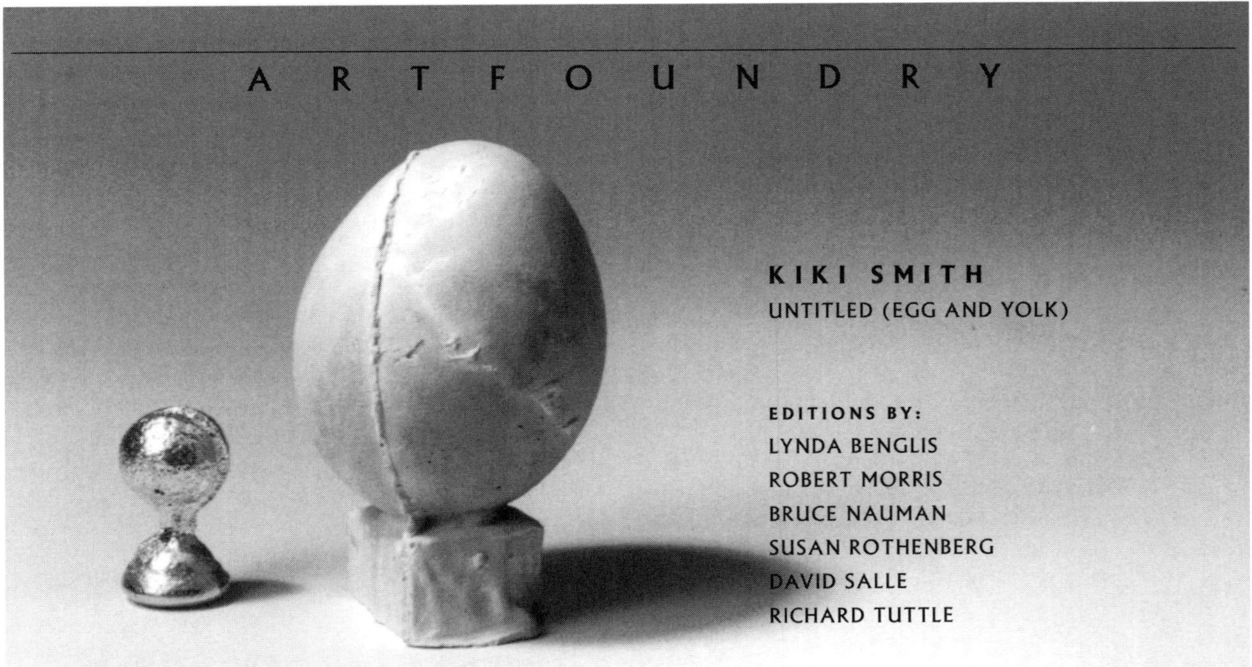

ARTFOUNDRY

KIKI SMITH
UNTITLED (EGG AND YOLK)

EDITIONS BY:
LYNDA BENGLIS
ROBERT MORRIS
BRUCE NAUMAN
SUSAN ROTHENBERG
DAVID SALLE
RICHARD TUTTLE

POST OFFICE BOX 8107, SANTA FE, NEW MEXICO 87504 USA   TELEPHONE: 505/471-7184   FAX: 505/471-6426

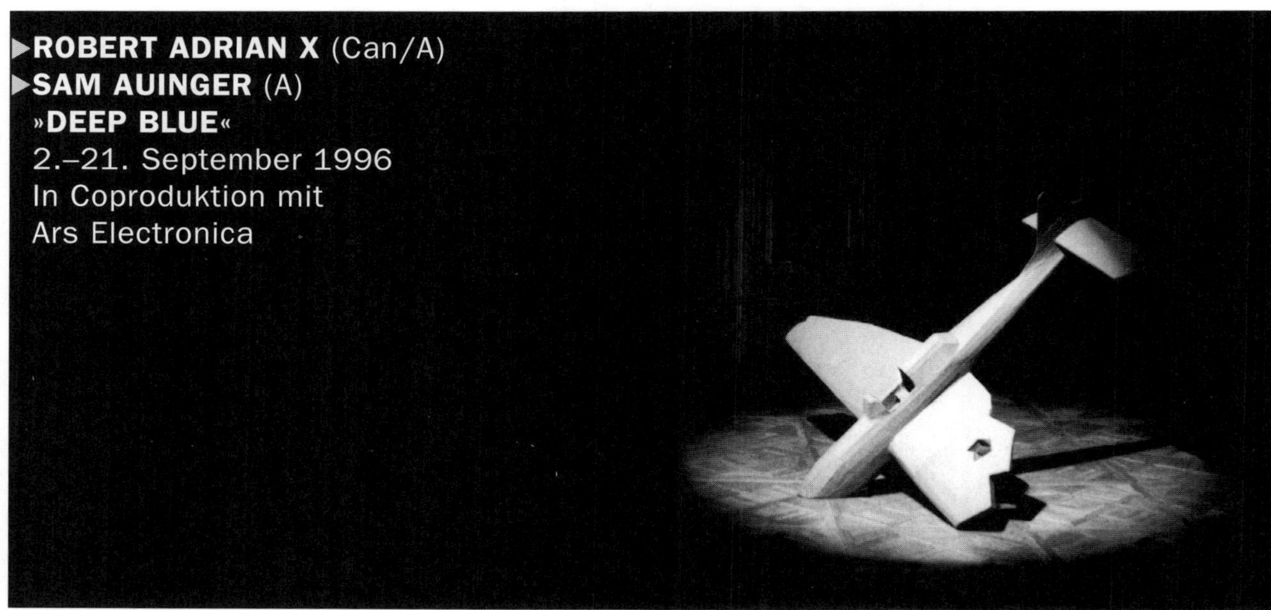

Castello di Rivara Center of Contemporary Art

21 september 1996

PITTURA

DIRK SKREBER PETER SCHMERSAL CARO SUERKEMPER JOHANNES HÜPPI
MONIKA BAER ANKE DOBERAUER MICHAEL VAN OFEN NIKOLAUS LIST BRIGITTE HALDER
KARIN KNEFFEL MICHAEL BACH ANDREAS SCHÖN PETER THOL WERNER WEFERS
ROBERT HAISS LUC TUYMANS MARLENE DUMAS CECILIA EDEFALK FRANCIS ALYS
BERT DE BEUL MIRIAM CAHN STEPHAN MELZL CHRISTIAN MACKETANZ
WALTHER OBHOLZER RAYMOND HAINS FABRICE HYBERT BERNHARD FRIZE
REZA FEYKONDEH STEPHEN SKIDMORE LISA MILROY JULIE ROBERTS ALESSANDRO RAHO
ALEXANDER GUY JOHN CURRIN RAY SMITH MAUREEN GALLACE ALBERTO CASTELLI
STEFANO PISANO PAOLA GANDOLFI MAURIZIO CANNAVACCIUOLO GUGLIELMO ASCHIERI
PIERLUIGI PUSOLE MARCO NERI ELKE WARTH BRUNO ZANICHELLI SALVO
THORSTEN KIRCHHOFF DANIELE GALLIANO GIAN MARCO MONTESANO ALDO DAMIOLI
ANDREA MANDARINO TOMAS MORELL JOSE MALDONADO
Progetto **Museo d'Arte Italiana 1985 - 1996...** LUISA LAMBRI

11 november 1996
PIA STADTBÄUMER

7 dicember 1996
WIEBKE SIEM

Castello di Rivara 10080 Rivara/To **t/f 0124 31122** sat-sun 10.00-12.00 14.30-18.30 (and by appoinment)

UIPT (T. Taub, vice-dispatcher)

Projet de niveau de subsistance minimum 1984 W - Phase IV

«Catabase sotériologique»

Collection André L'Huillier

Musée Rath, Genève
Ouvert de 10 à 17 heures
Mercredi, ouverture continue de 12 à 21 heures
Fermé le lundi

Ville de Genève
Département des affaires culturelles

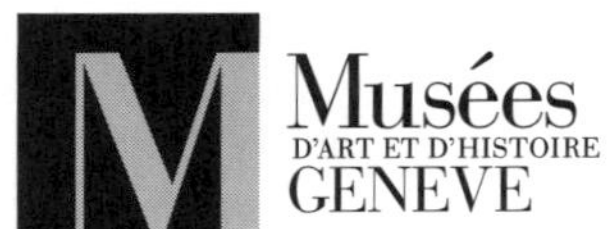

27 septembre - 17 novembre 1996

MUSEUM MODERNER KUNST STIFTUNG LUDWIG WIEN

MMK SLW

LUCIO FONTANA
Retrospektive

25.9.1996 – 6.1.1997

Palais Liechtenstein

Fürstengasse 1
1090 Wien

Mehr Informationen über diese Ausstellungen finden Sie im Internet!
Internet: http://www.MMKSLW.or.at/MMKSLW/
E-mail: museum@MMKSLW.or.at
Web-Design by MISSING LINK

ÁKOS BIRKÁS
Im Kopf

21.9.1996 – 10.11.1996

ABSTRAKT/ REAL

21.11.1996 – 12.1.1997

20er Haus

Schweizer Garten · 1030 Wien

Art supports Art: Das Museum moderner Kunst Stiftung Ludwig Wien stellt dem Obala Art Centar Sarajevo kostenlos Anzeigenraum zur Verfügung:

OBALA ART CENTAR

JONAS MEKAS
8.9.1996 – 13.10.1996

EDIN NUMANKADIĆ
November 1996

INÉS LOMBARDI

Parkett Artists' Editions på Louisiana Museum for moderne kunst

fra den 11, september til den 13. oktober 1996 Grafik, multiples og værker af:

Richard Artschwager John Baldessari Stephan Balkenhol Matthew Barney Georg Baselitz Ross Bleckner Alighiero e Boetti Christian Boltanski Louise Bourgeois Sophie Calle Vija Celmins Francesco Clemente Enzo Cucchi Martin Disler Marlene Dumas Eric Fischl Peter Fischli / David Weiss Günther Förg Katharina Fritsch Franz Gertsch Gilbert & George Robert Gober Felix Gonzalez-Torres Andreas Gursky David Hammons Damien Hirst Jenny Holzer Rebecca Horn Ilya Kabakov Alex Katz Mike Kelley Martin Kippenberger Imi Knoebel Jeff Koons Jannis Kounellis Wolfgang Laib Sherrie Levine Sarah Lucas Brice Marden Mario Merz Juan Muñoz Cady Noland Bruce Nauman Meret Oppenheim Tony Oursler Raymond Pettibon Sigmar Polke Richard Prince Markus Raetz Charles Ray Gerhard Richter Tim Rollins & K.O.S Susan Rothenberg Thomas Ruff Ed Ruscha Thomas Schütte Cindy Sherman Roman Signer Hiroshi Sugimoto Philip Taaffe Rirkrit Tiravanija Rosemarie Trockel James Turrell Jeff Wall Andy Warhol Lawrence Weiner Franz West Rachel Whiteread Robert Wilson Christopher Wool

Louisiana Museum for moderne kunst Humlebæk Danmark +45 4919 0719

Susan Inglett 100 Wooster Street New York, New York 10012 Phone 212.343.0573 Fax 212.343.0574

RONA PONDICK

I WANT

A limited edition artist's book published by I.C. Editions.

An exhibition of books, related prints and drawings

31 October 1996 - 14 December 1996

VIJA CELMINS

Paintings and Drawings 1964-1995

Institute of Contemporary Arts, London *November 1-December 22, 1996*

Museo Nacional Reina Sofia, Madrid *January 21-March 23, 1997*

Kunstmuseum Winterthur, Switzerland *April 12-June 15, 1997*

Museum Fur Moderne Kunst, Frankfurt *June 27-September 28, 1997*

Represented by McKee Gallery 745 Fifth Avenue NY 10151

Seit 50 Jahren Ihr diskreter Partner für Kunsttransporte

Transport à la carte

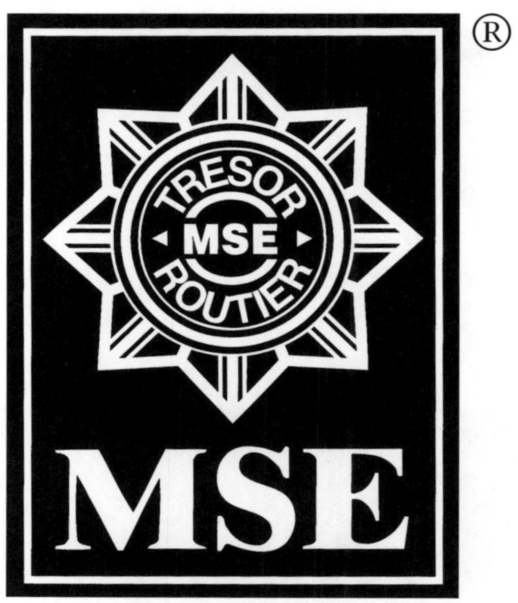

1945 – 1995

MAT SECURITAS EXPRESS AG

Kloten-Zürich	01 /814 16 66	Fax 01 /814 20 21
Basel	061/271 43 80	Fax 061/271 43 18
Chiasso	091/683 75 51	Fax 091/683 98 08
Genève	022/827 18 22	Fax 022/827 18 33

Ein Unternehmen der VIA MAT Holding AG

3rd ArtistBook International

The world's finest publishers and dealers of Artists' Books

15 - 17th. of November 1996, 12 am - 9 pm

Hotel Im Wasserturm, Kaygasse 2, Cologne

Information: ABI, 46, rue de Sévigné, 75003 Paris, Tel +33-1-42775894, fax 42777427

ARTYEAR

THE INTERNATIONAL GUIDE
TO EXHIBITIONS OF ART AND
ARCHITECTURE IN MUSEUMS

ARTYEAR

KEEPS YOU IN TOUCH WITH **1000**

MUSEUMS THE WORLD OVER

REPORTING ON EXHIBITIONS

ADDRESSES COLLECTIONS

CURATORIAL STAFF

OPENING HOURS...

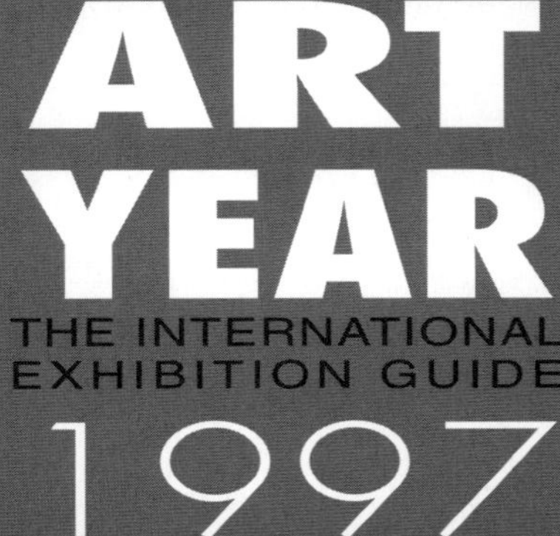

ARTYEAR

THE INTERNATIONAL GUIDE
TO EXHIBITIONS OF ART AND
ARCHITECTURE IN MUSEUMS

ARTYEAR

TWO SPECIAL SECTIONS

PREVIEWS FOCUSES ON

THE MOST IMPORTANT EVENTS

PROFILES TAKES A CLOSE LOOK

AT NEW MUSEUMS

hopefulmonster editore
via Santa Chiara 30 10122 Torino Italia phone 39.11.4367197 fax 4369025

WIENER SECESSION

A–1010 WIEN, FRIEDRICHSTRASSE 12, TEL 43–1–587 53 07, FAX 43–1–587 53 07–34

MARTIN WALDE   27. 9.–3. 11. 1996

LARRY CLARK   27. 9.–3. 11. 1996

HANS SCHABUS   27. 9.–3. 11. 1996

PHILIP TAAFFE   23. 11. 1996–12. 1. 1997

DOROTHEE GOLZ   23. 11. 1996–12. 1. 1997

SUSANNA MORGENSTERN   23. 11. 1996–12. 1. 1997

3rd ArtistBook International

The world's finest publishers and dealers of Artists' Books

15 - 17th. of November 1996, 12 am - 9 pm

Hotel Im Wasserturm, Kaygasse 2, Cologne

Information: ABI, 46, rue de Sévigné, 75003 Paris, Tel +33-1-42775894, fax 42777427

Kunst

96

Zürich

Internationale

Kunstmesse

27.–30. September

ABB-Industriegelände

Zürich-Oerlikon

Freitag, Samstag

und Montag

11–20 Uhr

Sonntag

10–20 Uhr

FIAC

2 - 7 october 96
Espace Eiffel Branly
Paris. International Contemporary Art Fair

Every day from 12 p.m. to 8 p.m.
Late evening Thursday 3 October from 12 p.m. to 11 p.m.
Saturday and Sunday from 10 a.m. to 8 p.m.
Monday 7 October from 12 p.m. to 6 p.m.

AIR DE PARIS (Paris) · ANGELA FLOWERS (Londres) · GALERIE DES ARCHIVES (Paris) · ARIEL (Paris) · ARLOGOS (Nantes) · ARNDT & PARTNER (Berlin) · ART CONCEPT (Nice) · ALFONSO ARTIACO (Naples) · BAGNAI (Sienne) · JACQUES BARBIER (Paris) · ALBERT BARONIAN (Bruxelles) · RAMIS BARQUET (Mex-Garza Garcia) · BAUDOIN LEBON (Paris) · GALERIE BEAUBOURG (Paris - Vence) · JEAN BERNIER (Athènes) · BISCHOFBERGER (Zurich) · MARC BLONDEAU (Paris) · BORZO KUNSTHANDEL (Hertogenbosch) · GILBERT BROWNSTONE ET CIE (Paris) · FERRAN CANO - 4 GATS (Palma de Mallorca) · LOUIS CARRE (Paris) · BERNARD CATS (Bruxelles) · CHOSUN ART (Seoul) · CLAUDE BERNARD (Paris) · CONTINI (Venise) · CRANE KALMAN (Londres) · PATRICIA DORFMANN (Paris) · LAURENT DELAYE (Londres) · DENISE RENE (Paris) · WILLY D'HUYSSER (Bruxelles) · DI MEO (Paris) · DINA VIERNY (Paris) · DONG SAN BANG (Seoul) · ERIC DUPONT (Toulouse) · ANTONI ESTRANY (Barcelone) · NIEVES FERNANDEZ (Madrid) · FERNANDO SANTOS (Porto) · JENNIFER FLAY-CAROLINE BOURGEOIS (Paris) · JEAN FOURNIER (Paris) · GALERIE DE FRANCE (Paris) · GALERIE DU JOUR (France) · FROMENT ET PUTMAN (Paris) · GALERIE MODERNE - SILKEBORG (Silkeborg) · GALERIE DE SEOUL (Seoul) · GANA ART (Seoul) · GENTILI (Florence) · GMURZYNSKA (Cologne-Marienburg) · MARIAN GOODMAN (New York) · KARSTEN GREVE (Paris-Cologne-Milan) · NOHRA HAIME (New York) · HANSUN (Seoul) · THESSA HEROLD (Paris) · ERNST HILGER (Vienne) · XAVIER HUFKENS (Bruxelles) · GHISLAINE HUSSENOT (Paris) · LEONARD HUTTON (New York) · HYUNDAI (Seoul) · CATHERINE ISSERT (Saint-Paul-de-Vence) · BERNARD JACOBSON (Londres) · RODOLPHE JANSSEN (Bruxelles) · JEANNE BUCHER (Paris) · JEAN ART (Seoul) · JGM. (Paris) · JOUSSE SEGUIN (Paris) · JO HYUN (Busan) · ANNELY JUDA (Londres) · KRIEF (Paris) · FRANS JACOBS (Amsterdam) · URSULA KRINZINGER (Vienne) · KRUGIER-DITESHEIM (Genève) · KUKJE (Seoul) · LAAGE - SALOMON (Paris) · LAHUMIERE (Paris) · YVON LAMBERT (Paris) · FRED LANZENBERG (Bruxelles) · LAROCK GRANOFF (Paris) · LELONG (Paris) · YVES LE ROUX (Montreal) · ALBERT LOEB (Paris) · JORGE MARA (Madrid) · MARLBOROUGH (New York) · MARWAN HOSS (Paris) · GABRIELLE MAUBRIE (Paris) · HANS MAYER (Dusseldorf) · JAMES MAYOR (Londres) · ANTHONY MEIER (San Francisco) · EVA MENZIO (Turin) · METEO (Paris) · MONTENAY-GIROUX (Paris) · NACHST ST. STEPHAN (Vienne) · ENRICO NAVARRA (Paris) · NATHALIE OBADIA (Paris) · ORANGERIE - REINZ (Cologne) · ROGER PAILHAS (Paris) · YVONAMOR PALIX (Paris) · CLAUDINE PAPILLON (Paris) · PARK RYU SOOK (Seoul) · ALICE PAULI (Lausanne) · EMMANUEL PERROTIN - MA GALERIE (Paris) · GILLES PEYROULET (Paris) · PIECE UNIQUE (Paris) · GUY PIETERS (Knokke-le-Zoute) · PLESSIS (Nantes) · POLARIS (Paris) · PUNTO (Valence) · PYO (Seoul) · RABOUAN-MOUSSION (Paris) · MICHEL REIN (Tours) · RHO (Seoul) · RIBBENTROP (Eltville-am-Rhein) · PHILIPPE RIZZO (Paris) · THADDAEUS J. ROPAC (Paris) · SAMTUH (Seoul) · SAMY KINGE (Paris) · SAPONE (Nice) · MICHAEL SCHULTZ (Berlin) · NATHALIE SEROUSSI (Paris) · TONY SHAFRAZI (New-York) · SCHIPPER & KROME (Cologne) · SOLLERTIS (Toulouse) · PIETRO SPARTA (Chagny) · SPERONE WESTWATER (New York) · SUN (Seoul) · MICHELINE SZWAJCER (Anvers) · TANIT (Munich) · TEGA (Milan) · DANIEL TEMPLON (Paris) · THOMAS (Munich) · TRIGANO (Paris) · SOPHIA UNGERS (Cologne) · GEORGE-PHILIPPE VALLOIS (Paris) · DANIEL VARENNE (Genève) · ALINE VIDAL (Paris) · VIDAL - SAINT-PHALLE (Paris) · ANNE DE VILLEPOIX (Paris) · VIVITA (Florence) · LESLIE WADDINGTON (Londres) · THEO WADDINGTON (Londres) · XIPPAS (Paris) · YEH (Seoul) · ZURCHER (Paris) ·

REED-OIP. 11, rue du Colonel Pierre Avia. BP 571. 75726 Paris cedex 15. France. Tel. 33 (1) 41 90 47 80. Fax 33 (1) 41 90 47 89

30. Internationale Messe für
Kunst des 20. Jahrhunderts

ART
COLOGNE

Internationaler
Kunstmarkt

10. – 17. November 1996

Veranstalter: Bundesverband Deutscher Galerien e.V. (BVDG)
Informationen: KölnMesse, Postfach 210760, D-50532 Köln
Telefon (0)221/821-0, Fax (0)221/821-3415

KölnMesse

ART FOCUS

Hugo Weber
Chicago — New York

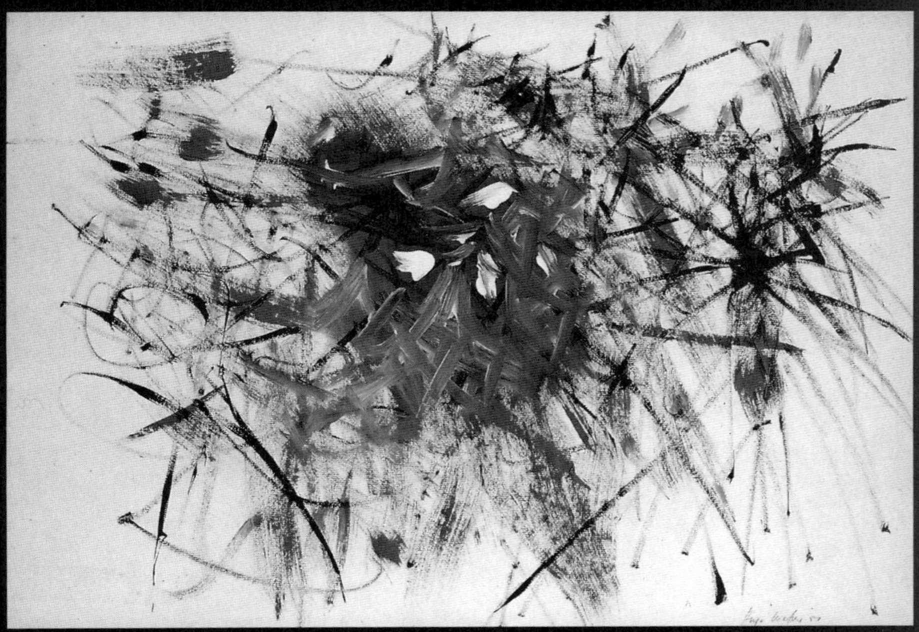

A Swiss Pioneer of
American Abstract Expressionism

September 20 – November 30, 1996

Tuesday–Friday 10.30 a.m. to 12.30 p.m.
                 3.00 p.m. to 6.30 p.m.
Saturday   11.00 a.m. to 4.00 p.m.

Talstrasse 16   CH-8001 Zurich   Phone 01 225 38 48

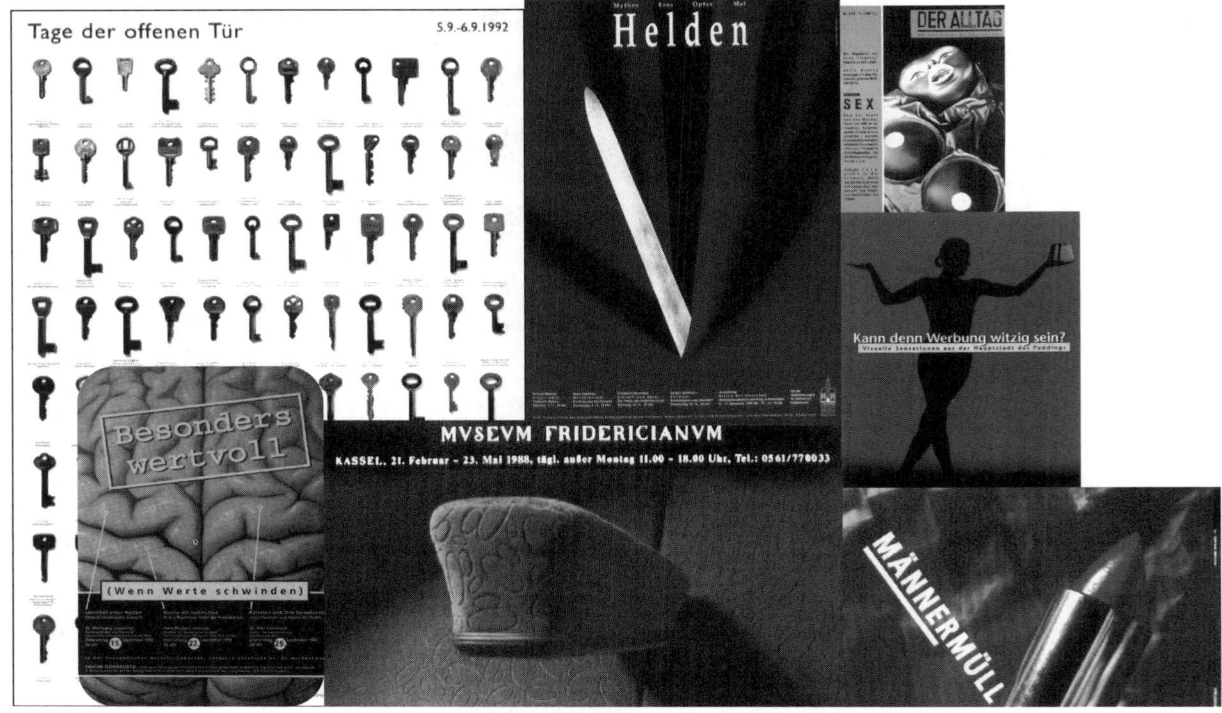

Kommunikationsdesign für Kunst und Kultur **MODERNE REKLAME** Hasengasse 5-7 _60311_ Frankfurt am Main
Telefon +49 69- 20 10 5 | Telefax +49 69- 29 05 62

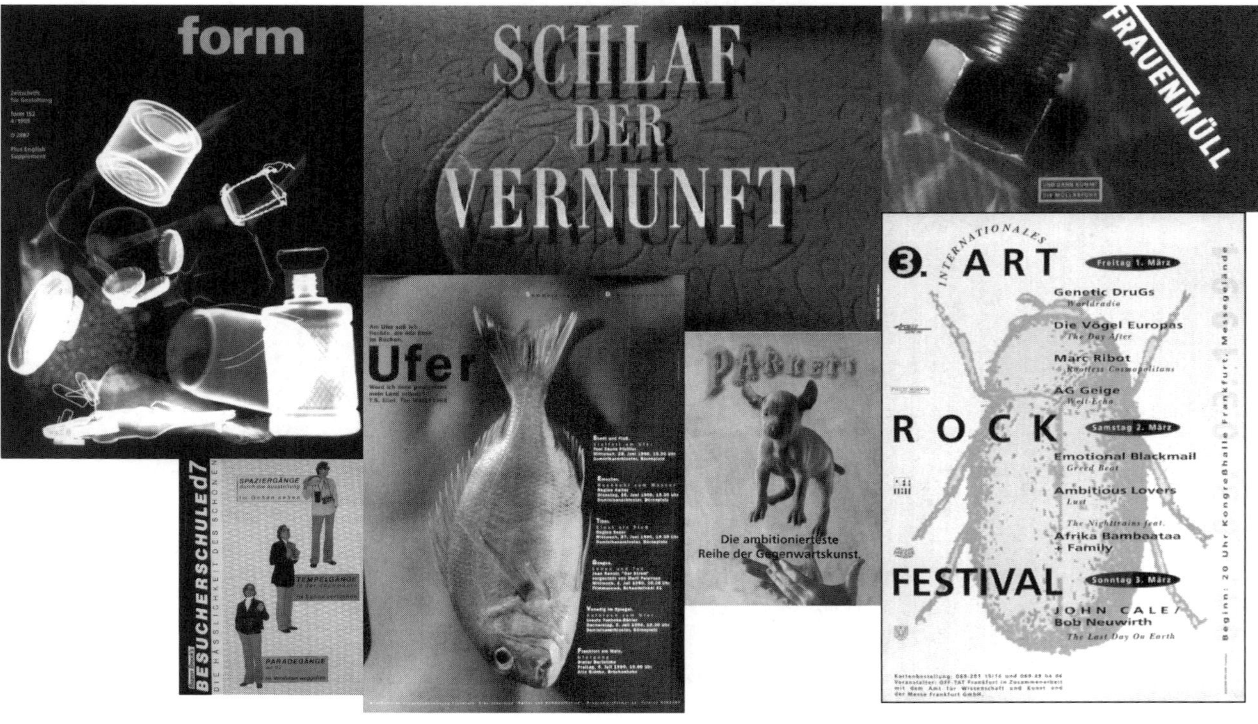

30.10.-3.11.96

Kunstmarkt
INTERNATIONAL
Düsseldorf

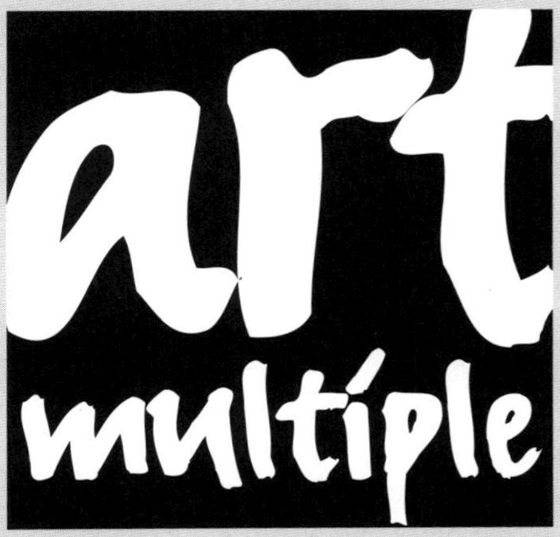

art
multiple

Graphik
Skulptur
Objekt

Täglich
11 bis 20 Uhr

Freitag,
1. November,
11 bis 22 Uhr

Messe Düsseldorf
Basis für Business

INTERMESS Dörgeloh AG
Obere Zäune 16 · 8001 Zürich · Telefon (01) 2529988 · Telefax (01) 2611151

FRANKFURT

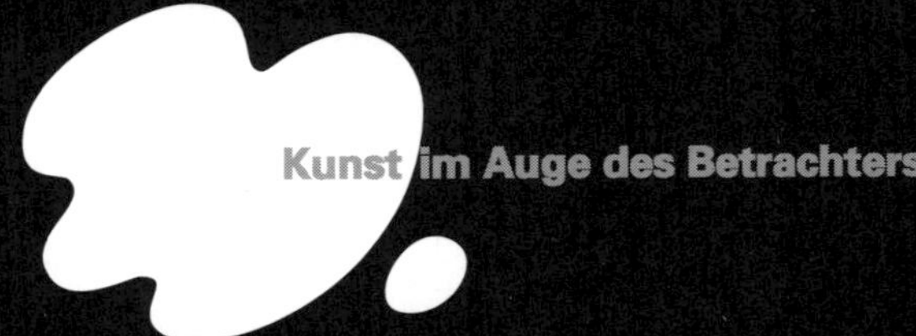

Messe Frankfurt
Halle 1 – Eingang City

Öffnungszeiten:
Sa. bis Mi. 11 bis 20 Uhr
Do. 11 bis 18 Uhr

Infos unter:
Telefon: (0 69) 75 75 - 66 64
Telefax: (0 69) 75 75 - 66 74
Internet:
http://www.messefrankfurt.de/art/

Aktion, Information, Diskussion –
aktuelle Kunst der Gegenwart,
präsentiert von Galerien aus aller
Welt, das Rahmenprogramm, die
Sonderschauen und die in ihrer
Art einmalige Besucherschule
machen die Begegnung mit der
Kunst auf der Art Frankfurt zu
einem inspirierenden Erlebnis.

ART Frankfurt
Die Messe zum Thema Kunst
26. April – 1. Mai 1997

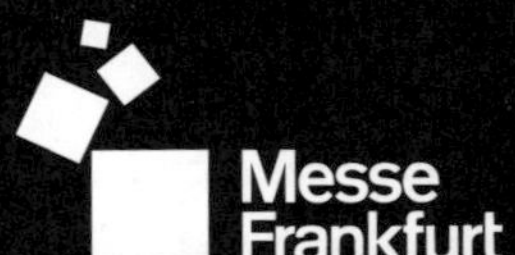

A printing collaboration
for 10 years and
38 Parkett issues:

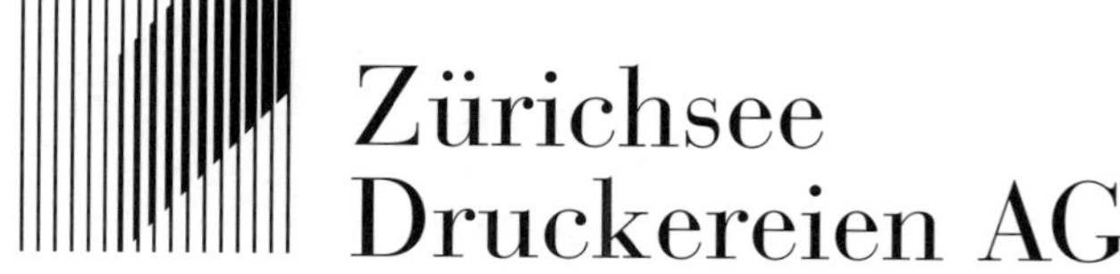

For an estimate of your next printing project please contact:
Zürichsee Druckereien AG, Seestrasse 86, 8712 Stäfa,
Telefon +41-1-928 53 03, Fax +41-1-928 53 10

Permutationen der zeitgenössischen Kunst

ABRAHAM — ABSALON — ARP — BASELITZ — BROODTHAERS — BROUWN
FABRO — FEDERLE — FÖRG — HIRST — IMMENDORFF — KAWAMATA
KIECOL — KIRKEBY — KOGLER — LANE — LOHSE — LÜPERTZ
MEYER-AMDEN — NAUMAN — NITSCH — PENCK — PETTIBON
POLKE — RAINER — SACCONI — SCHWITTERS — SOUTTER
TAEUBER-ARP — TORONI — WEINER — WEST — WÖLFLI

Chaos Wahnsinn

Eine Ausstellung von Johannes Gachnang

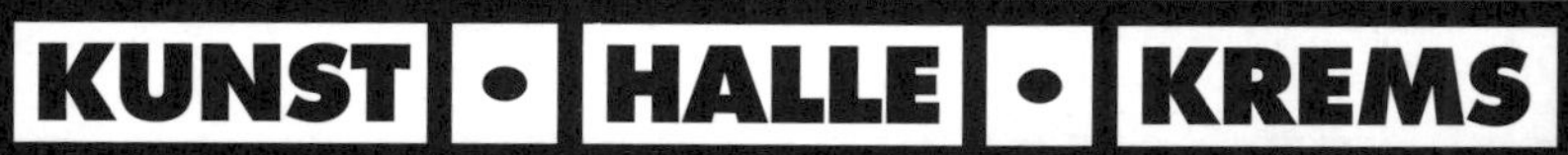

20. Juli bis 27. Oktober 1996
Dienstag bis Sonntag 10 bis 18 Uhr
Kunsthalle Krems, Steiner Landstraße 8 und Minoritenplatz 4, 3504 Krems-Stein, AUSTRIA
Tel. +43 (02732) 826 69, Fax DW 16

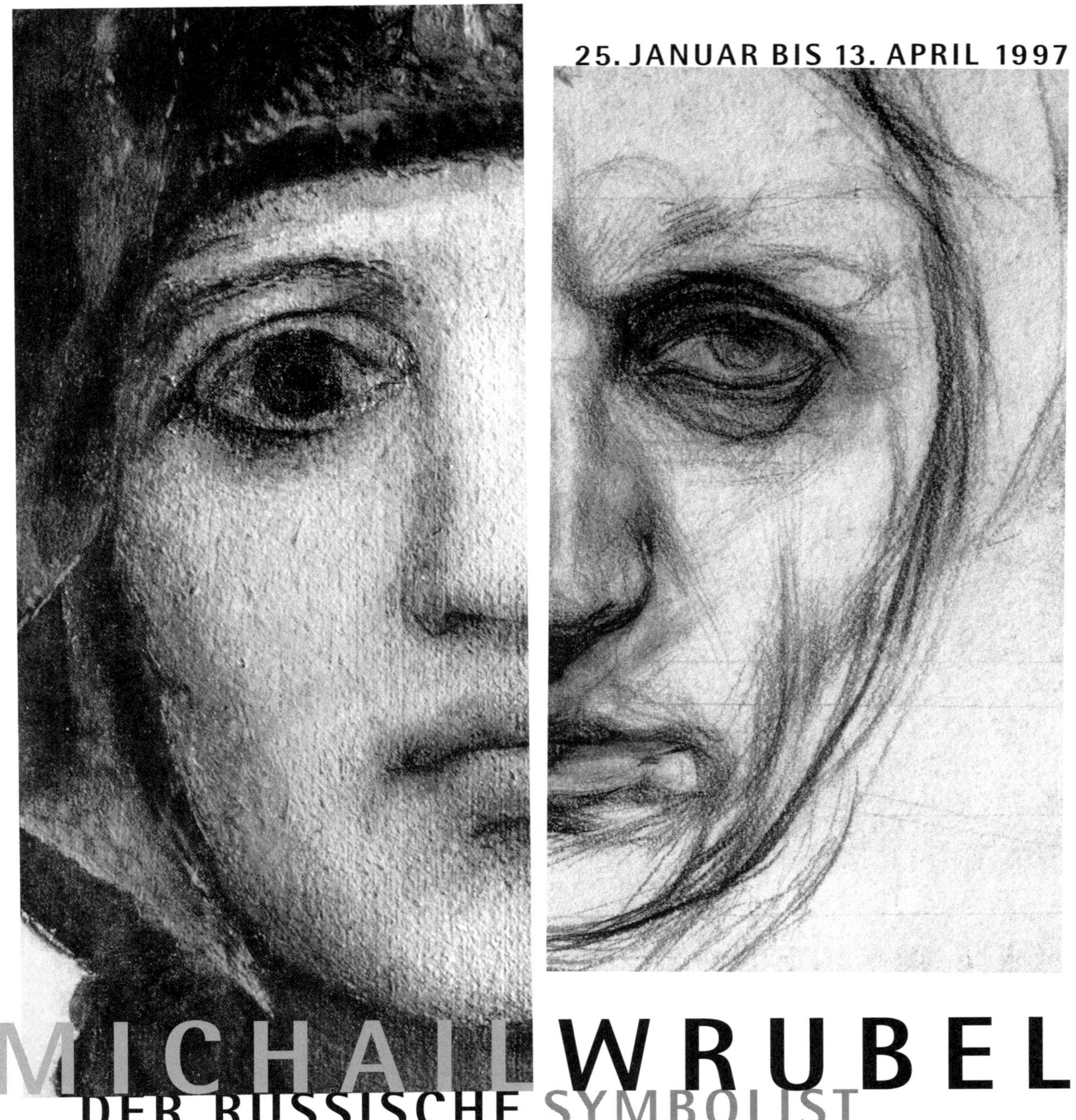
KUNSTHALLE DÜSSELDORF, GRABBEPLATZ 4, TELEFON 02 11/899 62 40
25. JANUAR BIS 13. APRIL 1997
MICHAIL WRUBEL
DER RUSSISCHE SYMBOLIST
HAUS DER KUNST MÜNCHEN, PRINZREGENTENSTRASSE 1,
TELEFON 0 89/21 12 70
10. MAI BIS 27. JULI 1997

Tony Oursler

Galerie Ghislaine Hussenot

5bis, rue des Haudriettes, 75003 Paris
Tél. 48 87 60 81, Fax 48 87 05 01

THOMAS AMMANN FINE ART AG ZURICH

BRICE MARDEN

June 10 – September 28, 1996

RESTELBERGSTRASSE 97   CH-8044 ZÜRICH   TEL. (411) 252 90 52   FAX (411) 252 82 45
ADDRESS OF EXHIBITION: KRÄHBÜHLSTRASSE 42   CH-8044 ZÜRICH

catherine lee

daemons & valentines

august 18 - september 21

robert rauschenberg

anagrams

october 4 - november 16

christian herdeg

light sculptures

november 23 - december 21

galerie jamileh weber

waldmannstrasse 6

ch-8001 zürich

telefon 01 252 10 66

telefax 01 252 11 32